Communications in Computer and Information Science 714

Commenced Publication in 2007
Founding and Former Series Editors:
Alfredo Cuzzocrea, Dominik Ślęzak, and Xiaokang Yang

More information about this series at http://www.springer.com/series/7899

Constantine Stephanidis (Ed.)

HCI International 2017 – Posters' Extended Abstracts

19th International Conference, HCI International 2017
Vancouver, BC, Canada, July 9–14, 2017
Proceedings, Part II

 Springer

Editor
Constantine Stephanidis
Foundation for Research & Technology –
  Hellas (FORTH)
University of Crete
Heraklion, Crete
Greece

ISSN 1865-0929   ISSN 1865-0937 (electronic)
Communications in Computer and Information Science
ISBN 978-3-319-58752-3   ISBN 978-3-319-58753-0 (eBook)
DOI 10.1007/978-3-319-58753-0

Library of Congress Control Number: 2017940246

Printed on acid-free paper

This Springer imprint is published by Springer Nature
The registered company is Springer International Publishing AG
The registered company address is: Gewerbestrasse 11, 6330 Cham, Switzerland

Foreword

The 19th International Conference on Human–Computer Interaction, HCI International 2017, was held in Vancouver, Canada, during July 9–14, 2017. The event incorporated the 15 conferences/thematic areas listed on the following page.

A total of 4,340 individuals from academia, research institutes, industry, and governmental agencies from 70 countries submitted contributions, and 1,228 papers have been included in the proceedings. These papers address the latest research and development efforts and highlight the human aspects of design and use of computing systems. The papers thoroughly cover the entire field of human–computer interaction, addressing major advances in knowledge and effective use of computers in a variety of application areas. The volumes constituting the full set of the conference proceedings are listed on the following pages.

I would like to thank the program board chairs and the members of the program boards of all thematic areas and affiliated conferences for their contribution to the highest scientific quality and the overall success of the HCI International 2017 conference.

This conference would not have been possible without the continuous and unwavering support and advice of the founder, Conference General Chair Emeritus and Conference Scientific Advisor Prof. Gavriel Salvendy. For his outstanding efforts, I would like to express my appreciation to the communications chair and editor of *HCI International News*, Dr. Abbas Moallem.

April 2017   Constantine Stephanidis

HCI International 2017 Thematic Areas and Affiliated Conferences

Thematic areas:

- Human–Computer Interaction (HCI 2017)
- Human Interface and the Management of Information (HIMI 2017)

Affiliated conferences:

- 17th International Conference on Engineering Psychology and Cognitive Ergonomics (EPCE 2017)
- 11th International Conference on Universal Access in Human–Computer Interaction (UAHCI 2017)
- 9th International Conference on Virtual, Augmented and Mixed Reality (VAMR 2017)
- 9th International Conference on Cross-Cultural Design (CCD 2017)
- 9th International Conference on Social Computing and Social Media (SCSM 2017)
- 11th International Conference on Augmented Cognition (AC 2017)
- 8th International Conference on Digital Human Modeling and Applications in Health, Safety, Ergonomics and Risk Management (DHM 2017)
- 6th International Conference on Design, User Experience and Usability (DUXU 2017)
- 5th International Conference on Distributed, Ambient and Pervasive Interactions (DAPI 2017)
- 5th International Conference on Human Aspects of Information Security, Privacy and Trust (HAS 2017)
- 4th International Conference on HCI in Business, Government and Organizations (HCIBGO 2017)
- 4th International Conference on Learning and Collaboration Technologies (LCT 2017)
- Third International Conference on Human Aspects of IT for the Aged Population (ITAP 2017)

Conference Proceedings Volumes Full List

1. LNCS 10271, Human–Computer Interaction: User Interface Design, Development and Multimodality (Part I), edited by Masaaki Kurosu
2. LNCS 10272 Human–Computer Interaction: Interaction Contexts (Part II), edited by Masaaki Kurosu
3. LNCS 10273, Human Interface and the Management of Information: Information, Knowledge and Interaction Design (Part I), edited by Sakae Yamamoto
4. LNCS 10274, Human Interface and the Management of Information: Supporting Learning, Decision-Making and Collaboration (Part II), edited by Sakae Yamamoto
5. LNAI 10275, Engineering Psychology and Cognitive Ergonomics: Performance, Emotion and Situation Awareness (Part I), edited by Don Harris
6. LNAI 10276, Engineering Psychology and Cognitive Ergonomics: Cognition and Design (Part II), edited by Don Harris
7. LNCS 10277, Universal Access in Human–Computer Interaction: Design and Development Approaches and Methods (Part I), edited by Margherita Antona and Constantine Stephanidis
8. LNCS 10278, Universal Access in Human–Computer Interaction: Designing Novel Interactions (Part II), edited by Margherita Antona and Constantine Stephanidis
9. LNCS 10279, Universal Access in Human–Computer Interaction: Human and Technological Environments (Part III), edited by Margherita Antona and Constantine Stephanidis
10. LNCS 10280, Virtual, Augmented and Mixed Reality, edited by Stephanie Lackey and Jessie Y.C. Chen
11. LNCS 10281, Cross-Cultural Design, edited by Pei-Luen Patrick Rau
12. LNCS 10282, Social Computing and Social Media: Human Behavior (Part I), edited by Gabriele Meiselwitz
13. LNCS 10283, Social Computing and Social Media: Applications and Analytics (Part II), edited by Gabriele Meiselwitz
14. LNAI 10284, Augmented Cognition: Neurocognition and Machine Learning (Part I), edited by Dylan D. Schmorrow and Cali M. Fidopiastis
15. LNAI 10285, Augmented Cognition: Enhancing Cognition and Behavior in Complex Human Environments (Part II), edited by Dylan D. Schmorrow and Cali M. Fidopiastis
16. LNCS 10286, Digital Human Modeling and Applications in Health, Safety, Ergonomics and Risk Management: Ergonomics and Design (Part I), edited by Vincent G. Duffy
17. LNCS 10287, Digital Human Modeling and Applications in Health, Safety, Ergonomics and Risk Management: Health and Safety (Part II), edited by Vincent G. Duffy
18. LNCS 10288, Design, User Experience, and Usability: Theory, Methodology and Management (Part I), edited by Aaron Marcus and Wentao Wang

HCI International 2017 Conference

The full list with the Program Board Chairs and the members of the Program Boards of all thematic areas and affiliated conferences is available online at:

http://www.hci.international/board-members-2017.php

HCI International 2018

The 20th International Conference on Human–Computer Interaction, HCI International 2018, will be held jointly with the affiliated conferences in Las Vegas, NV, USA, at Caesars Palace, July 15–20, 2018. It will cover a broad spectrum of themes related to human–computer interaction, including theoretical issues, methods, tools, processes, and case studies in HCI design, as well as novel interaction techniques, interfaces, and applications. The proceedings will be published by Springer. More information is available on the conference website: http://2018.hci.international/.

General Chair
Prof. Constantine Stephanidis
University of Crete and ICS-FORTH
Heraklion, Crete, Greece
E-mail: general_chair@hcii2018.org

http://2018.hci.international/

Contents – Part II

Learning, Games and Gamification

Health, Well-Being and Comfort

Mobile Interaction

Visual Design and Visualization

Social Issues and Security in HCI

Contents – Part I

Psychophisiological Measuring and Monitoring

Perception, Cognition and Emotion in HCI

Ergonomics and Models in Work and Training Support

Interaction in Virtual and Augmented Reality

Factors of Cybersickness

Patricia Bockelman$^{(\boxtimes)}$ and Deanna Lingum

Institute for Simulation and Training at the University of Central Florida,
Orlando, FL, USA
{pbockelm, dlingum}@ist.ucf.edu

Abstract. As virtual reality (VR) applications expand in private and public sector contexts, so do reports of sickness elicited within VR systems. Users of head mounted VR displays frequently report symptoms similar, but not identical, to those of motion sickness and simulator sickness. Because of this distinction, the symptoms are collectively classified as symptoms of cybersickness. While researchers and tech developers alike acknowledge VR's propensity for inducing cybersickness, there is no symptom prediction tool. The present paper describes a research agenda which will culminate in a cybersickness prediction tool. First, the authors clarify nomenclature relevant to the VR, virtual environments (VE), and cybersickness. The preliminary literature review resulted in a test Cybersickness Index Matrix (CIM), with three cybersickness trigger categories: System, Task, Individual Differences. Researchers conducted a validation test of the CIM in a pilot study conducted in conjunction with an energy industry training program. The paper presents those preliminary results and provides a discussion including CIM refinement and future implementation potential.

Keywords: Cybersickness · Virtual reality · Human factors

1 Clarifying Cybersickness

1.1 Common Language for Common Ground

In November of 2015, a The Telegraph Health News headline read, "Cybersickness: The new 'illness' sweeping the nation" [1]. Briefly, the article proposed a pandemic of nausea, headache and some blanket of malaise triggered by the things people viewed—especially their electronic devices, like cell phones. While the sensational headline likely hooks the interest of a reader, it fails to capture the phenomenon that virtual reality(VR) developers and human factors researchers are seeking to understand when considering cybersickness (CS). It is neither "new" nor "sweeping" the UK or any other nation.

CS is not new, especially if it is defined as a physiological illness like motion sickness (MS) triggered by atypical visual stimuli. For decades, researchers have examined visually induced MS, considering the relationship between the optical, vestibular, and proprioceptive systems. Aeronautic research had established a compelling relationship between MS and spatial perception [2]. US investment in space exploration compelled NASA scientists to consider the physiological catalysts of MS

© Springer International Publishing AG 2017
C. Stephanidis (Ed.): HCII Posters 2017, Part II, CCIS 714, pp. 3–8, 2017.
DOI: 10.1007/978-3-319-58753-0_1

from a variety of sources, including optical perception. While obvious sources like zero gravity and high-rate rotations could make a body respond to genuine motion-induced sickness, researchers also observed that visual exposure to angular accelerations altered the experience of MS [3].

Further, it would be difficult to argue that it is spreading rampantly. Rather, people are placing themselves in situations that are more apt to trigger visually induced MS through frequent use of digital displays. There is simply no evolutionary precedent for the regular consumption of light-emitting visual stimulation as many humans currently experience.

But, something *is* going on. VR headsets come with warnings about experiencing symptoms of MS during use. National Science Foundation and other scientific sources fund CS research. Newspapers are running articles warning people of the cybersickness epidemic. Yet, as long as we cannot define the phenomenon, we cannot move toward a solution. The present work aims to contribute to a clearer working definition of CS and offer a framework for analyzing and predicting CS risk.

In order to examine what cybersickness is and determine how best to address it, we must settle on a definition. Does it include any digital display (like a desktop or cell phone), is it limited to virtual reality, or is further limited to head-mounted display? Is it to be considered as a product of vection displacement or perception of any motion? Is it only cyber if the body isn't moving? Is it distinct from motion sickness and simulator sickness?

While we will propose answers to each of those questions so that we may work toward addressing the problem, we start with the final question, as it requires a conceptual clarification between three tightly related constructs: CS, motion sickness, and simulator sickness (SS).

Although the researchers who first shaped the notion of have mapped a cogent distinction between CS and SS, research on CS continues to be conducted using the metrics of SS. They argue that the profile of CS symptoms emphasizes disorientation, diminishes oculomotor discomfort relative to SS, and presents with three times the severity of symptoms over SS [4]. The authors assert that CS and SS are types of motion sickness, but distinct from one another. Nonetheless, numerous studies examining CS use the simulator sickness questionnaire (SSQ) as the metric [5–7].

This brings the discussion to a point that requires clarification of CS symptoms and the conditions under which CS occurs. To this end, we offer four points to clarify our use of the term "cybersickness":

1. CS symptoms include: Disorientation, dizziness, eyestrain, headache, sweating, fatigue, stomach discomfort, nausea/stomach discomfort, vertigo, blurred vision.
2. CS symptoms emerge from exposure to cyber sources.
3. Although CS shares symptoms with motion sickness, it is not a type of motion sickness.
4. Individual differences, task features, and cyber/technical system features contribute to risk of experiencing CS symptoms.

Just as a cold is not the flu, the symptoms of CS may resemble motion sickness, but because the root causes are distinct, the present work requires a distinction. For the purpose of our research, motion sickness, as the name implies, is triggered by *motion* and it involves the vestibular system with or without a visual stimulus. While Stanney et al. [4] propose CS as distinct from SS and both as types of motion sickness; we assert that it is more helpful to categorize SS as one subset or type of CS when triggered by cyber display. This means that simulators that are not cyber-based (such as the original Link Trainer) may elicit SS, but without a cyber display would not be eliciting CS. Likewise, motion-based simulators elicit may elicit a type of motion sickness.

These distinctions matter, as they help to establish the categories by which we can begin to not only understand, but also predict the incidents of CS. The following sections moves beyond the cyber/motion distinction sketched above to examine the contributions from individual differences and the technical cyber system. These contributions then form the theoretical justification for the Cybersickness Index Matrix (CIM).

2   Contributors to CS

In the preceding section, we mapped our rationale for isolating the CS discussion to include VR, virtual environments, and other potential CS-inducing cases to the ones that are distinctly *cyber*, and not necessarily motion-based or simulation-based. Now, we provide examples of the other factors and features that may contribute to CS. These factors come from three key sources: the context, the individual, and the technical system.

2.1   Contextual Contributions

Context contributors to CS risk include contextual constraints such as:

- Environmental conditions: temperature, humidity, ambient noise
- Performance requirements: physiological, psycho-cognitive, affective (as determined by appropriate measures of effort, duration, complexity, and resonance)
- Human-in-system factors: habituation, exposure duration

While the environmental contributions may be evident (for example, one will likely see an increase in the symptom of sweat and fatigue in hot, balmy conditions), the other contextual contributors are equally important. For performance requirements, the physiological stress symptoms rise during physically, mentally, or emotionally difficult tasks. However, other aspects of the performance, such as whether one must move one's head, could inadvertently increase risk [8]. Other studies suggest that habituation may reduce CS symptoms.

2.2   Individual Differences

Individual differences contributing to the risk of CS include:

- Bodily traits: binocular disruption, body mass index (BMI), general health, migraine propensity

- Behavioral conditions: time since eating, sleep patterns
- Symptomatic propensity: motion sickness history, prior negative experiences
- Psychological traits: Risk taking, openness, motivation

As one may expect, the individual differences research in CS runs a gamut from fairly well-established factors to more highly disputed. Stanney and associates studied susceptibility to these symptoms in a virtual environment finding a significant correlation with self-reported history of motion sickness [9].

In respect to individual differences, we face a challenge to find a balance between reducing risk from some individual sources For example, the connection between BMI and oculomotor symptoms in a virtual environment are clear [9]. However, a high BMI may be related to the reason one should be in a virtual environment. Case in point would be a study from Riva et al. [10], where the researchers were using VR technology as body-image therapeutic treatment. Participants demonstrated positive benefits from the therapy, but they also demonstrated high symptoms as measured on the SSQ. A higher BMI clearly would not justify exclusion from such a treatment, but researchers should consider it as a factor (as it was in that study) so treatments could be employed in the safest fashion.

2.3 Technical System

Some variance in CS symptom risk is due to aspects of the cyber system, such as:

- Hardware: type of display (e.g. head mount, projection, desktop), comfort of design,
- Visual experience: 2D vs 3D, scene oscillation, navigation speed, navigation control, vection
- Hardware/software interaction: delay, locus of control

In this category, research has demonstrated that hardware and software features trigger CS. For example, display type influences CS, with head mounted displays contributing the most risk [11, 12]. Further, researchers are confident that dimensionality and vection influence CS [13, 14]. The interactions between the hardware and software can also introduce CS risk, as studies involving the locus of control [12, 15] suggest.

3 Known Unknowns

While our comprehensive literature review suggests that the three categories of contribution are adequate for framing CS, the lack of research employing this framework at high granularity suggests that there are more sub-factors that remain to be studied. For example, psychological traits have been correlated with MS and SS [16], but how do they relate to CS, specifically? Further how do these factors relate to one another?

Further, because these constructs (MS, CS, and SS) have been collapsed in much of the research, it is unclear whether the affects observed are applicable when the stimulus changes by display, task, and so forth. Take the role of gender, clearly an individual difference, but the impact of gender on CS remains disputable. Some research suggests that female gender increases susceptibility to CS [9, 17, 18], where another study suggests males are more succeptible to MS [19] whereas other studies suggest that there is no significant risk associated with gender [17]. Gender is not the only contributing factor in dispute. Similar conflicting research results abound for age and ethnicity. We propose that future studies should be clearer about what construct is under investigation (CS/MS/SS), what tools are being used to measure the construct, and clarify any mitigating/moderating variables within the study.

4 Toward CS Prediction

Appreciation of the complex interactions among and between contributing factors can lead to the development of a predictive model. The authors of this paper are currently working on the Cybersickness Index Matrix (CIM) to provide guidance for cyber users. By taking those relationships into account prior to cyber exposure, users can reduce risk in entertainment, training, and work contexts. The final goal is to establish an open-source tool using fuzzy metrics to give users a "quick and dirty" evaluation of risk given a unique set of circumstances from context, individuals, and systems. A verification and validation study is under way testing the model on an international sample of trainees using virtual reality training for the energy industry.

References

1. Agency: Cybersickness: The new 'illness' sweeping the nation, 17 November 2015. http://www.telegraph.co.uk/news/health/news/12001743/Cybersickness-The-new-illness-sweeping-the-nation.html. Accessed 23 Mar 2017
2. Steele, J.E.: Motion sickness and spatial perception. A theoretical study, November 1961
3. Reason, J.T., Diaz, E.: Effects of visual reference on adaptation to motion sickness and subjective responses evoked by graded cross-coupled angular accelerations. In: Fifth Symposium on the Role of the Vestibular Organs in Space Exploration, pp. 87–97, August 1970
4. Stanney, K.M., Kennedy, R.S., Drexler, J.M.: Cybersickness is not simulator sickness. In: Proceedings of the Human Factors and Ergonomics Society Annual Meeting, vol. 41, no. 2, pp. 1138–1142, October 1997
5. Bruck, S., Watters, P.A.: Estimating cybersickness of simulated motion using the simulator sickness questionnaire (SSQ): a controlled study. In: Sixth International Conference on Computer Graphics, Imaging and Visualization, CGIV 2009, pp. 486–488 (2009)
6. So, R.H.Y., Lo, W.T.: Cybersickness: an experimental study to isolate the effects of rotational scene oscillations. In: Proceedings IEEE Virtual Reality (Cat. No. 99CB36316), pp. 237–241 (1999)
7. Vinson, N.G., Lapointe, J.-F., Parush, A., Roberts, S.: Cybersickness induced by desktop virtual reality. In: Proceedings of Graphics Interface 2012, Toronto, Ontario, Canada, pp. 69–75 (2012)
8. Howarth, P.A., Finch, M.: The nauseogenicity of two methods of navigating within a virtual environment. Appl. Ergon. 30(1), 39–45 (1999)

9. Stanney, K.M., Hale, K.S., Nahmens, I., Kennedy, R.S.: What to expect from immersive virtual environment exposure: influences of gender, body mass index, and past experience. Hum. Factors **45**(3), 504–520 (2003)

10. Riva, G., Bacchetta, M., Baruffi, M., Cirillo, G., Molinari, E.: Virtual reality environment for body image modification: a multidimensional therapy for the treatment of body image in obesity and related pathologies. Cyberpsychol. Behav. **3**(3), 421–431 (2000)

11. Bando, T., Iijima, A., Yano, S.: Visual fatigue caused by stereoscopic images and the search for the requirement to prevent them: a review. Displays **33**(2), 76–83 (2012)

12. Sharples, S., Cobb, S., Moody, A., Wilson, J.R.: Virtual reality induced symptoms and effects (VRISE): comparison of head mounted display (HMD), desktop and projection display systems. Displays **29**(2), 58–69 (2008)

13. Keshavarz, B., Hecht, H.: Stereoscopic viewing enhances visually induced motion sickness but sound does not. Presence **21**(2), 213–228 (2012)

14. Keshavarz, B., Riecke, B.E., Hettinger, L.J., Campos, J.L.: Vection and visually induced motion sickness: how are they related? Front. Psychol. **6**, 472 (2015)

15. Cl, L.: A neuro-fuzzy warning system for combating cybersickness in the elderly caused by the virtual environment on a TFT-LCD. Appl. Ergon. **40**(3), 316–324 (2009)

16. Golding, J.F.: Predicting individual differences in motion sickness susceptibility by questionnaire. Personal. Individ. Differ. **41**(2), 237–248 (2006)

17. Graeber, D.A., Stanney, K.M.: Gender differences in visually induced motion sickness. In: Proceedings of the Human Factors and Ergonomics Society Annual Meeting, vol. 46, no. 26, pp. 2109–2113, September 2002

18. Parsons, T.D., et al.: Sex differences in mental rotation and spatial rotation in a virtual environment. Neuropsychologia **42**(4), 555–562 (2004)

19. Klosterhalfen, S., Kellermann, S., Pan, F., Stockhorst, U., Hall, G., Enck, P.: Effects of ethnicity and gender on motion sickness susceptibility. Aviat. Space Environ. Med. **76**(11), 1051–1057 (2005)

Effects of Short Exposure to a Simulation in a Head-Mounted Device and the Individual Differences Issue

David Hartnagel$^{(\boxtimes)}$, Marine Taffou, and Patrick M.B. Sandor

Département Action and Cognition en Situation Opérationnelle,
Institut de Recherche Biomédicale des Armées,
BP 73, 91223 Brétigny-sur-Orge, France
david.hartnagel@defense.gouv.fr

Abstract. Virtual Reality (VR) displays have been developed for years; lots of technological challenges are still remaining to improve presence and hopefully avoid oculomotor trouble, eyestrain and sickness. Although the technology is not mature enough to avoid discomfort, the market already proposes devices to a large public, especially head-mounted devices. Many questions arise: Will customers adapt to those unnatural technologies? Could exposure to those kinds of devices be a public health trouble? Is it safe to drive a real vehicle afterwards? Motion sickness, simulator sickness and cyber sickness in VR are symptoms linked to a wrong (biased) multisensory integration, where visual fluxes and vestibular information are not coherent. As the VR images differ from real world by focus, anamorphic fluxes, image characteristics (rate of flickering, luminance....), vision, balance and oculomotor issues may be involved. Our concerns are focused on short time exposure (less than 10 min) to a VR display. We developed a brief test battery to quickly evaluate 3 dimensions: cognitive style using Rod and Frame Test (RFT), oculomotor modification (AC/A) and balance (vestibular tests). Here we present a pilot study to evaluate the hypothesized influence of a short time exposure to a roller coaster simulation using Oculus Rift DK1™. Participants were tested before and after 3 cycles of roller coaster simulation, they were allowed to freely move head and body. A few number of participants asked to stop the experiment before the third cycle of roller coaster, some of the participants felt a bit uncomfortable after the exposure. Global data analysis showed no significant effect of short time exposure on a series of tests but individual differences remain.

Keywords: Perception · Virtual Reality · Vision · Vestibular · Multisensory integration · Test · Head-mounted display

1 Introduction

Head-mounted devices (HMD) are in the focus of market for a couple of years but they are studied for decades in laboratories [1]. Cybersickness induced by those devices was classified as a sort of Visual Induced Motion Sickness [2]. The main hypothesis proposed to explain this sickness is based on the "sensory conflict theory" of Reason and

© Springer International Publishing AG 2017
C. Stephanidis (Ed.): HCII Posters 2017, Part II, CCIS 714, pp. 9–16, 2017.
DOI: 10.1007/978-3-319-58753-0_2

Brand [3], which considers that the sickness is due to the mismatch between sensory information from visual, vestibular and somatosensory systems. If the brain is able to deal with new sensory interaction rules (multisensory reweighting process) [4], those new rules could afterwards produce wrong perception in the real world (disorientation, reminiscence, negative training…). Facing the large diversity of environments inducing this sickness, researchers have mainly used the Simulator Sickness Questionnaire to psychometrically evaluate simulation side effects [5]. In this questionnaire participants have to rate their feelings (dizziness, nausea, cold sweating, disorientation and eye-strain), however those feelings could be biased by motivation and the will to adapt. Subjective evaluation alone may not be enough when security and life span health are at stake. Question is about evaluating synthetic environment effects on multisensory integration without subjective filter. Nalivaiko et al. [6] studied cybersickness provoked by HMD focusing on physiological online reaction. They were also interested about effects on cognitive performance and noticed the lack of publications addressing this issue. Yet, it is of tremendous importance to provide a reliable and fast test battery to objectively evaluate undesirable impacts of synthetic environment on human perception in order to help prevent side effects linked to VR exposure. Here we propose and tested a brief test battery to measure VR exposure effects on basic perceptions.

2 Methods

2.1 Participants

14 volunteers (2 women, mean age = 40.7, range = [22–56]) participated in the study. Participants were instructed not to drive during the 3 h following the experiment. Five participants had already experienced a VR head mounted device before, but only to try. For participants wearing glasses, the head mounted device was adjusted using one of the provided lenses (A, B, C from Oculus Rift DK1).

2.2 Tests Battery

To assess the effect of VR exposure four tests were selected. SSQ focuses on three main effects of VR exposure: nausea, oculomotors and disorientation. We selected our tests to investigate the influence of VR exposure on oculomotors effects, balance (supposed to take part of disorientation) and cognitive style.

Oculomotor tests consisted in measuring the accommodation/vergence ratio (at far & near distances) to evaluate the amount of the oculomotor modification. The participants viewed the Bernell Muscle Imbalance Measure (MIM) card with a Maddox plate in front of their right eye. They had to report the position of the Maddox red rod produced by the flashing spotlight (2 Hz) placed at the center of the MIM card [7]. This heterophoria assessment was done before and after exposure for near (40 cm) and far (3.05 m) viewing distance.

Balance board tests consisted in measuring the balance with a platform of a seesaw (stabilometer, SATEL balance board) when participants were standing upright static or standing on a cylindrical curved base board (pitch: forward/backward or roll: left/right) with their eyes open or closed [8]. Balance ability was assessed using the surface area (in cm^2) of the mass center's movements. In static conditions participants had to stand without moving for 51.2 s, in dynamic conditions they had to stand without moving for 25.6 s.

WOFEC i.e. Walk On Floor Eyes Closed, test consisted in «walking» heel-to-toe steps with eyes closed and arms folded against chest [9] The WOFEC score is calculated on 30 points corresponding to 3 times 10 perfect steps over 5 trials of 10 steps.

Rod-and-Frame test: This test measures the effect of frame orientations on the perception of the vertical subjective. It consisted in putting a rod vertically relative to gravity in a square frame displayed in different orientations to evaluate field dependence/independence considered as the cognitive style [10].

Tests orders were the same for all participants: they first completed oculomotor tests, then balance tests, then the WOFEC and finally the Rod and Frame test. Participants passed all the tests before and started again the series immediately (less than 30 s) after the VR exposure.

2.3 Head-Mounted VR Device

The VR exposure used an Oculus Rift DK1 TM. This device permits to display image over a 110° horizontal field of view, the resolution per eye is 640 × 800 pixels, the refresh rate is at 60 Hz and the persistence around 3 ms. Sensors (Gyroscope, Accelerometer, Magnetometer) are update at 1000 Hz. Three types of lens were provided in order to cope with participant's ametropia. We used a VR software a replica of the Helix roller coaster of Liseberg amusement park created by ArchiVision. The software is free online (Virtualrealityreviewer 2014) [11].

2.4 Exposure Scenario

The VR software scenario was the same for each participant; before the roller coaster simulation sequence started, the avatar was sitting on a sofa with a popcorn box and a drink on the left side and glasses on the right side. At this time, the experimenter invited the participant to move the head around to feel how the head mounted display works. Participants were sitting on a rotating chair. The experimenter asked them to first look at the popcorn box, then at the glasses and to turn themselves to look at a written sentence on the wall behind them. Then, participants were invited to turn the head 45° towards the right hand side to activate a green button which triggers the roller coaster sequence. To enhance the experience a head set was put on the ears of the participant to improve presence sensation with a loud music and sounds of the rollercoaster; the experimenter could keep on talking to the participant but needed to speak louder.

Then, the roller coaster sequence started. During the ride, participants were free to do what they wanted and to comment on their own free will. At the end of the first roller coaster round, the trolley slows down. At this moment, the experimenter checked how the participant was feeling, and invited him/her to turn his head around. The experimenter also asked the participant about the other characters in the trolley in order to improve presence. If the participant was fine, he/she was invited to launch another round. At the end of the 3rd round participant was invited to quit the game.

3 Results

3.1 Oculomotor Results (AC/A)

Results showed no significant differences (Paired T-Test, p = 0.2622) (Fig. 1a). At individuals level pre-post differences were very small (Fig. 1b).

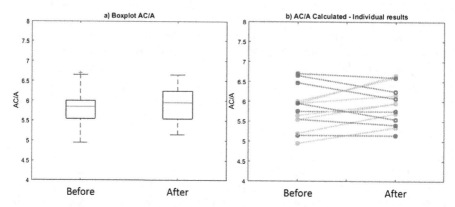

Fig. 1. AC/A Scores. (a) Boxplot before and after exposure. (b) Individual scores before and after exposure, decreasing scores in red, increasing scores in green. (Color figure online)

3.2 Balance Board Tests Results

Due to technical problem for one participant, data analysis was done on 13 participants only.

Differences of surface area between static and dynamic conditions were large (static: 207.38 cm^2; dynamic: 1008.2 cm^2). In static condition (Fig. 2a), mean surface area increased after exposure whether the participants were eyes opened (before: 148.71; after: 233.46) or closed (before: 188.2; after: 259.1). However differences were not significant in the eyes opened condition (paired T-Test p = 0.1185) and only tended to be significant in the eyes closed condition (paired T-Test p = 0.0559). In the pitch condition (Fig. 2b), mean surface area increased after exposure when the participants were eyes opened (before: 271.4; after: 299.7) but not when they were eyes closed (before: 1410.9; after: 1202.6). However, in both cases pre-post differences were not significant (eyes opened: paired T-Test p = 0.5296; eyes closed: paired T-Test p = 0.4787). In the roll condition (Fig. 2c), mean surface slightly decreased after exposure when the participants were eyes opened (before: 634.15; after: 520.15) and slightly increased with eyes closed (before: 1818.4; after: 1908.4). The pre-post differences were significant only in the eyes opened condition (paired T-Test p = 0.0467; eyes closed: paired T-Test p = 0.7318).

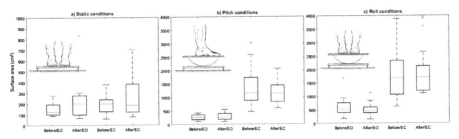

Fig. 2. Surface area boxplot before and after exposure, eyes opened (EO) and eyes closed (EC). (a) standing static, (b) standing on a moving board in pitch rotation, (c) standing on a moving board in roll rotation. Note the scale difference between static and dynamic conditions.

3.3 WOFEC

Pre-post VR exposure differences were not significant (before: 21.61 (SD: 6.4); after: 21.23 (SD: 6.8)). Paired T-test showed no significant difference due to the exposure (p = 0.7419) (Fig. 3a).

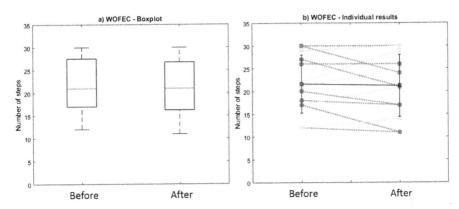

Fig. 3. WOFEC scores. (a) Boxplot before and after exposure. (b) Individual scores before and after exposure, decreasing scores in red, increasing scores in green. (Color figure online)

Looking at individuals scores, two types of participants can be grouped, some improve their scores, others decline (Fig. 3b). The fact that five individuals improved their scores compensates the global decrease of the other participants' scores. It is worth noting that this test is very simple for a non-pathological population. Thus, with repetition effect the scores should have increased for everyone if the exposure had no effect.

3.4 Cognitive Style Results (RFT)

Due to technical problem one participant was not able to perform this task. Data analysis was performed on 13 participants.

Mean results are coherent with literature; vertical subjective estimation varies with frame orientation (Fig. 4). Before VR exposure the main effect of the frame orientation was at ±28°. In contrast, after the exposure the curve is smoother and the largest effect is observed when the frame was tilted at ±18°. After VR exposure, response variability got smaller and frame effect weaker, participants seem to be less sensitive to the orientation of the frame but differences were not statistically significant.

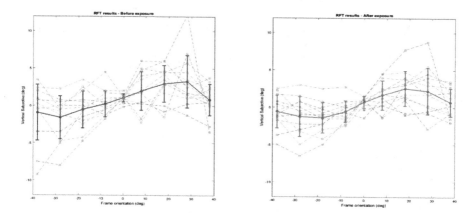

Fig. 4. RFT test results, individual (dash) and mean (plain) data. Vertical subjective estimation varies with frame orientation for tests before and after exposure to VR.

3.5   Behavioral Observations

During the first part of the exposure the participants were invited to move and enjoyed possibilities of HMD. Participants were free to move during the rest of the exposure time. Some participants really enjoyed all the VR exposure, they moved their head and chest (still sitting on the chair) to follow the track, they made noises, they smiled. A part of the participants enjoyed the first round but the good feelings decreased with time and they expressed bad sensations during the remaining exposure. A third part of participants moved the head only when the experimenter invites them to explore around, otherwise they stayed still. Most of the discomforts feelings raised by participants were linked to gastrointestinal sensations (only one felt real nausea), sweat and vertigo during the exposure.

4   Discussion

Our goal was to easily assess the main sensory systems involved in the sensory conflict theory proposed by Reason and Brand. The present tests battery duration is less than 25 min and participants performed all the tests easily. Results showed no large differences due to a 10 min VR rollercoaster simulation exposure using an HMD. It is known that HMD devices produce dissociation between convergence and accommodation [12]; but 10 min exposure seems to have no significant effect on oculomotors parameters tested here. RFT results showed also no significant effect of exposure but it is also a tool to characterize participants and investigate interindividual differences. With more participants we would be able to define field dependency groups and look at score differences to the other tests. We could prefer long duration exposure [13] to reveal stronger effects, but we assumed that subtle consequences could happen as participants already report discomfort within 10 min. In addition our tests are probably biased by learning effects. In the dynamic conditions (roll, eyes opened) the mean surface area and variance significantly decreased after exposure. Standing upright on a moving board is not a common condition; improvement on second run could be due to a learning effect. On the other hand, standing upright on a static plan is quite easy; in those conditions surface area and variance increased after exposure and differences are close to be significant. Increasing score is also found for WOFEC test although this test is probably strongly dependent on learning effect also.

Even though our study does not evidence any significant effect of short VR exposure, the findings indicate several directions of interest. By enlarging our sample of participants, we could link the interindividual differences in the response to multisensory conflict linked to VR exposure with behavioral differences during exposure.

References

1. Fuchs, P.: Les casques de réalité virtuelle et de jeux vidéo. Presses des MINES, Collection Mathématique et informatique (2016)
2. Kennedy, R.S., Drexler, J., Kennedy, R.C.: Research in visually induced motion sickness. Appl. Ergon. **41**(4), 494–503 (2010)
3. Reason, J.T., Brand, J.J.: Motion Sickness. Academic Press, Cambridge (1975)
4. Di Cesare, C.S., Macaluso, T., Mestre, D.R., Bringoux, L.: Slow changing postural cues cancel visual field dependence on self-tilt detection. Gait Posture **41**(1), 198–202 (2015)
5. Kennedy, R.S., Lane, N.E., Berbaum, K.S., Lilienthal, M.G.: Simulator sickness questionnaire: an enhanced method for quantifying simulator sickness. Int. J. Aviat. Psychol. **3**(3), 203–220 (1993)
6. Nalivaiko, E., Davis, S.L., Blackmore, K.L., Vakulin, A., Nesbitt, K.V.: Cybersickness provoked by head-mounted display affects cutaneous vascular tone, heart rate and reaction time. Physiol. Behav. **151**, 583–590 (2015)
7. Hirsch, M.J.: Clinical investigation of a method of testing phoria at forty centimeters. Optom. Vis. Sci. **25**(10), 492–495 (1948)
8. Golomer, E., Dupui, P., Monod, H.: The effects of maturation on self-induced dynamic body sway frequencies of girls performing acrobatics or classical dance. Eur. J. Appl. Physiol. **76**(2), 140–144 (1997)
9. Fregly, A.R., Graybiel, A., Smith, M.J.: Walk on floor eyes closed (WOFEC): a new addition to an ataxia test battery (No. NAMRL-1144). Naval Aerospace Medical Research Lab, Pensacola, FL (1971)
10. Oltman, P.K.: A portable rod-and-frame apparatus. Percept. Mot. Skills **26**(2), 503–506 (1968)

11. http://www.virtualrealityreviewer.com/DEMO-detail/helix-oculus-rift-coaster/
12. Neveu, P., Philippe, M., Priot, A.E., Fuchs, P., Roumes, C.: Vergence tracking: a tool to assess oculomotor performance in stereoscopic displays. J. Eye Mov. Res. **5**(2) (2012)
13. Ortiz de Gortari, A.B., Griffiths, M.D.: Altered visual perception in game transfer phenomena: an empirical self-report study. Int. J. Hum.-Comput. Interact. **30**(2), 95–105 (2014)

Projection Simulator to Support Design Development of Spherical Immersive Display

Wataru Hashimoto[✉], Yasuharu Mizutani, and Satoshi Nishiguchi

Faculty of Information Sciences and Technology, Osaka Institute of Technology,
1-79-1 Kitayama, Hirakata City, Osaka 573-0196, Japan
{wataru.hashimoto,yasuharu.mizutani,
satoshi.nishiguchi}@oit.ac.jp

Abstract. This research aims to develop a simulator that supports the construction of a spherical immersive display, which is a system that can provide a realistic presence, as if the user exists in another space. In general, when developing a display, it is necessary to perform optical design of the projection system in considering special distortion correction on the dome screen. However, accuracy of the optical system that is actually manufactured is not guaranteed to be when it is simulated, and fine adjustment is again necessary when the display is used. In this research, we report on the development of a projection simulator that can perform optical system adjustment and distortion correction simultaneously during optical design of the projection system.

Keywords: Spatially immersive display · Optical design · Image registration · Distortion correction

1 Introduction

Immersive projection display is one of the most powerful systems for enhancing spatial presence and experienced realism. Cave-like immersive displays are increasingly being used for immersive Virtual Reality(VR) applications. A major problem with immersive displays is that they cannot be installed easily, due to the large amount of space required by the surrounding screens. In order to consider the space utility and reduce the volume, a fisheye lens and convex mirror, for example, are utilized to shorten the projection distance. An ultra-short focus projector is also an appropriate device for decreasing spatial cost. It is necessary to simulate the optical system of the projection display; however, optical simulation with certain special lenses is too complex to be easily implemented. Since the optical system is delicate in terms of installation precision, the designed projection cannot always be obtained. After assembling several pieces of display equipment, fine adjustments on the screen are necessary to correct the error due to the optical system for accurate projection. Furthermore, it is necessary to apply the distortion of the image as a result of the optical system to the display content.

The purpose of this research is to achieve design of an immersive display without difficulty, and to develop an environment that can correct error due to the optical system. We focus on the spherical immersive display (Fig. 1), which can be realized on an average room size scale among immersive displays, and organize the spherical

© Springer International Publishing AG 2017
C. Stephanidis (Ed.): HCII Posters 2017, Part II, CCIS 714, pp. 17–24, 2017.
DOI: 10.1007/978-3-319-58753-0_3

immersive display's development flow to extract problems that are obstacles to its development. Moreover, we aim to develop a simulator that can build a device without requiring special knowledge or experience.

Fig. 1. Spherical immersive display

2 Spherical Immersive Display Features

A planetarium is one of the most similar systems to a spherical immersive display. Since the projection technology of the planetarium was established, many technical resources [1] have been discussed for projecting onto the half-spherical dome. Recently, there have been several examples of the DIY planetarium, due to the widespread use of projectors or other such optical devices. Although the planetarium can be classified as a spherical immersive display, the display utilized in the VR field has the following features.

- *Interactivity*

The user can interact with the image; therefore, the projected image is not pre-rendered like those in movies, but must be generated immediately.

- *Rear projection*

Rear projection is suitable for surrounding the user completely with a screen, and can also prevent the user from casting a shadow on the screen.

- *Viewpoint position dependency*

As the curvature radius of the spherical screen is shortened, the user begins to feel the distortion of the projected image on the screen's surface; therefore, the viewpoint position dependency results in restriction of the user's movement.

Based on the above features, we organize the development flow of the spherical immersive display.

3 Spherical Display Development Flow

The development flow classification of the spherical display can be roughly divided into the following four areas.

1. Optical design

Optical simulation is necessary in order to project the image onto the spherical surface correctly. The simulation determines, among others, the size, shape, and placement of the screen, as well as the direction and focus distance of the projector. Points to consider in optical design include whether the projected image is focused on the screen, the projector light is blocked by the user or structure, and the projector pixels are used effectively. It is also necessary to focus on the seam of the projected image when multiple projectors are utilized simultaneously. Since the optical simulation can also predict the distortion of the projected image onto a curved screen, a corresponding table for distortion compensation, utilized in flow 4, is generated through the simulation.

2. Spherical screen prototype

A spherical screen and its optical system are built based on the results of flow 1. It is extremely difficult to form a spherical screen with precision. In general, FRP molding or a scraping of polystyrene mass is adopted to form a large curvature radius for the spherical screen.

3. Adjustment

The prototype display optical system usually contains undesirable manufacturing error. Since the optical system is delicate in terms of error, it is impossible to obtain an ideal design result. Figure 2 shows the grid (latitude/longitude) computed by the optical design described in flow 1. The grid in the left-hand image is clearly shifted from the ideal position shown in right-hand picture, due to manufacturing error in the optical system. Therefore, it is necessary to physically move the screen or projector and adjust the grid position on the screen in order to approach the ideal state shown on the right. Several studies (for example, [3]) use external cameras to observe the projection state for automatically adjusting the grid position.

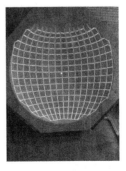

Fig. 2. Result of fine alignments for domed screen, shown on the right. Manufacturing error causes some misalignments, as shown on the left

4. Visual content creation

In order to project visual content onto the spherical surface accurately, a pre-distorted image must be generated, for which the two-pass rendering method is a suitable approach. The rendering requires the use of a corresponding table, obtained by the adjustment described in flow 3. A rendering method using a game engine such as Unity has also been proposed [4].

The adjustment mentioned in flow 3 is an essential process, due to the error involved in the manufacturing and assembly of the optical system described in flow 1. As the number of points in the adjustment grid increases, the distortion correction accuracy increases. However, adjustment becomes troublesome with a very large number of points.

In this research, we propose a simulator that can perform optical design and adjustment simultaneously, so as to reduce the cost of adjustment while maintaining sufficiently high distortion correction accuracy. In particular, we aim to fine-adjust all parameters related to placement by confirming the distortion correction result. This involves estimating the actual parameters, including manufacturing error, from the state of the distortion correction that is actually displayed. If the all parameters are precisely estimated, it is easy to increase the number of points in the distortion correction grid.

4   Simulator Design

The projection of omnidirectional images can take several formats: the dome master format can cover the projection range of the fisheye lens; the equirectangular projection format extends a 360-degree image to a rectangle, as with a world map; and the cube-map format covers all user directions with a cube, as shown in Fig. 3. We opted to use the cube-map, which can also be applied to the resulting display during the adjustment process. With this approach, it is only necessary to render images in all six directions and map their textures onto the spherical shape.

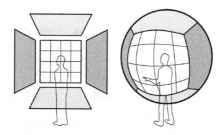

Fig. 3. Omnidirectional image rendering with cube-map

To realize the cube-map rendering, distortion correction is performed based on the relationship between the light ray $\overrightarrow{PI}$ of the projector and the projection point S, as shown in Fig. 4. Point S, which is located on the spherical screen, is the extension of a straight line from the ideal viewpoint V to the feature point M of the cube-map. In the case of Fig. 4, $\overrightarrow{PI}$ reaches point S after being reflected by the convex mirror C. Given the convex mirror's position, orientation, and curvature, S can be obtained from the reflection from P at C. However, although S and P are already known, it is difficult to determine the intersection point C of $\overrightarrow{PI}$; that is, it is easy to follow the projector's ray in the forward direction, but difficult to calculate the inverse.

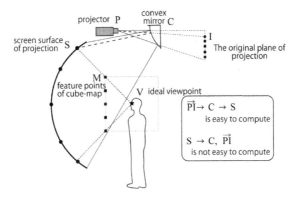

Fig. 4. Calculated points on projector-projected image plane, corresponding to feature points of cube-map

The correspondence between the original plane of projection (I) and the feature points (M) of a cube-map positioned on the ideal viewpoint is required for distortion correction. If the correspondence cannot be determined by the inverse calculation, another method must be considered. We decided to calculate all valid pixels displayed on the projection's screen surface in the forward direction, such as $\overrightarrow{PI} \rightarrow C \rightarrow S$. Then, the nearest point S is searched using the intersection point of the line VM and the screen surface, to obtain the relationship between M and I. In order to reduce the number of searches for the nearest point, we applied the hill-climbing method as a search algorithm. Since all of these ray trace calculations are independent of another, this method is easy to apply to parallel computation.

5   Simulator Implementation

Figure 5 provides an overview of the developed projection simulator. Several parameters related to the screen and projector configuration can be changed in the upper-right windows. The result of the ray tracing process is reflected immediately in the left window. The result of the distortion correction process is rendered in the lower-right window as the feature point of the cube-map. Projecting the lower-right window onto the full screen enables us to confirm the actual projection condition while changing parameters.

We applied this projection simulator to two spherical screen environments. Figure 6 shows a hemispherical screen with a diameter of 1800 mm, projecting by means of diffuse reflection with a convex mirror. Figure 5 shows the result obtained by fine adjustment of the parameters through observing the distortion correction. The result of projecting the distortion correction image onto the screen is shown in Fig. 7.

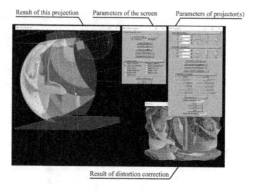

Fig. 5. Overview of projection simulator. The left window indicates the result of projecting a normal image onto the spherical screen. The lower-right window is the distortion corrected image. If the image is projected onto the screen, the viewer can see properly

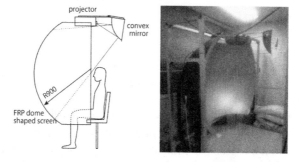

Fig. 6. Projection simulator applied to environment 1: this environment consists of a hemispherical screen of 1800 mm in diameter, projector, and convex mirror with a curvature radius of 259 mm

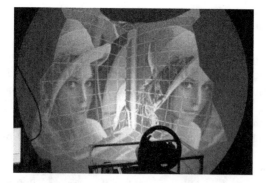

Fig. 7. Result of distortion correction in environment 1 (captured approximately 2 m behind the ideal viewpoint)

The distortion correction process requires a maximum of 0.21 s to complete the calculation in system equipped with an Intel CPU (Core i7-4710MQ, 16 GB main memory) when the total number of feature points is 121. If a full search algorithm is applied instead of the hill-climbing method, the process requires 7.05 s to complete the calculation. This means that the projection simulator using the hill-climbing method can follow the results in almost real time, and the user can verify the pixel distribution in the design or adjust the alignment at any time.

The second environment, shown in Fig. 8, consists of an acrylic dome screen with a diameter of 1000 mm and an ultra-short focus projector behind the screen. Figure 9 shows the distortion correction result of the cube-map on the actual screen. It can be confirmed that the left and right faces of the cube-map are displayed without distortion. The total time required for the distortion correction process was 6.8 s using a full search, 2.78 s using the optimized all-point search by OpenMP, and 0.17 s using a combination of the hill-climbing method and OpenMP.

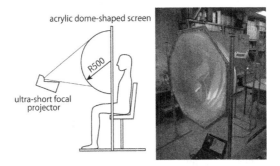

Fig. 8. Projection simulator applied to environment 2: this environment consists of a spherical screen of 1000 mm in diameter and an ultra-short focal projector behind the screen.

Fig. 9. Result of distortion correction in environment 2 (captured approximately 1 m behind the ideal viewpoint)

6 Conclusion

We have developed a projection simulator that can simultaneously perform optical design and adjustment of a spherical display. This simulator enables us to estimate substantive parameters related to the optical system by observing the projection state. The obtained parameters aid in increasing the number of feature points of the cube-map, for high distortion correction accuracy. The obtained distortion correction result is converted to the OBJ format, so that visual contents can be easily created with a game engine such as Unity.

The current simulator corresponds only to parametric shapes; therefore, in future work we will aim for our simulator to be able to support non-parametric shapes captured by devices such as a depth camera. In addition, further improvements in the computation time are expected when GPGPU is applied to the simulator.

Acknowledgments. This work was supported by JSPS KAKENHI, Grant Number 15K00290. We also appreciate Prof. Corchado and Dr. De la Prieta at the University of Salamanca for assisting with this research.

References

1. IMERSA (2017). http://www.imersa.org/
2. International Planetarium Society (2017). http://www.ips-planetarium.org/
3. Raskar, R., van Baar, J., Willwacher, T., Rao, S.: Quadric transfer for immersive curved screen displays. In: EUROGRAPHICS, vol. 23, no. 3 (2004)
4. Bourke, P.: Dome: immersive gaming with the unity game engine. In: Proceedings of CGAT 2009, pp. 265–272 (2009)

Immersive Virtual Experience: An Effort to Increase the Interest for Reading on First-Time Readers

Luis Hernández-Zavaleta, Jaime Espinoza-Martínez,
Diana Morón-González, Alba Núñez-Reyes(✉), Carlos Rivero-Moreno,
Octavio Mercado-González, and Alejandra Osorio-Olave

Maestría en Diseño, Información y Comunicación (MADIC),
División de Ciencias de la Comunicación y Diseño,
Universidad Autónoma Metropolitana (UAM) Unidad Cuajimalpa,
Mexico City, Mexico
lahzavaleta@gmail.com, jaime.trt@gmail.com, moronnita@gmail.com,
ar.nunezreyes@gmail.com, carlosj.rivero@gmail.com, omercado@gmail.com,
alitaosorio@gmail.com

Abstract. From the Analysis of the results obtained from surveys conducted worldwide by the Organization for Economic Cooperation and Development (OECD) in May 2005, it is possible to observe, the low level of reading ability of Mexicans, compared to other countries. The average of books read per year in Mexico is 2.9 per person.

In this research we propose, the use of technology to increase the interest in reading in first time readers. We pretend to use Immersive reality for generating new bonding experiences between children and stories. Studies and reading habits surveys show that the ideal stage to receive motivation and generate interest for reading is childhood. That's why we focus on first time readers which cover a range of age from 8 to 12 years old, according to standards of some publishers in Mexico.

Keywords: Reading ability · Technology · First time readers · Immersive reality · Interest

1 Introduction

The reading habit should be encouraged since childhood, at home and school, according to an analysis of the National Survey of Reading 2015 applied by Arts and Culture National Council (CONACULTA Spanish acronym). Several organizations are focused on creating and promoting programs useful to build material to improve the levels of reading, but probably one of the biggest challenges faced by these governmental and non-governmental organizations (NGOs) is the disinterest of the population, which is due to family, cultural, economic, political, media, etc., factors.

In some countries, the reading promotion is guided through reading campaigns in bookstores and libraries with dynamic activities for attendees, in order

© Springer International Publishing AG 2017
C. Stephanidis (Ed.): HCII Posters 2017, Part II, CCIS 714, pp. 25–31, 2017.
DOI: 10.1007/978-3-319-58753-0_4

to observe, analyze and draw conclusions for further suggest recommendations system improvements. There are also methods based on technology, as e-books or interactive applications. The reading promotion in social media is very accessible and it helps to create a link with new generations.

From the analysis of the data obtained from the National Survey of Reading 2015 we detect the main reasons why people do not read, the main reason is lack of interest, motivation or enjoyment of reading, followed by lack of time, health issues, other activities and finally lack of money among others.

Environment construction is directly linked with digital technology, it becomes a main axis in development which Prensky calls "Digital Natives". Prensky takes this term, since all are born and are formed using video-games, video and web "digital language", all kids are born as digital natives have expectations in new teaching ways by their teachers, so this way can bond their own learning process. In this way is being created a multiple ways, chains, open textually walkthroughs infinite net, described as node, web, plot and path; all this is called hypertext, Theodor Nelson defines it as "A set of text blocks interconnected by links, which form different routes for the user".

This set of interactive and multimedia systems create hypermedia multidirectional communication, is a complex communication system that works censorial expressions development they increase the five senses physiological immersion, as well as psychological attention upon narrative discourse or transmitted message. Interaction should be developed through predefined associations known as hyperlinks, they become multimedia expressive substance relating interface and hyperlinks in an open way.

Content makers, fiction, scientific or informative stories think on a wider spectrum production spreading platforms. This new spectrum is called trans-media.

Actually we can frequently see, books, toys, shirts, comic books, video games, board games, etc., they all are related to a common story, perhaps not directly but always related to the main story. Here is where trans-media and hypermedia storytelling are pertinent, this name has being given to this parallel and sometimes infinite worlds.

Nevertheless, trans-media storytelling matter is based in inter-semiotic translation concept, where a meaning migration is required, it entails an interdisciplinary vision, where meaning migration could be done through many creation ways decision and different ways of seeing the world.

Roman Jakobson points inter-semiotic translation or, transmutation, as a linguistic signs interpretation kind through non linguistic systems. Román Gubern says that every trans-codification is just an optimal semantic equivalence selection taken from an expression different subjects sign set.

This way we can see these expressions in a content interactive shaping, represented in still images, sounds, moving images, etc. Really the story content can be selected, transformed even built in reader-author group, through mind images (or as said "seeing with the mind's eye", "head voices", "sense imagination") almost perceptual images and resembling perceptual experience.

The term "full immersion" determines the entering in a closed environment capability, in this world we can handle objects, even modifying the environment. Is a simulation that allows the experimentation with an alternate reality.

The data of the first "National Survey on Consumption of Digital Media and Reading" (IBBY 2016) helps us to draw conclusions about how much time young people, between 12 and 17, spent in Internet, and the device used for this purpose, where approximately 30% of respondents remain four hours surfing the Internet on weekdays, while at least 25% spends up to three hours on weekends. For which 77% of the population uses smart-phones.

When we mention "first readers" we refer to children in ages from 0 to 10, therefore we include people who can't read words, people in learning process and people who can read in basic levels, they need an adult intervention and their language characteristics are different (Cerrillo 2016). In this stage the children begin reading their surrounding world and with the introduction to the literary world we contribute in building a reading sense, the readers give this sense according to their development context.

We pretend to generate interest in reading, through devices that allow the experience of Immersive reality. The visual motivation complements the text, which by its nature increases the sense of a multisensorial experience. We are developing a prototype of a visual storytelling using Immersive reality for Cardboard, based on the book "El enigma del hoyo en el pantalón" of the publishing house SM, from Barco de Vapor series. We won't tell the full story, we will show the context in which the story unfolds and a clue of the most interesting part of the book. We are creating 3D characters based on the illustrations in the book, the animation of the script and the interaction between the application and users, with the main objective of generate an engagement between first time readers and books.

The rest of the paper is organized as follows. Section 2, Related Work describes recent results of researches in the use of immersive reality. Section 3, Methodology explains our experimental methodology, and Sect. 4, Results presents some resent results. Finally Sect. 5, Conclusions depicts our conclusions and what we are doing nowadays, as well as future work.

2   Related Work

Mexico's city management has different reading promotion programs for its people such as "Libro Club" network, it has activities such as book lending, reading out loud among others; "Subway reading network", this project is held in Mexico city's subway there are reading spaces.

Culture budget grew 4 times since 2000 year in spite of this reading levels have not increased, applied surveys don't consider electronic devices reading, there are not 100% confidence data, Mexico has not numbers for first time readers. There are not background on immersive reality use in reading promotion, nevertheless the amount of available apps is growing fast.

An example of this applications are studies devoted to the distraction of phantom limb pain following limb amputation, in which encouraging results have been reported for the treatment of the condition. In education area a system for teaching surviving abilities in handicap people has been developed, this app teaches them how to act in vulnerability situations. This kind of tools is increasing in numbers and giving encouraging results for a paradigm change in actual technological development.

Some of these studies investigate the effects of Immersive Reality in users; Analysis of brain function during the stimulation process; Qualitative observations of their behavior and reaction when using Immersive Reality (IR) or Virtual Reality (VR) tools; Subsequent observation of behavior, etc., however there is still much to study and know.

Bailey and Bailenson made an experiment and observation series, to determine the link between children mind development and technology use. In those studies they discovered that one of the reasons for this kind of technology being so appealing to children is the control they have over their avatar. Nowadays practically any platform counts on representations of the consumer through an avatar.

As mentioned before, within the on-line environment (mobile apps, web sites, video games, etc.) is very common users represent themselves through avatars, this helps to create a connection between user and system. In movies, the characteristics of a character, personality, history, weaknesses and abilities, create a link between user and story. In the case of children, this bond becomes so strong that most of them develop parasocial relationships with emotional tones with these characters, treating them as faithful and trusting friends (Bond and Calvert 2014).

This kind of interaction is used in TV educative shows, for example: some research has proved that children can learn mathematical concepts when taught by a TV or movie character, if they experienced a previous interaction with a toy of that character (Calvert et al. 2014; Howard et al. 2013).

Parents also play an important role in children interaction with elements of Immersive Reality and Virtual Reality, they are those who authorize or limit the use of this type of devices, in addition to analyze from an objective point of view what the children can use or see. Parents determine the means of communication to which they have access and act as mediators between technology, it's content and children's understanding of the information presented. (Strouse et al. 2013) The mediator role as a parent, in the interaction of their children with Immersive Reality or Virtual Reality sometimes allows a healthier and more useful approach.

It is true that many studies remain to be done, to know the reaction of children towards specific stimulus. For example, controlled learning spaces, where the teacher and the assessment type are specific to personal, mental and cognitive development of each child. But to make it possible, is necessary to follow the tool development in formats like VR, and make the relevant observations, since a market study refers only to the novelty that a new app may result, it cannot allow us to know the real effect in people's life, specifically in children's.

3 Methodology

Our research methodology results from three research lines involved in the project, Information Design, Interaction Systems and Communication Strategies and their own solving problems methods. Our goal is to generate an interdisciplinary solution to this problem.

3.1 Analysis

Our goal in this stage is to define and delimit the problem, research about the state of art and the results obtained in previous work, setting goals and decide our reach, analyze our alliances and look for the aid by experts.

3.2 Solution Architecture

Here we will proof our practical, empiric and technical knowledge. We'll test our problem solution ideas and define the proposal of a technological solution, we also will define our testing and result collection tools. In this stage we make a deep analysis on technological requirements.

Besides we finish legal processes, licensing, authorization, budget (if needed) or any project support process.

3.3 Production and Development

On this stage we will develop our solution final prototype and all activities for info gathering about the solution proposed in our project.

3.4 Release

Here we will publish our app so our users or people interested will be able to experiment it.

Our solution includes the use of operative system iOS and Android mobile devices, so in this stage the app should be released in their respective download sites.

3.5 Evaluation

The stage's goal is to test our solution, and our complementary activities for an integral solution cycle to the research problem.

This stage consists of the following activities:

1. Prototype evaluation.
2. Results gathering in user experience.

4   Results

The project development goes hand in hand with the monitoring and evaluation, in order to drive, learn and document at all times the results that are being obtained. The evaluation is not only done at the end, but also during the project to make adjustments opportunely. In the project we have used both quantitative and qualitative instruments since the Analysis phase, during the development and we will apply them to test our proposal.

The results register follows a logical framework, which is a set of activities and products that focus on the overall objectives of the project, this includes the resources needed, the activities to be carried out, the groups with which the evaluation is carried out and the results.

For the final evaluation will be developed a series of playful activities that allow our users (first readers) to experiment with creating their own device of immersive reality (cardboard). After experimenting with our prototype we will ask them to share the ideas they imagine, no matter when they read the book, we want to know what other stories they imagine after using this technology, to collect these answers we will use a web page.

5   Conclusions

It is a fact that children or as Prensky calls them "Digital Natives" already dominate the majority of the digital media, because they were born with it and they enjoy it. The approach of an hypermedia medium linked to the books is only a proposal to create a bridge back to texts whether printed or digital.

Our recent results and the current research had shown us, that this approach is viable, and it could generate profitable benefits. The next step of the investigation is the experimentation stage, where we are going to test our prototype with kids from 8 to 12 years old. To evaluate this we are considering the use of mechanics where technological and traditional didactic tools through us material to improve the prototype.

The use of immersive reality is booming because mobile applications allow the use of this technology in a fast, easy and economical way, thereby encouraging the growth of this industry, which in turn encourages the development of new apps and new uses in different science fields.

References

Bailey, J., Bailenson, J.: Considering virtual reality in children's lives. J. Child. Media **11**, 103–107 (2017)

Bond, B.J., Calvert, S.L.: A model and measure of US parents' perceptions of young children's parasocial relationships. J. Child. Media **8**, 286–304 (2014)

Calvert, S.L., Richards, M.N., Kent, C.: Personalized interactive characters for toddlers' learning of seriation from a video presentation. J. Appl. Dev. Psychol. **35**, 148–155 (2014)

CERLALC (Centro Regional para el fomento del Libro en América Latina y el Caribe). Comportamiento de Lector y Hábitos de Lectura: una comparación de resultados en algunos países de América Latina (2012)

Cerrillo, P.C.: El lector literario. Fondo de Cultura Económica, México (2016)

El Universal, México lee 3.8 libros al año, indica encuesta del Inegi. En El Universal (2016). Recuperado de: http://www.eluniversal.com.mx/articulo/2016/04/16/mexico-lee-38-libros-al-ano-indica-encuesta-de-inegi

Google Cardboard, En Google Cardboard (2015). Recuperdado de: https://www.google.com/get/cardboard/

Howard, G., Richards, M., Lauricella, A., Calvert, S.L.: Building meaningful parasocial relationships between toddlers and media characters to teach early mathematical skills. Media Psychol. **16**, 390–411 (2013)

IBBY México: (International Board on Books for Young People), Primera Encuesta Nacional sobre Consumo de Medios Digitales y Lectura (2016)

Mora: La interfaz hipermedia, el paradigma de la comunicación interactiva: Modelos para implementar la inmersión juvenil en multimedia interactivos culturales. Datautor, Madrid (2004)

Perales-Blanco, V.: Creatividad y Discursos Hipermedia: Isidro Moreno. Narrativa Hipermedia y Transmedia, España, Editum (2012)

Prensky, M.: Nativos e inmigrantes digitales. Distribuidora SEK (2010)

Strouse, G.A., O'doherty, K., Troseth, G.L.: Effective coviewing: preschoolers' learning from video after a dialogic questioning intervention. Dev. Psychol. **49**, 2368–2382 (2013)

Correcting Distortion of Views into Spherical Tank in Aquarium

Yukio Ishihara[1(✉)] and Makio Ishihara[2]

[1] Shimane University, 1060 Nishikawatsu-cho, Matsue-shi, Shimane 690-8504, Japan
iyukio@ipc.shimane-u.ac.jp
[2] Fukuoka Institute of Technology,
3-30-1 Wajiro-higashi, Higashi-ku, Fukuoka 811-0295, Japan
m-ishihara@fit.ac.jp
http://www.fit.ac.jp/~m-ishihara/Lab/

Abstract. In this study, we discuss a way of correcting the distortion of views that look into spherical tanks. It is widely known that those views are all seen distorted due to light distortion. That is, light rays traveling inside the tank straight towards an observer make a change to their course when passing the boundaries between different media: water, glass and air. Therefore, those rays come away from the observer, which are however necessary for creating the observer's view without distortion. To capture the rays, a camera is placed at specific positions in advance and takes a set of photos. Finally, the observer's view is constructed from those photos.

Keywords: Distortion correction · Spherical tank · Aquarium · Light distortion

1 Introduction

In aquariums, there are various kinds of tanks used to display sea creatures. Those tanks are mainly made of flat and round glass walls. Although the tanks give a lot of views of things such as fish, plants and rocks, it is known that those views are all seen distorted due to light distortion. Technically, this phenomenon stems from light refraction, or the fact that light rays bend as travelling through the boundaries between different media: water, glass of the tank and air. Light distortion more badly affects the views as you get closer to the tank. You may feel dizziness and faintness at the time. Therefore we previously presented a way of correcting the distortion of such views, or constructing views without distortion [1]. A set of photos are taken at specific positions outside the tank and a distortion-free view is constructed from those photos using the image based rendering technique [2]. In that study we focused on simple rectangular tanks while we are focusing on spherical tanks in this study.

There have been various studies dealing with light distortion. Treibitz et al. study a way of measuring underwater objects with accuracy [3]. Photos taken

© Springer International Publishing AG 2017
C. Stephanidis (Ed.): HCII Posters 2017, Part II, CCIS 714, pp. 32–37, 2017.
DOI: 10.1007/978-3-319-58753-0_5

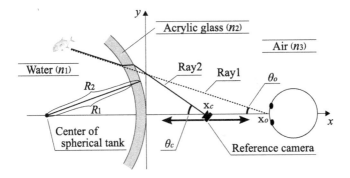

Fig. 1. Our approach to correct the distortion of an observer's view.

by an underwater camera are affected by light distortion in the same way as mentioned above. It leads to inaccuracy of measurement on the photos. To deal with this problem, correspondence from each pixel on the photos to a light ray, called ray-map, is created during the calibration process. The map enables accurate measurement of objects on the photos even though the objects are seen distorted. In contrast, Sedlazeck et al. study a way of creating photo-realistic underwater images by modeling light refraction, light scattering and light attenuation [4]. So far, no studies are found attempting to construct observer's views without distortion. 3D structure estimation of underwater objects studied in [5] could construct those views using the extracted geometric information, but it seems inappropriate to create underwater atmosphere by including drifting dust, ascending air bubbles, tiny creatures and the like. Therefore, in this study, we exploit the image based rendering technique and construct observer's views without distortion.

The rest of this manuscript is organized as follows. In Sect. 2, a basic idea of correcting the distortion of observer's views, which look into a spherical tank, is explained. In Sect. 3, it is shown that the distortion is successfully corrected in a real world environment. Finally, we give concluding remarks in Sect. 4.

2   Correction of Distortion

Figure 1 shows the sectional top view of a spherical tank and illustrates how the distortion of an observer's view is corrected. The observer stands right in front of the straight line Ray1 coming from a fish. Ray2 represents the actual light path. In this situation, the observer does not see the fish in that direction represented by Ray1. Thus, the distortion-free view from the observer needs to be comprised of a set of rays represented by Ray2 rather than Ray1. In order to capture the rays, a camera (hereinafter referred to as a reference camera) is placed at a series of positions and takes photos. Finally, those photos are merged as a single image without distortion.

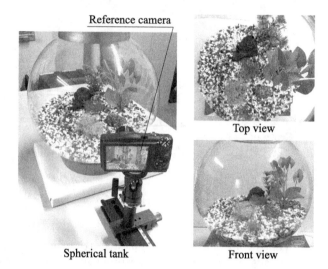

Fig. 2. A spherical tank made of acrylic glass. Note that no water in the tank to see the right positions of the rocks and plants inside. (Color figure online)

To be more specific, let (x_o, θ_o) be the position of the observer and the orientation of Ray1. Let (x_c, θ_c) be the position of the reference camera and the orientation of Ray2. n_1, n_2 and n_3 are refractive indices of water, acrylic glass and air, respectively. R_1 and R_2 are the inside and outside radius of the spherical tank. Given (x_o, θ_o), (x_c, θ_c) is obtained as follows.

$$x_c = (x_o + R_2) \frac{n_1}{n_3} \frac{\sin \theta_o}{\sin \theta_c} - R_2 \tag{1}$$

$$
\begin{aligned}
\theta_c = \theta_o &- \arcsin\left(\frac{x_o + R_2}{R_1} \sin \theta_o\right) \\
&+ \arcsin\left(\frac{n_1}{n_2} \frac{x_o + R_2}{R_1} \sin \theta_o\right) \\
&- \arcsin\left(\frac{n_1}{n_2} \frac{x_o + R_2}{R_2} \sin \theta_o\right) \\
&+ \arcsin\left(\frac{n_1}{n_3} \frac{x_o + R_2}{R_2} \sin \theta_o\right)
\end{aligned}
\tag{2}
$$

Using (1) and (2), each ray represented by (x_o, θ_o) traces back to another ray represented by (x_c, θ_c), thus each pixel on the observer's view can be drawn by picking up the color of the corresponding pixel on the reference camera's view.

In the next section, we confirm that the observer's view is drawn without distortion.

3   Experiment on Correction of Distortion

Figure 2 shows an experimental setup and Fig. 3 shows the sectional top view. The spherical tank is 300 mm in outside diameter and 3 mm in thickness. To find the effect of light distortion easily, it was decorated with gravel, rocks and artificial plants. The observer stood 50 mm to the surface of the tank and looked in 15° off-center. The reference camera was placed at 24 to 35 mm to the tank. It was also angled 40° off-center for 24 to 31 mm and 0° for 32 to 35 mm. At each position one reference camera's view, or one reference photo, was taken, therefore a total of 12 reference photos were obtained.

Figure 4(a) shows a view into the empty tank from the observer's position. Figure 4(b) shows a view at the same position but the tank is filled with water. As expected, the view is distorted compared to (a). Specifically the objects in (b) are skewed towards the right. Figure 4(d) to (f) are three of the 12 reference photos. Note that these photos are all affected by light distortion. Finally as shown in Fig. 4(c), the desired view from the observer was constructed from the reference photos. Enclosed regions in (d), (e) and (f) contributed to the corresponding parts in (c). Thus, (c) is comprised of partial regions of the reference photos.

Finally, it is obviously shown that the distortion found in (b) was successfully corrected in (c), but not totally. Some peripheral part was left gray background. The light gray could be drawn if reference photos at 1 to 23 mm positions were available as well as upward/downward ones. In reality, however, reference photos up to 23 mm positions were unable to be obtained because of no room to place the reference camera closer to the tank. It should also be mentioned that only rightward reference photos were taken and used for simplicity in this experiment. As for the dark gray, none of reference photos was obtained due to total internal reflection. That is, light rays coming from that dark gray region towards the observer cannot penetrate through the acrylic glass, but reflect back inside.

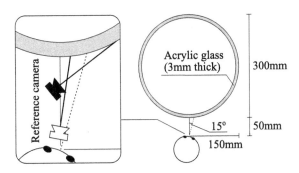

Fig. 3. An experimental setup (sectional top view).

(a) The observer's view when no light distortion affects it or no water is filled with.

(b) The observer's view when water is filled with, in which the objects are skewed towards the right compared to (a).

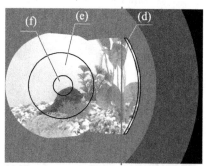

(c) The constructed view from the observer, which is comprised of the reference views represented by (d) to (f).

(d) The reference photo taken by a camera that is placed at 24mm to the tank and angled 40° off-center.

(e) The reference photo taken by a camera at 34mm and 0° off-center.

(f) The reference photo taken by a camera at 35mm and 0° off-center.

Fig. 4. Views from the observer and photos taken by the reference camera in a real world environment. The vertical lines help understand to what extent (b) is distorted, also corrected.

4   Conclusions

In this study, we discussed a way of correcting the distortion of views that look into spherical tanks. It is widely known that those views are all seen distorted due to light distortion. That is, light rays traveling inside the tank directly towards an observer make a change to their course when passing the boundaries between the different media: water, acrylic glass and air. Therefore, those rays come away from the observer. To capture the rays, a reference camera is placed at specific positions and takes photos. Finally, those photos are merged as the observer's view without distortion. We conducted an experiment in a real world environment and confirmed that the observer's view was successfully constructed. However, a peripheral part of the view suffers from total internal reflection, resulting in a blank space.

In future work, we will seek another approach to fill in the blank space by capturing light rays that cannot penetrate through the acrylic glass of the tank due to total internal reflection.

References

1. Ishihara, Y., Ishihara, M.: Correcting distortion of views into aquarium and its accuracy. IEICE Trans. Inf. Syst. **E97.D**(9), 2552–2553 (2014)
2. Gortler, S.J., Grzeszczuk, R., Szeliski, R., Cohen, M.F.: The lumigraph. In: Proceedings of SIGGRAPH 1996, pp. 43–54 (1996)
3. Treibitz, T., Schechner, Y., Kunz, C., Singh, H.: Flat refractive geometry. IEEE Trans. Pattern Anal. Mach. Intell. **34**(1), 51–65 (2012)
4. Sedlazeck, A., Koch, R.: Simulating deep sea underwater images using physical models for light attenuation, scattering, and refraction. In: Proceedings of Vision, Modeling, and Visualization Workshop 2011, pp. 49–56 (2011)
5. Kang, L., Wu, L., Yang, Y.-H.: Two-view underwater structure and motion for cameras under flat refractive interfaces. In: Fitzgibbon, A., Lazebnik, S., Perona, P., Sato, Y., Schmid, C. (eds.) ECCV 2012. LNCS, vol. 7575, pp. 303–316. Springer, Heidelberg (2012). doi:10.1007/978-3-642-33765-9_22

A Study on VR Sickness Prediction of HMD Contents Using Machine Learning Technique

Jae Beom Kim and Changhoon Park[✉]

Department of Game Engineering, Hoseo University, 165 Sechul-ri,
Baebang-myun, Asan, Chungnam 336-795, Korea
rehomik@imrlab.hoseo.edu, chpark@hoseo.edu

Abstract. Recently, the price of HMD for virtual reality has been popularized, and the technology related to virtual reality and the market have been actively growing. But, the popularization of HMD is rapidly increasing, scientific studies on the side effects of HMD and countermeasures for improving the safety are not enough. In this paper, we propose an evaluation model that quantitatively predicts the VR sickness induced by HMD using machine learning technique. This approach will provide an evaluation model for predicting VR sickness caused by contents for HMD objectively and in real time without any additional user experiment. We expect this approach to support the stability and quality improvement of VR content based on HMD.

Keywords: Virtual reality sickness · Head mounted display · Machine learning · Prediction model

1 Introduction

Recent advances in hardware technology have led to the production of consumer appropriate head-mounted displays (HMDs) such as the Oculus Rift, which is theoretically ideal for personal use in immersive virtual reality (VR) applications including gaming, simulation, and film. As the virtual reality is expected to converge with other industries, worldwide sales of HMDs will increase to 39.8 million units by 2018 and the number of users will reach 171 million. Although the popularization of HMD is rapidly increasing, scientific studies on the side effects of HMD and countermeasures for improving the safety are not enough.

Most VE-related sickness definitions describe it as a type of motion sickness. According to Burdea and Coiffet, cyber sickness is a form of motion sickness that results from interaction with or immersion in VEs [1]. visually-induced motion sickness (VIMS) refers to sickness experiences evoked by immersion in computer-generated virtual environments without the use of mechanical simulators. [2–4] Because of the lack of real motion in VIMS, it has been suggested that stimuli-related features such as vection, lag, and image quality are the main contributors to VIMS symptoms [5].

In addition to the direct symptoms just listed, several other phenomena are closely associated with motion and VR sickness, and potentially persist long after usage. One of the most troubling aspects of VR sickness is that symptoms might last for hours or even days after usage [6] (Fig. 1).

© Springer International Publishing AG 2017
C. Stephanidis (Ed.): HCII Posters 2017, Part II, CCIS 714, pp. 38–41, 2017.
DOI: 10.1007/978-3-319-58753-0_6

Fig. 1. (Left) The 'French Revolution 2 VR', which is the first Korean theme park to be worn on HMD in 2016, has opened. This can be an adventure experience by combining VR technology with the thrill of a roller coaster. (Right) Universal Studio Japan introduced XRRide in 2016, which synchronize the speed and the sense of gravity of a theme park ride with astonishing advances in virtual reality that transport you to brand new real world through sight and sound, stimulating the six senses.

2 Problem

HMD provides 360-degree stereoscopic image to the user using head tracking and wide viewing angle display technology, while blocking real-world perception and perception. This maximizes the immersion and realism of the user. But, the problem of VR sickness is expected to be serious. VR sickness is one of the physiological side effects that occur when experiencing a virtual environment, and it shows symptoms like real-life motion sickness such as dizziness, eye fatigue, and nausea. Negative experiences such as VR sickness may lead to aversion learning to the virtual environment and may result in users distancing access to the virtual environment. Therefore, the study on VR sickness is essential for the expansion and quality improvement of virtual reality related business using HMD in the future (Fig. 2).

> Immediately discontinue use if anyone using the Gear VR experiences any of the following symptoms: seizures, loss of awareness, eye strain, eye or muscle twitching, involuntary movements, altered, blurred, or double vision or other visual abnormalities, dizziness, disorientation, impaired balance, impaired hand-eye coordination, excessive sweating, increased salivation, nausea, light-headedness, discomfort or pain in the head or eyes, drowsiness, fatigue, or any symptoms similar to motion sickness.

Fig. 2. Part of "gear VR product use warnings"

In this paper, we propose an evaluation model that quantitatively predicts the VR sickness induced by HMD using machine learning technique. This approach will provide an evaluation model for predicting VR sickness caused by contents for HMD objectively and in real time without any additional user experiment.

3 Main Idea

For this purpose, we will study a model for predicting VR sickness using semi-supervised learning techniques, which is a class of machine learning using both labeled and unlabeled data for training. Typically, a small amount of labeled data with a large amount of unlabeled data. We perceive the relative motion between the camera and the subject as the main characteristic of the VR sickness due to the nature of the HMD that provides the first-person view. In order to extract these features from the image, we introduce optical flow, which is the pattern of apparent motion of objects, surfaces, and edges in a visual scene caused by the relative motion between an observer and a scene.

And, the desired output value for a given input data is classified into five levels according to the degree of comfort. For labeled training data, experiments are performed to measure VR sickness for subjects. That is, the subjects are stimulated by using the same image as the machine learning, and the subjects' reaction are analyzed through subjective self-report and physiological measurement. The basic concept of physiological measurement of VR sickness is that a psychological change causes a physiological change, and a change pattern of a physiological response changes according to a specific psychological state (Fig. 3).

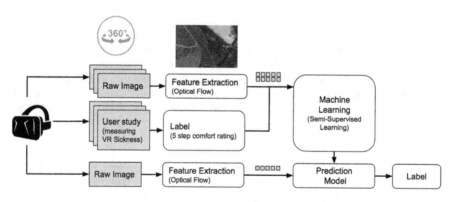

Fig. 3. System overview

4 Implementation

We used NoLimit2 to generate roller coaster content to create stimuli for HMD-based virtual environments. The user wears an HMD and rides on a virtual roller coaster track. At this time, we store the image at the point of view of the user. And we use openCV's optical flow algorithm to extract features from this image. Machine learning is performed using the information extracted from the image and the motion estimation information acquired through the user experiment. At present, the core technology for machine learning has been secured in relation to this research, and systematic experiments will be conducted based on this.

5   Conclusion

The prediction model proposed in this paper will not only quantify the VR sickness caused by the HMD contents without additional user experiments, but also predict in real time. The predicted VR sickness is an objective criterion for users to choose the content suitable for them and will be used as a guideline for developing VR contents to developers. We expect this approach to support the stability and quality improvement of VR content based on HMD.

Acknowledgments. This work was supported by the National Research Foundation of Korea Grant funded by the Korean Government (NRF-2012S1A5A2 A03034747).

References

1. Burdea, G., Coiffet, P.: Virtual Reality Technology. Wiley, Hoboken (2003)
2. Regan, E.C., Price, K.R.: The frequency of occurrence and severity of side-effects of immersion virtual reality. Aviat. Space Environ. Med. **65**, 527–530 (1994)
3. Ellis, S.R.: Nature and origins of virtual environments: a bibliographic essay. Comput. Syst. Eng. **2**, 321–347 (1991)
4. Howarth, P.A., Hodder, S.G.: Characteristics of habituation to motion in a virtual environment. Displays **29**, 117–123 (2008)
5. Stanney, K.M., Mourant, R.R., Kennedy, R.S.: Human factors issues in virtual environments: a review of the literature. Presence: Teleoperators Virtual Environ. **7**, 327–351 (1998)
6. Stanney, K.M., Kennedy, R.S.: Aftereffects from virtual environment exposure: how long do they last? In: Proceedings of the Human Factors and Ergonomics Society Annual Meeting, vol. 48, no. 2, pp. 1476–1480 (1998)

Physically-Based Clay Art Rendering with HMD VR

Donghwe Lee, Hyunmin Choi, and Seongah Chin[✉]

Division of Media Software, XICOM LAB,
Sungkyul University, Anyang City, South Korea
{ehdgn13546, chyw000}@naver.com,
solideo@sungkyul.ac.kr
http://xicomlab.re.kr

Abstract. In this paper, we propose an efficient physically-based rendering method for clary art materials. To do this, we develop an efficient method to calculate the optical parameters of some clay materials using only spectrophotometer and algorithmic approach without going through optical parameter extraction process accompanied with HDRI physical measurement process. It also provides a VR environment that can be experienced using HMD VR to add user's interest and interaction. In order to verify this study, we compared and evaluated our results with the HDRI sampling, and the BRDF methods.

Keywords: Optical parameters · Physically-based rendering · Clay art · VR

1 Introduction

Physically-based rendering (PBR) is basically a lighting technique that simulates a photo-realistic scene with high fidelity for a computer game, virtual reality, cinematic view, and design applications. More concretely, a scene is composed of a set of pixels with color values that can be determined by combination of quite complicated procedures such as a location of light, material property, smoothness of surface, and a location of viewer etc. To accomplish PBR, material rendering parameters have to be measured in real [1]. In usual, a task for extracting optical parameters basically require critical processes including taking of High Dynamic Range Image (HDRI) and extracting optical parameters. Each clay material has its own material-rendering properties such as scattering, absorption, Fresnel and roughness etc.

In addition, virtual reality (VR) has been gradually highlighted recently in lots of applications like an educational content, entertainment areas and various games. PBR plays a significant role in boosting immersion in VR, in which PBR helps a user to feel more realistic while running applications.

To our knowledge, no literature has been found that deals with PBR and clay art rendering. Hence, in this paper, authors propose an efficient physically-based clay art rendering scheme that reduces the execution time of acquiring optical parameters. To this end, we actually measure only a clay color using spectrophotometer and compute optical parameters without going through acquiring a raw HDRI and a sampling process that seems to be daunting tasks because it is likely a time-consuming process [2, 3].

© Springer International Publishing AG 2017
C. Stephanidis (Ed.): HCII Posters 2017, Part II, CCIS 714, pp. 42–47, 2017.
DOI: 10.1007/978-3-319-58753-0_7

Finally, we synthesize a few virtual clay models that are rendered by our physically-based approach. Also, we have carried out the comparisons of experiments to validate the method.

2   Method

2.1   Clay Materials

There are various kinds of clay used in clay art depending on the composition and properties. The mud clay, which is composed of basic particles, is highly viscous and flexible, and can be deformed by various models. Paper clay is made of clay material with paper fiber added. The initial color is white and color can be painted. Color clay has very high viscosity between clays. Cork clay is composed of materials using bark, not clay, and has similar texture to wood.

In addition, ball clay is composed of styrofoam particles and is painted with colors. Icing clay is a very low viscosity material and is suitable for expressing soft parts such as cream. The shape of the individual clay is shown in Fig. 1.

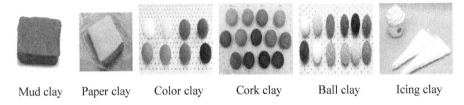

Mud clay   Paper clay   Color clay   Cork clay   Ball clay   Icing clay

Fig. 1. Clay classification (Color figure online)

2.2   Optical Parameters Computation

In order to create a photo-realistic synthetic image, we must actually observe and reflect the interaction of light with the physical properties of the material that constitutes the object when the light is illuminated by the material. The light and interaction are different depending on the materials such as opaque material, translucent material, transparent material, perfect reflector, and complete absorber. PBR is a technique to calculate the color value of a pixel observed in our eyes at the end of the rasterization process. At this time, there are objects constituting a scene, and each object is made of a material. The input values of PBR include light position, normal vector of surface, optical parameter (Fresnel, scattering coefficient, absorption coefficient) which represents physical characteristic of material. The input value is used to calculate the color value of the pixel finally observed in the user's field of view. Generally, PBR performs rendering using optical parameters of objects.

In order to extract the optical parameters, several Low Dynamic Range Images (LDRI) are photographed using a spectrophotometer and optical imaging equipment, which is a customized camera, and a single HDRI is created by sampling, and optical parameters are calculated by curve-fitting. However, this method requires a complicated process and a lot of calculation time. Thus, we need to find a way to efficiently calculate optical parameters.

The following Eq. (1) is the formula to calculate the intrinsic color of an object using extracted optical parameters [4].

$$
\begin{aligned}
R_d &= (1 - F_{dr,t})(\int_0^d (1 - \sigma_a x)^2 dx + F_{dr,b}\left(1 - \sigma_a d - \sigma_s' P(g)d\right)^2) \\
&= (1 - F_{dr,t})\left(\sigma_s' P(g)(d - \sigma_a d^2 + \frac{1}{3}\sigma_a^2 d^3) + F_{dr,b}\left(1 - \sigma_a d - \sigma_s' P(g)d\right)^2\right)
\end{aligned}
\tag{1}
$$

where σ_a and σ_s' are the absorption and reduced scattering coefficients of the material respectively. $P(g)$ is the integration of the phase function for backward scatter, and d is the depth. $F_{dr,t}$ represents the diffuse Fresnel reflectance at the upper boundary. $F_{dr,b}$ represents the diffuse Fresnel reflectance at the lower boundary.

We transform the Eq. (1) into the Eq. (2) in terms of σ_a, the absorption coefficient and σ_s', the reduced scattering coefficient.

$$
\alpha \sigma_s'^2 + \beta \sigma_s' + \gamma \sigma_s' \sigma_a + \delta \sigma_a = \varepsilon,
\tag{2}
$$

where

$$
\begin{aligned}
\alpha &= d^2 P(g)^2 F_{dr,b}, \\
\beta &= P(g)d(1 - 2F_{dr,b}), \\
\gamma &= P(g)d(2F_{dr,b} - d + \frac{1}{3}\sigma_a d^2), \\
\delta &= F_{dr,b}d(-2 + \sigma_a d), \quad \varepsilon = \frac{R_d}{(1 - F_{dr,t})} - F_{dr,b}
\end{aligned}
$$

We can use the spectrophotometer to measure the value of the material's unique color, $R(d)$. In this case, $F_{dr,t}$ and $F_{dr,b}$ can be obtained by using the formula derived from $R(d)$. The value of $R(d)$ in Eq. (2) is known from the spectrophotometer, $F_{dr,t}$ and $F_{dr,b}$ can also be derived. $P(g)$ and d are also known variables. Therefore, σ_a and σ_s' can be obtained by using a minimum mean square error (MMSE) estimator.

Table 1. Reduced scattering coefficient σ_s' and absorption coefficient σ_a

Method	Clay	σ_s'			σ_a		
		Red	Green	Blue	Red	Green	Blue
Sampling	Clay1	0.7650	0.7290	0.7230	0.0001	0.0001	0.0003
	Clay2	0.7620	0.7300	0.7180	0.0921	0.1222	0.0291
	Clay3	1.2130	1.0910	1.1060	0.0059	0.2441	0.1746
	Clay4	0.7730	0.7290	0.7340	0.0743	0.0086	0.1347
Ours	Clay1	0.7640	0.7280	0.7230	0.0001	0.0001	0.0002
	Clay2	0.7620	0.7300	0.7180	0.0920	0.1222	0.0291
	Clay3	1.2130	1.0910	1.1060	0.0059	0.2441	0.1746
	Clay4	0.7720	0.7280	0.7340	0.0743	0.0086	0.1347

Table 1 below shows the optical parameters extracted by directly shooting and sampling the HDRI and the optical parameters obtained by the proposed method. As shown in Table 1, we carried out experiments on four clay materials. Optical parameters from the sampling method were obtained through a curve-fitting of samples on HDRI. We discover that the numerical values of the optical parameters between the sampling method and our method do not seem differentiable.

3   Experiments

The following environment was set up to evaluate the proposed method. A desktop computer installed with Windows 10 64-bit and a GeForce GTX 1060 as graphics card was used. An Oculus Rift DK2 model was used for the VR HMD. Unity 5.4.1f. and shader code was used to implement rendering results while C# was used to compute optical parameters and to develop user interface and HMD VR facilities shown in Fig. 2.

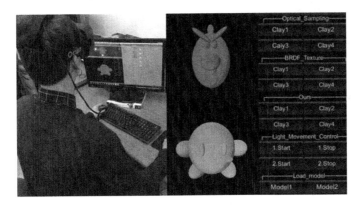

Fig. 2. Clay rendering interface with HMD VR

3.1   Comparisons of the Rendering Results

To validate our method, we have carried out the comparative rendering experiments that show BRDF (Bidirectional Reflectance Distribution Function), the sampling and our methods. Four clay materials were tested to obtain optical parameters. For BRDF rendering [6], four texture images were acquired from taking photos of four clays. And the rendering equation [4] with optical parameters as input values shown in Table 1 was employed to synthesize PBR character models. Our findings are both the sampling and ours are quite similar while BRDF rendering results are less resemble as shown in Table 2.

Table 2. The comparisons of rendering results from BRDF, sampling and ours

Clay	Texture	BRDF	Sampling	Ours
Clay1				
Clay2				
Clay3				
Clay4				

3.2 Analysis of the Execution Time for Optical Parameter Calculation

An optimization strategy was investigated in Ref. [2] by showing that four LDRIs was good enough to create one HDRI to sample and extract optical parameters. Exposure Fusion [5] algorithm was used to build a HDRI on which a focusing light point was found. The radius from the center to the boundary was 5 mm with 20 pixels/mm, of which total samples was 300 samples (RGB). Given the sample points, a curve-fitting algorithm was computed to acquire optical parameters.

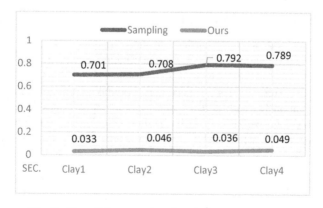

Fig. 3. Plot of the execution time between two methods

The proposed method as mentioned before is not necessarily going through some daunting processes such as taking LDRI and a sampling procedure to obtain optical parameters.

As shown in Fig. 3, the execution time to compute optical parameters is found about 0.040 s on average while the sampling method take 0.748 s on average that does not even include some tasks for taking LDRIs and merging them into HDRI. In short, this indication represents the proposed method enhances technical merits for PBR without losing high fidelity rendering results as well.

4 Conclusion

In the previous research, the preprocessing process, which is a daunting task, is indispensable to measure optical properties of materials and extract optical parameters from acquired HDRI. This preprocessing process must take the steps of HDRI imaging, sampling, and optical parameter extraction. Therefore, in this study, we proposed an efficient method to calculate the optical parameters of an object using spectrophotometer and algorithm without going through optical parameter extraction process accompanied with physical measurement process. In order to add the interest and immersion of the user, we provided a HMD VR facility to experience clay art rendering as well.

Acknowledgements. This research was partially funded by National Research Foundation, NRF (No. 2015R1D1A1A01057725).

References

1. Iglesias-Guitian, J.A., Aliaga, C., Jarabo, A., Gutierrez, D.: A biophysically-based model of the optical properties of skin aging. In: Computer Graphics Forum, vol. 34, pp. 45–55 (2015). Proceedings of Eurographics 2015
2. Lee, W., Chin, S.: Optimal model of optical parameter extraction for material rendering. Imaging Sci. J. **64**, 131–139 (2016)
3. Shenoy, M.R., Pal, B.P.: Method to determine the optical properties of turbid media. Appl. Opt. **47**, 3216–3220 (2008)
4. Choi, T., Lee, S., Chin, S.: Method of combining spectrophotometer and optical imaging equipment to extract optical parameters for material rendering. J. Sens. **2014**, 8 p. (2014). Article ID 803710
5. Mertens, T., Kautz, J., Reeth, F.V.: Exposure fusion: a simple and practical alternative to high dynamic range photography. Comput. Graph. Forum **28**, 161–171 (2009)
6. Walter, B.: Notes on the Ward BRDF. Technical report PCG-05-06 Cornell Program of Computer Graphics (2005)

Feasibility of Integrated GNSS/OBD-II/IMU as a Prerequisite for Virtual Reality

J.H. Lim, K.H. Choi, W. Yoo, L. Kim, Y. Lee,
and Hyung Keun Lee[✉]

Korea Aerospace University, Goyang City, Republic of Korea
hyknlee@kau.ac.kr

Abstract. To build accurate GIS (Geographical Information System) in urban area for advance virtual reality, accurate positioning is one of most important prerequisites. For this purpose, GNSS (Global Navigation Satellite System) is attractive since it can provide absolute coordinates to any object located on earth. However, accurate positioning is not a simple problem since any single GNSS cannot provide sufficient the number of visible satellites in urban area. To improve positioning availability in urban area for advanced virtual reality applications, this paper proposes a hybrid positioning method integrating a GPS/BeiDou receiver, an OBD-II (On-Board Diagnostics-II) device, and a MEMS IMU (Micro Electro Mechanical Systems-Inertial Measurement Unit). By an experiment result with field-collected actual measurements, the feasibility of the proposed method is evaluated.

Keywords: GIS · Virtual reality · Positioning · Urban · GNSS · OBD · IMU

1 Introduction

To build accurate GIS (Geographical Information System) in urban area for advance virtual reality, accurate positioning is one of most important prerequisites. For this purpose, GNSS (Global Navigation Satellite System) is attractive since it can provide absolute coordinates to any object located on earth. However, accurate positioning is not a simple problem since any single GNSS cannot provide sufficient the number of visible satellites in urban area.

To improve the positioning availability in urban area, more GNSS constellations need to be utilized. Undoubtedly, more constellations we use, better availability can be obtained. In addition, improved accuracy, integrity, and continuity can also be obtained.

As widely known, no matter how many constellations we use, shortage of visible satellites is unavoidable due to the limitation of radio signals depending on signal paths. To overcome this limitation, GNSS should be integrated with other aiding sensors.

To improve positioning availability in urban area for advanced virtual reality applications, this paper proposes an efficient hybrid positioning method integrating a GPS/BeiDou receiver, an OBD-II (On-Board Diagnostics-II) device, and a MEMS IMU (Micro Electro Mechanical Systems-Inertial Measurement Unit).

© Springer International Publishing AG 2017
C. Stephanidis (Ed.): HCII Posters 2017, Part II, CCIS 714, pp. 48–53, 2017.
DOI: 10.1007/978-3-319-58753-0_8

In the proposed method, only the two constellations of GPS and BeiDou are considered since three constellations are far more expensive than the two constellations for common users for the time being with no significant improvement in urban area. By the simple OBD-II interface unit, moving speed can be obtained conveniently. By the MEMS IMU, attitude information can be continuously tracked.

2 Integrated GNSS/OBD-II/IMU

2.1 Embedded Linux Platform

This study utilizes a BBB (Beagle Bone Black) board [1, 2] to collect GNSS, MEMS-IMU, and OBD-II measurements with time synchronization information. Figure 1 shows the configuration of the proposed system integration utilizing the BBB board. It can support Linux and Android operating systems.

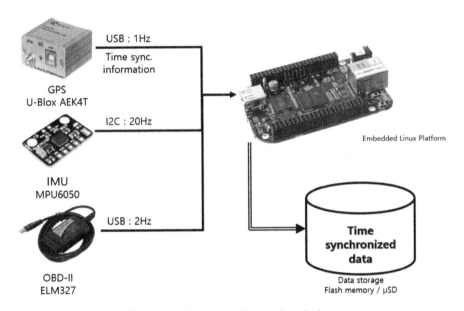

Fig. 1. Configuration of integration platform

The GNSS receiver and the OBD-II unit are connected via USB. The IMU is connected via GPIO-pin. To merge all the sensor measurements, the PPS (Pulse Per Second) information from the GNSS receiver is utilized. At first, the time synchronization information is derived from the PPS information. Next, it is utilized for different sampling rates of the three sensors. The sampling rates of the GNSS receiver, the OBD-II device and the MEMS-IMU are 1 Hz, 2 Hz and 20 Hz, respectively. In this way, the proposed method can collect the time synchronized measurements from the three different sensors.

2.2 OBD-II

OBD-II is the standard to diagnose all types of land vehicles [3, 4]. The OBD-II specification provides unified hardware interface to the vehicles from difference manufacturers. By OBD-II, state of vehicle can be checked by MIL (Malfunction indicator Lamp). OBD-II provides messages classified by PIDs (Parameter IDs). PIDs consists of 6 modes. Among them, mode 1 provides vehicle information including fuel system status, engine RPM (Revolution Per Minute), and vehicle speed. Typically, a user can obtain the messages with a scan tool. The procedure is summarized by the following steps.

(1) A user enters the PID.
(2) The PID is fed to the vehicle's controller–area network (CAN) bus through a scan tool.
(3) A device on the CAN bus recognizes the PID and returns the response to the PID.
(4) The scan tool reads the response message and displays it to the user.

2.3 Integration

The proposed method consists of four functional parts. The first part processes GPS/BeiDou measurements and extracts GPS PPS (Pulse Per Second) signal for the time synchronization, the second part collects MEMS IMU measurements, the third part extracts the speed of a vehicle by OBD-II, and the last part merges all the outputs from the former three parts based on the time synchronization information.

To integrate GNSS, OBD-II, and IMU, a loose-coupled Kalman filter is designed. The designed Kalman filter consists of 15 states to account for position errors, velocity errors, attitude errors, gyro drifts, and accelerometer biases. The filter is based on the conventional dynamics model [5, 6] for time propagations. For measurements updates, only the two types of measurements are considered. One is the position information combining GPS and BeiDou and the other is the OBD velocity. To generate position measurement, an iterated least square method is utilized considering five variables; three receiver coordinate values, a GPS clock bias, and a BeiDou clock bias. The OBD velocity measurement is modeled to consider the effects of attitude errors for the transformation from the body frame to the navigation frame.

3 Experiment

To evaluate the feasibility of the proposed method, an experiment was performed in the area where surrounding buildings form urban canyons. The experiment was performed in Teheran-ro, Gangnam-gu, Seoul, Korea. Figure 2 shows typical appearance of the experiment area. Figure 3 shows the experiment trajectory plotted by *Google Earth*.

For the experiment, three sensors were utilized; a Novatel ProPak6 as the single frequency GNSS receiver, an MPU-6050 as the MEMS-IMU, an ELM327 as the OBD-II device and a BBB board as the embedded Linux platform.

Fig. 2. Typical appearance of the experiment area

Fig. 3. Experiment trajectory

Figure 4 compares the two trajectories generated by the two different methods, respectively. The triangles correspond to the GNSS-alone method and the circles correspond to the proposed GNSS/MEMS-IMU/OBD-II integration method. By comparing the two trajectories, it can be observed that the proposed method provides more continuous and available positioning results against the urban canyon environment. Note that the proposed method compensates IMU velocity with OBD-II speed measurements even when GNSS measurements are not available. Whereas, the GNSS-only method shows unavailable periods where positioning results cannot be provided due to insufficient number of visible satellites.

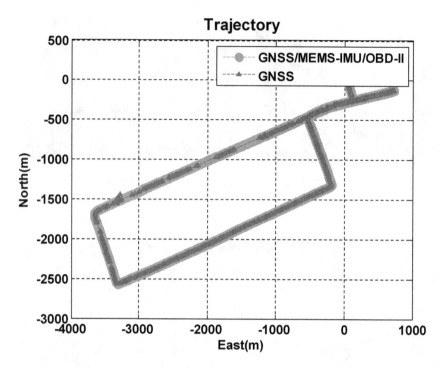

Fig. 4. Comparison of trajectories generated by the proposed method and the GNSS-only method

4   Conclusions

This paper proposed a GNSS/MEMS-IMU/OBD-II integration method against GPS-denied environments to build accurate vector maps for advance virtual reality. Since the propagation of accurate position requires accurate velocity, the proposed method utilized OBD-II speed to correct the velocity continuously. By the result, the accuracy degradation of the velocity could be mitigated even when GPS measurements were not available.

To evaluate the feasibility of the proposed integration method, an experiment was performed in the area where surrounding buildings form deep urban canyons. By the experiment result, it was shown that the proposed method is feasible to provide more accurate and reliable positioning results. However, more experiments are required to obtain meaningful performance statistics.

Acknowledgements. This research was supported by Basic Science Research Program through the National Research Foundation of Korea (NRF) funded by Ministry of Education, Science and Technology (NRF-2016R1D1A1B01009881).

References

1. http://www.probotix.com/wiki/index.php/BeagleBone
2. http://beagleboard.org/BLACK
3. Lin, J., Chen, S.C., Shih, Y.T., Chen, S.H.: A study on remote on-line diagnostic system for vehicles by integrating the technology of OBD, GPS, and 3G. World Acad. Sci. Eng. Technol. **56**, 435–441 (2009)
4. https://en.wikipedia.org/wiki/OBD-II_PIDs
5. Lee, H.K., Lee, J.G., Roh, Y.K., Park, C.G.: Modeling quaternion errors in SDINS: computer frame approach. IEEE Tr. Aerosp. Electron. Syst. **34**(1), 289–300 (1998)
6. Kim, S.B., Bazin, J.C., Lee, H.K., Choi, K.H., Park, S.Y.: Ground vehicle navigation in harsh urban conditions by integrating inertial navigation system, global positioning system, odometer and vision data. IET Radar Sonar Navig. **5**(8), 814–823 (2011)

Presence and Usability Do Not Directly Predict Procedural Recall in Virtual Reality Training

Bradford L. Schroeder[1]([⊠]), Shannon K.T. Bailey[2],
Cheryl I. Johnson[2], and Emily Gonzalez-Holland[1]

[1] StraCon Services Group, LLC, Orlando, FL, USA
{bradford.schroeder.ctr,
emily.gonzalezhollan.ctr}@navy.mil
[2] Naval Air Warfare Center Training Systems Division, Orlando, FL, USA
{shannon.bailey,cheryl.i.johnson}@navy.mil

Abstract. The goal of this experiment was to compare the effectiveness of training a procedural task in two simulated environments (desktop and virtual reality [VR]) and to examine the impact of different interaction methods in VR (gesture-based and voice-based). Traditional desktop-based computer simulations may create learning environments different from VR systems due to differences in task presentation (i.e., 2D versus 3D) and interaction method (i.e., clicking a mouse versus physically moving), which may influence presence and usability. Previous theoretical work purports that simulations that are more immersive, such as VR, should foster a sense of presence and lead to higher learning outcomes (see Witmer and Singer 1998), but these claims remain largely untested. Therefore, we compared two VR conditions and a desktop training condition to determine and examine the influence of presence and usability on recall. Seventy-five college students learned how to replace an alternator in one of three training conditions. Following the training, participants completed a presence questionnaire, usability questionnaire, and written recall test to assess how well they learned the procedure. We found no significant differences among the groups on presence, usability, or recall performance. Furthermore, we found no relationship between presence and recall, but a moderated mediation analysis indicated that usability predicted recall, but only for those receiving low immersion (i.e., desktop) training. That is, for desktop training, those who rated usability lower recalled fewer procedural steps. Contrary to theory, our results suggest that presence is not predictive of learning outcomes in more immersive simulations.

Keywords: Maintenance training · Human-Computer interaction · Procedural knowledge · Presence · Usability · Virtual reality

---

Disclaimer: The views expressed herein are those of the authors, and do not necessarily reflect the official position of the Department of Defense or any of its components.

© Springer International Publishing AG 2017
C. Stephanidis (Ed.): HCII Posters 2017, Part II, CCIS 714, pp. 54–61, 2017.
DOI: 10.1007/978-3-319-58753-0_9

1   Introduction

Early work on Virtual Reality (VR) speculated that the high-fidelity immersive environments generated by VR systems can foster a sense of "presence," such that users feel as though they are physically present in the virtual environment (VE) [1, 2]. At the time, it was generally assumed that a sense of presence would be an unconditional boon to learning [2–5], though later studies found evidence that presence is not particularly predictive of conceptual knowledge acquisition [6], procedural knowledge acquisition [7], or spatial knowledge acquisition [8]. Others have indicated that presence contributed to improvements in learning, cognitive task performance, or therapeutic outcomes [9]. Importantly, previous work has highlighted that presence and usability factors may be interrelated, such that one's sense of control over a VE may foster a sense of presence [2, 10, 11]. It is also possible that one's sense of control (i.e., usability or level of interactivity) over a VE may first require presence to be fostered [12, 13]. Before the relationship between presence and performance can be accurately understood, it is critical to disentangle usability factors from presence.

Thus, the goal of this experiment was to determine the extent to which presence influences learning in VR environments. To address this, we compared the effectiveness of training a maintenance procedure in both 2D desktop and 3D VR environments to observe whether greater presence was perceived in more immersive systems and to observe the effect of presence on recall and training. We also examined the impact of different interaction methods in VR (gesture- vs. voice-based interaction), as well as perceptions of usability to investigate what factors may influence perceptions of presence. Based on the literature that predicts more immersive environments (e.g., 3D vs. 2D environment) will lead to increased perceived presence and positive effects on learning, we predicted that people experiencing the VR conditions would recall more on a procedural task than participants trained in the desktop environment. Additionally, we predicted that more natural system interaction, such as gesture-based versus voice-based interaction, would also lead to increased presence and subsequent learning.

2   Methodology

2.1   Equipment

Testbed. The Unity 3D game engine was used to develop both desktop and VR trainers for this study, which trained participants how to complete a procedural maintenance task on a virtual shore-based E-28 arresting gear. An arresting gear is a machine that stops an aircraft at the end of a short runway or aircraft carrier. In the present study, participants performed a procedure to remove and replace a virtual alternator on the arresting gear, which also served as the training task for this experiment (Fig. 1). Participants learned the maintenance task using either a desktop-based trainer with a mouse, keyboard, and monitor, or a VR-based trainer using a Microsoft Kinect V2 motion tracker and Oculus Rift DK2 Head-Mounted Display (HMD). Conditions were identical except for the method of user interaction.

Fig. 1. E-28 arresting gear alternator from the maintenance training task

Interaction. There were three conditions that differed based on method of computer interaction: a desktop-based training group (desktop), a VR-based training with gesture group (gesture), or a VR-based training without gesture group (voice). In the desktop group, participants used a mouse and keyboard to interact with the environment, which was displayed on a computer monitor. In both VR groups, participants viewed the VE through the Oculus HMD. Participants were able to move around in the VE by walking and they could interact with virtual objects using their right hand. We utilized Kinect's body, head, and gesture motion-tracking capabilities to enable participants to interact with the VE. In the gesture group, participants were trained during a tutorial and practice session to use five gesture-based actions to interact with the system (Table 1).

Table 1. List of gestures, actions, and descriptions for interacting with the system

Action	Gesture
Select	Hover hand to highlight object and close fist
Open	Raise arm up, make a 90° angle at the elbow
Close	Drop arm down past hip
Remove	Move arm from chest out to the side, keep arm parallel to ground
Replace	Bring arm to outside of the shoulder and keep elbow in, close to chest

Note. Voice group spoke actions aloud; Desktop group clicked a mouse for all actions.

In the voice group, participants were trained by completing a tutorial and practice session to use the same five actions as voice commands to interact with the system. Although the testbed could recognize gestures, it was not technologically feasible to develop an accurate voice recognition system. Thus, the researcher manually triggered participants' voiced actions on a computer system linked to the HMD. In every condition, the researcher monitored the experiment on a linked computer to ensure smooth system operation. For the VR conditions, we calibrated the VE for every person's height, such that the same visual scene was displayed for all participants.

2.2   Participants

Seventy-five students from a large southeastern United States university participated in this study (55% female, M_{age} = 21.4 years, SD_{age} = 3.6 years). Students received $15 an hour for up to three hours of participation. Participants were assigned randomly to one of three conditions: VR training with gesture (n = 25), VR training without gesture (n = 25), or desktop training (n = 25).

2.3   Materials

A subset of the materials administered during the experiment is included in this section and the following analyses. Additional measures were collected that are outside the scope of the current research question, such as demographic questions.

Mental Effort Rating Scale. After each training scenario, participants were asked to indicate their level of mental effort on the task they just performed on a scale of 1 ("Low") to 9 ("High") [14].

Presence Questionnaire (PQ). The PQ (α = .76) [15] is a 19-item measure that assesses participants' experience within the VE on four subscales: involvement (α = .85), sensory fidelity (α = .73), adaptation/immersion (α = .60), and interface quality (α = .50). Participants responded on a scale of 1 ("Not at All") to 7 ("Completely") to each item.

System Usability Scale (SUS). The SUS (α = . 69) [16] has 10 items with statements relating to usability rated on a scale of 1 ("Strongly disagree") to 5 ("Strongly agree").

Recall Measure. Participants were asked to list the steps for the maintenance procedure, including tools and parts where appropriate, within five minutes.

2.4   Procedure

Participants were recruited through an online research participation system. After participants consented, they completed a demographic questionnaire. Participants then read a PowerPoint tutorial that familiarized them with the VE and the interaction method for their condition. In the tutorial, all participants received general information about the task environment, interface, and the E-28 arresting gear. The tutorial also provided different instructions for the interaction method depending on which condition was randomly assigned (gesture, voice, or desktop). Once participants completed the tutorial, their understanding of the tutorial content was assessed and any questions about the task and interaction instructions were clarified.

Next, participants in the desktop condition were seated at the computer and instructed to complete the practice phase in the experimental testbed. Participants in the gesture and voice conditions practiced the five gesture or voice commands, respectively. Participants in the VR conditions were then directed to a mark on the floor and were told how to adjust the HMD, and the researcher calibrated the VE. In the practice phase (i.e., replacing an engine cage), participants were told they would receive narrated instructions with relevant arresting gear parts highlighted in green to guide them. For example, to remove the exhaust pipe, participants would first hear a verbal narration to equip the pipe wrench tool, and then the exhaust pipe was highlighted in green to direct the participant to the part requiring interaction. Depending on the assigned group, participants interacted by clicking a mouse, speaking voice commands, or enacting gestures to select the appropriate tool and then perform the "remove" action. Throughout the practice phase, participants were permitted to ask questions about interacting with the task, but questions were not permitted during subsequent scenarios.

Participants completed three training phases involving the task of replacing the alternator. The training scenarios provided scaffolding (e.g., narration and highlighting part location) that was reduced in each subsequent scenario. The first training scenario provided participants with narrated instructions and green highlights to guide them. In the second training scenario, only narrated instructions were provided. In the final recall scenario, neither narrated instructions nor green highlights were provided, such that participants were required to perform the maintenance task without guidance. At the end of each scenario, participants were asked to rate their level of mental effort on the scenario. Following the training scenarios, participants were asked to complete several measures, a subset of which included the PQ, SUS, and a five minute free recall measure of the procedural steps in replacing the alternator. Participants were debriefed upon conclusion of the study.

3 Results

Prior to examining the relationship among presence, usability, mental effort, and procedural recall performance, we examined preliminary group differences and correlations among our variables. We performed several one-way ANOVAs to examine the differences among groups (gesture, voice, desktop) for presence, usability, mental effort, and recall performance, but there were no significant group differences for any of these variables (all $ps > .50$). However, bivariate correlation analyses revealed that usability was positively related to performance ($r = .29, p = .01$), and mental effort was negatively related to performance ($r = -.40, p < .001$). Presence was not related to performance ($r = -.01, p = .96$), but it was correlated with usability ($r = .60, p < .001$).

Because several of our variables of interest were significantly related to performance, and due to the potential confounding nature of presence and usability (as indicated by their high correlation with one another), we conducted a more comprehensive post-hoc analysis to examine the simultaneous effects of these variables on procedural recall performance for each condition. We tested a moderated mediation model where presence score was the predictor variable, usability was the mediating variable, condition (gesture, voice, or desktop) was the moderating variable, and recall performance was the outcome variable. Usability mediated the relationship between presence and performance, and condition moderated the relationship between usability and performance. Additionally, participants' subjective ratings of mental effort were included as a control variable (see Fig. 2 for a conceptual diagram of this model). It should be noted that we tested this same model with usability as the predictor and presence as the mediator, but it was not significant.

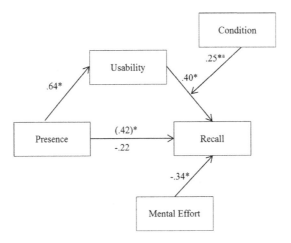

Fig. 2. Conceptual diagram for moderated mediation model predicting procedural recall performance. Standardized regression coefficient (β) values are provided on each line; estimated indirect effect is provided in parentheses. [a]β value for condition by usability interaction. *$p < .05$

The overall model was significant, $(F[5, 69] = 6.89, p < .001, R^2 = .33$; see Table 2), accounting for 33% of the variance in procedural recall performance, with usability and the interaction between usability and condition as significant positive predictors, and mental effort as a significant negative predictor (such that lower subjective mental effort corresponded to greater recall performance). The direct effect of presence on performance was not statistically significant ($p = .09$), but the indirect effect of presence on performance through usability was statistically significant for only the desktop condition ($\beta = 0.41$, 95% CI = 0.21, 0.68; index of moderated mediation = 0.16; 95% CI = 0.06, 0.27). Specifically, any benefit to recall that could have been conferred by presence was better explained through usability, but only for the desktop condition. Although presence and usability were highly correlated, participants in the desktop condition who reported poor usability recalled the fewest procedural steps, regardless of their feelings of presence.

Table 2. Standardized regression coefficients predicting recall performance.

	β	t	95% CI (β)	
			LL	UL
Usability	0.40**	3.11	0.14	0.66
Presence	−0.22	−1.70	−0.48	0.04
Condition	−0.13	−1.32	−0.33	0.07
Usability*Condition	0.25*	2.87	0.08	0.43
Mental effort	−0.34**	−3.31	−0.55	−0.13

Note. **$p < .01$, *$p < .05$. CI = Confidence Interval, LL = Lower Level, UL = Upper Level. Condition was dummy coded in the regression model.

4 Discussion

Examining the group-level statistics, it is of note that there were no differences among any of our variables – particularly presence. Theory would suggest that our most immersive condition (i.e., gesture-based VR) should have fostered a significantly greater sense of presence than our desktop condition, but our analyses indicated that presence was equivalent across conditions. Usability was highly related to presence in our analyses, but was stronger than presence in predicting recall performance. The moderated mediation model indicated that the presence and usability questionnaires may be assessing the same cognitive mechanism that relates to performance; however, usability appears to measure it more accurately. Although the overall reliability of the PQ was acceptable, the reliability scores of two subscales was unsatisfactory. It is possible that some aspects of the PQ may not accurately assess sub-constructs of presence. In short, we contend that any claims of learning or training benefits due to presence may actually be better explained by usability.

5 Conclusion

Contrary to theory, our results suggest that presence is not predictive of learning outcomes in more immersive simulations. We recommend that developers and researchers consider prioritizing usability before fostering immersion in simulation-based training, as presence may not be the underlying cognitive mechanism by which simulation-based training is effective. Although the current study used gestures that were representative of real-world interactions, system limitations required the gestures to be gross and discrete, instead of fluid, natural gestures. Future researchers may want to consider investigating the role of other design features which may influence recall, such as interactivity (e.g., natural gestures) or sensory feedback (e.g., haptic feedback).

References

1. Regian, J.W., Shebilske, W.L., Monk, J.M.: Virtual reality: an instructional medium for visual-spatial tasks. J. Commun. **42**, 136–149 (1992). doi:10.1111/j.1460-2466.1992. tb00815.x
2. Sheridan, T.B.: Musings on telepresence and virtual presence. Presence-Teleop. Virt. **1**, 120–126 (1992). doi:10.1162/pres.1992.1.1.120
3. Krueger, M.: Artificial Reality II. Addison-Wesley, Reading (1991)
4. Lombard, M., Ditton, T.: At the heart of it all: the concept of presence. J. Comput.-Mediat. Commun. **3**(2) (1997). doi:10.1111/j.1083-6101.1997.tb00072.x
5. Rheingold, H.: Virtual Reality. Summit Books, New York (1991)
6. Moreno, R., Mayer, R.E.: Learning science in virtual reality multimedia environments: role of methods and media. J. Educ. Psychol. **94**, 598 (2002). doi:10.1037/0022-0663.94.3.598
7. Bliss, J.P., Tidwell, P.D., Guest, M.A.: The effectiveness of virtual reality for administering spatial navigation training to firefighters. Presence-Teleop. Virt. **6**, 73–86 (1997). doi:10. 1162/pres.1997.6.1.73

8. Singer, M.J., Allen, R.C., McDonald, D.P., Gildea, J.P.: Terrain appreciation in virtual environments: spatial knowledge acquisition. Technical report No. 1056, ARI. U.S. Army Research Institute for the Behavioral and Social Sciences, Alexandria, VA (1997)

9. Schuemie, M.J., Van Der Straaten, P., Krijn, M., Van Der Mast, C.A.: Research on presence in virtual reality: a survey. CyberPsychol. Behav. **4**, 183–201 (2001). doi:10.1089/109493101300117884

10. Held, R.M., Durlach, N.I.: Telepresence. Presence-Teleop. Virt. **1**, 109–112 (1992). doi:10.1162/pres.1992.1.1.109

11. Witmer, B.G., Singer, M.J.: Measuring presence in virtual environments: a presence questionnaire. Presence **7**, 225–240 (1998). doi:10.1162/105474698565686

12. Riva, G.: From virtual to real body: virtual reality as embodied technology. J. Cyber Ther. Rehabil. **1**, 7–22 (2008). doi:10.3389/fpsyg.2016.01839

13. Riva, G., Mantovani, F.: From the body to the tools and back: a general framework for presence in mediated interactions. Interact. Comput. **24**(4), 203–210 (2012). doi:10.1016/j.intcom.2012.04.007

14. Paas, F., van Merriënboer, J.J.G., Adam, J.J.: Measurement of cognitive load in instructional research. Percept. Mot. Skill. **79**, 419–430 (1994). doi:10.2466/pms.1994.79.1.419

15. Witmer, B.G., Jerome, C.J., Singer, M.J.: The factor structure of the presence questionnaire. Presence-Teleop. Virt. **14**, 298–312 (2005). doi:10.1162/105474605323384654

16. Brooke, J.: SUS: a "quick and dirty" usability scale. In: Jordan, P.W., Thomas, B., Weerdmeester, B.A., McClelland, I.L. (eds.) Usability Evaluation in Industry, pp. 189–194. Taylor & Francis, London (1996)

Webizing Interactive CAD Review System Using Super Multiview Autostereoscopic Displays

Daeil Seo[1], Yongjae Lee[1,2], and Byounghyun Yoo[1,3(✉)]

[1] Center for Imaging Media Research,
Korea Institute of Science and Technology, Seoul, South Korea
xdesktop@kist.re.kr, 11109342@seoultech.ac.kr,
yoo@byoo.net
[2] Department of Computer Science and Engineering,
Seoul National University of Science and Technology, Seoul, South Korea
[3] Department of HCI and Robotics, University of Science and Technology,
Daejeon, South Korea

Abstract. A glasses-free super multi-view display has emerged alongside the development of optical technologies. However, the display is not yet widely used because its content remains in the early stages of only image or video without user interaction. Expanding the display market would require content that can take advantage of the display. In this paper, we propose a webized interactive CAD review system that uses super multi-view autostereoscopic displays with an application facilitating the popularization of super multi-view displays. The content for the display is described by web technologies such as HTML5, CSS, and JavaScript. The proposed system renders the content through a web browser and handles user interactions via JavaScript. A user can view autostereoscopic images with a sense of depth through motion parallax using the display and control the content remotely using gesture interaction devices. We present an example of content using a prototype implementation to verify our approach's usefulness.

Keywords: CAD · Super multiview display · Remote interaction · Webizing

1 Introduction

As CAD applications such as Onshape [1] and Tinkercad [2], run on the web, CAD designers can design and review modeled products through a web browser without specific software. CAD designers use a two-dimensional display for the design process. However, there is a difference between a CAD model and an actual product, because it is difficult to express the depth information of a 3D CAD model via a 2D display. Although designing a 3D CAD model on a 2D display is less intuitive, CAD designers are accustomed to viewing 3D product designs with spatial information such as width, height, and depth using 2D displays. However, CAD reviewers who do not have empirical knowledge experience difficulties when examining the model design and making important decisions using 3D-projected CAD model with 2D displays.

© Springer International Publishing AG 2017
C. Stephanidis (Ed.): HCII Posters 2017, Part II, CCIS 714, pp. 62–67, 2017.
DOI: 10.1007/978-3-319-58753-0_10

Various types of stereoscopic 3D display such as 3DTVs, autostereoscopic multi-view displays, and autostereoscopic super multi-view (SMV) displays have emerged [3]. People can view 3D content on autostereoscopic displays without a wearable device; however, these displays are not widely used because the amount of content available for them is currently small and they mostly use images or videos without user interaction. Facilitating the use of autostereoscopic displays will require content that can take full advantage of the medium. Seo et al. [4] proposed a webizing SMV content rendering method that renders 3D content according to various types of SMV display profile on the web to create an emergent 3D content ecosystem. However, their method focuses on rendering content without various types of user interaction. In this paper, we propose a webized interactive CAD review system using SMV autostereoscopic displays that provides an immersive CAD model review environment. The content for the display is described by web technologies such as HTML5, CSS, and JavaScript, and the proposed method supports hand gestures-based user interaction for the SMV display environment. The proposed system renders the content on a web browser and handles user interaction using JavaScript.

2   Our Method

We design a system architecture for an interactive CAD review system on the web, as shown in Fig. 1. The webized content renderer is implemented based on the webized SMV content rendering system [4] and the CAD review web application has two user interfaces: the webized 3D annotation editor and the webized SMV CAD viewer. The CAD designer uses the webized editor to add a text, image, or video annotation to a CAD model. The CAD reviewer uses the CAD viewer to check or review the CAD models with various annotations.

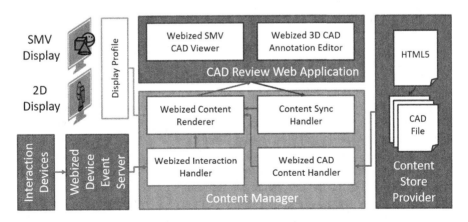

Fig. 1. Overview of the architecture

The CAD files are stored in the content store provider and linked in HTML documents that have various types of annotations for the CAD files. The content manager loads the CAD files and HTML documents, and the webized content renderer renders a final scene based on the display profile that describes characteristics of the SMV or 2D displays.

To support user interaction, the proposed system webizes interaction events according to the webized interaction method [5]. The user interaction events are synchronized between the webized 3D annotation editor and the webized SMV CAD viewer in real-time. The proposed system provides two types of interaction: mouse/keyboard and hand gesture interaction, according to the display type as shown in Table 1. We chose four basic interactions from TC184 Visualization Requirements [6]: selection (requirement 5), zooming (requirement 7), camera rotation (requirement 8), and transformation (requirement 16).

Table 1. User interaction for the CAD review system based on the TC184 requirements [6]

		Selection (TC184 Req. 5)	Zooming (TC184 Req. 7)	Camera Rotation (TC184 Req. 8)	Transformation (TC184 Req. 16)
User Interaction	2D Display				
		Left click	Wheel up/down	Drag	Drag axis helper
	SMV Display				
		Point	Swipe	Move with two fingers	Swipe while pointing

A user selects a 3D object in 2D display mode by clicking the left button of the mouse on the 3D object. When the user points a 3D object using a finger in SMV display mode, the 3D object is selected. The user can zoom in and out to change the scale of the CAD scene by scrolling up and down with the mouse wheel in 2D display mode or swiping a hand from left to right or from right to left in SMV display mode. The user can also rotate the camera viewing perspective by dragging the mouse with a left click in 2D display mode or move their hand with two fingers in SMV display mode. Moving a 3D model first requires a preceding selection interaction. In 2D display mode, the system shows an axis helper and the user drags the axis helper along the x-, y-, or z-axis to move the selected object. In SMV display mode, the system highlights the selected object and the user swipes their hand to a new position while pointing at the object.

3   Experimental Results

We present an example scenario of a prototype implementation to verify our approach's usefulness, as shown in Fig. 2. In this scenario, the CAD designer on the left side uses the webized 3D CAD annotation editor with a mouse device on the 2D display. The CAD reviewer on the right side checks the CAD model using a webized SMV CAD viewer with hand gestures for the SMV display. The system uses the leap motion controller to recognize hand gestures. When the reviewer has an idea and and suggestion with which to improve the model, the CAD designer adds an annotation to the model using the CAD annotation editor. The designer can use all resources on the web for annotations, and although the CAD designer and reviewer are located together in this experiment, they can be located remotely. They discuss and comment on the CAD model and add their opinions via annotations. The annotation editor and CAD viewer in the proposed system synchronize 3D models, their annotations, and the camera viewing perspective and position in real-time when the designer or reviewer changes the CAD scene via user interactions.

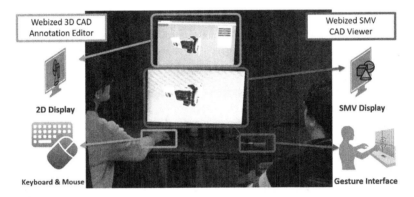

Fig. 2. Prototype implementation of the proposed system

Figure 3 depicts examples of the annotation editor on the 2D display. The annotation editor shows CAD models and their annotations in the middle of the scene. The menu bar is located at the top right-hand corner of the editor to add, remove, and update CAD models and their annotations. The annotation editor loads an initial engine CAD model, as shown in Fig. 3(a). The "Model tree" menu bar shows a list of the CAD models and their annotations in the CAD scene. The CAD designer can select an "Add assembly" button on the "Tools" menu bar to add a propeller CAD model, as shown in Fig. 3(b), the CAD designer can add an annotation for the propeller assembly by clicking the "Add comment" button, at which point the editor shows a WYSIWYG HTML editor, as shown in Fig. 3(c). After an annotation is added, it is attached to the scene. The CAD designer can toggle the visible status of all annotations by clicking the "Show/Hide annotations" button at the top left-hand corner of the editor. The user interaction events change the scene of the annotation editor, and the webized SMV CAD viewer also synchronizes interaction events in real-time.

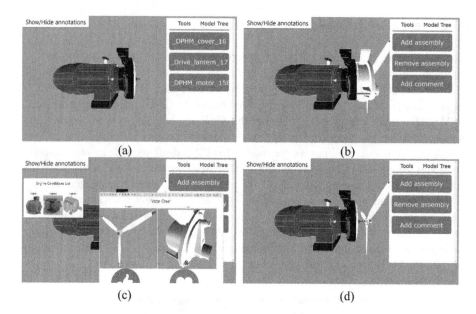

Fig. 3. Examples of the webized 3D CAD annotation editor: (a) loads an engine CAD model, (b) adds a propeller assembly CAD model, (c) adds an annotation for the propeller assembly, and (d) hides all annotations.

The CAD reviewer views an autostereoscopic image with a sense of depth through motion parallax using the SMV CAD viewer on a SMV display and changes the position, rotation, and scale of the content via hand gesture interactions, as shown in Fig. 4. The reviewer can watch different rendering results for the 3D CAD models and their annotations seamlessly in the viewing zone using the motion parallax of the SMV display. Thus, the CAD reviewer, a non-CAD expert without experience in CAD applications, can intuitively understand the CAD model through the SMV display using motion parallax.

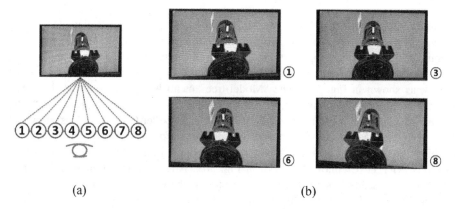

Fig. 4. Review examples using the webized SMV CAD viewer by moving viewpoints: (a) the movement trajectory of the CAD reviewer and (b) reviewer's views at each position.

4 Conclusion

In this paper, we have proposed a webized interactive CAD review system that uses SMV autostereoscopic displays to provide an immersive review environment through motion parallax. The proposed system uses all resources on the web for annotations, and it supports suitable hand-gesture-based interaction methods for SMV autostereo-scopic displays at a long viewing distances. As a result, non-CAD experts can intu-itively understand 3D CAD models. In the future, we will conduct a user study to evaluate our proposed system.

Acknowledgments. This work was supported in part by the Korea Institute of Science and Technology (KIST) Institutional Program (Project No. 2E27190) and 'The Cross-Ministry Giga KOREA Project' Grant from the Ministry of Science, ICT and Future Planning, Korea.

References

1. Onshape: Onshape (2012). http://www.onshape.com. Accessed 20 Mar 2017
2. Autodesk: Tinkercad (2011). http://www.tinkercad.com. Accessed 20 Mar 2017
3. Urey, H., Chellappan, K.V., Erden, E., Surman, P.: State of the art in stereoscopic and autostereoscopic displays. Proc. IEEE **99**, 540–555 (2011)
4. Seo, D., Yoo, B., Choi, J., Ko, H.: Webizing 3D contents for super multiview autostereoscopic displays with varying display profiles. In: International Conference on Web3D Technology, pp. 155–163. ACM, Anaheim (2016)
5. Seo, D., Kim, D., Yoo, B., Ko, H.: Webizing human interface devices for virtual reality. In: ACM Conference on Virtual Reality Software and Technology, pp. 367–368. ACM, Munich (2016)
6. ISO/TC184: TC184 Visualization Requirements for X3D CAD (2009). http://www.web3d.org/wiki/index.php/TC184_Visualization_Requirements_for_X3D_CAD. Accessed 20 Mar 2017

Webizing Virtual Reality-Based Interactive Interior Design System

Daeil Seo[1], Jongho Lee[1,2], and Byounghyun Yoo[1,3(✉)]

[1] Center for Imaging Media Research, Korea Institute of Science
and Technology, Seoul, South Korea
xdesktop@kist.re.kr, ow0707@seoultech.ac.kr,
yoo@byoo.net
[2] Department of Computer Science and Engineering, Seoul National University
of Science and Technology, Seoul, South Korea
[3] Department of HCI and Robotics, University of Science and Technology,
Daejeon, South Korea

Abstract. The virtual reality (VR)-based interior design systems have the
advantage of cost reductions and can support multiple users without spatial or
temporal constraints. Recently, various head-mounted display (HMD) applications for VR using smartphones have become popular, and WebVR technology
has been introduced to implement VR applications on the web. However,
WebVR is still its early stages for use in the development of VR applications.
Interaction methods for WebVR are limited compared to traditional VR
development environments. In this paper, we propose an interactive VR system
for interior design based on web technologies with a system that supports 3D
and VR views with various interaction methods on the web.

Keywords: Virtual reality · HMD · Webizing · Interior design · Multimodal
interaction

1 Introduction

Web technologies have recently become widely used because they take advantage of
cost reductions and the ability to support multiple users without space or time constraints. Interior design systems that use web technologies have emerged; Floorplan [1]
is a web-based indoor interior design system that provides a 2D floor plan and 3D
modeling results based on the 2D floor plan. Valkov et al. [2] implemented an
immersive virtual reality (VR) space using a projector on the screen, and de Guimarães
et al. [3] proposed a method to leverage web technology on mobile devices to arrange
furniture. Recently, various head-mounted display (HMD) applications for VR that use
smartphones have become popular, and WebVR [4] technology has been introduced to
implement VR applications on the web. However, WebVR is still the early stage and
interaction methods for WebVR are limited compared to traditional VR development
environments. We propose an interactive VR system for interior design based on web
technologies with a system that supports 3D and VR views via various interaction

© Springer International Publishing AG 2017
C. Stephanidis (Ed.): HCII Posters 2017, Part II, CCIS 714, pp. 68–72, 2017.
DOI: 10.1007/978-3-319-58753-0_11

methods. The interaction devices are webized and connected to the system to handle interaction events through a web browser.

2 Our Method

We have designed a system architecture as shown in Fig. 1. The proposed system provides a 3D view to determine an interior layout and the stereoscopic VR view to look around the interior immersively. The content manager provides web content such as HTML documents, multimedia contents, and 3D model data to the webized content renderer on the web browser. The system deals with users' interaction events based on the webized interaction method for human interface devices and events [5]. The webized interaction method provides a device-independent interface between VR applications and physical peripherals, and the interaction method uses an event negotiation mechanism to provide different abstraction types of user interaction events. When a user triggers an event using interaction devices, the webized device event server generates a message for the event and sends the event message to the webized device event library, which is written in JavaScript. The communication handler sends the user's events to other users and receives events from other users. The webized content renderer then applies its own events and other's events on the content. The renderer visualizes a final rendering result according to the rendering mode.

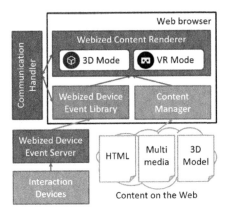

Fig. 1. Overview of the architecture

We define gesture-based user interaction events as shown in Table 1 to interact with the content in a HMD VR environment. In the VR view, a user uses hand gesture interactions to select menu items and place 3D furniture models, and the user can walk around the designed space using foot gesture interactions. The user can also clench and open his/her hand to open a menu. When the user touches a menu item with any finger, the item is selected. Pinch and drag interactions allow a user to move furniture around. The user can navigate the designed space by moving his/her center of gravity, which is carried out changing his/her foot position.

Table 1. User gestures and interaction events in HMD VR environment

	Hand gesture			Foot gesture
User gesture				
	Clench and open	Touch	Pinch and drag	Press
Event	Open a menu	Select an item	Move furniture	Navigate the space

3 Experimental Results

We present an example of an interior design using a prototype implementation to verify the usefulness of our approach. Figure 2 shows a 3D view of an example scenario through a desktop environment. In this scenario, a bride designs an interior of her marital house and shares this with the bridegroom. She uses a mouse to declare a virtual interior design space by moving boundary points on the 2D floor plan view as shown in Fig. 2(a) and selects a menu to arrange interior furniture models using the top view as shown in Fig. 2(b). When she chooses the 3D front view to view the immersive interior design, the system changes its view, as shown in Fig. 2(c). She can change the position of furniture in the interior space. She can share the designed space with the bridegroom by clicking on the e-mail button on the menu, as shown in Fig. 2(d), and the system then sends an e-mail to the bridegroom.

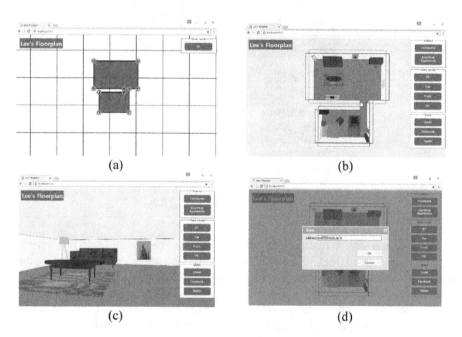

Fig. 2. Prototype examples of the desktop environment: (a) the 2D floor plan view, (b) the 3D top view, (c) the 3D front view, and (d) sharing the floor plan with others via e-mail.

To view the shared interior design as shown in Fig. 2(d), the bridegroom reads the e-mail from his bride and clicks on a link within it to view the interior design using a HMD VR environment. The prototype system uses the leap motion controller to recognize hand gestures and the Wii balance board to collect pressure position input according to foot gestures, as shown in Fig. 2(a). When he wears a HMD VR device on his head, he can see the interior design and his virtual hand to interact with the design, as shown in Fig. 3(b).

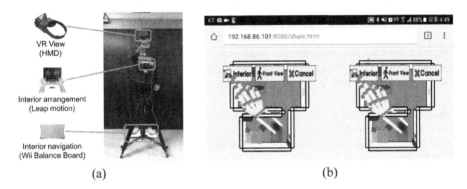

(a)   (b)

Fig. 3. Overview of HMD VR environment: (a) interaction devices for hand and foot gestures and (b) a screenshot of the VR interior design content with a hand gesture.

The bridegroom navigates the interior design with foot gestures and changes the space by hand gestures, as shown in Fig. 4. He can call up a menu widget and touch a button to place additional furniture, as shown in Fig. 4(a). He can touch an item on the list to choose furniture, as shown in Fig. 4(b). He can arrange selected furniture in the

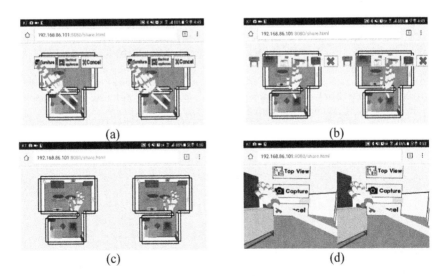

(a)   (b)

(c)   (d)

Fig. 4. Prototype implementation of the proposed system in a HMD VR environment

interior space, as shown in Fig. 4(c). After such the arrangement, he can change to a front view to navigate the designed space, as shown in Fig. 4(d).

4 Conclusion

In this paper, we proposed an interactive VR system for interior design based on web technologies. The proposed system provides 3D and immersive VR views with various types of interaction event through hand and foot gestures on the web. Web developers can use the proposed system to create VR applications easily and share applications by delivering a URL such as by sharing a webpage over a social network or instant messaging without any bothersome processes. In the future, we will conduct user studies to evaluate our proposed system, and we will then support real-time content and view synchronization to create collaborative work.

Acknowledgments. This work was supported in part by the National Research Council of Science & Technology (NST) grant by the Korea government (MSIP) (No. CMP-16-01-KIST) and the Korea Institute of Science and Technology (KIST) Institutional Program (Project No. 2E27190).

References

1. Floorplanner: Floorplanner (2007). https://www.floorplanner.com. Accessed 5 Dec 2016
2. Valkov, D., Steinicke, F., Bruder, G., Hinrichs, K.H.: Traveling in 3D virtual environments with foot gestures and a multi-touch enabled WIM. In: Virtual Reality International Conference, pp. 171–180, Laval, France (2010)
3. de Guimarães, M.P., Gnecco, B.B., Stephanin, A., Teubl, F.: Virtual home decoration in web and mobile platforms. In: Murgante, B., Misra, S., Rocha, Ana Maria A.C., Torre, C., Rocha, J.G., Falcão, M.I., Taniar, D., Apduhan, Bernady O., Gervasi, O. (eds.) ICCSA 2014. LNCS, vol. 8579, pp. 796–807. Springer, Cham (2014). doi:10.1007/978-3-319-09144-0_55
4. Vukicevic, V., Jones, B., Gilbert, K., Wiemeersch, C.V.: WebVR. World Wide Web Consortium (2016)
5. Seo, D., Kim, D., Yoo, B., Ko, H.: Webizing human interface devices for virtual reality. In: Proceedings of the 22nd ACM Conference on Virtual Reality Software and Technology, pp. 369–371. ACM, Munich, Germany (2016)

Error Monitoring and Correction Related to the Sense of Presence in Virtual Environments

Boris B. Velichkovsky$^{(\boxtimes)}$, Alexey N. Gusev, Alexander E. Kremlev,
and Sergey S. Grigorovich

Moscow State University, Moscow, Russia
velitchk@mail.ru

Abstract. Error monitoring and correction system in humans is responsible for the resolution of errors and conflicts in cognitive activity. As virtual reality conflicts with reality per definition, error monitoring and correction may be involved in the emergence of the sense of presence. Here we show that error monitoring and correction is indeed related to various aspects of presence. Specifically, it was shown that effective error monitoring and correction is able to counteract the emergence of negative somatic effects during virtual reality exposure. It is also related to higher perceived naturalness of a virtual scenario, possible due to better suppression of contradictions in the virtual scenario. However, it was shown that better error monitoring and correction may be related to less presence due to a more critical evaluation of virtual environments at least for low-immersion settings. Implications of these findings for user selection procedures and design of virtual environments are discussed.

Keywords: Virtual reality · Presence · Cognitive control · Error monitoring and correction · Anterior cingulate cortex

1 Introduction

The sense of presence is an important aspect of interaction with virtual environments. It refers to the subjective illusion of the "realness" of virtual reality [1, 2]. Achieving a high level of presence is an important goal in the development of virtual reality applications as it may promote the effectiveness of user interaction in virtual environments. Presence is a multidimensional construct determined by a host of factors [3]. Quite obviously, presence is strongly influenced by technological factors like frame rate and immersion level. However, presence is a psychological phenomenon and today's research focus shifts to the study of the psychological determinants of presence [4]. These includes demographic, cognitive and personality variables. In this study, we assess the influence of error monitoring and correction functions on the sense of presence in virtual environments.

Error monitoring and correction is a subsystem within human cognitive control [5]. Cognitive control is a set of meta-cognitive process responsible for the tuning of specialized cognitive processes towards achieving a specific goal in a given context [6].

© Springer International Publishing AG 2017
C. Stephanidis (Ed.): HCII Posters 2017, Part II, CCIS 714, pp. 73–80, 2017.
DOI: 10.1007/978-3-319-58753-0_12

Within cognitive control, error monitoring and correction is responsible for the detection of conflicts and for the subsequent re-configuration of cognitive processes with the aim of reducing the conflict. A conflict is conceptualized as the deviation of the expected cognitive activity from the actual cognitive activity. In the famous Stroop paradigm, conflict is produced in incongruent trials when the font color does not match the meaning of the color word. In this case, the error monitoring subsystem detects the conflict and activates cognitive control system which inhibits the inappropriate response and reduces conflict. An error (faulty actions) is a form of conflict as it clearly implies a difference between the expected and the observed. Errors are therefore detected and corrected by the same system which is employed for the control of conflicts [5].

Error monitoring and correction may be involved in the emergence of presence as virtual reality exposure clearly has strong conflict generating potential. Virtual reality is based on an illusion and presents the user with artificially constructed perceptual inputs which substitute for the "real" reality. Simulator sickness observed in many cases is an obvious consequence of the conflict between the virtual sensory input and the sensory-motoric expectancies of the users habituated to the real environment. On a more abstract level, error monitoring signals to the user that the virtual environment is not real even if the perceptual evidence strongly advocates for the contrary. Thus, error monitoring and correction is an important component in the process of presence formation. This study aims to research the relationship between error monitoring and correction and subjective feeling of presence. To this end, we assess error monitoring and correction functions in a sample of VR users and their feeling of presence during interaction with a virtual environment.

2 Error Monitoring and Correction

Error (conflict) monitoring and correction is a subsystem within cognitive control – a set of meta-cognitive processes responsible for the fine-tuning of regular cognitive processes aimed at achieving of specific goals in a given context [6]. The error monitoring and correction subsystem is responsible for the detection of errors committed by the human and for the subsequent reorganization of regular cognitive processes in order to increase the quality of cognitive activity [5]). Neuroscientific data clearly associates error monitoring and correction with a part of medial frontal cortex – the anterior cingulate cortex (ACC). This brain structure is thought to be responsible for the detection of conflicts – the difference between the expected and the observed – with errors being a particularly strong special case of conflict. According to the dominating "control loop" hypothesis [5, 7], error monitoring in the ACC detects conflicts and errors and activates prefrontal cortex associated with cognitive control which in turn modulates the workings of regular cognitive processes.

2.1 Post-error Slowing

The workings of error monitoring and correction is reflected in two behavioral effects: post-error slowing and conflict adaptation. Post-error slowing [8] refers to the increase of reaction time in the correct probe which follows an erroneous probe. This increase in reaction time may be quite substantial (30–50% of average reaction time) and it dissipates gradually over several subsequent probes. This increase in the reaction time is usually interpreted as reflecting the intervention of the error monitoring and correction system as a reaction to the perceived error. This interpretation is supported by the observation that post-error slowing is reduced via the increase of the inter-trial interval. Thus, the size of post-error slowing reflects the efficiency of error monitoring and – more importantly – error correction.

2.2   Conflict Adaptation

Conflict adaptation is another behavioral effect of error monitoring and correction. Conflict adaptation refers to the decrease of conflict interference in incongruent probes if the previous probe also was an incongruent one [9]. This effect means that if the error (conflict) monitoring and resolution system was already activated for the resolution of the conflict in the previous probe, it may more efficiently resolve the conflict in the current probe. Conflict adaptation is observed in several cognitive tasks where the performance in conflict inducing incongruent probes is contrasted with the performance in no-conflict congruent probes. On the whole, conflict adaptation is interpreted as indicative of strategically operating conflict resolution associated with the workings of error monitoring and correction subsystem of cognitive control.

Below, we study how error monitoring and correction is related to the sense of presence by correlating aspects of presence with indices of post-error slowing computed for an error-inducing task (the letter-digit switching task) and conflict adaptation computed for a conflict-inducing cognitive task (the Eriksen flanker task).

3   Method

3.1   Subjects

39 students of Moscow State University, 20 females, aged 18–23, participated in the study in exchange for a course credit.

3.2   Virtual Scenario

Subjects had to explore a virtual space (20 × 20 m) and to traverse a series of randomly placed digits in correct numerical order. The presentation medium was either a full-immersion CAVE system or a standard 19-inch computer display. The CAVE system has four large flat screens (Barco ISpace 4), which were connected into one cube consisting of three walls and a floor. The length of each screen side was about 2.5 × 2.2 m. Shutter eye glasses were made by Volfoni. Projection system was based on BarcoReality 909. The projector's matrix resolution was 1280 × 1024 with 100 Hz update frequency. Tracking system produced by ArtTrack2, include Flystick, Finger-tracking, Motion Capture. Graphic Cluster for 5 PC was based Quadro FX 5800. 3Dvia

Virtools was used for software developing. There was a training session (with digits from 1 to 5) and two experimental session (with digits from 1 to 9). The total exposure to the virtual scenario was about 10 min.

3.3   Presence Inventory

Aspects of presence were assessed via a Russian version of the ITC-SOPI inventory. ITC-SOPI is a cross-media presence inventory with four dimensions. These are Spatial Presence, Naturalness of Virtual Scenario, Emotional Involvement, and Negative Effects [3].

3.4   Post-error Slowing

Post error slowing was computed for a demanding cognitive task involving task switching (the letter-digit task). The task involved the random presentation of a letter-digit pair with the task being either an odd/even judgement task or a vowel/consonant judgement task. The task was specified by a color cue aligned with stimulus onset. The subjects had thus to switch between tasks on approximately the half of the trials. Post-error slowing was computed individually as the ratio between average RT on correct trials following an incorrect trial to average RT in correct trials following a correct trial. Higher values of this variable are indicative of effective error monitoring and correction.

3.5   Conflict Adaptation

Conflict adaptation was computed for a conflict inducing selective attention task (the Eriksen flanker task). The task required the subjects to identify the direction of an arrow surrounded by four arrows (two arrows on each side). The flanker arrows could be either congruent or incongruent to the central arrow but should in any case be ignored by the subject. Conflict adaptation was computed as the ratio of average RT in incongruent trials following a congruent trial to average RT in incongruent trials following an incongruent trial. Lower values of this variable are indicative of effective conflict monitoring and resolution.

3.6   Procedure

The subjects first performed the cognitive tasks within a computerized battery in a group session. Virtual scenario was presented individually with the order of CAVE and display presentations counterbalanced across participants. After the presentation of the virtual scenario in each medium, the subjects completed the presence inventory.

4   Results

Pearson correlation coefficients were computed between poste-error slowing and conflict adaptation and dimensions of presence for both presentation mediums (Table 1).

Table 1. Correlations between aspects of presence and error monitoring/correction indices in a full-immersion (CAVE) and a low-immersion (display) environments (PSE – post-error slowing, CA – conflict adaptation, SP – spatial presence, EI – emotional involvement, NVS – naturalness of the virtual scenario, NE – negative effects). Significant (p < 0.05) correlations in bold.

| | Presence | | | |
	SP	EI	NVS	NE
Full-immersion				
PSE	0.055	0.094	0.176	−0.295
CA	0.038	−0.145	−0.278	0.126
Low-immersion				
PSE	−0.163	−0.374	−0.047	−0.381
CA	0.036	0.095	−0.285	0.078

For the full-immersion CAVE environment two significant correlations were found. First, post-error slowing was significantly inversely related to negative somatic effects. This indicates that efficient error monitoring and correction leads to less experience of negative vestibular symptoms which may arise as a consequence of exposure to virtual reality. A result like this has a simple explanation as negative effects arise from sensory-motor errors during virtual exposure and effective error correction may be an obvious remedy for this. Second, conflict adaptation was significantly and inversely related to perceived virtual scenario naturalness. This indicates that more effective conflict resolution is related to more scenario naturalness. Such a result may be related to the fact that scenario naturalness may be compromised by scenario's inconsistencies and violations of user's expectations which are conflict-inducing experiences. Effective conflict suppression my counteract this, leading to more presence.

For the low-immersion display environment three significant correlations were observed. Post-error slowing was inversely related to negative effects, and conflict adaptation was inversely related to virtual scenario naturalness. These results are exact replicas of that obtained for the high-immersions CAVE environment indicating a sufficient generalizability of the positive relationship between presence and efficient error monitoring and correction. Additionally, post-error slowing is inversely related to emotional involvement. This means less presence with effective error monitoring and correction indicating that it may have different effects on the sense of presence at least in low-immersion environments. Specifically, effective error monitoring is related to a stronger critical stance towards virtual scenario which may undermine the illusion of "realness" and prevent emotionally comforting interaction with the virtual environment.

5   Discussion

This study was aimed at exploring the role of error (conflict) monitoring and correction meta-cognitive system in the emergence of the sense of presence during exposure to a virtual environment. It was found that error monitoring and correction is indeed related to the subjective sense of presence.

First, post-error slowing was inversely related to the emergence of negative somatic effects which reflect sensory-motor discoordination typical of virtual environments. Effects like nausea emerge in virtual environment because visual input is to some extent misaligned with proprioceptive input. This clearly produces a sort of error, and it is not surprising that effective error correction (as indicated by post-error slowing) may be involved in effectively combating this error. Effective error control is thus a remedy for negative effects produced by virtual environment. The absence of negative effects promotes presence by inducing more subjective comfort and preventing negative symptoms from distracting attention from the interaction with the virtual environment. Thus, effective error monitoring and correction has the potential to increase presence. This effect was found both in high- and low-immersion environments which suggest generality of this result.

Second, conflict adaptation was consistently found to be related to virtual scenario naturalness in both high- and low-immersion scenarios. The naturalness factor of the ITC-SOPI refers to the extent to which the virtual scenario is understandable, predictable, and free of contradictions. If a virtual environment is considered as "natural" is allows for the construction of a mental model on which interactions with the virtual environment and interpretations of virtual stimuli and events may be based. The importance of mental models in the emergence of presence has been long acknowledged in presence research [10, 11]. The construction of a coherent mental model for a virtual environment may be hindered by the inconsistences of the virtual scenario and its high "artificiality". These inconsistences may be effectively suppressed by an efficient mechanism of conflict resolution which may be the reason why empirical correlations between conflict adaptation and scenario naturalness are observed. For instance, a specific mechanism of the link between efficient conflict suppression and scenario naturalness may be the increased ability to "suspend disbelief" (which is a strong determinant of presence, [12]) in people with increased conflict processing abilities. Thus effective conflict monitoring and control may advance presence via better conflict resolution, corroborating the results observed for the negative somatic effects.

Third, it was found that in low-immersion conditions post-error slowing may be inversely related to the emotional involvement dimension of presence. We see this as an indication that strongly developed error detection may have differential effects on presence. While – as seen from the discussion above – effective error control may suppress errors and conflicts induced by a virtual environment – it may also undermine presence due to increased sensitivity to conflicts/errors. Specifically, effective error monitoring and control may be related to critical thinking. The ability to think rationally would clearly suggest the user of a virtual environment that the displayed reality is only an illusion. This would be especially strong if inadequacies of the virtual environment are clearly perceptible. Sensitivity to conflicts may thus promote a more critical stance towards virtual environments and thus diminish presence. This is especially true of low-immersion virtual environments where the sophistication of the virtual environment is severely limited due to technological factors.

The results obtained above have consequences for the development and usage of virtual environments. These include:

- User selection for better cognitive control
- Understanding of presence mechanisms related to cognitive control
- Maintaining appropriate level of cognitive control
- Objectively measuring presence

User selection procedures may include error monitoring and correction assessment in order to select users more capable of developing a strong sense of presence in a virtual environment. Given the above result, selecting potential users based on post-error slowing data may lead to a decrease of negative somatic symptoms experienced during VR exposure. This is especially relevant for dynamic virtual scenarios with a lot of simulated motion. User selection for better conflict adaptation may be especially relevant for optimizing presence in highly artificial virtual scenarios in which it is important to suspend disbelief and to suppress conflicts.

Understanding the mechanics of the relationship between error monitoring and correction and presence may also help to develop more sophisticated virtual environments. For instance, our results make a strong case for the reduction or error and conflicts produced by virtual environments. This refers, for instance, to the conflicts between visual and proprioceptive sensory inputs (via better visual stimulation or appropriate proprioceptive feedback). On a more conceptual level, this refers to making virtual scenarios as coherent as possible avoiding the need for conflict suppression.

The individual level of error monitoring and correction is the product of complex long-term development and cannot be directly manipulated. Still, some factors may influence the efficiency of error monitoring and correction. For instance, cognitive control has been shown to depend on cognitive resources [13] which may be depleted in the state of fatigue or illness. Exposure to virtual environments in a less than optimal functional state may lead to less effective cognitive control, less ability to compensate for errors and conflicts, and less presence. Thus, it is advisable to refrain from employing user in non-optimal functional states as they will not be able to exert full cognitive control over their interactions with a virtual environment.

Finally, the present results may be used to drive the development of new objective measures for presence. Specifically, error monitoring and correction is related to the activity of the ACC. It is now widely believed that ACC activity has a distinct electrophysiological index – the fronto-medial theta rhythm [14]. Thus, measuring bursts of fronto-medial theta during virtual exposure may be used to assess aspects of presence.

6   Conclusions

Error monitoring and correction is a subsystem within human cognitive control. Better errors/conflicts processing was related to less negative somatic effects during virtual reality exposure and more naturalness of a virtual scenario both in high- and low-immersion virtual settings. In a low-immersion environment, error processing was also related to less emotional involvement which reflects a critical stance towards virtual stimulation. The explication of cognitive mechanisms of presence can be used to better recruit users and to better develop virtual reality applications. *This work was supported by Russian Foundation for Basic Research, grant no. 15-06-08998.*

References

1. Lombard, M., Ditton, T.: At the heart of it all: the concept of presence. J. Comput. Mediat. Commun. **3** (1997)
2. Witmer, B., Singer, M.: Measuring presence in virtual environments: a presence questionnaire. Presence: Teleoperators Virtual Environ. **7**, 225–240 (1998)
3. Lessiter, J., Freeman, J., Keogh, E., Davidoff, J.: A cross-media presence questionnaire: the ITC-sense of presence inventory. Presence: Teleoperators Virtual Environ. **10**, 282–297 (2001)
4. Coxon, M., Kelly, N., Page, S.: Individual differences in virtual reality: are spatial presence and spatial ability linked? Virtual Real. **20**, 203–212 (2016)
5. Botvinick, M.M., Braver, T.S., Barch, D.M., Carter, C.S., Cohen, J.D.: Conflict monitoring and cognitive control. Psychol. Rev. **108**, 624–652 (2001)
6. Lorist, M.M., Boksem, M.A., Ridderinkhof, K.R.: Impaired cognitive control and reduced cingulate activity during mental fatigue. Cogn. Brain. Res. **24**, 199–205 (2005)
7. Van Veen, V., Carter, C.: Conflict and cognitive control in the brain. Curr. Dir. Psychol. Sci. **15**, 237–240 (2006)
8. Dutilh, G., van Ravenzwaaij, D., Nieuwenhuis, S., van der Maas, H., Forstmann, B., Wagenmakers, E.: How to measure post-error slowing: a confound and a simple solution. J. Math. Psychol. **56**, 208–216 (2012)
9. Ullsperger, M., Bylsma, L., Botvinick, M.M.: The conflict adaptation effect: it's not just priming. Cogn. Affect. Behav. Neurosci. **5**, 467–472 (2005)
10. Sheridan, T.B.: Descartes, Heidegger, Gibson, and God: towards an eclectic ontology of presence. Presence **8**, 551–559 (1999)
11. Shubert, T.: A new conception of spatial presence: once again, with feeling. Commun. Theory **19**, 161–187 (2009)
12. Blake, E., Nunez, D., Labuschagne, B.: Longitudinal effects on presence: suspension of disbelief or distrust of naive belief? In: Presence 2007. The 10th Annual International Workshop on Presence, 25th–27th October 2007, Barcelona, Spain, pp 19–27. Starlab, Barcelona (2007)
13. Baumeister, R.F., Bratslavsky, E., Muraven, M., Tice, D.M.: Ego depletion: is the active self a limited resource? J. Pers. Soc. Psychol. **74**, 1252–1265 (1998)
14. Kovacevic, S., Azma, S., Irimia, A., Sherfey, J., Halgren, E., Marinkovic, K.: Theta oscillations are sensitive to both early and late conflict processing stages: effects of alcohol intoxication. PLoS ONE **7**, e43957 (2012)

3D Route Planning Within a Stereoscopic Environment Based on 2D Mouse Interaction

Leonhard Vogelmeier[✉], Christoph Vernaleken, and Peter Sandl

Airbus Defence and Space, 85077 Manching, Germany
leonhard.vogelmeier@airbus.com

Abstract. Stereoscopic displays have reached a level of maturity sufficient for professional applications. At Airbus, an evolutionary approach is fostered to integrate such displays in existing mission planning systems for airborne use. One necessary building brick is to provide interaction with the stereoscopic content in a way users are familiar with from common (two-dimensional) human-computer interaction.

This paper describes an approach to provide three-dimensional interaction within a stereoscopic environment based on standard mouse and keyboard using interaction metaphors.

Keywords: Mission planning · Stereoscopic visualization · Virtual reality · Mixed reality · Interaction

1 Introduction

Today's mission planning systems rely on a two dimensional map for the primary mission planning task. Consequentially, the route planning process is divided into two steps, the first of which, dealing with the lateral component of the route, is carried out on a traditional map, assuming constant altitude. Afterwards, the vertical component is elaborated, refining the altitudes, aided by a profile view. This is an effective method for planning high altitude routes of low complexity. However, when topography has a major impact on mission success, e.g. for air to ground attacks, this planning method becomes inefficient, since the user has to mentally integrate both the lateral and vertical components, a very demanding task.

Planning tools based on stereoscopic, three-dimensional visualization can help to solve this issue because they relieve the user from the mental integration task. But they can only be efficient if user interaction with the 3D scene is adequately implemented.

It is intended to use the stereoscopic route planning application in conjunction with a common 2D screen, as the mission planning process requires a lot of text based and two-dimensional information to be entered and processed. To enable seamless interaction in the entire mission planning system, a basic requirement is to rely exclusively on standard mouse and keyboard, also for interaction with the stereoscopic environment. This necessitates that the handling of the mouse and the keyboard in the stereoscopic environment shall follow the expectations of users arising from their experience with the default 2D environment.

© Springer International Publishing AG 2017
C. Stephanidis (Ed.): HCII Posters 2017, Part II, CCIS 714, pp. 81–87, 2017.
DOI: 10.1007/978-3-319-58753-0_13

In the following, a corresponding interaction method is developed and realized inside a stereoscopic route planning demonstrator. The implementation is subsequently tested and further developed until acceptable interaction results are achieved. The improvement of the method was supported by informal user tests.

2   Problem Statement

One basic metaphor for working with a mouse and a two-dimensional mouse cursor is moving the cursor over an object to interact with it; this requires the cursor to be always the topmost object. This metaphor can easily be transferred to non-stereoscopic 3D-visualizations where the three-dimensional content is projected onto an arbitrary image plane, as visualized in Fig. 1, the content of which is then visualized on a screen. This projection reduces the *cursor over object* problem to a 2D problem that can easily be solved. By contrast, in a stereoscopic 3D-visualisation, two projections are applied, one for each eye, cf. Fig. 2. As a consequence, for all virtual 3D-objects which are not placed directly on the screen plane, two pictures are displayed on the screen, one for each eye. Trying to move the 2D cursor over a 3D symbol not in the screen plane may therefore result in placing it between the two projected pictures. This could only be solved by the user by closing one eye which would reduce the picking problem again to a 2D problem. This not an acceptable solution. First tests also showed that cursors moving only in the screen plane cause unacceptable eye strain in many cases. Moving it in the line of sight of a virtual 3D object located in front of or behind the screen plane will result in two objects on the same spot with a different depth impression for the user. Only one of the two objects can be fused to a depth image and the other one generates a hard to interpret double picture which implies unacceptable stress to the human visual perception system. This problem will be called *depth perception problem* in the following.

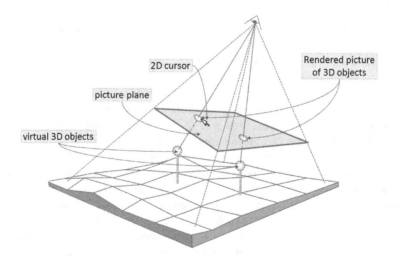

Fig. 1. Standard non-stereoscopic projection of 3D content to a 2D picture plane

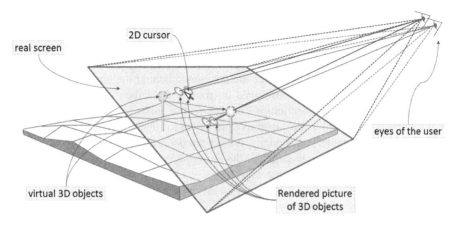

Fig. 2. Stereoscopic projection of 3D content to the screen

To provide an adequate interaction, a solution for the *cursor over object* problem must be found for use inside the stereoscopic environment. With an adequate solution, other two-dimensional interaction metaphors like *left click on object* for selection, or *mouse over* for additional information can be easily transferred.

3 Proposed Solution

As solution for this problem we introduced a virtual 3D cursor as displayed in Fig. 3. The 2D cursor is replaced by a 3D geometry which starts its movement in the screen plane at the position of the 2D cursor, the visual representation of which is hidden (see number one in Fig. 3). An intersection line is calculated, starting from a position in the middle between the user's eyes and heading through the 2D mouse position of the

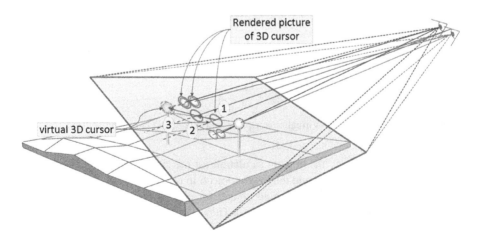

Fig. 3. Behavior of virtual 3D cursor for picking virtual 3D objects

screen. For each movement of the mouse, it is calculated if the intersection line hits virtual objects. If this is not the case, the 3D cursor moves attached to the mouse position in the screen plane (see 2 in Fig. 3). If an intersection occurs, the 3D cursor jumps to the position of the related 3D object (see 3 in Fig. 3). Tests showed that this technique works well for objects which are positioned behind the screen in relation to the user. For objects which are positioned in front of the screen the cursor has to be moved behind the object an then jumps from behind the object towards it. This violates the user expectation to move the cursor over an object for interaction, and has therefore been rated as unacceptable. Additionally, it has been detected that for objects which are located far away from the screen plane, the *depth perception problem* appears again when moving the cursor close to the objects.

To overcome these problems, the authors invented a virtual plane and transferred the cursor movement from the screen plane to the virtual plane. The virtual plane is oriented parallel to the 3D map, and the distance to the map is defined by the highest 3D object in the scene as shown in Fig. 4. The 3D cursor now always moves atop all 3D objects. In Fig. 4, it starts moving behind the screen (number one), moves out of the screen (number two) and jumps to the virtual 3D-object (number three). First tests showed that while this method was acceptable in most cases, it fails when some 3D objects are located very high above the others. This moves the virtual 3D cursor plane very high above any 3D objects placed lower, which again leads to the depth impression problem described above.

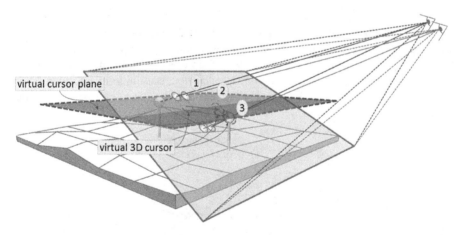

Fig. 4. Visualization Virtual cursor plane and related 3D cursor movement

To attenuate this effect, the height calculation for the cursor plane was changed to be located between the highest and the lowest object. In order to prevent a recurrence of the problem of moving the cursor behind objects for picking them, virtual intersection areas as displayed in Fig. 5 has been invented. They start at the intersection point of the plumb line of an object with the cursor plane, and reach up to object itself. They are always oriented towards the user, and their width equals the width of the object. With every movement of the cursor, it is checked if the intersection line intersects with an intersection area. If no (see Fig. 5 number one), the cursor is placed on the cursor plane. If yes, the cursor is placed on the intersection position between intersection line and intersection area (see Fig. 5 number two). If an intersection with an object occurs, the cursor is place on the object see (Fig. 5 number three).

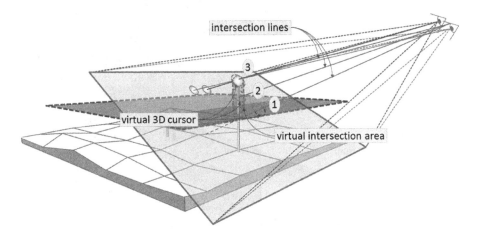

Fig. 5. Visualization of virtual intersection area for 3D cursor control

In some cases, this picking method produces the sensation of the cursor 'crawling up' to the 3D object, which is an unexpected behavior at the start, but it has been rated as acceptable after a short familiarization phase by the test users.

With this last adaption an acceptable *move cursor over object* method has been found and implemented in an route planning demonstrator described in the following.

4   Demonstrator Setup

A photograph of the realized demonstrator is shown in Fig. 6. It consists of a screen capable of providing an active stereo[1] picture, a tracking system, tracked active stereo shutter glasses, a standard keyboard and a standard mouse. The content, an interactive three-dimensional map and a three-dimensional route, is rendered in a way which gives the user the impression that the map is just lying on the table. The screen acts in this case like a window providing a view into a showcase.

To achieve this effect, the eye-position of the user is continuously measured by the tracking system to render the correct perspective regarding the position of the users eye, the position of the screen and the position of the table. To keep the negative effects of the de-coupling of convergence and accommodation[2] implied by the stereoscopic

---

[1] For an in detail description of *active stereo* see [1].
[2] For an in detail description of *de-coupling of convergence and accommodation* see [2].

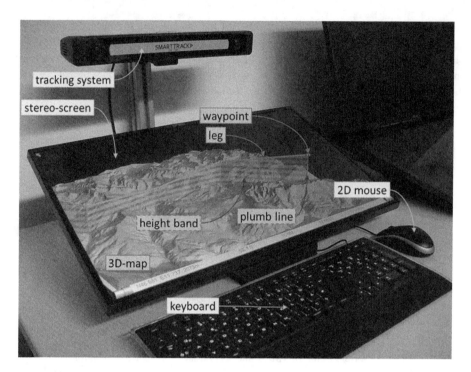

Fig. 6. Photograph of demonstrator with declaration of hardware (orange) and content (blue) (Color figure online)

visualization low, the screen has been tilted to an angle of 30° relative to the table, to keep the to be visualized content near to the screen.

The intractable objects of the demonstrator are the 3D-map and the waypoints and legs of the 3D-route (see Fig. 6). The plumb line and the height band are only for visualization. The defined needs for interaction are listed in Table 1.

Table 1. Defined needs for interaction for 3D-map and 3D-route

Interaction with 3D-map	Interaction with 3D-route
Move map	Select waypoint
Scale map	Add waypoint at end of route
Rotate map	Insert waypoint between two existing waypoints
Tilt map	Move waypoint in all three dimensions
	Delete waypoint

Using the developed *cursor over object* method, the means for interaction listed Table 2 have been implemented. The discrimination between map and object interaction is done by analyzing if a *mouse over object* occurs or not. If not map interaction is applied if yes object interaction. During map interaction e.g. moving the map the

Table 2. Defined means for interaction for route manipulation

Interaction mean	Interaction with 3D-route
Left mouse button click on waypoint	Select waypoint
Right mouse button click on 3D-map	Add waypoint at end of route
Left mouse button drag on leg	Insert waypoint between two existing waypoints
Left mouse button drag	Move waypoint parallel to ground
mouse wheel while cursor on object	Change height of waypoint
Delete-key while cursor on object	Delete waypoint

search for intersection with objects is deactivated. A special case is the interaction *add waypoint at end of route*. In this case the intersection of the actual intersection line with the 3D-map is calculated and the waypoint is placed at the intersection point with the height of the preceding waypoint.

First user tests proved the method to be usable for 3D route manipulation; further quantitative test are planned.

5 Summary and Way Ahead

The Authors propose an interaction method for a stereoscopic environment which utilizes standard mouse and keyboard and interaction metaphors derived from the well-established two-dimensional interaction.

The method has been implemented inside a stereoscopic route planning demonstrator and improved to provide suitable interaction. Qualitative, informal user tests have been applied to assist the improvement of the method. In a next step qualitative measurements shall be applied, to evaluate interaction performance and failure rate to compare it to standard two-dimensional interaction.

References

1. Wikipedia. https://en.wikipedia.org/wiki/Active_shutter_3D_system
2. Patterson, E.P.: Human Factors of Stereoscopic 3D Displays. Springer, London, Heidelberg, New York, Dordrecht (2015). doi:10.1007/978-1-4471-6651-1

The Implementation of Instructional Strategies for Training in a Virtual Environment: An Exploratory Investigation of Workload and Performance

Elizabeth Wolfe, John Granger, Natalie Alessi, Lauren Farrell, and Crystal Maraj[✉]

Institute for Simulation and Training,
University of Central Florida, Orlando, FL, USA
{ewolfe,jgranger,nalessi,lfarrel,cmaraj}@ist.ucf.edu

Abstract. This study expanded upon the use of Simulation-Based Training (SBT) to enhance kinesic cue detection in military operations. The research investigated three SBT instructional strategies: Massed Exposure (ME), High-lighting, and Kim's Game. An additional Control condition was included as a validity measure for the tested instructional strategies. Each strategy provided a separate perceptual experience for learning how to detect the target kinesic cues specified: aggressiveness and nervousness. The subjects' workload scores from the NASA-Task Load Index (NASA-TLX) subscales of performance, effort, and frustration provided greater understanding of each strategy's impact on per-ceptual skill improvement. For each instructional strategy, this research increased understanding of workload efficiencies and highlighted potential applications. Examination of descriptive statistics revealed that Kim's Game scored the lowest in detection accuracy, and exceeded both Highlighting and ME in terms of effort, performance, and frustration on the NASA-TLX. High-lighting scored highest in detection accuracy, but lowest in effort, performance, and frustration. The Control and ME scored neither highest nor lowest for all NASA-TLX subscales and detection accuracy. Given the results, the instruc-tional strategies may be implemented individually or used in combinations for a desired training effect. Kim's Game may be suited for training experts, whereas Highlighting and ME may be suited for novice trainees. Additional fields, such as baggage screening, healthcare, and education may benefit from implemen-tation of workload-appropriate perceptual training strategies within a virtual environment.

Keywords: Simulation-Based Training (SBT) · NASA-TLX · Workload · Virtual environment · Kinesic cues

1 Research Foundation

A Warfighter must accurately detect and interpret threats in the field. One type of threat is in the form of kinesic cues, here nonverbal body movements communicating one's intent [1]. The target kinesic behavior cues conveyed in this study were either

© Springer International Publishing AG 2017
C. Stephanidis (Ed.): HCII Posters 2017, Part II, CCIS 714, pp. 88–94, 2017.
DOI: 10.1007/978-3-319-58753-0_14

aggressive or a nervous behaviors signifying a potential threat. Aggressive behaviors included clenching one's fists or slapping one's hands, while nervous behaviors included checking one's "six o'clock" or wringing one's hands (i.e., clasping and rubbing the palm of one hand with the other hand). Currently, a need exists to increase accuracy in detecting threats in a Warfighter context. This need has inspired the use of instructional strategies in a virtual environment for training perceptual skills.

1.1 Instructional Strategies

Instructional strategies were sought to aid knowledge acquisition of target cues in a virtual environment. The instructional strategies included Kim's Game, Highlighting, and Massed Exposure (ME). Kim's Game was adopted from Rudyard Kipling's book titled *Kim*, where the former focused on teaching change detection and recall. Adopting the premise behind Kim's Game allowed for the creation of a virtual version presented in the form of an instructional strategy. The strategy presented a discrete task whereby the trainee had to identify a change (or no-change) in a virtual scene. Specifically, the trainee observed a scene of non-target cues for 8 s, a blank screen for 1 s (i.e., an interstimulus interval), and a second scene of cues for 8 s. The second scene required change detection, as one cue may have changed from a non-target to a target cue. Following, the trainee chose whether a change had occurred or not within final scene. This tasks the trainee with recalling the first stimuli, and then detecting whether a change has occurred [2].

Another instructional strategy used in this study was Highlighting, which is the use of a non-content stimuli within the simulated environment to orient the trainee's attention toward the target cue. A translucent blue box appeared over the target cues, leaving the user to classify the presence of an aggressive or nervous cue. ME involves the saturation of practice opportunities by presenting a higher amount of the target cues to the user, in comparison to the Control group. A Control condition was incorporated as a continuous task with no formal training (i.e., the absence of an instructional strategy). Overall, each strategy requires the selective attention of the trainee, in order for the trainee to accurately detect the target cue among non-target cues [3].

1.2 NASA-Task Load Index

This research utilized the NASA-Task Load Index (NASA-TLX) survey, which is a subjective tool used to assess perceived workload for a given task. The full survey consists of six subscales, including mental demand, physical demand, temporal demand, performance, effort and frustration [4]. Each subscale is comprised of 100 points, with a 5-point interval step. For this report, the survey comprises effort, frustration, and performance subscales. Specifically, effort referred to how much physical and mental strength was needed to accomplish the task. Frustration examined the level of stress, versus relaxation, felt during the task. Finally, performance described the level of confidence the participant had in their performance of the task. Unlike the other subscales, performance was scored as '0' to represent perfect performance and '100' to represent lowest performance. The mental demand subscale, as well as a global demand scale, were evaluated and presented in research by [5] and will not be duplicated in this research effort.

1.3   Detection Accuracy

For selecting correct target cues, detection accuracy was logged and scored. The score was measured by the percentage of correctly detected targets cues out of the total number of target cues presented.

1.4   Research Questions

This research explores the impact of workload responses (i.e., effort, frustration, and performance) using a between-subjects design for the instructional strategies (i.e., Kim's Game, ME, Highlighting and Control). Changes in cognitive demands and resource allocation may result in differences reported for workload, and ultimately detection accuracy. This has inspired an investigation into the following research questions:

1. Which strategy will score highest or lowest for effort, frustration, performance, and detection accuracy?
2. How do the strategies differ in workload and detection accuracy?
3. Which strategy is most effective in yielding an appropriate amount of workload?

2   Data Collection

The experimenter greeted each participant and verified that he or she met the inclusion requirements (i.e., the participant was a U.S. citizen, was at least 18 years of age, had normal or corrected vision, and had not participated in prior Simulation-Based Training experiments). After entering the experiment room, the experimenter obtained the participant's signed consent and administered the color blindness test [6]. If the participant passed the color blindness test, he or she was assigned to one of the four conditions.

Next, the experimenter asked the participant to view a scenario (on a 22-inch desktop computer) which familiarized him or her with the user interface and the testbed's Virtual Battlespace 2 (VBS2) software. Following this event, the experimenter requested that the participant complete a pre-test scenario, using prior experience to detect and classify cues as exhibiting either aggressiveness or nervousness. After, the experimenter presented a PowerPoint training on behavior cue detection with explanations for aggressive and nervous cues. The presentation also highlighted non-target cues (such as idle talking and cross arms) as well as instructions for completing the task. Next, the experimenter displayed one of the four conditions (i.e., Kim's Game, ME, Highlighting or Control) on the desktop and asked the participant to complete the scenario. Following the scenario, which was displayed for approximately

15 min, the experimenter requested that the participant complete the on-line version of the NASA-TLX.

After the NASA-TLX was completed, a final PowerPoint with instructions to complete the post-test was presented by the experimenter. Afterwards, the participant completed the post-test, which tested knowledge acquisition and logged the detection accuracy scores used in the present analysis. Following this, the participants were debriefed, compensated (with either $10 per hour or class credit), and dismissed. The total duration of the experiment was roughly 3 h.

3   Results

Preliminary analyses indicated that the age ranges of the participants were 18–38 ($M = 22.12$, $SD = 3.44$). The number of both male and female participants was 65, with a sample size of 130. Closer inspection of the data showed that the distribution was non-normal, or nonparametric, in nature. Therefore, it was more meaningful to examine the medians for the NASA-TLX subscales (i.e. effort, frustration and performance) and detection accuracy. Observing the median distribution for all the conditions, Kim's Game had the highest median scores for effort (60), performance (35), and frustration (45) subscales, and had the lowest detection accuracy score (85.94%). Highlighting had the lowest median scores for the three workload subscales of effort (14), performance (3), and frustration (5), and had the highest score for detection accuracy (96.71%). ME scored neither the highest nor lowest in effort (47), performance (24), frustration (30) or detection accuracy (94.19%). Finally, the Control was neither highest nor lowest in effort (53), performance (17), frustration (26), or detection accuracy (94.57%).

As previously mentioned, the non-normal distribution prompted an inspection of the data to identify extreme outliers. A closer look at the detection accuracy scores revealed extreme outliers in three out of the four groups: select ME, Highlighting, and Control scores were beyond the lower outer fence. Additionally, Kim's Game's effort subscale showed extreme outliers beyond the lower outer fence. Finally, Highlighting's performance subscale displayed extreme outliers beyond the upper outer fence.

4   Discussion

Based on the results, responses to the following research questions are provided.

4.1   Which Strategy Will Score Highest or Lowest for Effort, Frustration, Performance and Detection Accuracy?

Kim's Game scored highest in effort, frustration, and performance; but lowest in detection accuracy. The discrete nature of the Kim's Game target cue presentation may have stimulated more attention, which increased effort and frustration levels. As a result, performance scores were impacted because the user felt challenged by Kim's Game. When examining detection accuracy, it appears that the Control had a higher positive impact than Kim's Game. In addition, the Control was comparable to ME in terms of detection accuracy. Overall, from a design perspective, a baseline helps determine if a strategy is warranted for downstream training acquisition.

Highlighting scored lowest in effort, frustration, and performance; but highest in detection accuracy. The subscale scores suggest that Highlighting was perceived as a simpler task than Kim's Game. Prompting towards the target cue in Highlighting may explain this perception, leading to lower scores in effort and performance. Thus, Highlighting may be beneficial for training users who require low-frustration learning environments. For example, children with autism may benefit from training that starts with the least intrusive approach [7].

4.2   How Do the Strategies Differ in Workload and Detection Accuracy?

Each set of workload and detection accuracy scores for the three instructional strategies differ, signifying distinct trends to inform future strategy selection. At first glance, Highlighting seems equivalent to the Control in terms of detection accuracy. However, there is a distinction between performance scores for the Highlighting and Control conditions (see results for an overview). The differences may be explained by increased task confidence, induced by the non-content stimuli. Highlighting, therefore, may be applied toward inexperienced trainees, to increase their confidence levels. Highlighting may be applied to first-year nurses to gain confidence in technical skills required for treating patients in stressful environments [8].

When ME is compared to Highlighting, considerable differences in workload exist for all subscale scores. Yet, differences in detection accuracy scores between the two strategies were minimal. Given the differences in workload subscales, but similarities in detection accuracy scores, ME can assist with training tasks that are neither too challenging nor too simplistic. ME may be suited for high-stake security fields that require a tax on effort, but need a high detection accuracy. To illustrate, ME may be introduced to baggage-screening training, which requires the screener to identify Improvised Explosive Devices (IEDs) [9].

4.3   Which Strategy is Most Effective in Yielding an Appropriate Amount of Workload?

The appropriate amount of workload for an instructional training strategy depends on the desired application. Tasks that entail a large amount of workload for adequate performance may use Kim's Game. Whereas training instances that demand execution of simple tasks may gear toward Highlighting. Alternatively, ME may be used as an intermediate training strategy that provides extensive amounts of practice, with moderate workload demands. The placement of instructional strategies within a training continuum can cater to specific trainee needs. For example, Highlighting may act as a simplified approach to train detection. Once the trainee has mastered basic task components, ME may be presented for practice purposes, to create repetition and moderate workload demands. Lastly, Kim's Game may act as a testing mechanism for detection skills. Kim's Game is an appropriate testing agent because it generates high workload demands expected in the real world. Therefore, the presence of high detection accuracy in Kim's Game suggests ideal performance under high-workload conditions.

5   Limitations

A limitation of this study was the discrete aspect of Kim's game, when compared to the continuous nature of Highlighting, ME, and Control. This ecological difference in design may have acted as an extraneous variable, given that the pre-test and post-test also used a continuous method. Furthermore, outliers were detected in all conditions, which may have skewed the data.

6   Conclusion

This study analyzed the descriptive statistics of three instructional strategies, for the NASA-TLX subscales of frustration, effort, and performance; and detection accuracy. Based on the research findings, recommendations were given to map strategies according to a training continuum. Potential applications include baggage screening, special education, and healthcare. Future directions of research includes a follow-up study to assess learning retention for detection skills, and assessing other subscales of the NASA-TLX. Finally, to improve the objectivity of the results, physiological measurements to assess trainee workload should be integrated.

Acknowledgments. This research was sponsored by Dr. Irwin Hudson of the U.S. Army Research Laboratory Human Research Engineering Directorate Advanced Training and Simulation Division (ARL HRED ATSD), under contract W911NF-14-2-0021. However, the views, findings, and conclusions contained in this presentation are solely those of the author and should not be interpreted as representing the official policies, either expressed or implied, of ARL HRED ATSD or the U.S. Government. The U.S. Government is authorized to reproduce and distribute reprints for Government. Special thanks to Mr. Jonathan Hurter for his time and contributions to the success of this paper.

References

1. United States Marine Corps. Combat Hunter profiling B2E2965/B2E2967 [Student handout] (n.d.). http://www.harisingh.com/Combat_Hunter_Profiling.pdf
2. Maraj, C.S., Hurter, J., Badillo-Urquiola, K.A., Lackey, S.J., Hudson, I.L.: Investigating performance of Kim's game for behavior cue detection. In: Proceedings of the Interservice/Industry Training, Simulation, and Education Conference (I/ITSEC). NTSA, Arlington (2016)
3. Salcedo, J.N., Lackey, S.J., Maraj, C.: Impact of instructional strategies on workload, stress, and flow in simulation-based training for behavior cue analysis. In: Lackey, S., Shumaker, R. (eds.) VAMR 2016. LNCS, vol. 9740, pp. 184–195. Springer, Cham (2016). doi:10.1007/978-3-319-39907-2_18

4. Hart, S.: NASA-task load index (NASA-TLX); 20 years later. In: Proceedings of the Human Factors and Ergonomics Society 50th Annual Meeting, vol. 50, no. 9, pp. 904–908. Sage Publications, Los Angeles (2006)
5. Maraj, C., Hurter, J., Aubrey, W., Wolfe, E., Hudson, I.: Contrasting instructional strategies suited to a detection task: examining differences in subjective workload. In: Proceedings of the 2017 Human Computer Interaction International Virtual, Augmented, and Mixed Reality Conference. Springer (in press)
6. Ishihara, S.: Ishihara's Tests for Colour Deficiency. Kanehara Trading, Tokyo (2013)
7. Yanardag, M., Birkan, B., Yılmaz, İ., Konukman, F., Ağbuğa, B., Lieberman, L.: The effects of least-to-most prompting procedure in teaching basic tennis skills to children with autism. Kinesiol. Int. J. Fundam. Appl. Kinesiol. 43(1), 44–55 (2011). http://hrcak.srce.hr/69602
8. Roh, Y.S., Issenberg, S.B., Chung, H.S., Kim, S.S., Lim, T.H.: A survey of nurses' perceived competence and educational needs in performing resuscitation. J. Continuing Educ. Nurs. 44 (5), 230–236 (2013). doi:10.3928/00220124-20130301-83
9. Schuster, D., Rivera, J., Sellers, B.C., Fiore, S.M., Jentsch, F.: Perceptual training for visual search. Ergonomics 56(7), 1101–1115 (2013). doi:10.1080/00140139.2013.79048180/00140139.2013.790481

Service Design of Intergeneration Home-Sharing System Using VR-Based Simulation Technology and Optimal Matching Algorithms

Taeha Yi, Jimin Rhim, Injung Lee, Amartuvshin Narangerel,
and Ji-Hyun Lee[✉]

GSCT, KAIST, 291 Daehak-Ro, Yuseong-Gu, Daejeon 305-701, Korea
{yitaeha, kingjimin, edndn, amartuvshin,
jihyun187}@kaist.ac.kr

Abstract. Services that allow Share house between elders and young adults are becoming more prevalent to fulfill various needs for different stakeholders. However, various difficulties among the residents who are strangers from different generations are likely to occur. Research aim is to solve this social phenomenon by applying interdisciplinary total design solution. This research suggests an integrative solution to support optimal matching of cohabitants by developing matching algorithm and then implementing spatial mapping and simulation system using VR technology. Service blueprint that represents total service design solution for seamless user experience is suggested. Our system has the potential for industrialization and field application through service packaging.

Keywords: Total service design · Home sharing · VR-simulation · Matching algorithm · Service blueprint

1 Introduction

Intergeneration home-sharing programs have emerged to fulfill the needs for accommodations for the elders who want to reduce loneliness [1], and young adults who want to minimize dwelling expenses. Such services are also called Shared Housing, in which seniors and college students share housings, where students provide maintenance and chore services for the elder homeowners who provide boarding [2]. The concept of shared housing among elders and students occurred since 1980s [3], but due to physical, social, psychological, economic and health consequences of living together, share house services have become more popular since 2000s [4]. The two generations have consensus for sharing living spaces because it is beneficial for both elders and college students. However, conflicts among the residents are likely to occur when sharing a house with strangers of different generations. To prevent conflicts between cohabitants, current home-sharing programs provide matching services [5]. Existing matching services collect inhabitants' profiles and ask questions about residency needs and then pair up people with similar responses [6]. Furthermore, these questionnaires

© Springer International Publishing AG 2017
C. Stephanidis (Ed.): HCII Posters 2017, Part II, CCIS 714, pp. 95–100, 2017.
DOI: 10.1007/978-3-319-58753-0_15

do not consider complex social traits of people nor spatial traits of the residency, which is not sufficient enough to solve fundamental problems. Although social interactions between the home shares are crucial, they are actually sharing living space. In the case of home sharing of elders and young adults, the house is pre-owned by the elders with furniture and living space arranged in the current dweller's lifestyles. The new comer is likely to have his or her own furniture with distinct lifestyles including living behaviors and preferences [7]. The moving patterns during daily activities or furniture arrangements caused by differences of life styles between users cannot be predicted by matching services, which are found while living together. Social phenomena caused by gaps in generations due to social structure exists. Our research team aims to provide total design solution by applying interdisciplinary methodologies, by applying technology to simulate home sharing experiences. This research suggests an integrative solution to support optimal matching of cohabitants by developing matching algorithm and then implement spatial mapping and simulation system using VR technology. Specific goals and solution directions will be discussed in the following section.

2 Total Design Solution for Integrative Home-Sharing System

The goal of the research is to provide milestone for developing a comprehensive total service design for potential home sharers including two generations; elders and young adults. The service solution is divided into social psychology aspect and spatial-technological aspect. This study aims to explore the service of home-sharing based on convergence between sociological and science technological approach. The aim of the service is to provide matching between co-habitants through thorough analysis of the potential dwellers, and to provide pre-living experiences through VR based simulation to provide more satisfactory living experiences. Figure 1 shows overall background and solution methods for each aspect that provides guidelines for the total service system.

2.1 Solve Social Problem Through Developing Optimal Matching Algorithm

Providing methods to match home sharers who can live harmoniously is essential. The social approach suggests an optimal matching algorithm which is based on multi-dimensional analysis considering their needs, characteristics, and lifestyle of each parties. Furthermore, a transportation network and residential area analysis is take in place for supporting the matching system more realistically since geographical preferences are crucial factor selecting an accommodation.

2.2 Solve Spatial Problem Through VR Based Interior Support System

Simulation technology will be developed upon human-behavior to carefully examine the matched individuals and provide them close to real experience before moving in.

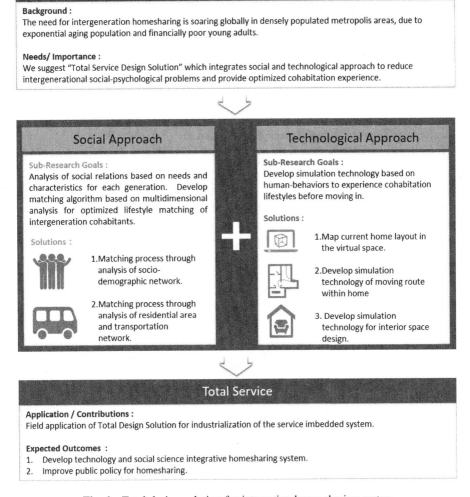

Fig. 1. Total design solution for integrative home-sharing system

And this approach designed in three parts. Augmented Reality based space design framework that arranges furniture will be developed upon the existing accommodation layouts. The simulation technology of moving route of both individuals will be also developed with the simultaneous consideration of furniture arrangement. Third, moving routes and the furniture placement greatly influenced from the matching algorithm and interaction of them. Furthermore, the simulation of a color and texture for the interior wallpaper is implemented to provide a lifelike experience for AR visualization.

2.3   Integrative Total Service System

The total service design for Home sharing service will be designed by integrating these above mentioned social matching and technological simulation approach. Final goal of designing Integrative total service design is for field application of service imbedded system. Expected outcome of implementing the service is development of technology and social science integrated home-sharing system which can lead to improving public policy for home sharing.

2.4   Service Blue-Print for Home-Sharing System

In order to describe more specific procedures of how the services will be implemented, a Service blue-print of total service design that combines matching algorithm system and simulation system based on VR is shown in Fig. 2. The service is targeted for potential homes-sharers. More specifically, the targets users are elders who own houses and young adults who needs residencies. This total service solution consists of four steps. First, user recruitment period to apply people who are interested in home sharing. In this step, people participate in surveys to find optimal pairing up of candidates for home sharing based on their lifestyles, social relationships, and geographical preferences. To implement this steps, the part of social relation and social network analyzes users to recognize their features of characteristic, hobby, ethnographical information, patterns of transportation and residential needs by developing matching system based on multidimensional analysis. Next part shows simulation of spatial interactions based on VR technology. To construct VR simulation for experiencing expected interactions, the simulation system needs to recognize user's flow in the home and interactive features. Then, the system analyzes house owned by the elders to retrieve interior information such as functionality of furniture, floor plan, and such. The second step is individual's home sharing selection period. After the result of best matched pairs is given, potential home sharer selects where and with whom he or she wants to live with. Then, users visit the candidate of selected home. After selecting homes, users experience their home-sharing experiences through VR simulation system constructed by the part of spatial interaction and modeling based on VR. While using tablet PC to simulate how the living will be with home owner and potential home sharer, they can place furniture on the virtual reality system and make consensus of how to use the living space. Furthermore, the system can recommend optimal placements of furniture or moving routes for both dwellers.

Third step is actual home sharing period. When the period of actual home sharing ends in the fourth step, they evaluate and give the feed-backs through the final questionnaire based on the P.O.E. (Post Occupancy Evaluation). Based on the feedbacks, matching algorithm based on life style evaluation and transportation network analysis can be improved. Furthermore, guidelines or methods for improving actual living space and expected living styles can be modified through spatial simulation systems.

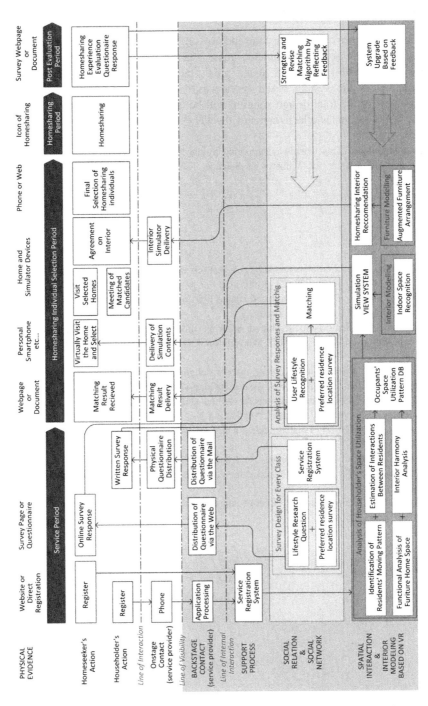

Fig. 2. Service blueprint for total solution for integrative home-sharing service

3   Conclusion and Future Work

This paper describes overall milestone and goals of the interdisciplinary service design, that aims to solve social phenomena; house sharing between the elders and young adults. Although this project is at an initial stage, further research results will be implemented in the system based service as described in the service blue print. Effectiveness of the total design solution will be tested through post occupancy evaluation, which evaluates effectiveness of dwellers' living experience [8].

Acknowledgement. This work was supported by the National Research Foundation of Korea (NRF) grant funded by the Ministry of Science, ICT & Future Planning (NRF-2016M3C 1B6949668).

References

1. Savikko, N., et al.: Predictors and subjective causes of loneliness in an aged population. Arch. Gerontol. Geriatr. **41**(3), 223–233 (2005)
2. Jaffe, D.J., Howe, E.: Agency-assisted shared housing: the nature of programs and matches. Gerontologist **28**(3), 318–324 (1988)
3. Sheranian, M.: Senior/student shared housing: model project. Report No. CG-019-795. Administration on Aging (DHHS), Washington, DC (1987). Retrieved from ERIC database (ED279986)
4. Ahrentzen, S.: Double indemnity or double delight? The health consequences of shared housing and "doubling up". J. Soc. Issues **59**(3), 547–568 (2003)
5. Rice, R., et al.: Computer-implemented method and system for matching a consumer to a home service provider, U.S. Patent Application No. 11/342,262, 17 August 2006
6. Pritchard, D.C.: The art of matchmaking: a case study in shared housing. Gerontologist **23**(2), 174–179 (1983)
7. Kahle, L.R., Beatty, S.E., Homer, P.: Alternative measurement approaches to consumer values: the list of values (LOV) and values and life style (VALS). J. Consum. Res. **13**(3), 405–409 (1986)
8. Zimring, C.M., Reizenstein, J.E.: Post-occupancy evaluation an overview. Environ. Behav. **12** (4), 429–450 (1980)

Learning, Games and Gamification

Application of Human Computer Interaction Interface in Game Design

Jing Cao[(⊠)] and Ying Cao

Huazhong University of Science and Technology,
Wuhan, People's Republic of China
1103575751@qq.com

Abstract. This article through the development process of the game, the game features, the current status of the design research, found that the current mode of electronic games there are serious problems. Smart phones, interaction design in the past, the display on the big screen display and data analysis and processing capacity and other factors will play the player's entertainment experience and interaction of freedom to have an impact. Based on the previous research and analysis, and through the electronic game interactive system, game players, game players, game behavior, game scenes, the technology of game design needed to explore the new requirements for the players to interact with the new The Conceptual Design of Electronic Game Interaction. In the interactive design of the game with the focus on considering the latest technology, by giving gamers the best user experience, it can bring the current mobile game interface design to some references.

Keywords: Interaction design · Games · Entertainment experience

1 Introduction

Game as the most important human life an entertainment, whether it is the traditional game, or the moment to digital technology as the carrier of the game, has shown a high degree of participation. "The game converts the world," the author Jane Mc Goniga described in the book: the game can make up for the real world deficiencies and shortcomings, the game can make the reality better. It hits the core of humankind well being, offering delightful rewards, irritating challenges and brilliant victories. However, a good human-computer interaction performance is the interface design and graphic design of the difference, thus the game team responsible for interactive de-signers to human-computer interaction theory in-depth study, thinking about the player's psychology, otherwise it is difficult to guarantee Designed to meet the player needs of the game interface [1].

2 Paper Preparation

Mobile phone game has become an important way for people to leisure and entertainment, according to the mobile game industry survey data show that in 2016 China's mobile game users to 90.31 million, an increase of 17.4% over 2015. It is expected that

© Springer International Publishing AG 2017
C. Stephanidis (Ed.): HCII Posters 2017, Part II, CCIS 714, pp. 103–108, 2017.
DOI: 10.1007/978-3-319-58753-0_16

the number of online game users in China will reach 100 million in 2017. These survey data illustrate a problem that online games have penetrated into people's lives and become an integral part of the number and the number has grown year by year. From another point of view, the popularity of online game entertainment also requires us to focus on the game interface design to ensure that users fully enjoy the fun of the game. The interface design is an important part in the game design, to understand the interface design work should first plan the interface design goals and principles. Constantine points out that a good user interface allows people to use the application without having to read the user manual or receive training [2]. A beautiful game interface, a reasonable interface operation process can give the user a very good first impression.

Therefore, in order to help people more in-depth understanding of the game industry, the growth of correct understanding; to create a high quality and enduring classic game, the benefit of hundreds of millions of players groups; for the occupation of the global market, to provide new growth points; Industrial health and sustainable development, research mobile game interface interaction design is particularly important.

3   An Analysis of Mobile Game Interaction Design Based on "Asphalt 8: Airborne"

3.1   Analysis of Application Effectiveness of Specific Interaction Design

Compared to click-based interactive experience converts to touch control based on changes in response to the touch area, can not provide tactile feedback; mode of operation: handheld, interactive design requires both ergonomic and consider the type of games, according to the type of the game selection Hand or hands operation; limited physical size, screen visibility range becomes smaller, in the information presented on the fundamental and secondary classification; also has a wealth of sensors, such as acceleration, gravity, compass, geographical location, suitable for more interesting, innovative, intelligent and efficient interactive design; Convenient, conducive to the exchange of players at any time to establish a huge social network, the highest users of those who sticky. Therefore, the mobile side of game on the interactive design of a higher demand for the characteristics of the platform set up user experience better game can greatly reduce the player to learn the cost of the game at the same time, but also bring the user a better sense of game immersion [3].

3.2   User-Centric Feedback

The user of the game is the player, and the game is designed for most players. Players can be divided into core players and regular players. Core players are also often referred to as "Hardcore" players. They are familiar with a game interface and rules, do not have too many tips to be able to proceed smoothly, and even feel that the existence of quite a few texts prompts are redundant [4].

Brice Morrison proposed game design based on five levels: the core experience (player game experience), the underlying mechanism (player and game interaction rhythm), reward and punishment system (player's behavioral consequences), long-term motivation Game goals) and aesthetic layout (the main screen effects and sound effects), the other four levels of the ultimate goal is to reach the core also experience. Quality assessment of other Internet products takes place from three main aspects of usefulness, usability, and emotional factors.

3.3   Analysis of Interactive Experiences of "Asphalt 8: Airborne" Emotions with Users

(Asphalt 8: Airborne) is produced by Gameloft issued racing game. Released on August 22, 2013, the App Store game included 131 cars, of which 80% were new model. Includes 9 seasons and 331 career mode games. The new exotic races, 9 environmental settings, including the Dragon Blood Tree, San Diego Port, Great Wall, Tokyo, Barcelona, the Alps, Venice, French Guiana, Iceland and Nevada, including exotic stimulation track The This is a game with real fantasy racing and phenomenal quality fans who are extremely passionate about street racing, and a game that will attract racing simulation game enthusiasts.

Game Music and the Combination of the Screen
The game is to meet everyone in daily life cannot meet the emotions, such as missile attacks such a scene, in daily life cannot drive such cars, or launch the bullet in front of these cars are destroyed. All of these points are based in these forms together. Game level and reasonable rhythm.

The game has some of the checkpoints in the design, including the arrangement for the bridge to meet such emotions. This is a picture of the player's brain waves. We measure the player's heart rate, heart rate changes, sweating some of the situation and brain waves, through the EMOI and SCL two indicators to judge. EMOI called the emotional index, and the higher the value represents (relative to the black part) mood is more excited, the lower represents a bit boring. SCL is the physiological index, the same relatively high value on behalf of his relatively high, relatively low is the mood is relatively low (Fig. 1).

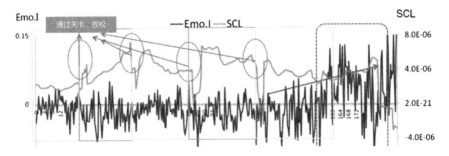

Fig. 1. The EMOI and SCL.

3.4   Exclude Non-Core Play Factors on the User's Interference

Virtually, this is still far from enough, follow-up and related to some experience, such as the use of stealth props when used, players over a number of dense cars will produce a perfect trigger will produce some nitrogen acceleration, so the accumulation is intensely strong.

The Use of Gray Layer
The teaching method uses a layer of mask, reducing the brightness of other controls, making the require doing to guide the principles is highlighted, and click on other controls is invalid [5]. And with the dynamic arrows, the guide ways are intensely direct, rarely the user presses the guide to operate in order to proceed to the next step. This method reduces the misuse to ensure that the user to the next step of the smooth operation with high availability (Fig. 2).

Fig. 2. Mask layer interface

"Asphalt 8: Airborne" through the perfect guidance system to play the game for the first time players brings a wonderful game experience while reducing a group of the game operating costs of the game. Nevertheless, the high-level players have either played the game before, provide that not just switched the version of the player, this part of the public doesn't need this guidance and tips.

Precise Control Design
Figure for the wild racing in the game selection interface, the bottom of the interface for the relevant options, from the page can be seen, the choice between the button is too narrow, the phone screen smaller users can not click on the filter, provide that the player there are many times the erroneous situation, it is bound to trigger the player's discontent. Additionally, the following "drivers" and the top of the "multiplayer" button, it is confused (Fig. 3).

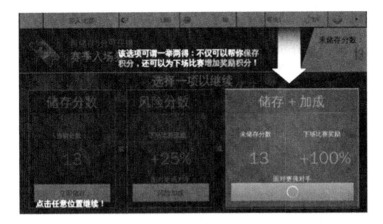

Fig. 3. Precise control design

Timely Information Feedback

For the players click on the skills after the game interface map, when the user clicks, the interface immediately emerged in the wind of the musical effect, as well as the enemy contribute to a wide range of damage [6].

Therefore it decided to mobile game in the operating process, and we must consider the length of available time for these players, as far as possible to set aside the player's time to improve the player's game efficiency, in a relatively short period of time, lest players get pleasant results, that is the priority, and the phone will be set on the difficulty of the PC side of the game is simple, to avoid an army of mental work, simple, easy game mode is the main promotion style (Fig. 4).

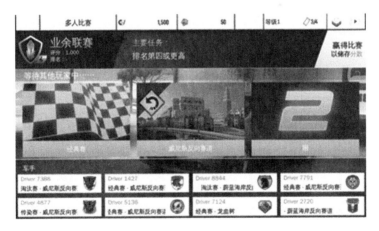

Fig. 4. The order of the performance interface

4 Summarize

This paper hopes to establish a reasonable explanation and quantitative evaluation method through the integration of documents, user research, design analysis, design of game interactive interface, and help users realize the immersion status of high-level player experience and hope to use it for other Field interface design, to help users more efficient and pleasant to achieve goals and challenges. The structure of interaction design is discussed from the mode of operation, information display and the feedback design. The construction of the interface style, the theme of the atmosphere and design specifications is aimed at exploring the style of visual design; from the dynamic loading and interesting design to explore the dynamic of performance design.

References

1. Deng, S.: Discuss on the gaming experience in interaction design use. Technol. Mark. 59–60 (2015)
2. He, S., Liu, Z.: The aesthetic transformation of visual culture in new media era. News Knowl. **6**, 12–16 (2015)
3. Xin, X.: Interaction design: from logic of things to logic of behaviors. Zhuangshi **1**, 58–62 (1985). (cial Psychol. 49(3) 607–627 (2015)
4. Lao, Q.: Application Research of App Interface Design Based on Context. Peking University, Beijing (2014)
5. Gaggioli, A., Cipresso, P., Serino, S., Riva, G.: Psychophysiological correlates of flow during daily activities. Health Technol. Inf. **191**, 65–69 (2013)
6. Wang, A.: New development of modern art design from the aesthetic pespective. Packag. Eng. **34**(18), 119–122 (2013)

Creating an Environment for Millennials

Bruce Gooch[(✉)], Nicolas Bain, and Taylor Day

College of Engineering, Texas A&M University, College Station, USA
BruceGooch@gmail.com

Abstract. Millennials, individuals born between the years 1978 and 2000, are advancing from colleges and universities to the workplace. The traits and characteristics of this generation are widely studied and categorized. Previous work demonstrates that Millennials have difficulty pursuing objectives that require critical thinking skills. We designed and deployed a one week program to aid Millennials in developing critical and free thinking skills. Our program scaffolds learning using a resource rich laboratory environment. We allowed them free reign over any and all available resources to work or build with as they pleased. Throughout the process, we followed progress, offered advice, and noted instances when group actions paralleled documented Millennial behaviors. Participants documented their learning process in a comic book style poster to further our ability to understand their progression.

1 Introduction

As technology advances and home environments shift throughout the years, generational learning styles and workplace skills alter along with the rising students that progress through the higher education environment. Most recently, Millennials, individuals born between the years 1978 and 2000, have been advancing through colleges, universities, and into entry level workplace positions, where they seem to have some difficulty adhering to conventional workplace policies and pursuing objectives that require critical thinking skills. These traits and characteristics of the incoming generation have been widely studied and categorized, and a general synopsis of the findings of other research groups has been included as background for our findings. In order to pinpoint any weaknesses and partially combat them, we as a computer science and emerging technology laboratory at Texas A&M University took part in an engineering camp, called ENGAGE (ENGineering Aggies Gaining Experience). The camp is based on knowledge gained through hands-on learning experiences, and its participants are chosen from a selection of applications received from high school students who meet eligibility qualifications, which outline that the students must have GPAs of 3.5 or above and must be entering 10th or 11th grade, though it is clearly stated that "... priority will be given to students of ENGAGE partner high schools and students from underrepresented groups..." (ENGAGE Summer Camp, n.d.). Our particular goals for the weeklong camp were to enrich the students' familiarity with new types of technology as well as allow them to develop critical thinking skills by placing them in a resource rich open-ended laboratory environment. Throughout the process, we

© Springer International Publishing AG 2017
C. Stephanidis (Ed.): HCII Posters 2017, Part II, CCIS 714, pp. 109–114, 2017.
DOI: 10.1007/978-3-319-58753-0_17

followed their progress, offered advice, and noted instances when the actions of a student group paralleled with behaviors, based on thorough research, that Millennials are known to demonstrate. We asked them to document their process in the form of a comic book style poster, and paired with our observations we were able to ascertain some faults as well as some strengths in the thought development of these students, all of which were in the upper end of the age range of Millennials. Our attempts to repair problem areas in student abilities and their reaction to these efforts were also under observation and provided insight into what kind of changes could be made in the educational and workplace environments in order to support student growth and achievement.

2   The Definition of Millennials by Birth Year

Generations by year			
Generation Y	Generation Z	Millennial	Source
		1982-present	Monaco and Martin (2007)
	1995–2012		Singh (2014)
1978–1990	1990–2000	1978–2000	Tulgan (2013)
		1982–2003	Keeling (2003)
		1982–2002	Roehl et al. (2013)
		1981–1999	Nicholas (2008)
1982–2004	2005-present	1982–2004	Strauss and Howe (1991)

Millennials are defined in various, depending on the experimental group involved, and this can be problematic when researching the generational learning and development styles of various age groups. In order to clearly define the birth years and ages of the students described in our research, we have taken the ages of Millennials to be those born between the years 1978 and 2000. This vast span is then subdivided into two categories; Generation Y, those born between 1978 and 1990, and Generation Z, born between 1990 and 2000. This definition, as described by Tulgan (2013), is useful for our purposes because it allows us to both generalize traits across the board as well as utilize more specific descriptions as described in other research articles. Below is a small set of sources and their internal demarcations of the generational spans, including the much-cited Strauss and Howe book, *Generations: The History of America's Future, 1584 to 2069*, which, while insightful into the mental processes of the generation, contrasts drastically in its classification of the generations.

3   Helicopter Parenting

When addressing the issues and strengths of the Millennial generation, it is worth noting the increasing phenomenon of helicopter parenting. This interesting occurrence "...refers to an overinvolvement of parents in their children's lives..." (LeMoyne and Buchanan 2011), especially during the formative years. This, in turn, creates a new breed of learners and students, as "...parent-driven scheduled lifestyles with little "free" time characterizes the childhood of Millennials. This regimented schedule of extra-curricular activities has decreased opportunities for independent creative thought and decision-making skills and provides challenges for both employers and educators..." (Monaco and Martin 2007). These heavily involved parents, and therefore the students themselves, demand more than ever that schools are held to the highest standards of accountability for the services they provide. (Keeling 2003) Students who have been monitored and hand-held through their entire childhood, and "...isolated and scheduled to a degree that children have never been..." (Tulgan 2013), may have a more difficult time transitioning to the lifestyle of a traditional college student, where self-direction and critical thinking skills are a must. This difficulty could be attributed to the massive amounts of "...protection and direction from parents, teachers, and counselors..." that students were exposed to prior to entering the higher education environment (Tulgan 2013).

4   Standardized Testing

Standardized testing, where tests are created to be taken by all students of a specific skill level and are then scored in a standard manner, have been implemented in all fifty states in the US. These tests are the basis of "...grade promotion and graduation to school funding. By degrees, standardized testing is becoming just about the only measure of academic quality that really counts in many school systems..." (Keeling 2003) Because of this, teachers are utilizing time in class to teach to the test, as well as educate students on test-taking abilities, which places a larger emphasis on the structure and learning goals associated with the test itself. This, in turn, fosters a type of learning that follows a list of skills to master and schedules the learning pattern of students into a streamlined path which must be followed in order to proceed. By organizing the educational system into a series of prewritten goals, independent learning, critical thinking, and free thinking skills are inhibited, leaving students at a disadvantage if they then enter into the higher education or workplace environments.

5   Millennial Traits

Due to external influences such as standardized testing and the integration of technology into everyday life, Millennials, especially Generation Z, have developed their own unique set of traits that characterize their generation. These traits are detailed by Strauss and Howe, and can be compressed down to a concise list; Millennials are special, sheltered, confident, team oriented, achieving, pressured, and conventional. By expounding on each of these traits, we can observe the byproducts of the internal strengths and weaknesses of this generation, and can possibly research strategies that attempt to adapt the higher educational environment in order to better suit incoming students.

As listed in *The Millennial Student: A New Generation of Learners* (pg. 44), each attribute of this generation plays a role in their performance in the classroom. They perceive themselves as special, and are accustomed to rewards for participation; they have been sheltered, and work best in a structured environment with a strict set of well-followed rules. While they may show signs of independence, they work well in groups and tend to be inherently socially active, a consequence of continuous inter-action through media and online resources. Though their high level of optimism due to their confidence causes them to want to have a hand in the creation of their own knowledge, they also require feedback every step of the way. They perform well when being judged, but if told they do not meet preset standards they will challenge the grading process and the validity of the verdict (Monaco and Martin 2007). These characteristics of the Millennial learner branch further into classroom applications and the consequences of removing or adding different applications.

Millennial students, as noted by workplace professionals and university level educators, are most well acquainted with being spoon-fed information (Keeling 2003). As a result, they have not been given the opportunity to develop a large range of critical thinking skills, and require clear instructions as well as feedback in order to continue their assignment or project, and as stated in Advising the Millennial Generation, "… these students may want a major chosen for them rather than by them… "…students demand that 'everything is spelled out' in detail and have trouble thinking for them-selves."…" Even when supplied the safety net of direction, Millennial students still "… thrive on constant feedback and become paralyzed, often unable to proceed forward, without feedback and direction…" (Monaco and Martin 2007). As a method meant to combat this paralysis, it has been highly suggested that educators give clear expecta-tions in the course syllabus regarding assignment due dates, test dates, evaluation methods, and required prerequisite knowledge.

6 Project Methods

Our project consisted of a weeklong camp centered on a technology rich lab envi-ronment. Twenty high-achieving high school aged students were selected to participate in the program. The technologies available to them included 3D printers, movement detectors, and remote controlled drones. Students were instructed to begin a self-directed group project given these technologies and to document their progress via comic book-style poster boards. As a bonus designed to promote motivation among the students, guest speakers were invited to talk about and demonstrate their own self-directed projects. These methods promoted an environment of self-rewarding behaviors centered around learning and research, and because we encouraged them to work in groups it also fostered a collaborative and cooperative aspect to the project. Because they were able to work hands-on with all the technologies being introduced to them, their learning environment required interaction, and their evaluation method of their own project was left open to interpretation, so long as they recorded their progress on the posters by the end of the week.

Classroom application	Did we?
Provide rewards for individual and group work	No
Provide feedback	Yes
Teach to self-reward	Yes
Learning centered syllabus	Yes
Clear instructions and expectations of assignments	Yes
Course calendar with test and assignment dates	No
Daily lesson learning outcomes	No
Collaborative learning	Yes
Cooperative learning	Yes
Interactive learning	Yes
Opportunities for in and out of class social learning activities	No
Provide clear definitions and paths to success in class	Yes
Include variety of technology in teaching and assignments	Yes
Link content to "real life" applications	Yes
Provide feedback in various forms including technological means	No
Timely feedback	Yes
Simulations and case work through technology and non-technology instructional delivery	Yes
Develop well defined grade appeals policy	No
Integrate a variety of valid evaluation methods	Yes
Utilize problem solving by integrating sociological situations from a variety of cultures	No

Classroom applications for Millennial students (Monaco and Martin 2007); italicized were not implemented during our research.

7 Project Results

Participants had difficulty beginning their projects, but with continuous feedback were able to confidently work in a self-directed environment. Allowing them to interact with completed past projects aided them in moving forward, and building a visual representation of their process helped support their faith in the trial-error method of production. During the first day, many students were notably "lost", and continuously requested step-by-step direction. By the end of the second day, about half of the students had formed groups around technologies that they found interesting or useful. A guest speaker, who had built a motorized longboard on his own time, came to speak on the third day; the motivation and excitement caused by the guest speaker were noticeable, and energy in the laboratory increased exponentially. Between the last two days, all students became somewhat engaged in at least one of the resulting self-directed projects, and on the last day, students were given a presentation centered on remote controlled drones our laboratory built using the 3D printers versus a commercially bought drone. The students put together their presentation posters, and most notably the majority of the posters centered on the comradery of the groups, the resulting discussions, and the guest speaker presentations. We noted that some students were reluctant to record their failures, which led us to believe that more positive feedback for failing and moving forward would be necessary for such an environment.

8 Conclusion

Throughout our experiment, we found that positive feedback for moving on after a failure and generalized feedback on students' methods were the best ways to create an environment in which students were able to thrive. Notably, working in groups to provide collaborative interaction suited the students well, and maintaining energy by providing examples of others' success were also key components of student success.

References

ENGAGE Summer Camp: Engineering Texas A&M University (n.d.) Web

Howe, N., Strauss, W.: Generations: The History of America's Future, 1584 to 2069. William Morrow & Company, New York (1991). ISBN 978-0-688-11912-6

Keeling, S.: Advising the millennial generation. NACADA J. 23(1–2), 30–36 (2003)

LeMoyne, T., Buchanan, T.: Does "hovering" matter? Helicopter parenting and its effect on well-being. Sociol. Spectr. 31(4), 399–418 (2011)

Monaco, M., Martin, M.: The millennial student: a new generation of learners. Athletic Train. Educ. J. 2(2), 42–46 (2007)

Nicholas, A.: Preferred learning methods of the millennial generation (2008)

Roehl, A., Reddy, S.L., Shannon, G.J.: The flipped classroom: an opportunity to engage millennial students through active learning. J. Fam. Consum. Sci. 105(2), 44 (2013)

Singh, A.: Challenges and issues of generation Z. IOSR J. Bus. Manag. IOSRJBM 16(7), 59–63 (2014). doi:10.9790/487x-16715963

Tulgan, B.: Meet generation Z: the second generation within the giant "Millennial" cohort. Rainmaker Thinking (2013)

Flexible Virtual Environments: Gamifying Immersive Learning

Neil Gordon[(⊠)] and Mike Brayshaw

University of Hull, Hull HU6 7RX, England
{n.a.gordon, m.brayshaw}@hull.ac.uk

Abstract. The availability of Virtual Reality (VR) and Virtual Environment (VE) equipment - with the launch of domestic technologies such as the Oculus Rift, Microsoft Hololens and Sony Playstation VR) - offer new ways to enable interactive immersive experiences [16]. The opportunities these create in learning and training applications are immense: but create new challenges. Meanwhile, current virtual learning environments are typically web or app based technologies, sometimes perceived as having little value added from a user perspective beyond improved User Interfaces to access some content [6]. The challenge is how the human computer interaction features of such VE platforms may be used in education in a way that adds value, especially for computer mediated instruction. This paper will outline some of the issues, and opportunities, as well as some of the open questions about how such technologies can be used effectively in a higher education context, along with a proposed framework for embedding a learning engine within a virtual reality or environment system.

Three-dimensional technologies: from work-walls, through CAVES to the latest headsets offer new ways to immerse users in computer generated environments. Immersive learning [1] is increasingly common in training applications, and is beginning to make inroads into formal education. The recent rise in such off-the-shelf technologies means that Augmented Learning becomes a realistic mainstream tool [13]. Much of this use is built in game environments using game engines, where these serious games provide learning effects as an intended consequence of playing.

Keywords: Gamification · Flexible pedagogy · Virtual environments

1 Introduction

The use of game mechanics in learning – known as gamification [9] – is becoming more established, with options such as multiple attempts at tests (akin to lives in a game), immediate feedback and reward (marks as a substitute for game scores) illustrate how game mechanics can reflect established and novel approaches to instruction [8]. Such mechanics are increasingly prevalent in modern Virtual Learning Environments (VLE), though these VLE systems are typically web based 2-dimension information repositories, supported with a range of learning and assessment tools, such as support for online tests, quizzes and other computer based assessment.

This paper will describe what is needed to combine such technologies so they can be effectively utilised to support higher education teaching, where the computer based

© Springer International Publishing AG 2017
C. Stephanidis (Ed.): HCII Posters 2017, Part II, CCIS 714, pp. 115–121, 2017.
DOI: 10.1007/978-3-319-58753-0_18

instruction is provided by a mix of suitable back-end intelligent and flexible learning system [5] alongside the immersive front end provided by the Virtual technology. An effective way to assess such systems can be offered through heuristic evaluation, as previously explored by the authors [7].

The paper concludes with a model for combining the computer-based instruction, gamification of the learning mechanics, along with the virtual environment itself to provide an engaging, practical and effective true virtual learning environment.

2 Of Being Virtual

The concept of virtual environments for work, education and relaxation is well established, though is evolving as new technologies improve the virtual experience. In the current context, there are some differing meanings of virtual that are explored in the following sections.

2.1 Virtual Environments

Virtual environments (VE) [10] have moved on from the large and research-lab style headsets, to now becoming a domestic home leisure device, with a variety of cheap smart-phone based devices (Google Cardboard and Samsung Gear for example), through medium price games-console accessories (PlayStation VR), to more expensive headsets that require a high-spec PC to support them (Oculus Rift). VE headsets such as those just listed shut out the physical world, though many include cameras to enable some element of inclusion of real world content. Augmented devices such as the Microsoft Hololens and short-lived Google-glass prototype provide facilities to overlay computer-generated content onto real-world objects and environments. These approaches to VE have provided individual views on virtual worlds, with a variety of uses. They have technical issues in terms of the usability and impact on users, with side effects such as nausea for some users, as well as a lack presence and self with the immersive headsets.

2.2 Immersive Learning

Immersive learning is concerned with the use of virtual worlds and/or environments in learning and training. This may be the use of a virtual world: such as Second Life [19], or the use of a other game engine such as Unity [4]. The immersion in this may be from a 2D viewpoint of the 3D world, rather than a fully immersive experience. However, the VR support of engines such as Unity, mean that they can offer truly immersive experience, this offering the potential for training and simulation activities where effectiveness depends upon realistic virtual environments [11] to support training. Immersive Learning is typified by its use of simulation and virtual worlds to provide interactive learning environments. Immersive learning can utilise game-based learning, where this use may be the environment itself, such as the example of using Unity and Second Life, to the mechanics within an environment, as described in the next section.

2.3 Gamification

As mentioned in the introduction, gamification is concerned with the application of game mechanics to a non-game activity [8]. In education, this can be around the way that assessment is used to provide rapid feedback on progress and proficiency, the way that learners can reattempt an activity, or the competitive nature of an activity. Such gamified approaches can also include personalization: with adaptive difficulty and a personalized experience. Whilst game engines are used to provide some immersive environments for learning, the linkage between playability and learning progress is not as transparent.

2.4 Virtual Learning Environments

Virtual Learning Environments (VLE) are the online version of traditional teaching and learning support. They do not typically offer virtual technologies, but are online platforms and use traditional GUIs and web technologies to support teaching and learning. The requirements of these is centered on traditional teaching and learning [6]. Often they borrow a direct classroom or school metaphor and map this into the virtual. In doing so they often implement a type of straight-jacket for teachers and learners that force a certain type of pre-ordained interaction. This means that it is often necessary for tools to be adapted to meet local needs rather than providing virtual support. We consider later how flexibility needs to play a vital role in the way ahead and that part of that flexibility can be to add an element of gameplay and personalization. Furthermore, we consider this misnomer in that existing VLEs do not utilise Virtual Learning Environments nor immersive learning, and would be better typified as Web-based Learning Environments.

2.5 Virtual Individuals and Virtual Teams

Working in a virtual environment is an increasingly common experience. The nature of modern internet connectivity means that as an individual the task of eLearning can be undertaken almost anywhere. For immersive learning, this might be either an individual or a group experience. Single roles, for example managing a particular incident, can be created. The user interacts with other scenario-based characters, which might be perceived like game non-playing characters and implemented via devices from state machines to artificial intelligences. The problems of working alone, potentially far away from others in terms of place or time, are those of loneliness and isolation. These provide motivating reasons as to why we consider the use of gamification as a means to address this isolation and generate inclusivity.

Alternatively, more than one person may be immersed within the same-shared space to make up a virtual team. This can immediately overcome some of the problems of working alone. Teams also provide an important new angle on learning from a pedagogic angle in that the task has to be managed and shared. The gamification of this process potentially provides immediate and sharable goals and motivations for the team. We naturally frequently compete as teams, so to do so in an immersive environment builds upon our background experiences and shared desires for success.

3   A Framework for True Virtual Environments in Higher Education

As we have seen in the previous sections, there are a range of technologies and pedagogic approaches that offer tools for enhancing learning and teaching, and complement the typical features of a VLE. Bringing these together into an actual virtual learning toolset requires a combination of content, assessment and delivery with support for the different forms of learning activity that are needed in Higher Education. Figure 1 links the various aspects identified as a framework for supporting learning and teaching, as well as training.

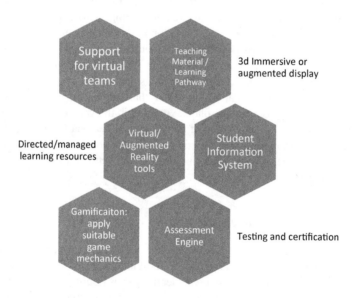

Fig. 1. A framework for a virtual environment for virtual learning.

One way to link these would be through utilizing interoperability standards, such as the Learning Tools Interoperability standard [12], which enable learning applications to interface to VLEs and other learning management systems. Enabling the embedding of learning content within a virtual world, enabling control (gateway) features to support personalized learning pathways, and linking assessment activities to virtual world activities would open up the potential for truly virtual learning environments that offer a personalized flexible learning experience.

4 Issues in Virtual Environments

4.1 Sense of Presence

One key issue is getting a believable interaction – users have to believe in the surroundings and what they are seeing. Most existing VR require an acceptance of the projected reality by the user. Indeed some do not feel real unless the user accepts them and accepts the story. In the game context, this is potentially easier to achieve, where the element of the VR that we are interested in is the most important part. Within a game context, the rendering of the body of the characters may be crudely and unrealistically done, but this does not matter; what is of interest here is the game elements of the interaction. In gamifying immersive learning, we can play a similar trick, where the game and the game dynamics are used to make any shortcoming of presence easier to overlook, as the game makes new goals more important.

4.2 Modalities

Modalities refers to different ways of communicating (e.g. text, speech, visual, audible, and tactile). The use of these technologies can greatly affect the interaction in different ways [14, 18, 20]. In a perfect virtual reality, we can expect interpersonal communication to behave as it would in the real world involving Face2Face interaction. However, in many practical shared virtual experiences a full real world experience is not available or would be too expensive, so participants interact by text, chat, phone, or video channel. These types of choice can have significant effects on the resultant communication in an immersive environment. This qualitative difference has to be allowed for when gamifying immersive learning. That people are effected by the modality of communication means that the type of immersion and the didactic content need to take special measure of these issues.

4.3 Inclusivity

Isolation is recognized as an issue for distance learning [3]. Designers of Internet Web based material need to consider ways to construct their material and activity for online learners. If we are to consider students from a full range of abilities then we have to also think about how this approach will scale to disability-aware software [15]. What are the consequences and realities of immersion and gamification for this class of students? This consideration must include what types of media interaction will work, what types of physical interaction in terms of game mechanics are practical, and are the cognitive requirements of special users fully addressed?

4.4 Evaluation

If Gamifying Immersive Learning is to be of any value then we need to measure that value. This places a particular burden on the evaluator in considering what aspects of such learning environment can be measured. High Sores or Time Taken will give a gross measure of engagement. The very fact that the game is immersive means that those immersed may not be the best people to evaluate their experience (other than to comment on the immersion). We have argued elsewhere [2] that one solution route to is Heuristic Evaluation. In this technique, expert software designers are given a set of basic heuristics and then are asked to evaluate the software according to these criteria. Such heuristic can be extended to cover any aspects of the immersive experience that are not already covered by the original or educationally extended heuristic set. This would thus give us a way of evaluating our games and specifically particular criteria that are of direct relevance.

4.5   Motivation and Engagement: Gamification

One of the explicit reasons to use immersive games in learning is that the very immersion the user finds in the game gives us the motivation and engagement that we are frequently striving for when designing online teaching environments. By taking a particular syllabus and adding the immersive game element, the aim is to produce educational material that is spell binding and leads to maximal engagement with the material by the game player/learner. Rigby and Ryan [17] note the way Video Games can hold our attention in a gripping manner. They look to see motivating factors and how they are used in games design. The concepts of self-autonomy and flexibility that come from games also fit with the notion of flexibility considered earlier. They also note that the self-motivation and gamification may not actually be purely about fun but other factors may drive our interaction with the game.

5   Conclusions

In this paper, we have contrasted the different meanings of virtual when considering education; in particular, in the he higher education context where independent learning and group collaboration are frequently important features, there are some real potential benefits from the use of true virtual learning environments to locate our learning activities. The potential for building a true virtual and immersive learning environment is clear, though requires the development of suitable interfaces to enable interoperability between VR and AR, and VLE along with appropriate pedagogic techniques, valuation of the effectiveness, from a HCI perspective, of any such environment can be problematic, but expert based heuristic evaluation may offer a solution here.

References

1. Appelman, R.: Designing experiential modes: a key focus for immersive learning environments. TechTrends **49**(3), 64–74 (2005)
2. Brayshaw, M., Gordon, N., Nganji, J., Wen, L., Butterfield, A.: Investigating heuristic evaluation as a methodology for evaluating pedagogical software: an analysis employing

three case studies. In: Zaphiris, P., Ioannou, A. (eds.) LCT 2014. LNCS, vol. 8523, pp. 25–35. Springer, Cham (2014). doi:10.1007/978-3-319-07482-5_3

3. Croft, N., Dalton, A., Grant, M.: Overcoming isolation in distance learning: building a learning community through time and space. J. Educ. Built Environ. 5(1), 27–64 (2010)

4. Dawley, L., Dede, C.: Situated learning in virtual worlds and immersive simulations. In: Spector, J.M., Merrill, M.D., Elen, J., Bishop, M.J. (eds.) Handbook of Research on Educational Communications and Technology, pp. 723–734. Springer, New York (2014)

5. Gordon, N.: Flexible pedagogies: technology-enhanced learning. Technical report. The Higher Education Academy (2014)

6. Gordon, N., Brayshaw, M.: Requirements capture analysis for MOOCS in higher education. In: Furthering Higher Education Possibilities through Massive Open Online Courses, pp. 107–124. IGI Global (2015)

7. Gordon, N., Brayshaw, M., Aljaber, T.: Heuristic evaluation for serious immersive games and M-instruction. In: Zaphiris, P., Ioannou, A. (eds.) LCT 2016. LNCS, vol. 9753, pp. 310–319. Springer, Cham (2016). doi:10.1007/978-3-319-39483-1_29

8. Gordon, N., Brayshaw, M., Grey, S.: Maximising gain for minimal pain: utilising natural game mechanics. Innov. Teach. Learn. Inf. Comput. Sci. 12(1), 27–38 (2013)

9. Groh, F.: Gamification: state of the art definition and utilization. Institute of Media Informatics Ulm University, p. 39 (2012)

10. Hale, K.S., Stanney, K.M.: Handbook of Virtual Environments: Design, Implementation, and Applications. CRC Press, Boca Raton (2014)

11. Herrington, J., Reeves, T.C., Oliver, R.: Immersive learning technologies: realism and online authentic learning. J. Comput. High. Educ. 19(1), 80–99 (2007)

12. IMS Global: Learning Tools Interoperability. http://www.imsglobal.org/activity/learning-tools-interoperability

13. Kidd, S.H., Crompton, H.: Augmented learning with augmented reality. In: Churchill, D., Lu, J., Chiu, Thomas K.F., Fox, B. (eds.) Mobile Learning Design. LNET, pp. 97–108. Springer, Singapore (2016). doi:10.1007/978-981-10-0027-0_6

14. Miller, H., Bugnariu, N.L.: Level of immersion in virtual environments impacts the ability to assess and teach social skills in autism spectrum disorder. Cyberpsychol. Behav. Soc. Netw. 19(4), 246–256 (2016)

15. Nganji, J.T., Brayshaw, M.: Facilitating learning resource retrieval for students with disabilities through an ontology-driven and disability-aware virtual learning environment. In: Special and Gifted Education: Concepts, Methodologies, Tools, and Applications, pp. 1668–1688. IGI Global (2016)

16. Pierce, D.: The future of AV displays. J. (Technol. Horiz. Educ.) 43(4), 26 (2016)

17. Rigby, S., Ryan, R.M.: Glued to games: how video games draw us in and hold us spellbound. ABC-CLIO (2011)

18. Schroeder, R.: Being There Together: Social Interaction in Shared Virtual Environments. Oxford University Press, Oxford (2010)

19. Second Life Education. http://wiki.secondlife.com/wiki/Second_Life_Education/

20. Wilkes, S.F.: Communication modality, learning, and second life. In: Learning in Virtual Worlds: Research and Applications (2016)

The Effect of Emotion in an Ultimatum Game: The Bio-Feedback Evidence

Yifan He[(⊠)] and Tiffany Y. Tang

Media Lab, Department of Computer Science,
Wenzhou-Kean University, Wenzhou, China
{heyif,yatang}@kean.edu

Abstract. In neoclassical economics, Rational Choice Theory states that individuals always make prudent and rational decisions provided with the greatest benefits. In Ultimatum Game, the proposer (Player I) proposes how to split a sum of money. The responder (Player II) decides to accept or reject the proposal. If the responder accepts, the sum is splitted as proposed; otherwise, neither player can receive money. One of the results shows that some "unfair" offers are often rejected, which implies the effect of emotion in an economic decision-making. In this research, a special Ultimatum Game has been designed to collect bio-feedback evidence for emotion in an economic decision-making using the Galvanic Skin Response (GSR) sensor. Also, an Ultimatum Game with computer simulation had been designed to collect bio-feedback results when the sum of money is in virtual points offered by a computer.

Keywords: Ultimatum Game · Emotion factor · Galvanic Skin Response · Economics

1 Introduction

Though economists have not denied the existence and significance of emotion in economical decision-makings, in the past, emotion were still left out of the analysis in an economical behavior modeling because of the unpredictability and complexity. However, recent research has shown the strong relation between emotion and economic decision-makings. The researchers reported that people's bargaining behavior, inter-temporal choices and decision-making under risk or uncertainty are strongly affected by the emotion [1].

Ultimatum Game, a famous economic experiment, has been widely used to prove the limitation on emotional factors of current standard economic models [2–5]. In Ultimatum Game, two players (one as a proposer; the other as a responder) are required to split a sum of money. The proposer will first give a proposal on how to split the sum and the responder will decide to accept or reject the proposal. If the proposal is accepted, the money will be split as proposed; otherwise, neither of the players can receive any money. Based on Rational Choice Theory, the expected result of Ultimatum Game is that the proposer splits most of the sum to leave it to himself/herself and the responder accepts the proposal. However, prior researchers reported two opposite results:

© Springer International Publishing AG 2017
C. Stephanidis (Ed.): HCII Posters 2017, Part II, CCIS 714, pp. 122–129, 2017.
DOI: 10.1007/978-3-319-58753-0_19

1. The most frequent outcome of the proposal is a fair share.
2. Some unfair proposals are often rejected by the responder.

One of the explanations such conflicting results are that the "benefits" in Rational Choice Theory also includes emotional benefits [5]. In other words, the experiment results showed the existence of emotion in Ultimatum Game.

Sensor technology has been widely applied in the prior research of emotion. GSR sensor can measure the electrical conductance of the skin. Strong emotion can cause stimulus to the nervous system, resulting more sweat being secreted [6]. Therefore, applying GSR sensor is an effective method to monitor emotion. In this research, a special Ultimatum Game has been designed, applying GSR sensor technology, to find the bio-feedback evidence for emotion in the game. Another experiment has been designed to test the bio-feedback results when the sum to split is in virtual points rather than real money. To improve the experimental effects, during the whole experiment, the players have been required to make decisions in a limited time, and "fair" split is not allowed. Before we present our studies, earlier works will be discussed in the next section.

2 Related Work

2.1 Emotion and Ultimatum Game

The Role of Emotion in Economic Decision-Making. Economists have been focus on emotion in a decision-making. For decades, different from physiologists who mainly studied immediate emotion, they turned their attention to anticipated emotions which are not experienced at the time of the decision-making. However, in 2000, it is reported that a kind of immediate emotion, more specifically, visceral factors, should be considered as significant factor in decision-making as well [1]. The researcher pointed out that visceral factors can grab people's attention and motivate their special behaviors. These behaviors are applied in almost all-domains but when it comes to economic behaviors, three categories are of special relevance: bargaining behavior which is easily affected by anger, fear and embarrassment, inter-temporal choice which is strongly influenced by multiple factors, and decision-making under risk and uncertainty which is easily influenced by factors like fear. In the following years, researchers and scientists continued to pay attention on the immediate emotion as a factor of decision-makings, including the famous Ultimatum Game.

Emotion in Ultimatum Game. The "irrational" decisions, especially the "irrational" rejection for the unfair proposals in Ultimatum Game have been discussed for a long period. Recent years researchers have started to find bio-evidence of emotion which has been considered to be the cause of "irrational" decisions. Researchers have found neural basis evidence of the economic decision-making in the Ultimatum Game, using magnetic resonance imaging (fRMI) technology in 2003 [2]. They scanned the brains of responders after responding to fair and unfair proposals. The magnetic resonance setting has detected the brain activity in the areas related to emotion (anterior insula) and cognition (dorsolateral prefrontal cortex) when responding unfair offers. They also reported the heightened activity in the anterior insula when a responder rejected an unfair offer. Besides the neural basis evidence, researchers also found electrodermal activity evidence. In 2006, researchers applied skin conductance amplifier in the Ultimatum Game [3]. The collected data revealed that skin conductance activity was higher for unfair offers and was associated with the rejection of unfair offers. However, this pattern only occurred for offers proposed by human.

2.2   GSR and Emotion Detection

To detect emotion, such technologies like speech recognition, face recognition and brain signal scanning are often applied [7, 8]. GSR value is another effective indicator for emotion activities. Also, GSR sensor is a more portable tool which can monitor the emotion of users compared to the skin conductance amplifier. Therefore, it is widely applied in the research on emotion and recognition. A research group built an emotion recognition system based on Electromyography (EMG) data and skin conductance signals which can be indicated by GSR data in 2005 [4]. They reported the model using Bayesian network and other methodologies to recognize user's emotion. In 2006, researchers developed a stress detection system based on physiological signals monitored by non-invasive and non-intrusive sensors [9]. The system performed supervised classification of affective states between "stress" and "relaxed" using a support vector machine based on the four kinds of data, GSR, Blood Volume Pulse (BVP), Pupil Diameter (PD) and Skin Temperature (ST).

3   Our Experiment

The entire experiment included an Ultimatum Game with a sum of real money and an Ultimatum Game with the sum of virtual points of simulated money. The first game was to collect the bio-feedback evidence in the Ultimatum Game. The second game was to probe whether the computer simulated game can reach the same goal.

3.1   Participants and Apparatus

10 participants (5 proposers and 5 responders) chosen from a local university were divided into two groups. Group I contained 6 participants (3 proposers and 3 responders) and Group II contained 4 participants (2 proposers and 2 responders). To collect the bio-feedback data, participants were required to wear a Seeed Grove - GSR sensor connecting to the Arduino (Fig. 1). The bio-feedback data would be shown as a line chart.

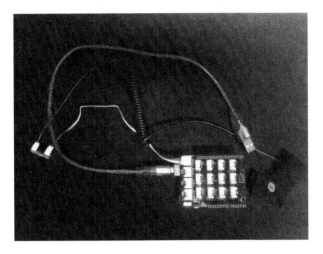

Fig. 1. Seeed Grove - GSR Sensor and Arduino used in the Ultimatum Game experiment.

3.2 Study Design

To improve the experimental effects, the experiment was designed based on these rules:

1. The participants need to make a decision in a limited time.
2. The proposers cannot propose a fair offer.
3. Every partition in a split should be integer multiples of 10%.

Ultimatum Game I. Two groups of participants were required to play Ultimatum Game with real money. Each pairs in Group I (3 proposers and 3 responders) were going to split the sums of 20 RMB (3 USD). Pairs in Group II (2 proposers and 2 responders) were instructed split the sums of 50 RMB (7.5 USD). Both proposers and responders were required to make decisions in 10 s.

Ultimatum Game II. All participants were required to play Ultimatum Game with virtual points. Each proposers were asked to propose an offer to split the sums of a random virtual points from 100 to 10, 000. Each responders were expected to make a decision among randomly generated proposals. Both proposers and responders were

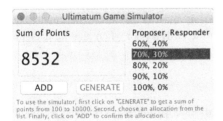

Fig. 2. Ultimatum Game simulators to generate random sums for proposers (left) and random proposals for responders (right).

required to make decisions in 10 s. The sums and proposals were generated by two separated programs (Fig. 2). The program for proposers would not generate a fair offer as well as an offer which the proposer receive less than half of the sum.

3.3 Experiment Procedure

Ultimatum Game I. Before the experiment, participants were allocated as proposers or responders randomly. Proposers in both groups were required to fill the form on how to split the sum of money in 10 s. After proposers filling the forms, the experimenter collected the form and allocated the forms to the responders randomly. The responders were also required to decide on accepting or not within 10 s. In this experiment, only the proposers were required to wear the GSR sensor when filling the form. The data collected by GSR sensor would be shown as line charts in Arduino Serial Plotter (Fig. 3).

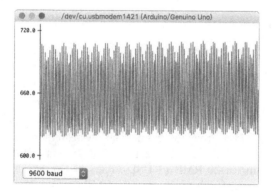

Fig. 3. A line chart of GSR sensor data of a participant who was taking a break shown in Arduino Serial Plotter.

Ultimatum Game II. Before the experiment, participants were randomly divided into groups of proposers and responders. Proposers were required to choose a proposal from among five proposals provided by the program in 10 s. And the sum of points to split was randomly generated. Responders were going to make decisions on whether to accept or reject the randomly generated proposals in 10 s. In this experiment, both proposers and responders were required to wear the GSR sensor when making decision.

4 Experiment Results and Analysis

In this research, the bio-feedback of emotion of each player was collected as quantitative data. The results of the first and the second Ultimatum Game are shown in the tables below.

4.1 Results of Two Ultimatum Games

The value variation of GSR sensor are shown in one or multiple "+" and "−". More "+" means a larger variation in GSR sensor value. "−" stands for no significant variation.

Table 1 shows the proposals of each proposers and corresponding GSR sensor value variations in the first Ultimatum Game experiment. Two of the proposers from Group I offered proposals that provided 60% of the sum to themselves and the rest 40% to their responders. Only one proposer (Proposer 3) in this group made a decision to provide 70% of the sum to himself and the rest 30% to his responder. In Group II, both two proposers decided to offer 60% of the sum to themselves and the rest 40% to their responders. Among the five proposers, the GSR value variations of Proposer 3 and Proposer 4 were largest (both of them reached "+ + +") during decision-making period. The variation of Proposer 2 ("+") was the least. The GSR value variations of rest two proposers were both "+ +".

Table 1. Proposals of proposers and corresponding GSR value variation in Ultimatum Game I.

Group number	Proposer	Proposal (proposer, responder)	GSR sensor value variation
I	1	60%, 40%	+ +
	2	60%, 40%	+
	3	70%, 30%	+ + +
II	4	60%, 40%	+ + +
	5	60%, 40%	+ +

Tables 2 and 3 show the experiment results of the second Ultimatum Game. Among the five proposers, Proposer 4 made a proposal on the largest sum of the points (8532). Proposer 3 made a decision on the minimum sum of the points (1009). Three proposers decided to split the sum as two partitions of 70% (for themselves) and 30% (for responders). One of the rest proposers proposed 60% for himself and the other proposed 90% for himself. The GSR sensor value variation of Proposer 1 is largest among the five proposers. Two of the proposers did not have significant variation in GSR value. Among the five responders, the largest percentage of the sum which a responder can receive if he/she accepted the proposal is 40% (Responder 3 and Responder 5). The largest amount of points which a responder can receive if he/she accepted the proposal is $6185 \times 40\% = 2474$ (Responder 3). The largest GSR value variation of five responders is "+" (Responder 2 and Responder 3). No significant variation of GSR value was found during the rest responders were making decisions.

Table 2. Proposals of proposers and corresponding GSR value variation in Ultimatum Game II.

Proposer	Sum of points	Proposal (proposer, responder)	GSR sensor value variation
1	4277	70%, 30%	+ +
2	1389	60%, 40%	+
3	1009	90%, 10%	+
4	8532	70%, 30%	−
5	4879	70%, 30%	−

Table 3. Proposals and GSR value variation of each responder in Ultimatum Game II.

Responder	Sum of points	Proposal (proposer, responder)	GSR sensor value variation
1	2342	90%, 10%	−
2	2082	90%, 10%	+
3	6185	60%, 40%	+
4	5027	70%, 30%	−
5	1722	60%, 40%	−

4.2   Discussion

In Ultimatum Game, when a proposer is required to propose an offer to split the sum of money, his/her emotion variation during the decision-making will be indicated by GSR data. On one hand, when a proposer makes decision on a large amount of money, he/she will have a larger variation of GSR value as well as emotion. On the other hand, the proposer will also have a larger variation of GSR value, when he/she is making decision to split more percentage of the money to him- or her- self. For example, in Ultimatum Game I, Proposers 1, 2, 4 and 5 offered a same splitting method (Proposer: Responder = 3: 2). Proposers 4 and Proposer 5 who were required to split 50 RMB, while Proposer 1 and Proposer 2 were required to split 20 RMB. The experiment result showed that the average GSR value variation of Proposer 4 and 5 is larger than Proposer 1 and 2. Proposer 3 was required to split 20 RMB and he offered a proposal that he would get 70% of the sum. Compared with Proposer 1 and 2, his GSR value variation was larger. However, in the second experiment, where players were required to making decisions on virtual points or proposals offered by computer, we failed to draw the same conclusion. Hence, we speculate that players will have a variation in emotion only when he/she is making decision on the real money. Further studies need to be conducted in order to explore such differences.

5   Future Study

In the current experiment design, the number of participants is limited. In Ultimatum Game I, only the data of proposers was recorded. Also, in both experiments, the acceptance statuses of each proposals were not recorded yet. Therefore, in the future, we are going to re-design a new experiment and test with more participants.

References

1. Loewenstein, G.: Emotions in economic theory and economic behavior. Am. Econ. Rev. **90**, 426–432 (2000). doi:10.1257/aer.90.2.426
2. Sanfey, A.G.: The neural basis of economic decision-making in the ultimatum game. Science **300**, 1755–1758 (2003). doi:10.1126/science.1082976
3. Van't, W.M., Kahn, R.S., Sanfey, A.G., et al.: Affective state and decision-making in the ultimatum game. Exp. Brain Res. **169**, 564–568 (2006)

4. Nakasone, A., Prendinger, H., Ishizuka, M: Emotion recognition from electromyography and skin conductance. In: Proceedings of the 5th International Workshop on Biosignal Interpretation, pp. 219–222 (2005)
5. Nowak, M.A.: Fairness versus reason in the ultimatum game. Science **289**, 1773–1775 (2000). doi:10.1126/science.289.5485.1773
6. Seeed Wiki. http://wiki.seeed.cc/Grove-GSR_Sensor/
7. Kim, S., Georgiou, P. G., Lee, S., et al.: Real-time emotion detection system using speech: multi-modal fusion of different timescale features. In: IEEE 9th Workshop on Multimedia Signal Processing, MMSP 2007, pp. 48–51. IEEE (2007)
8. Savran, A., Ciftci, K., Chanel, G., et al.: Emotion detection in the loop from brain signals and facial images (2006)
9. Zhai, J., Barreto, A.: Stress detection in computer users based on digital signal processing of noninvasive physiological variables. In: 28th Annual International Conference of the IEEE Engineering in Medicine and Biology Society, EMBS 2006, pp. 1355–1358 (2006)

Motion Recognition Interactive Game Activity for Early Childhood

Hyung-Sook Kim[✉] and Seong-Hee Chung

Inha University, Incheon, Korea
khsook12@inha.ac.kr, yellow8100@naver.com

Abstract. The purpose of this study is to experience the elements of science, cognitive, art, relationship, fitness through physical activity in connection with ICT skills. It provides the content of brain development, personality development, creativity and social development through physical activity. It can also to increase the interest and fun of the children by applying type of game. It suggests 36 contents construction grouped for children motion recognition interactive game activities, the concept of mobile interactive projector and application algorism. The subjects and activities are made up by peculiarities of development of children. Activities via subjects are consisted of 3 steps which are DO THINK, DO ACTIVITIES, DO COMMUNICATION. Mobile Interactive Projectors are designed considering variety environments and utilizing mobile PC, Beam projector, KINECT. KINECT is available to detect user movement and collecting activities data related with location and routes of children on the floor by depth camera. We purpose providing creative contents focusing utilization of developed technologies in fields instead of developing brand new technologies. Such approach may offer an opportunity to experience more easily skills in the users. In addition, the development content can be used in child institutions and facilities, as well as educational institutions.

Keywords: Kinect · Interactive game · Motion recognition · Education contents

1 Introduction

Future society is a fusion age and creativity is a core competence. The education field emphasizes convergence talent education (STEAM) for future human resources development. Various health monitoring application services are continuously increasing in the health and physical education industry, and production of practical contents is expected to spread. As such, it is competitive with advanced ICT infrastructure, contents, digital technique, and creative ability. And development of experiential services for fun and education are required. For this purpose, gamification should be applied to education to increase user's interest and participation. Also, contents production utilizing advanced ICT technology should be activated. Therefore, it is necessary to develop experiential physical activity contents that can be applied to actual education field.

© Springer International Publishing AG 2017
C. Stephanidis (Ed.): HCII Posters 2017, Part II, CCIS 714, pp. 130–135, 2017.
DOI: 10.1007/978-3-319-58753-0_20

2   Interactive Game Activity

2.1   Direction of Development

The purpose of this study is to experience the elements of science, cognitive, art, relationship, fitness through physical activity in connection with ICT skills. It provides the content of brain development, personality development, creativity and social development through physical activity. It can also to increase the interest and fun of the children by applying gamification in a method of providing active content. In particular, factors such as computer graphics, music, speech guidance can induce continued participation by increasing the engagement of the children. Thus, the visually perceived, thinking and activity expressed through the body can develop reasoning, memory, problem solving and cognitive skills.

Korea applies the national curriculum 'Nuri Curriculum' to kindergarten. It consists of five domains: physical exercise and health, communication, social relations, artistic experience, and natural exploration. The contents of education by age and area are presented considering the developmental characteristics of children aged 3 to 5 years. The Nuri curriculum emphasizes the need to organize five areas per day in a balanced manner and to include physical exercise time. Through this, children can relieve stress and form pro-social relations with their friends. In addition, the content of the education is organized around the play considering the developmental characteristics and experience of the child, and it is possible to deepen and expand according to the class time. In this study, we designed and constructed child physical activity contents based on Nuri curriculum.

2.2   Method of Development

This study suggests 36 contents construction grouped for children motion recognition interactive game activities and the concept of mobile interactive projector and application algorism. Contents consisted of a total of 36 classes modular (12 classes per module) considering the developmental characteristics per age based on nuri curriculum. And the composition of the classes were extended and deepened by topic so that kindergarten and day cater center teachers can optionally be utilized in physical activity-related classes. In this study, we selected topics that can be linked with real life in the natural exploration domain among the five domains of Nuri Curriculum. And it is designed to do interesting physical activity of gamification by linking physical fitness

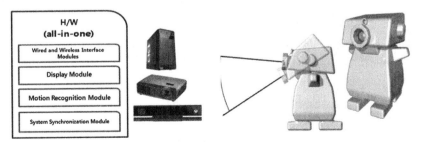

Fig. 1. The concept of interactive projector

elements of physical exercise and health domain with ICT technology. Mobile Inter-active Projectors are designed considering variety environments and utilizing mobile PC, Beam projector, KINECT (Fig. 1). KINECT is available to detect user movement and collecting activities datas related with location and routes of children on the floor by depth camera (Fig. 2).

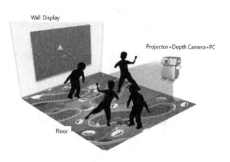

Fig. 2. The concept of physical activity

2.3   Contents of Development

The subjects and activities are made up by peculiarities of development of children. Activities via subjects are consisted of 3 steps which are DO THINK, DO ACTIVITIES, DO COMMUNICATION (Table 1). DO THINK is a stage that understands the basic knowledge of the subject and induces interest. This allows you to enjoy animation using characters. DO ACTIVITIES uses ICT technology to understand and experience subjects. It can be configured as an interactive game activity and can be adjusted in the way and difficulty according to age. In addition, activity contents are composed by PC and beam project to minimize the influence of environment for ICT technology implementation. Through interactive game activities that utilize the beam project, children will be able to participate in activities by raising their interest and commitment. Through such visual recognition, thinking, and expression through the body, brain development and physical fitness can be achieved at the same time. DO COMMUNICATION emits energy and improves physical fitness by inducing fun and exciting physical activity through avatars. This will enable the maximization of education effect and continuous health management. And the children shares the activities of the class with his friends and gives feedback to each other. An example of activity in one class is presented in Table 2.

Table 1. Physical activity content organization

Module theme	Activity		
	Step 1	Step 2	Step 3
	Do Think	Do Activities	Do Communication
Movement Play: I Imaginative Play: You Creative Play: We	Animation display	Motion recognition interactive game activity	Activity sharing

Table 2. Activity example

Module	Imaginative Play : You	Age	4-5years
Subject	You & Me Ⅱ : Shape story making body		
Purpose	- It understands different shapes. - It recognizes shapes of the objects associated with the life to take advantage of the application. - By expressing a variety of shapes to the body and improves muscle strength and muscle endurance.		
Stage	Activity		
Do Think	**[Animation Display]** 		
Do Activities	**[Motion Recognition Interactive Game Activity]** - Shape Recognition - Shapes Distinguish 		

Table 2. *(Continued)*

- Find a Shape around the Living

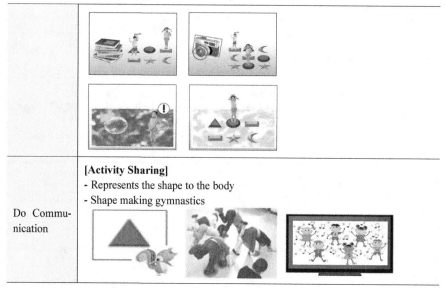

Do Communication	[Activity Sharing] - Represents the shape to the body - Shape making gymnastics

3 Conclusion

The program developed in this study can develop physical development, health promotion, brain development, creativity and personality development, and social development through play and movement. Based on this experience, we can achieve our goal of developing convergent talent through imagination and creativity. And we purpose providing creative contents focusing utilization of developed technologies in fields instead of developing brand new technologies. Such approach may offer an opportunity to experience more easily skills in the users. In addition, the development content can be used in children institutions and facilities, as well as educational institutions.

Acknowledgement. This work was supported by INHA UNIVERSITY Research Grant.

References

1. The Ministry of Education, The Ministry of Health and Welfare. 3–5 years old Nuri Curriculum for Teachers (2012)
2. Korea Institute of Child Care and Education. Comparison of the Actual Conditions and Analysis of Needs of Kindergartens and Day Care Center (2014)

3. Korea Institute of Child Care and Education. A Study on the Quality Management of Teaching Materials in Kindergarten (2014)
4. Vega, L., Ledezma, G., Hidalgo, A., Ruiz, E., Pinto, O., Quintero, R., Zepeda, L.: Basic elements on game design for interactive museum exhibitions. In: ACM SIGGRAPH Posters, p. 47 (2010)
5. Tremblay, M.S., et al.: Canadian physical activity guidelines for the early years (aged 0–4 years). Appl. Physiol. Nutr. Metab. **37**(2), 345–356 (2012)

Development of Gesture Recognition-Based Educational Dance Game for Children with Intellectual Disability

Hyung Sook Kim[1,2], Yonghyun Park[1(✉)], Sunghee Hong[1],
and Junghwan Hwang[1]

[1] Major in Human Art and Technology, Graduate Program,
Inha University, Incheon, Republic of Korea
khsook12@inha.ac.kr, yhpark81@gmail.com,
hongsungh22@hanmail.net, jdydec23@naver.com
[2] Major in Dance, Department of Kinesiology,
Inha University, Incheon, Republic of Korea

Abstract. The purpose of this study is to develop an educational dance game for children. Successful experience on the stage improves the confidence of the participants. People with intellectual disabilities also have personal satisfaction and confidence as they finish the stage with dance and theater. However, during the process of explaining the movement, it is not easy to maintain a constant interest for the children with intellectual disabilities in the dance class. Children with intellectual disability are struggling with participating in dance class because of their low ability of body awareness. This makes children with the intellectual disability more inactive in dance class. Gesture recognition-based interface is an excellent educational tool to make students more active. This game contains 40 different dance pose images. The children match their head, hands, and legs to the images' pose. The game was conducted at the intellectual disability child education center of the Lords of the Republic of Korea. The following results were obtained after conducting the dance lesson using a game. When children align their poses with the pose of the photo, they give auditory feedback as a means of praise and score the number of poses matched. In the dance lesson using these games, the children with intellectual disabilities were very interested in the appearance of their own images on TV. In addition, the children were more interested and actively participated in the class than the existing dance class. The use of Kinect in the dance lessons of children with intellectual disabilities is a good tool to increase students' interest and excitement

Keywords: Gesture recognition-based game · NUI · Dance education · Intellectual disability · Contents design · Kinect

1 Introduction

Successful experience on the stage improves the confidence of the participants. People with intellectual disabilities also have personal satisfaction and confidence as they finish successfully the stage with dance and theater. However, it is not easy to maintain

© Springer International Publishing AG 2017
C. Stephanidis (Ed.): HCII Posters 2017, Part II, CCIS 714, pp. 136–140, 2017.
DOI: 10.1007/978-3-319-58753-0_21

constant interest and during the process of explaining the actions and attitudes for artistic activities to the people with intellectual disabilities in dance class.

Intellectual Disability Students' ability to adjust their body movements is less than that of regular students. Not only choreography but also activity in everyday life, the degree of motion development is insufficient and below average. Therefore, in the instructional style in which teachers demonstrate and follow the dance teaching time, the children with the intellectual disability take more time to learn choreography than the general children. As the choreography takes more time, children with intellectual disabilities also become less distracted and more distracted.

In addition, teachers are well aware of these difficulties because they show very slow movements of dance lessons and behave in a way that they cannot concentrate on their intellectual disabilities. In particular, children with disabilities often fail to follow the dance movement when they learn to dance. To help with this difficulty, a game that can give feedback to immediate audiovisual stimulation can be effectively used. It is expected that the TV screen will provide feedback on the choreography movement and the identity of oneself, and if it poses correctly, it will lead to a positive attitude by giving praise through effect sound. The purpose of this study is to introduce an application that helps the mild intellectually disabled people to practice dancing choreographed using KINECT for the work "Les Miserables" in a dance education class.

2 Educational Dance Game Using KINECT

The KINECT used in this study uses only body movements as a controller without any other devices such as keyboard, mouse, and joystick. In this game, after taking a dance action with a camera, the still image is used to make a pose image, as shown in Table 2 (Green shape). In the game, it proceeds by moving the body along with the pose image that is stopped. The KINECT camera reflects the participant's movements on the screen. This makes it easy to use the technique used by the Chroma key with KINECT. By linking the actions learned through this content, dance performances can be completed naturally as a stage performance.

3 Game Program Scheme

The works used for the dance performances were based on "Les Miserables", which is widely known to the public. It is a famous musical work intended to induce the interest of people with intellectual disabilities. The inducement of interesting is necessary for active participation. In the Korean version of the musical "Les Miserables", two rhythmic songs were selected for the background music, and the scenes from the movie were captured were used for the background (Table 1).

The first screen was adapted from a poster of "Les Miserables". It starts when the teacher clicks the screen. Every time a person with intellectual disabilities aligns his or her movements, the 'action' sound provides feedback. The dance motion images

Table 1. Screen shots of dance education game

Start Screen	On-going	Result

Table 2. Dance pose composition and sample pose image

Types of Dance pose		
Moves only the upper body	Upper and lower bodies must move together	Balanced by one foot

contains 40 different poses. Each time provides 3 min of game/dance play, and their score is shown after. The result show up the total number of actions taken correctly. The difficulty level does not change during the game. However, the game mode was applied differently according to the level of disability of children with intellectual disabilities before game start. If the level of intellectual disability is severe, the option is changed to a mode that provides more visual cues.

The choreography (40 poses) used in the game was based on the opinions of teachers in the Center for Children with Intellectual Disabilities and dance instructors. The athletic ability of children with intellectual disabilities is very large, at the level similar to that of the general public to the level where they can not recognize the positions of their arms and legs. Therefore, when composing choreography movements, easy movement and difficult movement were classified by level. Easy dance moves begin with a simple pose that moves only the upper body. Somewhat difficult movements consist of a pose with the upper and lower body moving together and a pose with the center with one foot. When the game starts, the user is presented in random order so that the order of poses cannot be determined. However, if a child with an intellectual disability does not act at all, he added the ability to move to the next action by the teacher's veneer.

4   Demonstration Class at the Center of Children with Intellectual Disability

The dance education game designed in this study was used for 4 days as an education program at a center for children with intellectual disability in Yeongju-city, Gyeongbuk-province, South KOREA. The total hours of education program was 20 h for mildly handicapped people. At first, they were awkward following the images and dance movements on the screen, but they gradually got used to it. In conclusion, the Chroma key technique using KINECT was very useful for inducing the interest of the people with intellectual disability (Table 3).

Table 3. The place where the training is conducted by the participants.

Unlike general dance lessons, the characteristics of children with intellectual disabilities appearing in dance lessons using games are as follows. Children with intellectual disabilities have had fun with the their appearance on the TV screen using chroma key effect. After a student with a disability matches his/her body's pose, he or she begins to perceive hearing sound feedback and score increases, and then the students begin to participate in the game harder to get high scores as well as motivation.

Particularly, the handicapped students were interested in concentrating on oneself in the pose matched while moving the body, concentrating on the dance movements. It can be seen that there are many differences from the passive figure of intellectual disability children participating in the traditional dance lesson. As an example, the dance movement was always difficult and burdensome. The accuracy of the dance movement was poor, and the students could see themselves around them, and they could not concentrate and appeared to have decreased self-confidence. As we progressed through the game, we became more focused on the fast-paced game and were able to work more happily because of immediate auditory feedback. In addition, I was able to know that I was confident when I showed my intention to show it to my friends around me whenever I set the motion for the students with disabilities.

Acknowledgement. This research was supported by the National Research Foundation of Korea (NRF) Grant funded by the Ministry of Science, ICT and Future Planning for convergent research in Development program for convergence R&D over Science and Technology Liberal Arts (2016929336).

References

1. Miller, N.: Games in the Classroom. Indiana Librar. **33**, 61–63 (2014)
2. Beetham, H., Sharpe, R.: Rethinking Pedagogy for a Digital Age: Designing for 21st-Century Learning. Routledge, Abingdon (2013)
3. Freeman, S., Eddy, S.L., McDonough, M., Smith, M.K., Okoroafor, N., Jordt, H., Wenderoth, M.P.: Active learning increases student performance in science, engineering, and mathematics. Proc. Natl. Acad. Sci. **111**, 8410–8415 (2014)
4. Miles, H.C., Pop, S.R., Watt, S.J., Lawrence, G.P., John, N.W.: A review of virtual environments for training in ball sports. Comput. Graph. **36**, 714–726 (2012)
5. Taylor, P.: Transformative steam education for the 21st century. In: Proceedings of the Australian Conference on Science and Mathematics Education (Formerly UniServe Science Conference)
6. http://en.wikipedia.org/wiki/Unity_%28game_engine%29

Development of Educational Application Using Standard Movement Code-Based on Human Behavior

Hyung Sook Kim[1], Chan-Ik Park[2], David O'Sullivan[3],
and Jeesun Lee[4(✉)]

[1] Department of Human Arts and Technology,
Inha University, Incheon, Republic of Korea
hksook12@inha.ac.kr
[2] Faculty of Healing Industry, Daegu Haany University,
Daegu, Republic of Korea
cipark@dhu.ac.kr
[3] Department of Sports Science, Pusan National University,
Busan, Republic of Korea
davidosullivan@pusan.ac.kr
[4] Center for Interactive Culture Technology,
Inha University, Incheon, Republic of Korea
jeesunlee11@gmail.com

Abstract. The aims of this study is to extract a standard movement code according to specific emotional behavior patterns in the human behavior information database and to develop educational applications composed of corresponding opposite behavior codes. Among the various behaviors of the human being, we focused on the behavior of the emotional behavioral disorder group and accumulated the motion data and extracted the specific behavior motion code from it. Finally, we suggest an educational program for emotional and behavioral difficulties using this motion code.

Keywords: Emotional and behavioral disorder · Standard movement code · Behavior · Labanotation · Motion-capture · Kinect

1 Introduction

The purpose of this study is to extract a standard movement code according to specific emotional behavior patterns in the human behavior information database and to develop educational applications composed of corresponding opposite behavior codes. A standard movement code is the basic unit of the behavior classification system used for motion analysis and recording. This type of data includes elements, such as cognitive, emotional, and non-categorical movement in the 'movement' as 'nonverbal behavior' and is critical for understanding interactive information. Therefore, a standard movement code is the basis for building a source technology for the communication between human and machine and vice-versa in our digital environment. In fourth

© Springer International Publishing AG 2017
C. Stephanidis (Ed.): HCII Posters 2017, Part II, CCIS 714, pp. 141–145, 2017.
DOI: 10.1007/978-3-319-58753-0_22

industrial revolution it is essential to construct a service platform environment through the Internet of things, artificial intelligence, and big data, to improve quality of life.

In this study, we used Labanotation software (LabanWriter) to analyze behavioral data which is commercialized in the field of motion research. We coded common behavioral characteristics from the notation data and designed interventional education contents by constructing opposite behavior code. In addition, among the various behaviors of the human being, we focused on the behavior of the emotional behavioral disorder group and accumulated the motion data and extracted the specific behavior motion code from it.

2 Behavioral Data Collection

The contents for the emotional behavioral items of the AMPQ-II (Adolescent Mental Health and Problem Behavior Screening Questionnaire-II) (Jung et al. 2008), were developed and verified by Korean behavioral experts. The emotional behavior scenarios were constructed to induce basic movements such as hand, clapping, arm movement, walking and running on the spot (see Table 2).

As a main group, 3 middle and high school students with emotional and behavioral disabilities (mood, depression, ADHD) who were accompanied by medication and adjunctive therapy were recommended from the doctor. As a control group, data from 7 university students majoring in drama and film were recorded. We extracted behavioral data by using motion capture and Labanotation recording, and extracted emotional behavioral characteristic movement codes through comparative analysis of interpersonal behavior data codes.

To analyze the behavior of the subject, we recorded their bodily movement with Labanotation and motion capture technique. The 50 markers were attached to the subject's head and body, and 3 Kinect cameras and 12 OptiTracks were installed. Three observers recorded object's behavioral observations at the experimental site, and after the experiment was completed, the Kinect video were recorded as LabanWriter[1] by the same observers. The notation information recorded by the LabanWriter of the patient and the normal group.

We selected one from each of the two groups for example. Their notations were compared with each other. Among the 7 items in Table 2, one example of comparison and derive the movement code from the notation data of 1-B as shown in Table 1. In AMPQ-II, the 1-B problem is related to the "Learning and Internet" question: "Do not concentrate when you need to focus and do not do anything else." And it was reconstructed as an interactive content that "give various shapes and applause when the stars are shiny". The behavior notation induced by the video was based on the Kinect video taken from the pilot. Notation is recorded in 1 s increments, and the notation results are summarized as Table 1 for parallel comparison of data. The interpretation of Labanotation data can be read from the bottom of the left line to the top and read to the right.

---

[1] Labanotation Software for Mac developed by Ohio State University.

Table 1. An example of encoding and decoding data comparison

No.	Behavior-based Application	Notation	Movement Code
1-B	Clap hands when shapes flash	Subject from Patient Group	(a)wrong reaction (b)mistiming (c)hesitation (d)passive
		Subject from Normal Group	

3 Educational Application with Opposite Behavioral Code

The subjects' responses to the 1-B contents were appropriately met with applause from both the normal group and the patient group, as in the notation recording. There is also a significant difference between the two groups. In Table 1(a), the normal group did not applaud, whereas the disability group showed the wrong reaction. In (b), the normal group responds clearly and distinctly when applauding, whereas the patient group cannot clap properly and cannot judge and timed when to applaud. (c), the normal group still applauds clearly, while the patient group can read the hesitant pattern of narrowing the gap between the reaction and the reaction and not clapping properly. (d) showed that the normal group had more detailed and clear behaviors, whereas the patient group had three sections of behavioral response, but the number of microscopic applause and execution was negatively occurring. Therefore, emotion behavior movement codes such as wrong reaction, mistiming, hesitation, and passive are extracted from behavior of disability group by comparison analysis of notation data of normal group and disability group.

In order to mediate the emotional behavior problems revealed in the notation, we designed action scenarios composed of opposite codes. Inverse codes of wrong reaction, mistiming, hesitation and passive should be composed of behaviors contrary to AMPQ-II's question content while including these behavioral characteristics with proper reaction, on-timing, immediate, simple and sharp. Based on these criteria, the scenario for each question was designed as follows.

- put the correct shape or color in the basket
- make shapes together
- make symbol of elements with own body
- exit the maze without stepping on the bottom line
- matchmaking, brick mining
- pausing and moving play
- mirroring, dance with myself

As shown in Table 2, the proposed application is a kind of educational behavior intervention program that expects emotional behavior intervention effect when applied for more than 12 weeks.

Table 2. Behavior-based application from selected questions of AMPQ-II and educational application designed with movement codes

| no | Paper-based Questionnaire | | | | Behavior-based Application | | Educational Application | |
| | DSM-V | | AMPQ-II | | A Type | B Type | Opposite Movement Code | Educational Regulation |
	Factor	Question	Factor	Question				
1	Inattention	1) Often fails to give close attention to details or makes careless mistakes in schoolwork, at work, or during other activities. 2) Often has difficulty sustaining attention in tasks or play activities. 4) Failure to follow directions or to perform missions in school work, chores, or workplace.	Learning and Internet	1) When I need to concentrate, I do not concentrate and do something else.	Focus on a various given shape	Clap hands when shapes flash	When I need to concentrate I concentrate well.	Put the correct shape or color in the basket.
2		3) Often does not seem to listen when spoken to directly	Mood and Suicide	10) I do not follow well because I have a sense of displeasure to the instructions of my parents or teachers.	Follow the Father Follow the Mother	Fallow the Teacher	Follow the instructions of the parents or teacher.	Make shapes together
3		5) Often has difficulty organizing tasks and activities 6) Often avoids, dislikes, or is reluctant to engage in tasks that require sustained mental effort.	Mood and Suicide	12) I have difficulties to understand what I'm learning in class.	Animal Habitat Matching	Contents of mathematics, Korean language, and science subjects	I understand what I learn in class.	Make symbol of elements with own body
4	-	-	Violation of Regulation	22) I am often subjected to serious rule violations.	Walk to traffic lights	Walk to traffic lights with sound effect	Keep the rules well.	Exit the maze without stepping on the bottom line
5	Hyperactivity & Impulsivity	2) Often leaves seat in situations when remaining seated is expected. 3) Often runs about or climbs in situations where it is inappropriate. 4) Often unable to play or engage in leisure activities quietly. 5) Is often "on the go," acting as if "driven by a motor"	Learning and Internet	25) I cannot wait and action is ahead of thoughts.	Walk or run along the virtual path	Walk or run along the virtual path with arms	think carefully and then act on it	Matchmaking, brick mining
6	Inattention	1) Often fidgets with or taps hands or feet or squirms in seat. 8) Often interrupts or intrudes on others.	Learning and Internet	28) I cannot sit still and I keep digging my hands or feet.	Listen to boring subject	Listen to boring subject and make a quiz	I can sit calmly with my hands and feet.	Pausing and Moving play
7	Hyperactivity & Impulsivity	6) Often talks excessively.	Worry and Thought	34) I am afraid to speak in front of people.	Express joy, sadness, depressed mood	Express joy, sadness, depressed mood in the audience	I speak confidently in front of people.	Mirroring, dance with myself

4   Future Study

The debate on the intervention program is now being further intensified, and the next pilot will accumulate action data by expanding the total number of subjects and the disabled population. Furthermore, by analyzing the data through the machine learning technique, we want to construct behavior classification system and standard motion code of the emotionally disabled children. It is our hope that this standard movement code and content research based on emotional behavior will be extended for general ICT use. It is important to develop an ICT system that can be applied for everyday life (emotional communication digital environment), engineering (motion recognition based health care), performing arts (mixed reality realization performance culture), sports science (intelligent motion analysis system), education (emotional communication ubiquitous education) and design (customized environment design).

Acknowledgement. This research was supported by the National Research Foundation of Korea (NRF) Grant funded by the Ministry of Science, ICT and Future Planning for convergent research in Development program for convergence R&D over Science and Technology Liberal Arts (2016929336).

References

Jung, S.A., Ahn, D.H., Chung, S.Y., Jeong, Y.G., Kim, Y.Y.: Development of screening test for adolescent mental health and problem behavior. J. Korean Neuropsychiatric Assoc. **47**(2), 168–176 (2008)
Adolescent Mental Health and Problem Behavior Screening Questionnaire-II

A Serious Game to Teach Computing Concepts

Devorah Kletenik[1(✉)], Florencia Salinas[1], Chava Shulman[1],
Claudia Bergeron[2], and Deborah Sturm[2]

[1] Brooklyn College, City University of New York,
2900 Bedford Avenue, Brooklyn, NY 11210, USA
kletenik@sci.brooklyn.cuny.edu, florenciabsalinas@gmail.com,
cshulman95@gmail.com
[2] College of Staten Island, City University of New York,
2800 Victory Boulevard, Staten Island, NY 10314, USA
klausebergeron@gmail.com, Deborah.Sturm@csi.cuny.edu

Abstract. In this work, we discuss our ongoing project to design a
serious game to teach advanced programming concepts in C++. These
concepts are challenging for students to learn; our game is a fun and
motivating way for students to learn and practice their understanding.
Our game, Point Mouster, was designed and developed by women Computer Science majors and is part of a study to examine whether games
with specific design elements can help recruit and retain female students.
We report on a pilot study of our game conducted at Brooklyn College
and the College of Staten Island. Students, including an unusually high
number of female participants, demonstrated educational effectiveness,
and reported high levels of motivation and engagement.

Keywords: Serious games · Digital game-based learning · Computer
science education · Gender

1 Introduction and Background

A flurry of research conducted over the last decade is geared at rethinking the
way we think about education. The long-standing formal lecture teaching mode
is less popular with students [1] and less effective than more interactive modes
of learning [2]. Educator Prensky has argued that today's generation of students are "Digital Natives" whose brains are wired fundamentally differently
than the previous generation of "Digital Immigrants" and should be taught in
dramatically new ways [3]. Guzdial and Soloway similarly argued that a heavily
text means of teaching programming is ill-suited to the "Nintendo Generation,"
which thrives on sounds, graphics, animation, and speed [4].

Research on *digital game-based learning* (also called *serious games for education*) show that students who learn through games have increased feeling of
alertness, activity, involvement in contrast to boredom during standard lecture
mode [5]. Game-based learning allows educators to tap into the enthusiasm that
students show for computer games and bring those attitudes to the classroom

© Springer International Publishing AG 2017
C. Stephanidis (Ed.): HCII Posters 2017, Part II, CCIS 714, pp. 146–153, 2017.
DOI: 10.1007/978-3-319-58753-0_23

as "interested, competitive, cooperative, results-oriented, actively seeking information and solutions" [6].

A number of serious games have been created for specific topics in CS education; for example, loops and arrays [7–9], binary trees [10], and object-oriented programming [11], along with a number of games created for teaching introductory programming [12–16] and other CS topics [17–19]. Experimental evaluations of these games have indicated that they are an effective and fun teaching tool. However, we do not know of any games developed for advanced programming topics needed to prepare students for the critical Data Structure courses. We have developed a game in Unity that teaches and assesses student knowledge of advanced programming topics; we focus on C++ pointers, which we find to be particularly confusing to students. In this work, we explain our game and report on feedback from students piloting the game.

2   Game Design

The game that we created is a side-scrolling platformer. Its storyline features rogue robots that have dismantled a critical government computer. An intrepid computer mouse is on a mission to rebuild it and save society. The game is composed of three levels; each part has two stages: a learning step and an assessment step. In the learning step, as the mouse jumps from platform to platform, it encounters a variety of scientists. Each scientist, when approached, shares a particular lesson in the use of pointers. At the end of the learning stage, a summary of the lessons learned is shown on the screen. The player then progresses to an assessment stage, during which s/he must correctly answer multiple-choice questions about the material just taught in order to defeat the enemy. After the player correctly answers all the questions, a missing part of the computer is displayed on the screen and the player progresses to the next level, which is both more challenging in terms of the gameplay and the material being taught. After the player completes all three levels, a picture of the fully assembled computer is shown, along with the message that the mouse has saved the world. Screenshots of our game are shown in Fig. 1.

Research has shown that there are fundamental differences in the ways that male and female players play computer games (see, e.g. [20–22]). For example, males tend to be more enthusiastic players than females [23]; males tend to play games more frequently and for longer durations than do their female peers [24]; male players have stronger desires for competition and tend to be more motivated by a "need to win," while female players prefer the within-game social dynamics between game characters [25]. Hence, effort must be invested to ensure that educational games are appropriate for both genders [26]. This game was designed by a team of women developers and we tried to make the game appealing to female players through the use of a storyline that included a meaningful goal, the use of facial expressions and human-like animations on our sprites, positive feedback, and rewards at the end of each level to motivate persistence. This is a "by women, for women" game that we hope will help all students, especially female ones, learn difficult Advanced Programming concepts.

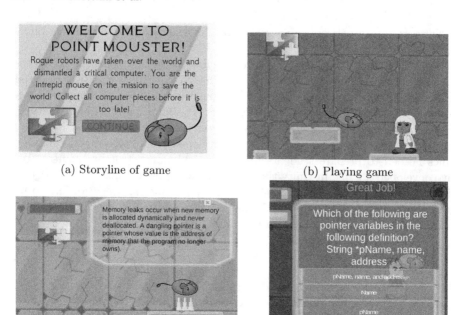

(a) Storyline of game

(b) Playing game

(c) learning a fact

(d) question and feedback

Fig. 1. Screenshots of the game

Our game conforms to the four principles of gamified learning given by Stott and Neustaedter [27]:

- **freedom to fail:** Players are allowed unlimited attempts to answer the multiple choice questions; answering them correctly increases their score but incorrect answers do not make the game end.
- **rapid feedback:** Immediately after answering a question, students are told if their answer is correct without needing to complete an entire set of questions. This is essential to good learning; "the more frequent and targeted the feedback, the more effective the learning" [28].
- **progression:** Student learning and assessment progresses from basic concepts of pointers to more advanced or complex topics. This aids students to build on their areas of knowledge and expertise and add to them.
- **storytelling:** Research such as [13] has shown that players are more engaged and persist for longer when they are motivated by meaningful goals. Our storyline attempts to draw players in through an appeal to their help to save the world.

Our game also incorporates principles of good learning of educator Gee [29] such as "just in time" directions to instruct users just when it becomes relevant, and a "pleasantly frustrating" gameplay.

3   Experimental Design

We piloted our game on undergraduate students of Brooklyn College and College of Staten Island (both senior colleges of City University of New York) to learn about our game's effectiveness. Each participant was asked to take a pre-test that tested their level of knowledge about pointers, play the game, and take a post-test that measured their knowledge of pointers again. The pre-test and post-test questions differed only trivially; questions were repeated with different variable names or values. In addition, the pre-test asked for basic demographic information (college attended, programming course currently taking, and gender). The post-test included a questionnaire measuring their levels of intrinsic motivation, shown in Fig. 2, based on [30], except that we used a 5-point Likert scale instead of a 7-point one. We also asked three additional questions about the user's thoughts about the game (Fig. 3) using the same 5-point scale, as well as a request for general feedback on the game design.

1. I played this game because I found it interesting.
2. I played this game because I found it pleasant.
3. I played this game because it is fun.
4. I played this game because I feel good when playing this game.

Fig. 2. Measuring intrinsic motivation

1. I would play this game for fun.
2. I would play this game to learn about pointers.
3. I would play this game to help assess my knowledge of pointers.

Fig. 3. Measuring engagement attitude towards game

Besides for the information mentioned here, no other personal information was collected, except for the participants' email addresses, which we used as their unique user IDs for the game. (We suggested that participants create anonymous email addresses if they did not want to be identified, but very few did this.) We used Google Forms to conduct the pre- and post- evaluations.

4   Results

Twenty-eight students played the game and completed both pre- and post-tests. (An additional six students completed a pre-test but either did not play the game or did not complete the post-test; they are excluded from our analysis.) Twelve participants are Brooklyn College students and 16 are College of Staten Island students. Twelve of the participants are female and sixteen male. Twenty-six of the participants are Computer Science majors or related (e.g. multimedia majors); two are non-CS majors who were interested in playing the game anyway.

Among the students who completed both tests, the average pre-test score was a 49, the average post-test score was a 60, and the average improvement was about 12%.

We calculated levels of intrinsic motivation using the standard approach, giving one point to all "strongly disagree," two points to "agree," and so on until "strongly agree." We computed the average across all four intrinsic motivation questions to get an "intrinsic motivation score" for each participant. A score of three indicates average levels of motivation (the equivalent of "neutral" responses for all questions). The average score for our participants was 3.5, indicating above-average levels of motivation. In total, 60% of participants reported above-average levels of motivation; 67% of female participants and 57% of male participants indicated high motivation.

We used a similar process to evaluate the questions about the engagement of the game. The average score for these questions was 4, indicating that students found the game a fun and effective learning tool. (The average score for "I would play for fun" was 3.6; the average scores for "I would play to learn about pointers" and "I would play to assess my knowledge of pointers" were 4.29 and 4.25, respectively, indicating that students would be more likely to play our game as a learning tool than as a fun tool, which is what we would have intuitively expected.) 83% of female participants and 94% of male participants gave the game an above-average score in this area.

When asked for feedback, participants pointed out a number of technical issues, which we plan to fix before our next release. They also gave a lot of positive feedback about the UI, graphics and music, with responses such as:

- "The graphic design is excellent. Very pleasant art style to look at."
- "Graphics are very pleasing and well thought out."
- "[I liked] the mouse, and layout of the game (how each stage gave you a puzzle piece)."
- "The visuals and music were great."
- "User friendly appearance, easy to use."

Participants also praised the educational aspect of the game:

- "The questions were a great way to test your knowledge or refresh yourself on pointers. Great way to have fun and learn at the same time."
- "The premise of the game is neat; Platforming while simultaneously learning about pointers while the music is playing offers a unique experience for those wanting to learn more or just wanting to play the game."
- "The questions were brief enough to not be annoying but also long enough to have useful content."

- "Testing your knowledge while fighting bosses is a great feature and really shows that the user understands what they learned throughout the level."
- "Its super fun, and it teaches you a lot about pointers."
- "It was very informative and certainly refreshed my memory on pointers and probably I would like to play this game before I walk into an interview. Also, I think the difficulty made me want to play much more so that was really good motivation to keep playing the game."

5   Discussion

Despite our small sample, our pilot study of this game shows a number of encouraging results. We attracted a large number of female testers. Despite the fact that female students represent well under a third of the CIS majors at these institutions, female students constituted 43% of the participants who played the game. Our game received positive feedback and it had a moderate effect on tested knowledge of pointers. Levels of motivation and interest in the game were high among our participants, and many of them reported enjoying the learning + playing experience.

We were a bit puzzled by five students whose post-test scores actually decreased by comparison to their pre-test scores and conjecture that students did not think carefully when responding and may have guessed or made random choices. We are attempting to figure out a better way to encourage careful thought in answering the questions in our next round of testing, perhaps by offering an incentive to students who do well.

We plan to test the game on a bigger pool of students from both institutions by the end of the academic year.

Acknowledgements. This project was funded by the Collaborative Research Experience for Undergraduates (CREU) program, sponsored by the Computing Research Association Committee on the Status of Women in Computing Research (CRA-W) in conjunction with the Coalition to Diversify Computing (CDC), funded by the National Science Foundation.

We thank Alex Aquino, Kwan Holloway, and Elina Shirani for sharing their GREat Escapes GRE vocabulary game with us.

References

1. Sander, P., Stevenson, K., King, M., Coates, D.: University students' expectations of teaching. Stud. High. Educ. **25**(3), 309–323 (2000)
2. Knight, J.K., Wood, W.B.: Teaching more by lecturing less. Cell Biol. Educ. **4**(4), 298–310 (2005)
3. Prensky, M.: Digital natives, digital immigrants part 1. On Horizon **9**(5), 1–6 (2001)
4. Guzdial, M., Soloway, E.: Teaching the nintendo generation to program. Commun. ACM **45**(4), 17–21 (2002)
5. Grimley, M., Green, R., Nilsen, T., Thompson, D., Tomes, R.: Using computer games for instruction: the student experience. Act. Learn. High. Educ. **12**(1), 45–56 (2011)

6. Prensky, M.: Digital game-based learning. Comput. Entertain. (CIE) **1**(1), 21 (2003)
7. Eagle, M., Barnes, T.: Wu's castle: teaching arrays and loops in a game. ACM SIGCSE Bull. **40**, 245–249 (2008). ACM
8. Eagle, M., Barnes, T.: Evaluation of a game-based lab assignment. In: Proceedings of the 4th International Conference on Foundations of Digital Games, pp. 64–70. ACM (2009)
9. Eagle, M., Barnes, T.: Experimental evaluation of an educational game for improved learning in introductory computing. ACM SIGCSE Bull. **41**, 321–325 (2009). ACM
10. Chaffin, A., Doran, K., Hicks, D., Barnes, T.: Experimental evaluation of teaching recursion in a video game. In: Proceedings of the 2009 ACM SIGGRAPH Symposium on Video Games, pp. 79–86. ACM (2009)
11. Zhang, J., Caldwell, E.R., Atay, M., Jones, E.J.: Learning the concepts of classes and objects in a game. In: Proceedings of the International Conference on Frontiers in Education: Computer Science and Computer Engineering (FECS), The Steering Committee of The World Congress in Computer Science, Computer Engineering and Applied Computing (WorldComp), p. 1 (2012)
12. Lee, M.J., Ko, A.J.: Personifying programming tool feedback improves novice programmers' learning. In: Proceedings of the Seventh International Workshop on Computing Education Research, pp. 109–116. ACM (2011)
13. Lee, M.J., Ko, A.J.: Investigating the role of purposeful goals on novices' engagement in a programming game. In: 2012 IEEE Symposium on Visual Languages and Human-Centric Computing (VL/HCC), pp. 163–166. IEEE (2012)
14. Lee, M.J., Ko, A.J., Kwan, I.: In-game assessments increase novice programmers' engagement and level completion speed. In: Proceedings of the Ninth Annual International ACM Conference on International Computing Education Research, pp. 153–160. ACM (2013)
15. Leutenegger, S., Edgington, J.: A games first approach to teaching introductory programming. ACM SIGCSE Bull. **39**, 115–118 (2007). ACM
16. Li, F.W., Watson, C.: Game-based concept visualization for learning programming. In: Proceedings of the Third International ACM Workshop on Multimedia Technologies for Distance Learning, pp. 37–42. ACM (2011)
17. Caulfield, C., Xia, J.C., Veal, D., Maj, S.P.: A systematic survey of games used for software engineering education. Mod. Appl. Sci. **5**(6), 28 (2011)
18. Connolly, T.M., Stansfield, M., Hainey, T.: An application of games-based learning within software engineering. Br. J. Educ. Technol. **38**(3), 416–428 (2007)
19. Debabi, W., Bensebaa, T.: Using serious game to enhance algorithmic learning ant teaching. J. E-Learn. Knowl. Soc. **12**(2), 127–140 (2016)
20. Boyle, E., Connolly, T.: Games for learning: does gender make a difference. In: Proceedings of the 2nd European Conference on Games Based Learning, pp. 69–75 (2008)
21. Steiner, C.M., Kickmeier-Rust, M.D., Albert, D.: Little big difference: gender aspects and gender-based adaptation in educational games. In: Chang, M., Kuo, R., Kinshuk, Chen, G.-D., Hirose, M. (eds.) Edutainment 2009. LNCS, vol. 5670, pp. 150–161. Springer, Heidelberg (2009). doi:10.1007/978-3-642-03364-3_20
22. Vermeulen, L., Van Looy, J., De Grove, F., Courtois, C.: You are what you play? A quantitative study into game design preferences across gender and their interaction with gaming habits. In: DiGRA 2011: Think, Design, Play, Digital Games Research Association (DiGRA) (2011)

23. Gorriz, C.M., Medina, C.: Engaging girls with computers through software games. Commun. ACM **43**(1), 42–49 (2000)
24. Connolly, T., Boyle, L., Stansfield, M., Hainey, T.: The potential of online games as a collaborative learning environment. J. Adv. Technol. Learn. **4**(4), 208–239 (2007)
25. Hartmann, T., Klimmt, C.: Gender and computer games: exploring females dislikes. J. Comput. Mediat. Commun. **11**(4), 910–931 (2006)
26. Luik, P.: Would boys and girls benefit from gender-specific educational software? Br. J. Educ. Technol. **42**(1), 128–144 (2011)
27. Stott, A., Neustaedter, C.: Analysis of gamification in education. Surrey, BC, Canada **8** (2013)
28. Kapp, K.M.: Games, gamification, and the quest for learner engagement. T + D **66**(6), 64–68 (2012)
29. Gee, J.P.: Learning by design: games as learning machines. Digit. Educ. Rev. **8**, 15–23 (2004)
30. Guay, F., Vallerand, R.J., Blanchard, C.: On the assessment of situational intrinsic and extrinsic motivation: the situational motivation scale (SIMS). Motiv. Emot. **24**(3), 175–213 (2000)

An Analysis of Students' Learning Behaviors Using Variable-Speed Playback Functionality on Online Educational Platforms

Toru Nagahama[1] and Yusuke Morita[2(✉)]

[1] Graduate School of Human Sciences, Waseda University, Mikajima 2-579-15,
Tokorozawa, Saitama 359-1192, Japan
[2] Faculty of Human Sciences, Waseda University, Mikajima 2-579-15,
Tokorozawa, Saitama 359-1192, Japan
ymorita@waseda.jp

Abstract. The goal of this study is to clarify how students' learning styles give effects to their learning experience and behaviors while visual contents presented at high speed. In our experiment, participants (10 visual learners and 9 verbal learners) categorized by Felder's index of learning styles learned information science by watching the video content composed of 6 slides. The participants watched the content on the YouTube and used variable-speed playback functionality: $0.5\times$; $1.0\times$; $1.25\times$: $1.5\times$; $2.0\times$ and we recorded participants' behaviors by using video cameras and measured how long they spent using the functionality. We applied ANOVA to the participants' scores on the comprehension test, mean responses for the questionnaire, and the mean percentage of functionality-usage time duration. The comprehension test results indicated no signify discrepancies between visual learners and verbal learners. Questionnaire survey showed that verbal learners felt significantly less difficulty on the slide 2. The functionality usage time duration indicated that verbal learners spent significantly longer time duration watching the video content at $2.0\times$ speed. Those findings suggest the possibility that verbal learners tend to use the hi-speed playback functionality longer than visual learners when they feel less difficulty on educational slides.

Keywords: Learning behaviors · Variable-speed playback functionality · e-Learning

1 Introduction

As the popularity of massive open online courses (MOOC) continues to grow worldwide in recent years, research efforts dedicated to studying the learning processes of course participants continue to increase. Guo *et al.* who analyzed a dataset containing some 7 million instances of students watching visual content on MOOCs [1]. Their results indicated that the number of course participants paying attention to an image-based content stream begins to decrease significantly when the content streams of duration are longer than 6 min and instructors' speaking rates are fairly slow. Nagahama and Morita studied the efficacy of using variable-speed playback

© Springer International Publishing AG 2017
C. Stephanidis (Ed.): HCII Posters 2017, Part II, CCIS 714, pp. 154–159, 2017.
DOI: 10.1007/978-3-319-58753-0_24

functionality to present visual content at high speed and indicated that content playback speed variation: 1.0×; 1.5×; 2.0× did not affect learning outcomes [2].

Felder's index of learning styles (F-ILS) is an online survey instrument used to assess preferences on four dimensions: active-reflective; sensing-intuitive; visual-verbal; sequential-global of a learning style model [3]. F-ILS has been used for researches that examine the relationship between learner characteristics and learner behaviors [4, 5]. To date, however, there have been few studies of clarifying the relation between students' learning styles and effects of using content playback speed variation functionalities. The goal of this study is to clarify how students' learning styles give effects to their learning experience and behaviors while visual contents presented at high speed.

2   Methods

2.1   Visual Content

The visual content was same as the one used in the experiment by Nagahama Morita [2]. The theme of the content was the network infrastructure of a high school information science department. The time required to play back the content was 8 min and 34 s (8:34). The content was composed of 6 educational slides and uploaded on the YouTube. YouTube has the variable-speed playback functionality and offers a choice of five playback speeds: 0.5×, 1×, 1.25×, 1.5×, and 2×. The following Table 1 gives a summary of the educational slides. Mora is a unit of Japanese words.

Table 1. Summary of educational slides.

Slide ID [Slide theme]	Number of letters	Number of moras	Time (s)	Speaking rate (moras/min)
Slide 1 [Network]	98	466	89.9	311.01
Slide 2 [Instruments]	83	262	51.9	302.89
Slide 3 [Protocol]	240	792	141.0	337.02
Slide 4 [IP address]	143	631	111.7	338.94
Slide 5 [DNS server]	114	230	40.3	342.43
Slide 6 [URL]	149	428	79.5	323.02

2.2   Experiment

In our experiment, participants (10 visual learners and 9 verbal learners) categorized by F-ILS. First, before presenting any visual content, we give students a comprehension test (the pre-lesson test) to assess their pre-existing knowledge of the educational material in the visual content. Next, participants practiced using variable-speed playback functionality watching the pre-video content so that they get used to the experimental environment. Then, they learned about the network infrastructure while we recorded they behaviors by using video cameras and measured how long they spent using the functionality. After viewing the visual content at various speeds, we set a post-lesson test and questionnaire. The questionnaire asked how much they felt difficulty to each slide.

3   Results and Discussion

3.1   Analysis of Comprehension Test

We determined the overall score and conducted a two-factor mixed-model ANOVA using the learning styles as one factor (F-ILS factor) and pre-lesson vs. post-lesson as the second factor (pre/post factor). Table 2 shows the mean scores on the comprehension tests with the ANOVA results.

Table 2. Mean scores (*SD*) on the comprehension tests with the ANOVA results.

	Visual		Verbal		F-Value		
	Pre	Post	Pre	Post	F-ILS	Pre/Post	Interaction
Score	3.40 (2.07)	12.30 (2.71)	3.22 (3.03)	12.20 (2.73)	0.13 *ns*	143.38 **	0.06 *ns*

**: $p < .01$, *: $p < .05$, +: $p < .10$

Here interactions were not significant ($F(1, 17) = 0.06$, n.s., *partial* $\eta^2 = 0.00$, *power* $= 0.07$). An analysis of primary effects indicated a significant trend toward the F-ILS factor ($F(1, 17) = 0.13$, n.s., *partial* $\eta^2 = 0.00$, *power* $= 0.07$). On the other hand, statistically significant differences were found with respect to the pre/post factor ($F(1, 17) = 143.38$, $p < .01$, *partial* $\eta^2 = 0.89$, *power* $= 1.00$).

3.2   Analysis of Educational Slides' Difficulty

We applied a single-factor ANOVA to the mean responses for the questionnaire (see Fig. 1). The results on the slide 1 indicated no significant discrepancies between groups ($F(1, 17) = 0.09$, n.s., *effect size* $f = 0.07$, *power* $= 0.06$). The results on the slide 2

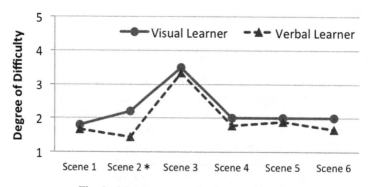

Fig. 1. Mean responses for the questionnaire

indicated significant discrepancies between groups ($F(1, 17) = 4.68, p < .05$, *effect size* $f = 0.52$, *power* $= 0.58$). The results on the slide 3 indicated no significant discrepancies between groups ($F(1, 17) = 0.12$, *n.s.*, *effect size* $f = 0.08$, *power* $= 0.06$). The results on the slide 4 indicated no significant discrepancies between groups ($F(1, 17) = 0.34$, *n.s.*, *effect size* $f = 0.14$, *power* $= 0.09$). The results on the slide 5 indicated no significant discrepancies between groups ($F(1, 17) = 0.04$, *n.s.*, *effect size* $f = 0.05$, *power* $= 0.06$).

3.3 Analysis of Functionality-Usage

We applied a single-factor ANOVA to the mean percentage of the functionality-usage time duration. Table 3 shows the mean percentage of the time duration (except for $0.5\times$ usage-time duration which lacked enough data). The mean percentage of $2.0\times$ usage-time duration (see Fig. 2) on the slide 2 indicated significant discrepancies between groups ($F(1, 17) = 5.21, p < .05$, *effect size* $f = 0.55$, *power* $= 0.62$).

Table 3. Mean percentage (*SD*) of time duration.

		Visual learner	Verbal learner	F-Value
Scene 1	2.0×	14.10 (14.63)	36.91 (45.59)	2.26 ns
	1.5×	23.90 (35.03)	19.11 (37.33)	0.08 ns
	1.25×	37.00 (40.03)	25.33 (35.62)	0.45 ns
	1.0×	24.90 (39.04)	15.78 (27.44)	0.34 ns
Scene 2	2.0×	3.90 (8.25)	36.89 (45.03)	5.21 *
	1.5×	33.30 (47.14)	22.89 (39.66)	0.28 ns
	1.25×	29.90 (44.35)	25.22 (34.90)	0.06 ns
	1.0×	31.5 (43.40)	9.0 (16.34)	2.14 ns
Scene 3	2.0×	8.90 (19.97)	22.67 (41.45)	0.88 ns
	1.5×	21.60 (41.46)	23.89 (41.97)	0.01 ns
	1.25×	31.20 (43.31)	32.33 (40.40)	0.01 ns
	1.0×	32.8 (40.72)	17.0 (31.93)	0.87 ns
Scene 4	2.0×	1.30 (4.11)	19.89 (39.51)	2.20 ns
	1.5×	48.20 (50.91)	25.44 (43.32)	1.09 ns
	1.25×	30.30 (44.98)	19.78 (36.34)	0.31 ns
	1.0×	18.70 (39.54)	26.78 (41.46)	0.19 ns
Scene 5	2.0×	3.6 (11.38)	20.44 (40.77)	1.58 ns
	1.5×	47.50 (50.32)	23.56 (43.52)	1.22 ns
	1.25×	21.70 (41.61)	28.78 (38.23)	0.15 ns
	1.0×	26.20 (43.44)	20.67 (38.37)	0.09 ns
Scene 6	2.0×	5.6 (11.84)	19.56 (38.89)	1.17 ns
	1.5×	40.40 (48.06)	22.22 (44.10)	0.73 ns
	1.25×	24.90 (41.26)	26.22 (38.27)	0.01 ns
	1.0×	27.40 (44.68)	24.11 (38.78)	0.03 ns

**: $p < .01$, *: $p < .05$, +: $p < .10$

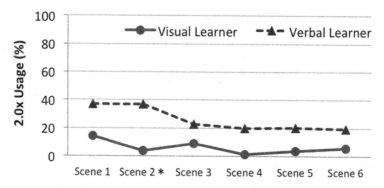

Fig. 2. Mean percentage of 2.0× functionality-usage

4 Conclusion

The goal of this study is to clarify how students' learning styles give effects to their learning experience and behaviors while visual contents presented at high speed.

In our experiment, participants (10 visual learners and 9 verbal learners) categorized by Felder's index of learning styles learned information science by watching the video content composed of 6 slides. The participants watched the content on the YouTube and used variable-speed playback functionality: 0.5×; 1.0×; 1.25×: 1.5×; 2.0× and we recorded participants' behaviors by using video cameras and measured how long they spent using the functionality.

We applied ANOVA to the participants' scores on the comprehension test, mean responses for the questionnaire, and the mean percentage of functionality-usage time duration. The comprehension test results indicated no signify discrepancies between visual learners and verbal learners. Questionnaire survey showed that verbal learners felt significantly less difficulty on the slide 2. The functionality usage time duration indicated that verbal learners spent significantly longer time duration watching the video content at 2.0× speed. Those findings suggest the possibility that verbal learners tend to use the hi-speed playback functionality longer than visual learners when they feel less difficulty on educational slides.

References

1. Guo, P.J., Kim, J., Rubin, R.F.: How video production affects student engagement: an empirical study of MOOC videos. In: Proceedings of the First ACM Conference on Learning, pp. 41–50 (2014)
2. Nagahama, T., Morita, Y.: An analysis of effects of learning with high-speeded visual contents. Jpn. J. Educ. Technol. **40**(4), 291–300 (2016)
3. Felder, R.M., Henriques, E.: Learnig and teaching styles in foreign and second language educatin. Foreign Lang. Ann. **28**(1), 21–31 (1995)

4. Morita, Y., Koen, V., Ma, G., Wu, Z., Johendran, A.: Pilot study of the relationship between learning progress and learning style in web-based PSI course. In: Proceedings of World Conference on e-Learning in Corporate, Government, Healthcare, & Higher Education (E-Learn), pp. 2243–2248 (2005)
5. Oyama, M., Murakami, M., Taguchi, M., Matsushita, K.: An analysis of students' learning behaviors using e-learning materials: focusing on students' learning styles. Jpn. J. Educ. Technol. **34**(2), 105–114 (2010)

Collaborative Learning Support System for Programming Education Using Gamification

Kohei Otake[1(✉)] and Tomofumi Uetake[2]

[1] Faculty of Science and Engineering, Chuo University, Tokyo, Japan
otake@indsys.chuo-u.ac.jp
[2] School of Business Administration, Senshu University, Kanagawa, Japan
uetake@isc.senshu-u.ac.jp

Abstract. Computer programming education is being given increasing importance in many universities in Japan. But conventional classes do not allow enough time to cultivate computer programming skills. One of the effective methods for cultivating computer programming skills is a collaborative learning method in voluntary community. However, it is difficult to maintain a student's motivation in such a voluntary community. On the other hand, Gamification has attracted much attention recently as a method to help users to maintain and improve their motivation. In this research, we propose a support system to emphasize collaborative learning in a voluntary community by using Gamification. The experimental results confirmed that our proposed system was effective in supporting the cultivation of computer programming skills.

Keywords: Computer supported collaborative learning · Computer mediated communication · Gamification · Computer programming education

1 Introduction

Computer programming course are being included as part of the curriculum at many universities in Japan. In a conventional class, students have to practice to describe program codes as well as study theoretical programming knowledge [1]. However, there is sometimes not enough time for them to do these activities. One of the effective methods for cultivating computer programming skills is a collaborative learning method in a voluntary community. However, it is difficult to improve student's skill and motivation in such a voluntary community, causing individual differences from person to person in their understanding and attitude. There are many e-learning systems such as MOOCs [2]. There has also been research done on communication assistance systems such as Wiki, chatting, or SNS [3, 4]. But there is very little research that discusses their learning attitudes and motivations.

© Springer International Publishing AG 2017
C. Stephanidis (Ed.): HCII Posters 2017, Part II, CCIS 714, pp. 160–166, 2017.
DOI: 10.1007/978-3-319-58753-0_25

2   Research Backgrounds

2.1   Activities in Voluntary Community

In our past research [5], it became clear that the following three activities are important to improve user's motivation in a voluntary community (Fig. 1).

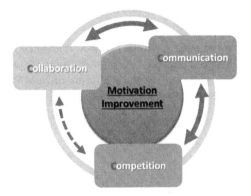

Fig. 1. Activities in voluntary community

- Communication activity: Share member's status, condition, problem and goal
- Collaboration activity: Work on common subjects to maintain their motivation
- Competition activity: Compete with other members to improve their motivation

Moreover, it is important to connect these activities seamlessly to improve student's motivation.

2.2   Gamification

Gamification has attracted much attention recently as a method to help users maintain and improve their motivation [6, 7]. Gamification is defined as "to use gaming elements, such as concept, design, and mechanics of a game, for social activities or services other than the game itself [8]". We think that Gamification is effective to maintain and improve member's motivation in voluntary communities.

3   Research Purpose

In this study, we targeted the voluntary community for programming learning. We propose a support system to emphasize collaborative learning in such a voluntary community by using Gamification.

4 Proposal of Collaborative Learning Support System for Programming Education

We propose a support system that has the following functions by applying the concept of Gamification.

- Peer Review Function to support Collaboration activity
- Competition Function (called Programming Challenge) to support Competition activity

Moreover, our system has the platform of the Communication Function such as "Bulletin Board" and "Message function". Communication Function supports activity in the voluntary community as well as the platforms of Peer Review Function and Competition (Programming Challenge) Function. These functions are connected seamlessly.

4.1 Peer Review Function

Our system consists of 15 exercises, each constituting a different level. Each exercise has 5 questions. Users are designated to have obtained level clearance when users have cleared these questions. The user who has finished solving the questions submits the outcome on the contribution page on our system. The submitted outcome is reviewed by the other users chosen by the peer review function (Fig. 2). But, reviewers are chosen from the users who have level clearance for that exercise. The contents of the review consisted of two fields, the judgment of the result of the exercise and comments on the outcome. Also the reviewer name is not specified. Peer Review can reinforce the learning by reviewing the outcome created by the other users. We think that it is important for users to help and teach each other when learning programming skills.

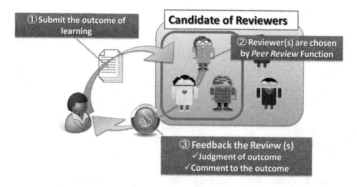

Fig. 2. Image of peer review function

4.2 Programming Challenge Function

We prepared the overall questions for the Programming Challenge (Fig. 3). The questions have two characteristics such as "There can be multiple descriptions" and "The difference is easily noticeable between the users". There is a submission time limit for an outcome. The administrators evaluate the outcome based on 3 items, earliness, correctness and easiness of reading. The competition function ranks the outcome based on these evaluations. Only the top 3 users are commended in the system after the competition. The program codes of those top 3 users are exhibited in the system, and everyone can read. The title is added to the top 3 users in the site as well as the commendation. Programming Challenge measured the check points of learning achievements. Moreover, this function was made for the purpose of improvement of the desire to learn by competing with the other users for the value of the outcome. Also we put the programming challenge into effect twice under the experiment.

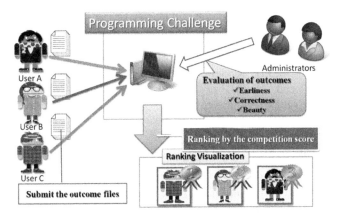

Fig. 3. Image of programming challenge function

4.3 Prototype System

To test the feasibility of our proposal, we made a prototype system. Screen hierarchy of our prototype system is shown Fig. 4.

Fig. 4. Screen hierarchy of our prototype system

5   Evaluation

To evaluate our system, we conducted the experiment targeted at the voluntary community aimed at programming learning for about 3 months. We set the subjects who belong to a science faculty department of the same university (between 21 to 22 years old, 5 males and 2 females). First we explained beforehand about how to use the proposed system. The account ID was given to each subject at the same time. The programming language learned during this experiment was Python. Furthermore, the authors made the teaching materials used for learning.

In order to verify the effectiveness of our system, we conducted interview survey about the whole system and each function, on 4th, 8th and 12th weekend. Moreover, we put the programming challenge in the 5th and 11th week. We handed out a questionnaire asking about learning situation, whole system and each function after the programming challenge.

5.1   Evaluation of Peer Review Function

We show a questionnaire about the validity of Peer Review function. We established two evaluation items for Peer Review, which were: "Q1: The reviews from other users to user's outcome" and "Q2: The reviews for the other user's outcome". The questionnaire asked the subjects to answer based on 5 stages of Likert scale (5: Useful, 1: Not useful). We show the average value of answers in Table 1.

Table 1. Evaluation of Peer Review function (average value)

Question	5th week	11th week
Q1: The reviews from other users to user's outcome	4.14	4.29
Q2: The reviews for the other user's outcome	4.00	4.14

From the results of Table 1, it became clear that the review activities are effective in learning for about 90% of the subjects in the experiment. Next, based on the result of the interview survey, we classified the effective reviews for motivation improvement after the experiment. The characteristics of an effective review were: "The contents of the submitted review are written clearly", "Improvement methods for the program are indicated clearly" and "There are descriptions about assumed errors". On the other hands, the characteristics of an ineffective review were: "Only a judgment result" and "There are no directions in detail on how to think". From the results of questionnaire and interview survey, the validity of the Peer Review system was confirmed. Moreover, the features of effective reviews became clear.

5.2   Evaluation of Programming Challenge Function

We compared the outcomes during the experiment. Specifically, outcome just after the course starting (1st week), outcome of first programming challenge (5th week) and outcome of second programming challenge (11th week) were used. Three teachers who participated in information education at the university evaluated these outcomes on a scale of 5. Furthermore, alphabets (A~H) are the user number. We considered 2 metrics for evaluation, correctness and easiness of reading. We show the result of evaluation of each item to Figs. 5 and 6.

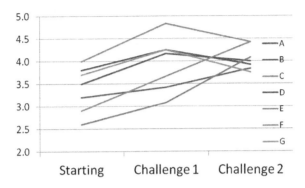

Fig. 5. Change in the evaluation value about correctness (average value)

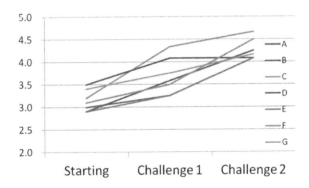

Fig. 6. Change in the evaluation value about easiness of reading (average value)

Figures 5 and 6 show that each evaluation metric is increasing from starting to challenge 1 or 2. Focusing on the correctness metric, about half of the users improved the evaluation value from challenge 1 to challenge 2. Big improvements were seen in the users whose starting evaluation values were low in particular. Focusing on the easiness of reading metric, most users improved the evaluation value from the challenge 1 to challenge 2. We think the improvement of subjective programming skill was confirmed from the above mentioned result.

6 Conclusion and Future Studies

In this paper, we proposed a support system to motivate students' individual learning in a voluntary community. We proposed three functions to support the three types (Communication, Collaboration and Competition) of activities based on the analysis of their current conditions. To examine feasibility of our proposal, we implemented a prototype system and conducted an evaluation. Through the practical use of our prototype system, the validities of our proposed functions were confirmed.

In our future studies, we revise the prototype system and evaluate it in actual uses.

References

1. Uno, K., Unekawa, M.: Development of the feedback system of learning situation in real time for a programming exercise. J. Fac. Manag. Inf. Syst. Prefectural Univ. Hiroshima **7**, 163–169 (2015). (in Japanese)
2. Fulton, K.: Upside down and inside out: flip your classroom to improve student learning. Learn. Lead. Technol. **39**(8), 12–17 (2012)
3. Strayer, F.J.: How learning in an inverted classroom influences cooperation, innovation and task orientation. Learn. Environ. Res. **15**(2), 171–193 (2012)
4. Otake, K., Shinozawa, Y., Uetake, T.: Proposal of the support tool for after-class work based on the online threaded bulletin board. Int. J. Adv. Comput. Sci. Appl. **8**(2), 219–226 (2017)
5. Otake, K., Komuro, M., Shinozawa, Y., Uetake, T., Sakurai, A.: A proposal of an SNS to support individual practices in a voluntary community. In: Stephanidis, C. (ed.) HCI 2015. CCIS, vol. 529, pp. 107–112. Springer, Cham (2015). doi:10.1007/978-3-319-21383-5_18
6. Zichermann, G., Linder, J.: Game-Based Marketing: Inspire Customer Loyalty Through Rewards, Challenges, and Contests. Wiley, Hoboken (2010). ISBN 978-0470562239
7. Zichermann, G., Cunningham, C.: Gamification by Design: Implementing Game Mechanics in Web and Mobile Apps. Oreilly & Associates Inc., Sebastopol (2011). ISBN 978-1449397678
8. Inoue, A.: Gamification: "Game" Changes Business. NHK Publishing Co, Tokyo (2012). (in Japanese). ISBN 978-4140815168

Personalizing Game by Using Social Network

Jaebum Park, Huitae Ryu, and Changhoon Park$^{(\boxtimes)}$

Department of Game Engineering, Hoseo University, 165 Sechul-ri,
Baebang-myun, Asan, Chungnam 336-795, Korea
{ppp4542,htryu02}@imrlab.hoseo.edu, chpark@hoseo.edu

Abstract. A social network game is a type of online game that is played through social networks. Users are now able to play games online, compare scores, and challenge each other among many other things. But, existing social network games encourage a user to forward a message to the friends of a user connected to the social network to promote the game. In this paper, we propose a personalized game using social network. To achieve this, the game reflects the update or activity of the relationship between friends in the social network. This approach not only enhances the immersion of the game by providing the game that reflects the reality to the user, but also promotes the participation of the social network by allowing the user to detect the situation of the social network while playing the game.

Keywords: Social network game · Personalization · Game interaction · Social interaction · Synchronous vs asynchronous interaction

1 Introduction

A social network game is a type of online game that is played through social networks. The social networking sites environment has provided a platform for online games to develop and expand in the virtual medium. Users are now able to play games online, compare scores, and challenge each other among many other things. The social games business has been growing fast and, in recent years, they have made headlines with promising estimations [1–3]. Facebook is the most popular social network service with over 1.1 billion active users. Recently Facebook announced that 20% of Facebook's daily users play social games [4]. These numbers suggest that games and play on Facebook have become very popular, and that it is the most popular platform for social games.

The beginning of the social games era can be set in 2007, when the social network service Facebook was opened for third-party developer applications with the launch of the Facebook Developer Platform [5]. [6] has proposed the following short definition for social games: "Online games that adapt your friendship ties for play purposes, while accommodating your daily routines." This definition emphasizes three distinct aspects: Social games are played online, they take advantage of the player's existing social network, and they support the sporadic and spontaneous cultural use of social network services, such as Facebook.

C. Stephanidis (Ed.): HCII Posters 2017, Part II, CCIS 714, pp. 167–171, 2017.
DOI: 10.1007/978-3-319-58753-0_26

But, existing social network games encourage a user to forward a message to the friends of a user connected to the social network to promote the game. This kind of spam message delivery is a problem that can cause displeasure among friends of social network. We will study a new type of social network game that can promote both social networks and game play.

2   Personalized Social Network Game

In this paper, we propose a personalized game using social network. To achieve this, the game reflects the update or activity of the relationship between friends in the social network. This approach not only enhances the immersion of the game by providing the game that reflects the reality to the user, but also promotes the participation of the social network by allowing the user to detect the situation of the social network while playing the game (Fig. 1).

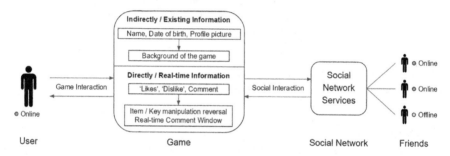

Fig. 1. Interaction of personalized social network game

2.1   Synchronous vs Asynchronous Interaction

There are two different way of interaction for the proposed social game. First is synchronous interaction between game and social network. This method exchanges data in real time between the game and the social network during gameplay to provide seamless connectivity between game players and friends on-line. For example, the game instantly reflects a friend's "likes" or "dislikes" updates on the social network to the game environment, affecting game play. Although they interact with each other in a heterogeneous way, they recognize each other's existence and become able to communicate in a new way.

The second is asynchronous interaction, which uses existing information in social networks to reflect on the game. Unlike the first, it does not provide real-time communication with users on social networks. For example, a game environment is constructed using public information accessible from a social network, such as a friend's birthday, a school of his or her birth.

2.2   Game System Reflecting Social Network

There are two ways to reflect the information acquired from social networks into the game. The first is to build the background of a game that uses information from social networks. The background of the game does not directly affect the game play, but it is easy for the user to recognize while playing the game. For example, it is possible to naturally inform the user who is playing the game, such as collecting photo information of friends who have reached birthday and playing billboard on the background of the game.

Second, we use information from social networks to influence game play directly. This can interfere with or help users play the game. To implement this, we automatically post a message to the social network when the game starts. If friends make a positive comment, such as "Like" in the message, the player will have an item that is favorable to gameplay. Or, negative reactions can be caused by obstacles in the game (Table 1).

Table 1. Using information of social network

	Existing information	Real-time information
Information interaction	Social Network → Game	Social Network ↔ Game
Influence on the game	Indirectly	Directly
Examples applied to the game	Background of the game	Item/Obstacles

3   Implementation and Results

3.1   Development Environment

We use Unity3D engine to implement a proposed social network game. Unity3D engine supports multi-platform, and it can be distributed to various operating systems such as Android and iOS. In particular, there are a variety of plug-ins that can be applied to social networks. And, tetris made with Unity3D was used as an example game. In the existing Tetris game, the game system will be modified to reflect the information of the social network. The social network API uses the Facebook API. The Facebook API supports the Unity3D plug-in and provides all of the social networking information for this study.

3.2   Main Function

We implemented a login window to connect to Facebook in a Tetris game using the Facebook API. If the login is successful, access to existing information in the social network is made to implement asynchronous interactions. And, the wallpaper of the Tetris game is created by using the name, profile picture and date of birth of a friend whose birthday is approaching. As a result, the game player naturally recognizes the information of the social network while playing Tetris. And since this information is used only as a background for the game, it does not directly affect the game.

To implement the synchronized interaction between the Tetris game and Facebook, "Likes", "Dislike" responses and comment information are used. When the Tetris game starts, a message is automatically posted to notify friends about the start of the game on the timeline of the logged-in Facebook account. Friends who are online on Facebook can respond to comments like "Like" or "Dislike" on the post while playing the game. We provide the game player with an item that can clear the Tetris block whenever there is a "Like" response, allowing the game to proceed advantageously. On the contrary, whenever there is a "Dislike" response, the direction of the key that manipulates the falling Tetris block is reversed for 3 s to make the game difficult.

As a result, the social interaction and the game interaction are linked in synchronous or asynchronous manner, and the game and the social network update are mutually reflected. We have implemented cases where the game does not have a direct impact on the game play, and that provides an obstruction or an aid factor when reflecting the social network updates in the game.

4   Conclusion

In this paper, we propose a new type of social network game that can make both social network and game play positive by utilizing information of friends of social network for game play. We divide the information of social network into two categories: existing information that the user has registered in the past, and real - time information that is updated and communicated in real time, and processed and applied to be used as an element of the game. As a result, the user can easily detect the situation of the social network while playing the game (Fig. 2).

Fig. 2. Exchange of information between Facebook API and Unity3D

However, there was a limit to the fact that friends of social networks could not know the user's game play situation in real time. Depending on the progress of the game, the responses of the friends can be changed, and the users who play the game should feel more immersed in the game and be influenced by the social network. Therefore, it is necessary to follow-up research to configure the system so that the friends of the social network know the situation of the game in real time.

Acknowledgments. This work was supported by the National Research Foundation of Korea Grant funded by the korean Government (NRF-2012S1A5A2 A03034747).

References

1. Business Wire. Social gaming is fastest growing sector in global video gaming market: Companiesandmarkets.com (2011). http://www.businesswire.com/news/home/2011060900 5704/en/Social-Gaming-Fastest-Growing-Sector-Global-Video
2. Gobry, P.-E.: The social gaming market will explode to $5+ billion by 2015. Business Insider, 21 February 2012. http://www.businessinsider.com/the-social-gaming-market-will-explode-to-5-billion-by-2015-2012-2
3. GP Bullhound. Social gaming: the fastest growing segment of the games market (2010). http://www.gpbullhound.com/researchpdf/GPB%20Social%20Gaming%20Report%20-%20March%202010%20%283%29.pdf
4. Crook, J.: Facebook now hosts 250M monthly gamers, paid out $2B to devs in 2012. TechCrunch, 26 March 2013. http://techcrunch.com/2013/03/26/facebook-nowhosts-250m-monthly-gamers-paid-out-2b-to-devs-in-2012/
5. Mäyrä, F.: Games in the mobile internet: understanding contextual play in Flickr and Facebook. In: Grawford, G., Gosling, V., Light, B. (eds.) Online Gaming in Context: The Social and Cultural Significance of Online Games, pp. 108–129. Routledge, London (2011)
6. Järvinen, A.: State of social in social games [Presentation slides], February 2011. http://casualconnect.org/lectures/community-social/state-of-social-in-social-games/

Learning to Code in a Community of Practice in Mozambique: The Case of MozDevz

Ivan Ruby[1(✉)] and Salomão David[2]

[1] Concordia University, Montreal, Canada
ivan.ruby@mail.concordia.ca
[2] Universitá Della Svizzera Italiana (USI), Lugano, Switzerland
cumbulas@usi.ch

Abstract. In this paper, we present and analyze the current computer science educational environment in Mozambique and the relationship between the activities undertaken by the Mozambican developers' community (MozDevz) and the objectives set on the Information and Communication Technologies (ICT) policies of the local Government. Data was collected over a 2-month period and consisted of document analysis, semi-structured interviews as well as observations from two training sessions organized by the community and from public forums used by members on social media platforms. ICT initiatives deployed in the Education sector in Mozambique were mainly geared towards providing access to the internet and delivering computer skills to students, teachers, and school administrative personnel. However, the skills provided to students were not at par with job market requirements. In light of these circumstances, MozDevz emerges as an alternative to fill the gap between the focus of government initiatives and the job market demands for knowledgeable and qualified professionals, by providing an informal learning environment, guided by socially-aware values.

Keywords: Informal learning · Technology-enhanced learning · Communities of practice · International development · ICT4D

1 Introduction

The recent outbreaks of economic crises in developed countries in the world (North) have given rise to an unprecedented movement towards finding alternative solutions. Small and medium companies from these countries, looked at the exceptional blossoming of the least developed countries (South) as a possible partner to contain their restricted consumption. In the most recent years, the South witnessed a strong migration of Information and Communication Technologies (ICT) and specialised personnel.

Mozambique witnessed during this period a rapid economic expansion, a speculative bubble fuelled by increasingly close and accentuated relations of credit and debt by external funding agencies. ICT companies from the South absorbed much of the local grants and ICT personnel, reducing the gap between capacity and demand.

© Springer International Publishing AG 2017
C. Stephanidis (Ed.): HCII Posters 2017, Part II, CCIS 714, pp. 172–177, 2017.
DOI: 10.1007/978-3-319-58753-0_27

Since the end of the Mozambican financial boom, the long-term players active in the market are large Mozambican Software developing companies and coalition of individuals. The Mozambican Developers' community (MozDevz) is an example of a coalition of individuals engaged in the development of software solutions for the community, maintaining high levels of engagement backed by an agenda focused on developing the local community. In this paper, we focus on the impact of MozDevz in the capacity-building of personnel aimed at the development of ICT solutions and how it is related to the overall ICT atmosphere in the country.

Our research takes as the founding philosophy that of a designer in the middle, hired by the North to produce solutions for the local government and private agencies of the South.

2 Methods

Data was collected over a 2-month period and consisted of document analysis, semi-structured interviews as well as observations from two training sessions organized by the community and from public forums used by members on social media platforms (Facebook and WhatsApp). Two researchers immersed in the community and engaged in participant observation taking field notes of events, observed interactions and facts deemed relevant in the context of this study. Participants consisted of administrative staff, founding members of the community as well as members in general. Data analysis comprised of a thematic analysis of the data collected from the different sources.

3 Mozambican Developers Community

The Mozambican Developers Community (MozDevz) was created in October 2013, aiming to sensitize and train students and ICT-enthusiasts and connect them to corporate and civil society organizations (MozDevz n.d). The MozDevz coalition soon became a driving force when the Minister of Science and Technology (MCT), in 2014 created conditions for the first hackathon, which gathered a major number of Mozambican developers. The coalition became an informal network of developers, creating sustainable ICT solutions for government agencies and private companies. Currently, the coalition has more than 1200 members, out of which 800 registered, an administrative staff comprised of 8 people. Most of the coalition members are undergraduate students from local and international universities at which most of the learning process is done using formal methods of learning.

During the Mozambican financial boom, most of the coalition members were recruited at the university to work on software development projects for the government. They experienced formal learning methods and provided to such organizations in-depth knowledge of cultural and local practices in usage and adoption of software.

The group promotes community empowerment, working spirit and knowledge sharing as key values to make Mozambique a regional reference in the production of technological solutions through collaboration, innovation and creation of local solutions to local problems.

3.1 When Formal Is Supported by Informal Learning

The MozDevz coalition started from the desire of young developers to gain recognition, establish friendship, discover opportunities and connect with other like-minded. The coalition started developing small applications aiming to become a pro-active consultant body for the community. The early days of the movement were not concerned with sustaining the movement and finding solutions for pressing social problems of the coalition members as the movement was concerned with the transference of knowledge and software development standards and practices.

Most of the members of the coalition are university students, who attend classes delivered using formal learning methods and reported that the process of formal learning delivers structured content in a long time-period.

What we learn at the university is something structured, based sometimes on old development approaches. You cannot ask to be given other type of classes and you are forced to attend even if it is not interesting (Interviewee 1 – Coalition Member).

In the community, members are provided the opportunity to complement what is learned in the traditional classroom. The informal learning process takes place online, in public places and any member of the coalition can seek out learning opportunities and ways in which they can share ideas with other learners. The coalition doesn't take a solitary learning approach instead it is more like a group which picks a topic and can change or alter during the process of learning.

The programming classes are mainly what we decide it will be, there will be some groups doing something specific we just share in some moments the same physical space but anyone can join at any time, we are all teachers and students (Interviewee 6 – Coalition Member).

Informal learning takes place at the grassroots level in a non-formal school setting, where technologies can be adapted to learning objectives with fewer constraints than formal learning processes at the university.

The above excerpts demonstrate how the community of developers linked both the formal and informal learning. They use the structure provided at the university classes and bridge with the student-centered, interest-guided approach of the informal learning that occurs in the context of participatory media, which offers significant opportunities for increased student engagement.

3.2 Negotiation as a Key Component in Achieving Shared Goals

As a social learning system, one of the defining characteristic of a community of practice is the ability of members to establish a sense of identity (Wenger 2010). By being allowed to take part in the goal-setting and decision-making processes, members foster a sense of ownership and participation. At MozDevz, this was enabled through collective decision-making. Although there are roles assigned to the administrative staff, there is no established hierarchy. This allows a greater flexibility and inclusion of member's opinions in the decision-making process. An example is the decision of what not to include in one of the member forums on social media. Members ask whether certain topics are suitable to be shared and others reply. There is no single authority who makes a decision, relegating all remaining members to lesser roles. Consensus is clearly achieved through open-dialogue and active participation of community members in the decision-making process.

3.3 Community Reach

The MozDevz community benefits from the usage of social media platforms to reach their target audience. Members actively use the forums on social networks Facebook and WhatsApp to engage with each other, exchanging links to tutorials, news articles and most noticeably asking questions and providing answers. Questions range from broad discussions regarding trends in the programming field to troubleshooting and suggestions for tools and services to use. Members also disseminate information regarding job opportunities, both long and short term.

Another avenue explored by the community is its *Ambassadors program*. Students who are members of the community can serve as the community representatives in their respective educational institutions, relaying information and providing a point of contact and physical presence of the community in the campus.

3.4 Partnerships as a Cornerstone for Progress

The establishment of the community was a result of a collective effort and well-supported intentions. However, growth and alignment of the community with the interests of prospective members and demands of the job market were out of the reach of the administrative staff. To achieve this goal, the coalition established strategic partnerships with public and private sector institutions, securing event venues and resources to conduct their events. This partnerships also provide an opportunity of members to reach prospective employers and vice-versa, which benefits and interests both.

4 Opportunities for Participation: Mozambique National ICT Policies and Digital Inclusion Goals

Approved in December 2000, Mozambique's ICT policy prioritizes, amongst other objectives, the ambition of making the country a producer and not merely a consumer of ICTs, listing Education, human resource development, health, universal access, national ICT infrastructure and governance as the priority areas (Isaacs 2007; Muianga et al. 2013) (Table 1).

Table 1. Some of Mozambique's education and ICT indicators

Indicator	Percentage	
	Male	Female
Youth (15–24 years) literacy rate (%) (2009–2013)*	80	57
Primary school net enrollment ratio (2009–2013)*	88.8	84.1
Secondary school net enrolment ratio (2009–2013)*	18.2	17.3
Households with a computer**	7.33	
Households with Internet access**	6.22	
Mobile phone users*	69.7	
Internet users*	5.9	
ICT Development Index Rank**	158/167	

Sources:
*United Nations Development Programme (UNDP) Human Development Report 2015
**International Telecommunication Union (ITU) 2015 Global ICT Development

ICT initiatives deployed in the Education sector so far were mainly geared towards providing access to the internet and delivering computer skills to students, teachers, and school administrative personnel.

A project denominated SchoolNet (FMFI 2007) was launched in 2002 to introduce computer literacy into secondary schools, to enhance learning and teaching. By July 2006, the project facilitated the establishment of Computer Labs in 75 schools, with 25 estimated to be connected to the internet. eSchools Mozambique (Farrell et al. 2007), is an initiative funded by the New Partnership for Africa's Development (NEPAD), implemented from 2006 on 6 Secondary schools, in cooperation with Hewlett Packard (HP) and Microsoft. In this project, each school was fitted with a lab comprising approximately 20 Personal Computers (PCs), a Server, a Printer and a Media Lab. In addition to the resources, teachers received training and learners were provided hands-on experience with the PCs. Another initiative launched in 2006 is the Mozambique Research and Education Network (MoReNeT) which links 25 education and research institutions in an attempt to improve the speed and quality of internet access between such institutions. The list of implemented initiatives aligned with the country's ICT Policy and Education sector objectives extends further but a common ground is the provision of computers and peripherals, access to the internet and capacity building.

However, although praised for the development that took place since its inception, the policy has been deemed outdated, no longer meeting the reality of needs and current development in the country as well as in the state of technology (Gaster et al. 2009). Gaster et al. (2009) also suggest the need to involve citizens in the discussion of ICT policies and strategies that will affect their lives.

5   Conclusion

The community of Mozambican software developers is a promising collective with a growth being catalysed by strategic partnerships and an ability to adapt to the medium, interests and resources available to existing and prospective members. Through the implementation of training programs and job-placement initiatives, MozDevz in effect contributes to achieving the goals set by the Mozambique's government national ICT policy by providing capacity building and opportunities for integration of its members in the job market.

We identified negotiation, community reach and strategic partnerships as the foundational and defining characteristics that drive the success of MozDevz as a software development community in Mozambique. With a growing user-base and increasingly positive reputation amongst public and private sector institutions, we project that MozDevz will continue playing a key role in complementing the government efforts in the ICT sector due to its ability to deliver learning in environments and through processes out of the reach of public policies.

A limitation of this study comprised of its duration and the number of training sessions attended. A larger time period of observation will allow a richer description of the community and its members, detailing their interests, motivations and perceptions of both members and outsiders of its effectiveness.

References

Farrell, G., Isaacs, S., Trucano, M.: The NEPAD e-Schools Demonstration Project: A Work in Progress, Vancouver (2007)

FMFI: SchoolNet Mozambique: project overview (2007). http://www.fmfi.org.za/wiki/index.php/Schoolnet_Mozambique:Project_Overview. Accessed 18 May 2016

Gaster, P., Cumbana, C., Macueve, G., Domingos, L.N.C., Mabila, F.: Digital inclusion in Mozambique: a challenge for all (2009). http://www.ngopulse.org/sites/default/files/FinalMozambiqueReport10July2009-English.pdf

Isaacs, S.: ICT in education in Mozambique (2007). http://www.infodev.org/infodev-files/resource/InfodevDocuments_419.pdf

MozDevz: Communidade de desenvolvedores mocambicanos (n.d). http://www.mozdevz.org. Accessed 10 Mar 2017

Muianga, X., Hansson, H., Nilsson, A.: ICT in education in Africa - myth or reality: a case study of Mozambican higher education institutions. Afr. J. Inf. Syst. 5(3), 5 (2013)

Wenger, E.: Communities of practice and social learning systems: the career of a concept. In: Blackmore, C. (ed.) Social Learning Systems and Communities of Practice, pp. 225–246. Springer, London (2010). doi:10.1177/135050840072002

"Free Will": A Serious Game to Study the Organization of the Human Brain

Deborah Sturm[1]([✉]), Jonathan Zomick[2], Ian Loch[1], and Dan McCloskey[1]

[1] College of Staten Island, City University of New York,
2800 Victory Boulevard, Staten Island, NY 10314, USA
{Deborah.Sturm,Dan.McCloskey}@csi.cuny.edu, Ian.Loch@cix.csi.cuny.edu
[2] Touro College, 1602 Avenue J, Brooklyn, NY 11230, USA
jzomick@student.touro.edu

Abstract. We report on a serious game that is designed to teach the functional anatomy of the human brain to undergraduate and graduate students in Psychology and Neuroscience courses. The game provides a unique, immersive, first-person experience for students to understand the discrete faculties of the human brain and the associated brain regions. In addition to our core designers and developers, we included design-feedback testers on our team to give us iterative feedback throughout the development process. Initial feedback from this group indicates that "Free Will" is effective as a game-based learning supplement.

Keywords: Serious games · Digital game-based learning

1 Introduction and Background

According to a Pew Research Center report, 97% of teenagers and 81% of adults between the ages of 18–29 years of age play video games [1]. Education in particular was found to be a significant factor, with 76% of students playing video games versus 49% of non-students. Traditionally, video games have been primarily designed for and played as a form of entertainment and recreation. However, in recent years researchers, educators, and employers have explored the potential benefits this medium can have on educational outcomes and employee training. Considering video games' broad appeal to students, researchers and educators have focused on harnessing the simulative, and interactive aspects of video games to better engage students and enhance comprehension and retainment of subject material. Educators have argued that our approach to educating today's students must differ significantly from that of previous generations because as "Digital Natives" they process information differently from the those of the last generation [2].

In a meta-analysis examining the effects serious simulation games have on instructional effectiveness, Sitzmann found that instructional games were effective in improving measures of self-efficacy, declarative knowledge, procedural

© Springer International Publishing AG 2017
C. Stephanidis (Ed.): HCII Posters 2017, Part II, CCIS 714, pp. 178–183, 2017.
DOI: 10.1007/978-3-319-58753-0_28

knowledge, and retention results [3]. Another study examining educational out-comes of gamified learning found that students who were provided with a gam-ified experience performed better in practical assignments and overall received higher grades than a control group [4].

Games that are not only interactive but also immersive present additional benefits in that they allow students to discover through highly effective Experi-ential Learning [5]. Experiential learning through immersive simulations of real world environments has been used widely for training in medical and military professions and has grown in business education [6]. However, application of immersive game based learning in the liberal arts is relatively novel, and appears to be unprecedented in the study of functional neuroanatomy.

Functional neuroanatomy, the study of how the brain is organized and which brain regions are necessary for different perceptions, thoughts and behaviors is fundamental to many courses in Psychology, Biology and Neuroscience. "Free Will" seeks to enhance learning outcomes of brain anatomy and functionality by presenting the material in an interactive, appealing, and immersive virtual environment. Game based learning presents the opportunity for students to sim-ulate how the world would be experienced without certain brain faculties thereby encouraging experiential learning.

2 Game Design

Free Will was designed by an interdisciplinary team of neuroscientists and com-puter scientists. We are developing the game in an iterative manner with input from undergraduate and graduate Psychology and Computer Science students. We used James Paul Gee's Principles of Learning as a framework for how to design the learning components of the game [7]. His principles include co-design, customizing, identity and presenting well-ordered problems. Gee emphasizes that the games should be pleasantly frustrating so that the player wants to play (and thereby learn) and persist. The game shouldn't be too easy so that the player is bored and stops playing, nor should it be too difficult to avoid quitting as a result of frustration. Instead the game should progress in difficulty at a pleas-ant pace to increase learning and persistence. The feedback to the player should be positive when learning is occurring and not overly negative when the player doesn't succeed. We also included his recommended "on demand" information and "just-in-time" instructions.

Our game, Free Will? is written in Unity3d with C# scripting, and applies many of these design principles in order to encourage learning in a fun interactive way. The opening scenes set up the storyline introducing our main character, Will. The premise is that an autopsy has mistakenly been performed on Will. He finds himself without much information of who he is or why the sensations available to him are so limited. Through game play, the player helps Will to reassemble his brain. Will still maintains his inner dialogue (his free will), which provides the player with clues and the ability to move around. The goal of the game is for the player to reassemble Will's brain by learning about brain regions and their function.

Parallel scenes within the game allow the player to explore and self-assess. In the exploration mode students are presented with a 3D model of the human brain containing 21 movable parts and an animated human model. This module encourages students to explore the various regions of the brain, with their spatial locations, names and functions, and visualize their contribution to normal human functioning through animations. Both sides of the brain are displayed and each can be rotated independently. As the player mouses over a region a probe appears, that part changes color, and the name is displayed. When the player presses the mouse on a region, the probe inserts into that area and information about the functionality is displayed. A sound clip of the name of the region is played so that the user learns how to pronounce the parts. For some regions, the human model animates a function. This is done to reinforce the textual message. For example in Fig. 1, the player has moused over and pressed down on the occipital lobe, the area of the brain responsible for processing visual information. The name is displayed and an animation of a boy looking around is played. There are two assessment levels; the first evaluates whether the player has mastered the structure (names and locations) of the regions of the brain. A grey-scale model of the brain is presented (in a morgue scene) and the names of individual brain regions are displayed in random order. If the player selects the correct position on the brain model, the part animates into place from off screen. In Fig. 2 several parts have already been correctly placed (the score is 6) and Cerebellum is displayed. The player can switch to the Explore scene to review the names and positions of the regions and then return to the morgue scene to choose the part. Along with the score, we give positive feedback when the player reaches key scores, such as "Good Job," "Half way there," "Almost done" and "You are a brain master!" Once the brain is complete the brain spins around and Will announces "I feel complete again."

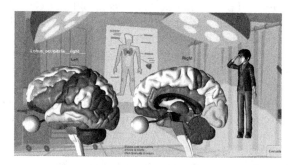

Fig. 1. Explore level (Color figure online)

The second assessment level evaluates the player's knowledge of the functionality of brain regions. Students are presented with a 3D brain template to fill and a puzzle to solve from the perspective of a human figure (representing Will). Brain parts are stored in specimen jars on shelves in the room. There are three ways that Will displays some deficit in brain functioning relating to specific brain regions; using animations, audio clues, or a displayed hint. For

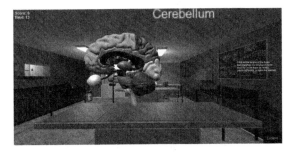

Fig. 2. Assessment level (Color figure online)

example, one animation shows Will off-balance and the player needs to drag the cerebellum (which plays an important role in motor control and balance) over to the correct place in the template in order for him to regain his balance. In another puzzle, an audio clip of a neurologist asks Will a question and Will struggles to speak using short phrases, which is symptomatic of Brocca's aphasia. To solve this puzzle, the player must drag over the region that contains Brocca's area. This module is ideal for demonstrating the interdependency of brain areas required for complex thought and behavior by simulating for the player how ones experience of the world differs with and without the function of specific brain regions.

3   Methods

In order to optimize the effectiveness and educational value of our game we sought design feedback from psychology undergraduate and graduate students and Computer Science majors. We asked the team testers to play the current version and to fill out a survey with their impressions and suggestions for improvement. The questions asked about the appeal, educational benefits, and design of the game. We also watched players while they played the game to assess whether it was intuitive. In addition to recording scores, we are using Google Analytics to keep track of milestones achieved by players, and which levels each player completed. A useful feature of Google Analytics is the summary data showing how many players viewed each level. For each level one can view the total and percentage of unique views (see Fig. 3). Google also provides the data on exits from scenes so one can determine when and how often player quit the game. We also added custom events to track when a player reaches certain scores and when they switch scenes.

We are particularly interested in determining how often the player switches to the explore mode to look up answers and how long they stay on each level. Figure 4 shows a snippet of the screens viewed by a particular player - showing that this player switched back and forth from the assessment to the explore levels.

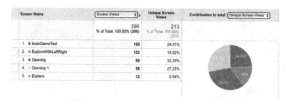

Screen Name	Screen Views ⬩⬇	Unique Screen Views	Contribution to total: Unique Screens Views ⬩
	396 % of Total: 100.00% (396)	213 % of Total: 100.00% (213)	
1. ▦ brainGameTest	195	24.41%	
2. ▦ ExploreWithLeftRight	102	15.02%	
3. ▦ Opening	69	32.39%	
4. ▦ Opening 1	58	27.23%	
5. ▦ Explore	12	0.94%	

Fig. 3. Google analytics - screen views

☐ 12:15 AM   ◉   Viewed **brainGameTest**

☐ 12:15 AM   ◉   Viewed **Explore**

☐ 12:14 AM   ◉   Viewed **brainGameTest**

☐ 12:14 AM   ◉   Viewed **Explore**

☐ 12:14 AM   ◉   Viewed **brainGameTest**

Fig. 4. Google analytics - single player feedback

4   Design Feedback

Here we report some important design feedback reported by several design-feedback testers. Most of our testers reported that they liked the game and all of them said that they feel this is a good way to learn about the parts of the brain. The majority felt that the game-play was intuitive and they liked the storyline and premise. Some players did not enjoy the background music especially during the assessment level where they found it distracting and suggested that we add a mute button (keeping the sound effects though). Most responded that their knowledge of the brain regions increased and said they would recommend the game to friends. When we observed testers playing the game, we noted that some did not notice the button to switch to the Explore scene or did not realize that one could toggle back and forth. They were also frustrated that they couldn't skip questions and come back to them (as one typically can during a traditional paper and many computer-based assessments). We are updating the game to incorporate their feedback.

5   Discussion

Immersing students in a 3D game environment where deficits in these discrete brain functions are experienced should provide an effective way for students to better comprehend and retain lessons in functional neuroanatomy and will provide a novel tool for students who struggle with a rote memorization approach to learning. Learning outcomes will be measured by comparing exam results posed to undergraduate and graduate students in these courses with and without our game-based learning supplement.

Acknowledgements. This project was funded in part by a Technology grant from the College of Staten Island. We thank Zhi Qui, and Kasie Okpala for their work on the graphics and animation.

References

1. Lenhart, A., Jones, S., Macgill, A.: Video games: adults are players too. Pew Research Center Publications, Pew Research Center (2008)
2. Prensky, M.: Digital natives, digital immigrants part 1. On Horizon **9**(5), 1–6 (2001)
3. Sitzmann, T.: A meta-analytic examination of the instructional effectiveness of computer-based simulation games. Pers. Psychol. **64**(2), 489–528 (2011)
4. Domínguez, A., Saenz-De-Navarrete, J., De-Marcos, L., Fernández-Sanz, L., Pagés, C., Martínez-Herráiz, J.J.: Gamifying learning experiences: practical implications and outcomes. Comput. Educ. **63**, 380–392 (2013)
5. Kolb, D.: Experiential Learning as the Science of Learning and Development. Prentice Hall, Englewood Cliffs (1984)
6. Freitas, S.: Learning in Immersive Worlds. Joint Information Systems Committee, London (2006)
7. Gee, J.P.: What video games have to teach us about learning and literacy. Comput. Entertain. (CIE) **1**(1), 20 (2003)

Purposive Game Production in Educational Setup: Investigating Team Collaboration in Virtual Reality

Olga Timcenko[✉], Lise Busk Kofoed, Henrik Schoenau-Fog,
and Lars Reng

Aalborg University Copenhagen, A.C. Meyers Vaenge 15,
2450 Copenhagen, SV, Denmark
ot@create.aau.dk

Abstract. With increasing amount of research and applications in Virtual Reality (VR), there is a growing need to educate future professionals in this field. Thus, it is crucial to motivate young persons to choose this career, especially as many developed countries report not enough interest for STEM educations in general.

In this poster, we will present an experiment conducted with undergraduate students on their final year of studying. The whole education is organized within Problem Based Learning paradigm (Aalborg model), and students work in groups to solve a problem chosen by themselves and only broadly defined by the semester theme. For this experiment, we have organized a special Production Group, of a size of three ordinary semester groups (21 persons), and required that within the semester theme "Audio-Visual Experiments" a meaningful problem using VR should be investigated, by developing and testing a VR application. The students were assigned specific roles, as if they were working on a real project in a real company – thus a bigger size of the group. Several Oculus Rift Development Kit 2 sets were available. After reviewing literature, the group formulated a research question: "Does virtual reality have an effect on group communication effort in a collaborative environment?" To answer this question, the group developed a 3D VR puzzle game with several levels. In order to solve puzzles, participants needed to collaborate and communicate in VR, which is a field that still requires research. The students tested several scenarios, using triangulation method of observations, screen recording and questionnaire, and developed ideas why something might work or not.

Three teachers were supervising the students, and the fourth was observing the whole process. During supervision hours, and interviews with the students after the production was finished, we were able to learn about their learning process and get information on their motivations and challenges in using this novel technology.

This poster will present both students work setup, testing process and conclusions, and teachers' observations on the process.

Keywords: Eduction for Virtual Reality developers · Purposive game development · Problem-based learning · Collaboration in Virtual Reality

© Springer International Publishing AG 2017
C. Stephanidis (Ed.): HCII Posters 2017, Part II, CCIS 714, pp. 184–191, 2017.
DOI: 10.1007/978-3-319-58753-0_29

1   Introduction

Virtual Reality (VR) is again becoming a hot topic among game developers and other technologists. Novel equipment is significantly better and cheaper than in nineties, so there is a real chance that VR will stick this time – which opens a need to educate professionals who could develop meaningful and useful VR applications. This poster will describe a case study of a large group of students (21) learning about Virtual Reality (VR) while developing a game to test human behavior during team building. The educational idea was to let students who do have some knowledge in programming, game development, sound computing and interaction design, but have never previously worked with VR, gain some experience in VR by challenging them to solve a problem that they find interesting. This is a variant of Aalborg University Problem Based Learning (PBL) pedagogical approach, but with a modification that the students, while developing a game in VR, should work in an environment that mimics small-to-medium size game company, both to motivate them, and prepare them better for future job-market. That is why three ordinary-semester groups (5–7 persons each) were joined in one so called Production Group. Effects of this mode of organizing project work and using game development process as motivator for learning are reported in [1]. Theoretical background for this approach, which is very close to design-based educational approach, could be found for example in [2–6], where different authors claim that placing the learners in active designer role enables them for deeper learning and understanding, and eases knowledge transfer, as the learners are placed in a situation very close to their future work environment. Observations that we have made during the project described in this poster support those claims.

In the first part of the poster, we will describe the students' group organization, working and learning process, as well as an experiment and the conclusion they have made. In the second, concluding part, we will note some of supervisors' observations and conclusions.

2   Purposive Game Production

2.1   Organization of the Group Work

By working in the Production group students should fulfill the requirements of their semester study plan, which is 15ECTS non-evenly distributed over the whole semester. The remaining 15ECTS are filled in by obligatory courses, with majority of the workload closer to the beginning of the semester. Working in a large group provides both advantages and challenges. The students might work longer and deeper in areas that interest them, as work division becomes necessary. More complex problems could be considered and solved. On the other side, some decision-making hierarchy is needed, and communication and planning could become an issue. Thus, before the project work had started, the supervisors have provided the students with some agile software development tools, such as sprints, backlogs, burn down charts, and daily scrum meetings among team members. In order to keep the team informed and under control, platforms for communication were Facebook, Google Drive and Slack, depending on purpose and kind of communication – from urgent info about absence to software organization. Meetings with supervisors were approximately once a week, and scheduled via e-mail.

The project timeline was also defined by supervisors – who, for the sake of this production, were called CEOs – to mimic company's set-up. It can be seen on Fig. 1. The numbers in the top row are dates from September to December. The important milestone was at the beginning of December, which denotes the end of production, when the game should be presented to external jury consisting of developers in several successful game companies. The jury should give feedback about the game, and that served as a huge motivational factor for the students. The remaining month of the semester was used to fulfill other academic requirements connected with the project work (using the developed game to test some scientific hypothesis), and that is beyond the scope of this poster.

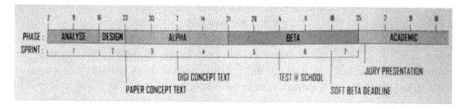

Fig. 1. Top-level timeline provided by "CEOs"

In order to fulfill the tasks and requirements of the project, the students have divided them into hierarchical teams, as can be seen from Fig. 2.

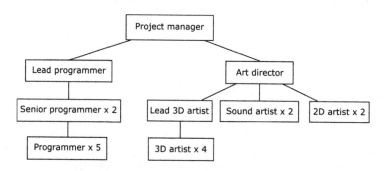

Fig. 2. Size and structure of the project team

2.2 Choosing the Purpose of the Game

The main idea of Aalborg University Problem Based Learning (PBL) is that the students should choose their own problem to solve, within the semester theme. As the theme of the semester where the Production group was organized was Audio-visual experiments, the students had to decide which kind of an experiment they would like to conduct using their developed game. After analysis and discussions, the students got interested into team building activities. Collaboration is a significant factor in well-functioning teams, so the students have chosen to work with the research question:

"To which extent does virtual reality impact team-collaboration during problem-solving"

At the moment when this production started, there have been very few multiplayer games in VR, and research in this field was very sparse, but the students really wished to challenge themselves, and the supervisors agreed (Fig. 3).

Fig. 3. Concept art for the environment

2.3 Design of the Game

The students had to delimit their ambitions to fit two months development period, during which they should also master technology they did not know. They were also limited with available equipment, which were three Oculus Rift head sets. So the decision was to develop three-persons puzzle game, where the players could solve the puzzles only if they collaborate – and then observe their behavior, communication, and time needed to solve the puzzles in VR environment and analogous 3D on-screen computer game, and see whether there are any differences.

The game mechanics was using headlights which players could focus and thus interact with the game objects. Thus, headlights should be used to solve the puzzles – but the puzzles were designed that no individual player could solve them – collaboration in combining several colored headlights, in order to produce a new color based on RGB scheme, was necessary.

The game consisted of three intro levels and three puzzle levels. The intention was also to give the players pleasant experience with HMD, so the game environment was designed to contain both large and small spaces, and provided an opportunity to perceive the depth of the virtual medium. Special attention was on in-game sounds, that should contribute to the feeling on presence in VR [7].

2.4   Testing Game Levels

The students used theoretical knowledge on game development and navigation/ interaction in VR to design game levels and reasoned why they had decided on certain elements. However, two usability tests early in the game development had shown that the users had difficulties in noticing relevant puzzle elements and figuring out what to do, even in much simpler one-person environment. Thus the re-design of certain puzzle elements was performed, mainly by making visual clues and auditory feedback more obvious. This was an important lesson for the students.

2.5   Example of a Puzzle in the Game

The second introductory level was created in order to train the players to create new light color by combining two headlights. For example, magenta is the result of a combination of red and blue. The location of the three color combination buttons was adjusted based on several usability tests, which had shown that the players did not understand the possibility of combining the colors because they thought that they each had their own, single function button.

This puzzle was designed with the idea to create a discussion about solving the problem. Optimally the players should discuss the possibilities for activating all the three buttons through combining the different colors. The players were able to see the color combinations throughout the whole game if they shined their light on the same spot, e.g. when red and blue player shined their lights on the same spot the combined color becomes magenta. If one or more of the players knew color theory they could share this information to the other players and thus succeed in solving the puzzle.

2.6   Using the Game to Set-Up an Experiment

Based on literature overview on team building and collaboration, the students had defined their own weighting scale (presented in Table 1) for observing the teamwork of the players playing the finalized game.

Table 1. Weighting factors for certain elements of collaboration

Teamwork	Weight
Did they communicate about the puzzle	2
Did they small-talk (not about the puzzle)	1
Did they share information (what they observe/do/understand)	2
Did they discuss their approach (discuss misunderstandings/their POV)	2
Did anyone take the role of leader	0
Did he dictate	-2
Did he listen to feedback	1
Did they negotiate/solve as a group	2
Did they refer to objects in the scene while explaining	1

The experiment was set up as follows:

The participants were randomly divided into two groups; VR and Non-VR. Further on, each group was divided into several sub-groups of 3 members each. All participants were provided with a computer, controller, headset, microphone, and all VR group participants additionally had an Oculus Rift Development Kit 2. Each group also had a Teamspeak setup that the participants communicated through verbally. During the test, one of test participant's computer screens was recorded, together with all the group's communication. Test observants were set to observe individual screens and take notes of their behavior on a checklist.

In order to avoid subjective opinions, four students had the task to observe and annotate the recorded data, and the average result for each of the groups was calculated. The result can be seen in Table 2.

Table 2. Average test results per group. Higher points denote better teamwork rating

Group	Group with Virtual Reality (G_VR)	Group without_Virtual_Reality (G_NVR)
1	3.44	3.89
2	4.19	3.75
3	3.86	2.92
4	2.61	3.69
5	3.42	3.83
6	4.03	3.72

Statistical analysis of the result, performed using Wilcoxon Rank-Sum Test (because the measurement level of the data was interval, but not continuous), showed that there was no significant difference between the experimental ($M = 3.591$, $SE = 0.233$) and control ($M = 3.633$, $SE = 0.145$) groups collaborative abilities (ranksum = 38, $p = 0.9372$, $h = 0$).

3   Supervisors' Observations and Conclusion

The production described in this poster is the second year of experimenting with the novel way of organizing project work in frames of Aalborg University Problem Based Learning. The students who were organized in a large group were challenged with technically significantly more complicated setup then would normally be expected for the corresponding semester. Neither the students nor the supervisors had any previous experience of working with Virtual Reality. The students additionally challenged themselves to produce a collaborative game in VR, which is generally a novel topics without enough published research work.

The results were somehow disappointing from the students' perspective, but very encouraging from teachers' perspective. The functional game, integrating VR, in-game sound communication system and believable sounds was programmed, however with some flaws. VR game was compared with equivalent non-VR game. The major disappointing factor for the students was that VR was not better than non-VR game – however, the fact that it was not worse is a valuable achievement, from teachers' perspective. Moreover, the students were motivated to work hard throughout the semester and overcome technical and organizational problems.

Although we did not conduct any formal research among the students during this production, weekly supervisions/observations confirm experiences from the previous year, reported in [1]:

- It is advisable to let students go though some kind of application process, in order to get the students, who are motivated and ready to work harder in the group.
- Maximum 20 students per group.
- Important roles: Game Designer (manages the design of game mechanics, challenges, balance etc.) and Game Director (directs the overall creative production of the game).
- Introduction course to overall game production as well as production management tools and SCRUM, so that the team know what it is, before the production starts.
- The design should be decided on and fixed at an early stage.
- Roles and responsibilities in the different departments should be clear.
- Students should be able to choose their own teams based on portfolios and early discussions.
- A good management tool is essential.
- Make sure all team-members maintain an early and high level of communication with other departments.
- Develop ideas across the different roles in the production.
- The Leads should have the power to decide (democracy is not always the solution).
- Project owners (supervisors) may help a lot by supervising the group closely and by setting clear goals, requirements and demands. It is essential that they make sure to give feedback often, and it is ok to be "bossy".
- Latest versions of the game ("builds") should be available all the time, so team-members can test the game continuously.
- The group should meticulously evaluate each member's skills before setting their ambitions.

Acknowledgment. The authors are thankful to all 5th semester Medialogy students of Aalborg University Copenhagen, who accepted the challenge to work in a Production group and who have produced and tested the game described in this poster. Moreover, their project report [8] was used as a reference while writing this poster.

References

1. Schoenau-Fog, H., Reng, L., Kofoed, L.B.: Fabrication of games and learning: a purposive game production. In: European Conference on Games Based Learning, p. 480. Academic Conferences International Limited, October 2015
2. Savin-Barden, M.: Using problem-based learning: new constellations for the 21st century. J. Excell. Coll. Teach. **25**, 197–219 (2014)

3. Ke, F.: An implementation of design-based learning through creating educational computer games: a case study on mathematics learning during design and computing. Comput. Educ. **73**, 26–39 (2014). Elsevier Ltd.
4. Robertson, J., Howells, C.: Computer game design: opportunities for successful learning. Comput. Educ. **50**(2), 559–578 (2008)
5. De Vries, E.: Students' construction of external representations in design-based learning situations. Learn. Instr. **16**, 213–222 (2006)
6. Lo, Q.: Understanding enactivism: a study of affordances and constraints of engaging practicing teachers as digital game designers. Educ. Tech. Res. Dev. **60**, 785–806 (2012)
7. Nordahl, R., Nilsson, N.: The sound of being there: presence and interactive audio in immersive virtual reality. In: The Oxford Handbook of Interactive Audio, pp. 213–233. Oxford University Press, New York (2014)
8. Production group project report, Medialogy 5th semester, Aalborg University Copenhagen, December 2015

Frustrating Interaction Design of *AS IF*, an Embodied Interaction Game for Perspective Taking Towards Physical Limitations

Servet Ulas[✉], Weina Jin, Xin Tong, Diane Gromala,
and Chris Shaw

Simon Fraser University, 250-13450 – 102nd Avenue, Surrey,
BC V3T 0A3, Canada
{eulas, weinaj, tongxint, gromala, shaw}@sfu.ca

Abstract. In this extended abstract, we discuss the interaction design of *AS IF*, a serious game that employs embodied interaction in order to facilitate perspective taking. The goal of this game is to offer non-patients an insight into what it may feel like to function with a body that is, at times, disabled or limited because of Chronic Pain. The interactor controls an avatar by means of skeletal tracking. In this way, the avatar mimics the interactor's movements and gestures in the virtual environment where they complete a series of tasks. The tasks require the interactor to reach out in physical space with their hands to have the avatar touch objects in the virtual space. During the game, we introduce range of motion limitations to the avatar, effectively making it more difficult to complete the motor tasks in the game environment. Through this "disabling" feature, the interactor's actions are deliberately mapped incorrectly to the avatar; the aim is to give the interactor a glimpse into what it may be like to live with constraints—a frustrating experience.

Keywords: Embodied interaction · Serious games · Perspective taking · Uncomfortable interaction

1 Introduction

Human-Computer Interaction (HCI) research traditionally has focused on making artefacts more usable [1]. However, in the cases where negative experiences are to be conveyed, making the system less accessible to the interactor could become a design choice that help communicate the "right" negative experience. Indeed, Halbert and Nathan suggest that it might even be inappropriate to engineer a positive experience where the context calls for a negative one [8]. To depict what it may be like to live with chronic pain and have movement limitations that may impede the sufferer from fulfilling social obligations, we devised a game-like environment. In this environment, the interactor has to bake a cake for their grandchild while going through episodes of pain that limit her movement.

AS IF features an avatar—an elderly woman who has chronic pain and is struggling with daily tasks. Through embodied interactions and audio recordings, the narrative exposes the thoughts of this avatar in ways that are often invisible. These thoughts are

© Springer International Publishing AG 2017
C. Stephanidis (Ed.): HCII Posters 2017, Part II, CCIS 714, pp. 192–198, 2017.
DOI: 10.1007/978-3-319-58753-0_30

captured from the perspective of a chronic pain patient and are intended to reveal what it may mean to try to do seemingly simple tasks while living with a condition that limits one's ability to perform them. In this extended abstract, we discuss the design decisions we have made to facilitate a disabling experience and how such frustrating interactions are vital in communicating a corporeal experience that is inherently frustrating. We will argue that it may be necessary to abandon practices that foster positive interactor experiences to devise an experience that may be negative yet vital to conveying the right kind of insight and provide a reflective space (Fig. 1).

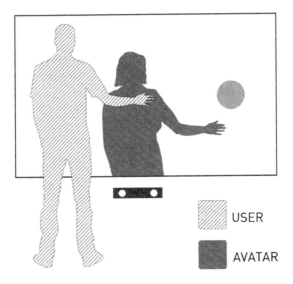

Fig. 1. The avatar in the virtual world mimics what the interactor does in the physical world. The red ball represents an object in the game world which the interactor needs to touch with the avatar's hands. (Color figure online)

1.1 Chronic Pain

Where nociceptive pain exists when actual tissue damage occurs or in the event of a threat, chronic pain may exist without any damage or visible injury. A widely used definition of Chronic Pain is pain that lasts more than a year [15]. A 2011 survey conducted in Canada showed that 18.9% of the adult population had chronic pain, more frequently found in older adults and females compared to males [14]. Affecting almost 1 in 5 of the adult population, chances are that most of us will experience CP ourselves or are close to someone who may be living with chronic pain. Because chronic pain is often invisible, is not well understood, and is termed "the silent epidemic" [11]. Because patients suffer from social stigma [5] it is essential to understand how this condition burdens the patient to create a supportive environment.

Although the aspect of pain itself is a dominant problem, it is not the only one side of the problem. Chronic pain interrupts behavior, interferes with functioning and negatively affects the quality of life [9].

The cause of and cure for chronic pain are unknown; however, the complexity of this condition is recognized by the biopsychosocial approaches that pain clinicians and health researchers have adopted [5]. For example, patients often also suffer from sequelae such as insomnia, depression, anxiety, cognitive impairment, decreasing mobility and social isolation [5]. Further, may affect a person's sense of self: patients compare "who they are now" to "who they have become" as the result of their degenerative condition, and often feel alienated from their body and themselves [11]. Moreover, patients face stigma from those who are unfamiliar with chronic pain, doubt its existence or feel helpless—from friends, co-workers and family to health care workers. Therefore, successful management of chronic pain requires more than only managing the sensation of pain, but requires multifaceted approaches in treatment as well as advocacy in educating the public.

AS IF provides an environment where the general public can "walk in the shoes" of a chronic pain patient – albeit briefly – to gain insight into what it may be like to live with similar constraints in a virtual environment.

1.2   Perspective Taking

Perspective taking refers to the individual going beyond their typically egocentric view of the world in order to consider a different point of view [12]. It is vital for the community – be it healthcare workers or relatives of the patient – to understand the unique and multiple difficulties that patients struggle with. In invisible illnesses like chronic pain, patients feel as if their close ones and even their doctors do not believe them [5]. Therefore, to foster empathy and a more understanding environment for the patients, perspective taking exercises might help.

1.3   Perspective Taking in Serious Games

Serious games are a category of applications that does not merely entertain but addresses real world problems such as raising awareness about a certain cause or issue, giving a more bearable context for painful physical rehabilitation or eliciting behavioral change. In the case of "games for change," the goal is to persuade, change or form an attitude or simply raise awareness regarding social issues [13].

Games often feature an avatar which the players control and experience the world through. This makes them a useful tool for showing interactors unique perspectives they might not have considered before. Traditionally in perspective taking studies the participant is merely asked to imagine themselves as the model they are briefly shown [6]. In the context of Immersive Virtual Environments (IVE), Groom suggests that viewing oneself embodied as an avatar is more visceral than simply imagining, resulting in greater understanding [6].

1.4   Simulated Disability

While *AS IF* portrays the struggle of a Chronic Pain patient, physical limitations that the illness brings may very well apply to a variety of conditions. From an HCI standpoint, the problem that needs to be mediated by the system and experienced by the interactor is analogous to many other ailments. Any range-of-motion reducing condition, be it chronic or acute creates a constraint for the person that may limit their day-to-day activities. Even seemingly easy and mundane tasks such as cooking or doing groceries may become difficult to perform, and can lower one's quality of life. The invisibility and changes in behavior can also easily be misunderstood. Charmaz, for example, describes a case where a middle aged woman's inability to prepare meals quickly and her overall slow movement caused her spouse irritation; he attributed her slowness to her attitude towards him [3].

Simulated disability exercises have been employed to help non-disabled populations improve attitudes towards a disability and improve their understanding and knowledge of specific handicaps by simulating the disability in real life with physical constraints [6]. By providing an embodied insight into what it is like to be disabled, a more understanding and supportive social environment may be fostered. Thus, we employed a simulated disability approach by introducing constraints on the avatar; this, in turn, creates a handicap for the interactor by limiting their ability to interact with the game world. See Fig. 2.

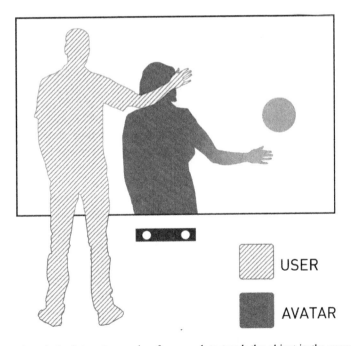

USER

AVATAR

Fig. 2.   Even though the interactor reaches far enough to touch the object in the gameworld, the avatar stops synchronizing her movements perfectly and the interactor fails to complete the task, causing frustration.

2   Uncomfortable HCI

Most of HCI research is focused on making interactions more "natural," fluid and effective. This is understandable since a majority of computer applications aim to elicit positive or productive experiences. In our case, however, to convey an experience that is in essence not-fluid and, not positive, our system had to reflect the frustrating nature of the limitations we are mimicking. Benford suggests that distorting the balance of control by making the user give up or conversely have an unusual degree of agency creates discomfort through control [1]. Similarly, in *AS IF,* we continually change how much the interactor has control over the avatar, not only to create discomfort and dissonance, but as a way to embody the perspective of the avatar, who simultaneously talks about how frustrating her limitations can be which creates an uncomfortable closeness, creating another level of discomfort as Benford proposes [1].

2.1   Frustrating the Interactor

AS IF employs bodily interaction with the system. The avatar mimics the interactor's actions with the help of a 3D camera that can detect and map the interactor's movements onto the avatar. While the avatar mimics the interactor's actions in the virtual environment, the interactor is tasked with making a virtual cake which can be done by controlling the avatar's upper body with her own to interact with objects in the game world.

The making of the cake is divided into a number of steps and to progress, the interactor has to complete a connect-the-dots puzzle that signifies the task. For instance, to put the cake in the oven, the interactor connects the dots by reaching them with her hands and trace the shape of an oven or place candles on the completed cake by tracing a candle. As the interactor completes each task we trigger voice-over narrations hinting on what to the in the next step as well as setting the tone with the patients' voice.

Prior research suggests that removing agency from the player may elicit feelings of anger and helplessness [2]. In the case of embodied interaction where the interactor's body is the instrument through which she interacts with the world, removing agency partially problematizes the body for the interactor. By merely not mapping the actions perfectly but in a limited way, the system can still be interacted by the interactor but the completion of the tasks have now become immensely more difficult.

Leder points to the taken-for-granted absence of the body in the nature of our experience; yet pain doesn't let our body disappear, but dys-appear, or appear in a "bad", "ill" way. With pain, a dys-representation of our body becomes central to the experience at hand [10].

When agency is disrupted, the interactor feels a dissonance with their body and the avatar, as if the avatar has gone beyond being a representation but a dys-representation. Merely gazing at a sculpture that depicts a body under distress results in felt activation of the muscles that mimic the sculpture [4]. We propose that embodying an avatar that is constrained and distressed the users can have an experiential understanding.

3   Conclusions

To convey an experience that has an unpleasant, negative nature – like illness or grief – and to render visible certain constraints through interaction, instead of designing for usability we may at times have to turn to designing more uncomfortable experiences through non-ideal interactions. *AS IF* aims to convey what it feels like to *not* be able to complete seemingly easy physical tasks by systematically robbing the interactor of her agency. Not translating the interactor's actions to the virtual world like the interactor expects in the game, creates frustration by rendering the interactor not as effective as they were before the simulated disability was induced on the avatar.

Embodied interaction affords the interactor the metaphorical shoes of the avatar for them to walk in. By unfairly removing the agency from the user causes them frustration since it is now harder to complete the objective, we deliberately make progress difficult for the user in order to convey a difficult experience.

Our preliminary study showed that our participants were frustrated with the interaction but this seemed to give them a better understanding of the context, resulting in increased willingness to help patients with chronic pain. Even though the experience was described to be frustrating and negative, the participants had left with newfound understanding and sympathy for the avatar's character.

References

1. Benford, S., Greenhalgh, C., Giannachi, G., Walker, B., Marshall, J., Rodden, T.: Uncomfortable interactions. In: Proceedings of SIGCHI Conference on Human Factors in Computing Systems, pp. 2005–2014. ACM, New York (2012). https://doi.org/10.1145/2207676.2208347
2. Bopp, J.A., Mekler, E.D., Opwis, K.: Negative emotion, positive experience?: emotionally moving moments in digital games. In: Proceedings of 2016 CHI Conference on Human Factors in Computing Systems, pp. 2996–3006. ACM, New York (2016). https://doi.org/10.1145/2858036.2858227
3. Charmaz, K.: Loss of self: a fundamental form of suffering in the chronically ill. Sociol. Health Illn. **5**(2), 168–195 (1983)
4. Freedberg, D., Gallese, V.: Motion, emotion and empathy in esthetic experience. Trends Cogn. Sci. **11**(5), 197–203 (2007). https://doi.org/10.1016/j.tics.2007.02.003
5. Gatchel, R.J., Peng, Y.B., Peters, M.L., Fuchs, P.N., Turk, D.C.: The biopsychosocial approach to chronic pain: scientific advances and future directions. Psychol. Bull. **133**(4), 581–624 (2007). https://doi.org/10.1037/0033-2909.133.4.581
6. Grayson, E., Marini, I.: Simulated disability exercises and their impact on attitudes toward persons with disabilities. J. Rehabil. Res. **19**(2), 123–132 (1996)
7. Groom, V., Bailenson, J.N., Nass, C.: The influence of racial embodiment on racial bias in immersive virtual environments. Soc. Influ. **4**(3), 231–248 (2009). https://doi.org/10.1080/15534510802643750
8. Halbert, H., Nathan, L.P.: Designing for negative affect and critical reflection. In: CHI 2014 Extended Abstracts on Human Factors in Computing Systems, pp. 2569–2574. ACM, New York (2014). https://doi.org/10.1145/2559206.2581241

9. Harris, S., Morley, S., Barton, S.B.: Role loss and emotional adjustment in chronic pain. Pain **105**(1–2), 363–370 (2003)
10. Leder, D.: The Absent Body, 1st edn. University of Chicago Press, Chicago (1990)
11. Moorman-Li, R., Motycka, C.A., Inge, L.D., Congdon, J.M., Hobson, S., Pokropski, B.: A review of abuse-deterrent opioids for chronic nonmalignant pain. Pharm. Therap. **37**(7), 412–418 (2012)
12. Osborn, M., Smith, J.A.: The personal experience of chronic benign lower back pain: an interpretative phenomenological analysis. Br. J. Pain **9**(1), 65–83 (2015). https://doi.org/10.1111/j.2044-8287.1998.tb00556.x
13. Peng, W., Lee, M., Heeter, C.: The effects of a serious game on role-taking and willingness to help. J. Commun. **60**(4), 723–742 (2010). https://doi.org/10.1111/j.1460-2466.2010.01511.x
14. Schopflocher, D., Taenzer, P., Jovey, R.: The prevalence of chronic pain in Canada. Pain Res. Manag.: J. Can. Pain Soc. **16**(6), 445–450 (2011)
15. Weiner, R.S.: Pain Management: A Practical Guide for Clinicians, 6th edn. CRC Press, Boca Raton (2001)

The Influence of Toy Design Factors on Children's Problem-Solving Skills

Tien-Ling Yeh[1(✉)] and Jo-Han Chang[2]

[1] Doctoral Program in Design, College of Design,
National Taipei University of Technology, Zhongxiao E. Rd., Taipei, Taiwan
tienling0303@gmail.com
[2] Graduate Institute of Innovation and Design,
National Taipei University of Technology, Zhongxiao E. Rd., Taipei, Taiwan
johan@ntut.edu.tw

Abstract. Nowadays, the issue which parents care about the most is how to improve their children's ability to solve problems in this constantly changing society. "Game-based learning" is a concept commonly identified in preschool education, developing children's key ability required in the future in the process of playing. This study explores the factors influencing children's ability to solve problems and elements of toy design. This study contains two parts: (1) Literature review. This part reviews the studies on the factors affecting children's ability to solve problems. (2) Analyses of current products. The qualitative analysis method and the software Atlas.ti6.0 is applied to analyze the design factors for parent-child interactions with children aged 2 to 6 years. The findings are summarized below: (1) Children's ability to solve problems is related to factors include "family background", "parent-child interaction", "emotion regulation", and "ability to process information". (2) Based on the result of the analysis of the current products, this study finds that the product elements can be categorized into those with "physical" influences, including facilitating sensorial development, facilitating fine motor development, and facilitating perceptual-motor skill development, and those with "psychological" influences, including cognitive ability and educational meaning.

Keywords: Parent-child · Toy · Problem-solving

1 Introduction

The recent reports on social events have reflected the importance of family communication and parent-child relationship. My previously published study with key works including "Marschak Interaction Method", "parenting time", and "children's growth and development" found no significant result with the various interactions, accompanying time interval, children's social competence, and problem-solving skills. Henggeler et al. (1986) suggested that positive and supportive communication helps children to lower their defense, improve their problem-solving skills, feel empathy for others and, learn to trust people. As a result, children can adjust their emotions toward a positive direction with high efficiency. For individuals, problem-solving is a process of thinking. In a parent-child interaction, it is about sharing experiences and is a part of

© Springer International Publishing AG 2017
C. Stephanidis (Ed.): HCII Posters 2017, Part II, CCIS 714, pp. 199–206, 2017.
DOI: 10.1007/978-3-319-58753-0_31

their interactive behaviors. Parents' open and positive communication and interactions and emotional support are associated with their child's problem-solving performance. Wood et al. (1976) found that once children develop a new behavioral portfolio while playing a game, they can use it to resolve real-live problems. Thus, if there can be more behavioral options in a game for children, it is possible that their problem solving skills in terms of flexibility can be advanced. The purpose of this study is to review the studies on the factors influencing children's problem-solving skills and to analyze the design factors of parent-child interaction toys for children aged 2 to 6 years.

2   Literature Review

2.1   Family Background

Some foreign studies on socio-economic statuses and problem-solving skills had pointed out that children of rather high socio-economic statuses have better problem-solving skills than those of rather low socio-economic statuses (Bermudez 1986; Cox 1985). However, a recent foreign study found no significant difference in problem-solving skills between children from complete families and those from broken families (Düşek and Ayhan 2014). Some domestic studies on family socio-economic statuses and problem-solving skills had also found a positive and significant relationship between socio-economic statuses and problem-solving skills. Those with higher family socio-economic statuses have better problem-solving skills. However, the percentage of variation explained by the variable "socio-economic status" is rather low. Thus, it is not appropriate to use this variable as a single predictor for problem-solving skills (Zhan 1989).

2.2   Parent-Child Interactions

Bandura's social learning theory (1986) suggested that the parent-child interactive process of observing and learning is the most important process for human socialization. Therefore, parents are important examples of right behaviors for their children. The affectional connection between parents and their babies is built on continuous mutual interactions of satisfying each other's needs. Building a mother-child dependence relationship is a learning process. This behavior is emitted, not innate (Mercer and Ferketich 1990). In a qualitative study on co-parenting for preschool children, parents play with their children by being their partners in a game, work together to teach their children rules of the game, and provide ideas to resolve problems encountered. A part of parent-child interactions is parent-child verbal communication. Some researchers had found a significant influence of parents' language use on their children's problem-solving skills (Jen 1989).

2.3   Emotion Regulation

Many scholars believe that specific emotions may trigger certain types of adaptive behavior. Izard (1991) and Renninger (1992) argued that being interested is the main emotion that encourages students to explore and solve problems (Hyson 2004). Chen (1999), a domestic scholar, also contended that among the factors influencing problem-solving, perception is closely related to problem-solving. In the cognitive aspect of emotion regulation, understanding of emotions is controlled by attention. Whether a problem can be solved successfully depends on the integration of many fundamental cognitive techniques, such as the components of attention (concentration, persistence, and patience). Kochanska et al. (2000) also found that preschool children no longer need adult to involve in their emotion and behavior regulation (Kalpidou et al. 2004). Thus, there is a close relationship between emotion regulation competence and problem-solving skills.

2.4 Domain Knowledge

Chen (1999), a domestic scholar, argued that among the factors influencing problem-solving skills, perception and memory are closely related to problem-solving skills. Children's memory capacity is limited, directly influencing the amount of knowledge they can access and showing that they may lack of strategies for information processing. "problem solving" is a process, when students encounter a problem, they would attempt to solve it with the knowledge they already have. If the problem cannot be solved, they would try to find a new way to solve it or ask for help. To help students learn efficiently, besides knowledge for a specific field, opportunities for situated learning, exploratory research, and deep consideration should also be provided to them (Su and Hsieh 2006).

2.5 Information Processing

Preschool children's problem-solving skills improve with their development and thus they can solve more complex problems when they grow up (Siegler 1976; Siegler and Chen 2002). According to a study, the balance scale task can provide children hints and help them to improve their skills to solve two-factor balance problems. Pine and Messer (2003) believed that giving children opportunities to play and to explore helps them to gain insight and learn to combine the distance information and the weight information to make a scale balanced. Individuals' knowledge concepts and problem-solving performances are related, as knowledge is the key to break the limit of thinking while solving a problem and is helpful for both adults and children (DeLoache et al. 1997). Thus, Pine

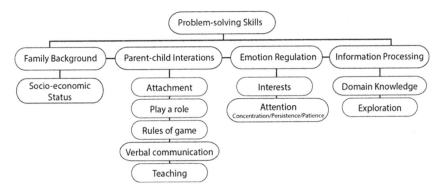

Fig. 1. Summarize the factors influencing children's problem-solving skills

and Messer (1999) explained children's skills to solve the two-factor balance problem using their knowledge representation (Fig. 1).

3 Research Methods

This study analyzed the currently available toy products from the Toy of the Year (TOTY) Award, which is like the Oscar in the toy business in the US. All toys participating in the Award must be available in toy stores in the US before the end of November of the year before the Award. All the toys are nominated by experts in the business, including people from large retailers, the academic circle, and toy media, and toy inventors. The members of the industry association in the US must review toys from 12 categories for 80 finals and cast their votes. The winners are determined based on the votes from consumers (25%), multiple retailers (40%), reporters and bloggers (20%), and the toy association (15%).

The qualitative grounded theory: This study selected the structural toys for children aged 2 to 6 years from the toys nominated for TOTY 2016 and performed a factor analysis based on their description contents and appearances. The software for qualitative data analyses Atlas.ti6.0 was used to perform the analysis. The collected product data were organized and the toys were categorized into three stages based on the factors. The design factors were named. Figure 2 shows the interface of the software. On the left is an image of the product scenario, while the coding process is shown on the right side. Through coding, the relationships were built. Then the networks were created based on the coding and the categories. Each network contains two or more stages connected to the related categories. Figure 2 also shows the coding hierarchies. Finally, a conceptual structure was obtained to display the corresponding relationships.

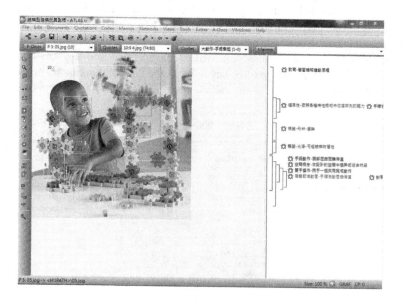

Fig. 2. The interface of the software

3.1   The Qualitative Analyses for the Currently Available Toy Products

According to the grounded theory, there are three stages of coding. The first stage is open coding. The 15 products coded and 29 factors were obtained as shown in Table 1. The second stage is axial coding. The products of similar appearances, description

Table 1. The coding for the toy factor analyses

Stage 3	Stage 2	Stage 1
Physiology	Facilitating sensual development	Visual – shape – a gear wheel Visual – image – a concrete object Visual – shape – a rectangle Visual – shape – a hexagonal screw Visual – shape – a radial shape Visual – shape – various shapes Visual – shape – a continuous long shape Touch – smoothness – something can be assembled and stuck together Touch – smoothness – something can be assembled without adhesion Touch – softness – something can be assembled with adhesion Hearing – a speaking voice
	Facilitating fine motor development	Wrist motion – bending, rotating, and stretching a wrist Metacarpophalangeal joint flexibility - bending and stretching a finger Opponens – holding a small object using fingers
	Facilitating perceptual motor development	Two-hand operation – a motion done with two hands together Hand-eye coordination – eyes gazing at hand operations and motions Big movement – a body movement Big movement – raising an arm Big movement – lifting an object with both arms
Psychological	Cognitive ability	Logical inference – constructing a logical inference based on perception or language comprehension Categorization ability – putting objects of the same characteristics into the same category Spatial concept – manipulating or assembling an object in a designed space Sequence – arranging objects of various characteristics in order
	Educational meaning	Education – learning the theory of mechanical interlocking Education – learning the theories of physics Education – human-machine interactions Education – STEM

contents, and forms were analyzed based on Hsieh's (2007) study on toy factor analyses, with four dimensions, namely the "facilitating sensual development", "facilitating fine motor development", "facilitating perceptual motor development", and "cognitive ability". However, during the process of induction, another dimension was discovered, "educational meaning". This study also performed further analyses for this dimension. The third stage is selective coding, with "physiology" and "psychology" (see Table 1).

According to the summarized information in Table 1, the factor with the most items is facilitating sensual development, followed by educational meaning, cognitive ability, facilitating perceptual motor development, and lastly facilitating fine motor development. Then Atlas.ti was used to create networks. Figure 3 shows the categorization based on the five dimensions of the networks.

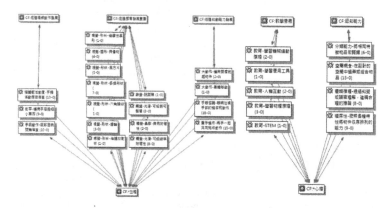

Fig. 3. The categorization based on the five dimensions of the networks

4   Analysis Results

The product factors include "physiological" and "psychological" ones, which are discussed separately below.

The physiological factors: Based on Hsieh's (2007) coding principle, the number of times of coding for "facilitating sensual development" (32 times) is obviously higher than others. Moreover, the influences of the toy design factors on the physiological aspect are summarized below:

- Regarding the coding for "facilitating sensual development", the number of times of coding for touch – smoothness (plastics) (8 times) is the highest, followed by visual – various shapes (7 times) and visual – a concrete object (4 times).
- Regarding the coding for "facilitating fine motor development", the number of times of coding for metacarpophalangeal joint flexibility – bending and stretching a finger (10 times) is the highest, followed by wrist motion – bending, rotating, and stretching a wrist (10 times) and opponens – holding a small object using fingers (9 times).

- Regarding the coding for "facilitating perceptual motor development", the numbers of times of coding for two-hand operation – a motion done with two hands together (15 times) and hand-eye coordination – Eyes gazing at hand operations and motions (15 times) are the highest, followed by big movement – a body movement, big movement – Raising an arm, and big movement – Lifting an object with both arms (1 to 2 times).

5 Conclusion and Discussion

Both foreign and domestic studies had suggested that children's problem-solving skills are related to their families. Although children's problem-solving skills are closely associated with their own cognitive development, whether their parents' disciplining methods are positive or negative is also an important factor. For individuals, problem-solving is a thinking process. In parent-child interactions, it is about sharing experiences and is a part of the parent-child dependency. If a child's parents are very open in bringing up the child and can offer sufficient emotional support, the child's problem-solving performances are influenced to a certain degree. In the cognitive aspect of emotion regulation, one's anxiety may interfere with components of his attention and thus influence his problem-solving skills. In a game, children can try many new behaviors and ways to play. With good communication, it would be a great help for them in future situations with real-life problems to be solved. There are many factors involved. It is not appropriate to discuss just one single factor.

This study analyzed the product design factors and came up with the influences in the physiological aspect (facilitating sensual development, facilitating fine motor development, and facilitating perceptual motor development) and the psychological aspect (cognitive ability and educational meaning). Thus, future research can focus on whether different game mechanisms can help to improve children's problem-solving skills and the influences on parent-child interactions.

References

Bandura, A.: Social Foundations of Thought and Action: A Social Cognitive Theory. Prentice Hall, Englewood Cliffs (1986)

Bermudez, A.: Examining the effects of home training on problem-solving styles. Paper presented at Annual Meeting of the Teachers of English to Speakers of Other Languages (1986)

Chen, L.C.: Cognitive Development and Counseling. Psychological Publishing Co., Ltd., Taipei (1999)

Cox, D.W.: The Purdue elementary problem-solving inventory (PEPSI), grade level, and socioeconomic status: a preliminary study. Gifted Child Q. 29(2), 72–73 (1985)

DeLoache, J.S., Miller, K., Rosengren, K.: The credible shrinking room: very young children's performance with symbolic and nonsymbolic relations. Psychol. Sci. 8, 308–313 (1997)

Düşek, G., Ayhan, A.B.: A study on problem solving skills of the children from broken family and full parents family attending regional primary boarding school. Procedia – Soc. Behav. Sci. **152**, 137–142 (2014)

Henggeler, S., Rodick, J.D., Hansen, C.L.: Multisystemic treatment of juvenile offenders: effects on adolescent behavior and family interactions. Dev. Psychol. **22**, 132–141 (1986)

Hyson, M.: The Emotional Development of Young Children, 3rd edn. Teacher College Press, New York (2004)

Kalpidou, M.D., Power, T.G., Cherry, K.E., Gottfried, N.W.: Regulation of emotion and behavior among 3- and 5-year-olds. J. Gener. Psychol. **131**(2), 159–178 (2004)

Mercer, R.T., Ferketich, S.L.: Predictors of parental attachment during early parenthood. J. Adv. Nurs. **15**, 268–280 (1990)

Pine, K.J., Messer, D.J.: What children do and what children know: look beyond success using Karmiloff-Smith's RR framework. New Ideas Psychol. **17**, 17–30 (1999)

Pine, K.J., Messer, D.J.: The development of representations as children learn about balancing. Br. J. Dev. Psychol. **21**(2), 285–301 (2003)

Su, H.L., Hsieh, H.Y.: The study of science game incorporated into elementary school natural science and technology instructions on problem-solving ability. J. Sci. Technol. Stud. **40**(1), 47–68 (2006)

Siegler, R.S.: Three aspects of cognitive development. Cogn. Psychol. **8**, 481–520 (1976)

Siegler, R.S., Chen, Z.: Development of rules and strategies: balancing the old and the new. J. Exp. Child Psychol. **81**, 446–457 (2002)

Wood, D.J., Bruner, J.S., Ross, G.: The role of tutoring in problem solving. J. Child Psychiatr. Psychol. **17**(2), 89–100 (1976)

Wyver, S., Spence, S.: Play and divergent problem-solving: evidence supporting a reciprocal relationship. Early Educ. Dev. **10**(4), 419–444 (1999)

Zhan, X.M.: Variables relating to creating thinking and problem-solving ability of elementary school students. Unpublished Master's thesis, National Taiwan Normal University, Taipei, Taiwan (1989)

Understanding Reading Comprehension in Multi-display Presenting System: Visual Distribution and Cognitive Effect

Xueqing Zhang[1] and Sanya Liu[2(✉)]

[1] Wuhan Huada National E-Learning Technologies Co., Ltd.,
Wuhan, Hubei, China
xqzhang@outlook.com
[2] National Engineering Research Center for E-Learning, Central China Normal
University, Wuhan, Hubei, China
lsy5918@mail.ccnu.edu.cn

Abstract. This study aims to investigate students' reading comprehension and cognitive load changes under multi-display presenting system in an experimental setting. It is part of the project that has been established in order to develop multi-display interaction system in real classroom for all students.

A dual-screen presenting system, two-adjacent screens for presentation, was utilized to facilitate students' reading compared to single-screen. The presentation was set up in the formats of text-only, text-image, and image-only. 34 participants were tested from Central China Normal University. Their visual distribution and attention levels were recorded by means of SMI's eye-tracking device and NeuroSky's EEG device.

The results proved that the attention levels were increased on the dual-screen system. The reading formats of text-only or text-image took more fixation time and attracted more attention on both single- and dual-screen system. Multi-display presenting system could have a positive effect on Chinese reading comprehension and increase the students' attention levels.

Keywords: Reading comprehension · Multi-display · Cognition · Instructional design

1 Introduction

Learning to read is one of the most important things people accomplish in their young ages because it is the foundation for most of their academic endeavors, as well as for the rest of their lives. Reading activities require people to comprehend and recall the main ideas or themes in text. Reading comprehension is a complex process that occurs as the reader builds a mental representation of a text message. It can be categorized into three levels: word level, sentence level and text level of mental representations [1]. The construction of text level, also called situation model, is the key psychological process in reading comprehension [2].

The comprehension skills could be improved by explicit instruction for students of all levels. In practice, instructors explain specific reading strategies or provide

© Springer International Publishing AG 2017
C. Stephanidis (Ed.): HCII Posters 2017, Part II, CCIS 714, pp. 207–214, 2017.
DOI: 10.1007/978-3-319-58753-0_32

independent practice with feedback when students find difficulties to comprehension in reading. It was reported that it could benefit their achievement of competent and self-regulated reading [3].

In real class, instructors demonstrate reading strategies using annotations or references to reading materials supported by printed handouts, handwriting chalkboard, or digital whiteboard. With the development of multimedia technology, there is a trend that the conventional learning environment is improved with advanced technology. Multimedia can improve both learning and education process [4]. Nowadays, a variety of multimedia technology has been utilized in modern classroom such as PowerPoint, animation by electronic projectors. However, the projector system, as well as additional software, is not user-friendly designed to implement due to the limited display area. Thus, a multi-display interaction system (Fig. 1), has been developed in order to facilitate educational instruction in classroom. This project aims to improve learning effectiveness with innovation technology for all students.

Fig. 1. Multi-display interaction system in real classroom.

This study was part of the project of multi-display interaction system. The purpose of this paper was to investigate students' visual distribution and cognitive attention level while they were reading in multi-display learning environment, in order to evaluate the effectiveness of multimedia learning. A dual-screen presenting system was designed as a prototype of multi-display interaction system for reading comprehension.

2   Related Work

This part explains the cognitive process of reading comprehension, and follows the instructional design based on cognitive theory.

2.1 Development of Reading Ability

Reading is that learning to understanding writing as well as one understands spoken language. It's related to linguistic abilities, relevant knowledge and general intelligence. At the beginning, children are learning to decode and identify words. This process requires less comprehension, no correlation with spoken language. As the improvement of reading skills, the correlations between reading comprehension and spoken language increase and then reach the maximum level by high school [5].

Comprehension is a complex process. Perfetti et al. [6] proposed a framework of the process of reading comprehension. Their model pointed out that the level of word representation includes two units: orthographic and phonological, that are the basic cognitive activities. Once it's been established, inferences occur between word and sentence level in reading process, which develops the foundation of text level of comprehension. The text level of reading process is related to general knowledge stored in human memory. Furthermore, they argued that the linguistic system has a big influence in all the process above.

2.2 Cognitive Process of Information

The beginning of this section will discuss information process in brain that determine the ability of reading comprehension, and follow the introduction of cognitive load and its measurement.

Information Process. Based on the dual-coding theory [7], cognitive model of human brain include visual and audio separated channels that are independent in function. Human sensory system, for instance eyes and ears, receives the stimuli of information outside world, such as text or image, and transmits into working memory. Then working memory integrates mental representations from stimuli into long-term memory. The long-term memory transfers mental representations into schema or automation [8]. Hence, knowledge is acquired through external information to internal schema.

Cognitive Load. However, the working memory has limited capacity and duration [9]. Thus, it could cause cognitive load when human integrate information. The cognitive load is mainly determined by the capacity of working memory. The schema in long-term memory can also affect the cognitive process in working memory that lead to changes of cognitive load. Human cannot process more information if the mental work is overloaded. That would decrease the effective of learning. There are three types of cognitive load: *intrinsic cognitive load, extraneous cognitive load, and germane cognitive load* [10]. *Intrinsic* load is directly related to the learning material (or task) and defined by the number of and interactivity of information elements that have to be processed. Information element is defined as "anything that needs to be or has been learned, such as concept or procedure". *Extraneous* load refers to those mental resources devoted to elements that do not contribute to learning and schema acquisition or automation. It is mainly related to the information presentation and the instructional format that could both increase the human's overall cognitive load while hinder lcarning gain. *Germane* load refers to the mental resources devoted to acquiring and automating schema in long-term memory.

Measurement of Cognitive Load. Subjective rating techniques are the most common method to measure cognitive load [11]. Physiological technology, like heart rate [12], eye-tracking [13], EEG [14], and near infrared spectroscopy [15], provides an alternation to measurements. Besides, performance-based method such as secondary-task method is the indirect measurement to test cognitive load [16]. This study utilized physiological method using eye-tracking technology and EEG device to measure cognitive load, as well as questionnaires.

2.3   Instructional Design

According to cognitive load theory, Sweller et al. [17] proposed several effects for instructional design that are goal-free effect, worked example effect, completion effect, split-attention effect, modality effect, redundancy effect, and variability effect. For instance, the worked example effect suggests the students gain better learning compared to no examples. Mayer [18] further investigated the multimedia learning and advised multimedia design principles such as signaling, spatial contiguity, temporal contiguity, etc. Hence, instructions of making annotations and references could reduce cognitive load to reading.

In summary, cognitive load could be a key indicator to cognitive process of reading comprehension. Both eye-tracking and EEG technology can measure cognitive load changes as well as subjective ratings. Annotations and references presented to students can decrease cognitive load and enhance learning gain when applied in educational instructions.

3   Methods

3.1   Participants

The participants were recruited from Central China Normal University. They were all postgraduate students, half males and half females. The participants were divided into control group and experimental group. The control group tested 18 students in the dual-screen presenting system, with the average age of 26.5 ± 3.7. However, two participants quit during the experiment that have been excluded of results analysis. The experimental group was tested in the single-screen presenting system. 16 participants, with the average age of 27.8 ± 3.1, were tested in total.

3.2   Apparatus

The prototype of dual-screen presenting system was developed for students. It consisted of two 27-inch screens. The software, named 'StarC', was developed to control both screens to present materials as well as annotations and references. Each screen could work independently and cooperatively. Reading strategies would be available by annotating and referencing tools. When students read, two screens simultaneously present the materials in different formats as needed.

The MindWave headset can report the wearers' metal state in the form of Neu-roSky's proprietary attention and mediation values, as well as raw brainwaves and EEG power spectrums. The attention level was recorded to represent the cognitive load of participants in the dual-screen condition as shown in Fig. 2.

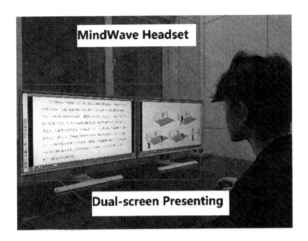

Fig. 2. Participants reading material in the dual-screen presenting system.

In the experimental group, both eye-tracking device (SMI RedN 250) and Mind-Wave headset were used to record the student's visual distribution and attention level in single-screen presenting system.

3.3   Procedures

Three reading materials were translated from [2, 19, 20] and presented in the order of the Latin square design. The participants were randomly assigned to each group. They were given an introduction of the experiment and asked to sign in the consent form at the beginning. Then they were required to wear the MindWave headset and play a game in order to be familiar with the testing environment. The eye-tracking device was calibrated if the participants were under the single-screen system. Three reading materials were presented in the Latin sequence of text-only, text-image, image-only formats. After each material, they were asked to answer one question related to the material contents. At the end, questionnaires adapted from NASA LTX were provided to participants, and their personal information were recorded. The whole experiment took about 15 min.

4 Results

Questionnaires. The ratios of correct answer to each material were 94%, 100% and 94% for text-only, text-image, image-only respectively in dual-screen system. On the other hand, the ratios were 100%, 88% and 75% in single-screen system. The results showed that the correction rates were all over 70%, especially in text-only situation, both groups reached over 90%. The reason was that the difficulties of tasks were rather simple, reported by participants, no matter under single- or dual-screen condition. However, most participants put more effort in reading in the single-screen system than dual-screen condition. Dual-screen system may increase the performance to reading when materials were presented in text-image or image-only format.

EEG Headset. According to MindWave's e-Sense Metric, attention data between 40 to 60 is indicated as natural state of cognition, 60 to 80 is slightly elevated and 80 to 100 is very elevated. The average attention levels were calculated for the duration of reading task. Figure 3 showed that half participants were 'slightly elevated' and one under 40 in dual-screen testing, whereas nearly 40% of participants' value ranged over 60 and two under 40 in single-screen testing. The attention level was slightly higher in the dual-screen system than single-screen. However, there was no significant difference between dual-screen and single-screen system (p-value = 0.66 according to two-sample t-test).

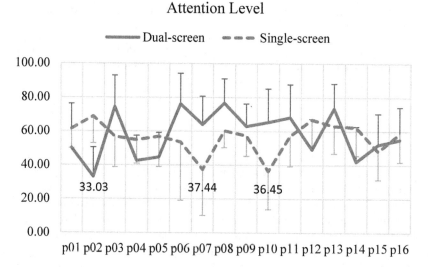

Fig. 3. A comparison of attention level between single-screen and dual-screen presenting system.

Eye-Tracking Device. In the experiment group, the testing was to evaluate the presentation formats of text-only, text-image and image-only with eyes' fixation time. The total fixation duration of participants in reading was captured by eye-tracking device under single-screen condition. The results were shown in Fig. 4. It can be seen that image-only presentation spend much less time for students to read compared to other two formats. The result of ANOVA test showed that, [$F(2, 45) = 1.8443$, $p = 0.17$], there was no significant difference among three reading formats.

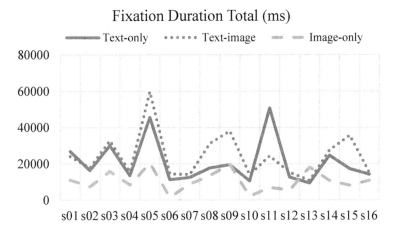

Fig. 4. Total fixation duration by eye-tracking device

5   Conclusion

This work was part of the project of development of multi-display interaction system in classroom. It was carried out to evaluate the dual-screen presenting system for students' cognition to reading comprehension. The attention of reading comprehension increased on dual-screen system. The reading formats of text-only or text-image took more fixation time and attracted more attention on both single- and dual-screen system. Further investigation is required to study the difference between text-only and text-image. Dual-screen system could have a positive effect in multimedia learning. However, there is no significant difference between single- and dual-screen conditions.

Acknowledgements. This research was funded by the Humanities and Social Sciences Foundation of the Ministry of Education (No. 16YJC880052).

References

1. Kintsch, W., van Dijk, T.A.: Toward a model of text comprehension and production. Psychol. Rev. **85**(5), 363–394 (1978)
2. O'Brien, E.J., et al.: Updating a situation model: a memory-based text processing view. J. Exp. Psychol. Learn. Mem. Cogn. **24**(5), 1200–1210 (1998)

3. Ness, M.K.: Reading comprehension strategies in secondary content area classrooms: teacher use of and attitudes towards reading comprehension instruction. Read. Horiz. **49**(2), 143–166 (2009)
4. Mayer, R.E.: Multimedia learning: are we asking the right questions? Educ. Psychol. **32**(1), 1–19 (1997)
5. Vidal, K.: A comparison of the effects of reading and listening on incidental vocabulary acquisition. Lang. Learn. **61**(1), 219–258 (2011)
6. Perfetti, C.A., Landi, N., Oakhill, J.: The Acquisition of Reading Comprehension Skill, pp. 227–247. Blackwell Publishing Ltd., Hoboken (2005)
7. Clark, J.M., Paivio, A.: Dual coding theory and education. Educ. Psychol. Rev. **3**(3), 149–210 (1991)
8. Sweller, J.: Instructional design consequences of an analogy between evolution by natural selection and human cognitive architecture. Instr. Sci. **32**(1), 9–31 (2004)
9. Baddeley, A.: Working memory. Science **255**(5044), 556 (1992)
10. Sweller, J.: Element interactivity and intrinsic, extraneous, and germane cognitive load. Educ. Psychol. Rev. **22**(2), 123–138 (2010)
11. Paas, F.G., Van Merrienboer, J.J., Adam, J.J.: Measurement of cognitive load in instructional research. Percept. Mot. Skills **79**(1 Pt 2), 419–430 (1994)
12. Backs, R.W.: Going beyond heart rate: autonomic space and cardiovascular assessment of mental workload. Int. J. Aviat. Psychol. **5**(1), 25–48 (1995)
13. Chen, F., et al.: Multimodal behavior and interaction as indicators of cognitive load. ACM Trans. Interact. Intell. Syst. (TIIS) **2**(4), 22 (2012)
14. lSezer, A., et al.: An investigation of university students' attention levels in real classroom settings with NeuroSky's MindWave mobile (EEG) device. In: International Education Technology Conference (2015)
15. Ferrer-Márquez, M., Belda-Lozano, R., Ferrer-Ayza, M.: Technical controversies in laparoscopic sleeve gastrectomy. Obes. Surg. **22**(1), 182–187 (2012)
16. Cierniak, G., Scheiter, K., Gerjets, P.: Explaining the split-attention effect: is the reduction of extraneous cognitive load accompanied by an increase in germane cognitive load? Comput. Hum. Behav. **25**(2), 315–324 (2009)
17. Sweller, J., van Merrienboer, J.J.G., Paas, F.G.W.C.: Cognitive architecture and instructional design. Educ. Psychol. Rev. **10**(3), 251–296 (1998)
18. Mayer, R.E.: Multimedia learning. Psychol. Learn. Motiv. **41**, 85–139 (2002)
19. Zwaan, R.A., Madden, C.J.: Updating situation models (2004)
20. Richards, E., Singer, M.: Representation of complex goal structures in narrative comprehension. Discourse Process. **31**(2), 111–135 (2001)

Health, Well-Being and Comfort

Improving Patient Satisfaction Using a Video-Based Patient Education Platform

Katharine T. Adams[✉], Alexander D. Walker, Eileen Searson,
John Yosaitis, Rita Owens, and Lowell Satler

MedStar Simulation Training & Education Lab (SiTEL),
MedStar Health, Columbia, USA
Katie.Adams@medicalhfe.org

Abstract. Patient education is a critical component in a patient's preparation for, and recovery from, a medical procedure. The research team utilized a novel approach in the development and presentation of patient education material in an effort to address gaps between health education and patient health literacy and to utilize the flexibility of technology in disseminating health education. Patient and healthcare provider responses were collected and analyzed to determine the feasibility of using this approach to create future education. Overall responses to the ease of use and educational experience of the patient education center were positive.

Keywords: Patient education · E-learning

1 Introduction

A patient's ability to understand and recall medical information is an important component of successful outcomes, and there is a current need to improve health literacy and memory among all patient populations. Health literacy is "the degree to which individuals have the capacity to obtain, process, and understand basic health information and services needed to make appropriate health decisions" [1]. Low health literacy has been consistently associated with poorer health outcomes and poorer use of healthcare services [2–5]. Additionally, the ability to recall medical information after leaving the hospital or doctor's office can be a challenging task, especially for older adults. Previous studies report that patients of all ages remember between 17.1% and 60% of the medical information their doctor provides [6–11]. One of these studies focused on middle-aged and older adults and found that the total recall of given information was only 40%, and of the 40% that is recalled, almost half of the information is recalled incorrectly [7].

One avenue for addressing the outcomes impacted by health literacy is through the use of patient education. Patient education is a critical component in a patient's preparation for clinical procedures, as well as recovery following those procedures [12–15]. Additionally, educated patients are more likely to use preventative services, manage their condition, and are less likely to be admitted to the hospital unnecessarily [16–20]. Unfortunately, despite the recognized benefits of effective patient education,

© Springer International Publishing AG 2017
C. Stephanidis (Ed.): HCII Posters 2017, Part II, CCIS 714, pp. 217–224, 2017.
DOI: 10.1007/978-3-319-58753-0_33

many patient facing materials available contain content that exceeds the recommended literacy levels for patient education [21–23].

While standardized written and verbal forms of education for patients can provide the basic information necessary, web-based technologies give patients the flexibility to view and interact with educational material how, when, and where they want. This flexibility can help address the issue of patients' poor memory for health information by serving as an external memory or performance support tool that can be used to recall the necessary information exactly when it is needed.

In addition to the flexibility in access provided by web-based technologies, they also provide a certain level of educational flexibility in the creation of the patient education content. This is of particular interest when providing information to patients about an upcoming medical procedure. Effective education has a wide variety of objectives including the provision of information about how to prepare for the hospital, what to expect when you are at the hospital, what the procedure is, the risks and benefits, and how to care for yourself when you go home. This variation in educational objectives necessitates more than the one-size-fits-all approach that is provided in most written and video based patient education materials. Instead, the design of patient education should attempt to match the format and style of the education to the particular objective that the materials are trying to achieve.

Previously, this matching has been difficult because patient education materials have been constrained by the delivery format available to healthcare systems (i.e., handbooks, pamphlets, DVDs). With the advent of online video platforms and the prominence of ultra-short form videos (i.e., microlearning), it is now possible to create short pieces of educational content that are designed to address a given educational objective (e.g., how to care for your procedure site) and that can be combined into an accessible online educational experience.

This current study describes research around the development of a new style of educating patients that combines microlearning videos with a web-based platform to create patient education experiences for acute medical procedures. Given the novel nature of this educational approach, the first step in evaluating this solution was to determine whether patients and clinicians would like education created in this way and integrate it into the overall medical procedure experience.

2   Methods

2.1   Development of the Education

The development of educational content focused on capturing the crucial elements of the entire patient experience around undergoing a medical procedure, specifically a cardiac catheterization. Initial development of the educational content began with eliciting knowledge from Subject Matter Experts (SMEs) familiar with the medical procedure and the preparation and recovery process in this health system's procedure lab. SMEs shared their knowledge of the entire patient experience, from hospital arrival to discharge home and beyond. Detailed SME input regarding how a patient needs to prepare for their procedure, what the patient will experience while in the hospital, and what the patient needs to do when they get home was incorporated into the content development. Additionally, SMEs provided the team with common questions patients ask, issues that most patients have, and issues that often lead to a patient returning to the hospital after their procedure.

Using the information gathered from the SMEs, the education development team created a detailed outline of content with achievable objectives and a clear intent supporting each piece of proposed content. Instructional designers with expertise in adult learning then created scripts for microlearning content (i.e., 30–90 s videos) that aligned with appropriate health literacy levels of the patient population, focusing on one or two objectives per script to keep the content short and concise. The goal for the education development team was to make each topic easy to search within the overall collection of videos.

The instructional designers and video production team collaborated to match the intent and feeling of the video with a production format that best suited the information, such as live video, animation, or a whiteboard-like graphic. The resulting content consisted of 28 videos that ranged from character based animations describing what to expect when you get to the hospital, to whiteboard style videos explaining the steps for caring for your procedure site, to live videos with real clinicians putting patients at ease about their upcoming experience. The final videos were reviewed by the hospital's patient and family advisory council to validate the content and usability of the platform.

2.2 Technology Platform

The education was hosted on a web-based patient education center (Mytonomy, Inc.) that was designed to provide microlearning-based patient education content. The research team collaborated with the developers of the online platform to design a user experience that would match the educational workflow of the medical procedure.

Below are two screenshots of the patient education center. Figure 1 displays the "After Discharge" section of the education content. The user can move between

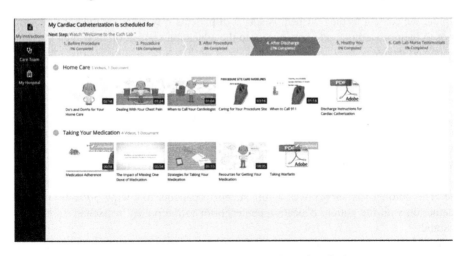

Fig. 1. Patient education center - section: after discharge

different content sections as they desire, but are visually cued as to which videos they've already watched and how much of each section they have completed. Figure 2 is an example of the video playback and closed captioning components of the education content.

Fig. 2. Patient education center – video playback

2.3   Procedure

The research team coordinated with the pilot hospital and staff members of the cardiac catheterization lab to identify the ideal location to integrate the patient education center into the clinical workflow. The majority of patients who consented to participate in the study received access to the education when they arrived for their procedure. In the hospital, patients were provided a tablet device and login information and were free to explore the content as they wished. A subset of patients was called by the hospital staff prior to their procedure and given access to the education content on their own internet connected device.

Nursing staff in the procedure lab encouraged patients to watch the pre- and post-procedure videos. Due to the nature of the clinical workflow, the patients often had more time to watch the videos following the procedure.

Members of the research team collected subjective feedback from the patients through a survey containing both quantitative questions in the form of a six-point scale ranging from 0 (strongly disagree) to 6 (strongly agree), and open-ended questions to capture qualitative responses. The survey consisted of questions regarding the patient's overall educational experience, as well as specific feedback on the platform's ease of use. The 20-question survey was administered to patients following 30 to 60 min of interaction with the patient education center, prior to the patient's discharge from the hospital.

Feedback from clinical providers regarding their impression of the content and its use in the procedure lab was collected at the end of the two-month pilot period.

3 Results

Over the course of a two-month period, 68 patients provided feedback on six survey questions related to their overall educational experience, and 29 patients provided feedback on fourteen survey questions related to the ease of use of the platform. Patient survey responses regarding both the overall educational experience and the ease of use of the patient education platform were overwhelmingly positive. As seen in Fig. 3, average responses to the six survey questions related to their educational experience ranged from a 5.5 - "I am confident that I understand how to care for myself as a result of the education" to a 5.75 - "If a friend needed to have the same procedure, I would tell them to go to this hospital".

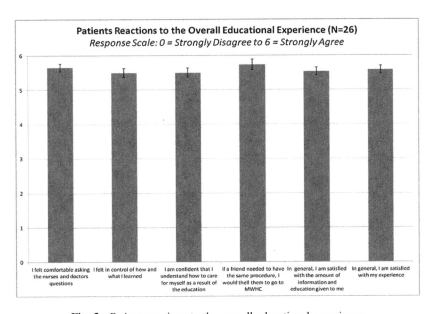

Fig. 3. Patient reactions to the overall educational experience.

Patient reactions to the ease of use of the platform are displayed in Fig. 4, below. Average responses to the fourteen survey scale response questions related to the use of the platform averaged between a 5.2 - "The Patient Education Center works the way I want it to work" and 5.6 - "I would recommend the Patient Education Center to a friend, if they were going to have this same procedure".

Additionally, 29 patients provided 37 free response comments that the research team analyzed for general themes. Nine patients reported that the education was informative, seven patients liked the education in general, and five patients praised the clinical staff. Four patients provided both positive and negative feedback on the usability of the education, and four patients commented positively on the ability to share the education with a family/caregiver. Three patients disliked the format of some

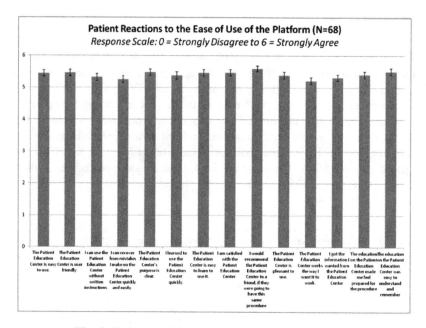

Fig. 4. Patient reactions to the ease of use of the platform

of the education, and one patient reported reduced anxiety because of their experience interacting with the education.

Eight members of the procedure lab nursing staff were surveyed to capture their impression of the education and how prepared and knowledgeable their patients were following the introduction of the education. The nursing staff expressed an appreciation for the concise, unique, and layman-focused content. Several nurses emphasized areas of improvement to make to the education regarding the accessibility for non-English speakers and the need to encourage the patient to watch the education content prior to arrival.

4   Conclusion

Patients had nearly universal positive responses regarding their interaction with the education content. They were generally enthusiastic about the technology-based style and content of the education, which is particularly important as the patient population included in this study consisted of primarily older adults who may be less familiar with this type of education delivery, but are more likely to have trouble remembering medical information. Nurses also had positive feedback for the education content, though highlighted areas of improvement for future iterations of the content and education delivery method.

One particularly important takeaway from the results is the patients' appreciation for the fact that the education could be shared with family members and caregivers. Often family members carry the burden of remembering their loved one's medical information and the complex patient instructions following a procedure. During this pilot projects, family members watched the education while their patient family member was undergoing the procedure or sleeping in the post-operative care area. A major benefit of at-your-own-pace, technology-based patient education like that developed for this pilot is the constant accessibility of patient information to anyone involved in the patient's care in a variety of environments, both at-home and on-the-go.

The pilot program was a successful first step in improving both the content of important medical information provided to patients concerning a procedure, and the method in which patients learn from and interact with that information.

4.1 Limitations

A limitation of this study was the lack of comparative data regarding patient and clinical staff responses to education already in use in this pilot hospital. The focus of this pilot was to collect feedback about our unique education platform and content, but we recognize that it would strengthen the positive patient responses if compared to patients' feedback on current education, and this will be an area of future work.

4.2 Future Directions

Our pilot study intended to capture the feasibility of and reaction to a novel way to provide health education to patients. Future steps will be taken to determine if the innovative patient education platform and content improves health literacy and impacts outcomes. Additionally, we hope to test this approach with other types of education, such as chronic care management.

References

1. U.S. Department of Health and Human Services: Healthy People 2010. U.S. Government Printing Office. Washington, DC (2000)
2. Berkman, N.D., Sheridan, S.L., et al.: Low health literacy and health outcomes: an updated systematic review. Ann. Intern. Med. 155, 97–107 (2011)
3. Scott, T., Gazmararian, J., et al.: Health literacy and preventive health care use among medicare enrollees in a managed care organization. Med. Care 40(5), 395–404 (2002)
4. Bennet, C., Ferreira, M., et al.: Relation between literacy, race, and stage of presentation among low-income patients with prostate cancer. J. Clin. Oncol. 16(9), 3101–3104 (1998)
5. Schillinger, D., Grumbach, K., et al.: Association of health literacy with diabetes outcomes. J. Am. Med. Assoc. 288(4), 475–482 (2002)
6. Cohen, G., Java, R.: Memory for medical history: accuracy of recall. Appl. Cogn. Psychol. 9, 273–288 (1995)
7. Anderson, J., Dodman, S., et al.: Patient information recall in a rheumatology clinic. Rheumatol. Rehabil. 18, 18–22 (1979)
8. Ley, P.: Doctor-patient communication: some quantitative estimates of the role of cognitive factors in non-compliance. J. Hypertens. 3(Suppl. 1), S51–S55 (1985)

9. McGuire, L.: Remembering what the doctor said: organization and adults' memory for medical information. Exp. Aging Res. **22**, 403–428 (1996)
10. Rice, E., Meyer, B., et al.: Using text structure to improve older adults' recall of important medical information. Educ. Gerontol. **15**, 527–542 (1989)
11. Shapiro, D., Boggs, S., et al.: The effect of varied physician affect on recall anxiety, and perceptions in women at risk for breast cancer: an analogue study. Health Psychol. **11**, 61–66 (1992)
12. Goodman, H., Peters, E., et al.: A pilot study using a newly devised manual in a programme of education and support for patients waiting for coronary artery bypass surgery. Eur. J. Cardiovasc. Nurs. **2**(1), 27–37 (2003)
13. Shuldham, C.: Pre-operative education for the patient having coronary artery bypass surgery. Patient Educ. Couns. **43**(2), 129–137 (2001)
14. Tooth, L., McKenna, K., et al.: The effects of pre-coronary angioplasty education and counselling on patients and their spouses: a preliminary report. Patient Educ. Couns. **32**(3), 185–196 (1997)
15. Veronovici, N., Lasiuk, G., et al.: Discharge education to promote self-management following cardiovascular surgery: an integrative review. Eur. J. Cardiovasc. Nurs. 1–10 (2013)
16. Center for Advancing Health: A new definition of patient engagement: what is engagement and why is it important?. CFAH, Washington, DC (2010)
17. Wennberg, D., Marr, A., et al.: A randomized trial of a telephone care management strategy. N. Engl. J. Med. **363**, 1245–1255 (2010)
18. Roter, D., Rudd, R., et al.: Patient literacy: a barrier to quality of care. J. Gen. Intern. Med. **13**, 850–851 (1998)
19. Vernon, J., Trujillo, A., et al.: Low Health Literacy: Implications for National Health Policy. George Washington University, Washington, DC (2007)
20. Berkman, N., Sheridan, S., et al.: Health literacy interventions and outcomes: an updated systematic review. Agency for Healthcare Research and Quality, Rockville, MD (2011)
21. Davis, T., Crouch, M., et al.: The gap between patient reading comprehension and the readability of patient education materials. J. Fam. Pract. **31**(5), 533–538 (1990)
22. Safeer, R.S., Keenan, J.: Health literacy: the gap between physicians and patients. Am. Fam. Physician **72**(3), 463–468 (2005)
23. Badarudeen, S., Sabharwal, S.: Assessing readability of patient education materials: current role in orthopaedics. Clin. Orthop. Relat. Res. **468**(10), 2572–2580 (2010)

Developing a Health-Enabling Service System Combining Wearable Device and Personal Health Records for Older Adults

Kuei-Ling Belinda Chen[(⊠)] and Peisan Lee

Institute for Information Industry, 8F., No. 133, Sec. 4, Minsheng E. Rd.,
Songshan District, Taipei City 105, Taiwan (R.O.C.)
{klchen,peisanlee}@iii.org.tw

Abstract. The use of wearable devices in health promotion service is less common among older adults. The goal of this project is to validate the health-enabling innovative service for seniors combining wearable device and personal health records ("My Health Bank") from National Health Insurance Administration (NHIA). ComCare, a health-enabling service system with an app, is built to integrate the medical records and physiological index data from three parts: data collected via wearable sensors, national personal health record storage ("My Health Bank" from NHIA), and a health management IoT cloud. The user-friendly ComCare service and app expects to provide the following two major benefits:

1. Health and Physical Assessment: With the help of wearable device and IoT cloud networks to collect activity (movement) records, daily physiological measurements (blood pressure, blood sugar, body temperature, BMI, heart rate), and medical records/prescriptions from NHIA, the family members and caregivers are fully aware of the senior's health conditions.
2. Healthcare Service Notification: ComCare provides real-time monitoring of the elderly's vital signs, and the corresponding care centers will be notified upon detection of abnormality. It ensures an instant healthcare and provides tracking and reporting service to promote healthy lifestyles among older adults.

This research provides an empirical study to explore and analyze the effectiveness of senior health promotion using data from wearable devices and "My Health Bank". The project will adopt a "one-group pretest-posttest" design and recruit 60 daycare seniors to participate in the next phase. Questionnaires will be completed and analyzed to generate knowledge of participants' subjective changes towards quality of life and evaluate the Technology Acceptance Model (TAM). The results of this study may benefit the Ministry of Health and Welfare for consideration in policy-making process and developing a business model for the senior care industry.

Keywords: Wearable device · Personal health records · IoT cloud networks · Healthcare Service Notification

© Springer International Publishing AG 2017
C. Stephanidis (Ed.): HCII Posters 2017, Part II, CCIS 714, pp. 225–231, 2017.
DOI: 10.1007/978-3-319-58753-0_34

1   Introduction

In recent years, wearable devices and IoT have become very popular. Portable wearable devices that can measure and record the amount of exercise, along with IoT, are being used as a tool to manage exercise systematically and scientifically in health promotion. Also, preventive medicine, companion diagnostics and big data analysis that incorporate sensor and data analysis technology have gradually become the mainstream in medicine. This has created business opportunities in the field of "precision medicine" that can ensure better efficiency and reduce waste of resources in the field of medicine. With the development of ICT and wearable devices, the traditional patient-centered model of healthcare has changed. Medical and healthcare industries now have access to a patient's health data via different ways. With that, the "continuous, symptom-centered medical care" model has emerged.

As many people need to have regular physiological measurements, the major wearable device companies such as Apple, Google, Samsung and Xiaomi have launched lightweight, easy-to-carry wearable devices so that the users can monitor their own health conditions continuously over a long period of time. At the same time, these companies hope to provide innovative services with the development of big data by incorporating physiological sensors into their products as well as by devising back-end application platforms and apps. The purpose is to promote the feasibility and convenience of wearable devices so that they will become an important part of future medicine. The major challenge is the lack of a platform which integrates such a huge amount of data collected via various devices. Thus these physiological statistics cannot be incorporated into one's health record, which undermines the effectiveness of health analytics. To tackle with the problem, this research has developed a platform called "ComCare" to integrate data and analysis collected from different devices in order to provide users with detailed health information.

2   Literature Review

The chapter includes three parts: (1) a brief introduction on the development of wearable devices in healthcare, (2) the current situations of Taiwan's National Health Insurance, and (3) an introduction on "My Health Bank".

2.1   The Development of Wearable Devices in Healthcare

According to a research conducted by III (Institute for Information Industry), people in Taiwan using wearable devices to record their health information will reach 930,000 in 2015 [1]. Currently the wearable devices are developed in three fields: exercise assistance, health management and medical assistance. The first two fields can be applied, for example, to help office workers keep themselves fit and reduce stress (e.g. weight control). The potential market of such use is huge yet lacks high demand since people tend to ignore the importance of body fitness unless they are experiencing deterioration in health or facing diseases.

On the other hand, the field of wearable devices as medical assistance (an extension of medical equipment) is mainly applied for symptom management, diagnosis or monitoring in elderly or patients with chronic disease. If adopted in medical institutes, wearable devices as medical assistance can cover a large population of users, which means the potential market is considerably huge.

According to a survey conducted by the Health Promotion Administration (under the Ministry of Health and Welfare), the percentage of Taiwanese population that exercise regularly has risen from 26.1% in 2010 to 33.4% in 2015. This is the result of the government's continuous promotion. In the past, smart bracelets were mainly defined as sport equipment that only measured statistics such as calories burned, steps or distance walked/run, etc. [2]. Since 2014, manufacturers have started to further collect users' more delicate movements and thus acquired users' daily behavior pattern as well. With such, after analyzing a certain user's daily routine behavior, the system can send notifications or reminders (e.g. Your working hours are too long, Please get up and stretch, etc.) in order to help the user manage his/her health conditions more easily. The built-in sensors that used to measure steps can now only measure physiological statistics such as pulse, blood pressure, blood oxygen, etc. [3]. Besides collecting physiological statistics, it is also expected that data collected via smart bracelets will be able to analyze users' mental status (e.g. stress index, fatigue, etc.). Through comprehensive analysis, the system can also send out reminders or "tips" to help users accommodate their own mental health conditions.

Wearable devices can make it easier for researchers to access the health-related data of the users, but the utilization of wearable devices in elderly is yet to be comprehensively planned. Due to the fact that current studies (regarding types of devices, users' habits and data collection) mainly focus on the utilization of wearable devices among younger adults in good health, it is expected that more research should be done to discuss how wearable devices can benefit the elderly in the future [4].

2.2 National Health Insurance in Taiwan

Launched in 1995, the National Health Insurance (NHI) program is a compulsory social insurance which provides healthcare coverage to all population in Taiwan. The purpose is to ensure that the economically disadvantaged can also receive fair and quality care at affordable costs.

The focus of NHI has shifted from universal healthcare coverage and medical readiness (availability of healthcare resources) to quality medical services. Firstly, transparency in healthcare information is made to protect people's right to know. Secondly, quality care for the disadvantaged in remote areas is enhanced. Finally, a patient-centered care focus is emphasized. Programs and projects were launched accordingly to upscale medical service quality and efficiency.

Through the collaboration of NHIA (National Health Insurance Administration), hospitals, clinics and the public, the NHI system currently covers over 99% of Taiwan's population [5]. The dedication has also elevated medical service quality and the quality of care, as well as enhanced electronic network services. Administrative efficiency and service quality are also bettered. More underprivileged people are assisted and taken care of.

2.3   Introduction on "My Health Bank"

"My Health Bank" is a cloud-based inquiry service from NHIA which provides 12 different kinds of data from cross-institute, including outpatient data, medication records, medical examination reports, etc. It provides an easy access and a convenient self-management tool for the insured to check on their personal information whenever needed. Using either a "citizen digital certificate" or a "password-registered NHI card" to log into "My Health Bank" system, the user can check on his/her personal data and even download it. NHIA hopes to make "My Health Bank" more accessible and convenient for the insured and to develop its functions to the fullest in the future [6].

3   Research Methods

The "ComCare Health Information Integration Platform (abbreviated as 'ComCare')" is established to collect the exercise data sent in via wearable and other IoT devices and concurrently download medical records from "My Health Bank" before the data is analyzed. With the analysis and evaluation of ComCare, users' personal health information can be presented in a clear, understandable fashion for the users and/or the caregivers (e.g. medical professionals, care center staff, family members, etc.). They will also receive personalized messages or tips that remind the users to pay attention to particular aspects of their health conditions.

3.1   Information Architecture of the ComCare Platform

The ComCare Platform has a multi-layered architecture (as illustrated in Fig. 1). It mainly consists of (1) external data retrieval APIs, (2) internal modules for smart health management and (3) data visualization APIs. Following is a more detailed introduction of the information architecture:

- External data retrieval APIs Layer collects the data from wearable and other IoT devices, "My Health Bank" and other open platforms. It offers a standardized interface for all kinds of data. It also integrates and anonymizes heterogeneous data (physiological measurements and statistics). Individual users can transmit their data to the ComCare Platform via wearable devices, physiological measurement devices, physiological signal collection gateways or private cloud services.
- Internal modules for smart health management consist of modules that function in the following aspects: Health Management, Health Warning, Healthy Lifestyle Planning, Behavioral Analysis, Commercial Promotion and Information Security. Based on the data transmitted via the external data retrieval APIs, this layer of architecture processes data for different kinds of value-add applications for the users.

- Data visualization APIs Layer, as the final layer, presents the processed data that caters to the needs of individuals, healthcare providers or other health-related product manufacturers. Before accessing any information, individuals or institutes first have to be authorized and certified by apps in order to ensure information security.

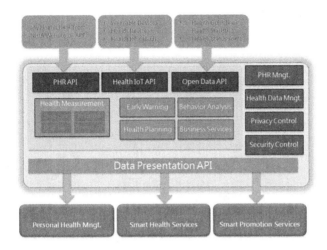

Fig. 1. Information architecture of the research

3.2 Functions of the ComCare Platform

Long-term care for elderly has shifted its main focus from traditional treatment for diseases to the prevention of mental illness and promotion of health. With its accessibility via ICT, integration capability and preventive nature, ComCare is expected to be applied to elderly care and boost the efficiency of elderly health management and quality of care via comprehensive integration of resources.

There are eight main functions on the ComCare Login Dashboard (illustrated in Fig. 2). The applications can be divided into two categories for users:

1. Application of data collected/analyzed: ComCare analyzes data differently based on different user groups. For example, blood pressure and blood sugar will be assessed based on users' age. If the result is abnormal, the system will signal to warn the user. As for chronic disease patients suffering from cardiovascular diseases or diabetes, the data will be instantly analyzed to help family members or caregivers to take timely action. The ComCare Platform not only allows the users to keep track of physiological records but also practice caution in advance when abnormality is detected.
2. Automatic mobile recording service: In the past, physiological data were measured by doctors or nurses and the paper/electronic medical records were kept in the hospitals/clinics. With the development of home measurement equipments, it has

become a trend to take physiological measurements at home for the youth. Yet the elders or patients usually have difficulties using such equipments by themselves. ComCare is user-friendly and efficient. It automatically collects and uploads data to the platform via the Internet, saving labor works and ensuring correctness (no typos in transcription).

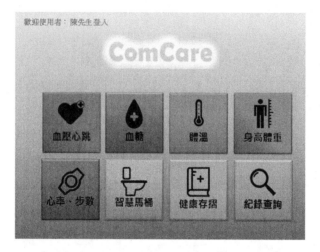

Fig. 2. ComCare login dashboard

4 Conclusion and Discussion

4.1 Future Prospect

A living lab will be designed to explore and analyze the data collected via wearable devices, physiological measurement devices and "My Health Bank". The data will be assessed to determine the effectiveness in health promotion. "One-group pretest-posttest" design will be conducted in a daycare center with 60 participants with collaboration of local medical institutes. The participants will experience the ComCare service in a time period of 12 weeks and fill out questionnaires at the end to find out their acceptance of the ComCare Platform. With such, the research can validate whether the experiment design in the living lab is favorable to promote users' health.

4.2 Conclusion

The wearable devices mainly target the public, among which smart watches, bracelets or collars are the dominant products in the market. However, smart wearables for medical use are becoming more popular and promising. This kind of medical devices helps people record and access their physiological signals more easily. The prevention, diagnosis, alleviation and treatment of diseases can be done in a more accurate and hassle-free manner. The Government is also advocating the use of "My Health Bank" to help the public better manage their medical and medication records, raise awareness of health among people and assist individuals to better manage their health.

Currently there are different apps and cloud services available in the market, but not a unified system that can integrate all the data information. The feature of ComCare aims to analyze the data collected in order to find out the correlation between disease and lifestyle. Once the correlation is established, it can help the medical professionals to provide professional advice. We believe this study will raise the awareness of health management in the public. In addition, with the long-term program of ComCare launched by the Ministry of Health and Welfare, the caregivers can plan their schedules and work assignments more efficiently and effectively. The result will also raise the overall quality of care noticeably and enormously.

References

1. Institute for Information Industry (FIND): An Investigation on the Current Situation and Demand of Broadband Application in Taiwan (2015). http://www.iii.org.tw/Press/NewsDtl. aspx?nsp_sqno=1653&fm_sqno=14
2. BI Intelligence: Forecasts for Annual Wearable Device Shipments (2014)
3. Bajpai, A., Jilla, V., Tiwari, V.N., Venkatesan, S.M., Narayanan, R.: Quantifiable fitness tracking using wearable devices. In: Proceedings of 37th Annual International Conference of the IEEE Engineering in Medicine and Biology Society (EMBC) (2015). doi:10.1109/EMBC. 2015.7318688
4. Schrack, J.A., Cooper, R., Koster, A., Shiroma, E.J., Murabito, J.M., Reieski, W.J., Ferrucci, L., Harris, T.B.: Assessing daily physical activity in older adults: unraveling the complexity of monitors, measures, and methods. J. Gerontol. Ser. A: Biol. Sci. Med. Sci. **71** (8), 1039–1048 (2016). doi:10.1093/gerona/glw026
5. National Health Insurance Administration. Ministry of Health and Welfare. http://www.nhi. gov.tw/
6. My Health Bank. https://myhealthbank.nhi.gov.tw/IHKE0002/IHKE0002S01.ASPX

FitViz: A Personal Informatics Tool for Self-management of Rheumatoid Arthritis

Ankit Gupta[1(✉)], Xin Tong[1], Chris Shaw[1], Linda Li[2], and Lynne Feehan[2]

[1] School of Interactive Arts and Technology,
Simon Fraser University, Burnaby, Canada
aga53@sfu.ca
[2] Department of Physical Therapy,
University of British Columbia, Vancouver, Canada

Abstract. Rheumatoid arthritis (RA) affects 1 in 100 adults in Canada. Self-management of this disease requires that the patients maintain an adequate level of daily physical activity, while not overdoing it; excessive physical activity can be harmful to RA patients. The RA patients receive regular physical activity recommendations from their clinicians, based on the condition of their disease. Current solutions for physical activity monitor do not satisfy the needs of the arthritis patients and their clinicians, as they do not allow the patients and the clinicians to know if the patients did the physical activity as recommended by the clinicians. Therefore, we developed a web application which monitors patient's daily physical activity, and generates visualizations to help the patients in the self-management of the disease. In this paper, we present the design of the application and the interim results of an ongoing pilot study that we are conducting to evaluate our prototype.

1 Introduction

Rheumatoid Arthritis (RA) is a chronic musculoskeletal disease that causes pain, and damage in muscles, and joints, resulting in decreased mobility and decreased functional independence. One of the important factors in successful management of arthritis is maintaining a physically active lifestyle. There is ample evidence that suggests that a physically active lifestyle can reduce pain, improve mobility and quality of life (QoL) [4,10,14,15]. However, patients' adherence to keeping an active lifestyle is poor, with fewer than half of the patients being active [1]. In 2011, the Canadian Community Health Survey reported that over 60% of adult arthritis patients, with age over 30 were physically inactive during their leisure time [13, p. 38].

One of the important contributors to the lack of exercise adherence among arthritis patients is lack of self-efficacy [5,18]. Self-monitoring has been shown to improve self-efficacy. Gleeson-Kreig has shown the effectiveness of self-monitoring in improving self-efficacy among type 2 diabetes patients [6]. In addition to improving self-efficacy, self-monitoring can also lower hospitalization [9] and reduce costs [2].

© Springer International Publishing AG 2017
C. Stephanidis (Ed.): HCII Posters 2017, Part II, CCIS 714, pp. 232–240, 2017.
DOI: 10.1007/978-3-319-58753-0_35

While adequate physical activity is necessary, it is also important that the patients do not over-exert themselves. Over-exertion can result in excessive joint pain, which in turn can act as a further barrier to adequate physical activity [5,18]. However, the current consumer-accessible wearable devices such as Fitbit® are not designed for arthritis patients. For instance, Fitbit does not take into account the disease activity of a patient when identifying active minutes. Further, when identifying non-sedentary hours—a feature that was added very recently[1]—requires that everyone, irrespective of their physical ability, perform 250+ steps in an hour.

Every arthritis patient has a different tolerance for physical activity, and different levels of disease activity. Based on their current condition, a clinician can help them set realistic goals that do not hurt them while still maintaining adequate physical activity. In this paper, we present the design of a web application that we have developed to help arthritis patients and clinicians customize goals based on parameters relevant for self-management of arthritis. We also present the intermediate results of an ongoing pilot study.

2   Related Literature

While previous research has focused on using accelerometers in a smartphone for arthritis detection [19] and disease activity prediction [12], there is a lack of research in understanding the effectiveness of physical activity tracking for self-management of patients with rheumatoid arthritis. However, there is previous research that focused on detection of arthritis. For example, Yamada et al. developed a smartphone application for detecting abnormal gait in arthritis patients [19]. However, their research focused on detection of abnormal gait, and not on the self-management.

Physical activity tracking has also been employed for other areas in the health domain. Nachman et al. developed "Jog Falls", a system designed for diabetes patients and their physicians [11]. Jog Falls monitored diet (via manual logging) and energy expenditure and helped the patients and physicians to analyze and reflect on their data. The authors found that Jog Falls was effective for weight loss. Lee et al. developed Asthmon, a ubiquitous toy for children [8]. The toy consisted of a virtual pet and peak flow meter. The virtual pet instructs the child to inhale and exhale, and displays behaviors based on the child's use of the device. Physical activity monitoring has also been used for monitoring mobility recovery in older patients after surgery [3]. However, it was not used for self-management, and used only for monitoring purpose.

Automatic measurement of physical activity is not influenced by reporting bias and issues with patient recalling past information. Therefore, there is a growing interest in using a patient's lifelog data in clinical practice [16]. West et al. conducted a study—literature review and vignette based role-play approach with clinicians—to explore the opportunities and limitations in using life log

---

[1] https://blog.fitbit.com/sit-less-move-more-with-hourly-activity-stationary-time-tracking, published in April, 2016.

data in clinical settings [17]. One of the findings, relevant to our case, is that the need for visual presentation of information that the clinicians can use to explore patient data. In another research, Kim et al. employed use of food logs and physical activity during a patient–clinician consultation [7]. The authors found that clinicians usefully employed this data to develop and recommend specific plans for their patients.

3 The FitViz App

We consulted with clinicians—3 physiotherapists, one of whom is also an arthritis patient—to determine the physical activity goals and parameters that were important to consider for supporting self-management of arthritis. We found that the clinicians were interested in 3 physical activity goals: number of minutes in a day spent doing bouts (continuous activity sessions of moderate-to-vigorous activity) including sessions of over-exertion, number of non-sedentary hours in a day, and sleep. We designed a prototype which was iteratively modified based on the feedback we received from the clinicians and the patients. The final prototype collected Fitbit data to visualize bouts, sleep, and non-sedentary behavior and allowed a clinician to set daily goals based on the patient's physical current condition.

3.1 Physical Activity Parameters

- **Bout.** A Bout is a session of continuous physical activity (PA), performed with a minimum average intensity for a minimum recommended duration. In addition, a bout can be "longer than recommended" if the patient exceeds the maximum recommended duration, "harder than recommended" if the patient performs the bout with higher than the maximum recommended intensity, and "sooner than recommended" if the patient does not take sufficient rest after the previous bout.
- **Non sedentary hour.** We defined an hour as non-sedentary if it has enough minutes with greater than 10 steps. We used a threshold of 10 steps – instead of 0 steps – because we found that Fitbit often overestimated the number of steps in a minute.

3.2 Clinicians Recommend Customized Patient Plan

When a clinician signs into FitViz, she sees a list of her arthritis patients. The clinician can change the settings that affect the detection of bouts and non-sedentary hour. FitViz allows the clinician to set daily goals for the number of minutes spent during a bout, and the number of non-sedentary hours. In addition, the clinician can adjust other parameters that are used to detect bouts for a patient. These parameters include the minimum and maximum recommended intensity for a bout, minimum and maximum duration for a bout, the duration to rest between bouts, and the minimum number of minutes a patient must move in an hour for it to be considered a non-sedentary hour. Figure 1 shows the interface that the clinicians can use to set a new plan for a patient. When a clinician moves the sliders the visualization updates to show how changing the parameters affects the visualization.

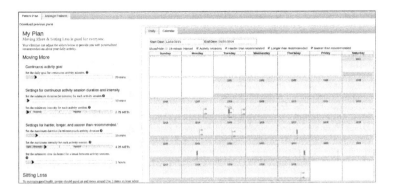

Fig. 1. A clinician can move the sliders to see how it affects the visualization and set a new plan for the patients.

3.3 Visualization of Bouts and Non-sedentary Behavior

When a patient signs into FitViz, she sees a visualization of her daily activities and progress towards her goals (see Fig. 2. The x-axis represents the day as 24 h. The y-axis represents the intensity of physical activity. The bouts are visualized as green bars. When a patient exceeds the recommended maximum intensity or duration during a bout, red heat marks—using a metaphor of radiation—and sweat drops appear on top the green bars respectively. When a patient performs two bouts without taking sufficient rest in between, a spring is drawn between the two green bars. Non-sedentary hours are visualized using a walking icon that appears below the x-axis. In addition, the patient can check her progress towards her daily goals (see Fig. 2(c)).

4 Pilot Study

4.1 Participants

To evaluate our system, we conducted a pilot study with 10 participants who have rheumatoid arthritis. So far 9 participants—8 female, 1 male between ages of 47 and 66—have been recruited and completed the pilot study (Fig. 3).

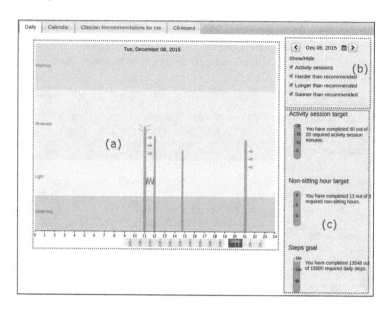

Fig. 2. FitViz Visualization for a single day. (a) Visualization of bouts, non-sedentary hours, and sleep in a day. The width of the bar represents the duration of the PA session, and the height of the bar represents the average intensity level of the physical activity; (b) The patient can change date; (c) Visualizations showing progress towards daily goals of minutes spent doing bouts, non-sedentary hours, and number of steps in a day.

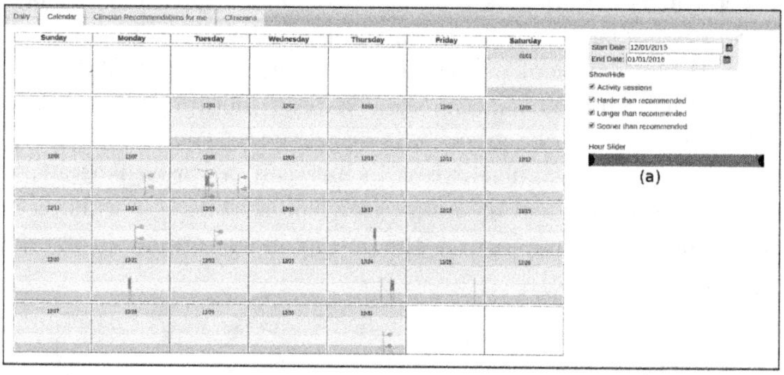

Fig. 3. A patient can select a range of days using the start date, and end date to see bouts performed in the past. (a) An hour range slider allows the patient to select a range of times in a day to visualize.

4.2   Procedure

Before the study, the participants were asked to wear Fitbit Flex for 4 days. This was followed by 1.5 h long education session where they received standardized education from a physiotherapist. The physiotherapist used the data collected during the 4 days to set goals for the patients. The research staff then setup FitViz and Fitbit for the patients to use. The participants then used FitViz and Fitbit app for 4 weeks. During this time, the participants consulted with their physiotherapist 3 times—in the beginning of the study (face-to-face), and at the end of 2nd and 4th week (over phone). At the end of 4 weeks, the participants filled a questionnaire containing questions from Fatigue Severity Scale, McGill Pain Questionnaire Short Form, and Partners in Health Scale. In addition, they filled a System Usability Score (SUS) form. This was followed by an interview, where the participants were interviewed about the intervention, and their experiences with the orientation session, using the FitViz application, and consultation with the clinicians. In this paper, we report the SUS score, and results from the interviews that are relevant to the design of the application. The interviews are still being transcribed. Therefore we report on the 5 interviews which are completely transcribed.

4.3   Results

All participants found the system engaging. Based on the responses from the 5 participants, who have completed the study, FitViz received a high usability score of 78 (SD = 17.2). We now report on the experiences expressed in the interviews.

Encouragement from Non-sedentary Successes. We found that the participants found the walking icons at the bottom of the visualization were helpful.

"Loved the walkers at the bottom."

"That's one thing that's actually very helpful."

The walking icons which represented the hours spent non-sedentary. Achieving a bout is much more harder than walking enough over an hour. Even if a patient is unable to perform enough bouts during a day due to pain, it is comparatively easier to meet non-sedentary goals. Getting success in keeping non-sedentary was a source of encouragement for the patients to continue moving. Another participant found it encouraging

"that you know you're moving every hour."

Supporting Reflection and Awareness. Visualizations which provide an overview of whether or not a goal was achieved is useful. However, detailed visualizations can be important for reflecting and gaining awareness about self. We found that visualizing bouts and non-sedentary hours over a 24-hour timeline presented an opportunity for the patients to get more aware of their physical activity behavior. One of the participant metnioned

"Well overall, the Fitbit kind of shows you stuff but if you set your goals, it, it might show you how many steps per goal but as people with arthritis of course we've got other goals like spreading things out, like, like the sitting each hour target. You know that was an eye opener for me is that sometimes I could go two, three hours and, especially with my work, and not necessarily get up, and this was a real reminder for me so and that's something that the Fitbit kinda shows you but doesn't really show you whether you've gotten too, done too much or not enough."

Disregarding Partial Successes Is Discouraging. One of the aspects of FitViz that the participants found frustrating was that FitViz does not recognize bouts even if they are only slightly lower than recommended intensity, duration, or have a break of more than one minute. This is caused due to strictly defined parameters for bout detection. For example, this strictness can result in not identifying a potential bout because the patient walking in an urban area had to stop multiple times at stoplights. One participant said,

"...it doesn't make sense to me when you're out for half an hour walk and you have to stop at lights, or you stop to do up your shoe or whatever, or you stop for, like that little bit of a stop but that it makes that much of a difference."

5 Conclusion

In this paper, we presented FitViz, a web application to facilitate self-management of arthritis and a data-based communication between the patients and their clinicians. FitViz was successful in enabling reflection and awareness, providing encouragement, and providing objective measurements of physical activity to clinicians. However, there are certain aspects such the calendar view which remained largely unused. Further, we found that strict definitions of success can be discouraging. Our visualizations need to be redesigned to account for partial successes. Another limitation of the system is that is not available on mobile platforms. Mobile platforms can act as better means of encouraging patients to move more and provide immediate feedback. In addition, our pilot did not explore the effect of using FitViz on long-term behavior change. In this pilot, we focused on the feasibility of the application, and understanding its use. In future, we plan to study how FitViz can support long-term behavior change.

References

1. Austin, S., Qu, H., Shewchuk, R.M.: Association between adherence to physical activity guidelines and health-related quality of life among individuals with physician-diagnosed arthritis. Qual. Life Res.: Int. J. Qual. Life Aspects Treat. Care Rehabil. **21**(8), 1347–1357 (2012). http://www.ncbi.nlm.nih.gov/pubmed/22038394

2. Bodenheimer, T., Lorig, K., Holman, H., Grumbach, K.: Patient self-management of chronic disease in primary care. JAMA. J. Am. Med. Assoc. **288**(19), 2469–2475 (2002). http://www.ncbi.nlm.nih.gov/pubmed/12435261

3. Cook, D.J., Thompson, J.E., Prinsen, S.K., Dearani, J.A., Deschamps, C.: Functional recovery in the elderly after major surgery: assessment of mobility recovery using wireless technology. Ann. Thorac. Surg. **96**(3), 1057–1061 (2013)

4. van den Ende, C.H.M.: Effect of intensive exercise on patients with active rheumatoid arthritis: a randomised clinical trial. Ann. Rheum. Dis. **59**(8), 615–621 (2000). http://ard.bmj.com/cgi/doi/10.1136/ard.59.8.615

5. Gecht, M.R., Connell, K.J., Sinacore, J.M., Prohaska, T.R.: A survey of exercise beliefs and exercise habits among people with arthritis. Arthritis Care Res. **9**(2), 82–88 (1996)

6. Gleeson-Kreig, J.M.: Self-monitoring of physical activity: effects on self-efficacy and behavior in people with type 2 diabetes. Diabetes Educ. **32**(1), 69–77 (2006)

7. Kim, Y., Ji, S., Lee, H., Kim, J.W., Yoo, S., Lee, J.: "My doctor is keeping an eye on me!": exploring the clinical applicability of a mobile food logger. In: Proceedings of the 2016 CHI Conference on Human Factors in Computing Systems, pp. 5620–5631 (2016)

8. Lee, H.R., Panont, W.R., Plattenburg, B., de la Croix, J.P., Patharachalam, D., Abowd, G.: Asthmon: empowering asthmatic children's self-management with a virtual pet. In: Proceedings of the 28th of the International Conference Extended Abstracts on Human Factors in Computing Systems - CHI EA 2010, p. 3583 (2010). http://portal.acm.org/citation.cfm?doid=1753846.1754022

9. Lorig, K.R., Sobel, D.S., Stewart, A.L., Brown, B.W., Bandura, A., Ritter, P., Gonzalez, V.M., Laurent, D.D., Holman, H.R.: Evidence suggesting that a chronic disease self-management program can improve health status while reducing hospitalization: a randomized trial. Med. Care **37**(1), 5–14 (1999). http://www.ncbi.nlm.nih.gov/pubmed/10413387

10. Minor, M.A., Webel, R.R., Kay, D.R., Hewett, J.E., Anderson, S.K.: Efficacy of physical conditioning exercise in patients with rheumatoid arthritis and osteoarthritis. Arthritis Rheum. **32**(11), 1396–1405 (1989). http://doi.wiley.com/10.1002/anr.1780321108

11. Nachman, L., et al.: Jog falls: a pervasive healthcare platform for diabetes management. In: Floréen, P., Krüger, A., Spasojevic, M. (eds.) Pervasive 2010. LNCS, vol. 6030, pp. 94–111. Springer, Heidelberg (2010). doi:10.1007/978-3-642-12654-3_6

12. Nishiguchi, S., Ito, H., Yamada, M., Yoshitomi, H., Furu, M., Ito, T., Shinohara, A., Ura, T., Okamoto, K., Aoyama, T.: Self-assessment tool of disease activity of rheumatoid arthritis by using a smartphone application. Telemedicine e-Health **20**(3), 235–240 (2014). http://online.liebertpub.com/doi/abs/10.1089/tmj.2013.0162

13. O'Donnell, S., Lagacé, C., McRae, L., Bancej, C.: Life with arthritis in Canada: a personal and public health challenge. Technical report, no. 3 (2011). http://www.phac-aspc.gc.ca/publicat/hpcdp-pspmc/31-3/ar-08-eng.php

14. Plasqui, G.: The role of physical activity in rheumatoid arthritis. Physiol. Behav. **94**(2), 270–275 (2008). http://linkinghub.elsevier.com/retrieve/pii/S0031938407005057

15. Stenström, C.H., Minor, M.A.: Evidence for the benefit of aerobic and strengthening exercise in rheumatoid arthritis. Arthritis Rheum. **49**(3), 428–434 (2003). http://www.ncbi.nlm.nih.gov/pubmed/12794800

16. Trost, S.G., O'Neil, M.: Clinical use of objective measures of physical activity. Br. J. Sports Med. **48**(3), 178–181 (2014)

17. West, P., Giordano, R., Van Kleek, M., Shadbolt, N.: The quantified patient in the doctor's office: challenges & opportunities. In: Proceedings of the 2016 CHI Conference on Human Factors in Computing Systems, pp. 3066–3078 (2016). http://doi.acm.org/10.1145/2858036.2858445
18. Wilcox, S., Der Ananian, C., Abbott, J., Vrazel, J., Ramsey, C., Sharpe, P.A., Brady, T.: Perceived exercise barriers, enablers, and benefits among exercising and nonexercising adults with arthritis: results from a qualitative study. Arthritis Rheum. 55(4), 616–627 (2006)
19. Yamada, M., Aoyama, T., Mori, S., Nishiguchi, S., Okamoto, K., Ito, T., Muto, S., Ishihara, T., Yoshitomi, H., Ito, H.: Objective assessment of abnormal gait in patients with rheumatoid arthritis using a smartphone. Rheumatol. Int. 32(12), 3869–3874 (2012)

A Crowdsourcing-Based Social Platform to Increase a Community's Sustainability and Well-Being

Kota Gushima(✉), Mizuki Sakamoto, and Tatsuo Nakajima

Department of Computer Science and Engineering,
Waseda University, Tokyo, Japan
{gushi,mizuki,tatsuo}@dcl.cs.waseda.ac.jp

Abstract. This study proposes enhanced *micro-crowdfunding*, which is a platform for improving subjective well-being and community sustainability. *Micro-crowdfunding* is a service designed to achieve the former. The study proposes a platform that improves well-being by automatically adding the "*Three Good Things in life*" exercise to enhance well-being to *micro-crowdfunding*. This exercise is effective for decreasing depression. Our preliminary experiment revealed some pitfalls in our approach.

Keywords: Crowdsourcing · Subjective well-being · Positive psychology

1 Introduction

Information technology as typified by smartphones has become necessary for our lives and it makes our daily lives more valuable [10]. For example, services for deepening people's connections such as Social Network Services (SNS) and services for maintaining health using wearable devices have appeared in recent years. Similarly, many services utilizing information technology exist to improve the quality of life. The spread of challenging attempts to improve subjective well-being has increased. For example, serious game and gamification techniques are used for mental health [13]. It is necessary to raise the well-being to realize a sustainable society because realizing a flourish society is important [3, 10, 11].

On the other hand, these attempts are focused on individuals. We believe that these services will bring better effects through mutual cooperation. This is because the existing services as SNSs and social games in recent years incorporate the connection among people as an important element, and cooperation with others might also be important for the services enhancing subjective well-being.

In this study, we propose a service that enhances the subjective well-being of the community through activities in a small community called a micro-community. The service is designed based on *micro-crowdfunding,* which refers to extended crowdsourcing. *Micro-crowdfunding* contains potential factors that enhance subjective well-being.

© Springer International Publishing AG 2017
C. Stephanidis (Ed.): HCII Posters 2017, Part II, CCIS 714, pp. 241–248, 2017.
DOI: 10.1007/978-3-319-58753-0_36

2 Micro-crowdfunding

2.1 Basic Design

Micro-crowdfunding is a new crowdsourcing infrastructure that focuses on increasing the recognition of the importance of society's sustainability[1]. It tries to address the free rider problem that hinders the realization of a sustainable society. Sustainability will be lost by the free riders who use a high level of public resources, such as natural resources and public facilities. This phenomenon is called the *tragedy of the commons* [1]. Especially in urban areas, many people use public facilities; as a result, the free rider problem appears clearly. This problem is caused by people's selfish pursuit of their own benefits. If everyone tries to maintain resources spending a little idle time, it will solve the problem efficiently. Even significant problems like environmental concerns can be solved by individual efforts. Psychological techniques for changing human behavior have become famous and social psychology has been used in public policies [2, 9].

However, it is difficult for some people in the community to perform socially good actions without incentives. *Micro-crowdfunding* provides social and economic incentives by applying a crowdsourcing-based approach. Using this platform, people can commit to solving many problems in the community, and furthermore can recognize the importance of community sustainability. It is expected that many social problems will be solved using a bottom up approach because the mindset of each community member changes.

Many crowdsourcing and crowdfunding services make use of real currency, but *Micro-crowdfunding* uses virtual currency. It is similar to the local currency that can only be used within a particular community. Using real currency has a limitation in that people who do not have money to spare cannot fund projects. However, using virtual currency, everyone can participate in *micro-crowdfunding* regardless of their economic situation.

2.2 Crowdfunding Activities in Micro-crowdfunding

Micro-crowdfunding is a crowdsourcing infrastructure implemented in the *micro-community*. *Micro-crowdfunding* consists of three phases: organizing, funding, and executing. Figure 1 shows an overview of *micro-crowdfunding*. First, one of the community members frames a problem within the community as a mission. Next, people who want to solve the problem fund the mission. Finally, someone pursues the mission and receives rewards. *Micro-crowdfunding* encourages participation by dividing the commitment to community problems into three stages. This section describes the three stages.

The mission proposed by community members is called a *micro-mission*. It is proposed when a member notices the problem. He or she is called a *mission organizer*. Any member in the community can propose a new *micro-mission*. It is desirable that

---

[1] More details about design and evaluation of *micro-crowdfunding* were reported in [7, 8].

Fig. 1. Overview of *micro-crowdfunding*

this *micro-mission* is simple enough to be manageable by anyone because all members who want to commit should be able to participate in the *micro-crowdfunding* activities. The goal of m*icro-crowdfunding* is to increase the awareness toward sustainability. To achieve this, many community members need to participate in *micro-crowdfunding* and solve their community problems. The organized *micro-mission* is released on a smartphone application, which can be accessed by community members.

In the next stage, when some members think that the proposed *micro-mission* should be solved, they can fund it using virtual currency. These members are called *mission investors*. The users can clarify how important the mission is by checking the amount of funded money for the mission. From another perspective, because everyone can propose a *micro-mission*, it will become difficult to recognize which mission is important in the absence of a *micro-crowdfunding* service that weighs a *micro-mission*. Funding makes it possible to weigh many missions using the power of the crowd.

When funded money reaches a sufficient level, the *micro-mission* becomes performable. After that, a member who has enough time performs it. This member is called the *mission performer*. After the member completes the *micro-mission*, he or she reports its completion to the *mission organizer*. If the *mission organizer* is satisfied with the quality of its accomplishment, the *mission performer* can receive the funded money as a reward.

3   A Way to Enhance Micro-crowdfunding

This section describes how to enhance *micro-crowdfunding* to make communities flourish. Table 1 shows activities that make our daily life flourish as advocated by Lyubomirsky [3]. As mentioned in Sect. 2.1, *micro-crowdfunding* promotes altruistic behavior and aims to solve community problems without free riders. *Micro-crowdfunding* can increase well-being because it promotes "Practicing acts of kindness" and "Nurturing relationships." Therefore, we aim to enhance the *micro-crowdfunding* platform to one that improves well-being.

Our proposal is to add a *micro-mission* that increases the well-being of *micro-crowdfunding* automatically. We focus on the *"Three Good Things in life"* exercise (TGT exercise) proposed by Seligman as a task to increase well-being [11]. This is a simple and effective exercise. In exercise, people write down three good events that happened on a particular day at the end of the day. In addition, they also write the reason why those good events happened. As a result of continuing this exercise, the subjective well-being is improved, and they tend not to become depressed. This writing activity is associated with "Counting your blessings," as shown in Table 1. Furthermore, it also involves "cultivating optimism" because it inculcates a positive approach.

The enhanced *micro-crowdfunding* regards the TGT exercise as a customized *micro-mission*. If it is a general *micro-mission*, the TGT exercise is completed by another user before being attempted by the current one. However, everyone can perform the exercise as the task is independent from other users.

Table 1. Lists of activities that make people flourish

Activities that make us flourish	
1.	Counting your blessings
2.	Cultivating optimism
3.	Avoiding overthinking and social comparison
4.	Practicing acts of kindness
5.	Nurturing relationships
6.	Doing more activities that truly engage you
7.	Replaying and savoring life's joys
8.	Committing to your goals
9.	Developing strategies for coping
10.	Learning to forgive
11.	Practicing religion and spirituality
12.	Taking care of your body

4 Experiment and Discussion

4.1 Experiment

We conducted a preliminary experiment to confirm the potential possibilities and pitfalls of enhanced *micro-crowdfunding*. This experiment was designed based on role-playing game-based method [6]. The method is mainly used when experimenting with the new currency system. In future research, we will conduct a field study in reference to the results of this preliminary experiment. We expect that the field study will yield better results by recognizing the potentials and limitations of our approach. In addition, we believe that this preliminary experiment will also serve researchers who try to increase well-being, because it identifies problems that need to be addressed and thus contributes to the common pool of knowledge.

In this experiment, we present the feasibility of enhanced *micro-crowdfunding* as a platform for increasing well-being when the *micro-mission* is performed. Therefore, we had all participants take on the role of the *mission performer*. We conducted this experiment on the assumption that the *mission organizer* and the *mission investor* existed virtually. The mission posted by the virtual *mission organizer* was "please count the number of instances of alphabet e." The participants were divided into two groups: Group A and Group B. Members of Group A only performed the above mention. Members of Group B additionally performed the TGT exercise after the counting mission. Figure 2 shows the experimental application we developed. The left screen is *micro-mission* and the right one is the TGT exercise implemented using Google Forms. After all the participants performed their own mission, they answered a questionnaire to measure well-being every day.

Fig. 2. Screenshots of the experimental application

This experiment is divided into 4 stages, and the displayed information on the first screen of the application changed according to the stage. At the first stage, it displayed "There is a simple mission." At the second stage, the *mission investors'* names were displayed. At the third stage, the social meaning of the mission was displayed. At the last stage, *mission investors'* names and their meanings are displayed. The duration of each stage was 2 days, while that of the whole experiment was 8 days.

The participants were 8 college students (2 females and 6 males, ranging from 21 to 24 years of age); 5 were in Group A and 3 in Group B. After 8 days of the experiment, all participants answered another questionnaire. In the questionnaire, we asked whether the motivation to perform *micro-missions* at each stage changed. In addition, we asked the members of Group B about the TGT exercise and the counting mission as follows: *"How important did you believe the counting mission and TGT exercises were?", "At what level did you perceive incongruence between the TGT exercise and counting mission?"* and *"How much did you feel like increasing your motivation for performing the micro-mission?"*

We also interviewed each participant to discuss the effects of the experiment. In an interview about each stage, three participants in Group A answered that their motivation was not affected by the *mission investor*. The other members of Group A and all members of Group B answered that the effectiveness in increasing their motivation was greater when the investor name was clearly displayed.

The results of the measuring well-being showed no clear difference between Groups A and B. However, in the interview, two members in Group B said they could feel the effect of the TGT exercise slightly. In order to strictly evaluate the effect of our approach, we need to conduct another long-period experiment. In addition, the all participants in Group B felt that the relationship between *micro-mission* and the TGT exercise was weak and said that the motivation to participate in the exercise was not high.

4.2   Discussion

In this section, we clarify potential pitfalls of our current approach. As a result of this preliminary experiment, it became clear that the following two pitfalls exist. The first relates to motivations for the TGT exercise. The second is that the TGT exercise is too weak to prevail over the effects of daily events.

We had predicted that the participants had enough motivation to perform the TGT exercise because it could increase well-being. However, participants said the motivation was low. This is because the exercise was a boring task like writing a diary. Therefore, the exercise needs to involve appropriate incentives. The simplest solution is that the system gives users virtual currency as a reward for performing the exercise. However, this approach has its limitations. Internal motivation is lowered by increasing external motivation. Therefore, we need to carefully design incentives.

The second pitfall is that the TGT exercise is insufficient as a task to increase well-being. We are influenced by various events in our daily lives. Of course, negative events lead to a depressed mood. The exercise is not powerful enough to prevail over such effects. The short experiment period can explain the lack of an apparent effect of the TGT exercise. However, to cater to a heterogeneous group of people, we believe that the platform design should involve various tasks and exercises that suit various personality types, rather than just the TGT exercise in isolation.

5   Related Work

In this section, we introduce past works related to crowdsourcing service. *MoboQ* is a real-time location-based question-answering crowdsourcing platform built on micro-blogging service [4]. People can help each other without spending much time. Users can ask location-based and real-time questions on the platform. For example, a user can ask "is the restaurant crowded?" and "does the bank have a long waiting queue?" These are difficult to answer using existing Q&A services.

UbiAsk [5] is also a mobile crowdsourcing platform on an existing social networking infrastructure to assist foreign visitors. On this platform, users can ask image-based questions. Local residents can answer rapidly because of the wide reach of existing social media. This platform enhances existing social media by focusing on the end-users' participation. While designing the community-based crowdsourcing service, we should also consider the motivation to participate.

6 Conclusion and Future Directions

In this study, we proposed enhanced *micro-crowdfunding* by adding TGT exercise. As a result, we discovered the pitfalls, namely, factors that hinder the motivation to perform the TGT exercise and the weakness of its effects. To address them, we should assign importance to building a platform with micro-crowdfunding, a well-being task, and well-being service.

We consider pitfalls found in this preliminary experiment to be fundamental. Future research should develop a new platform to enhance well-being using community currency with *micro-crowdfunding*. This platform should have characteristics of *micro-crowdfunding*, comprising a mechanism to enhance internal motivation, and designed to further increase well-being, and should have three elements: *micro-crowdfunding*, a well-being task, and well-being service. It should use existing *micro-crowdfunding*. The well-being task should aim to increase well-being as did the TGT exercise. In this preliminary experiment, we used only the TGT exercise. The new platform, however, should comprise several types of well-being tasks. After performing the well-being task, users can receive community currency as a reward issued by the system. This can increase the motivation to perform well-being tasks as mentioned in the previous section. For designing the platform, we should discuss the balance between psychological and economic incentives.

The challenge with community currency is identifying a way to exchange its value. For example, the virtual currency in a social game has value in that it is possible to purchase in-game items. Therefore, the use of the currency determines its value. The use of the virtual currency on this platform should enhance well-being, through, for example, the purchase of collection items that may increase satisfaction like social games. By designing a platform that satisfies these requirements, we will achieve a flourishing society.

We also should discuss the relationship between economic and psychological incentives. For designing a new platform, we need to examine the appropriateness of an incentive scheme first. After that, well-being tasks and services should be considered.

Acknowledgements. This work was supported in part by the Program for Leading Graduate Schools, "Graduate Program for Embodiment Informatics" of the Ministry of Education, Culture, Sports, Science and Technology (MEST) of Japan.

References

1. Hardin, G.: The tragedy of the commons. Science **162**, 1243–1248 (1968)
2. Institute of Government "MINDSPACE: Influencing Behaviour through Public Policy", Cabinet Office (2010)

3. Layous, K., Lyubomirsky, S.: The how, why, what, when, and who of happiness: mechanisms underlying the success of positive activity interventions. In: Gruber, J., Moskowitz, J. (eds.) Positive Emotion: Integrating the Light Sides and Dark Sides, Oxford University Press (2014)
4. Liu, Y., Alexandrova, T., Nakajima, T.: Using strangers as sensors: temporal and geo-sensitive question answering via social media. In: Proceedings of the 22nd International Conference on the World Wide Web, pp. 803–814 (2013)
5. Liu, Y., Lehdonvirta, V., Alexandrova, T., Nakajima, T.: Drawing on mobile crowds via social media. Multimed. Syst. 18(1), 53–67 (2012)
6. Powell, J.: The community currency role play. http://www.complementarycurrency.org/ccLibrary/asia/thailand/ccroleplay.html. Accessed 16 Mar 2016
7. Sakamoto, M., Nakajima, T.: Micro-crowdfunding: achieving a sustainable society through economic and social incentives in micro-level crowdfunding. In: Proceedings of International Conference on Mobile and Ubiquitous Multimedia (2013)
8. Sakamoto, M., Nakajima, T.: Gamifying social media to encourage social activities with digital-physical hybrid role-playing. In: Proceedings of the 6th International Conference on Social Computing and Social Media (2014)
9. Sakamoto, M., Nakajima, T., Akioka, S.: Gamifying collective human behavior with gameful digital rhetoric. Multimed. Tools Appl. (2016). doi:10.1007/s11042-016-3665-y
10. Sakamoto, M., Nakajima, T., Alexandrova, T.: Enhancing values through virtuality for intelligent artifacts that influence human attitude and behavior. Multimed. Tools Appl. 74(24), 11537–11568 (2015). Springer
11. Seligman, M.E.P.: Flourish: A Visionary New Understanding of Happiness and Well-being. Free Press, New York City (2011)
12. Seligman, M.E., Steen, T.A., Park, N., Peterson, C.: Positive psychology progress. Am. Psychol. 60, 410–421 (2005)
13. Fleming, T.M., Bavin, L., Stasiak, K., Hermansson-Webb, E., Merry, S.N., Cheek, C., Lucassen, M., Lau, H.M., Pollmuller, B., Hetrick, S.: Serious games and gamification for mental health: current status and promising directions

Estimation of Floor Reaction Force During Walking Using Physical Inertial Force by Wireless Motion Sensor

Atsushi Isshiki$^{(\boxtimes)}$, Yoshio Inoue, Kyoko Shibata,
and Motomichi Sonobe

Kochi University of Technology, Miyanokuchi 185,
Tosayamada, Kami, Kochi, Japan
9nine.apple@gmail.com, {inoue.yoshio, shibata.kyoko,
sonobe.motomichi}@kochi-tech.ac.jp

Abstract. Floor reaction force is widely used to evaluate walking. Generally, floor reaction force is measured by a floor reaction meter. However, floor reaction meter is not suitable for clinical practice due to the limitation in walk condition, measurement range and device size. This study suggests a simple method to estimate floor reaction force by processing dynamic acceleration information to be provided from small wireless motion sensors. In the experiment, optical motion capture and the floor reaction meter were used. The result shows that the sum of the inertial force of the whole body and gravity equal floor reaction force obtained through an experiment using optical motion capture. We consider that physical inertial force of the whole body could be estimated from the dynamic acceleration of the lower trunk and right/left thighs. A similar result obtained with the motion sensor. An estimation of floor reaction force by measuring the inertial force is effective, and much simpler walk analysis could be possible with using appropriate signal handling of wireless motion sensor information. This method can be applied to biofeedback.

Keywords: Floor reaction force · Physical inertial force · Gait analysis · Wireless motion sensor · Signal handling

1 Introduction

People walking every day. Reaction force by gait analysis is widely used in walk analysis in medical care and field sports [1]. Representative walk analysis is a combined system of floor reaction meter and optical motion capture. However, this system is not suitable for clinical practice due to the limitation in walk condition, measurement range and device size. Simpler system without floor reaction mater and optical motion capture is needed for a simple walk analysis. This study group suggests new analytical method to estimate of floor reaction force without the floor reaction meter [2]. This method uses only three motion sensors. This estimated system supposes that inertial force of the whole body equals floor reaction force. In the experiment, optical motion capture and the floor reaction meter were used. Estimate floor reaction force by processing dynamic acceleration information to be provided from small wireless motion sensors.

© Springer International Publishing AG 2017
C. Stephanidis (Ed.): HCII Posters 2017, Part II, CCIS 714, pp. 249–254, 2017.
DOI: 10.1007/978-3-319-58753-0_37

2 Methods

Figure 1 shows a split plot design of physical. That estimates an inertial force from that mass and dynamic acceleration. Multiply physical mass coefficient by whole physical mass and the product is each physical mass. Table 1 shows physical mass coefficient. This coefficient used the Estimation of Inertia Properties of the Body Segments in Japanese Athletes [3].

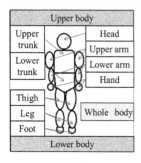

Fig. 1. Physical constitution.

Table 1. Physical information.

Body part	Mass ratio	Vertical direction acceleration	Movement direction acceleration
Head	0.069	$A_{hez}1$	$A_{hey}1$
Upper arm	0.027	$A_{uaz}2$	$A_{uay}2$
Lower arm	0.016	$A_{laz}3$	$A_{lay}3$
Hand	0.006	$A_{haz}4$	$A_{hay}4$
Upper trunk	0.302	$A_{utz}5$	$A_{uty}5$
Lower trunk	0.187	$A_{ltz}6$	$A_{lty}6$
Thigh	0.11	$A_{thz}7$	$A_{thy}7$
Leg	0.051	$A_{lez}8$	$A_{ley}8$
Foot	0.011	$A_{foz}9$	$A_{foy}9$

Dynamic acceleration a_z and a_y (Table 1) twice differentiates the vertical and movemant direction positional information. The dynamic acceleration of left/right part the sum of the right and left dynamic acceleration. A measurement interval equal h and a position (speed) of the time in the next expression i(i = 0–n) equal fi. (1) is a start point, (2) is differential calculus type of other time, (3) is endpoint.

$$f_0' = (-3f_0 + 4f_1 - f_2)/(2h) \tag{1}$$

$$f_i' = (-f_{i-1} + f_{i+1})/(2h) \tag{2}$$

$$f_n' = (f_{n-2} - 4f_{n-1} + 3f_n)/(2h) \tag{3}$$

Measurement dynamic acceleration included a high-frequency not to be included the normal walk. So make Butter worth digital filter in a Matlab, and to perform low-path handling of interception frequency 9 Hz for smooth [4].

Floor reaction force of the whole body F_w, Upper body F_u, and lower body F_l estimated all physical mass, dynamic acceleration of fifteen parts and acceleration of gravity. A coefficient including the gravity that the total of the consider body parts.

$$F_{uz} = M(0.069a_{hez} + 0.027a_{uaz} + 0.016a_{laz} + 0.006a_{haz} \\ + 0.302a_{utz} + 0.187a_{ltz}) + 0.656Mg \tag{4}$$

$$F_{lz} = M(0.11a_{thz} + 0.051a_{lez} + 0.011a_{foz}) + 0.344Mg \tag{5}$$

$$F_{wz} = F_{uz} + F_{lz} \tag{6}$$

Suppose that the upper body part ignores the dynamic acceleration of the arms as symmetric movement, the dynamic acceleration of a head and the body can represent dynamic acceleration of the lower trunk that is a center of gravity position from whole body, the dynamic acceleration of a lower body can represent dynamic acceleration of the right/left things that is lower part of the body centroid. Estimated floor reaction force of the representative upper body F_{repu}, the representative lower body F_{repl}, the representative whole body F_{repw}.

$$F_{repuz} = 0.558Ma_{ltz} + 0.656Mg \tag{7}$$

$$F_{replz} = 0.162Ma_{thz} + 0.344Mg \tag{8}$$

$$F_{repwz} = F_{repuz} + F_{replz} \tag{9}$$

As for The estimated floor reaction of vertical direction, (4)–(9) by replace vertical direction and movement direction (Table 1), expression for the acceleration of gravity.

Figure 2 shows two floor reaction meters (Tec Gihan Co.,Ltd. TF-4060) and ten motion captors (Motion Analysis Co.Ltd.) which uses walk experiment. Figure 3 shows the reflexive marker sticking position. The research participants measured three times of each three male physically unimpaired people in twenties at sampling frequency 100 Hz. Instruct them one leg instructed floor reaction maters adding up like Fig. 2 and to do a normal walk. The positional information that obtained from motion captors converts a plumb, a line into acceleration used expression (1)–(3). Let substitute smoothing acceleration and mass for (4)–(9) and let estimated floor reaction force. Compare the estimated floor reaction force from whole body, estimated floor reaction force and floor reaction force from reaction maters. Furthermore, experimented three motion sensors.

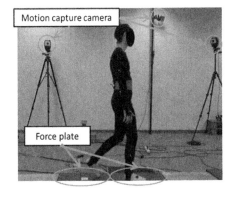

Fig. 2. Motion analysis system.

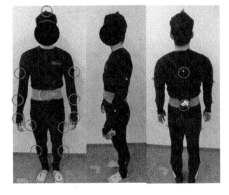

Fig. 3. Marker position.

3 Results

Figures 4 and 5 shows estimate floor reaction force by upper body F_u and the estimate floor reaction force by represent upper body F_{repu}. The result shows that the F_u displays similar amplitude cycle to the F_{repu}.

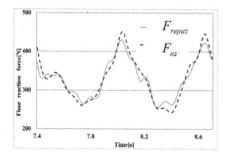

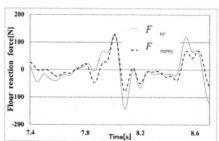

Fig. 4. Floor reaction force of vertical direction by the upper body.

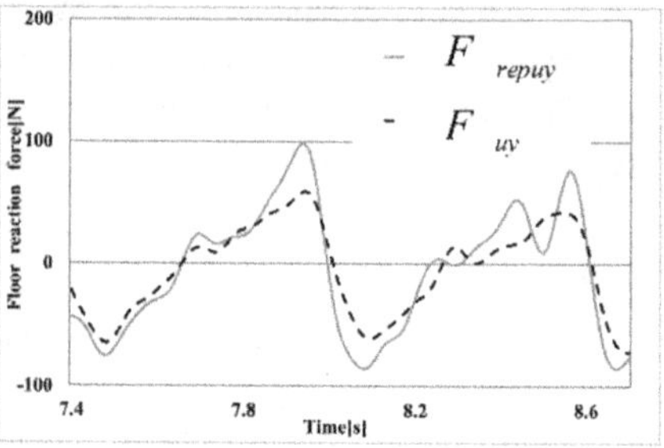

Fig. 5. Floor reaction force of movement direction by the upper body.

Figures 6 and 7 shows estimate floor reaction force by lower body F_l and the estimate floor reaction force by represent lower body F_{repl}. The result shows that the F_l displays similar amplitude cycle to the F_{repl}.

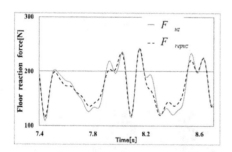

Fig. 6. Floor reaction force of vertical direction by the lower body.

Fig. 7. Floor reaction force of movement direction by the lower body.

Figures 8 and 9 shows estimate floor reaction force by whole body F_w, the estimate floor reaction force by represent whole body F_{repw} and floor reaction by floor reaction maters. The result shows that the F_w displays similar amplitude cycle to the F_{repw}.

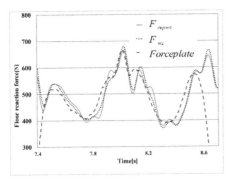
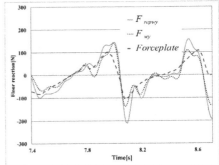

Fig. 8. Floor reaction force of vertical direction by the whole body.

Fig. 9. Floor reaction force of movement direction by the whole body.

Next is the same experiment result using motion sensors. Figures 10 and 11 shows the estimate floor reaction force by represent whole body F_{repl} and three motion sensors. The result shows that the motion sensors displays similar amplitude cycle to the motion captures.

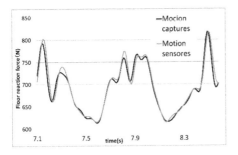
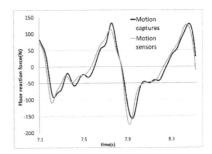

Fig. 10. Floor reaction force of vertical direction by the whole body.

Fig. 11. Floor reaction force of movement direction by the whole body.

4   Discussion

The result shows that the sum of the inertial force of the whole body and gravity equal floor reaction force obtained through an experiment using optical motion capture. We consider that physical inertial force of the whole body could be estimated from the dynamic acceleration of the lower trunk and right/left thighs. The same result was obtained by wireless motion sensor. This study suggests that an estimation of floor reaction force by measuring the inertial force is effective, and much simpler walk analysis could be possible with using appropriate signal handling of wireless motion sensor information.

References

1. Perry, J.: Gait Analysis Normal and Pathological Function. Medicine tooth medicine publication stock company (2007). (in Japanese)
2. Katsu, T., et al.: Estimation of ground reaction force during walking using a small number of inertial sensors. Jpn. Soc. Mech. Eng. Lect. Collect. Pap. **54**, 802-1–802-2 (2016)
3. Ae, M., et al.: Estimation of inertia properties of the body segments in Japanese athletes. Biomechanisms **11**, 22–33 (1992)
4. Ehara, Y., et al.: Introduction to Clinical Gait Measuring, pp. 65–67. Medicine tooth medicine publication stock company (2008)

Development of Content for an ICT Screening Program Based on the Emotional and Behavioral Disorder Questionnaire

Hyung Sook Kim[1], Chan-Ik Park[2], David O'Sullivan[3],
and Jeesun Lee[4(✉)]

[1] Department of Human Arts and Technology,
Inha University, Incheon, Republic of Korea
hksookl2@inha.ac.kr
[2] Faculty of Healing Industry,
Daegu Haany University, Daegu, Republic of Korea
cipark@dhu.ac.kr
[3] Department of Sports Science,
Pusan National University, Busan, Republic of Korea
davidosullivan@pusan.ac.kr
[4] Center for Interactive Culture Technology,
Inha University, Incheon, Republic of Korea
jeesunleell@gmail.com

Abstract. The purpose of this study is to recognize the limitations of the self-report text based Emotional and Behavioral Disorder (EBD) questionnaire and to develop the interactive behavioral screening program through ICT. For this purpose, seven representative items of the Adolescent Mental Health and Problem Behavior Screening Questionnaire-II (AMPQ-II) developed by Korean researchers were selected and their contents were reproduced as interactive video contents. To narrow down to the 7 representative items objectively, the common factors of items was compared with Attention-Deficit/Hyperactivity Disorder (ADHD) which is one of major problems consist in the broad area of EBD in the Diagnostic and Statistical Manual of Mental Disorder 5th edition (DSM-5). Each of questions were represented A/B type by level, and the contents were supported by various guidance to stimulate the behavioral reaction. The pilot study was applied to 10 subjects and the behavioral response data were coded as Labanotation to analyze the behavioral characteristics of subjects.

Keywords: Emotional and behavioral disorder · Screening · AMPQ-II · ICT · Behavior · Labanotation · Motion-capture · Kinect

1 Introduction

Emotional and behavioral problems are emerging as a serious social problem all over the world and they lead to high suicide rates and academic stress for Korean elementary, junior and high school students. Korea is reported to be the highest among OECD countries and the rate has increased for the past 12 years since 2003 (Korea

© Springer International Publishing AG 2017
C. Stephanidis (Ed.): HCII Posters 2017, Part II, CCIS 714, pp. 255–260, 2017.
DOI: 10.1007/978-3-319-58753-0_38

Institute for Health and Social Affairs 2015). Therefore, the Ministry of Education of Korea conducts annual emotional behavior test for elementary and middle school students to cope with emotional behavior problems and related developmental problems at an early stage.

The AMPQ-II (Adolescent Mental Health and Problem Behavior Screening Questionnaire-II) developed and tested by Korean researchers (Jung et al. 2008) has been used to as a simplified the Achenbach and Edelbrock (1983)'s CBCL (Child Behavior Checklist), which is widely used as a diagnostic tool for emotional and behavioral disorders internationally. The AMPQ-II is self-reported online and available to elementary school students, parent and teacher, and middle and high school students alike.

However, despite the pioneering development and application of tools, self-report testing through online has many problems of effectiveness, such as a false reporting, etc. Therefore, this study aims to recognize the limitations of the self-report type online survey and to develop an audio-visual interactive screening program using the Information and Communication Technology (ICT).

2 From the Paper-Based to the Interactive Behavior-Based Questionnaire

The seven out of thirty-eight items of the AMPQ-II that are easy to induce external behavior were selected and designed as behavior-based video question items. Also, to narrow down to the 7 representative items objectively, the common factors of items was compared with diagnostic criteria of Attention-Deficit/Hyperactivity Disorder (ADHD) which is one of the major problems in a broad group of EBD. The criteria referred from the Diagnostic and Statistical Manual of Mental Disorder 5th edition (DSM-5).

Each video item was composed of a form with minimal cognitive ability, that can induce an immediate behavioral response, and a form requiring comprehensive assessment of body reaction and cognition. Also, according to the degree of difficulty, two versions per item were specified and a total of 14 videos were completed. Content organization consisted of language, action, images, and sound guidance to promote entertainment and active participation, and to minimize the errors by interacting immediate behavioral response with video content (see Tables 1 and 2). The content design validity of the presented behavior-based Questionnaire was secured through consultation between the medical staff of neuropsychiatry department of Hanyang University Seoul Hospital who developed AMPQ-II and the researchers.

3 The Pilot Study

The designed contents were applied to 3 patients (mood, depression, ADHD) and 7 normal subjects in order to examine suitability of emotional behavior problem screening. For the normal, the seven university students majoring in theater were selected as a control group for data collection and methodological review at the pilot

Table 1. Behavior-based content from selected 7 questions of AMPQ-II

n o	Paper-based Questionnaire				Behavior-based Application	
	DSM-V		AMPQ-II		A Type	B Type
	Factor	Question	Factor	Question		
1	Inattention	1) Often fails to give close attention to details or makes careless mistakes in schoolwork, at work, or during other activities. 2) Often has difficulty sustaining attention in tasks or play activities. 4) Failure to follow directions or to perform missions in school work, chores, or workplace.	Learning and Internet	1) When I need to concentrate, I do not concentrate and do something else.	Focus on a various given shape	Respond to flashing shapes
2	Inattention	3) Often does not seem to listen when spoken to directly	Mood and Suicide	10) I do not follow well because I have a sense of displeasure to the instructions of my parents or teachers.	Follow the Father Follow the Mother	Fallow the Teacher
3		5) Often has difficulty organizing tasks and activities 6) Often avoids, dislikes, or is reluctant to engage in tasks that require sustained mental effort.	Mood and Suicide	12) I have difficulties to understand what I'm learning in class.	Animal Habitat Matching	Contents of mathematics, Korean language, and science subjects
4	–	–	Violation of Regulation	22) I am often subjected to serious rule violations.	Walk to traffic lights	Walk to traffic lights with sound effect
5	Hyperactivity & Impulsivity	2) Often leaves seat in situations when remaining seated is expected. 3) Often runs about or climbs in situations where it is inappropriate. 4) Often unable to play or engage in leisure activities quietly. 5) Is often "on the go," acting as if "driven by a motor"	Learning and Internet	25) I cannot wait and action is ahead of thoughts.	Walk or run along the virtual path	Walk or run along the virtual path with arms
6	Inattention	1) Often fidgets with or taps hands or feet or squirms in seat. 8) Often interrupts or intrudes on others.	Learning and Internet	28) I cannot sit still and I keep digging my hands or feet.	Listen to boring subject	Listen to boring subject and make a quiz
7	Hyperactivity & Impulsivity	6) Often talks excessively.	Worry and Thought	34) I am afraid to speak in front of people.	Express joy, sadness, depressed mood	Express joy, sadness, depressed mood in the audience

Table 2. Application eample: detail scenario concept flow of question no. 1

N o	AMP Q-II Question	T y p e	Contents Scenario Flow
1	When I need to con-cen-trate, I do not	A	1st scene — Show the various moving shapes randomly → 2nd scene — Show the various moving shapes in color randomly → 3rd scene — Mix the first concept with second → 4th scene — Show the third concept again and shapes turn into character at the end
	con-cen-trate and do some thing else.	B	1st scene — Show 1st scene of A again → 2nd scene — Show 3rd scene of A again → 3rd scene — Show the third concept again and shapes turn into character at the end → 4th scene — Show 3rd scene of A again but behavioral task added, 3 times repeat in variation. **Language Guidance** "Clap your hand, when star shape flash" **Sound Guidance** Sound effect when star shape flash

study because they were judged to be easy and clear to collect and analyze the behavioral induction and mechanical data compared to the general student. In order to confirm the validity of the developed program contents, the patient group responded to the 7 selected AMPQ-II questionnaires before the experiment.

To analyze the behavior of the subject, we recorded their bodily movement with Labanotation and motion capture technique. The 50 markers were attached to the subject's head and body, 3 Kinect cameras and 12 OptiTracks were installed. Three observers recorded object's behavioral observations at the experimental site, and after the experiment was completed, the Kinect video were coded as LabanWriter[1] by the same observers (Fig. 1).

---

[1] Labanotation Software for Mac developed by Ohio State University.

Fig. 1. Pilot study HW/SW setting

4   Discussion and Future Study

As a result of reviewing the behavior data obtained from the pilot test, the following significant meanings are found. First, subjects showed more active participation and behavioral responses than traditional online text-based self-test tools. The emotional behavioral items consisted of videos rather than simple sentences, which stimulated and interacted with the interest of the subjects, thereby inducing positive behavior. Second, behavior-based items have the advantage of identifying the emotional behavioral problem of a subject by examining specific and natural behavior patterns of the item, compared to text-based items approaching that problems with abstract and situational questions. Third, the notation analysis through behavior data accumulation coded the behavior information into a series of abstract symbols, so that the complex behavior patterns can be grasped clearly and symbolically. Analysis of notation data showed that students with emotional and behavioral disabilities were slower in responding to questions, more hesitant, more unnecessary behaviors, and less capable of coordinating their hands and feet.

In the future research, we intend to further study the effectiveness of the behavioral data test tool by applying the behavior based test contents to the immersive display environment platform. This immersive display based emotional and behavioral disorder test tool can be applied to many people at a low cost by utilizing ICT and can be commercialized as a general tool. Especially, it will spread to the Wee[2] class, Wee

---

[2] **Wee** (We + education, We + emotion) is a multi-integrated support service network that links schools, education offices, and local communities to support students' healthy and enjoyable school life. From 2008, **Wee class**, **Wee center** for local education office, and **Wee school** for municipal and provincial office of education are running schools for students who are not only poor in learning and maladjusted students but also for general students.

center and Wee school which is systematically operated in the government in order to prevent and manage emotional behavioral problems of students in Korea, and will lay the foundations for social problem solving, behavior database construction and research bases.

Acknowledgement. This research was supported by the National Research Foundation of Korea (NRF) Grant funded by the Ministry of Science, ICT & Future Planning for convergent research in Development program for convergence R&D over Science and Technology Liberal Arts (2016929336).

References

Kim, M.S.: The subjective well-being of Korean children and its policy implications. Health Welf. Forum. **220**(2), 14–26 (2015)

Jung, S.A., Ahn, D.H., Chung, S.Y., Jeong, Y.G., Kim, Y.Y.: Development of screening test for adolescent mental health and problem behavior. J. Korean Neuropsychiatric Assoc. **47**(2), 168–176 (2008)

Bhang, S.Y., et al.: Adolescent Mental Health and Problem Behavior Screening Questionnaire-II (AMPQ-II) (2011)

Achenbach T.M., Edelbrock, C.: The Child Behavior Checklist (CBCL) (1983)

Development of a Human-Seat Cushion Finite Element Model for Sitting Comfort Analysis

Xianxue Li[1,2], Li Ding[2(✉)], Xianchao Ma[1], Baofeng Li[1],
and Haiyan Liu[1]

[1] Shanghai Aircraft Design and Research Institute, No. 5188 JinKe Road,
Pudong New District, Shanghai 201210, China
[2] Key Laboratory for Biomechanics and Mechanobiology of Ministry
of Education, School of Biological Science and Medical Engineering,
Beihang University, No. 37 XueYuan Road, Haidian District,
Beijing 100191, China
li361011120@126.com

Abstract. With the development of civil aviation market, more and more people travel by plane and sitting comfort during the flight attracts increasing attention. In this study, a biomechanical human-seat cushion finite element model with spine, pelvis, thigh, buttocks and seat cushion was established along with seat comfort experiment to study the sitting comfort. The results show similarity in both pressure distribution and value between simulation and experiment. So the finite element model was validated.

Keywords: Civil aviation · Finite element · Comfort

1 Introduction

With the development of civil aviation market, more and more people travel by plane and sitting comfort during the flight attracts increasing attention. So it's very important to find how to evaluate the sitting comfort during the flight in order to supply more comfortable flight experience for the passenger.

In this study, a biomechanical human-seat cushion finite element model with spine, pelvis, thigh, buttocks and seat cushion was established along with seat comfort experiment to study the sitting comfort. The finite element model is based on a standard Chinese pilot's computer tomographic scan.

2 Methods

Firstly, a volunteer that fit the 50th percentile Chinese male's dimensional data was recruited and the informed consent was obtained. CT scans from T1 to pelvis and femur were obtained and then imported in Mimics software to reconstruct the geometry of spine, pelvis and femur.

For each piece of bone, such as vertebrae, hip, femur and so on, the initial geometry models were imported into reverse engineering software Geomagic Studio 2013 to

© Springer International Publishing AG 2017
C. Stephanidis (Ed.): HCII Posters 2017, Part II, CCIS 714, pp. 261–266, 2017.
DOI: 10.1007/978-3-319-58753-0_39

construct a detailed geometric model. In this step, poor quality triangular facet was remodified and the geometry was smoothed and optimized. Then we get the non uniform rational B spline (Nurbs) surface model, the surface model is saved as *.iges format to be meshed by finite element mesh generation method in Hypermesh. The Nurbs surface model of vertebrae, sacrum, hip and femur is as shown in Fig. 1.

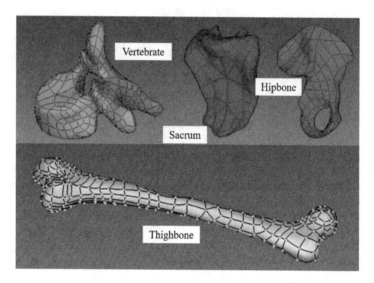

Fig. 1. Nurbs surface model of the bone

Then the above established Nurbs surface models were imported into the finite element pre-processing software Hypermesh 12. The Nrubs surface model contains only a layer of the surface and is not solid, therefore, the first step was to generate entity model, then the 3D finite element mesh was generated. The skeleton model was meshed in 4 node tetrahedron element, and the element size was about 5 mm for the vertebrae, 10 mm for the hip and femur.

The intervertebral disk model was generated based on the part of adjacent vertebral endplate in Hypermesh. Firstly the Nurbs surface model on the adjacent vertebral endplate surface part was extracted based on the upper and lower surfaces of intervertebral disk endplate and enclosed intervertebral disk surface model was generated. Finally, the surface model of the intervertebral disk was filled and 3D finite element model was generated. The model of intervertebral disk was divided into 4 node tetrahedral elements, and the size of the element was about 3 mm. The finite element models of bone and intervertebral disk were shown in Fig. 2.

In this study, the geometry model of the hip and thigh soft tissue was established based on a previous 3D geometry model of the human body. Part of the 3D model of human body was rotated to sitting posture after segmentation and the Nurbs surface model of the sitting human body was generated. The process of establishing the sitting posture human body model is shown in Fig. 3. The 3D finite element mesh model was shown in Fig. 4.

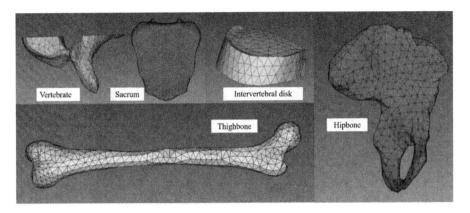

Fig. 2. Finite element model of the bone and intervertebral disk

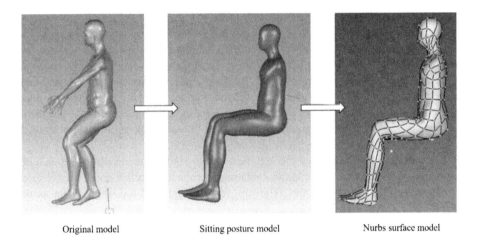

Fig. 3. Process of establishing sitting posture human body model

There are main 7 ligaments around the spine winch are relative with the spine's movement.

The seat cushion model was meshed in four layers with 8-nodes elements. The other parts of human such as head, neck, limbs and trunk were modeled by mass point and connected with relative vertebra and femur bones. The mass of each vertebra segmental of the human truck referred Pearsall's work (Pearsall et al. 1996). Ligaments on the spine were modeled using axial elements and their stress-strain relationship referred Shirazi-Adl's work (Shirazi-Adl et al. 1986).

Since the whole human model consists different body parts and the method of establish is different that different body parts have different coordinates, so the assembly of different body parts is an important work. The assembly consists of location and

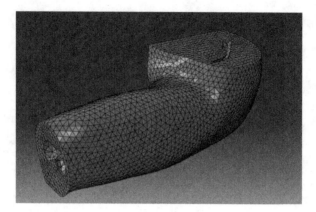

Fig. 4. Finite element model of hip and thigh

constraint relationship. The assembly of location is performed in Hypermesh and the assembly of restraints is performed in ABAQUS.

The mass points of head, neck and upper limb segment were constrained by beam element with the reference point of T1 vertebral endplate. The constraints between the vertebra and the various mass points of the trunk segments were defined as follows: firstly a reference point in front of each vertebrae center position was established that this reference point was constrained with the outer nodes of relative vertebrae through rigid coupling, then the reference points were connected with relative mass points of the truck segments by beam element, so the weight of each truck segments was applied to the corresponding vertebrae.

The contact surface between the vertebrae and the intervertebral disc is set as a tie constraint. According to the anatomical relationship, the appropriate nodes are selected on the sacrum and the hip bones. The hip, femur, thigh and hip are also set as tie constraint.

The constitutive laws for the bones in the model are considered as linear elastic. The intervertebral discs are modeled using a Mooney-Rivlin hyperelastic model which is expressed in the form of the polynomial strain energy potential. The soft tissue was modeled using a non-linear visco-hyperelastic material model. A second order polynomial strain energy potential was used to describe the hyperelastic portion. The viscoelastic portion was described by the Prony-series model and the viscoelastic parameters were set as $G_1 = 0.05$, $K_1 = 0.5$ and $\tau_1 = 0.8\,\text{s}$. Seat cushion was assumed to be made of SAF 6060 polymer foam with rate-independent hyperelastic and viscoelastic behaviors. The hyperelastic portion of the seat cushion is expressed in the form of the second order Odgen strain energy potential and the viscoelastic portion is expressed by the Prony series.

The established whole finite element model is shown in Fig. 5.

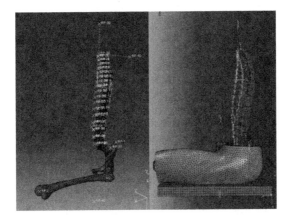

Fig. 5. The whole finite element model

3   Validation and Conclusion

Finally, seven volunteers with mean weight: 64.4 kg which were similar with the human model were recruited to perform the sitting pressure experiment. Then the sitting pressure distribution between simulation and experimental results were compared and the results shows similarity in both pressure distribution and value, as shown in Fig. 6.

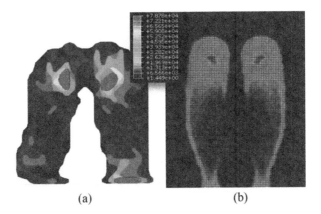

(a)   (b)

Fig. 6. Sitting pressure distribution (a) experimental result; (b) simulation result.

Based on previous analysis, we can think the finite element model is validated at this point.

References

Shirazi-Adl, A.A., Ahmed, A.M., Shrivastava, S.C.: Mechanical response of a lumbar motion segment in axial torque alone and combined with compression. Spine **11**, 148–163 (1986)

Belytschko, T., Schwer, L., Privitzer, E.: Theory and application of a three-dimensional model of the human spine. Aviat. Space Environ. Med. **49**, 158–165 (1978)

de Looze, M.P., Kuijt-Evers, L.F., van Dieen, J.: Sitting comfort and discomfort and the relationships with objective measures. Ergonomics **46**, 985–997 (2003)

Dooge, D., Cabane, C., Marca, C., Dwarampudi, R., Cohen, D., Pearson, S.: Utilizing finite element tools to model objective seat comfort results. SAE International (2012)

Grujicic, M., Pandurangan, B., Xie, X., Gramopadhye, A.K., Wagner, D., Ozen, M.: Musculoskeletal computational analysis of the influence of car-seat design/adjustments on long-distance driving fatigue. Int. J. Ind. Ergon. **40**, 345–355 (2010)

Bhonge, P.S., Thorbole, C.K., Lankarani, H.M.: Computational modeling and performance evaluation of a dax-foam aircraft seat cushion utilizing high loading rate dynamic characteristics. In: ASME 2010 International Mechanical Engineering Congress and Exposition (2010)

Makhsous, M., Lim, D., Hendrix, R., Bankard, J., Rymer, W.Z., Lin, F.: Finite element analysis for evaluation of pressure ulcer on the buttock: development and validation. IEEE Trans. Neural Syst. Rehabil. Eng.: Publ. IEEE Eng. Med. Biol. Soc. **15**, 517–525 (2007)

Pearsall, D.J., Reid, J.G., Livingston, L.A.: Segmental intertial parameters of the human trunk as determined from computed tomography. Ann. Biomed. Eng. **24**, 198–210 (1996)

Study on the Interactivity of Medication Behavior in Children's Group Environment

Miao Liu$^{(\boxtimes)}$, Zhaoyang Sun, and Tao Xiong

East China University of Science and Technology, Shanghai, China
183787975@qq.com, 775660337@qq.com, 472353860@qq.com

Abstract. In order to confirm and clarify the inference that preschool teachers and peers would play an important role in the process of social development, this study adopted the method of event sampling to observe the behavior of children in kindergarten. By observing the children's behavior in group environment, this paper provides quantitative analysis and specifies in 5 aspects. Combined with the study of statistical results and genetic analysis, the author summarized characteristics of young children's medication compliance behavior in group environment, as well as different types of drugs on the impact of young children to accept the elements. This study provides a new approach for the optimization of medication assisted technology for children, and enrich the index system of children health care, which is of prime importance to provide the methodological guidance for children's drug design.

Keywords: Children's group environment · Medication behavior · Interactive responses · Event sampling · Natural observation

1 Introduction

In December 2007, the World Health Organization(WHO) initiated "Better Medicines for Children" campaign to raise awareness among policy makers, medicine manufacturers, researchers, health care professionals and the public. And to promote the proper usage of medication for children, WHO issued the first Model Lists of Essential Medicines subsequently.

According to statistics, 90% of the medicines on domestic market didn't have equivalent formulas designed for children in China, and of more than 3,000 kinds of medicines, less than 2% are developed exclusively for children over the past decade. As a result, there has been a serious shortage of medicines for children. Even worse, among the small amount of children medicines, the procedures and instructions are ambiguous as to their proper uses. The problem of children medication has been neglected for decades, and now it requires immediate actions.

2 Research Methods

To identify the characteristics of the interactive objects, the elements of interaction behaviors and children's preference to pills or doses of varied colors, this paper examined children's interactive behaviors in the daily medicine-taking situation with

© Springer International Publishing AG 2017
C. Stephanidis (Ed.): HCII Posters 2017, Part II, CCIS 714, pp. 267–274, 2017.
DOI: 10.1007/978-3-319-58753-0_40

method of naturalistic observation and sampling. The selected group of kindergarten children was observed by three discontinuous periods, 7 days for each, with a length of 15 days valid, and 92 valid event samples recorded.

2.1   Experimental Subjects

The subjects of this study were 369 children from 3 different kindergartens or extracurricular interest classes, namely Affiliated Kindergarten of China University of Mining and Technology in Xuzhou, Jiangsu Province, Fugou County Kindergarten and Art Base of Qiushi Education in Zhoukou, Henan Province, among which there were 174 children from senior classes (75 males and 99 females), with an average age of 5.45, 158 children from intermediate classes (66 males and 92 females), with an average age of 4.70, and 37 children from primary classes (19 males and 18 females), with an average age of 3.72.

2.2   Research Procedure

Defining "Interactive Behaviors" During Medicine-Taking and the Objects of Observation

According to children's behavioral characteristics in communal environment, interactive behaviors can be defined as a series of behaviors when interacting with the surrounding objects and environment in the course medicine-taking (external use or internal use). Specifically, children's interactive behaviors during medicine-taking may include sharing, helping, cooperation, consolation and social moralities.

Defining the "4 Dimensions" of Interactive Behaviors and Designing Log Sheets

In this study, each interactive behavior was recorded in reference to four dimensions: the behavior's initiator's name and gender, the behavior's target receiver' name and gender, the behavior's details and types, the behavior's feedback, or responses by the receiver.

Observation

The observers carried out a preparatory observation on the aforementioned kindergartens for 2 days (each observer in charge of one class), in order to prepare themselves for the observation. The observation was immediately commenced on the end of pre-observation. The observation lasted for 3 weeks, starting at 8:00 (when the class begins) and ending at 15:30 (when the children leaves the kindergarten) for each day, among which 15 days had valid record in the end. The scope of the observation was the children's interactive behaviors during medicine-taking, also including first-aid or treatment of accidental injuries.

3   Results of Observation

With the aid of observer reliability analysis and SPSS processing, 92 valid samples of interactive behaviors were kept in record, which were analyzed in 6 different aspects.

3.1 Genders of the Children in Interactive Behaviors During Medicine-Taking

Genders of children engaged in interactive behaviors in 3 different grades, namely senior classes, intermediate classes and primary classes were shown in Table 1, which were checked by X^2 algorithm in SPSS. The result showed there was no perceptible difference in terms of gender when it comes to interactive behaviors ($X^2 = 0.39$, df = 1, P > 0.05). However, when the same statistics were checked by X^2 algorithm in the form of crosstab 3 × 2 (grades × genders), the result showed that there is considerable difference in terms of grades when it comes to interactive behaviors ($X2 = 0.34$, df = 2, P > 0.05).

Table 1. Genders of children engaged in interactive behaviors

Gender	Grade		
	Senior	Intermediate	Primary
Male	19	16	8
Female	22	20	7

3.2 Target Receivers of the Interactive Behaviors During Medicine-Taking

The target receivers of children's interactive behaviors might be other children (their peers), adults or ones hard to spot. Target receivers of the interactive behaviors in 3 different grades were shown in Table 2, which were checked by X^2 algorithm. The result showed that there is noticeable difference in terms of target receivers when it comes to children's interactive behaviors ($X2 = 119.30$, df = 2, P ≤ 0.01).

The target receivers of interactive behaviors were checked by X^2 algorithm respectively on the basis of each different grades, and the results showed there is also a noticeable difference in terms of targets receivers for children of different grades ($X2 = 77.56$, $X2 = 26.00$, $X2 = 17.29$, df = 2, P ≤ 0.01).

Table 2. Target receivers of the interactive behaviors

Grade	Receiver(s)		
	Peers	Adults	Not spotted
Senior	46	3	1
Intermediate	22	4	2
Primary	12	1	1

3.3 Genders of Children's Interactive Behaviors' Initiators and Receivers During Medicine-Taking

Of the 92 valid samples of interactive behaviors, 80 interactive behaviors were between peers. The numbers of different types of behaviors in consideration of gender (male to male, male to female, male to both male and female, and the same is true for female) in 3 different grades respectively are shown in Table 3. The numbers of interactive behaviors targeted at the same gender/the opposite gender were checked by X^2 algorithm in the form of 2×2 crosstab (initiator(s)' gender $\times$ target receiver(s)' gender). The result showed that the there is a noticeable difference in frequency between the interactive behaviors targeted at the same gender and those targeted the opposite gender (X2 = 24.36, df = 2, P $\leq$ 0.01).

The numbers of interactive behaviors targeted at the same gender/the opposite gender were checked by X^2 algorithm on the basis of 3 different grades. The result showed that there was no perceptible difference between numbers of interactive behaviors targeted at the same gender and the opposite gender as for children in primary and intermediate classes (the relatively younger ones) (X^2 = 5.05, X^2 = 1.53, df = 2, P > 0.05), whereas there was a noticeable difference as for children in senior classes (the relatively elder ones) (X^2 = 19.69, df = 2, P < 0.01).

Table 3. Genders of children's interactive behaviors' initiators and target receivers

Initiator		Target receiver		
		Male	Female	Male and female
Senior	Male	15	4	2
	Female	3	21	1
Intermediate	Male	8	2	1
	Female	3	7	1
Primary	Male	3	2	1
	Female	1	3	2

3.4   Types of Children's Interactive Behaviors During Medicine-Taking

The numbers of different types of children's interactive behaviors are shown in Table 4, which were checked by X^2 algorithm and the result showed that there is a noticeable difference in frequency between different types of interactive behaviors (X^2 = 82.35, df = 4, P < 0.01).

In order to find out whether there is a correlation between the distributional proportion of different types of interactive behaviors and children's ages (grades), statistics from Table 3 were re-examined by X^2 algorithm in the form of 3×5 crosstab (grade $\times$ types of behavior), and the result showed that there is a remarkable difference between senior classes and intermediate classes between proportions of different types of interactive behaviors, (X^2 = 71.00, X^2 = 14.50, df = 4,P < 0.01) besides, there is a noticeable difference as well for children in primary classes (X^2 = 9.57, df = 4, P < 0.05).

Table 4. Types of children's interactive behaviors

Grade	Types				
	Sharing	Helping	Cooperation	Consolation	Public moralities
Senior	10	4	33	1	2
Intermediate	5	8	12	1	2
Primary	2	5	6	0	1

3.5 Target Receivers' Responses to Children's Interactive Behaviors During Medicine-Taking

Of the children's interactive behaviors targeted at peers and adults, target receivers' feedback (response) is shown in Table 5, which were checked by X^2 algorithm in the form of 2 × 3 crosstab (target receiver(s) × nature of feedback). The result showed that there is no perceptible difference between peers and adults in their responses to children's interactive behaviors.

In order to find out if there is a correlation between types of interactive behaviors and the nature of responses, being it positive, neutral or negative, 4 types (out of 5) of interactive behaviors and 3 types of responses were examined by X^2 algorithm in the form of 4 × 3 crosstab (Table 6), and the result showed that responses changed as types of interactive behaviors varied.

Further X^2 examinations indicated that there are significantly more neutral responses than either positive responses or negative responses as to peer-to-peer interactive behaviors of sharing, helping and consolation,(X2 = 14.00, X^2 = 12.18, X^2 = 3.50, df = 2, P < 0.01) and positive responses are significantly more than either negative or neutral responses as to peer-to-peer cooperative behaviors. (X^2 = 70.57, df = 2, P < 0.01) Children's interactive behaviors targeted at adults and nature of responses of adults are shown in Table 6.

Due to the scarcity of children's cooperative and consolatory behaviors targeted at adults, only adults' responses to behaviors of helping and sharing were examined by X^2 algorithm. The result showed there was no noticeable difference between adults' positive responses and neutral responses to children's interactive behaviors of helping and sharing (X2 = 0, X2 = 2, df = 1, P > 0.05).

Table 5. Target receivers' responses tochildren's interactive behaviors

Target receiver(s)	Nature of responses of target receiver(s)		
	Positive	Neutral	Negative
Peer(s)	51	28	1
Adult(s)	5	3	0

Table 6. Target receivers' responses to varied types of children's interactive behaviors

Target receiver(s)	Types of behaviors	Nature of responses of target receiver(s)		
		Positive	Neutral	Negative
Peer(s)	Sharing	4	12	0
	Helping	2	9	0
	Cooperation	44	4	1
	Consolation	1	3	0
Adult(s)	Sharing	2	0	0
	Helping	2	2	0
	Cooperation	0	0	0
	Consolation	1	1	0

4 Analysis and Deduction

Based on the aforementioned statistics and analysis, it was concluded that there was no difference in interactive behaviors during medicine-taking between children of opposite genders, no matter in primary classes, intermediate classes and senior classes in kindergartens, which was contrary to what questionnaires found out about children's interactive behaviors previously done by many Chinese parents and teachers. Many of previous studies on this issue subjectively presumed that, as expected in traditional biased eyes, girls were supposed to play the roles who have more interactive behaviors with others than boys were supposed to do. In many other cultures, girls are also expected to be more compassionate, sympathetic and sensitive, and therefore have more interactive behaviors, e.g. offering consolation to their friends who suffer from illness or proactively asking for caring when they themselves get sick. The stereotype has largely influenced Chinese teachers and parents when evaluating children's interactive behaviors. However, in practice, the difference in interactive behaviors caused by the difference of gender is far more less than people have expected.

The largest proportion, 86.96% of the young children's interactive behaviors were targeted at their peers of similar ages, while only 8.69% were targeted at adults and 4.69% were not clearly targeted, the chief reason of which is that the interactive behaviors this paper deals with mainly occur during medicine-taking. Children's direct interactive objects during medicine-taking are mainly their peers, and they are of the same social status, similar calibers and similar interests, so their interactive behaviors are more likely to be directed to their peers. On the other hand, the adults(teachers) have more "authority" over them in children's eyes, which leads to a sense of inequality. In daily life, as the youngsters who are supposed to follow their supervisors' instructions, children tend to behave submissively rather than proactively initiate an interactive behavior towards adults. So there are much fewer children's interactive behaviors directed to adults than those directed to peers.

Among all the children's interactive behaviors targeted at their peers, there are ones targeted at those of the same gender and ones targeted at those of the opposite gender, the proportion between which changed as the children grow older. In senior classes where the children are relatively elder, interactive behaviors targeted at the same gender are significantly more than those targeted at the opposite gender, while in intermediate classes and primary classes, there is no noticeable difference. This phenomenon illustrates the close relationship between the characteristics of interactive behaviors in regard of age and the development of gender role cognition. Psychologist Nancy Eisenberg (Ph.D., University of California) noted in her researches on the development of gender role cognition that the younger children before the age of 5 can only recognize his/her own gender, and they are in the development stage of gender identity. Children of the age of 5–7 can not only properly recognize his/her own gender, but also identify other humans' gender, thus reaching the maturity of gender recognition. Children's gender role behaviors are subject to their gender cognitive level. Judith G. Smetana (Ph. D., University of Rochester) also found that girls who have gained gender cognition maturity are more likely to choose children of the same gender as their playmates than those who are experiencing the development stage of gender identity. In this study, children in primary classes and intermediate classes are experiencing the development stage of gender identity, therefore they won't choose their interactive behaviors' subjects in reference to gender, which explains why there was no perceptible difference between the numbers of interactive behaviors targeted at the same gender and those targeted at the opposite gender. On the contrary, children in senior classes are psychological old enough to gain gender role cognitive maturity, so they are more likely to direct their interactive behaviors to their peers of the same gender.

There are many types of children's interactive behaviors, among which the behaviors of cooperation take up the largest proportion, while the occurrence of the other types of interactive behaviors has a much lower frequency. In this study, frequencies of different types of children's interactive behaviors vary remarkably, cooperative behaviors having the highest frequency 55.43%, sharing and helping behaviors with the same percentage 18.48%, behaviors of public moralities, 5.43%, and behaviors of consolation, 2.17%. There is a difference in distributions of different types of interactive behaviors between primary, intermediate and senior classes, which are largely illustrated by the fact that the percentage of cooperative behaviors among senior class children is significantly higher than those among intermediate class and primary class children. During observation it was noted that children's cooperative behaviors are nearly all spontaneous, and the increase uncooperative behaviors is due to the increase of cooperative games in daily communal environment where they live in. Restricted by psychological development level, primary class children have less sense of cooperation and awareness of self-discipline, plus the teachers' strict supervision during children taking medicine can also interfere with the communication and interaction among children. With more developed yet not so mature sense of cooperation and awareness of self-discipline, intermediate class students are more likely to be engaged in cooperative behaviors, but not as much as senior class children are. It can be deduced that as children grow older, cooperative behaviors among them tend to increase, and take up more and more proportion in daily behaviors.

5 Conclusions

This study has found out several characteristics of children's interactive behaviors in medicine-taking scenario in the context of communal life in kindergartens.

- There is no difference in interactive behaviors during medicine-taking between two opposite genders.
- Most of children's interactive behaviors during medicine-taking are targeted at their peers, and very few of them are targeted at adults (or can't be spotted).
- There is a difference between different age groups in frequencies of interactive behaviors during medicine-taking targeted at peers of the same gender and those targeted at the opposite gender. There is no perceptible difference between frequencies of interactive behaviors targeted at peers of the same gender and those targeted at the opposite gender among primary class children and intermediate class children (the relatively younger ones). But as children grow old, interactive behaviors targeted at peers of the same gender increase while those targeted at the opposite gender decrease.

- In the communal environment, different types of interactive behaviors occur at remarkably different frequencies, among which cooperative behaviors take the lead, and increase instantly as children grow older. Behaviors of helping and sharing follow as the second place and the third place, while behaviors of consolation and public moralities are the rarest to be seen.
- Frequencies of adults' positive and neutral responses to children's interactive behaviors during medicine-taking are close to each other, while peer's responses depend on the types of interactive behaviors. Specifically, peers respond positively towards cooperative behaviors, and respond neutrally towards behaviors of helping, sharing and consolation.

By statistical analysis and reasoning, this research summarized characteristics and elements of children's interactive behaviors during medicine-taking in communal life, and children's preferences to pills of varied colors. The results could be used as guidelines on the development of pediatric pharmaceutical technology, the perfection of children health management system, and development of better medicines tailor-made for children.

References

Yau, J., Smetana, J.G., Metzger, A.: Young Chinese children's authority concepts. Soc. Dev. **18**, 210–229 (2009)

Siegler, R.S., Deloache, J., Eisenberg, N., Miller, P.A.: How Children Develop. Worth Publishing Ltd., Duffield (2007)

Damon, W., Eisenberg, N.: Handbook of Child Psychology, Social, Emotional, and Personality Development. Wiley, New York (2006)

Berryman, J.C., Smythe, P.K., Taylor-Davies, A., Lamont, A.: Developmental Psychology and You. Wiley, New York (2002)

Framework of Health Monitoring Service for the Elderly Drivers Community

Se Jin Park[1,2,3](✉), Murali Subramaniyam[1,2](✉), Seunghee Hong[1,2], and Damee Kim[1,2]

[1] Korea Research Institute of Standards and Science, Daejeon, South Korea
{sjpark,hsh82622,dameeing}@kriss.re.kr,
murali.subramaniyam@gmail.com
[2] Electronics Telecommunication Research Institute, Daejeon, South Korea
[3] University of Science & Technology, Daejeon, South Korea

Abstract. Stroke is the most common causes of death in the elderly community. It is the second leading cause of death, accounting for a 6.24 million deaths in 2015. The stroke population, as well as world population, is aging. Stroke onset while driving threatens driver and public safety on roads. Already automakers are paying more attention to developing cars that could measure and monitor drivers' health status to protect the elderly population. The automobile is rapidly becoming a "thing" in the Internet of Things (IoT).

The purpose of this study is to successfully detect and generate alarms in cases of stroke onset while driving. The goal is achieved through the development of an elderly health monitoring system, which is controlled by hyper-connected self-machine learning engine. The components of the system are big data, real-time data monitoring, network security, and self-learning engine. A proactive elderly health monitoring system is involved with the active capture of the brain, cardio and body movement signals, signal analysis, communication, detection and warning process. This system has been considered as one of the main application areas of pervasive computing and biomedical applications. The method mentioned above and its frameworks will be discussed in this paper.

Keywords: Stroke onset · Elderly · Prediction · Wearable sensors

1 Introduction

Aging results from increasing longevity, and most importantly, declining fertility [1]. Population aging is taking place in nearly all the countries of the world. As age increases, older drivers become more conservative on the road. Age-related decline in cognitive function threatens safety and quality of life for an elder. As the population in the developed world is aging, so the number of older drivers is increasing [2–4]. Research on age-related driving concerns has shown that at around the age of 65 drivers face an increased risk of being involved in a vehicle crash. Three behavioral factors, in particular, may contribute to these statistics: poor judgment in making left-hand turns; drifting within the traffic lane, and decreased ability to change behavior in response to an unexpected or rapidly changing situation [5–8].

© Springer International Publishing AG 2017
C. Stephanidis (Ed.): HCII Posters 2017, Part II, CCIS 714, pp. 275–279, 2017.
DOI: 10.1007/978-3-319-58753-0_41

Stroke is the sudden death of brain cells due to lack of oxygen, caused by blockage of blood flow to the brain or rupture of blood vessels [9, 10]. Stroke is the second leading cause of death above the age of 60 years, and its population is increasing [10, 11]. The stroke symptoms are a weakness in the arm or leg or both on the same side, loss of balance, sudden headache, dizziness, coordination problems, vision problems, difficulty in speaking, and weakness in the face muscle [12–14]. Sudden stroke onset during driving poses a serious threat to the other drivers and the general public.

The Internet of Things (IoT) plays an important role in the development of connected vehicles, which offers cloud connectivity, vehicle-to-vehicle connectivity, smartphone integration, safety, security, and healthcare services. Recent developments show already automakers are paying attention to develop cars that could monitor driver's health status. Both luxury automakers and key global original equipment manufacturers are integrating healthcare services into their next-generation products [15]. The purpose of this study is to successfully detect and generate alarms in cases of stroke onset while driving. This paper focused on briefly explaining the conceptual idea and related information of the elderly healthcare services in-vehicle using IoT.

2 Framework of Health Monitoring Service

Hyper-connected self-machine learning engine controls an elderly health monitoring system (Fig. 1). The components of the system are big data, real-time data monitoring, network security, and self-learning engine. The knowledge base would have risk factors, medical health records, psychological factors, gait and motion patterns, and bio-signals. The old peoples' activities, physiological, and bio signals are monitored in real-time through wearable sensors. The self-machine learning engine would include multi-model learning and model generator. If the proposed system predicts stroke

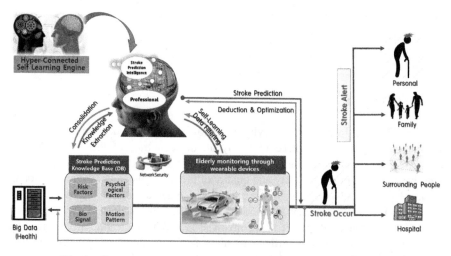

Fig. 1. Components of the proposed elderly health monitoring system

symptom above 90%, it will generate an alarm to family, the victim, people around the victim, and healthcare professionals. Then the victim will get the timely medical assistance.

Our proposed system is designed to get the rapid measurements required to monitor health status in a critical situation and in a cost effective way. The health status likes blood pressure, body temperature, heart rate, muscle activity, human brain activity, cardio activity, motion tracking, etc. are all very important to track down the healthcare status [16–18]. An IoT-based system is drastically reducing the costs and improving health by increasing the availability and quality of care [19–22]. Also, advancement in mobile gateway integrated with healthcare sensor can preferably be offered on a small, wearable and portable device, suitable for daily and continuous use, such as a smartphone or personal digital assistant [23–26]. Therefore, we employed specialized wearable sensors to monitor senior citizens physical and physiological activities. The portable sensors include motion sensors, EMG sensors, ECG sensor, and insole type foot sensors.

Already there are many developments in the wearables and embedded sensors to measure physiological and bio signals. Some of them are summarized here. An ECG monitoring system was introduced [27] comprised of six wearable textile-based electrodes are capable of providing e-health service via Bluetooth. An automotive seat [28] developed by Faurecia detects traveler's heart rate and breathing rhythm through unique types of embedded sensors. The Nottingham Trent University [29] developed a car seat with a capacitive sensor to detect traveler's heart rhythm. IPPOCRTE [30] proposed a steering wheel could measure vital parameters including body temperature, ECG, eye gaze, and pulse rate. Toyota also developed a smart steering wheel to monitor the driver's ECG [31].

3 Summary

The purpose of this study is to successfully detect and generate alarms in cases of sudden stroke onset while driving. The conceptual design of the elderly health monitoring system presented in this paper. The proposed system could predict stroke symptoms and generate an alarm. Thereby, the stroke victim will get the timely medical assistance.

Acknowledgments. This work was supported by the National Research Council of Science & Technology (NST) grant by the Korea government (MSIP) (No. CRC-15-05-ETRI).

References

1. Park, S.J., Subramaniyam, M., Kim, S.E., Hong, S.H., Lee, J.H., Jo, C.M.: Older driver's physiological response under risky driving conditions–overtaking, unprotected left turn. In: Duffy, V. (ed.) Advances in Applied Digital Human Modeling and Simulation. AISC, vol. 481, pp. 107–114. Springer International Publishing, Heidelberg (2017). doi:10.1007/978-3-319-41627-4_11

2. Statistics Korea (KoSTAT).: Korea's Population. http://kostat.go.kr
3. Andrews, E.C., Westerman, S.J.: Age differences in simulated driving performance: compensatory processes. Accid. Anal. Prev. **45**, 660–668 (2012)
4. Cohen, J.E.: Human population: the next half century. Science **302**, 1172–1175 (2003)
5. Park, S.J., Subramaniyam, M., Kim, S.E.: Psychophysiological characteristics of older drivers on highway using driving simulator. In: International Symposium on Affective Engineering, Kitakyushu, Japan (2016)
6. Park, S.J., Min, S.N., Lee, H., Subramaniyam, M.: A driving simulator study: elderly and younger driver's physiological, visual and driving behavior on intersection. In: IEA2015, Melbourne, Australia (2015)
7. Park, S.J., Subramaniyam, M., Moon, M.K., Kim, D.G.: Physiological Evaluation of Older Drivers' Emotional States While Driving with and Without Navigation in a Driving Simulator. SAE World Congress & Exhibition, Detroit (2013)
8. Moon, M.K., Subramaniyam, M., Park, S.J.: Older Driver's Physiological Responses During Last-Minute Braking in a Driving Simulator. SAE World Congress & Exhibition, Detroit (2013)
9. Hong, K.S., Bang, O.Y., Kang, D.W., Yu, K.H., Bae, H.J., Lee, J.S., Heo, J.H., Kwon, S.U., Oh, C.W., Lee, B.C., Kim, J.S., Yoon, B.W.: Stroke statistics in Korea: part 1, epidemiology and risk factors: a report from the Korean stroke society and clinical research center for stroke. J. Stroke **15**, 2–20 (2013)
10. Park, S.J., Subramaniyam, M., Kim, S.E., Hong, S., Lee, J.H., Jo, C.M., Seo, Y.: Development of the elderly healthcare monitoring system with IoT. In: Duffy, Vincent G., Lightner, N. (eds.) Advances in Human Factors and Ergonomics in Healthcare. AISC, vol. 482, pp. 309–315. Springer, Cham (2017). doi:10.1007/978-3-319-41652-6_29
11. Korea National Statistical Office. Annual Report on the Cause of Death Statistics (2008)
12. Yavuzer, G., Kucukdeveci, A., Arasl, T., Elhan, A.: Rehabilitation of stroke patients: clinical profile and functional outcome. Am. J. Phys. Med. Rehabil. **80**, 250–255 (2001)
13. Yavuzer, G., Gok, H., Ergin, S.: Spatiotemporal and kinematic gait characteristics of stroke patients. J. Rheum. Med. Rehabil. **12**, 148–152 (2001)
14. Kramers de Quervain, I.A., Simon, S.R., Leurgans, S., Pease, W.S., McAllister, D.: Gait patterns in the early recovery period after stroke. J. Bone Joint Surg. **78**, 1506–1514 (1996)
15. Park, S.J., Subramaniyam, M., Hong, S., Kim, D., Yu, J.: Conceptual design of the elderly healthcare services in-vehicle using IoT. SAE Technical paper (No. 2017-01-1647) (2017)
16. Abbate, S., Avvenuti, M., Light, J.: Usability study of a wireless monitoring system among Alzheimer's disease elderly population. Int. J. Telemed. Appl. **2014**, 1–8 (2014)
17. Chakraborty, S., Ghosh, S.K., Jamthe, A., Agrawal, D.P.: Detecting mobility for monitoring patient with Parkinson's disease at home using RSSI in a wireless sensor network. In: The 4th International Conference on Ambient Systems, Networks and Technologies, the 3rd International Conference on Sustainable Energy Information Technology, vol. 19, pp. 956–961 (2013)
18. Noureddine, B., Fethi, G.R.: Bluetooth portable device for ECG and patient motion monitoring. Nat. Technol. **4**, 19 (2011)
19. Sannino, G., Pietro, G.: An advanced mobile system for indoor patients monitoring. In: 2nd International Conference on Networking and Information Technology IPCSIT, 17, pp. 144–149 (2011)
20. Lustrek, M., Gjoreski, H., Kozina, S., Cvetkovic, B., Mirchevska, V., Gams, M.: Detecting falls with location sensors and accelerometers. In: Proceeding of the Twenty-Third Innovative Applications of Artificial Intelligence Conference, pp. 1662–1667 (2011)

21. Kaczmarek, M., Ruminski, J., Bujnowski, A.: Multimodal platform for continuous monitoring of elderly and disabled. In: 2011 Federated Conference on Computer Science and Information Systems (FedCSIS), pp. 393–400 (2011)
22. Yu, M., Rhuman, A., Naqvi, S.M., Wang, L., Chambers, J.: A posture recognition-based fall detection system for monitoring an elderly person in a smart home environment. IEEE Trans. Inf. Technol. Biomed. **6**, 1274–1286 (2012)
23. Nasution, A., Emmanuel, S.: Intelligent video surveillance for monitoring elderly in home environments. In: IEEE 9th Workshop on Multimedia Signal Processing, pp. 203–206 (2007)
24. Huang, Y., Miaou, S., Liao, T.: A human fall detection system using an omni-directional camera in practical environments for health care applications. In: MVA2009 IAPR Conference on Machine Vision Applications, pp. 455–458 (2009)
25. Webber, S., Porter, M.: Monitoring mobility in older adults using Global Positioning System (GPS) watches and accelerometers – a feasibility study. J. Aging Phys. Act. **17**, 455–467 (2009)
26. Shahriyar, R., Bari, M.F., Kundu, G., Ahamed, S.I., Akbar, M.M.: Intelligent mobile health monitoring system (IMHMS). Int. J. Control Automation **2**, 13–28 (2009)
27. Yang, C.M., Wu, C.C., Chou, C.M., Yang, T.L.: Vehicle driver's ECG and sitting posture monitoring system. In: Proceedings of the 9th International Conference on Information Technology and Applications in Biomedicine (2009)
28. http://www.faurecia.com/en/innovation/discover-our-innovations/active-wellness
29. Nottingham Trend University. https://www4.ntu.ac.uk/apps/news/160600-15/Car_seats_which_detect_when_drivers_are_falling_asleep.aspx
30. Parti, D.: Ippocrate: a new steering wheel monitoring system (2015). https://www.politesi.polimi.it/
31. Hutchings, E.: Toyota's ECG steering wheel monitors your heart rate as you drive. PSFK Innovation (2011)

Adaptation Monitoring System Preventing Fall Down from a Bed for Individual Difference of Behavior

Hironobu Satoh[1(✉)] and Kyoko Shibata[2]

[1] Kochi National College of Technology, Monobeotsu 200-1,
Nangoku, Kochi, Japan
satoh@ee.kochi-ct.ac.jp
[2] Kochi University of Technology,
Miyanokuchi 185, Tosayamada, Kami, Kochi, Japan
shibata.kyoko@kochi-tech.ac.jp
http://www.kochi-ct.ac.jp, http://www.kochi-tech.ac.jp

Abstract. Elderly sometime fall down from a bed and fractured their femur. Fall accident must be avoided to improve the quality of life. To solve this problem, we proposed monitoring system preventing fall down using DBN (Deep Belief Network) and Kinect.

However, there is a problem that the proposed system was not able to adapt individual difference of behavior leading to fall down from a bed for social deployment.

In this paper, it is proposed that monitoring system preventing fall down from a bed is adapted for individual difference of behaviors. Therefore, we proposed a learning method to adapt for individual difference of behaviors. In other words, distinctive behaviors are learned by monitoring system. The point of the discussion of this paper is behavior recognition of target. It does not the discussion about how to prevent fall down after dangerous behavior detected.

In the experiment, capability of the proposed learning method is evaluated.

Keywords: Awaking behavior detection system · Deep learning · Kinect

1 Introduction

Elderly sometime fall down from a bed and fractured their femur. Fall accident must be avoided to improve the quality of life. According to the health care workers, the subject individual specifically behaves before monitored person fall out of bed. To solve this problem, we have proposed a system using Web camera [1–5]. In the dark room at night, the detection ability of previous system is low, because the brightness adjustment processing of a Web camera is not able to adjust brightness of the dark room. It is a problem that the previous system is not able to use in the dark room at night.

© Springer International Publishing AG 2017
C. Stephanidis (Ed.): HCII Posters 2017, Part II, CCIS 714, pp. 280–284, 2017.
DOI: 10.1007/978-3-319-58753-0_42

Therefore, we proposed monitoring system preventing fall down using DBN (Deep Belief Network) [6] and Kinect [7]. The purpose of this research is appreciating conceptually human behaviors. From the previous studies, it had obtained a high detection rate with respect to individuals. However, there is a problem that the proposed system was not able to adapt individual difference of behavior leading to fall down from a bed for social deployment.

In this paper, it is proposed that monitoring system preventing fall down from a bed is adapted for individual difference of behaviors. Therefore, we proposed a learning method to adapt for individual difference of behaviors. In other words, distinctive behaviors are learned by monitoring system. The point of the discussion of this paper is behavior recognition of target. It does not the discussion about how to prevent fall down after dangerous behavior detected.

In the experiment, capability of the proposed learning method is evaluated.

2   Behaviors of Monitored Person

In this research, the behavior of monitored person is classified into two states. One is safe behavior. Another is dangerous behavior. A state of lie on a bed is defined as a safe behavior. A state of all fours, sitting, flapping feet and flapping arm is defined as a dangerous behavior. Figure 1 shows examples of safe behaviors. Figure 2 shows examples of dangerous behavior. Figures 1 and 2 is measured by Kinect.

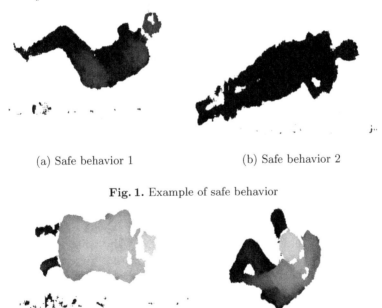

(a) Safe behavior 1   (b) Safe behavior 2

Fig. 1. Example of safe behavior

(a) Dangerous behavior 1   (b) Dangerous behavior 2

Fig. 2. Example of dangerous behavior

3   Monitoring System

3.1   Detection Processing

Figure 3 shows proposed monitoring system flow.

The proposed system is consisted with a PC (personal computer) and Kinect. Kinect, which measured distance between Kinect and monitored person, is developed by Microsoft. Target's behavior is measured by Kinect and send a PC via USB (universal serial bus). The program of proposed system is running on a PC. The program converts measured data to input data of DBN and detects dangerous behaviors. A target's body is extracted by the preprocessing using a threshold, which is set height of bed. The extracted data by preprocessing are normalized at one between two thresholds. The normalized data are inputted in DBN to recognize monitored person's behaviors.

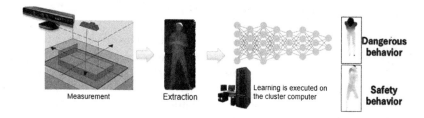

Fig. 3. Installation of Kinect

3.2   Proposed Learning Method

The proposed learning method is described as follows. First, initial learning is executed, in order to learn the variation of physique and basic behavior of targets. Second, user's distinctive behavior is collected from the individual monitoring system. Where, the collected data is consisted of data suggested by user and monitoring system using learned DBN with initial leaning data. And, learning data is constructed for each user using a collected data. Finally, continuous learning is executed using constructed learning data for each user.

4   Experiment

The proposed learning method is evaluated. Five subjects participate in the experiment. Each five subjects behave distinctively on a bed. And, behavers of subjects are measuring by Kinect. DBN, that Initial learning is completed, is used for the continuous learning. Where, collected data by the proposed procedure is used for the continuous learning. From the experimental results are shown as follows. When the initial learning is completed, correctly rate of the dangerous behavior is 83.2%(208/250) and rate of the safe behavior is 84.8%(212/250) (Table 1). After proposed learning method is executed, correctly rate of the dangerous behavior is 81.6%(204/250) and rate of the safe behavior is 91.2%(212/250) (Table 2).

Table 1. Detection rate (initila learning)

Subject	Dangerous behavior [%]	Safe behavior [%]	Total [%]
a	80.0(44/55)	64.0(32/50)	76.0(76/100)
b	94.0(47/55)	84.0(42/50)	89.0(89/100)
c	58.0(29/55)	92.0(46/50)	75.0(75/100) 1
d	76.0(38/55)	96.0(48/50)	86.0(86/100)
e	100.0(50/55)	88.0(44/50)	94.0(94/100)
Total	83.2(208/250)	84.8(212/250)	84.0(420/500)

Table 2. Detection rate (proposed learning method)

Subject	Dangerous behavior [%]	Safe behavior [%]	Total [%]
a	70.0(35/55)	92.0(46/50)	81.0(81/100)
b	90.0(45/55)	92.0(46/50)	91.0(91/100)
c	68.0(34/55)	78.0(39/50)	73.0(73/100) 1
d	80.0(40/55)	96.0(48/50)	88.0(88/100)
e	100.0(50/55)	98.0(49/50)	99.0(99/100)
Total	81.6(204/250)	91.2(228/250)	86.4(432/500)

5   Conclusion

In order to prevent a fall down from a bed, we have been developing the monitoring system. However, there is a problem that the proposed system was not able to adapt individual difference of behavior leading to fall down from a bed for social deployment. To solve this problem, we proposed learning method of the monitoring system.

From the experimental results, ability of the proposed learning method is confirmed. It was confirmed that the monitoring system can adapt to the characteristic behavior of each individual.

References

1. Ikeda, R., Satoh, H., Takeda, F.: Development of awaking behavior detection system nursing inside the house. In: International Conference on Intelligent Technology 2006, pp. 65–70 (2006)
2. Matubara, T., Satoh, H., Takeda, F.: Proposal of an awaking detection system adopting neural network in hospital use. In: World Automation Congress 2008 (2008)
3. Satoh, H., Takeda, F., Shiraishi, Y., Ikeda, R.: Development of a awaking behavior detection system using a neural network. IEEJ Trans. EIS 128(11), 1649–1656 (2008)

4. Yamanaka, N., Satoh, H., Shiraishi, Y., Matsubara, T., Takeda, F.: Proposal of the awakening detection system using neural network and it's verification. The 52nd The Institute of Systems, Control and Information Engineers (2008)

5. Satoh, H., Takeda, F.: Verification of the effectiveness of the online tuning system for unknown person in the awaking behavior detection system. In: Omatu, S., Rocha, M.P., Bravo, J., Fernández, F., Corchado, E., Bustillo, A., Corchado, J.M. (eds.) IWANN 2009. LNCS, vol. 5518, pp. 272–279. Springer, Heidelberg (2009). doi:10. 1007/978-3-642-02481-8_39

6. Yoshua, B., Pascal, L., Dan, P., Hugo, L.: Greedy layer-wise training of deep networks. Adv. Neural Inf. Process. Syst. **19**, 153–160 (2006)

7. Satoh, H., Shibata, K., Masaki, T.: Development of an awaking behavior detection system with kinect. In: Stephanidis, C. (ed.) HCI 2014. CCIS, vol. 435, pp. 496–500. Springer, Cham (2014). doi:10.1007/978-3-319-07854-0_86

Development of an Interactive Social Tool for Mexican Young Adults to Lower and Prevent Overweight and Obesity

Diana M. Sepúlveda$^{(\boxtimes)}$, César Delgado, Luis Alvarado, and Sergio Zepeda

Master in Design, Information and Communication, Universidad Autónoma Metropolitana – Cuajimalpa, Mexico, Mexico
dcg.disb@gmail.com, cdelgado.adc@gmail.com, luis0@outlook.com, jzepeda@correo.cua.uam.mx

Abstract. In this paper we analyze qualitative factors that are affecting employees from 29 to 35 years old that work in Santa Fe, a corporate sector located in Mexico City, that are leading to overweight and obesity problems. The research phase got as a result that there is a lack of information appropriation towards alimentary matters, mainly caused by their lack of spare time and heavy work loads. Having this in consideration, the proposal is an interactive social tool to aim this lack of information appropriation. Based on User-Centered Design, Information Visualization, Situated and Significant Learning, the tool displays interactive messages on a table, through sensors and video mapping, allowing corporate employees to assimilate information while eating at their work spaces. Methods used in prototyping and testing were helpful to evaluate not only the tool as in its hardware, also the relevance of the messages displayed and the graphic solution chosen to show them (infographics, diagrams, text).

Keywords: Media-based social interaction · User-Centered Design · Information visualization · Usability · Health information technologies · Health communication · Obesity · Interdiscipline · Information appropriation

1 Introduction

Overweight and obesity are health problems that are affecting life quality of mexicans and national economic development. They are also risk factors to develop chronic non communicable diseases and are responsible of millions of deaths annually. World Health Organization (WHO), defines these terms as an abnormal or excessive fat accumulation that present a risk to health.

In Sect. 2, we analyze the State of the Art related to campaigns to lower and/or prevent overweight and obesity in Mexico and Latin America; also strategies and tools used to aim these problems, such as technologic devices, apps, online programs and even traditional mass media approaches.

The Sect. 3 concerns to the contextual study and the qualitative research. This section explains the process and methodology followed for gathering information, understanding corporate employees needs and coming up with a proposal.

© Springer International Publishing AG 2017
C. Stephanidis (Ed.): HCII Posters 2017, Part II, CCIS 714, pp. 285–292, 2017.
DOI: 10.1007/978-3-319-58753-0_43

In Sect. 4, we present the prototype and content developing, technical specifications and design considerations.

Next section explains first results of the evaluation phase: Usability and User Experience (UX) testing, with final users. Finally, conclusions and future work.

2 Background and Related Work

In 2014, the OCED[1] Health Statistics [10] shown that Mexico was the country with more cases of obesity around the world. In November 2016, Secretaría de Salud, a Mexican Federal Institution of Public Health Care, launched a countrywide epidemiologic warning because of obesity. Most of actual national campaigns are built with massive communication messages that hampers information appropriation from specific groups population.

According to WHO's 2016 Global Report on Urban Health [13], there are some factors related to urbanization that affect and increase overweight and obesity cases: transportation issues (use of motorized vehicles because of distance or geographic inaccessibility); longer commutes and work days; replacement of home made meals by industrialized and street foods.

In a first approach to the problem, we reviewed the State of Art, mainly with Mexican population, but also researches and papers from abroad, that could gave us a glance of how overweight and obesity affected other countries. Also the reviewing of public and federal strategies and a selection of existing tools commonly used[2].

Most of the researches [1–3, 5, 8] urge Mexican Government to promote effective and efficient strategies to prevent overweight and obesity and to evaluate their results. One of the problems is that every federal prevention campaign that has seen light in Mexico falls into oblivion because of the change of political parties in Government. There is no concern for evaluating past strategies and campaigns.

Statistics from Mexican and International entities show the importance of the problem and its constant growth, but most of the researches are based on quantitative approaches [3, 4, 6, 9] difficulting the understanding of the problem in differents contexts. This generalization of information based on quantitative results, leads to strategies and campaigns based on mass-communication, difficulting messages appropriation from specific groups. Qualitative approaches in research are needed to understand specific groups behaviours and problems to propose functional tools and messages for them.

3 Contextual Study and Qualitative Research

We integrated a research team from different disciplines: Information Technologies, Information Design and Communication. We worked with 58 corporate employees from 29 to 35 years old with medium-high socioeconomic status with jobs at a

---

[1] Organisation for Economic Co-operation and Development.

[2] Fitness Apps, Weight Watchers and coaching programs, gadgets.

corporative sector from Mexico City, Santa Fe, an urban area that went from being the city's dumping site to one of the most exclusive and wealthy sectors. We selected this geographic and demographic sample because of the raising of the problem in this group, according to mexican federal inquiries[3], and the urban factors described by WHO in the background section.

The research methodology was divided in two stages: the research phase and the prototyping phase. In the research phase, we used ethnographic techniques for qualitative information gathering through interviews, surveys, discourse analysis, contextual and participatory observation. After that, we analyzed information to detect which factors were more relevant for corporate employees, where we identified cognitive, affective, physical and social factors involved in alimentary decision making. In spite of the multi-variable problem we were facing, some variables were highlighted by almost all participants.

Results obtained showed which variables were the most important for alimentary decision making, such as time (subordinated to amount of work load and an average of 10–12 h worked daily) and peatonal accessibility to food establishments (made in a delimitation of a block from the office location). Also, times spent for food consumption, usually less than 1 h (not only for eating, as well for finding an establishment, ordering and returning to office). Corporate employees perceive that they have poor/regular knowledge in alimentary matters and they feel they can't learn by themselves because online information is too chaotic and they don't have time to invest in their alimentary education. They consider their close social circles important to achieve behavioral changes, especially the ones that involve food (Fig. 1).

Fig. 1. Informal street vendors are a popular way to get food in Santa Fe.

---

[3] Young adults with medium/high income at urban locations, mainly Mexico City, *Health and Nutrition National Inquiry 2012.*

4 Prototype

Once, factors and needs were detected, we were able to propose a tool. Our hypothesis is that communicating relevant messages through pertinent design and interactive technologies, could be more valuable for people to appropriate information. Our objective was to develop a tool to help them to learn about alimentary matters so they could prevent or lower overweight and obesity, but keeping in mind their lack of time due to their job responsibilities.

Our proposal focuses in the lack of alimentary information appropriation and the need of collaborative work to achieve goals, like information dissemination through community-guided strategies adapted to their lifestyles, specially in their tight schedules because of their workload and their geographic delimitation.

Through an interactive table with video mapping at their work space, we help corporate employees to learn about alimentary matters, to identify their own alimentary patterns and to relate them with their own everyday situations. Guided by User-Centered Design (UCD), User Experience (UX) and Data Visualization techniques, we worked in an iterative process with users to develop messages according to their needs, interests and their previous knowledge about alimentary information [7, 11]. This last part was really important to consider according to situated and significant learning, so the users can actually appropriate information. It doesn't matter how well messages are presented if people don't have cognitive references to link with the new information.

In terms of implementation, we divided the tool in two sections, the first one is the Electronic Technology, and this includes all the electronic elements that allow the interactivity on the table through wires and sensors. We used Arduino One, as the center of the system because of its open source nature. The arduino board controls all activities and events of our device.

The software that controls the arduino board its activated from a computer attached to the table. The code lives inside the computer in an integrated development environment (IDE) and is loaded into the Arduino board to enable events coded. The interaction is possible through pressure sensors attached inside of 3D printed, custom made tablecloths, and connected to the Arduino, and give the signal that someone put a dish over the table. This action triggers the displaying of the information using the same table as the projecting surface. The sensors connected to the Arduino, allow the communication through MIDI language between the Arduino software and the display technology.

The second section, the Display Technology, is used for information visualization and consists in the usage of a projector device to allow the projection over uncommon surfaces, called video mapping, a technique usually used in arts and entertainment. The projector is set with a vertical orientation to enable the displaying of the information over the table, and creating a multimedia environment, while corporate employees have their meals. The information is controlled and distributed using VDMX5, a specialized software for video and visual arts. This software allows an easy mapping of the table's surface and distributes the graphic elements in a practical way, allowing users to control and interact with the messages displayed. Any kind of projector can be used, specially if it connects via Bluetooth to avoid more wires.

As part of the prototype, we also designed and constructed the table were the tool was implemented on, so we considered special slots to place hardware and wiring but it is planned to fit in any kind of table (Fig. 2).

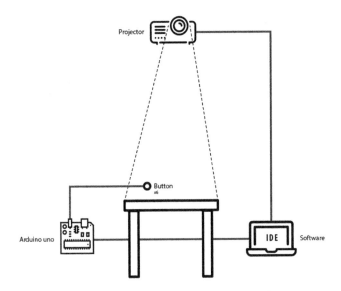

Fig. 2. Connection diagram for implementation.

4.1   Visualization

Based on findings in the research process, we worked with Nutrition specialists to develop a database of messages grouped according to objectives of habits modification: (a) To increase plain water intake, (b) To increase fresh fruits and vegetables intake, (c) To decrease industrialized meals and fast food consumption, (d) To decrease sugar consumption, (e) To increase homemade traditional food preparation, (f) To learn alimentary terms, meanings and portions, (g) To reduce frustration while trying to change alimentary habits.

Using Natural Language Processing (NLP) techniques [12] we identified some linguistic characteristics our population shared, such as commonly used vocabulary, slang, emojis, punctuation marks and symbols, such as the hashtag symbol. With this information we gathered a dictionary to establish they way we had to design messages, in order to be meaningful for corporate employees. NLP was also helpful to determine the length of sentences measured in amount of words[4].

---

[4] Between 7 and 12 words per sentence.

Seventy two messages were made for the prototyping phase that were displayed in different ways, depending on their purpose: infographics, charts and tables, text, animation and diagrams. Graphic styles of messages were determined based on interests and trends detected on the research phase, giving every message a particular personality. In Table 1 we show some examples of messages proposed. Slang and popular sayings are lost in English translation, but they explain the general idea.

Table 1. Examples of messages proposed.

Message in Spanish	Message in English
Intenta un cambio de hábito a la vez. Cuando seas master en ese, incorpora uno nuevo. Puede ser semanal, quincenal o cuando estés listo. #JustDoIt	Try changing one habit at a time. When you master that one, you can try a new one. It can be weekly, every 15 days or whenever you are ready. #JustDoIt
Desayuno Ganador: Menos azúcar, más poder. Échate mejor unos huevitos, unas tostadas con aguacate o frijolitos.	Winner's Breakfast: Less sugar, more power. It is better to eat some eggs, toasts with avocado or beans.
Que tus tortillas sean de maíz para que la fuerza esté contigo. May taquitos be with you.	Your tortillas must be made with corn so the force may be with you. May taquitos be with you.

5 First Results

To place the tool on a working space where corporate employees do routinary activities was perceived as a good decision, mainly because it adapts to their lifestyle. At a first evaluation, people wished they could interact more with messages, not only to select going to the next or previous message. They found messages to be appealing and easy to remember, and probably to learn, through using the tool in a repetitive way. Also, people evaluated messages timing (if they were displayed enough time). Time spent in each message needs to vary dependending on how complex information on them is; infographics, for example, needed more time due the amount of elements and abstraction. We have to consider that some users read slower than others. In few seconds, messages in hashtags were easier to remember that longer sentences. Dividing messages in bullets helped for a better idea assimilation.

We also tested the tool in a prototype table made by us and with capacity for two persons, but we intend the tool to be adaptable for any kind of table, specially for more users to enrich interactions between them and to spread what they learned mouth-to-mouth with their immediate circle (Fig. 3).

We need to solve some problems, like avoid using wires to connect the device to a computer and to the projector. There are new devices, such as projectors for smartphones, that could help us with wireless connections.

Individual silicone tablecloths were suggested to contain the pressure sensors because of their material's flexibility and heat resistance.

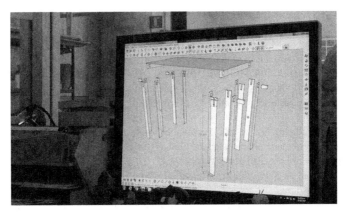

Fig. 3. Table prototyping with Medium-density fibreboard (MDF).

6 Conclusion

We conclude that lifestyles focused on professional responsibilities have affected other personal areas, such as health care, mainly in a preventive way. Alimentary decision making is based in consensus, this means, they decide what to eat with their colleagues. This lateral influence is an important factor to consider when trying to enhance alimentary habits or to disseminate information. Spatial appropriation through interaction and teamwork as a community is helpful in learning processes.

At the beginning of the research we thought an app could be a helpful tool, but through the ethnographic exercises we noticed that corporate employees didn't want that, mainly because it required an extra effort from them to use it and also required time from them, so it could really work.

We strongly believe more qualitative studies are needed to solve mass problems by aiming specific population at a time. It is vital for developing effective strategies to know the user in every way: their needs, habits, wishes, feelings.

Our prototype is a first approach to a different kind of strategy, besides the ones used by Government towards health care, no only in the tool by itself, but also in approaching an specific group usually ignored by alimentary campaigns. Everything was developed specially for them to fulfill their particular needs.

In a future work, we want to enhance hardware so it can be easier to merge with the dining spaces, and not to require special features in the furniture. Also to develop a website to gather all information there, so if someone wants to learn more, he or she could access that information anytime and anywhere.

References

1. Amancio, O., Ortigoza, J., Durante, I.: Obesity. Seminar: Medicine's Actual Practice. Universidad Nacional Autónoma de México. Mexico (2007). http://www.facmed.unam.mx/sms/seam2k1/2007/may_01_ponencia.html

2. Barquera, S., Campos, I., et al.: Obesity Prevalence in Mexican Adults, ENSANUT 2012. Salud Pública de México, vol. 55, 2nd supplement. Mexico (2013)
3. Comisión Federal de Mejora Regulatoria. The Problem of Obesity in Mexico: Diagnosis and Regulatory Actions to Deal with it. Mexico (2012). http://www.cofemer.gob.mx/Varios/Adjuntos/01.10.2012/COFEMER_PROBLEMA_OBESIDAD_EN_MEXICO_2012.pdf
4. Dimitropoulos, G., Toulany, A., et al.: A qualitative study on the experiences of young adults with eating disorders transferring from pediatric to adult care. Eat. Dis. **23**(2), 144–162 (2015)
5. Gómez, H., Fullman, N., et al.: Dissonant health transition in the states of Mexico, 1990–2013: a systematic analysis for the Global Burden of Disease Study 2013. The Lancet (2016). http://dx.doi.org/10.1016/S0140-6736(16)31773-1
6. Instituto Nacional de Salud Pública. Health and Nutrition National Inquiry, Mexico (2012). http://ensanut.insp.mx/
7. Lazar, J., Heidi, J., Hochheiser, H.: Research Methods in Human Computer Interaction, 1st edn. Wiley, Glasgow (2010)
8. Radilla, C., Vega, S., et al.: Prevalence of Risky Alimentary Behaviour and Its Association with Anxiety and the Nutritional Status in Teenagers from Technical-Junior Highs in Distrito Federal. Communal Nutrition Spanish Magazine, Mexico (2015)
9. Secretaría de Salud. National Strategy for Overweight, Obesity and Diabetes Prevention and Control. Mexico (2013). http://promocion.salud.gob.mx/dgps/descargas1/estrategia/Estrategia_con_portada.pdf
10. Organisation for Economic Co-operation and Development. OECD Health Statistics 2014 (2014). https://www.oecd.org/centrodemexico/medios/Briefing%20note%20-%20Mexico%202014.pdf
11. Pérez, S.: User Interfaces: Human-Computer Interaction. Universidad Autónoma Metropolitana, Cuajimalpa. Mexico (2014). http://computacion.cs.cinvestav.mx/ ∼ sperez/cursos/ui/Interaccion.pdf
12. Torres, J., Sánchez, C., Villatoro, E.: Online laboratory for document automatic processing. J. Res. Comput. Sci. **72**, 23–36 (2014). http://www.rcs.cic.ipn.mx/2014_72/Laboratorio%20en%20linea%20para%20el%20procesamiento%20automatico%20de%20documentos.pdf
13. World Health Organization. Global report on urban health: equitable, healthier cities for sustainable development. Geneva (2016). http://www.who.int/kobe_centre/measuring/urban-global-report/ugr_full_report.pdf

Wellness Programs: Wearable Technologies Supporting Healthy Habits and Corporate Costs Reduction

Marcos Souza, Taynah Miyagawa$^{(\boxtimes)}$, Paulo Melo,
and Francimar Maciel

Samsung SIDIA, Manaus, Brazil
{marcos.muniz, taynah.mello,
paulo.melo, francimar.m}@samsung.com

Abstract. Studies suggest improvements in the employees' quality of life, as well as costs reduction with health and absenteeism, and productivity increase. This article investigates the main characteristics of workplace wellness programs, their prevalence, impact on employees' health and medical costs, facilitators of their success, and the role of incentives in such programs. Presenting case study results from the use of wearable devices in support of a corporate wellness program, which through a chatbot manual and a simple competition system managed to promote engagement and satisfaction by participants, and signals opportunities for further study Use of these devices as a tool for health promotion within companies.

Keywords: Wellness · Wearable · Health · Habit

1 Introduction

Wearable devices are gadgets, or technological artifacts, that can be worn by users [1]. They are deeply associated to the connected-self idea, normally using Bluetooth technology to pair with smartphones and built with a great number of sensors. These sensors are able to collect various types of data from the user's body and the environment. Recently, wearable devices have been used to support common people achieve well-being goals, such as: staying active, losing weight or even keeping track of their current habits [2].

In recent times, there has been some debate about workplace health promotion programs [3] – also known as wellness programs – and whether they represent a good investment or not for the companies that sponsor them. In fact, some programs are successful while others fail but, most of the times, those results are related to how these programs are designed and executed. Furthermore, research shows that it is necessary to identify solutions that encourage employees to seek healthier habits – this is motivated by the high maintenance costs of health insurance, and the high number of medical clearance by employees [4].

There is a great expectation from the market for such problems to be improved by a higher application of wearable technology. Digital health can help with the challenges

© Springer International Publishing AG 2017
C. Stephanidis (Ed.): HCII Posters 2017, Part II, CCIS 714, pp. 293–300, 2017.
DOI: 10.1007/978-3-319-58753-0_44

of achieving a healthier lifestyle because it is cheap, scalable, and mainly because it has the audience's approval. Even if this involves privacy issues, the majority of people are willing to share data for personal and public health, including health history, physical activity, and genetic information [5]. Thus, it is believed that the employers' engagement will increase with the use of wearable devices, assuming that this is the main challenge to the successful application of wellness programs [6].

This work investigates the adoption of wearable technologies are useful as a tool for improving participants' engagement and building a healthier corporate culture. The focus is to bring an analysis of the literature by pointing out advantages, needs and strategies for the development of successful wellbeing programs. The study's main hypothesis is that the usage of wearable technologies are powerful tools for wellness pro-grams in companies because they are less intrusive and allow greater interaction among stakeholders, higher information accuracy and a better performance visualization for those involved.

2 Wearable Devices

Most wearable devices are wrist worn, but an increasing number of devices have emerged in the market with a less intrusive technology format, even taking the form of clothes and jewelry [2]. Currently, wearable devices are found in the following formats: smartwatches, fitness trackers, sport watches, head-mounted displays, smart clothing and smart jewelry. Those devices are equipped with several sensors that allow them to measure a great amount of data, such as: number of steps, heartbeat, body temperature and cardiorespiratory fitness. Furthermore, products that have motion sensors can even monitor full sessions of physical activities. When connected to a smartphone, wearable devices can capture even more data.

By providing this kind and quantity of data, wearable devices are considered to be a powerful tool for chronic patients that suffer from cancer or epilepsy, for instance. Additionally, due to its appealing product design, wearable devices have become a promising tool for regular users (without any health impairment) in wellness programs on large companies.

3 Health Promotion

According to findings from 2015, the United States is struggling with an epidemic of chronic diseases caused by unhealthy lifestyles [5]. Inactivity, poor nutrition, tobacco use, and frequent alcohol consumption are among the behaviors that contribute to higher rates of cardiovascular disease, diabetes, arthritis, and cancer. In this scenario, wellness programs pose as an important tool to improve people's wellbeing. The study also shows that if the interest in wellness programs continues to grow, employees may stay more engaged in the long term (if the program is not mandated or too intrusive).

Health insurance companies are also interested to enhance employees' wellness. The health insurance market is one of the largest in the world with an estimated 618 million people covered by private and/or corporate health insurance alone [6]. This number is projected to grow to 920 million by 2020 [7]. However, the high costs related to chronic diseases are putting financial pressure on healthcare and insurance providers, with costs growing worldwide. By the year 2020, it is expected to have 70% of healthcare expenses coming from chronic diseases, and 30% will be up to health insurance companies to cover [8]. This represents an untenable scenario for this market, demonstrating the need to seek tools to provide scalable programs for reducing costs and increasing their return of investment.

4 Corporate Wellness Experiment

With the assumption that social interaction can function as an effective design strategy in encouraging individuals to be more physically active [10], an experiment was conducted. This experiment was planned by SIDIA[1]'s Usability Lab team in order to evaluate – through two groups of employees – the difference between the participants' engagement levels. For this, one group used wearable devices and smartphones and the other used only smartphones.

The experiment's first steps were to define the number of participants and their profiles, and to decide the experiment duration (7 days). After this, an online survey was shared with SIDIA's employees to identify possible participants. The survey's introduction made it clear that, although shared through a corporate e-mail, this was an experiment made by the UX team and not a real wellness action made by the company. Answered by 115 employees, the survey was open for two business days and after it was closed, participant profiles were mapped (Table 1).

Table 1. Online sample of self-assessment by healthy profile

Considering your eating habits and physical activities, do you consider yourself a healthy person?		
Options	Percentage	Number of users
Totally healthy	6,1%	7
Healthy	25,2%	29
Partially healthy	45,2%	52
Unhealthy	23,5%	27
Total answers		115

Highlights from this phase results were:

- 30% of employees say that they do not engage in physical activities and claim to have no interest in healthy food.
- Most users claim that time and costs are the main difficulties for those looking to have healthier eating habits or to perform physical activities.

---

[1] Samsung R&D Institute Brazil, located in Manaus.

- The lack of time is the main factor that makes it difficult or impossible to maintain healthy habits.
- 30% of employees say do not perform physical activities.
- 23% have a nutritionist's specialist support.
- 48% read blog and websites about healthy eating.

Through the online survey, it was possible to identify five groups:

- Group 1 - Unhealthy people that are not interested in changing their habits.
- Group 2 - Unhealthy people that are willing to change their habits.
- Group 3 - Healthy or partially healthy people that are not interested in a corporate wellness program.
- Group 4 - Healthy or partially healthy people that are interested in a corporate wellness program.
- Group 5 - Totally healthy people that are interested in a corporate wellness program.

In order to select groups, the participants profile and interest in healthy habits were considered. Groups 1 and 3 were the immediately excluded because of the lack of interest in changing habits. This decision was made because people that lack awareness of how their lifestyle habits affect their health have little reason to put themselves through the misery of changing the bad habits they enjoy [11]. We also believed that Group 5 would contribute less to the experiment's results because they already had a completely healthy lifestyle, making it difficult to identify changes related to a wellness program. Therefore, Groups 2 and 4 were selected because they met the study's requirements and were believed to be the most appropriate profile for the experiment.

After the profile selection, the task was to send an email for the participants from Groups 2 and 4 to confirm their interest in participating in the experiment, to show the study's schedule and explain what would be the next steps. After confirming their interest, 12 employees (6 from each group) were invited to an individual conversation where they received information regarding the experiment's routine and daily challenges.

All participants had 4 daily goals that health experts claim can bring health benefits: walk 6.000 steps [12], drink 2 L of water [13], perform 30 min of exercise [12] and have at least 6 h of sleep at night [14]. These tasks had to be fully completed so the user could receive individual points. The completion of each goal was worth 10 points, and the partial completion or non-completion was not scored.

It was defined that the report should be sent through the Whatsapp messaging application, since all users had access to it and were familiarized with the service. Users should send a screenshot from Samsung's health application (S Health) main screen – with the data that was synchronized with their wearable device or by the application itself – every morning during 7 days. The idea was to collect the results of the users' previous day so they could receive virtual medals for each achieved goal (Figure 1).

The same program was applied for both groups, with benefits and prizes, but only six people received one smartwatch (either Samsung Gear S2 or Samsung Gear Fit2) for pairing with their smartphone and S Health account. The other participants would only use the smartphone with an S Health account (Fig. 2).

Fig. 1. Program's handbook.

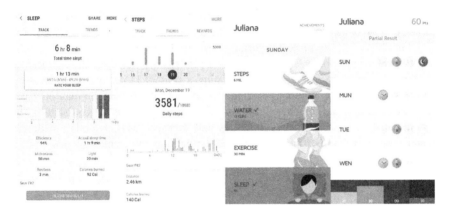

Fig. 2. Daily screenshots received from users. They represent hours of sleep, number of steps, milestones achieved, and partial score.

The devices' models choice as well as the use of Samsung's S Health application – a service that makes it possible to synchronize the activities monitored by a wearable devices as well as manually register activities through the smartphone application – was also done thinking about the possible application of a real wellness program in the company.

Furthermore, the distribution of wearable devices' models made after the analysis of the participants' profile. Participants from Group 4 received a Gear Fit2 for being more active, since the device is mostly focused in this audience. However, both devices offered the same use conditions necessary for the study (Table 2).

Table 2. Equipment and service distribution

Distribution of the equipment and services by employees and groups			
Groups	Wearable + S health	Only S health	Device model
Group 2	3 employees	3 employees	(3) Gear S2
Group 4	3 employees	3 employees	(3) Gear Fit2

5 Manual Chatbot

According to our research, there were no tools to monitor the activities proposed by this study that would offer support for Samsung's wearable and mobile devices. Also, it was not possible to structure the experiment within the company's applications ecosystem or to use third-party services/applications. It was necessary to create a method that would allow monitoring and support in the least intrusive way possible and with the minimum amount of effort from the participants during the 7 days of the experiment. For this reason, the idea was to create a manual chatbot using the participants' preferred messaging service as an avant-garde system to mediate communication and represent the project's virtual assistant.

All communication between researcher and participants was done through the app WhatsApp–as chosen by participants, simulating a chatbot [15]. Aiming to create an impartial communication, without association with a specific person the mascot Master Yoda from the Star Wars franchise was chosen to represent the virtual assistant. Using classic movie quotes through text messages and images, "Master Yoda" made recommendations, gave support, and recognized the participants' achievements.

6 Results

By the end of the experiment, 9 participants were fully engaged in the program even though some had failed to meet daily goals. The other 3 participants said that family problems directly affected their participation.

On the experiment's last day, participants were invited to answer a program satisfaction survey, which results highlighted important points:

- 100% of participants - (including those who could not keep up with program) expressed interest in participating in similar wellness programs in the company.
- 100% loved the experience of receiving incentives from "Master Yoda".
- Activities' gamification encouraged competitiveness in the program.
- They stated that the program did not weight heavily on their routine and it was fun to interact with "Master Yoda".
- Participants suggested that the program as it was could be implemented in the company.
- Some participants identified opportunities to change their habits in order to achieve a healthier lifestyle.

- The encouragement provided through "Master Yoda" and the incentives given for a healthier lifestyle were the experiment's main highlights (Table 3).

Table 3. Experiment's final ranking

Groups	Wearable + S health	Only S health
Group 2	110pts	180pts
Group 4	250pts	50pts
Group 2 + Group 4	360pts	230pts

7 Conclusions

Although results indicate that the program had a high level of acceptance, some points must be considered:

- All participants were SIDIA's employees.
- Group 2 had higher scores on goals related to water intake and sleeping, which are manual inputs of S Health and could not be validated.
- These results are not enough to ensure that employees would get engaged in a corporate wellness program.

In contrast, results demonstrate that the use of a more relaxed and fun communication can promote the engagement in corporate wellness programs. Furthermore, the use of a wearable device provides greater visibility to healthy activities performed throughout the day (that previously went unnoticed), and healthy competitiveness stimulates the groups' development as a whole.

It is in the interest of those involved in this research that a new phase with external participants should be performed considering a observation cycle of no less than 30 days, the option of choosing the virtual assistant and improvements regarding the visibility of the group's activities for all involved.

References

1. Sung, D.: What is wearable tech? Everything you need to know explained. Wareable 2016. http://www.wareable.com/wearable-tech/what-is-wearable-tech-753. Accessed 10 Oct 2016
2. Evenson, K., Goto, M., Evenson, F.R., et al.: International journal of behavioral nutrition and physical activity. Int. J. Behav. Nutr. Phys. Act. **12**, 159 (2015). doi:10.1186/s12966-015-0314-1
3. Torre, H., Goetzel, R.: How to Design a Corporate Wellness Plan That Actually Works. https://hbr.org/2016/03/how-to-design-a-corporate-wellness-plan-that-actually-works. Accessed 10 Oct 2016
4. Baicker, K., Cutler, D., Song, Z.: Workplace wellness programs can generate savings. Health Aff. **29**(2), 304–311 (2010)
5. Gandhi, M., Wang, T.: Digital Health Consumer Adoption: Rock Health. https://rockhealth.com/reports/digital-health-consumer-adoption-2015/. Accessed 19 Oct 2016

6. Limeade. More than participation: how to engage employees in well-being. http://www.limeade.com/wp-content/uploads/2016/05/Limeade-How-to-solve-the-wellness-program-participation-problemFINAL.pdf. Accessed 20 Oct 2016

7. Greenspun, H., Wald, R., Korba, C., Korenda, L.: Surveys of Em-ployers and Health Care Consumers. Deloitte Center for Health Solutions. http://www2.deloitte.com/us/en/pages/life-sciences-and-health-care/articles/employers-still-bullish-on-wellness-programs.html, http://www.boundlss.com/blog/insurers-are-bleeding-24-trillion-in-claims. Accessed 10 Oct 2016

8. The world health report 1998. Life in the 21st century: a vision for all. Geneva, World Health Organization (1998)

9. Report Healthcare Costs: Key Information on Healthcare Costs and Their Impact. https://kaiserfamilyfoundation.files.wordpress.com/2013/01/7670-03.pdf. Accessed 20 Oct 2016

10. Warraich M. Wellness Routines with Wearable Activity Track-ers: A Systematic Review. http://aisel.aisnet.org/cgi/viewcontent.cgi?article=1035&context=mcis2016. Accessed 20 Oct 2016

11. Bandura, A.: Health promotion from the perspective of social cognitive theory. Psychol. Health **13**, 623–649 (1998)

12. Tudor-Locke, C.: Steps to better cardiovascular health: how many steps does it take to achieve good health and how confident are we in this number? Curr. Cardio. Risk Rep. **4**, 271–276 (2010). doi:10.1007/s12170-010-0109-5

13. EFSA Panel on Dietetic Products Nutrition and Allergies (NDA): Scientific opinion on dietary reference values for water. EFSA J. **8**(3), 1459–1507 (2010)

14. Robertson, E.M., Pascual-Leone, A., Press, D.Z.: Awareness modifies the skill-learning benefits of sleep. Curr. Biol. **14**, 208–212 (2004)

15. Bayan, A., Atwell, E.: Chatbots: are they really useful? LDV-Forum **22**(1), 29–49 (2007)

Participatory Design of Vaccination Services with Less-Literate Users

Shyama V.S.[1](✉), Ulemba Hirom[1], Sylvan Lobo[1], Sujit Devkar[1],
Pankaj Doke[1], and Nikita Pandey[2]

[1] Tata Consultancy Services Limited, Mumbai, India
{shyamav.s,ulemba.h,sylvan.lobo,sujit.devkar,
pankaj.doke}@tcs.com
[2] Tata Institute of Social Sciences, Mumbai, India
nikita.pandey2015@tiss.edu

Abstract. Participatory Design (PD) in an ICTD context can be challenging due to various constraints of lesser literacy, exposure to technology, infrastructure, socio-cultural factors and power distances amongst others inhibiting users to participate. In this paper, we explored this phenomenon with Vaccination and Immunization as a case study. Our team in the field comprised of two Designers and a student of Public Health Policy who is also a qualified Dentist. We recruited users who were migrants to the city, less literate, and had a child within the past 18 months. We used Contextual Inquiry (CI) as a probing method. The team visited the users at their convenient time to conduct the PD sessions with individual users. We anticipated users to face difficulties in participating, designing and expressing critical and creative opinions, as they would have less formal awareness of the processes and systems. This paper discusses outcomes of the PD process, and shares the insights about conducting PD with users in an ICTD context.

Keywords: Participatory design · Less literate users · Healthcare · Service design · ICTD

1 Introduction

A multitude of definitions and views exist within design practitioners on what constitutes Design [1]. Traditionally the profession which was centered around Industrial production has moved into an approach which is applied to fields like software engineering, services, policymaking amongst others. Participatory design (PD) originated in the Nordic countries as a political approach to shaping democratic workplace [2]. Since then it has found its place in the design and business community as an approach for knowledge building and user empowerment [3]. PD has its roots in the developed countries and has been anecdotally practiced there. On the other hand, PD with marginalized users has been under investigated.

Due to the increase in ICT accessibility in India, there will be a significant ICTD intervention in India. On the other hand, these interventions will seemingly lack the practice of PD due to probable low awareness and challenges faced. Hence from a

© Springer International Publishing AG 2017
C. Stephanidis (Ed.): HCII Posters 2017, Part II, CCIS 714, pp. 301–308, 2017.
DOI: 10.1007/978-3-319-58753-0_45

design perspective we would like to investigate the phenomenon. We would like to situate this context within the domain of healthcare.

The Constitution of India places emphasis on improving Public health as a duty of the State [4]. Vaccination is one of the most cost-effective child survival interventions [5]. Universal Immunization Program (UIP) for children, which includes 6 vaccines: BCG (Bacillus Calmette–Guérin), DPT (Diphtheria, Tetanus toxoids and Pertussis), polio, measles, DT and TT (diphtheria and tetanus toxoids) is provided free of cost through the Indian Government Healthcare. In India, vaccination has a national coverage of 61% [6]. WHO aims a national coverage of 90% for its member states by 2020 [5]. We feel the compliance rates can further improve if there is co-creation of services with PD.

2 Literature Study

PD is used to model users' intrinsic knowledge and empower them in decision-making [2, 7]. Several challenges have been identified while designing with PD like contextual constraints [7] and literacy level of the participants [8]. Engaging participants with a meaningful PD problem statement and building relationship with the participants [9] are explored in PD literature. To conduct PD, it is advised to ensure participant's access to relevant information [10]. Bowen et al. [11], identifies how users in PD find it easier to find solutions to problems which are visible than finding lateral solutions to non-obvious problems. Participant's ability for decision-making [9] is also a factor, which affects PD. Yet PD does not have an established way of evaluating the output and there are conflicting views on debated the output of PD [3]. PD is used as a tool to find solutions to the problem or as an approach to understand the problem itself [7]. For the purpose of this study we have followed Sanders' [12] framework of PD tools and techniques of Priming, Probing and recording experiences using Making – making tangible things, Telling – tools and techniques that support verbally oriented activities, and Enacting – acting and playing.

3 Method

3.1 Objective

The aim of the study was to explore the phenomenon of PD with ICTD users. We have situated our context in healthcare service design. The PD sessions were conducted to co-create Customer Journey Maps of vaccination services with users.

3.2 Participants and Setting

Our team in the field comprised of two Designers and a student of Public Health Policy who is also a qualified Dentist. The Designer was expected to bring in the perspective of PD, while the public healthcare student was expected to bring in the perspective of public healthcare. In addition to the participants, the sessions were observed by an

Industrial Designer who remained as a passive observer. The focus of the Industrial Designer's work is not within the scope of this paper, but we would like to mention his presence.

We recruited users who were migrants to the city, less-literate [13], and had a child within the past 18 months from the urban poor wards of Chembur and Govandi, Mumbai. We arrived at the criteria of 18 months as vaccination which is part of UIP [6] is done frequently within this. We assumed an operational definition of less-literate as not more than standard 8 education in India [13]. Users were chosen through door-to-door convenient sampling. Prior to the PD sessions, a Contextual Inquiry was conducted with 11 users to gather insights about user's experience with vaccination. Based on the insights from CI, we decided to attempt PD with users who met our research criteria (Table 1). We arrived two types of users—User type A was compliant to the National Immunization Schedule and User type B had home births and was not fully compliant to the national Immunization Schedule through Contextual Inquiry (CI). We conducted PD sessions with both the user types. As part of the PD session, we situated the context in their recent past consumption of the vaccination service and triggered their participation into co-creation of such a service.

Table 1. List of users

Session	Location	Number of children	Demographic description
1	Chembur/Mumbai/India	3	Not employed. Institutional delivery. Fully immunized children
2	Chembur/Mumbai/India	2	Not employed. Institutional delivery. Fully immunized children
3	Chembur/Mumbai/India	1	Two users. Both unemployed, Institutional delivery and has Fully immunized children
4	Govandi/Mumbai/India	3	Unemployed. Non-institutional delivery. Partially immunized children
5	Govandi/Mumbai/India	4	Unemployed. Unimmunized children

3.3   Participatory Design Session

The participants included a Designer, Public Health Policy student and the User. The PD session was planned and executed within a timespan of two weeks. The session duration varied between thirty minutes to ninety minutes. Sessions were held at user homes and were scheduled based on user convenience. There was a constraint of space within most homes, so sessions were conducted on the available space like bed or floor, amidst the household activities. We would like to make a fair disclosure that we anticipated our users to have difficulties in expressing themselves creatively and critically. Hence, PD was held with individual users and we dressed down to suit the users environment. The only exception to this was a session where a houseguest met our user criteria and was our user's sister-in-law. We could not exclude her from the session due to the power structure within the family.

3.4 Procedure

Prior to the sessions the team developed an outline for conducting the sessions. This was based on Sanders et al. [12] framework of PD tools and techniques such as visual triggers (making), verbal triggers (telling) and roleplaying (acting).

The artifacts we used for PD were A4 size colour prints of (1) set of emoticons for empathy mapping, (2) photographs of vaccination process in India, (3) sketches with animals hidden in a forest (4) photographs of making tea. We collected images from the Internet due to shorter time window to create our own. The photographs of vaccination were chosen based on visual similarity to vaccination service in Mumbai. We also carried ruled notebooks and sketch pen sets. All of the stationery was purchased from the user's neighborhood to ensure they would be commonplace to the user.

The sessions contained different phases meant to understand user's experience and generate alternatives to the existing scenario. The introductory activity was based on verbal triggers and it captured users' daily life, vaccination experience and difficulties they face with vaccination process. In the subsequent activity discussion took place around customization with an example of customizing food to their children's liking. Our aim was to establish how experiences could improve when it is tailor-made for the user. The next phase user was primed for the generative phase through lateral thinking activities. The activities include identifying circular objects by shifting point of views and spotting the hidden animals from the image provided. While the former activity proved ineffective, the later became an icebreaking session user gained confidence from. At this phase we introduced pen and paper to the user. The subsequent activity was intended as process mapping using collage making. User had to map the process by which she prepares tea. Due to the environmental constraints, the activity was altered into a story telling exercise by making use of the photographs we provided. The next phase was generative which started with an activity to elicit users happy experiences and brainstormed to layer their qualities [14] on vaccination service. Subsequently, a process map of the vaccination service was captured through verbal triggers, sketches and artifacts like sketch pens. Further, we captured stakeholder maps by charting all the stakeholders mentioned in the process map. Assigning hierarchies to the stakeholder maps followed this activity. Further, we used photo elicitation to capture emotions user experienced during the vaccination service. We used emoticons to initiate discussions on emotions experienced by the user through the vaccination journey. Final activity was roleplaying where the user enacted how service providers are at points of service breakdown. User then generated alternatives scenarios to these scenarios.

4 Discussion

4.1 Need for Flexibility

Despite planning PD sessions in advance, researchers need to accommodate user context by altering the activities on the fly. Since users were also engaged with work we altered our methods and tools to suit their context. We could not photograph and sketch frequently, and engage with her in ways other than verbal and gestural due to the contextual constraints (lack of physical space available and as it affected their natural participation). So we used images to elicit responses on the existing process and to generate ideal processes. Personalizing the stakeholder maps helped increase user's enthusiasm levels. For example, in the illustrated stakeholder map we always referred to the baby by user's child's name. This often made the user smile and become visibly enthusiastic to contribute. During session 1, we illustrated the service providers and processes using simple illustrations that user spoke of. These sketches became a starting point for discussions in the further activities. During another session we provided the user with colored sticks to build process maps and stakeholder maps. Even though it provided an opportunity for user to record experiences, it was ineffective in furthering discussions. We eventually discovered that it is easier to build the process map and build stakeholders map and elicit users emotions using it as a foundation. But the interdependency of these activities also meant lesser opportunities to discover radically new information. Mapping emotions to the stages of vaccination journey was initially difficult. Users did not know how to describe in detail how they were feeling through various stages of the vaccination journey. To overcome this, we let the user assess the emoticons provided and interpret what emotions they represent. At times our users enacted the expression of the emoticon without us prompting. Users then matched the emoticons to the process map and elaborated on what it felt like to be at various stages of the vaccination journey.

During photo elicitation, users pointed out inconsistencies in the photograph with their experiences. For example, during the process mapping activity for preparing tea, users would point out inaccuracies in the photographs we showed and described their process in detail. Users often corrected us without hesitating, but the real challenge was to get in-depth descriptions. We constantly had to reassure the users since initially they doubted PD to be like a school examination. Such doubts were often expressed during the 'making' activities. The photographs of vaccination process during photo elicitation depicted service provider and user seemingly happy. Upon seeing them, the users mentioned how the depiction is inaccurate. They proceeded to tell us how they expect the service providers to be more empathetic towards children.

4.2 Communicating Intangible Concepts

Preparing a strategy to communicate common PD terminology to less-literate, non English speaking user could increase time spent on PD activities. It was relatively easy to probe for experiences, emotions and to generate alternatives for very specific problems within the service. PD was ineffective in generating suggestions for a holistic system design. We often found it difficult to communicate what a service is and where it begins and ends. User considered vaccination service to be only about the point where she walks into the ASHA workers station and gets the injection done. Whereas we believed information dissemination, preparation for the upcoming vaccination, post vaccination care also to be part of the service. Sketching the user stories provided an easier means of capturing intangible aspects of a service and initiate discussions. Users assumed sole responsibility for getting their child immunized. Yet they never considered themselves to be important enough to have opinions about the service. Often there was difficulty in explaining technical terms. Even a translation to Hindi was not effective for words like 'involvement' or 'process'. Concept behind each word had to be explained in-depth.

4.3   Creating a Meaningful Experience for the User

The commute, weather and the intensive sessions were exhausting. It was difficult to keep the user focused on the activities due to the physical constraints and the constant interruptions. We constantly adapted the activities and the narrative to keeping the user interested. Our Users and the Designer were non-native Hindi speakers. These lead to fragmented transitions between activities. We spend a significant part of the time to explain concepts to users. In order to improvise on the activities the Team needed to communicate within us. Users indicated discomfort as we switching from Hindi to English to speak to each other. Since our users initially expressed doubts that they were being tested, we had to minimize discussions within the team. Communicating within the team while putting the user at ease was especially hard in sessions where distractions like dependent members were not present. Vaccinations are not a daily affair and this could have contributed to our users not participating in PD with seriousness.

At times during the probing for experiences activity users described experiences of discrimination, abuse and of being deceived during the vaccination process. This combined with our time constraints, often created an ethical dilemma on whether to proceed with PD sessions. As a result, sometimes we cut short activities and spend more time listening to the user speak. It was especially hard with Users who had non-institutional delivery and partly immunized children.

4.4   Creative and Critical Opinions

We could barely convince the user that her opinions and ideas matter. Users believed they were powerless to influence the process. For example, when asked to generate solutions for service breakdowns a user responded by saying that she just follows what the doctor says for the benefit of her child.

User was introduced to pen and paper during 'spot the hidden animals' activity. Upon seeing the pen and paper one user responded that she does not know how to write. Even though the activity did not require her to write, it still intimidated her. During the process mapping, the Designer and the Student sketched to record the users story. User hesitated to even hold the pen later and required a lot of coaxing.

4.5   Insights About Vaccination

PD indicated a preference for woman as a service provider in vaccination. Women were more empathetic, gentle and playful to the child according to the users. Users expressed a lot of concern on a crying child being injected. They feared the child would faint from exhaustion. Users also suggested a need for Doctor's presence at the point of Immunization. This was because of experiences where the users were denied immunization service after the health worker felt the child could be sick. Users would then be asked to get of certificate from doctor. There was comparison between Hospitals or Camps being Immunization center. Users mentioned familiarity, ease of access and lower indirect cost in favor of camps. But they believed hospitals provided better care and service providers at hospital attempted to build better rapport with the child. Certain users who had partially or unimmunized children were under the belief that the child was fully immunized. They were not aware of immunization as a process, which involves multiple doses at intervals. Their experience with the vaccination process was limited to one or two events. Another User was under the impression that the mother-child protection card [15] needs to be completely filled for enrolling the child in school. To her, immunization was only a way to enroll her child in school. In such cases, PD activities we had designed for the sessions had little relevance to the user scenario. It was interesting to note that all of the suggestions were centered around the child and the user never considered her difficulties worthy of solving. Our users faced economic difficulties and did not have refrigerators in their homes. They buy Rupee 1 Frozen Cola sachets for cold compression.

5   Challenges and Limitations

Two weeks were a shorter time window to build relationship with our users. Sessions were often interrupted by external factors. We did not provide any monetary compensation to the users; instead we gifted the children with stationery and candy as a token of appreciation for participation. It was also our first experience conducting PD.

Since the users had several social commitments, it was difficult to conduct the sessions despite taking prior appointment. Many a times sessions happened while the user was cooking lunch, amidst crying children or houseguests. At times, users could not keep the appointment because of last minute interventions from older members of the family. We observed that users participated better in the absence of older dependent members, mother in law for example. We observed our users being comfortable with telling and enacting methods. We suggest caution during 'making' activities to minimize connotations of schooling. During PD with a single user within user setting, it is challenging to convince the user to participate formally. Transitioning between activities has to be planned carefully such that the user stay focused and finds PD meaningful. Further research is required to situate PD activities and terminologies within ICTD context when there is a constraint of physical space and users with little exposure to former schooling.

Acknowledgments. We thank all the users, volunteers, and all publications support and staff, who wrote and provided helpful comments on versions of this document.

References

1. Evbuomwan, N.F.O., Sivaloganathan, S., Jebb, A.: A survey of design philosophies, models, methods and systems. Proc. Inst. Mech. Eng. Part B J. Eng. Manuf. (2016). doi:10.1243/ PIME_PROC_1996_210_123_02

2. Spinuzzi, C.: The methodology of participatory design. Tech. Commun. **52**(2), 163–174 (2005)
3. Bossen, C., Dindler, C., Iversen, O.S.: Evaluation in participatory design: a literature survey, pp 151–160. ACM (2016)
4. Constitution of India. http://lawmin.nic.in/olwing/coi/coi-english/coi-4March2016.pdf
5. WHO – Immunization coverage. In: WHO. http://www.who.int/mediacentre/factsheets/fs378/en/. Accessed 24 Mar 2017
6. Universal Immunisation Programme. https://www.nhp.gov.in/sites/default/files/pdf/immunization_uip.pdf
7. Frauenberger, C., Good, J., Fitzpatrick, G., Iversen, O.S.: In pursuit of rigour and accountability in participatory design. Int. J. Hum.-Comput. Stud. **74**, 93–106 (2015). doi:10.1016/j.ijhcs.2014.09.004
8. Oyugi, C., Nocera, J.A., Dunckley, L., Dray, S.: The challenges for participatory design in the developing world, pp 295–296. Indiana University (2008)
9. Participatory design with marginalized people in developing countries: challenges and opportunities experienced in a field study in Cambodia. In: International Journal of Design. http://www.ijdesign.org/ojs/index.php/IJDesign/article/view/1054/455. Accessed 1 Dec 2016
10. Kensing, F., Blomberg, J.: Participatory design: issues and concerns. Comput. Support. Coop. Work CSCW **7**, 167–185 (1998)
11. Bowen, S., Dearden, A., Wright, P., et al: Participatory healthcare service design and innovation. In: Proceedings 11th Biennial Participatory Design Conference, pp 155–158. ACM (2010)
12. Sanders, E.B.-N., Brandt, E., Binder, T.: A framework for organizing the tools and techniques of participatory design. In: Proceedings of 11th Biennial Participatory Design Conference, pp 195–198. ACM (2010)
13. Doke, P., Joshi, A.: Mobile phone usage by low literate users, pp 10–18. ACM (2015)
14. Ideation Method: Mash-Up - IDEO U. http://www.ideou.com/pages/ideation-method-mash-up. Accessed 23 Mar 2017
15. Mother and Child Protection Cards. http://pib.nic.in/newsite/PrintRelease.aspx?relid=89740. Accessed 24 Mar 2017

Affordance of Real-Time Personalization and Adaptation of Hearing Aid Settings

Qi Yang[✉], Shira Hahn, Bill Chang, Almer van den Berg, and Greg Olsen

GN Hearing A/S, Glenview, IL 60026, USA
{qyang,shahn,bchang,avdberg,olseng}@gnresound.com

Abstract. Hearing aids are becoming increasingly reliant on interaction with personal mobile computing devices such as smartphones. However, the affordance of these "connected" hearing aids (typically with a remote interface on a user's smartphone) can be poor, particularly for the geriatric population, which comprises the majority of hearing aid users. In this work, we present several prototypes and preliminary results that explore novel interaction methods allowing users to personalize sound settings on hearing aids which are connected to smartphones and wearable devices while engaging with an environmentally-aware adaptive system. This work addresses both the affordance issues observed among hearing aid users, as well as the lack of HCI research on personalization of hearing aid sound settings for different listening environments.

Keywords: Hearing aid · Aging · Mobile phone · Wearable · Human computer interaction

1 Background

As personal mobile computing devices become more popular across age groups, hearing aids (HAs) allow more and more interaction with these devices. Many hearing aids now allow sound settings to be personalized through an intermediate accessory device such as a smartphone or smartwatch. Yet there is a surprising lack of research on interactions between users, hearing aids, and these accessory devices for personalization of hearing aid sound settings.

Traditionally, hearing aids have several *programs*, which are bundles of sound processing settings. Typically, these include a default (sometimes called "all-around") program set to an omnidirectional microphone mode, where sound is amplified equally in all directions, as well as programs intended for noisy environments, which often include a directional microphone mode and added noise reduction. While a "noisy environment" program might be beneficial to a user in certain difficult listening environments, hearing instrument users generally fail to change to this hearing aid program manually. This may be partly due to (a) a lack of knowledge about the benefits of the program change and (b) the effort required to interact with the physical switches on hearing aids, or with software interfaces on connected mobile devices.

© Springer International Publishing AG 2017
C. Stephanidis (Ed.): HCII Posters 2017, Part II, CCIS 714, pp. 309–316, 2017.
DOI: 10.1007/978-3-319-58753-0_46

In order to make it more likely that users are in the best program for their current location, commercial hearing aids have implemented automated systems that change settings in response to the characteristics of the sound environment. Machine learning methods for automatically classifying sound environments for adaptation of hearing aid settings is an active area of research [1,2]. Previous work [3] also explored methods to use the computing power of connected personal mobile devices for automatic adaptation and personalization of hearing instruments.

Although prior work [4] found that user adjustments were reliable for individual fine-tuning of gain-frequency response preferences in different acoustical conditions in a lab setting, there is large variation among users in their preferences for sound settings [3]. As a result, even when the environment is classified correctly, it is not clear what settings should be chosen for that environment without taking into account user intent/input.

Compounding the problem of variation in sound setting preferences, the affordance of both mobile devices (e.g. smartphones) and hearing aids can be poor for the geriatric population, which comprises the majority of the hearing aid users. Aldaz et al. [5] found that the user experience of training a hearing personalization system is dependent on user's affinity to technology. The interaction model for personalization is still an under-explored area of study.

This work envisions and explores a semi-automated system that can potentially prompt users and recommend self-adjustments, and offer opportunities for users to intervene if needed. In the following sections we outline several works in progress and preliminary results approaching this from multiple angles.

2   Work in Progress

2.1   User Interface for Hearing Aid Setting Self-Adjustment

Existing interfaces for self-adjustment of hearing aid settings consist of physical switches on the hearing aids themselves, sometimes coupled with software on connected smartphones. Physical switches, which can be set to control amplification or step-wise program changes, are often too small to be operated reliably by geriatric users. To sidestep this problem, we focused on interactions on the smartphones connected to hearing aids. In this work, we explore high-affordance interfaces that allow for program selection as well as finer adjustment within programs. In doing so, we increase the number of setting adjustments available without sacrificing the ability for geriatric users to personalize the sound of their hearing instruments.

We applied the process of iterative user-centered design to arrive at three alternative designs (Fig. 1) after two iterations. In the first iteration, static prototypes are tested using an iPhone with mounted camera ($n = 6$, age from 45 to 84 years. See Fig. 2). In the second iteration, functional prototypes are developed as native iOS applications and tested on the same apparatus ($n = 8$, age from

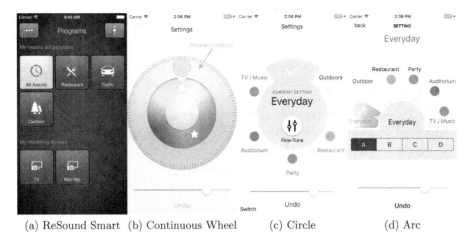

(a) ReSound Smart (b) Continuous Wheel   (c) Circle   (d) Arc

Fig. 1. Existing ReSound iPhone app, shown as a baseline, and three prototype interfaces for smartphone-based self-adjustment (Color figure online)

51+, 4 are 81+). The functional prototypes also made use of Bluetooth connectivity to remotely control ReSound Made-for-iPhone hearing aids, allowing participants in the study to hear the sound adjustments that they made.

Figure 1 shows the current ReSound app for adjusting hearing aid settings, along with three of the alternative designs after two design iterations. The idea at the core of the *Circle* and *Arc* designs (Fig. 1(c) and Fig. 1(d)) is the use of color as a mnemonic for referencing program settings. Both designs use a spectrum of discrete colors to represent the six available programs instead of icons with program names. Both designs contain both colored buttons and text labels. We found in user testing that text labels were crucial to understanding the function of the colored button. When both color and text are present, the confusion is resolved, and color can act as a memory aid. However, we found that text labels were not needed in the *Continuous Wheel* design (Fig. 1(b)). This design features a label-less rotatable control wheel marked by a continuous spectrum of colors. In the *Continuous Wheel* prototype, hearing aid sound settings are changed gradually and continuously whenever the user rotates the wheel, selecting from a large continuum of sound settings. Participants were initially confused about the functionality of the wheel, but quickly learned to operate the wheel and listen to the gradual

Fig. 2. iPhone with camera mounted to record and observe user interaction with the phone screen.

sound feedback to find their desired sound settings. They also naturally started to use the colors to talk about specific unlabelled sound settings.

While the iterative design cycle is ongoing, we found improved affordance in discovery and learning. We found so far that color can be helpful as a memory aid to represent sound settings without relying on inconsistent labels or technical jargon, as long as responsive sound feedback is present. This allows potential self-adjustment among potentially many more settings than what is possible on a traditional program switching interface.

2.2   Affordance of In-Situ User Notification

To complement the work on user-driven hearing aid adjustment mobile interfaces, we also considered situations where self-adjustment using mobile phone interfaces is inconvenient or socially undesirable (e.g. when the user is engaging in physical activity, or at a dinner party). Inspired by the recent popularity of wearable devices like the Apple Watch, we want to explore the efficacy of a system that allows guided and discreet self-adjustments with lower effort than waking and using one's smartphone. In this system, an automated algorithm can predict suitable hearing aid settings based on the current sound environment, and either change hearing aid settings automatically or notify the user and recommend a program to use. A connected wrist-worn device such as an Apple Watch allows discreet notifications and glance-like interactions which can be suited for this purpose.

Instead of implementing a full system with environmental sound classification and recommendation, we use a Wizard-of-Oz style experiment to isolate and study the user interactions with such a system (See Fig. 3). In addition to connected Made-For-iPhone hearing aids, an Apple Watch is connected to the iPhone so that notifications can be forwarded and displayed on the participant's wrist, and recommendations can be accepted or rejected on the watch. We made use of multipeer networking (which uses WiFi or Bluetooth) to connect the experimenter's iOS devices to the participant's phone as remote controls, allowing experimenters to "fake" a smart, automatic recommendation system without the awareness of participants. This approach allows rapid prototyping of interactions and validation of interaction designs without implementing the actual recommendation algorithms or waiting for such systems to mature and perform accurate, useful recommendations.

To understand how effective or irritating a notification/recommendation system can be in realistic environments, we are conducting ongoing user studies where older participants with hearing impairments are fitted with hearing aids and given the iPhone and Apple Watch, and are then engaged in conversation and social activities in several common real-world environments. We drove our participants to a local shopping mall, and talked with them while walking through a noisy store, a coffee stand, and a courtyard area with a waterfall. The interior of the shopping mall allowed us to sample a variety of environments with different noise levels, and also permitted participants to easily transition among these environments. During the transition of environments (e.g. walking

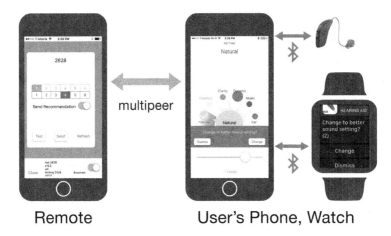

Fig. 3. Connected wearable/smartphone remote control system for notifying and recommending hearing aid settings in a Wizard-of-Oz style experiment. ReSound hearing aids are connected to the iPhone. One or more iOS devices can connect to the participant's phone using multi-peer WiFi/Bluetooth network, enabling the experimenter to send recommendation notifications to participants. An Apple Watch is paired to participant phones so that notifications are forwarded to the watch.

from a quiet parking lot into a loud store), and also while in the environments, one accompanying experimenter would discreetly push recommendation notifications to the participant's devices while the other experimenters engaged them in casual conversation and also acted as observers. Data collection was done through notes taken by experimenters and by the participant's phone, which logged every interaction by the user.

Preliminary results from 4 participants (2M, 2F, age 71–80) suggest that the common habits of placing one's phone in a purse or jacket pocket greatly reduces the chance that the participant will notice a notification on the phone. When a notification is pushed to an Apple Watch, the chance of being noticed increased substantially in most participants. We found that some participants quickly adapted to interacting with the recommendation system on the Apple Watch, and rated the interaction as being very helpful. Even though one participant did not respond to most of the notifications sent on the watch, they still reported in the post-study survey that recommendations were recognized. The fact that the user could notice recommendation notifications without having to look at or acknowledge them suggests that interactions with wearable devices such as the Apple Watch can be truly discreet, since it was not noticed by the other experimenter observing the interaction.

2.3   User Sound Preference

Prior work [3] showed that individual preferences for hearing aid settings were variable. We extended this work to investigate whether the preferences had high-level similarities across listeners, whether there are sound settings that are strongly favored over others by most people, and whether a user's preferred program improves their ability to understand speech and quality of sound.

Table 1. List of hearing aid settings tested: 18 programs cover a combination of these settings.

Noise Reduction	Directionality	Loudness/Equalization
Off	Omnidirectional	+6 dB across frequencies
Moderate	Adaptive directionality	+3 dB across frequencies
Very Strong	Fixed directionality	-3 dB across frequencies
		-6 dB across frequencies
		-6 dB below 1500 Hz ramping to +6 above 1500 Hz

To answer this question, we conducted a listening study with 11 participants with hearing impairment (6F, 5M, age 55–85) in a simulated speech-in-noise environment in a sound booth. Participants used a simple grid interface in an iPad application to audition 18 programs and then select, rank, and rate their top three programs. The application remotely controls a pair of hearing aids that the participants wear to switch among the 18 programs (See Table 1). Speakers in the sound booth played recorded speech directly in front of the participant, and cafe noise containing speech babble and impulsive dining noise at 45° to the left of the participant, with a SNR of about −5 dB. After the top three programs were selected and quality ratings recorded, we measured intelligibility of the top-ranked program versus a default program with omnidirectional sound and no noise reduction using Coordinate Response Measure (CRM) sentences. These sentences are commonly used to test the ability to understand speech in situations where speech comes from multiple sources [6].

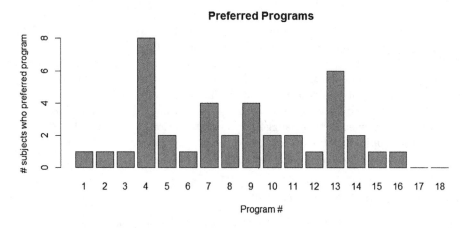

Fig. 4. Sound preferences show a broad variation in preferences. Nearly every program was chosen as one of the top three by at least one of the 11 participants.

Results of this study show a wide variety of user preferences, where almost all 18 programs are chosen at least once as a top choice by participants (See Fig. 4). Interestingly, some programs are favored more than others (e.g. program 4 and 13). Both of these programs used a fixed directional microphone mode, a finding that merits further investigation. Not all participants received intelligibility benefit from the program they chose over the default program. We also checked retest reliability with three of the participants after several weeks, and found that participant preferences were not reliable: all of the top three programs for all three participants changed, except for one top choice from one participant. These results suggest that users may have very different sound preferences and provides motivation for a personalization system that gives the user multiple sound setting options.

2.4   Daily Hearing Aid User Video Diary

The process of adapting to a hearing aid is more complex than simply finding the sound settings that work best for the individual user. New habits need to be formed, counseling is needed to address issues with social stigma and the physical handling of the device, and physical adjustments are sometimes needed to address the fit of the device in the ear. Although every hearing aid user must go through an adaptation period when they are first fitted with a hearing aid, research addressing user needs during this adaptation period is limited.

Prior work showed the feasibility of applying ecological momentary assessment (EMA), a method of sending users short surveys at regular intervals, to assess the everyday experiences of hearing aid users [7]. We adopted a similar methodology with new HA users to assess difficulties related to listening experiences and the hearing aids themselves during this adaption period. In this ongoing study, we recruited new hearing aid users (either new to hearing aids or receiving replacement new devices), and gave them an iPhone for a 2-week period. During this time, participants received a survey question via text message at a predefined time in the morning and evening, and were asked to record a video response to the question. We used an automated workflow[1] to simplify the video response process, and automatically uploaded the video to online storage for backup, which also allowed us to quickly review their answers.

Preliminary responses from two participants showed that users encounter a variety of difficult environments in their first weeks of usage, from luncheons to organized dinners and noisy sports events. Self-reported behavior matches data gleaned from the hearing aids' built-in usage logs, which shows that users seldom adjust their hearing aids or hearing aid programs using either physical controls on the hearing aid or on connected smartphones, regardless of the sound environment.

---

[1] Workflow, an automation application for iPhone: https://www.workflow.is.

3 Summary and Future Work

This paper has outlined work in progress to assess the affordance of methods for personalizing hearing aid settings. In one study, we are developing a mobile phone interface to enable user-driven self-adjustment among multiple settings, many more than are available through a traditional program switch interaction model. We also used a networked system to conduct Wizard-of-Oz style experiments to study user interaction with an automatic environmentally-adaptive system which notifies users about new recommended hearing aid sound settings. A second study to assess user preferences for hearing aid settings in various environments found a wide range of personal preferences, and prompts questions regarding the reliability of these preferences. We will repeat the sound preference test in different sound environments to potentially derive candidate settings for personalization. A third study, documenting user adaptation to hearing aids through video diaries, takes a holistic approach to understanding everyday listening challenges.

Together, these three studies demonstrate the value of three unique applications of HCI methodology to better understand how users interact with hearing aids and connected devices.

References

1. Büchler, M., Allegro, S., Launer, S., Dillier, N.: Sound classification in hearing aids inspired by auditory scene analysis. EURASIP J. Adv. Sig. Process. **2005**(18), 387845 (2005)
2. Xiang, J., McKinney, M.F., Fitz, K., Zhang, T.: Evaluation of sound classification algorithms for hearing aid applications. In: 2010 IEEE International Conference on Acoustics, Speech and Signal Processing, pp. 185–188 (2010)
3. Aldaz, G., Puria, S., Leifer, L.: Smartphone-based system for learning and inferring hearing aid settings. J. Am. Acad. Audiol. **27**(9), 732–749 (2016)
4. Dreschler, W.A., Keidser, G., Convery, E., Dillon, H.: Client-based adjustments of hearing aid gain: the effect of different control configurations. Ear Hear. **29**(2), 214–227 (2008)
5. Aldaz, G., Haydell, T., Szafer, D., Steinert, M., Leifer, L.: User experience in training a personalized hearing system. In: Marcus, A. (ed.) DUXU 2014. LNCS, vol. 8519, pp. 3–14. Springer, Cham (2014). doi:10.1007/978-3-319-07635-5_1
6. Brungart, D.S., Simpson, B.D., Ericson, M.A., Scott, K.R.: Informational and energetic masking effects in the perception of multiple simultaneous talkers. J. Acoust. Soc. Am. **100**, 2527–2538 (2001)
7. Galvez, G., Turbin, M.B., Thielman, E.J., Istvan, J.A., Andrews, J.A., Henry, J.A.: Feasibility of ecological momentary assessment of hearing difficulties encountered by hearing aid users. Ear Hear. **33**(4), 497–507 (2012)

Design and Implementation of Smartphone Application for Measurement and Management of Depressive Emotions in Adolescents Using Cognitive Behavioral Therapy

Jung-Sun Yoo[1], In-Sook Kim[1], and Jung-A Gwon[2(✉)]

[1] Science of Education, Soonchunhyang University, Asan, Korea
[2] Youth Education and Counseling, Soonchunhyang University, Asan, Korea
hellogwon@gmail.com

Abstract. This follow-up study examines the development of smartphone application content for measuring and managing youth depression (Park et al. 2016) by designing and implementing a smart phone application that measures and manages depressive emotions in adolescents. This app facilitates specific, individualized analysis of depressive symptoms and a simple, continuous self-check. By avoiding one-time or comprehensive analysis and diagnosis of depression, the app will allow for continuous management of the psychological states. We also aim to provide practical counseling services. To achieve this goal, we examined not only existing studies on youth depression, but also depression-related applications that can be integrated as components of the mobile application. The smartphone application consists largely of tools to facilitate emotional management, anxiety and tension relaxation, changes in negative thinking, and consultation linkage.

Keywords: Smartphone · Application · Youth mental health · Depression · Cognitive behavioral therapy

1 Introduction

Prevention and appropriate intervention are crucial in addressing the mental health issues of adolescents because the impacts of such issues typically extend into adulthood. Nonetheless, according to the results of a study by the Korea Youth Policy Institute, the number of adolescents with mental health problems is gradually increasing, and the system is currently failing to provide them adequate support. Furthermore, adolescent depression weakens the thinking, planning, and performance of those who suffer its symptoms, resulting in limited self-motivation. Thus, patients struggle to approach the treatment scene with self-motivation. In this study, we propose an appropriate intervention method that emphasizes user-centered convenience and daily use—specifically, the development of smartphone applications that incorporate psychiatry into engineering. This study follows-up on a previous study of the

© Springer International Publishing AG 2017
C. Stephanidis (Ed.): HCII Posters 2017, Part II, CCIS 714, pp. 317–323, 2017.
DOI: 10.1007/978-3-319-58753-0_47

development of smartphone application content for measuring and managing youth depression (Park et al. 2016) for wellness, which incorporated psychoanalysis into engineering technology. This earlier study was limited in several ways: first, the application was difficult to use in the actual counseling scene because the content was developed from a prototype; secondly, the application was developed to be used as an auxiliary means of group counseling, and it was therefore difficult for all youth to use it. The purpose of this study is to provide a practical and continuous counseling service with simple and continuous self-examination, as well as specific, individualized analysis of depression. We developed smartphone content for a possible Android environment. In addition, as a result of examining existing domestic and overseas smartphone applications related to depression, we identified three common features: first, pathological diagnosis smartphone applications predominate; second, virtually all of them charge for consecutive use online; and, third, designs are monotonous. In this study, we tried to address the above issues by differentiating our application from existing ones in the following ways:

- First, because depression has emerged as the most pressing youth mental health concern, we aimed to develop an application that is both pathological diagnosis-centered and easy for youth with a propensity toward depression to use.
- Second, we developed the application to facilitate continuously symptom monitoring and management by building a database so that changes in individual emotional states can be tracked weekly and monthly.
- Third, the application provides instruction in skills for coping with depression as well as immediate access to help through a program that 4.7.8 your breathing style, your own thinking style records, and free counseling.
- Finally, we added design elements to maintain youth interest and ensure continued use of the application.

2 Application Content for Prevention and Improvement of Youth Depression

This study developed an application that treats depression using cognitive behavioral therapy methods with proven effectiveness in a number of previous studies. The structure of cognitive behavior therapy include of persuasion and controversy as a process to change irrational thoughts, and to give specific action tasks to correct individual misperceptions and interpretations of major life events. In cognitive behavior therapy, the subject should play an active role in this process. Therefore, we judged that, in combination with therapy, the characteristics of the application that enable users to take the lead in their own treatment would have a positive effect. The application is designed to enable continuous, everyday use, taking into consideration the tastes and interests of adolescents, and each available area is intended to be mutually complementary within one activity of depressed emotional management.

2.1   Emotion Management

- The emotion management functions of the application include the Emotion Diary and the Anger Coping Method Tree.
- Adolescents with depressive symptoms tend to lack understanding of their current emotional states and have the difficulty of finding appropriate ways to address negative emotions. Through 'emotional management', adolescents can compare how they feel about their emotions, and they can also better understand their current emotional states.
- The Emotion Diary uses a total of 60 emotion-identifying words including joy, anger, sadness, fear, likes, dislikes, winds, seven major emotions and subordinate emotions. By keeping track of emotions that were felt on a given day, emotional states contained in glass bottles can be evaluated weekly and monthly, which makes it is possible to more effectively evaluate their periodic emotional states and to understand the flow of accumulated emotions.
- Writing 'the things that I want to be comforted about' and 'the experience of helping' makes it possible to identify emotional events, recognize the individual causes of depression, and practice better self-control.
- By getting users to write about how to cope with anger-inducing issues or situations, the Anger Management Method Tree helps users identify positive ways to act. Click 'Add' to create a leaf, and when you are finished, you can move the leaf to the desired location via 'Move'.
- To appeal to teenagers who tend to emphasize personality and individuality, the application allows users to decorate their own trees and add design elements to mirror their interests.
- I added 'Relaxation' and 'Accidental Conversion' in the lower part so that I could immediately see what kind of action I had in addition to the way I coped.

2.2   Anxiety and Relaxation of Tension

- Various body relaxation techniques that aim to eliminate or mediate the various forms of tension encountered in everyday life and lay the foundation for efficient and productive mind and body have been implemented in the application.
- To appropriately address and manage anxiety that deepens feelings of depression, we have embodied the process of using emotional relaxation through physical relaxation.
- Following a brief sequence of steps, you can move to a quiet, stable location. When you press the play button, the number of runs and how to run along with the narration comes up.

2.3   Change Negative Thinking

- To help adolescents with depressive tendencies improve their maladaptive attitudes, cognitive errors, and negative self-perceptions, the application enables users to examine life events by writing about their own experiences.
- Users think about the negative emotions they felt during the day and record the events that caused them. Recording the incidents allows users to name the incident through 'cognitive error' in order to search for an accident that made him or her worse in the situation.
- After searching for cognitive errors in automatic thinking, it is possible for users to record alternatives for positive adaptation thinking, and to recognize that their automatic thoughts and beliefs are irrational, thereby actively participating in the process of changing their thought processes.
- Once users are able to compare negative and alternative thoughts at a glance, they will be able to visually confirm the transition of the accident.

2.4   Consultation Linkage

- We added phone counseling and cyber counseling to this application, gaining permission to use these services in order to help the youth who might be burdened by the expenses of visit the counseling room.
- Both cyber counseling and telephone counseling are supported and operated by the Korea Youth Counseling and Welfare Development Institute, a semi-governmental organization. The services are free of charge and available 24 h a day, 365 days a year (Figs. 1, 2, 3 and 4).

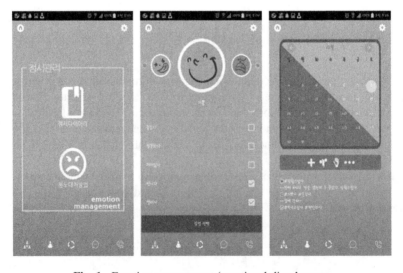

Fig. 1. Emotion management 'emotional diary' screen

Fig. 2. Emotion management 'Anger Coping Method Tree' screen

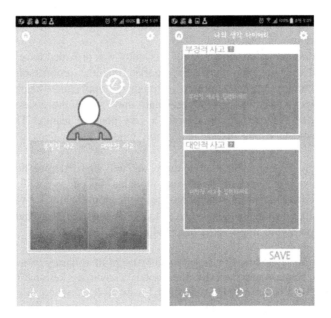

Fig. 3. Change negative thinking screen

Fig. 4. Consultation linkage screen

3   Conclusion

This study focuses on the prevention and management of depression using a mobile application that enables continuous management of depressed mood in everyday life. In addition, by exploring an adolescent's perception of situations that cause depressive emotions, we were able to see how he coped by using the application in various situations including communication.

The application under consideration in this study was provided to seven university students for pilot testing and the users reported that the process of continuously recording and confirming their emotions through the application helped them more closely examine their emotions. In particular, they found the access to practical counseling services via phone and internet a very positive feature. Throughout the process, supplementary bug fixes, application guides, and videos were added as needed.

For the future development of this study, we will first examine how to provide immediate feedback on users' dysfunctional thoughts. Second, we will integrate various additional content including video into the application. Finally, we will continue to solicit and consider user evaluations in order to clarify the usefulness and effectiveness of the application and to improve its practicality.

Acknowledgements. This research was supported by the MSIP (Ministry of Science, ICT, and Future Planning), Korea, under the ITRC (Information Technology Research Center) support program (IITP-2016-H8601-16-1009) supervised by the IITP (Institute for Information & communications Technology Promotion).

References

Kim, K.-N., Choi, D.-S., Lee, K.-M., Lee, M.-J.: Analysis on interesting element of mobile application using user reviews. Korea Digit. Contents Soc. **13**(3), 431–438 (2012)

Park, J.-S., Cho, J.-S., Ham, S.-H., Park, J.-S., Gwon, J.-A.: Smart-phone application content development for the measurement and management of adolescents' depression. Korea Soc. Wellness, **11**(2), 319–329 (2016)

Ha, E.-B., Lim, C.-M., Choi, J.-H.: Determinants of continuous use of mobile healthcare applications. Hum. Comput. Interact. Korea, **2014**(2), 645–650 (2014)

Ha, T.-H., Baek, H.-G.: Design and implementation of an application to cure wounded heart of the youth using color. Korea Digit. Contents Soc. **14**(4), 597–604 (2013)

Shen, N., Levitan, M.J., Johnson, A., Bender, J.L., Hamilton-Page, M., Jadad, A.A.R., Wiljer, D.: Finding a depression app: a review and content analysis of the depression app marketplace. JMIR mHealth and uHealth **3**(1), 16 (2015)

Smart Environments

Rist: An Interface Design Project for Indoor Navigation

Meeshu Agnihotri, Reema Upadhyaya, Katherine Kenna[✉],
and Chen-Dah Chiang

Georgia Institute of Technology, Atlanta, USA
kkenna3@gatech.edu

Abstract. This poster presents the findings from a semester long project that explored interface design for indoor wayfinding. In the project called RIST, we designed and evaluated the usability of a wayfinding interface within the context of a grocery shopping application. Through a formative study consisting of remote surveys, contextual interviews and observations, we identified the challenges in navigating in an indoor space. Next, we evaluated user preference and comfort for the navigation experience using a Smartwatch. We also evaluated the advantages and disadvantages of using a watch interface to that of a head mounted device. Using feedbacks through lab and in-context user testing, we iteratively optimized the presentation of complex information on the interface. We understood the parameters essential to optimize grocery shopping navigation experience, and concluded the project with a high-fidelity prototype. For example, we found that the relative direction guidance was more preferred over exact Cartesian mapping. In the poster, we discuss factors- such as usage of multiple devices and device sharing behavior-that influenced our decisions throughout the iteration process. Here we present such guidelines abstracted from our observation and findings that can help inform designers and researchers on the presentation of information rich tasks such as navigation and content browsing on small screen devices.

Keywords: Wayfinding · Smartwatch application · Indoor navigation · Human computer interaction · Interface design

1 Introduction

Wayfinding under time constraint can be a challenging experience. While research has shown that successful signage could be one potential solution (Cooper 2010), it doesn't cater to a user's specific goals. Using wearable interfaces can can also go a step further from signage systems in offering an individually targeted hands free guidance. Our formative research has helped identify an existing need for personal navigational interfaces for indoor wayfinding. This is especially relevant in public spaces such as shopping malls and hospitals where people under varying constraints come to achieve personal tasks and obtain services. Store-induced stress has also been shown to contribute to the consumer's overall experience and consequently on purchase likelihood (Albrecht et al. 2017). Prior research has shown that multitasking has a negative cost in the quality of task

© Springer International Publishing AG 2017
C. Stephanidis (Ed.): HCII Posters 2017, Part II, CCIS 714, pp. 327–334, 2017.
DOI: 10.1007/978-3-319-58753-0_48

performance (Menneer et al. 2010), which is further affected when presented with rich information on multiple interfaces. Therefore, it is imperative to study and design for specific contexts to avoid visual cognitive overload when delivering relevant information. In that regard, we designed and evaluated the usability of a wayfinding interface within the context of a grocery shopping application. The goal of this project was to help inform designers and researchers on the presentation of information rich tasks such as navigation and content browsing on small screen devices. We identified the challenges in navigating in an indoor space, and evaluated user preference for the navigation experience using a smartwatch. Using feedback through lab and in-context user testing, we iteratively optimized the presentation of complex information on the interface.

2   Related Work

Studies on navigation design for small screen devices have identified challenges (Baudisch and Rosenholtz 1993; Ekman and Lankoski 2002), navigation design principles (Levine et al. 1984) and have explored design for different scenarios (Baudisch and Rosenholtz 1993; Rukzio et al. 2005; Timmerman et al. 2013). Timmerman et al. (2013) explore time based navigation wherein the designed system highlights routes per the time desired to reach the destination. While such a system may be useful when a person is shopping without a time constraint, most of our users expressed shopping under time constraints.

Rukzio et al. (2005) design a multi device navigation system for public spaces that maps provided navigation information to the real world context. The public display points a compass needle in the desired direction at the same time the user's personal device vibrates. This cue helps the user navigate without looking at the mobile device. While providing a similar public navigation display in a grocery store may make it easier to find relevant aisles, it may require extra hardware installation for the store which may not be feasible. With respect to the design, a redundancy in encoding navigation directions through haptics and visuals may lead to a richer experience especially if parents are unable to see the direction on their personal devices.

Ekman and Lankoski (2002) highlight the importance of designing effective and likeable navigation interfaces. In a comparative study, they tested two interfaces with users - one consisting of rich contextual information along with an arrow for direction while the other consisting of just the arrow. The interface with just an arrow was reported easier to use and resulted in fewer mistakes due to confusion or misinterpretation. However, users reported liking the system with contextual information more as it was more familiar and credible.

3   Formative Study

3.1   Methods and Results

Contextual Interviews and Observation: We interviewed 13 shoppers at Walmart over two days and 4 at Target on a day. The semi-structured conversations revolved around questions such as: "What goes into planning for a shopping trip?", "What is difficult about shopping?", "What is easy or enjoyable about shopping?" and "What is something that may improve your experience?". Most shoppers were entire families (mother, father, and children), but some included older children or other relatives while others were alone. Of the 6 shoppers present with children, only one was male.

There were no big differences in answers whether the parent was shopping alone or not, except 40% of parents shopping together mentioned they plan for a quick shopping trip, while no other groups mentioned speed outside of checkout time. We received similar answers but noticed trends like parents wanting reduced time in the store or means to entertain their kids. We categorized answers into 3 groups (difficulties with children, difficulties with shopping experience and difficulties with checkout) based on frequency. 50% of our shoppers expressed difficulties during the shopping experience which included problems such as finding an item etc. After each participant told us what they found difficult, we asked what they might do to remedy their issues. 20% of our interviewees said that they wanted a technology to find items faster while other suggestions were toys for keeping kids entertained and day care.

Surveys: The online survey was carried out as a follow up to interviews to get opinions from a wider user base. The questions centered around similar topics as the ones discussed in interviews but collected additional demographic data as well as deeper understanding of their planning process. A significantly larger number of non-parents (82% of 96 responses) responded to the survey and about 10% of the respondents were not currently residing in the US. Shoppers expressed a wide range of problems which can be grouped as problems in finding and comparing items, remembering to shop for all the items in the list, slow checkout lines, limiting shopping within a budget and distance and commute from the store. Another problem was doubling back in an aisle to search for a product.

3.2   Discussion

Role of Children During Shopping: Parents shopping with children have specific needs such as childcare especially given that 40% of the parents we interviewed, planned for a quick shopping trip. Kids who were brought shopping to pick out their own items were much happier. In other words, time-consuming processes such as the locating of merchandise and checkout becomes stressful with the risk of a child running off and if the child presents opposing opinions.

4   Design and Evaluation

To address the need found in our user research, we decided to build a navigational application, specifically for grocery shopping. We evaluated several devices to explore the physical functionality, then evaluated design iterations with experts and users. Below is an overview of our evaluations and the design decisions made throughout the process.

4.1   Usability Specifications

The way users use an app evolves with time and hence the app needs to have features which would be equally usable as well as useful for a novice and an expert user. For example, users unfamiliar with the store will require more guidance with exact location of aisles within the store. In contrast, frequent users will simply be looking for the next aisle number they need to go to. Our design decision to have a single screen that provides both pieces of information appealed to the wider user base. Our usability specifications included:

- Learnability: App should be easy to learn and predictable
- Errors and Recoverability: User should be able to avoid errors and if they occur, recover from them
- Efficiency: Once the user has learned the app, it should be efficient
- Memorability: Easy to remember for even casual users
- Satisfaction: Easy to use and aesthetically pleasing

4.2   First Iteration

Our first design iteration consisted of 2 interfaces focused on navigating a grocery store. They were designed for a smartwatch and heads-up display, specifically Apple Watch and Google Glass. Mock-ups can be seen in Fig. 1 below.

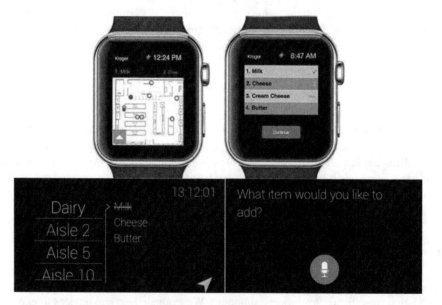

Fig. 1. Navigation, list view, and adding items in the first iterations on Apple Watch (above) and Google Glass (below).

Evaluation: To determine what device and features were idea, we conducted expert evaluations with human-computer interaction specialists. We had mock-ups of both a Google Glass and Apple Watch interface, viewed on their respective devices and worn by each expert. We asked the experts to think aloud while they used each interface and comment on the design, flow, content, and most importantly, the device used specifically for navigating a store. In order to better compare both designs, we asked the users to imagine wanting to add an item to their grocery list.

Results: In regards to the device itself, most users preferred a device on their wrist, as they felt the heads up display was too intrusive. In both cases, users felt that they could imagine being more comfortable with the features if the technology is more universal. For the watch interface, experts commented on the small font and graphics, something we struggled with when prototyping for a small screen. They were confused about the meanings of icons and the inconsistencies. Based on their feedback, we needed to work on how the user can progress through the items in different scenarios and making a functional prototype. We concluded that the characteristic features of the Apple Watch made it more learnable, reliable, and memorable to use.

4.3 Second Iteration

Using the feedback from the first iteration, we improved the smart watch interface design and conducted a heuristic evaluation with more UI experts. Our prototype was designed to use the scroll, tap, animation, and force touch gestures frequently used on Apple Watch. The design, in Fig. 2, featured a compass-like navigation, where the next aisle would be placed on the outer circle relative to the position of the user. List items are viewed by clicking on the aisle number and removed by swiping. Items can be added through voice command by accessing the menu with force touch.

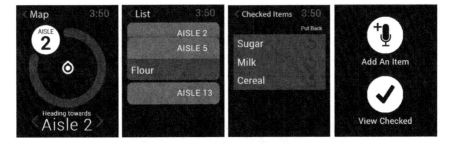

Fig. 2. Second interface iteration of navigation, list view, undo action, and adding items on Apple Watch

Evaluation: The expert users were asked to imagine they were carry out a shopping task. The task involved starting the application, using the navigation, identifying specific list items, and adding, removing, and re-adding (undo) items. We designed the interface based on this task so there would be minimal screens to prototype. As they completed the task, we wrote down the errors they made, and recorded them. After the completion of every user evaluation, we asked a set of questions to get heuristic feedback on the prototype.

Results: The following are the usability heuristic issues we found during this second user testing session.

- Visibility and affordance to transition from the list view to menu
- Learnability and intuitiveness for novice users and system visibility
- Predictability of icons and mapping of gestures
- Universal design and designing for users with impairments
- Feedback and accessibility is not immediate

Experts suggested that the map page should have an overview of the items in the displayed aisle and that being in the aisle will automatically check off the items. We chose not to integrate automatic-checking in case users decide not to get an item. The experts also expressed concern in understanding and imagining the motion design aspects of the map view.

Many participants did not use the compass provided in the app, instead, they looked at the compass to identify which aisle is next, switched to the list screen, then started heading toward that aisle. Some also assumed that the list would be in order from front to back of the aisle (ours was alphabetical). Finally, we received feedback to add a preview of the items needed in the next aisle before navigating there. These were all valuable insights integrated into our third and final prototype.

4.4 Third Iteration

Our third prototype (see Fig. 3) removed the directional navigation completely because we found users only wanted to know the aisle number of the item about the in-store signage. Users also have the option to to view the entire list ("ALL") or specific aisles, depending on how they like to shop or the length of their list. Items are listed in the order they appear in the aisle and on the same page as the aisle number to reduce steps. Adding items is still done through force touch, which is the default method of accessing the menu on Apple Watch.

Fig. 3. Final iteration on the Apple Watch

Evaluation: We chose to have users complete the same shopping tasks outlined in the second iteration's evaluation, but this time in the context of a specific store. Before completing the task, users were asked about their familiarity with the store, Apple Watch, iOS, their comfort level using voice commands in public, and the number of times they usually grocery shop in a week. Familiarity and comfort was measured on a Likert scale, 1 being very unfamiliar or very uncomfortable, and 5 being very familiar or very comfortable. Most users were familiar or very familiar with the store and iOS, but not very familiar or comfortable with the Apple Watch or voice control. Users were then asked to complete tasks that involved finding items on their list, checking off items, and undo checking off items. We observed them using the app, errors made, and noted any comments or questions they had. Afterwards, users were asked to complete 5 usefulness Likert scale questions regarding the overall app, adding items, aisle numbers, checking off items, and undoing actions. We also conducted semi-structured interviews with each participant about what was intuitive, helpful, relevant, distracting, or desired about the application.

Results: Force touch was an unfamiliar method of accessing the menu to add items, which was expected for users unfamiliar with the watch. Users spent some time looking on the screen for a button to add an item until accessing the menu. One user seemed to prefer using the "All Aisles" list to shop while the other made the point that he'd appreciate the segregation for longer lists that could become cluttered otherwise, cementing our idea of a multifunctional list for a variety of users. Finally, it was suggested to use a quick gesture for the undoing of an item that is checked off and an option for clearing all the checked items at once, as doing it individually would take a lot of time. Users found most of the functions and overall app to be useful to the task, except adding items. This may be because the menu was hidden and it is difficult to add items without voice command. We believe it will make more sense for users to add items onto the list with a smartphone or desktop, then use the watch app to navigate and cross off items. Users gave the most positive feedback about the aisles listed in the order of navigation and not having to go back and forth through the store.

4.5 Discussion

Motion design plays a pivotal role for users to accurately grasp and understand the functionality of a feature in an app and appreciate its value. We initially hypothesized that prototyping and testing on an Apple Watch would emulate the experience of the final product better and users would be able to relate how the app functions and fits in with their shopping experience. However, we soon observed that the watch prototype's inability to perform basic gestures such as swipe and force touch caused users to be frustrated with these limitations and they were unable to focus on the function of the app or the shopping experience.

Our decision to frequently test the app in the store with target and non-target users provided beneficial insights about user behavior and interactions with the device and the app in the store, and allowed us to apply a rapidly iterative design process to assess whether our design was evolving in the right direction.

5   Conclusion and Next Steps

From the beginning of our evaluation to the end, we iterated rapidly on our prototype to incorporate feedback from our users. We quickly assessed two alternatives as our interface's platform, allowing us to focus on the issue of navigation and refine the functionality and navigation. There are many features for our app that we wish to include but were not prototyped. For example, store coupons or promotional codes, item prices, sale recommendations, and brand recommendations. There were also high fidelity interactions that we wished to adopt but were not prototyped because they did not fit into the functionality of our interface. This includes Apple's force touch technology, location-based haptic notifications native to the Apple watch, and GPS location services.

Issues such as scalability, generalizability, the dialog initiative, and predictability can be addressed in future iterations. Not to mention other miscellaneous details such as the orientation of the Apple Watch screen relative to a user's arm position when pushing a grocery cart. We plan to develop a higher fidelity prototype to include the additional features and address the newer concerns. The complete system would require a companion iPhone app to import grocery lists and manage the Apple Watch app, as well as secure connections to the inventory database of respective grocery stores.

References

Albrecht, C.M., Hattula, S., Lehmann, D.R.: The relationship between consumer shopping stress and purchase abandonment in task-oriented and recreation-oriented consumers. J. Acad. Market. Sci. 1–21 (2017)

Baudisch, P., Rosenholtz, R.: Halo: a technique for visualizing offscreen location. In: Proceedings of the Conference on Human Factors in Computing Systems, CHI 2003 (1993)

Cooper, R.: Successful signage: how hospitals have solved wayfinding challenges. Health Facil. Manag. 23(11), 27–30 (2010)

Ekman, I., Lankoski, P.: What should it do? Key isssues in navigation interface design for small screen devices. In: CHI 2002 Extended Abstracts on Human Factors in Computing Systems, pp. 622–623. ACM (2002)

Levinew, M., Marchon, I., Hanley, G.: The placement and misplacement of you-are-here maps. Env. Behav. 16(2), 139–157 (1984)

Menneer, T., Donnelly, N., Godwin, H.J., Cave, K.R.: High or low target prevalence increases the dual-target cost in visual search. J. Exp. Psychol.: Appl. 16(2), 133 (2010)

Rukzio, E., Schmidt, A., Krüger, A.: The rotating compass: a novel interaction technique for mobile navigation. In: CHI 2005 Extended Abstracts on Human Factors in Computing Systems, pp. 1761–1764. ACM (2005)

Timmermann, J., Poppinga, B., Pielot, M., Heuten, W., Boll, S.: TimedNavigation: a time-based navigation approach. In: Proceedings of the 15th International Conference on Human-Computer Interaction with Mobile Devices and Services, pp. 476–479. ACM (2013)

Mobile App for a GPS-Based Location-Specific Communication System

"Ninja Messenger"

Riya Banerjee[✉] and Yugo Takeuchi

Graduate School of Integrated Science and Technology,
Shizuoka University, Hamamatsu, Japan
riya.banerjee.15@shizuoka.ac.jp,
takeuchi@inf.shizuoka.ac.jp

Abstract. This paper gives a detailed explanation of the proposal to build a mobile application for the purpose of communicating with other users of the mobile app who are in the vicinity of the communication initiator. This app enables the user to send text messages which may contain location-specific information.

Keywords: Android app · Smartphone · GPS · Location-based communication · Messaging service · Computer mediated communication · Mobile social computing and social media · Social media software

1 Introduction

Text-based communication is very popular in today's generation as it is quick, context-free and recordable. However, in order to communicate via text, one must have the receiver's contact information, such as their phone number or email address. Therefore, messages cannot be sent to an indefinite number of people. In case of location-aware apps, it may be useful if one can send a message to all those present in a particular area.

The system is an Android mobile application which, upon installation, can be used to send messages to those in the vicinity of the user as long as the receiver or receivers themselves have the same application. Thus, its main purpose is to provide location-specific information in real-time.

This is comparable to natural human communication in the real world, where one can even approach strangers for help or to know more about the location. In such a case, one can even know the response of the person immediately by observing their facial expressions, which is not possible with text-based communication. Thus, the system combines the advantages of verbal and text-based communication to provide a convenient means of communication among people in a specific area.

This app facilitates communication among those who have met for the first time and are at a similar location, without the need for exchanging contact information first. Thus, this method has been developed for extremely short exchanges. Moreover, the information provided in the messages will be kept as a record and can be used later.

C. Stephanidis (Ed.): HCII Posters 2017, Part II, CCIS 714, pp. 335–340, 2017.
DOI: 10.1007/978-3-319-58753-0_49

Thus, the focus is on the receipt of useful information rather than on the sender-receiver relationship or on the socializing aspect which is still possible in case there are some interested parties. Even if communication may have been initiated via the cyber-space, since the users are within eyeshot of each other in the real world, they may use this initial contact to further communicate verbally as well. Therefore, this system can be used to supplement verbal communication or provide an alternative to it in case verbal communication is not convenient or desired.

2 Features of the Ninja Messenger

This app has been created using native Android code, that is, using Android studio, the recommended IDE for Android app developers. The main language used for the code is Java, with XML being used for the GUI. We have incorporated the latest Android material design concepts and suggestions into the app. The SQLite database is used to store the messages for later reference.

There are three methods by which a user can send messages. Each method can be used in different situations as they serve different purposes.

1. Shuriken mode

In this mode, the sender can send a message to another user who is in their direct line of sight by pointing the mobile device in the direction of the intended receiver and sliding one's finger across the screen after the message is typed. This method is helpful for direct, context-free, short-term communication.

2. Noroshi mode

This mode is for sending the same message simultaneously to all users within a certain radius of the sender's device. Upon writing the message, the sender must aim the mobile device at the sky and perform the sliding gesture. One can think of this as the messaging equivalent to making an announcement on a loudspeaker, without the noise.

3. Makibishi mode

In this mode, after the message is typed, the sender directs his or her mobile device at the ground. The message is received by any user who passes that point during the life span of the message (Fig. 1).

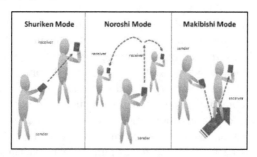

Fig. 1. A pictorial representation of the three modes of message transmission

3   Applications

The applications of this mobile app may vary depending upon the mode being used. One general application for all 3 modes would be advertising. This app could be convenient for sending location-specific advertisements such as information about nearby shops, restaurants, tourist spots, et cetera or available special offers and discounts in those places (Table 1).

Table 1. Information on the effects of the power of sliding

		Power of sliding	
		Weak (slow)	Strong (fast)
Shuriken	Reaching range (distance)	Near	Far
Noroshi	Reaching range (area)	Small	Large
Makibishi	Remaining time span (life-time)	Short	Long

1. Shuriken mode

The advantage of this form of communication is that it can be used for a one-time communication with a stranger without having to provide one's own contact information.

For example, when asking for directions, the user could use this app to receive the directions in writing in case they forget or get confused and need to double-check. In this case, the user is more interested in the information than developing a relationship with the sender.

Another situation is when the sender does not want to disrupt the peace of the area by calling out to the receiver or does not want those around to hear the message intended only for the receiver. In such a situation, a text could be more convenient than speech-based communication.

2. Noroshi mode

In any specific room such as a classroom or an office, a user may send a text to all those in the room to ask if anyone has some time to help the sender with some project or assignment.

Another case could be to raise awareness or send notices which concerns everyone in a particular location. This could be useful in case of any sudden news of possible danger in an area.

3. Makibishi mode

This mode can also serve the purpose of providing area-specific information. However, it is different as its focus is a specific location point. Since the message will be received by anyone who passes a particular point, there may be different kinds of messages left at different points by the sender even in the same room.

One interesting application would probably be to construct treasure-hunt type activities. Other applications include providing information or route guides at points where the road branches off or at the entrances or exits of shops, malls, offices, et cetera.

4 GUI of the App

The following are some screenshots of the application (Fig. 2).

5 System Requirements

Firstly, the user must own a smartphone which has an Android OS, preferably version 5 or above with the app installed (Fig. 3).

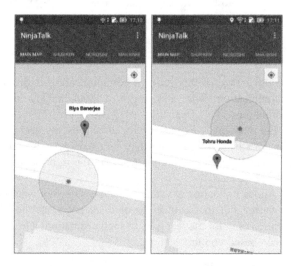

Fig. 2. The login page

Fig. 3. This is an example of what will show on the map when two devices are near one another.

Secondly, the app requires location permissions since the tracking of those in the nearby areas is mainly done using the GPS (Fig. 4).

Thirdly, the app should have access to the Internet so that the messages can be transmitted. This can be in the form of Wi-Fi, GPRS, etc. (Fig. 5).

Lastly, for the determination of the orientation and intensity of the sliding gesture, a 3D acceleration sensor and magnetometer must be present in the mobile device.

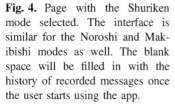

Fig. 4. Page with the Shuriken mode selected. The interface is similar for the Noroshi and Makibishi modes as well. The blank space will be filled in with the history of recorded messages once the user starts using the app.

Fig. 5. Upon pressing the floating action button, the screen shown on the left will appear and upon pressing the "done" button, the message is displayed in the form of a cardview which can then be swiped in order to send the message. Also, depending upon the mode, some relevant instructions about the direction in which the user needs to swipe will appear.

6   Conclusion and Future Work

Thus, this app has the potential to provide a convenient means of communicating even with strangers for a brief moment without the need for exchanging contact information. Moreover, the information provided in the messages will be kept as a record and can be used later.

Apart from incorporating the basic functions described in this paper, there is scope for many more added features, the most important being the security features. It is possible that certain persons may try to misuse the app. They may send spam mail or advertise aggressively through the app. In such a case, we would like to add the feature of reporting such behavior or straightaway blocking such a user.

Secondly, in the Makibishi mode, when a person receives a message by passing through a specific location point, he or she may want to find out more about the contents of the message. For this purpose, they may want to directly contact the sender of the message. Hence, an option to send a direct message to the concerned person may be facilitated.

Apart from modifications, we also plan to test the app practically. This means that volunteers will be asked to install the app and use all of its features. Then they will be questioned about the ease of understanding and maneuvering of the app and what questions arose during its use. We would also like to find out what scenarios the users felt they could use the app in. Also, we hope to receive feedback about the user interface.

The feedback will help with the analysis of the comfort and convenience of using this app. After receiving feedback from the volunteers, some modifications might be required.

The potential users of the app may be anyone with a smartphone running the Android OS. Although the iOS version of the app may be developed in the future to reach a larger group of smartphone users.

References

1. Zeng, J., Li, M., Cai, Y.: A tracking system supporting large-scale users based on GPS and G-Sensor. Int. J. Distrib. Sens. Netw. **11**(5), 862184 (2015)
2. Shahzad, A., Landr, R., Lee, M., Xiong, N., Lee, J., Lee, C.: A new cellular architecture for information retrieval from sensor networks through embedded service and security protocols. Sensors **16**(6), 821 (2016)
3. Rizos, C.: Trends in GPS Technology & Applications. In: 2nd International LBS Workshop (2003)
4. Lane, N., Miluzzo, E., Lu, H., Peebles, D., Choudhury, T., Campbell, A.: A survey of mobile phone sensing. IEEE Commun. Mag. **48**(9), 140–150 (2010)
5. Miluzzo, E., et al.: Sensing meets mobile social networks: the design, implementation, and evaluation of the CenceMe application. In: Proceedings of 6th ACM SenSys, pp. 337–350 (2008)
6. Korel, B., Koo, S.: A survey on context-aware sensing for body sensor networks. Sci. Res. Publishing: Wireless Sens. Netw. **2**(8), 571–583 (2010)
7. Foerster, F., Smeja, M., Fahrenberg, J.: Detection of posture and motion by accelerometry: a validation in ambulatory monitoring. Comput. Hum. Behav. **15**, 571–583 (1999)
8. Cho, Y., Lee, J., Neumann, U.: A multi-ring color fiducial system and a rule-based detection method for scalable fiducial-tracking augmented reality. In: Proceedings of First International Workshop on Augmented Reality (IWAR) 1998, San Francisco, CA (1998)

Design for Indoor Navigation: *CROSSFLOW* for Multiple Simultaneous Pedestrians in Public Spaces

Han Cao[✉]

College of Arts and Media, Tongji University, Shanghai 201804, China
scimus88@hotmail.com

Abstract. The provision of navigational support for multiple simultaneous pedestrians visiting unfamiliar complex indoor pubilc spaces is challenging. The conventional methods (architectural design, signage, maps, and verbal and written instruction) and many mobile and pervasive computing approaches suffer one or more drawbacks. We developed *CROSSFLOW*, a Crossmodal Display to address the problems through exploiting human multimodal perception, especially crossmodal interactions and utilizing a low-cognitive load combination of public and personal displays. We identified in the design process that *CROSSFLOW* could facilitate navigation within an unfamiliar complex indoor environment, support multiple simultaneous pedestrians accessing personalized navigational information without resorting to location tracking and impose lower mental workload demands on users. This paper mainly presents the design principles of *CROSSFLOW* and the design spaces of the components of *CROSSFLOW* so as to inspire people to come up with the better design of the system or the better solutions to the problems associated with indoor navigation.

Keywords: Indoor navigation · Human-computer interaction · Multimodal interfaces · Crossmodal Displays

1 Introduction

The problems of negotiating large complex public spaces in modern society such as airports, hospitals and shopping malls has resulted in the indoor navigation problem becoming the prototypical application domain for ubiquitous computing and mobile interaction researchers, with typical approaches center around the provision of expensive and novel spatial localization technologies. Navigation or wayfinding in unfamiliar indoor environments become more of a challenge for people. Dogu and Erkip [1] documented the many costs associated with having wayfinding problems such as loss of time, decreased safety, stress, and discomfort.

There are three aspects to the indoor navigation problem: the user, environment, and task. We are interested in multiple nomadic users who have no previous knowledge of the spatial environment. The indoor environment we are concerned with will typically be large, complex and crowed spaces, which may have structural similarities to

© Springer International Publishing AG 2017
C. Stephanidis (Ed.): HCII Posters 2017, Part II, CCIS 714, pp. 341–348, 2017.
DOI: 10.1007/978-3-319-58753-0_50

functionally related environments. Experience has shown that in many situations, users struggle to find/locate appropriate navigational information using traditional signage and maps (especially when placed under time pressure), which gives rise to the need to design more effective navigational aids. Even where navigational information is provided by an environment, it is not personalized, it is not efficient (e.g. suggest generally applicable paths) and it usually places a significant cognitive load on the user.

Navigation in indoor environments is most commonly supported by the conventional methods (architectural design, signage, maps, and verbal and written instruction). However, wayfinding signs have a number of well know limitations. Dogu and Erkip [1] identify that although putting up signs is a universally acknowledged approach to prevent people from getting lost, the language or pictographs used in the signs are not always well understood. Locating wayfinding signs in itself can be difficult for people in modern commercial public spaces where there are high levels of visual noise, such as advertisements in the form of posters or digital displays. Conventional handheld paper maps, as well as stationary embedded representations of the environment (e.g. poster maps or physical models), require users to identify their locations and the locations of their destinations in order to formulate navigation plans. Furthermore, people have significant (and well documented) problems understanding spatial layout and wayfinding performance decreases with increases in floor plan complexity [2].

Although a number of mobile and pervasive computing technologies have been proposed to support indoor and outdoor navigation (i.e. location-based guidance systems) in recent years, most of solutions (e.g. [3–8]) generally seek to present maps and spatial information using multiple modalities, and in a manner sensitive to a user's needs and spatial context. However, such systems generally suffer one or more the following shortcomings:

- High attention and cognitive load demands;
- Relying on expensive and unreliable sensing and tracking technologies;
- Not supporting users undertaking multiple concurrent tasks while navigating;
- Small user capacity;
- Weak protection for user's privacy.

In order to address the drawbacks above, we applied the framework of Crossmodal Displays [9, 10] to the application area of indoor navigation, that is, we explored the design of *CROSSFLOW*, a novel navigation system which exploited the human multimodal perception, especially crossmodal interactions [11–13] and utilized the synergy of both existing public displays and personal displays. Based on these features, *CROSSFLOW* could facilitate navigation within an unfamiliar complex indoor environment, support multiple simultaneous pedestrians accessing personalized navigational information without resorting to location tracking, and impose lower mental workload demands on users. Few navigation system found has these features and advantages. This paper mainly presents the design principles of *CROSSFLOW* and the design spaces of the components of *CROSSFLOW* so as to inspire people to come up with the better design of the system or the better solutions to the problems associated with indoor navigation.

2   *CROSSFLOW* Design Principles

CROSSFLOW shows multiplexed visual directional information (the public cues) publicly corresponding to all the destinations at each decision point using the public displays (e.g. projected dynamic signs), and presents the personalized vibrotactile and/or auditory cues (the private cues) via the personal displays (e.g. smartphones combining with earphones) to different users timely to indicate the particular directional information that corresponds to their destinations.

Here, visual public information and auditory/vibrotactile private cues are used because *CROSSFLOW* is designed for multiple simultaneous users. For this reason, the disturbance to other occupants of the public space, including those who are not using the system, should be minimized. The private cues presented through the vibrotactile or auditory (through headphones) modalities are essentially private to the users. Although there are ambiguities in the public cues, the private cues such as buzz or beeps for the user could resolve such ambiguities. The way of using auditory or tactile cues to resolve ambiguity in a visual display is closely related to the observations and experimental design of Sekuler et al. [13] and the *bounce-inducing effect* [13].

The implications for multimodal interface design that we inferred from the neuroscientific literature on multimodal integration and crossmodal interaction in humans [10] indicate that when the spatially incongruent multimodal cues from the spatial incongruent displays are temporally combined and presented in parallel, a user may be able to integrate the spatially incongruent but temporally synchronized multimodal information into a meaningful new percept, e.g. an intuitive directional information indication relevant to their destinations. Moreover, the perception of visual public information may be enhanced by a simultaneous auditory and/or vibrotactile private cue regardless of the spatial disparity between the cues from different modalities. Therefore, instead of having to comprehend the configuration of a public space (as when using a map), a visitor to a public space can enter his destination on his personal device, and in response, his device receives a time slot schedule (cue mapping) which defines the time slot when the visitor's directional information corresponding to his destination would be shown in the space. Whenever the directional information is "valid", the personal device indicates this using the private cue.

3   *CROSSFLOW* Prototype

Figure 1 provides the schematic diagram of a prototype of *CROSSFLOW* indoor navigation system we developed, which embodied our conceptual design of *CROSSFLOW*. The system components and functions are as follows:

Public Displays. The public display used in the prototype are projections displayed by digital projectors connected to a networked PC server. Several different designs of the visual public directional information (e.g. the fish-flow pattern) can be projected on the floor of an indoor environment.

Note: Users can download a destination list and cue mapping corresponding to a navigational environment during synchronization between their personal displays and the server.

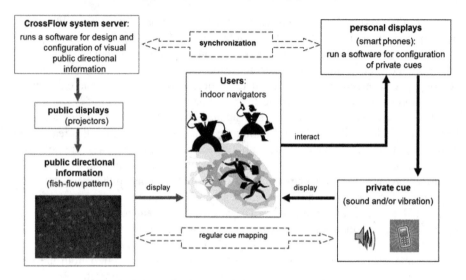

Fig. 1. Schematic diagram of the *CROSSFLOW* prototype

Personal Displays. *CROSSFLOW* uses smartphones (including earphones) as personal displays through which the private cues such as sound and vibration can be displayed privately.

Cue Mappings. We define that cue mapping as the spatio-temporal relation between the public cues and private cues. The design of cue mapping can be motivated by the different paradigms and techniques for the integration of information across the sensory modalities. Two types of cue mappings, a regular cue mapping and a random cue mapping, have been created.

Duration of Cue and Time Slot. The durations of the cue and the time slot (800 ms visual directional information, 800 ms vibration and/or 150 ms beep sound) were explored based on the findings of [14–16].

Public Directional Information (Public Cues). More than four visual design alternatives of directional information were designed including the rotating arrows shown at all decision points, highlighted markers showing all possible routes, and abstract ambient patterns covering the complete floor of the indoor environment (see Fig. 2).

Private Cues. A private cue should induce/invoke a subtle switch of a *CROSSFLOW* user's attention to the corresponding public directional information that is (concurrently) displayed. The private cues in *CROSSFLOW* could be abstract signals or explicit information such as a vibration coordinated with the onset of a time slot; or, an audible high pitch sound (i.e. a "beep") coordinated with the onset of a time slot. In our initial design we explored the combination of sound and vibration.

Fig. 2. The design of public cues: pointers (upper left), floor lights (upper right), ambient patterns (lower two)

Software for Visual Public Directional Information Configuration. *CROSSFLOW* includes a software tool, as a component of the central server, to support the design and configuration of the visual public directional information. The software tool enables a designer to graphically and interactively configure the directions of graphical elements of visual public directional information corresponding to different destinations (see Fig. 3) and specify the parameters that control the size, quantity, density, distribution areas (see Fig. 4) and dynamic properties of the individual graphical elements (rate of movement and visual persistence), as well as the duration and number of time slot within a cycle. The tool in turn generates a configuration file saved on the central server. For example, when configuring the fish-flow pattern using this software, a designer can steer the flow tendencies around obstacles and away from sites that are not intended to lie on the path to a destination through rotating a set of influential arrows (see Fig. 5), and can also add or scale the influential arrows to attain the desired patterns of flow (see Fig. 6).

Software for Private Cue (Auditory and Vibrotactile) Configuration. *CROSS-FLOW* also includes a software component installed on the smartphone, with which a user can configure the private cue. For example, the user can select a destination from a destination list, change the mode of private cue (vibration, sound, both or none) and the sound volume, and switch on/off private cues.

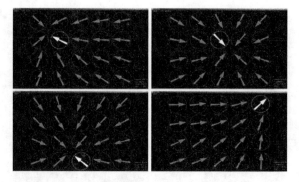

Fig. 3. Influential arrows for configuring the directions of graphical elements of the visual public directional information corresponding to different destinations

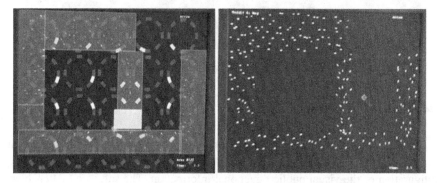

Fig. 4. An example of how to configure the distribution areas of the ambient pattern

Fig. 5. An example of how a designer steers ambient pattern flow tendencies around the central area of the screen

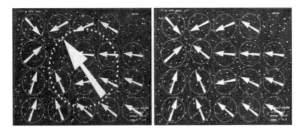

Fig. 6. An influential arrow (in red) added and scaled down for configuring the fish-flow pattern (Color figure online)

3.1 Usages

A user could be guided to his destination by simply selecting a numerical identifier of his destination in the destination list on his smartphone. The smartphone may either be pre-configured to synchronize with the *CROSSFLOW* central server, or it may communicate with the server via a wireless connection to receive the cue mapping and to synchronize the timing of the private cues. There is no need for the user's personal mobile device to communicate with the central server once this synchronization has been achieved.

4 Conclusions and Future Works

We present our initial design exploration of *CROSSFLOW*, a navigation system that has potential to avoid numerous drawbacks associated with many previous indoor navigation approaches, systems and technologies. Based on the design implications of multimodal integration and crossmodal interaction for interface design, *CROSSFLOW* could facilitate navigation within an unfamiliar complex indoor environment, support multiple simultaneous pedestrians accessing personalized navigational information without resorting to location tracking, and impose lower mental workload demands on users. It is a relatively low-cost navigation system because the digital public displays and smartphones are common devices and featured in many common public spaces such as shopping malls and art galleries. In the initial user study on our first prototype, individual participant was given dual tasks to perform using either *CROSSFLOW* prototype or hand-held paper map (more details were reported in [17, 18]). The initial results are encouraging.

However, because of the nature of *CROSSFLOW*, the users need to use both public cues and private cues to navigate. Besides this system limitation, some others were discussed in [10, 17, 18]. Further limitations, such as the way in which the system deals with errors, as well as the usability and the user experience afforded by *CROSSFLOW* need to be investigated and evaluated through formal user studies in the future. Moreover, the advantages *CROSSFLOW* should also be validated via a user study in which multiple simultaneous users would navigate in an unfamiliar complex physical indoor public space.

References

1. Dogu, U., Erkip, F.: Spatial factors affecting wayfinding and orientation: a case study in a shopping mall. Environ. Behav. **32**, 731–755 (2000)
2. O'Neill, M.J.: Effects of signage and floor plan configuration on wayfinding accuracy. Environ. Behav. **23**, 553–574 (1991)
3. Baus, J., Cheverst, K., Kray, C.: A survey of map-based mobile guides. In: Meng, L., Reichenbacher, T., Zipf, A. (eds.) Map-Based Mobile Services-Theories, Methods, and Implementations, pp. 193–209. Springer, Heidelberg (2005). doi:10.1007/3-540-26982-7_13
4. Ciavarella, C., Paternò, F.: The design of a handheld, location-aware guide for indoor environments. Pers. Ubiquitous Comput. **8**, 82–91 (2004)
5. Bejuri, W.M.Y.W., Mohamad, M.M., Sapri, M.: Ubiquitous positioning: a taxonomy for location determination on mobile navigation system. Int. J. Sig. Image Process. **2**, 15 (2011)
6. Liu, H., Darabi, H., Banerjee, P., Liu, J.: Survey of wireless indoor positioning techniques and systems. IEEE Trans. Syst. Man Cybern. Part C Appl. Rev. **37**, 1067–1080 (2007)
7. Kray, C., Kortuem, G., Krüger, A.: Adaptive navigation support with public displays. In: Proceedings of the 10th International Conference on Intelligent User Interfaces, IUI 2005, pp. 326–328. ACM (2005). doi:10.1145/1040830.1040916
8. Vanclooster, A., Van De Weghe, N., De Maeyer, P.: Integrating indoor and outdoor spaces for pedestrian navigation guidance: a review. Trans. GIS **20**(4), 491–525 (2016). doi:10.1111/tgis.12178
9. Cao, H., Olivier, P., Jackson, D.G.: Enhancing privacy in public spaces through crossmodal displays. Soc. Sci. Comput. Rev. **26**, 87–102 (2008). doi:10.1177/0894439307307696
10. Cao, H.: Crossmodal displays: coordinated crossmodal cues for information provision in public spaces. Doctoral dissertation. University of Newcastle Upon Tyne (2013)
11. Sarter, N.: Multimodal information presentation: design guidance and research challenges. Int. J. Ind. Ergon. **36**, 439–445 (2006)
12. Driver, J., Spence, C.: Crossmodal spatial attention: evidence from human performance. In: Spence, C., Driver, J. (eds.) Crossmodal Space and Crossmodal Attention, pp. 179–220. Oxford University Press, Oxford (2004)
13. Sekuler, R., Sekuler, A.B., Lau, R.: Sound alters visual motion perception. Nature **385**, 308 (1997)
14. Geldard, F.A.: Some neglected possibilities of communication. Science **131**(3413), 1583–1588 (1960). doi:10.1126/science.131.3413.1583
15. Brown, L.M.: Tactons: structured vibrotactile messages for non-visual information display. Doctoral dissertation. University of Glasgow (2007)
16. Gunther, E., O'Modhrain, S.: Cutaneous grooves: composing for the sense of touch. J. New Music Res. **32**, 369–381 (2003)
17. Olivier, P., Cao, H., Gilroy, S.W., Jackson, D.G.: Crossmodal ambient displays. In: Bryan-Kinns, N., Blanford, A., Curzon, P., Nigay, L. (eds.) Proceedings of HCI 2006, People and Computers XX – Engage, pp. 3–16. Springer, London (2007). doi:10.1007/978-1-84628-664-3_1
18. Olivier, P., Gilroy, S.W., Cao, H., Jackson, D.G., Kray, C.: Crossmodal attention in public-private displays. In: Proceedings of ACS/IEEE International Conference on Pervasive Services (ICPS06), pp. 13–18. IEEE (2006). doi:10.1109/PERSER.2006.1652201

Human-House Interaction Model Based on Artificial Intelligence for Residential Functions

Brendel Francisco Lima Santos$^{(\boxtimes)}$, Iury Batista de Andrade Santos,
Maurício José Miranda Guimarães, and Alcides Xavier Benicasa

Department of Information Systems - DSI, Federal University of Sergipe - UFS,
Itabaiana, SE, Brazil
brendelsantos@gmail.com, iurybas@gmail.com,
mauriciojosemirandaguimaraes@gmail.com, alcides@ufs.br

Abstract. The scenarios as smart homes and its devices requires novel ways to perform interactive actions. In this work we explore and develop a model to interact, in a natural, easy learning and intuitive manner, with a smart home, without use special sensors or another controllers, based on interpretation of complex context images captured with a trivial camera. We use artificial intelligence and computer vision techniques to recognize action icons in a uncontrolled environment and identify user interact actions gestures. Our model connects with well know computational platforms, which communicate with devices and another residential functions. Preliminary tests demonstrated that our model fits well for the objectives, working in different conditions of light, distance and ambiances.

Keywords: Human-house interaction · Artificial intelligence · Computer vision · Residential automation

1 Introduction

Forms of interaction between humans and computers have been evolved to new and diverse objects and environments of our day-to-day life. Advances in technologies, as miniaturization of devices, tools for no wired communications, and others, have provided the design of applications for smart homes, turning casual activities more simple, comfortable and intuitive. Residential automation is composed by a set of sensors, equipments, services and diverse technological systems integrated with the aim of assist basic necessities of security, communication, energetic management and housing comfort [1–3].

Those scenarios demand ways of interaction more dynamic, natural and easy learning. Several works presents novel interaction solutions based on voice commands, facial expressions, as well capture and interpretation of gestures, the

C. Stephanidis (Ed.): HCII Posters 2017, Part II, CCIS 714, pp. 349–356, 2017.
DOI: 10.1007/978-3-319-58753-0_51

last a point of investigation of this work. Systems that use free gestures interpret actions naturally realized by persons to communicate, giving the possibility of a more easy and intuitive way of interact to users, reducing the cognitive overload of information, training and learning [4]. Such type of interaction was perceived by researches in Human-Computer Interactions as relevant since the firsts investigations [5].

Therefore, we propose a model of interaction for smart homes without use of sensors or controllers, based on artificial intelligence techniques and computer vision. These methods are applied to recognizing actions of interaction with targets dynamically distributed in a residence, using capture of images from a trivial camera, in a manner similar to a touch area. This approach aims a more cheap, efficient and simple manner of interact with a smart home and its electric devices, using representative symbols and artificial intelligence techniques, recognizingly interactions from the user. Our work connect these techniques with well known computational platforms, which communicate with devices and another residential functions.

This work is organized as follow: in the next section, we present related works in residential automation. Our model, the techniques used and methodology is explicated in the section Methodology. Experiments and results are showed in section Experiments and Results. Finally, we conclude discussing the results and possible future improvements and researches to be explored.

2   Related Work

Capture of the gestures can be performed through the use of special devices, such as sensors, accelerometers and gloves. These accessories facilitate interpretation, however, the total cost of the system is increased [6]. In this sense, the work developed in Bharambe et al. [7] presents a system composed of an accelerometer to capture the gestures, a microcontroller responsible for identifying the information collected, a transmitter and an infrared receiver. It is worth mentioning that there is a limitation regarding distance, in addition to the fact that the infrared transmitter and receiver must be fully aligned.

In contrast to the use of special accessories, the methods based on computer vision require only a computer camera to capture images and automatically interpret complex scenes [8]. Therefore, Dey et al. [9] proposed a work where the capture and interpretation of gestures is performed using the camera of a smartphone. A binary signal is generated from the captured image, which is graphically analyzed and transmitted using bluetooth to a control board responsible for activate the devices in the residence.

Still referring to methods based on computer vision, Pannase [10] developed a research that focused on quickly detecting hand gestures. For this, algorithms of segmentation and detection of the positioning of the fingers were used, and, finally, the classification of the gesture through the neural network. Another aspect of this study is the limited amount of gestures, as well as the hand should be positioned exactly in front of the camera.

In this work, we propose a model of interaction between a human and a residential environment using gestures, dispensing especial sensors or another devices, providing a interaction solution more natural and intuitive to control the functions of a smart home as, for example, switch on and switch off electronic devices, lamps, open and close doors and windows etc. The system must be able to operate in both daytime and nighttime conditions. For this, a webcam was adapted to see infrared light.

In the next section will be presented the main characteristics of the proposed model.

3   Metodology

For the development of this project, techniques of artificial intelligence and computer vision, as well complex contexts images, have been adopted to identify interaction targets and actions of the user with the ambiance.

Our model is composed as presented in Fig. 1. An application located in a main computer is responsible for the execution of all procedures involving the techniques of artificial intelligence and computer vision. These procedures are applied upon a image captured from a webcam located in the environment, directed to where the target icons are placed. The action icons are disposed in the ambiance as desired by the user. The application in the main computer identifies if a user interaction action occurred. If positive, the respective action command is send to the control board, which is connected with the devices and another interactive functions of the residence.

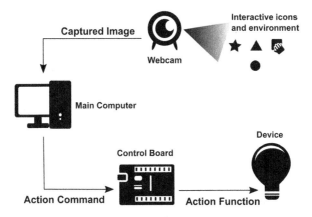

Fig. 1. Scheme of the model being proposed in this work, with it components and flux of information

To illustrate the operation of the proposed model was used a miniature of a residence. Is possible notice the triggering of a light as the interaction with an object occurs, as seen in the Fig. 2.

Fig. 2. Illustration of model working in a miniature

3.1   The Computer Vision Model

The application in the main computer incorporate a model developed in previous researches made by our research team. This model integrate different techniques of artificial intelligence, computer vision and image processing to discovery and classify specific objects (in this case, target icons of interaction) in a complex and low controlled environment. From a captured image of the ambiance, a pre-processing is performed for saturation of red-colored pixels, then we apply visual attention to identify interest areas in the image and discard any other visual information. In this step we have modified the classic method of visual attention as proposed in Itti et al. [11], simplifying it to respond only for color stimulus. The areas of interest are marked as seeds, which are used as input in the segmentation process. For segmentation we have used the method Watershed, as developed by Klava [12]. The segmentation step is responsible for generating individual elements of the target icons from the input image. These elements are classified using neural networks, were a action of interaction is attributed in respect with the type of each icon.

In follow, the interaction routines are started, continuously capturing images and searching for possible interact actions performed by the user. Interactions are recognized as changes in the coefficient of dissimilarity between the histograms of the regions where icons of interaction has been found. The dissimalirity $dSim_{cos}$ is calculated using an adaptation of the cosine similarity defined by:

$$dSim_{cos}(h_{ini}, h_{acq}) = 1 - \frac{\sum_{i=1}^{n} h_{ini_i} \cdot h_{acq_i}}{\sqrt{\sum_{i=1}^{n}(h_{ini_i})^2} \cdot \sqrt{\sum_{i=1}^{n}(h_{acq_i})^2}}, \qquad (1)$$

where $n = 255$, h_{ini} corresponds to the histogram of the red channel obtained from an initial capture and h_{acq} is the histogram of the red channel acquired from subsequent captured images.

The scheme of the computer vision model is show in Fig. 3.

3.2   The Human-House Interaction Model

The Human-house interaction model is composed as previously show in Fig. 1. The interactive icons placed in the environment was designed considering its function, simplicity and intuitive meaning. The icons are tested in diverse ambiances, with different conditions of light, distance from the webcam, and elements in the surrounds, to assure its correct recognizability by the computer

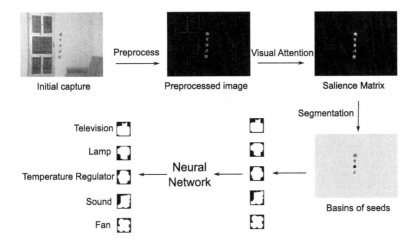

Fig. 3. Scheme of the computer vision model implementing artificial intelligence techniques (Color figure online)

vision model. The interactive functions are elected by its pertinence and utility. In Fig. 4 there is five icons of interaction used by our model, presented with their names and related functions.

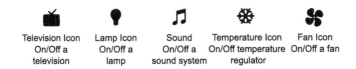

Television Icon	Lamp Icon	Sound	Temperature Icon	Fan Icon
On/Off a	On/Off a	On/Off a	On/Off temperature	On/Off a fan
television	lamp	sound system	regulator	

Fig. 4. Icons set of actions of interaction

Its is pertinent mention that our model is expansible and more icons can be introduced in the application.

4   Experiments and Results

The experiments were realized in several residential environments varying the positioning of the camera and with different levels of luminosity, including total absence of light. The process occurred through the attempt of interactions and the answers obtained as results. The environments where the tests were performed can be seen as in Fig. 5.

In total, 530 interactions were executed in ambiances with luminosity, being divided into 106 interactions attempts per option. The results in these conditions are presented through a confusion matrix, unsuccessful interactions (UI) and individual accuracy, as seen in Table 1. In addiction, the total accuracy was calculated, with a result of 96.04%.

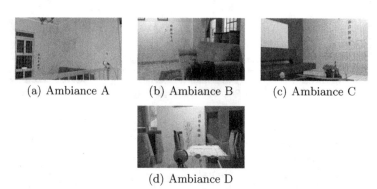

(a) Ambiance A   (b) Ambiance B   (c) Ambiance C

(d) Ambiance D

Fig. 5. Environments used in the tests

Table 1. Confusion matrix and individual accuracy of interaction in environments with luminosity

Actions	Fan	Lamp	Temperature	TV	Sound	UI	Accuracy
Fan	103	0	0	0	0	3	99.41%
Lamp	0	105	0	0	0	1	99.80%
Temperature	0	0	101	0	0	5	99.03%
TV	0	0	0	103	0	3	99.41%
Sound	0	0	0	0	97	9	98.26%
UI	0	0	0	0	0	0	0%

According with the objectives of this work, which refers to operation in nocturnal conditions, have been realized specific tests for these settings. Were executed the total of 205 interactions, distributed in 41 attempts per option. As done previously, the results are showed through confusion matrix, unsuccessful interactions (UI) and individual accuracy. The Table 2 exposes the results. In this case, the total accuracy obtained was 96.59%.

Table 2. Confusion matrix and individual accuracy of interaction in dark environments

Actions	Fan	Lamp	Temperature	TV	Sound	UI	Accuracy
Fan	38	0	0	0	0	3	98.50%
Lamp	0	41	0	0	0	0	100.0%
Temperature	0	0	40	0	0	1	99.49%
TV	0	0	0	39	0	2	99.00%
Sound	0	0	0	0	40	1	99.50%
UI	0	0	0	0	0	0	0%

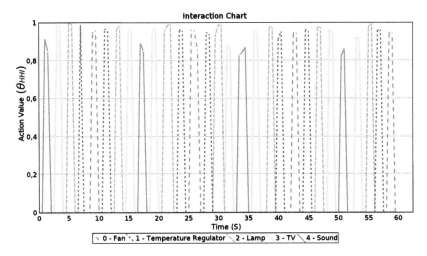

Fig. 6. Graphic of interaction in relation of the function action to the respective value of θ_{HHI}

In Fig. 6 is presented a graphic where interaction actions can be seen with its respective coefficient of dissimilarity, obtained using the Eq. 1, representing the human-house interaction value (θ_{HHI}). Only θ_{HHI} values above 0.8 are considered as a interaction by the user, triggering the send of the command of action. In the test execution of the Fig. 6 was intended the execution of twenty-nine interactions, with different functions icons, which all of them been recognized correctly.

The tests presented consistent results in both settings of light and scenarios, reaching high accuracy values. It is remarkable that none action have been triggered instead of another, corroborating the efficiency of the computer vision model adopted. Also, it is noteworthy that unsuccessful interactions are defined as the no recognized user interaction by the model, and not a interaction action executed arbitrarily, the last case being a more problematic situation.

Lastly, the interactions actions have been detected with confortable margins, with values of θ_{HHI} close of one, for the actions actually desired, and zero for the others, demonstrating robustness of the model.

5   Conclusions

In this work, a model of interaction based on artificial intelligence techniques and computer vision was proposed for smart homes without use of sensors or controllers. The proposed model was able to detected and recognized the icons of interaction correctly in a uncontrolled environment, with different distances from the camera used and the target icons, and different luminosity variances in the ambiance, rarely being necessary parameters changes or any type of calibration.

As presented in the previous section, the results exposed that interactions made by the user have been correctly identified in almost every action of interaction, which reinforces the confidence in the model been proposed.

Additionally, our model works in day and night conditions, only using a ordinary camera, dispensing special sensors or another controllers, with allows a low cost, easy learning and more natural form of interaction only using gestures. These characteristics was possible by the use of artificial intelligence and computer vision techniques, directing the complexity and cognitive enforces to the model and not to the users.

Conclusively, the model demonstrated satisfactory results, concretely offering a new option to control a residence. As future works, improvements in the method for detect interactions can be investigated, applying more intelligent approaches. Furthermore, a segmentation technique, providing a lower computational cost, and better segments quality, could be developed.

Acknowledgments. The authors would like to thank the Brazilian National Research Council (CNPq/PIBIC/UFS/PVE47492016) for the financial support provided for this research.

References

1. Chan, M., Hariton, C., Ringeard, P., Campo, E.: Smart house automation system for the elderly and the disabled, systems, man and cybernetics. In: IEEE International Conference on Intelligent Systems for the 21st Century, vol. 2, pp. 1586–1589. IEEE (1995)
2. Lee, K.Y., Choi, J.W.: Remote-controlled home automation system via bluetooth home network. In: SICE 2003 Annual Conference, pp. 2824–2829. IEEE (2003)
3. Ahmim, A., et al.: Design, implementation of a home automation system for smart grid applications. In: 2016 IEEE International Conference on Consumer Electronics (ICCE), pp. 538–539. IEEE (2016)
4. Valli, A.: Natural interaction white paper (2007). http://www.naturalinteraction. org/images/whitepaper.pdf
5. Aggarwal, J.K., Cai, Q.: Human motion analysis: a review. In: Proceedings of Nonrigid and Articulated Motion Workshop. IEEE (1997)
6. Erol, A., et al.: A review on vision-based full DOF hand motion estimation. In: IEEE Computer Society Conference on Computer Vision and Pattern Recognition-Workshops, CVPR Workshops. IEEE (2005)
7. Bharambe, A., et al.: Automatic hand gesture based remote control for home appliances. Int. J. Adv. Res. Comput. Sci. Softw. Eng. **5**(2), 567–571 (2015)
8. Jain, A.K., Dorai, C.: Practicing vision: integration, evaluation and applications. Pattern Recogn. **30**(2), 183–196 (1997)
9. Dey, S., et al.: Gesture controlled home automation. Int. J. Emerg. Eng. Res. Technol. **3**, 162–165 (2015)
10. Pannase, D.: To analyze hand gesture recognition for electronic device control. Int. J. **2**(1), 44–53 (2014)
11. Itti, L., et al.: A model of saliency-based visual attention for rapid scene analysis. IEEE Trans. Pattern Anal. Mach. Intell. **20**(11), 1254–1259 (1998)
12. Klava, B.: Segmentação interativa de imagens via transformação watershed. Dissertation Masters thesis, Instituto de Matemática e Estatística-Universidade de São Paulo (2009)

A Proposal for the "Cariño Index": A New Coordination Index Based on Weather Conditions

Akari Fujiwara[✉] and Katsuhiko Ogawa

Keio University, 5322 Endo, Fujisawa-shi, Kanagawa 252-0882, Japan
{sl4734af, ogw}@sfc.keio.ac.jp

Abstract. Deciding "What to wear today" is an oftentimes pleasurable part of most people's routine. However, especially at the turn of the season, wardrobe coordination often fails, leaving the individual feeling overly exposed or unnecessarily covered up. This premise is the basis of our proposal for the "Cariño index", which provides a reliable basis of coordination in any season or weather; using the "Cariño equation" to calculate the optimal index. The paper introduces the concept and procedures which inform the Cariño index and equation. The data, methodology, processes and results are described and the effectiveness of the "Cariño equation" and future issues are discussed.

Keywords: Life log · Weather · Clothes · Statistical analysis

1 Introduction

Getting up in the morning and deciding what to put on is a necessary and, sometimes, even fun, task. Especially for women attentive to current fashion trends, clothing and attire can be an important choice that could affect their moods and dispositions during the day. However, typically at the turn of the season, (e.g. from spring to summer or from autumn to winter), dressing and garb tend to be uncoordinated with the weather. An example of this would be putting on a short sleeve shirt when the weather is still too cold for that sort of clothing.

With regards to this specific issue, the Japan Meteorological Agency also publishes a "clothing index" on its homepage (see Ref. [2]) to respond to this problem. Thus, for instance, if the clothing index is 20, a one-point advice "muffler and gloves are indispensable" is displayed. Nevertheless, a full body coordination is not covered by this index. To address this specific issue, we devised the "Cariño index" which is an index that ensures better coordination in any season and weather, and the "Cariño equation" to calculate its optimal index.

This paper introduces the concept and structure of the "Cariño index" and the "Cariño equation", based on long-term observations in the Tokyo metropolis. The results of the evaluation experiments show the effectiveness of the "Cariño index" and the "Cariño equation". Also, future work is considered.

Note: Cariño means affection in Spanish.

© Springer International Publishing AG 2017
C. Stephanidis (Ed.): HCII Posters 2017, Part II, CCIS 714, pp. 357–365, 2017.
DOI: 10.1007/978-3-319-58753-0_52

2 Concept

The "Cariño index" is the total number of points (total score) assigned to a collection of items belonging to each of five groups of clothing articles, including; outer, tops, bottoms, shoes, and the other (see Fig. 1). Figures 2 and 3 show the score table in detail.

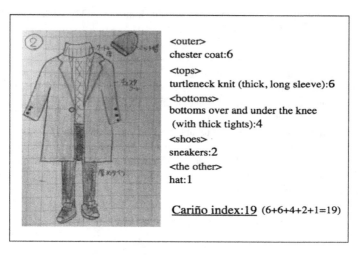

Fig. 1. Calculation example of Cariño index

<outer>
1 Short sleeve cardigan, short sleeve parka, gillet, vest, bolero
2 cardigan (thin), hoodies (thin), shirt (thin), stole
3 Blouson (thin), G jean, jacket (thin), Parker (thick), shirt (thick), long cardigan (thin), trench coat (thin and short), down vest, wind breaker
4 Cardigan (Thick), Trench Coat (Thick), Cordigan, Poncho, Short Coat, Blouson (Thick), Jacket (Thick)
5 half coat, leather jacket, down jacket, Mouton jacket
6 Long coat, Duffle coat (long), Chester coat, gown court
7 Fur coat, down coat, Mouton coat

<tops>
1 Tank top, camisole, sleeveless cut
2 T-shirt (short sleeve), cutaway (short sleeve), blouse (short sleeve), shirt (short sleeve)
3 T-shirt (thin · long sleeve), cutaway (thin · long sleeve), blouse (thin · long sleeve), shirt (thin · long sleeve), knit (thin · sleeveless · short sleeve), sweat (short sleeve)
4 V neck knit, (thin · long sleeve), V neck knit (thick · short sleeve), round neck knit (thin long sleeve), round neck knit (thick · short sleeve), turtleneck knit (thin · short sleeve), turtleneck knit · Sleeveless), shirt (thick · long sleeve), turtlenecked saw (long sleeve), sweat trainer
5 V neck knit (thick · long sleeve), round neck knit (thick · long sleeve), turtleneck knit (thin long sleeve), turtleneck knit (thick · short sleeve), sweat parka (with hood)
6 Turtleneck knit (thick, long sleeve)

Fig. 2. Outer and tops score

<bottoms>

1 bottoms over the knee (stockingless leg)

2 bottoms under the knee (stockingless legs)

3 bottoms over and under the knee (with stockings), bottoms with ankle length (no socks, no tights)

4 bottoms over and under the knee (with thick tights), long pants (generally longer than the ankle length)

<shoes>

1 sandals (stockingless legs)

2 sandals (socks) pumps (no heel, heel), sneakers, loafers,

3 short boots

4 long boots, mouton boots

<the other>

1 items for cold weather (muffler, snood, earmuff, hat, gloves)

Fig. 3. Bottoms, shoes, and the other scores

In accordance with the weather on a given day, the formula for deriving the optimum "Cariño index" is the "Cariño equation".

3   Observation Experiment

We conducted an observation experiment for 365 days (encompassing four seasons) to gather the data which informs the basis of the "Cariño equation".

3.1   Observation Method

Our observations involved drawing full-body sketches of 5 young women at a station in Tokyo every day. At the same time, we recorded weather data for the observed day. The experiment period lasted from October 7, 2015 to October 22, 2016. The specific site of the experiment was near the ticket gate of the station, which is a main thoroughfare in the center of Tokyo. Figure 4 shows an observation record note.

In addition to sketches of five people, the weather data of the day is cited from information found on the homepage of the Meteorological Agency website. Also, the "Cariño index" and its breakdown for the five persons are recorded at the bottom of the page. The weather data include, temperature, humidity, precipitation, wind direction, wind speed, and clothing index.

Fig. 4. Observation record note

3.2   Experimental Results

Over the course of this experiment, we gathered data for 1898 persons' coordination as well as weather data for a one year period. Based on data from the observation experiment, Fig. 5 presents the average of the "Cariño index" for each month. The monthly average for the "Cariño index" was highest between December and February, and lowest from July to August.

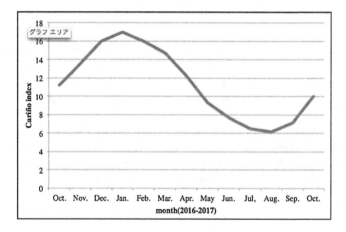

Fig. 5. Transition of Cariño index in 1 year

For each number in the "Cariño index", Table 1 summarizes the number of samples recorded and the main month and main coordination based on the data from the observation experiment.

Table 1. Month and coordination corresponding to each Cariño index number

Cariño index	The number of samples	Main month	Main coordination
3	8	Jul./Aug./Sep.	No sleeve + short length
4	35	Jun./Jul./Aug.	Short sleeve + short length
5	97	May/Jun./Jul./Aug./Sep./ early Oct.	Short sleeve + short length
6	136	May/Jun./Jul./Aug./Sep./ early Oct.	Long sleeve + short length, short sleeve + long length
7	160	May/Jun./Jul./Aug./Sep./ Oct.	Long sleeve + short length, short sleeve + long length
8	175	in late Apl./May/Jun./Jul./ Aug./Sep./Oct.	Outer (cardigan, parker)
9	107	Apl./May/Jun./July./Aug./ Sep./Oct.	Outer (cardigan, parker)
10	128	Apl./May/Jun./Sep./Oct.	Outer (jacket). long sleeve + long length
11	138	Mar./Apl./May/Sep./Oct./ Nov.	Outer (jacket)
12	134	Mar./Apl./May/Oct./Nov.	Outer (trench coat, jacket)
13	119	Feb./Mar./Apl./May/Oct./ Nov./Dec.	Outer (trench coat, jacket), tights, muffler
14	131	Mar./Apl./Oct./Nov./Dec.	Outer (trench coat, short coat), thin knit, tights
15	115	Jan./Feb./Mar./mid-Apl./ Nov./Dec.	Outer (thick coat), thick knit, tights
16	141	Jan./Feb./Mar./Apl./Nov./ Dec.	Outer (thick coat), turtle neck knit, muffler, tights
17	136	Jan./Feb./Mar./Dec.	Outer (thick coat), turtle neck knit muffler, tights
18	82	Jan./Feb./Mar./Dec.	Outer (thick coat), turtle neck knit, muffler, tights
19	42	Jan./Feb./Dec.	Outer (thick coat), turtle neck knit, muffler, tights
20	10	Feb.	Outer (thick coat), turtle neck knit, muffler, tights
21	3	Feb./Mar.	Outer (thick coat), turtle neck knit muffler, tights

4 The Cariño Equation: Calculating the Optimal Cariño Index

The "Cariño equation" is the formula for deriving the optimal "Cariño index" under certain weather conditions based on the observation data. For this equation, consider the following multiple regression model consisting of multiple explanatory variables to explain and predict the "Cariño index".

$$y_i = \beta_0 + \beta_1 x_{i1} + \beta_2 x_{i2} + \beta_3 x_{i3} + \ldots + \beta_p x_{ip} + \varepsilon_i$$

Multiple regression analysis was carried out using weather conditions such as humidity and temperature of a given day as explanatory variables ($x_{i1} \sim x_{ip}$) and the "Cariño index" of the day as an objective variable (y_i); the variables were then selected repeatedly to obtain the following "Cariño equation".

$$y = 21.04 - 0.48x_1 - 0.02x_2 + 0.09x_3 \tag{1}$$

y: Cariño index
x_1:   Temperature (°C)
x_2:   Humidity (%)
x_3:   Wind speed (m/sec)

The explanatory variable adopted the temperature, humidity, and wind speed. The value of R-squared (coefficient of determination) which is an indicator of the explanatory power of this regression equation was 0.774. There is no clear criterion for the coefficient of determination, but it is said that the explanatory power of the formula is high if it is generally 0.7 or more. The t-value of each explanatory variable are shown in Table 2. If the absolute value of the t-value is 2 or more, it is judged that the explanatory variable is significantly effective for the objective variable.

Table 2. The t-value of each explanatory variable

Explanatory variable	t-value
Temperature	−74.025
Humidity	−9.742
Wind speed	2.926

So, the formula (1) can be adopted as the "Cariño equation" for forecasting optimal "Cariño index" of the day.

5   Evaluation Experiment

To verify the accuracy of the "Cariño equation", evaluation experiments were carried out by spending several days with coordinated clothes predicted from the "Cariño equation".

5.1   Methods

The subject (in this case, myself) decided the coordination of the daily clothing for 10 days in January 2017, per the optimal "Cariño index" calculated from the "Cariño equation". The temperature comfort for everyday is then evaluated.

5.2   Results

Table 3 shows comparison records of optimal indices and self-indices for all 10 days. The optimal index means the "Cariño index" of the day calculated from the "Cariño equation". The self-index is the "Cariño index" of one's actual coordination on that day based on the optimal index. The difference is a value obtained by subtracting the optimal index from the self-index, with a margin for error/deviation of ± 3 kept in mind. In addition, the individual's evaluation/opinion of temperature (Sensible temperature) with regards to personal comfort was assigned based on a description of 5 stages (cold, somewhat cold, comfortable, somewhat hot, and hot) for the day (Fig. 6).

Table 3. Result of evaluation experiment

Date	Optimal index	Self index	Difference	Evaluation of sensible temperature
Jan. 10	15.7	16	0.3	Cold
Jan. 11	17.1	17	−0.1	Comfortable
Jan. 12	18.7	18	−0.7	Comfortable
Jan. 16	21.7	19	−2.7	Somewhat cold
Jan. 17	20.1	19	−1.1	Comfortable
Jan. 18	19.8	18	−1.8	Somewhat cold
Jan. 19	19.3	19	−0.3	Somewhat cold
Jan. 23	20.8	20	−0.8	Comfortable
Jan. 24	20.1	19	−1.1	Comfortable
Jan. 30	16.7	17	0.3	Comfortable

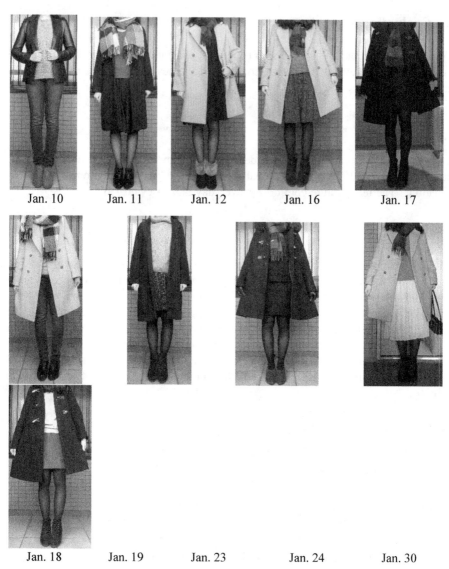

Fig. 6. Coordination of each 10 days

5.3   Considerations

There was no significant failure recorded due to the coordination comparison between the optimal index and the self-index.

The optimal index is usually obtained in the morning before leaving the house. Thus, it was comfortable from morning to noon for all 10 days, but by dusk/nighttime, thicker garments became necessary. Also, while it was comfortable outside, temperatures were understandably warmer indoors. Ultimately, there was better coordination compared to the people around the subject, who had not applied the "Cariño index".

6 Summary and Future Studies

This paper proposes the concept and the generation procedure of the "Cariño index", which becomes the basis of clothing-weather coordination with little to no failure instances in any weather and or season; along with the "Cariño equation" to calculate the optimal index. A one year observation experiment and results demonstrate the effectiveness of the "Cariño index" and the "Cariño equation".

Given the validation of the equation to a certain degree, with regards to the experiment carried out on myself, we intend to conduct similar evaluation experiments with women of the same age as subjects for future studies.

Furthermore, the system to calculate and reference the "Cariño index" will be improved upon. Specifically, by using the sketches of the record notes of the observation experiment, we will display sketches of the same coordination as the optimal index of the day. In so doing, not only numerical values but also visual reference of the day's coordination can be used.

References

1. Japan Meteorological Agency. http://www.jma.go.jp/jma/indexe.html. Accessed 08 Mar 2017
2. Clothing index. Japan Meteorological Agency. http://www.tenki.jp/indexes/dress/. Accessed 8 Mar 2017
3. Kogure, A.: Introduction to Statistical Data Analysis by R. Asakura Shoten, Tokyo (2013)
4. Multiple regression analysis. http://www.wakayama-u.ac.jp/~wuhy/am8.pdf. Accessed 08 Mar 2017
5. Sika Corporation. What is multi-collinearity? http://xica.net/vno4ul5p/. Accessed 08 Mar 2017
6. Sika Corporation. How about the coefficient of determination in multiple regression analysis? http://xica.net/x76kqwwo/. Accessed 08 Mar 2017
7. Market's storybook, marketing and multiple regression analysis part 2. http://xica.net/magellan/marketing-idea/stats/statistics-words/. Accessed 08 Mar 2017

Proposal of Internet Radio Walking Around Street While Listening to Voice of Virtual Idols

Shiori Furuta$^{(\boxtimes)}$ and Katsuhiko Ogawa

Keio University, 5322 Endo, Fujisawa-shi, Kanagawa 252-0882, Japan
{s13791sf, ogw}@sfc.keio.ac.jp

Abstract. When walking around the city with another person, there are many interesting things that are much more noticeable than if one is alone. However, nobody can always walk with another person. This research proposes a location based internet radio walking program together with virtual idols. There are two versions of the radio program: voice only and voice with vibration. This research describes design and experiments for both the voice version and voice and vibration version. It also clarifies future research directions.

Keywords: Walking · Internet radio · Vibration

1 Introduction

When walking around the city with someone, there are many interesting things that are much more noticeable than if one is walking alone. As a substitute for walking with another person, it may be possible to use a smartphone that is not a person. Like RPG games, virtual idols appear in smartphones, and you can walk while watching them on the smartphone. For example, Pokémon GO [1], released in 2016, corresponds to this, although no RPG messages were displayed.

However, "walking smartphone," or using smartphones while walking, has become a social issue; it involves hitting people walking without looking around. In a survey announced in 2015 [2], 91% of participants in the survey were bothered by others walking with smartphones. Serious accidents have occurred even in Pokémon GO.

In this research, we propose a service—"Walking with Virtual Idols (WaVIs)"—for people walking alone by offering voice together with virtual idols of speech using internet radio. The purpose of this service is to rediscover the charm of the city even when people are walking alone with the help of virtual idols.

As conventional studies of street walking services using radio demonstrate, there are "Podwalk" services [3]. This service is based on the premise that podcast voices are downloaded to playback equipment in advance, and one can walk while watching the printed map. Since the voice is determined by time flow, the walking speed and voice do not match. In addition, they refer to the podwalk from past experience rather than for present time.

This research proposes a service that allows for walking while watching the sceneries in the town by listening to voice guidance by virtual idols, walking at the pace of users.

© Springer International Publishing AG 2017
C. Stephanidis (Ed.): HCII Posters 2017, Part II, CCIS 714, pp. 366–373, 2017.
DOI: 10.1007/978-3-319-58753-0_53

2   Concept of "Walk with Virtual Idols (WaVIs)"

Women are generally sociable and often walk in groups, but men often walk alone. For this reason, women as virtual idols often appear in games. In addition, because there are many female college students in our laboratory, and considering the convenience in the making of the audio content, WaVIs used female college students as virtual idols.

This service creates the effect that when you walk around the city listening to the voice of virtual idols, you can imagine someone virtual from the voice and have a sense of walking together in the city. By doing this, we believe that awareness of a new viewpoint can be gained through the virtual idol pointing out places.

In WaVIs system, voice comments of virtual idols are mapped onto Google Maps before use [4]. Looking at Google Maps on the browser of the smartphone, we automatically acquire location information, and this becomes a mechanism that automatically sounds when it comes to the place of the voice comments. As shown in Fig. 1, it is possible to listen to the voice of the virtual idol independent of the walking speed of the user.

Fig. 1. Map to voices

To use WaVIs, open the page mapped on the smartphone and listen to the sound with the earphone. The user can walk along the route only from the starting point; so, the user walks along the street along with the voice.

3   Walk with Virtual Idols Ver.1 - WaVIs1

3.1   Design of WaVIs1

WaVIs1 (Walk with Virtual Idols ver. 1) is a town-walking service where only the voice of virtual idols flows. The recording is monophonic. We do not set the character of virtual idols, whose voice is designed to mimic a general female college student using the voice of one author. One voice speaks for around 5 to 15 s, and these voices are mapped in front of the intersection, the turning point, and the store, in order to introduce them. Information on the road is also made by a virtual idol voice. The route is fixed and requires walking in one direction.

3.2   Experiment

WaVIs1 experiments were conducted around Roppongi in Tokyo. To create voice comments, we first conducted a "survey." We walked in the town and determined what content would be used. We then "recorded" the content decided in the "survey." Finally, we "pasted" the sound "recorded" on the map. Figure 2 is a map-to-voice in Roppongi.

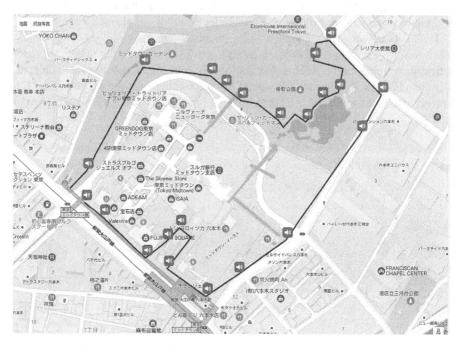

Fig. 2. Map to voices in Roppongi

Method. The purpose of this experiment was extraction of improvement points. After four subjects walked using WaVIs1, comments and impression were sought via interview.

Result. There were no problems in length and placement place. It seems that individuals felt as if they walked together, as the sound matched the pace of walking. Interviewees claimed it was not an image of a general Japanese female student that they imagined, but rather a calm voice like a radio personality. Interviewees also noted that because virtual idols spoke in an explanatory style, they felt that the virtual idols and distance cannot be measured. They seemed to want to engage with the voice like they would a friend. Also, it seems that emotion was hard to understand because there was no intonation in the voice. Interviewees felt virtual idols and a sense of distance, and seemed to not understand with much familiarity. Thus, they were less likely to feel emotions toward a virtual entity. However, it is convincing that this virtual idol is calm if a female college student's radio personality has been used.

Discussion. WaVIs1 could not create virtual idols. There are two main reasons for this. One is that the interviewees did not feel familiar with the virtual idols. Like a newscaster in a news program, the lack of tone makes explanation difficult; therefore, it is hard to understand emotions because there is no intonation in the voice, as there would be for a machine voice. This made it difficult to feel emotions towards virtual idols.

The second reason was due to a gap with regard to the female college student that each person thought. For example, one person might think of a bright and energetic female college student as a general female college student, while another might imagine a calm female college student thereby resulting in the voice and the female college student imagined not matching.

To solve these problems, WaVIs2 decided to make three improvements. The first was to use binaural recording to create a spatial sound. The second was to set up characters to eliminate the imaginary virtual idol gap. The third was to use a vibration device that uses a sense other than hearing.

4 Walk with Virtual Idols Ver.2 - WaVIs2

4.1 Design of WaVIs2

Based on the experiments in the previous chapter, we improved the WaVIs1 so that it included binaural recording, a virtual idol character setting, and a vibrating device known as the "Whispering Street Vibration Device (WSVD)".

Binaural Recording. Since there were many opinions that WaVIs1's virtual idols were unfamiliar with, leaving a gap, we adopted binaural recording as an improvement measure. When binaural recordings are heard with the human ear, they become a sound with a three-dimensional feeling, so it is as if the sound is moving. Experiments were conducted to determine whether users had the effect of feeling familiarity with virtual idols through this binaural recording.

In the experiment, eight subjects (male and female university students) who were subjects heard a sound for about 30 s. The content included a voice, wherein virtual idols walked together while completing a tour of the city, and also included a voice that whispered when approaching the ears of the subject on the way. As a result of listening to this sound, subjects felt their heart beating when approaching their ears and the result was that they felt a sense of intimacy.

Pattern of Virtual Idols. In order to eliminate the virtual idol gap imagined by the user, we provided the virtual idols with characters. About 50 persons participated in the experiments. These participants listened to the sound of WaVIs1 and wrote comments about the virtual idols on research. The experimental results are as shown in Table 1.

Table 1. Result of workshop

Appearance	• Normal • Some fleshy • Not too cute • Small • Face that looks everywhere • Black hair, with bangs • I do not make a face like RINNA [5], but behind the scenes it is attractive
Catch copy	•"Mimidoru"
Personality	• People who are popular with grandpa and grandma •Gentle • Positive • Smiling
Hobby	• Virtual idol is traveling around a fashionable café • There is a stylish commitment store (get going)
Image episode	• Carrying goods • Honors student • Observes traffic rules • Moves in a red bicycle • She is playing with little girls in the park • She brings a lunch box for lunch • Sento (Japanese bathroom) bytes • Meet at any time • Go to city hall • From the area • Common to shopping districts • Go to local cafes • She is familiar with the area • Grandpa is good for grandpa • The virtual idol's parent's store is a bakery/rice store • Signboard girl
Ideal plan	• Tsundere. I hope there is a zone to be drawn when walking. • I want you to follow one step behind • Breath rising on a slope • I am a clerk • Small enough to place in the palm of your hand • Show your face as far as possible from the telephone pole

We picked up some of the comments made, and the images were developed as per the five below.

The first image uses the catch phrase "Mimidoru." The second is of a cute female college student. The third is of a girl who thinks that simple is best. The fourth is of a girl familiar with the urban environment. The fifth is of a girl who likes fashionable items like cafes.

The first catchphrase has a role related to making friends through greetings. This girl feels familiar with the way the talent speaks on television gourmet programs concerning the second and third items. The fourth and fifth items are focused on selecting a route with shops within the city.

Vibration Device. In WaVIs2, we thought that virtual idols would be easier to imagine if we were to stimulate the user's five senses in addition to the voice of virtual idols. For example, two of Japan's most famous virtual idols, Hatsune Miku [6], are used to provide visual (visual) and voice/song (auditory) aids. Based on this, we decided to combine the other five senses and create a vibrating device (WSVD) to make use of the tactile sense. We also thought of using the olfactory sense, but decided to instead use the tactile effect with the least impact, so as not to disturb the user's own experiences, such as their smelling bakeries on street corners. As a reference, there is a device called "Buru-Navi 3 [7]" by Nippon Telegraph and Telephone Corporation. This is a device that creates a feeling as if one is being pulled on when it is held in the hand, and it is used as a navigation device that shows the direction of travel. This time we made a prototype of a wristwatch-type vibration device WSVD with Arduino. Figure 3 shows an image used when actually going to the town.

Fig. 3. Vibration device on left hand

4.2   Experiment

WaVIs2 conducted a physical experiment of WSVD. We experimented with the author mapping the pattern of three vibrations. This time, the device was set to Kanagawa, a neighboring city of Tokyo. The reason for choosing this town is that the author knows the area well because there are universities to which the author belongs.

Method. The purpose of this experiment was to select the mapping pattern of vibration. We tested which mapping patterns were easiest to imagine the largest number of virtual idols. There were three patterns. Pattern A is a pattern that adds vibration to every-thing before the mapped sound is reproduced (Fig. 4). Pattern B vibrates between the mapped voice and voice (Fig. 5). Pattern C adds vibrations before voices that are desired to be focused on among the mapped voices are reproduced (Fig. 6).

Fig. 4. Pattern A

Fig. 5. Pattern B

Fig. 6. Pattern C

Result. Pattern A was too frequent at the point where contents were dense, but in places where there was time between contents, it created the attitude that sound would come. Pattern B vibrated every time, so it got in the way of being disturbed when enjoying one's time. The vibration was just right for Pattern C. This vibration provided the sensation that the virtual idols had something to share and that they imagined someone virtual.

Discussion. We felt that Pattern C was good, out of the three patterns we experienced. The reason for this is that the sound of the vibrated place could be clearly understood as being something that the virtual idol wanted to convey. Pattern C was divided into hours to enjoy virtual idols and town walking and time to enjoy walking alone by one's self, and we were, in that pattern, able to experience and enjoy both varieties. Patterns A and B were associated with a small amount of discomfort. The reason for this is that there is a lot of vibration and it is disturbed by one person's time. However, both patterns A and B were considered to be usable patterns when meaning was applied to the vibration.

5 Conclusion

In this research, we proposed and developed "Walk with Virtual Idols (WaVIs)" which allows a person to walk with the virtual idol of a female college student when walking alone in the city. In WaVIs1, we used only voice to extract problems. There were two problems associated with this approach. The first is that one could not develop a feeling of familiarity. Another was that the general Japanese female student imagined by each user was different. To solve these problems, WaVIs2 produced a binaural recording, a workshop for making virtual idol settings, and a vibrating device "Whispering Street Vibration Device (WSVD)." Several small experiments were conducted using these.

Future research ought to improve WSVD. For example, the appearance of the device could be improved. For instance, it could be worn like a necklace, like a wrist-watch, and could be transformed into various shapes. Repeat prototype production, experimentation and improvement will enable completion of WaVIs.

References

1. Pokémon GO. http://www.pokemongo.com/. Accessed 14 Mar 2017
2. General Association of Telecommunications Carriers Association, "Survey on Walking Smartphones" (2015). http://www.tca.or.jp/press_release/pdf/150123sumahochosa.pdf. Accessed 14 Mar 2017
3. Kato, F.: Capture, share, and experience: "Podwalk" as a medium for flaneurs. In: PICS (Pervasive Image Capture and Sharing) Workshop, UbiComp2006, Orange Coungy, CA, 18 September 2006
4. Utsumi, S., Ogawa, K.: The Experiment of Vicarious Experience by Using Place's Second Sound Channel Media, "Whispath", The institute of electronics information and communication engineers, LOIS2015-94, pp. 181–185 (2016)
5. Microsoft Japan – RINNA. http://rinna.jp/. Accessed 14 Mar 2017
6. Hatsune Miku official. http://miku.sega.jp/. Accessed 14 Mar 2017
7. Nippon Telegraph and Telephone Corporation (2014) - Buru-Navi 3. http://www.kecl.ntt.co.jp/human/burunavi3/. Accessed 14 Mar 2017

Classification of Synchronous Non-parallel Shuffling Walk for Humanoid Robot

Masanao Koeda[1(✉)], Daiki Sugimoto[1], and Etsuko Ueda[2]

[1] Osaka Electro-Communication University, Kiyotaki 1130-70,
Shijonawate, Osaka 575-0063, Japan
koeda@osakac.ac.jp, mt15a003@oecu.jp
[2] Osaka Institute of Technology, 5-16-1, Omiya, Asahi-ku,
Osaka 535-8585, Japan
etsuko.ueda@oit.ac.jp

Abstract. Humanoid robot is one of the best solution to interact and utilize in our life space. We focus on shuffling walk for humanoid robots. Shuffling walk is expected to have an advantage in moving around the narrow area with constrained posture. In this study, we describe the classification of the motion of the shuffling walk and propose new classification in synchronous non-parallel shuffling walk which focused on the load point of the sole of the robot.

Keywords: Humanoid robot · Motion control · Slip · Sole · Load point

1 Introduction

We expect humanoid robots to interact and collaborate on many tasks in daily life. In our life space, most of tasks are performed stably in a narrow space with constrained posture. For example, in a kitchen task, constrained postures such as turning in place, forward stooping, knee bending, and knee stretching are required for cooking, dishes washing or placing to cupboard in a narrow space. For another example, in an elder-care situation, forward stooping to lift up a patient from the bed, turning in place to make the patient sit in a chair, and knee bending to have the patient shoe is needed in a narrow space.

Many other situations of constrained posture movements for humanoid robots. There are many researches about a continuous stepping walk for the humanoid robot movement. However, it is not suitable to perform in a narrow area because the knees are hit to the wall and the stepping walk becomes out of control in the situation of knee bending or stretching. Therefore, we have been studying a shuffling walk for a possible solution.

2 Categorization of Shuffling Walk

The shuffling walk is generated by stepless and slipping soles. The shuffling walk is categorized in [1, 2] (Fig. 1).

© Springer International Publishing AG 2017
C. Stephanidis (Ed.): HCII Posters 2017, Part II, CCIS 714, pp. 374–381, 2017.
DOI: 10.1007/978-3-319-58753-0_54

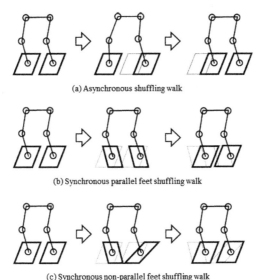

(a) Asynchronous shuffling walk

(b) Synchronous parallel feet shuffling walk

(c) Synchronous non-parallel feet shuffling walk

Fig. 1. Categorization of shuffling walk (adapted from [1, 2])

(a) Asynchronous shuffling walk

The asynchronous shuffling walk is generated by slipping one foot at a time (Fig. 1-(a)). It can take a long step. However, it is relatively unstable because the center of gravity needs to be shifted dynamically. Kojima [3] proposed a control method for this motion and demonstrated using a life-size humanoid robot.

(b) Synchronous parallel feet shuffling walk

The synchronous shuffling walk is generated by slipping both feet simultaneously and parallel (Fig. 1-(b)). It is relatively slow and needs to be control weight distribution in each foot. Therefore, it is unstable because of same reason in asynchronous shuffling walk. This motion was studied in [1, 2, 4–6].

(c) Synchronous non-parallel feet shuffling walk

The synchronous non-parallel feet shuffling walk is generated by slipping both feet simultaneously and non-parallel (Fig. 1-(c)). It is relatively stable because the change of the center of gravity during movement is relatively small than the previously described two methods. This motion was studied in [7, 8]. However, these studies do not mention the distribution of soles force. In this study, we first categorize this motion in focus on the load distribution of soles.

3   Categorization of Synchronous Non-parallel Feet Shuffling Walk

We categorized the synchronous non-parallel feet shuffling walk according to the load point and pressure gradient of soles. In a generally used rectangular foot sole shape, when loading to the sole corner and moving to the rightward, it is limited to only following four patterns; inner side, outer side, left side and right side (Fig. 2).

Load point		Center of gravity
Inner side	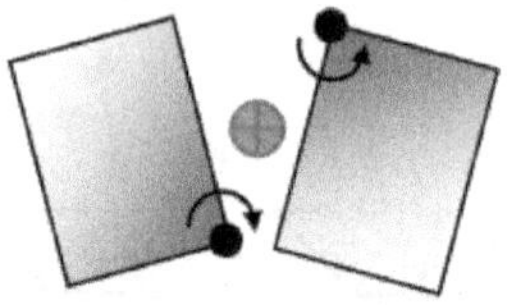	center
Outer side	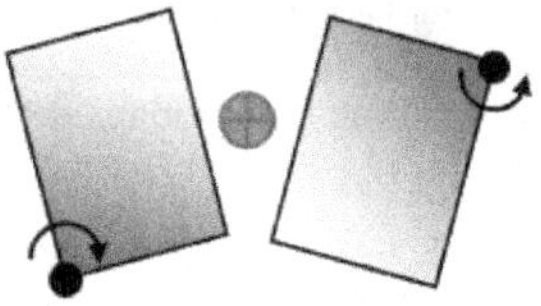	center
Left side	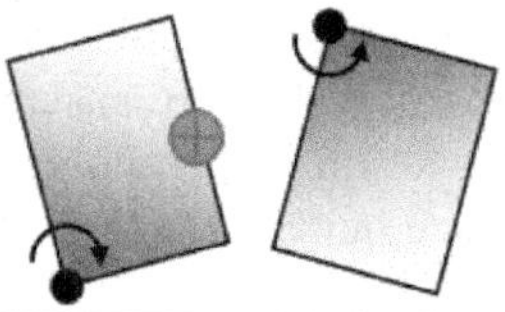	slightly left
Right side	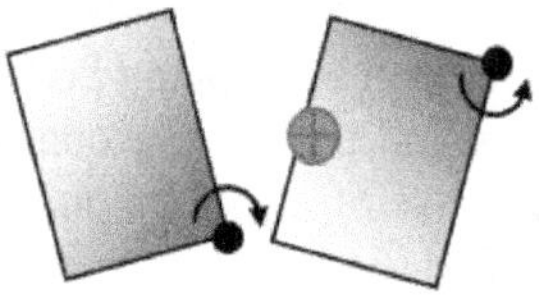	slightly right

Fig. 2. Classification of synchronous non-parallel shuffling focusing on the load point (rightward movement)

4   Motion Flow and Calculated Moving Distance

Figure 3 shows the motion flows of each categorized motion while moving rightward. In the case of move to another direction, the motion flow can be generated by the similar way. In each motion, moving distance in one step can be calculated in the following;

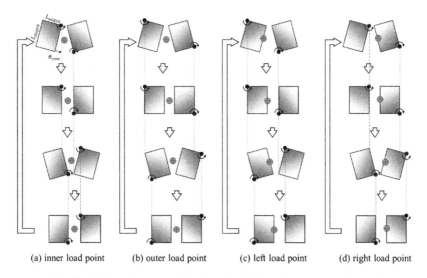

(a) inner load point   (b) outer load point   (c) left load point   (d) right load point

Fig. 3. Motion flow in each load point (rightward movement, 1 step)

$$L_{move} = 2L_{depth} \sin \theta_{yaw} \tag{1}$$

where L_{depth} is the depth length of sole of the robot and θ_{yaw} is the rotation angle in vertical axis of foot.

5 System Overview

We used Robovie-X PRO (manufactured by Vstone Co., Ltd.) for the following experiments (Fig. 4). The robot has 19 degrees-of-freedom (DOF) (1 [DOF] in the head, 3 [DOF] in each arm, and 6 [DOF] in each leg), dimensions of 380 (height) × 180 (width) × 73 (depth) [mm], and a weight of 2 [kg], approximately. The size of foot sole is 72 (width) × 123 (depth) [mm], approximately. We used RobovieMaker2 to create

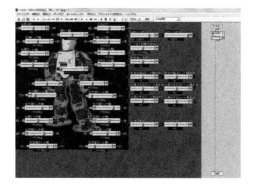

Fig. 4. Robovie-X Pro

Fig. 5. RobovieMaker2

robot motions (Fig. 5). We used LL Sensor (manufactured by Xiroku Inc.) for distributed pressure sensor. The sensor has 45 (width) × 37 (depth) measurement points in the dimensions of 540 (width) × 480 (depth) [mm] in 100 [Hz] (Fig. 6). By using the companion software, the distributed pressure can be measured as color map (Fig. 7).

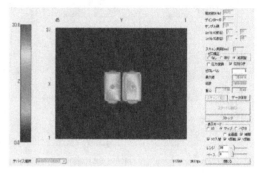

Fig. 6. LL Sensor

Fig. 7. Measured pressure using the companion software when the robot is standing on LL sensor (Color figure online)

6   Experiment and Result

Each shuffling motion was generated by adjusting load points measured by the distribution pressure sensor so as to follow each pattern. The shuffle motion was started from the state where the robot was upstanding at the center of the distribution pressure sensor (Fig. 8). In our experiment, $L_{depth} = 123$ [mm] and $\theta_{yaw} = 5$ [deg] was used. In this condition, the calculated travel distance is $L_{move} = 21.4$ [mm/step].

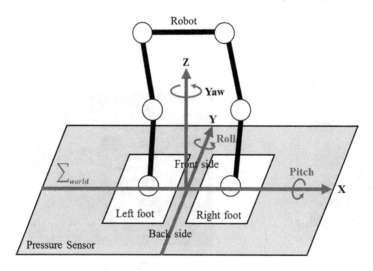

Fig. 8.   Coordination system

In our pressure sensor, the measurement value varies depending on the conductivity of the target object and the material of the covering sheet. Figure 9 shows the result of measuring the color against the input pressure using the same material (aluminum) and size as the sole of the robot. Figure 10 shows the distribution pressure measured during each motion.

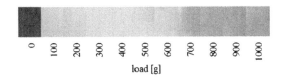

Fig. 9. Pressure-color mapping of the distribution pressure sensor in following experiments (Color figure online)

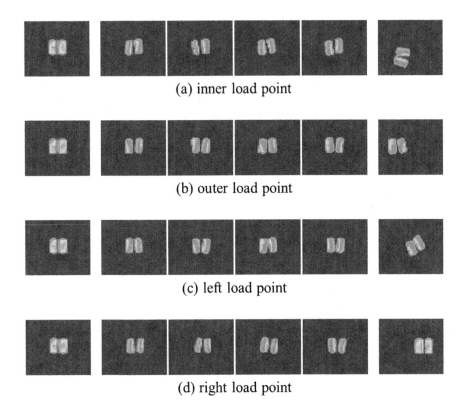

Fig. 10. Transition of distributed pressure in each load point while moving rightward (The first image is initial state, the next four images are first and second step, and the last image is final state.)

The movement trajectory was read from the coordinates of the center of gravity indicated by the measurement software. The measured trajectory is shown in Fig. 11. The travel distance and the angle of rotation are shown in Figs. 12 and 13 respectively.

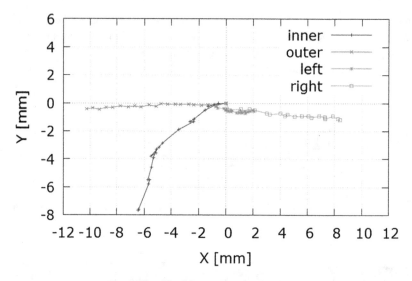

Fig. 11. Measured trajectory

As a result of the experiment, there was a big difference in trajectory, amount of movement and amount of rotation in each motion. In the pattern of inner load point (Fig. 3-(a)), it moved greatly to an unintended direction, and an unintended large rotation occurred. In the pattern of outer load point (Fig. 3-(b)), it also moved greatly to an unintended direction, but an unintended rotation was small. In the pattern of left load point (Fig. 3-(c)), it slightly moved to the intended direction, but unintended rotation was occurred. In the pattern of right load point (Fig. 3-(d)), it moves to the intended direction and no rotation occurs. However, the actual travel distance was 8.5 [mm] and it remained at 40% of the calculated travel distance. This loss is thought to be due to the slip on the floor.

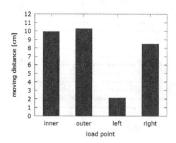

Fig. 12. Travel distance

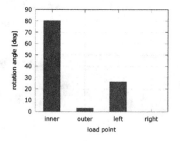

Fig. 13. Angle of rotation

7   Conclusion

In this paper, we proposed a classification focused on the load position of the sole on the synchronous non-parallel feet shuffling walk. When loading on the corner of the rectangular foot sole, it is only the four patterns of inner side, outer side, left side and right side. Uneven pressure distribution occurs on the soles of the feet due to the difference of these load positions, and the frictional force varies depending on places. Due to these effects, it seems that the experimental results showed a large difference in the traveling distance and the rotation angle. The right load point was the most desirable result with traveling distance and straightness.

For future works, we will model the dynamics of the sole and take into account the friction between the floor and the sole.

Acknowledgement. This research was supported by Grants-in-Aid for Scientific Research (No. 15K00369) from the Ministry of Education, Culture, Sports, Science and Technology (MEXT), Japan.

References

1. Koeda, M., Uda, Y., Sugiyama, S., Yoshikawa, T.: Shuffle turn and translation of humanoid robots. In: Proceedings of the 2011 IEEE International Conference on Robotics and Automation, pp. 593–598 (2011)
2. Koeda, M., Uda, Y., Sugiyama, S., Yoshikawa, T.: Side translation by simultaneous shuffle turn for humanoid robots. In: Proceedings of the 8th Asian Control Conference, pp. 1346–1351 (2011)
3. Kojima, K., Nozawa, S., Okada, K., Inaba, M.: Shuffle motion for humanoid robot by sole load distribution and foot force control. In: Proceedings of the 2015 IEEE/RSJ International Conference on Intelligent Robots and Systems, pp. 2187–2194 (2015)
4. Miura, K., Nakaoka, S., Morisawa, M., Kanehiro, F., Harada, K., Kajita, S.: A friction based "twirl" for biped robots. In: Proceedings of the 8th IEEE-RAS International Conference on Humanoid Robots, pp. 279–284 (2008)
5. Miura, K., Nakaoka, S., Morisawa, M., Kanehiro, F., Harada, K., Kajita, S.: Analysis on a friction based "twirl" for biped robots. In: Proceedings of the 2010 IEEE International Conference on Robotics and Automation, pp. 4249–4255 (2010)
6. Hashimoto, K., Yoshimura, Y., Kondo, H., Lim, H., Takanishi, A.: Realization of quick turn of biped humanoid robot by using slipping motion with both feet. In: Proceedings of the 2011 IEEE International Conference on Robotics and Automation, pp. 2041–2046 (2011)
7. Koeda, M., Murayama, R., Nishimura, M., Minato, I.: Analysis of shuffle traveling and verification by real humanoid. In: The 8th International Conference on Humanoid, Nanotechnology, Information Technology, Communication and Control, Environment, and Management 2015 (2015)
8. Sugimoto, D., Koeda, M., Ueda, E.: ZMP-based shuffling walk control for humanoid robot. In: Proceedings of the 25th IEEE International Symposium on Robot and Human Interactive Communication, pp. 904–905 (2016)

Case Representation of Daily Routine Data Through the Function Behavior Structure (FBS) Framework

Injung Lee, Taeha Yi, Jimin Rhim, Amartuvshin Narangerel,
Danial Shafiei Karaji, and Ji-Hyun Lee$^{(\boxtimes)}$

GSCT, KAIST, 291 Daehak-ro, Yuseong-gu, Daejeon 305-701, Korea
{edndn,yitaeha,kingjimin,amartuvshin,dshafiei,
jihyun187}@kaist.ac.kr

Abstract. Recently, a vast number of devices including home appliances and personal devices are surrounding most of the people. In the consequence, large amount of futile data is generated incessantly in daily basis. In order to make a system capable of using those sporadic data, which derived from the devices, should be manipulated and managed properly. Therefore, we suggest an integrative framework to design a case, out of the sporadic data in daily lives in this paper. The research team determined three data concepts to enable more suitable management of sensor values to a rigid form of daily life; (1) device usage log data, (2) quantified-self data, and (3) contextual data. Furthermore, our team proposes a new method for case representation that consists of three parts: function, behavior and structure. additionally we categorize aforementioned data into this framework as well, such that function represents device usage log data, behavior representing quantified-self data and structure representing contextual data. The ultimate goal of this research is to build a CBR based AI that recommends usage of a particular device - among a variety of devices surrounding the user- to the user in specific situations.

Keywords: Case-based reasoning (CBR) · Case representation · Function behavior structure framework · Internet of things · Artificial intelligence

1 Introduction

Weiser introduced the concept of ubiquitous computing which portrays a vision of people and environments augmented with computational resources that provide constant and seamless information and services [1]. Now we are living in a ubiquitous world where numerous devices such as home appliances and smart devices are connected to each other. Large amount of personal data are being produced and are used as both input and output data for computers to provide personalized and adaptive services for the users. Amazon Alexa, Amazon Echo, Amazon Echo Dot, Google Home and other smart devices are some examples of smart home assistant products.

Ambient intelligence involves integrating sensors into everyday objects or devices to make them 'smart', which can explore their environment and allow users to intuitively interact with them to help them cope with new tasks [2]. However, there are

© Springer International Publishing AG 2017
C. Stephanidis (Ed.): HCII Posters 2017, Part II, CCIS 714, pp. 382–389, 2017.
DOI: 10.1007/978-3-319-58753-0_55

challenges in managing sporadic personal input data from multiple devices into a single integrated system. Furthermore, it is difficult to fully understand a user's routine by analyzing digitized data due to differing personal patterns, contexts, and unexpected variables. Therefore, our research attempts to propose an integrative framework that includes cases from multiple inputs, which can be applied in actual AI-based personal assistants that connect with other smart home appliances to design more user adaptive system.

2 Literature Review

2.1 Data in Daily Lives

Introduction of various devices, including smartphones, tablet PC and wearable devices and so on, provided researchers with an understanding of human. Among data from devices, log data has primarily been used in research to figure out statistical inferences from users [3]. Numerous researchers, such as Ørmen and Thorhauge [4], and Oliver [5] analyzed smartphones log data to understand users' practices and norms when using smartphones. More precisely, Xu et al. learned the pattern of users' tap events [6].

Furthermore, embedded sensors - including accelerometer, digital compass, gyroscope, GPS, microphone and camera - enabled automatic tracking and monitoring multiple dimensions of human behavior and encompassing both physical and mental status of the user [7]. Several researchers analyzed data from smartphones to understand people's body postures and motions [8]. Also, other researchers analyzed the activity recognition of users tracking the various features of physical data. [9] Data from various sensors also led us to comprehend the mental status of the user. User's facial expression and related emotions were driven from the image data of digital camera embedded into smart devices [10]. Some of the emotions are detectable in visual appearance such as anger, happiness, surprise and dislike while emotions such as sadness and fear are audio dominant [11]. De Silva et al. examined users' emotion by means of combination of visual and vocal expression and suggested a hybrid approach that uses multi-modal information for emotion recognition. The digital camera of a smartphone was also used to measure heart rates in order to associate with sentimental states [12].

Recently, research of understanding human through digit data has been active under the term 'quantified-self [13, 14].' It means analyzing human through the self-tracking of the biological, physical, behavioral, or environmental information. Tapia et al. recognized user's presence and activity in home environment using data from set of small sensors [15]. In addition, the terminology quantified holistic self extended the range of detected personal data by including the context and needs of individuals [16]. In this flow, attempts to understand users thoroughly including their context of daily routine have been increasing, to be the recent trend of research about using data from devices.

2.2   Case-Based Reasoning and FBS Framework

There have been numerous efforts to develop AI that can echo human intelli-gence system by mimicking human extensive web of intelligence and reasoning paradigm. to that end, case-based reasoning (CBR) solves new problems by adapting previously successful solutions to similar problems [16]. As Schank elaborates, human's knowledge about the world is organized as memory packets holding our previous experiences that we use when facing similar problems in our life [17], CBR adapts similar method in which a case represents a packet. In CBR, the cases are stored in a case base and accessed to solve new problems. When a new problem arises, the system finds the most similar cases to offer a viable solution. To do so, CBR has a cycle of four tasks called retrieve, reuse, revise and retain in its system [18].

A case is a "contextualized piece of knowledge representing an experience that teaches a lesson fundamental to achieving the goals of the reasoner" [19]. Therefore, determining how a person's experience is arranged as an information - the content and structure of the case - is very critical [20]. There are several methods to represent a case. Feature vector approach that represent a case as a vector of attributes paired with values. Structured vector approach which is developed around a frame-based formalism and textual approach which is represented as sets of linguistic items [21]. Hierarchical case representation offers multiple representations at different levels of abstraction possibly using multiple vocabularies [22], which consequently allows the adaptation of new approaches into the case representation such as FBS framework.

The Function Behavior Structure (FBS) framework is an extension of the FBS ontology that represents the process of designing as a set of transformations among function, behavior and structure [23, 24]. The original attempt was to rep-resent artificial objects which later extended to include process of design [25]. In the FBS framework, the Function is defined as teleology; "what the artifact is for". The Behavior is defined as artifact's attributes that can be derived from its structure ("what the object does"), and Structure of an object is defined as its components and their relationships ("what the object consists of") [26]. Definition of structure can cover any physical, virtual or social artefact [27], which means that application of FBS model is not only limited to physical artefacts but also to cases which will be used for further interactions with the users.

The FBS framework has been used not only in design domains but also in building case-based reasoning systems. Table 1. shows several attempts that have applied the concept of Function Behavior and Structure into CBR. Rosenman et al. made cases of

Table 1. Previous researches that applied FBS framework into CBR

Authors	Description of research
Rosenman et al. 1992 [28]	Used FBS framework to make cases of precedent design knowledge. Those cases are added into knowledge bases and CAD databases
Maher et al. 1995 [29, 30]	Used FBS to structurize design cases. They eventually create a case-based design system that aids design process
Kim et al. 2015 [31]	Used FBS to reconfigure the assets of weapons to model the weapon systems. They analyzed the components of missiles into FBS attributes

room design using FBS framework [28]. Maher et al. used the FBS framework to classify variables in design processes [29, 30]. Kim et al. used function, behavior, and structure as elements to figure out the components of weaponries [31]. In overall, we can recognize that previous research utilized FBS to describe physical outputs of design products.

3   Case Representation Framework Using FBS

This section introduces our method of designing a case by applying the concept of Function-Behavior-Structure framework. First, we arranged daily data which are generated from daily lives' devices to make them in a manageable way to construct a case. Second, we explain the overall concept of our case according to FBS concept.

3.1   Data Concepts of Daily Lives

The ultimate goal of this research is to build a CBR based AI that recommends usage of a particular device - among a variety of devices surrounding the user- tailored to user's specific situations. We expect the AI to be used in a ubiquitous environment where every devices including smartphone, wearable devices, home appliances and etc. are connected to the AI agent. Considering that devices people possess vary from person to person, the explicit data types and their structures cannot be rashly determined. Moreover, data that are generated by devices surrounding users exist in a complex form in terms of their usage. A single string of sensor value can be interpreted differently or several sensor values from diverse devices can be used to determine a single status of the user. For these reasons, the sensor values derived from various devices should be arranged into conceptual data forms in order to be prepared to build a case out of them. In order to manage those sporadic sensor values, our research team tried to arrange those values with the natural notion of daily lives of a person. The data generated in daily lives' multiple devices can be classified into three concepts; (1) device usage log data, (2) quantified-self data, and (3) contextual data of the environment. Definitions of each data type and examples are provided in the following Fig. 1.

First, the concept of device usage log data takes account the details of devices when a user uses them. This data concept includes the power status, type of function, type of mode, the value of certain mode, timestamps of every transition, and so on. Second is the concept of user's quantified-self data. Like the general definition of quantified-self [12, 13], our team defined this concept as data tracked by the user, that describes the user's biological, physical, emotional and other statuses. Concept of contextual data includes every data that informs the environmental status. It covers data about environment surrounding the user. Our research team expect the data concepts - device usage log data, quantified-self data, and contextual data - to enable the management the sensor values to a rigid form of daily life, even in situations where additional devices are introduced in user's environment.

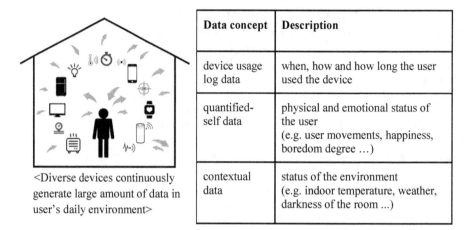

Data concept	Description
device usage log data	when, how and how long the user used the device
quantified-self data	physical and emotional status of the user (e.g. user movements, happiness, boredom degree …)
contextual data	status of the environment (e.g. indoor temperature, weather, darkness of the room …)

\<Diverse devices continuously generate large amount of data in user's daily environment\>

Fig. 1. Data concepts generated by devices in daily lives

3.2   Applying FBS Framework in Case Representation

This section introduces our method of integrating the FBS framework into the case representation. Traditional conventional case is represented through a set of features and attributes paired with a value. However, our team proposes a new method for case representation through which a case is comprised of three parts: function, behavior and structure (Fig. 2). Furthermore, we categorize our data into this framework as well, such that function represents device usage log data, behavior representing quantified-self data and structure representing contextual data.

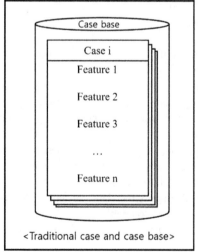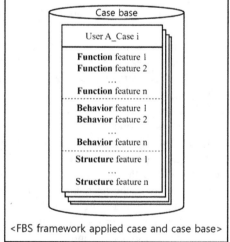

Fig. 2. Case represented through feature vector representation (left), and our FBS applied method (right)

As for the case representation, function expresses the service provided to the users. This part is linked to the device usage log data. The feature of the function represents elements, such as the status of device and information about how users control the devices. This data can deal with the features of device (such as name, size, and etc.), the timestamp when users use the device, and features of setting that can be controlled by users (such as power, mode and etc.) Second, behavior expresses the status of users through quantified-self data, that means the result of calculating raw data from sensors or devices. It does not however include the process of calculation. In our progress, quantified-self data is stored in database to save and derive the meaningful information of raw data (such as, heart beat, pedometer, and etc.) From the result, AI can recognize the status of users. For example, facial expression shows emotional features of users. Also, if the raw data is meaningful enough itself, it can come under the this part. Third, structure expresses the contextual data like the status of environment. It can be divided into two aspects. First aspect is the outdoor status around users. It includes the weather of the day, current temperature, and others. Second one is the indoor status, such as the illumination, humidity of inside space, location, and etc. This part can be used to recognize the environmental context compared with them. Therefore, through these procedures, a user's daily life activities that is somewhat broad and abstract can be structuralized. This has the advantage of integrating data from multiple input devices.

4   Conclusion

This paper reviewed the CBR utilized in artificial intelligence, and the Function Behavior and Structure framework to integrate it into our CBR based AI. We also introduced the method of representing daily data derived from various devices into a case. For case representation, we defined three data concepts to manage the sporadic data of daily routines: device usage log data, quantified-self data, and contextual data. These data concepts are used as function, behavior, and structure features that compose a case. Through this process our team could arrange the series of sensor values into meaningful information. Moreover, we designed a represented case by integrating our own data concept and the idea of FBS framework. For future work, we will implement the actual cases and CBR system with the consideration of FBS framework. The real time demonstration and in-situ tests will take place once testbed is completed. Through this phase, we will examine our framework with the real life problems. Therefore, the research will progress into the stage of improving for more accurate and well-defined services with the consideration of user's situation, condition, and habit through our system.

Acknowledgements. This work was supported by ICT R&D program of MSIP/IITP. [R7124-16-0004, Development of Intelligent Interaction Technology Based on Context Awareness and Human Intention Understanding].

References

1. Weiser, M.: The computer for the 21st century. Sci. Am. **265**(3), 94–104 (1991)
2. Bohn, J., et al.: Social, economic, and ethical implications of ambient intelligence and ubiquitous computing. In: Weber, W., Rabaey, J.M., Aarts, E. (eds.) Ambient Intelligence, pp. 5–29. Springer, Heidelberg (2005)
3. Ørmen, J., Thorhauge, A.M.: Smartphone log data in a qualitative perspective. Mob. Media Commun. **3**(3), 335–350 (2015)
4. Oliver, E.: The challenges in large-scale smartphone user studies. In: Proceedings of the 2nd ACM International Workshop on Hot Topics in Planet-scale Measurement, p. 5. ACM, June 2010
5. Xu, Z., Bai, K., Zhu, S.: Taplogger: inferring user inputs on smartphone touchscreens using on-board motion sensors. In: Proceedings of the Fifth ACM Conference on Security and Privacy in Wireless and Mobile Networks. ACM (2012)
6. Lane, N.D., et al.: Bewell: a smartphone application to monitor, model and promote wellbeing. In: 5th International ICST Conference on Pervasive Computing Technologies for Healthcare (2011)
7. Lai, X., Liu, Q., Wei, X., Wang, W., Zhou, G., Han, G.: A survey of body sensor networks. Sensors **13**(5), 5406–5447 (2013)
8. Kwapisz, J.R., Weiss, G.M., Moore, S.A.: Activity recognition using cell phone accelerometers. ACM SIGKDD Explor. Newsl. **12**(2), 74–82 (2011)
9. Yang, X., You, C.-W., Lu, H., Lin, M., Lane, Nicholas D., Campbell, Andrew T.: Visage: a face interpretation engine for smartphone applications. In: Uhler, D., Mehta, K., Wong, J.L. (eds.) MobiCASE 2012. LNICSSITE, vol. 110, pp. 149–168. Springer, Heidelberg (2013). doi:10.1007/978-3-642-36632-1_9
10. De Silva, L.C., Miyasato, T., Nakatsu, R.: Facial emotion recognition using multi-modal information. In: Proceedings of 1997 International Conference on Information, Communications and Signal Processing, ICICS 1997, vol. 1, pp. 397–401. IEEE, September 1997
11. Lakens, D.: Using a smartphone to measure heart rate changes during relived happiness and anger. IEEE Trans. Affect. Comput. **4**(2), 238–241 (2013)
12. Swan, M.: The quantified-self: fundamental disruption in big data science and biological discovery. Big Data **1**(2), 85–99 (2013)
13. Singer, E.: The Measured Life. MIT Press, Cambridge (2017)
14. Tapia, E.M., Intille, S.S., Larson, K.: Activity recognition in the home using simple and ubiquitous sensors. In: Ferscha, A., Mattern, F. (eds.) Pervasive 2004. LNCS, vol. 3001, pp. 158–175. Springer, Heidelberg (2004). doi:10.1007/978-3-540-24646-6_10
15. Yoon, H., Doh, Y.Y., Yi, M.Y., Woo, W.: A conceptual framework for augmented smart coach based on quantified holistic self. In: Streitz, N., Markopoulos, P. (eds.) DAPI 2014. LNCS, vol. 8530, pp. 498–508. Springer, Cham (2014). doi:10.1007/978-3-319-07788-8_46
16. Watson, I.: An introduction to case-based reasoning. In: Watson, I.D. (ed.) UK CBR 1995. LNCS, vol. 1020, pp. 1–16. Springer, Heidelberg (1995). doi:10.1007/3-540-60654-8_18
17. Schank, R.C.: Dynamic Memory: A Theory of Reminding and Learning in Computers and People. Cambridge University Press, Cambridge (1982)
18. Aamodt, A., Plaza, E.: Case-based reasoning: foundational issues, methodological variations, and system approaches. AI Commun. **7**(1), 39–59 (1994)
19. Kolodner, J.L., Leake, D.: A tutorial introduction to case-based reasoning. In: Leale, D. (ed.) Case-Based Reasoning: Experiences, Lessons and Future Directions, pp. 31–65. AAAI/MIT Press, Cambridge (1996)

20. Maher, M.L., de Silva Garza, A.G.: Case-based reasoning in design. IEEE Expert **12**(2), 34–41 (1997)
21. Bergmann, R., Kolodner, J., Plaza, E.: Representation in case-based reasoning. University of Trier, Business Information Systems II, 54286 Trier, Germany
22. Bergmann, R., Wilke, W.: On the role of abstraction in case-based reasoning. In: Smith, I., Faltings, B. (eds.) EWCBR 1996. LNCS, vol. 1168, pp. 28–43. Springer, Heidelberg (1996). doi:10.1007/BFb0020600
23. Gero, J.S., Kannengiesser, U.: The situated function-behaviour-structure framework (2002, in progress)
24. Gero, J.S., Kannengiesser, U.: The situated function–behaviour–structure framework. Des. Stud. **25**(4), 373–391 (2004)
25. Gero, J.S., Kannengiesser, U.: A function–behavior–structure ontology of processes. Artif. Intell. Eng. Des. Anal. Manuf. (AI EDAM) **21**(04), 379–391 (2007)
26. Gero, J.S., Kannengiesser, U.: A function-behaviour-structure ontology of processes. In: Gero, J.S. (ed.) Design Computing and Cognition 2006, pp. 407–422. Springer, Netherlands (2006)
27. Gero, J.S., Kannengiesser, U.: The function-behaviour-structure ontology of design. In: Chakrabarti, A., Blessing, L.T.M. (eds.) An Anthology of Theories and Models of Design, pp. 263–283. Springer, London (2014)
28. Rosenman, M.A., Gero, J.S., Oxman, R.E.: What's in a case: the use of case bases, knowledge bases and databases in design. In: CAAD Futures 1991: Computer Aided Architectural Design Futures: Education, Research, Applications, p. 285 (1991)
29. Maher, M.L., Balachandran, M., Zhang, D.M.: Case-Based Reasoning in Design. Psychology Press, Abingdon (1995)
30. Maher, M. L.: Casecad and cadsyn. In: Issues and applications of casc-based reasoning in design, pp. 161–185 (1997)
31. Kim, D., Seo, Y., Sheen, D.M.: Dynamic component reconfiguration system using case-based reasoning for weapons system in DM&S: guided weapon case. In: Modelling Symposium (EMS), 2015 IEEE European, pp. 9–13. IEEE, October 2015

Indoor Navigation Aid System Using No Positioning Technique for Visually Impaired People

Yeonju Oh, Wei-Liang Kao, and Byung-Cheol Min(⊠)

Computer and Information Technology, Purdue University,
West Lafayette, IN 47907, USA
{oh132,kaow,minb}@purdue.edu

Abstract. We propose a novel navigation aid system that assists the visually impaired to travel in unfamiliar indoor environments independently. The main idea of the proposed system is that it does not employ any of indoor positioning techniques. Instead, the system generates shoreline based optimal paths including a series of recognizable landmarks and detailed instructions, which enables the visually impaired to navigate to their destinations by listening the instructions on their smartphones. The paths and instructions are generated on a computer installed on an indoor kiosk where the visually impaired enters his or her destination, and then the generated instructions are wirelessly transfered to the user's smartphone. To validate the proposed system, we developed an Android-based smartphone App and conducted the user study with three visually impaired participants. The study shows that the proposed idea is feasible, useful and potential.

Keywords: Blind · Visual impairment · Indoor navigation · Smartphone based navigation · Orientation and Mobility (O&M)

1 Introduction

Globally, it is estimated that there are 285 million people who are blind or visually impaired [1]. For many, traveling to unfamiliar environments is one of the most difficult challenges for visually impaired people [7]. Although numerous studies have attempted to address such navigation challenges by using a smartphone, mobile robots, etc., still they do not adequately address the needs of people who are blind or visually impaired due to limited accuracy, accessibility, and adaptability. For example, blind travelers may not fully depend on the existing indoor navigation technologies because it would include 1–2 m localization error [2]. Because of such issues, the blind often participates in mobility training sessions with O&M (Orientation and Mobility) instructors in order to become familiar with a new place. However, such training is time consuming and expensive. Furthermore, it is often challenging for the blind to memorize all the steps necessary to independently navigate in a new location [6].

© Springer International Publishing AG 2017
C. Stephanidis (Ed.): HCII Posters 2017, Part II, CCIS 714, pp. 390–397, 2017.
DOI: 10.1007/978-3-319-58753-0_56

The objective of this study is to develop new, low-cost, and accessible navigation aid tools that do not employ any localization nor indoor positioning techniques and not require a direct interaction and training with O&M instructors for blind and visually impaired people to travel safely and independently in unfamiliar environments. To this end, we propose a system that generates optimized paths and very detailed instructions on a computer installed at an indoor kiosk and wirelessly transfers the generated instructions to the user's smartphone. The paths and the instructions are generated based on a shoreline approach that is a strategy used by O&M instructors when they teach independent navigation skills to people who are visually impaired. With the shoreline approach, blind people could continuously follow recognizable landmarks such as walls, doors, and intersections with his or her traditional white cane until they reach their destination. The judgment of the arrival of each landmark is the responsibility of the visually impaired, and accuracy of judgment can be improved by providing an easily recognizable landmark to the visually impaired. We envision this system being available in public spaces, more specifically at indoor kiosks to assist those needing help with navigation (like an audio guide tour system in museums).

This paper consists of 5 sections, including this introductory section. The rest of the paper is organized as follows. In Sect. 2, we present related works to this study including indoor positioning techniques and smartphone-based navigation systems. We then described the proposed system in Sect. 3. In Sect. 4, the user study procedures conducted, results and analysis are included. Section 5 summarizes the conclusions and future scope of this study.

2   Related Work

Numerous researchers have attempted to find adequate navigation aids for blind and visually impaired people. These related assistive technologies include a wide range of navigation tools such as devices utilizing indoor positioning techniques (Wi-Fi fingerprinting [8,14] and dead reckoning [3,11]), physical infrastructure in the building (RFID tags) [12], or mobile devices, for example multiple sensors, smartphones [13], and wearable devices [4,9].

Since GPS (Global Positioning System) is unavailable in the indoor situation, the indoor localization techniques mentioned above have been widely used to keep track the user's position. Wi-Fi fingerprinting is the system that utilizes wireless access points (APs) to obtain the location information. On the other hand, dead reckoning is another indoor localizing method that more relies on the computation, which calculates the estimated position with the velocity and starting point of the user. Also, some research attempted to combine these techniques together for enhancing the route planning algorithm effectively [8]. However, Wi-Fi fingerprinting is still inaccurate to calculate the position of the user. Additionally, several studies that addressed the dead reckoning showed several accuracy issues because this localization technique requires the computational overhead during traveling and the error in this method easily grows as time passes [3].

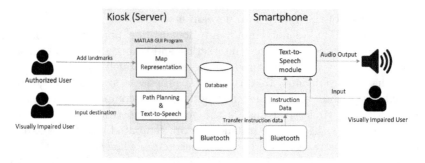

Fig. 1. Overall architecture of the system - The server contains two user interfaces which are for authorized users and visually impaired users. The server and smartphone communicate via Bluetooth. The smartphone receives generated instructions. Depending on a user input, it plays the instructions step by step using TTS.

A smartphone takes advantage of flexibility and functionality due to its accessibility. However, most research using the smartphone concentrated on the outdoor navigation [13] or had relatively lower accuracy in indoor situations [5]. Those systems are creative and effective for sighted people, but they are not suitable for blind people for their reliable navigation, because the suggested systems entail a considerable error (1–2 m) and low success rates which make users get confused and sometimes frustrated. For the higher accuracy, another study installed the physical infrastructure such as RFID [12]. Its main drawback is the high cost and long time taken to install these tags in the building.

Previous research has certain limitations such as error-prone systems, additional infrastructure, and inconvenience. Therefore, it is more restricted to a constrained use. On the other hand, our work involves the use of simplicity for the users in terms of a form factor, size, usability, robustness, and safety. Also we use a smartphone along with three simple gestures (left/right swipe, double tap) to achieve a navigation device capable of being held in hand or working with the user's cane.

3   System Design

The overall architecture of the navigation system is depicted in Fig. 1, and the user interface is shown in Fig. 2(a). The software is divided into two parts. One part is designed for authorized users such as building managers and O&M instructors to create a database on the interesting environment [10]. The traditional way to instruct blind people to navigate new paths is that instructors usually explore the requested location and find features around the routes in advance. They then teach the determined paths, which is finalized by many simulations. Likewise, this software is operated to add potential features by authorized users, which can be stored in the database and used for the path planning. This concept can update a software and the path planning in real-time when

(a) Computer user interface (Upper: for authorized users, Lower: for blind users)

(b) Screen captures of smartphone app

Fig. 2. User interface for the software.

authorized users enter a new landmark. Based on the collected information, the system creates a directed graph. A tuple indicates a node of the directed graph, and tuples are connected with the near feature (edge of the graph). Each edge has various weights in order to reflect difficulties in finding the next landmark at the current position. For example, following an adjacent wall is much easier than crossing to the hall way. In this case, when a user needs to cross the hall way, the edge has a higher cost than just following an adjacent wall. Thus, the weights are different depending on types of current feature and the next node.

Another part of the software is designed for the blind or visually impaired who mainly uses this software in a real-world situation. When a user comes to a kiosk in the building, the user will be required to enter their destination. After receiving the destination from users, the software generates the optimized paths to the destination using a shoreline-based path planning. The generated paths come from the directed graph which was generated by the first part of the software, and the software uses a Dijkstra algorithm for path planning. In order to give a detailed instruction, the system provides a direction, a distance, and the number of doors that a user has to pass. An example of the generated instruction is "Go straight until the corner. The distance is almost 15 ft. And you will pass 2 doors."

Last, we developed an Android App that enables users to listen to voice instructions while traveling with their existing navigation aid tools such as a white cane. Once smartphone receives the instructions generated by the kiosk, the App then (Fig. 2(b)) plays them by converting into speech using TTS. In addition, considering the interaction factors, the user can simply operate the App by three simple gestures (left/right swipe and double tap). Each gesture plays the next, previous, and current instruction. With this proposed system, users do

Fig. 3. User study - Three visually impaired participants navigating unfamiliar indoor environments with the help of the proposed system.

not need to memorize the entire paths in order to reach their destination. The arrival at each landmark is determined by the user, and if the user determines that he or she has reached the landmark, the user plays the next instruction to move to the next landmark.

4 User Study

In order to evaluate the feasibility and usefulness of the system, we recruited three blind and visually impaired participants as shown in Fig. 3 (P1, P3 - totally blind, P2- partially blind who can potentially recognize lights, all males)[1]. Before starting the actual experiment, each participant participated in the two tutorial sessions which made users comfortably operate the device and Android App.

Then, the participants conducted three predefined tasks that consist of different difficulty levels (See Fig. 4). The total travel distance of each path increases as the difficulty level gets higher. After finishing the tasks, we got user feedback from each participant. The questions (Table 1) are related to perceived usefulness and ease of use of the system.

4.1 Results and Analysis

Time and Trajectory. Investigators measured the time (Table 2) and recorded trajectories while the participants were traveling from the starting point to the destination. Overall, each participant followed the tutorial sessions safely and finished the three tasks well. One remarkable observation is that each participant used the smartphone in a totally different way. P1 played instructions step by step as we expected. On other hand, P2 put the smartphone in his pocket and played one by one. For a right handed person, it is hard to carry both a white cane and the smartphone at the same time. It shows that P2 took a long time to finish the first task, but he finished the other two tasks much faster than the other two participants in the task 2. In addition, P3 played all instructions at once and created a virtual map in his mind. Because of that, P3 took a relatively

---

[1] This study was approved through the Purdue Institutional Review Board (IRB) office (IRB protocol# 1603017357).

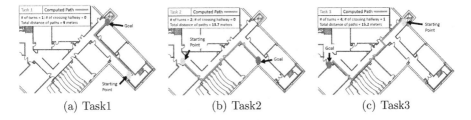

(a) Task1   (b) Task2   (c) Task3

Fig. 4. Map representation and numerical information of predefined tasks.

Table 1. Survey questions.

No.	Question
1	"An indoor navigation system would help me travel new place"
2	"An indoor navigation system is an effective assistive technology for people with visual impairment"
3	"The device is easy to carry and has a high usability"
4	"I learned to use the device quickly"
5	"I easily remember how to use the device"
6	"The navigation instructions helped me reach the destination"
7	"Overall, I recommend this device"

longer time to arrive at the destination. However, most of the time he spent was when he was playing all the instructions, and therefore the actual travel time was the fastest among all the participants. It was also observed that some participants had trouble with finding landmarks (particularly doors). Due to this issue, P1 failed to find the destination in the task 2 although he was able to move around the destination, and P3 had to repeat the previous instructions and correct his position. Figure 5 shows the trajectories that P1 and P2 explored. All participants did not deviate the desired paths over 3 m, and they were confident that they could arrive at the right destination. This result shows that blind and visually impaired users can arrive in unfamiliar spaces with the proposed system.

Experiment video is available at: https://goo.gl/VARGvY.

User Feedback. Most of them evaluated the system as useful and easy to use (see Table 3). All the participants strongly agreed that the proposed system would help visually impaired people travel a new place, and the generated instructions helped them reach their destinations. Therefore, they all recommend this device.

Q1 and Q3 scored relatively lower than other questions. This system mainly utilizes the walls in the building. Thus, the participants delineated some situations when they need to travel an open space, which does not include any wall. Also, they suggested potential improvements of the system. For example, if the

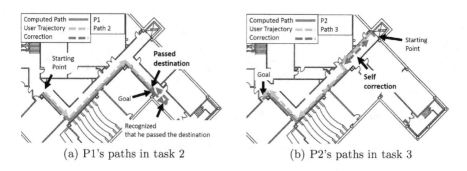

(a) P1's paths in task 2   (b) P2's paths in task 3

Fig. 5. Trajectory results of the user study.

Table 2. Travel time - Only P1 failed to find a destination during Task 2.

Participant	Task		
	1	*2*	*3*
P1	0:51	2:01 **F**	1:23
P2	1:58	1:26	1:48
P3	2:03	2:08	2:31
Avg	1:25	1:44	2:14
SD	0:35	0:16	0:15

Table 3. Survey results - We used Likert scale (1: Strongly disagree, 2: Disagree, 3: Neutral, 4: Agree, 5: Strongly agree).

	P1	P2	P3
Q1	4	4	5
Q2	4	5	5
Q3	3	5	5
Q4	4	5	5
Q5	5	5	5
Q6	5	5	5
Q7	4	5	5

user gets lost, the only way to get corrected is repeating the previous and current instructions by themselves. This can be improved by applying more various type of landmarks to the system.

5   Conclusion and Future Work

In this paper, we suggested a cost-effective indoor navigation aid system for people who are blind or visually impaired that uses no indoor navigation techniques. The user study shows that each step of the generated path instructions is clear enough for a user to reach the destination. Furthermore, the system gives shoreline-based instructions, such as by indicating walls and corner information, so that blind and visually impaired users can easily use the proposed system along with their traditional navigation aids, such as a white cane or a guide dog. The results show that the participants could follow the instructions easily, and the system could generate safe and effective paths for the user.

Future works will be related to the improvement of usefulness. First, the current system cannot generate paths and instructions in open spaces because the system is based on a wall in the building. Therefore, we will attempt to broaden the scope of the system using other landmarks, such as a chair, phone booth, or scent. This feature will be a good key for giving information about obstacles to users. In addition, we will include a recalibration feature to cope with situations where the user deviates from the desired paths.

References

1. WHO | Visual impairment and blindness. http://www.who.int/mediacentre/factsheets/fs282/en/
2. Al Nuaimi, K., Kamel, H.: A survey of indoor positioning systems and algorithms. In: 2011 International Conference on Innovations in Information Technology (IIT), pp. 185–190. IEEE (2011)
3. Apostolopoulos, I., Fallah, N., Folmer, E., Bekris, K.E.: Integrated online localization and navigation for people with visual impairments using smart phones. ACM Trans. Interactive Intell. Syst. (TiiS) **3**(4), 21 (2014)
4. Dakopoulos, D., Bourbakis, N.G.: Wearable obstacle avoidance electronic travel aids for blind: a survey. IEEE Trans. Syst. Man Cybern. Part C (Appl. Rev.) **40**(1), 25–35 (2010)
5. Fallah, N., Apostolopoulos, I., Bekris, K., Folmer, E.: The user as a sensor: navigating users with visual impairments in indoor spaces using tactile landmarks. In: Proceedings of the SIGCHI Conference on Human Factors in Computing Systems, pp. 425–432. ACM (2012)
6. Halder, S., Ghosal, A.: Mobility-assisted localization techniques in wireless sensor networks: issues, challenges and approaches. In: Koubaa, A., Khelil, A. (eds.) Cooperative Robots and Sensor Networks 2014, pp. 43–64. Springer, Heidelberg (2014)
7. Hollinger, K.: O&M for independent living: strategies for teaching orientation and mobility to older adults. J. Vis. Impairment Blindness **110**(2), 33–39 (2016)
8. Kannan, B., Kothari, N., Gnegy, C., Gedaway, H., Dias, M.F., Dias, M.B.: Localization, route planning, and smartphone interface for indoor navigation. In: Koubâa, A., Khelil, A. (eds.) Cooperative Robots and Sensor Networks, vol. 507, pp. 39–59. Springer, Heidelberg (2014)
9. Lee, Y.H., Medioni, G.: RGB-D camera based wearable navigation system for the visually impaired. Comput. Vis. Image Underst. **149**, 3–20 (2016)
10. Min, B.C., Saxena, S., Steinfeld, A., Dias, M.B.: Incorporating information from trusted sources to enhance urban navigation for blind travelers. In: 2015 IEEE International Conference on Robotics and Automation (ICRA), pp. 4511–4518. IEEE (2015)
11. Pratama, A.R., Hidayat, R., et al.: Smartphone-based pedestrian dead reckoning as an indoor positioning system. In: 2012 International Conference on System Engineering and Technology (ICSET), pp. 1–6. IEEE (2012)
12. Tsirmpas, C., Rompas, A., Fokou, O., Koutsouris, D.: An indoor navigation system for visually impaired and elderly people based on radio frequency identification (RFID). Inf. Sci. **320**, 288–305 (2015)
13. Yatani, K., Banovic, N., Truong, K.: Spacesense: representing geographical information to visually impaired people using spatial tactile feedback. In: Proceedings of the SIGCHI Conference on Human Factors in Computing Systems, pp. 415–424. ACM (2012)
14. Yuan, Z.: A cyber-human interaction based system on mobile phone for indoor localization. arXiv preprint arXiv:1503.08398 (2015)

SmartResponse: Emergency and Non-emergency Response for Smartphone Based Indoor Localization Applications

Manoj Penmetcha, Arabinda Samantaray, and Byung-Cheol Min[(✉)]

Computer and Information Technology, Purdue University,
West Lafayette, IN 47907, USA
{mpenmetc,samantar,minb}@purdue.edu

Abstract. In this paper, we present an Android based application that uses Wi-Fi fingerprinting technique to locate a person in an indoor environment with an accuracy of 1–2 m in 70% and 2–3 m in 30% of the test runs. This application can run in the background and whenever the individual requires assistance, their exact location along with a floor map image can be communicated to the appropriate authorities through an SMS, which is activated by pre-defined gestures such as swipe on a smartphone. We envision that the proposed application will assist people who are blind or visually impaired in navigating an indoor environment and in requesting assistance from other individual during their independent navigation.

Keywords: Emergency assistance · Indoor localization · Wi-Fi · Android programming · Visually impaired

1 Introduction

An important conclusion drawn during a series of interviews with first responders was that possessing accurate information about the exact location of a victim is of primary importance [1]. Obtaining such detailed information from victims suffering from visual impairment is very challenging as they use very specific landmarks (such as the number of turns, doors, etc.) to navigate, which cannot be easily understood by first responders leading to inefficient problem redressal.

As the visually impaired community attempts to take a more active part in the society, they face multiple challenges ranging from reading a sign on the road to evacuating a building in case of a fire. To address these issues, many applications based on computer vision, smart-phones, sensors (talking OCR, GPS, radar canes, etc.) have been developed [2–5], but most of them have very specific functionalities which renders them useless in many complex situations due to which a visually impaired person may require assistance from other individuals.

To ensure that assistance is provided as quickly as possible, it is extremely important that the location, description and the nature of the emergency is conveyed to the appropriate authorities. However, obtaining the location of a

© Springer International Publishing AG 2017
C. Stephanidis (Ed.): HCII Posters 2017, Part II, CCIS 714, pp. 398–404, 2017.
DOI: 10.1007/978-3-319-58753-0_57

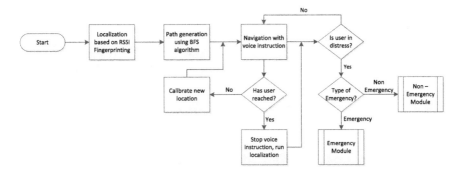

Fig. 1. A flowchart for the proposed smartphone application.

person in an indoor environment is a difficult problem. Various technologies such as sonar [6], beacons [7], vision [8], and Wi-Fi, have been explored to answer this problem. The easy availability of Wi-Fi makes it a lucrative proposition for many researchers who have used it for localization in indoor environments, through fingerprinting [9,10].

Our primary objectives in this research are first, to utilize the already existing Wi-Fi based localization techniques to build an indoor navigation application and second, to use this indoor navigation application as a basis to build an emergency and non-emergency based response system for providing assistance to people with visual impairment in the least amount of time possible. Through this app, we intend to overcome the absence of an emergency response system [11–13] specifically targeted for visually impaired individuals.

The application is built on the hypothesis that using this application will help people suffering from visual impairments in navigating in an indoor environment and whenever required they can request assistance from the concerned authorities, and it would be delivered to them in the shortest amount of time possible.

2   Approach and Methods

The application has two primary functions. First, it is to accurately localize an individual in an indoor environment, thus assisting him/her in navigation. Secondly, the application is to request assistance in an emergency or non-emergency situation. The flowchart for the proposed application is shown in Fig. 1.

2.1   Localization and Path Planning

We developed a reference coordinate system by dividing the entire floor plan into a grid. Subsequently, we fingerprinted each and every grid cell on the floor map and stored the Wi-Fi RSSI (Radio Signal Strength Indicator) strength range from all the concerned access points into a database. These values would help

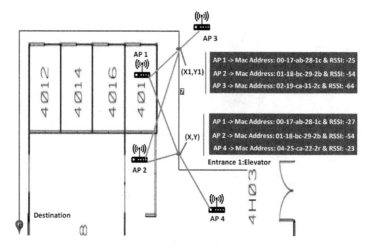

Fig. 2. An example of nodes and its corresponding stored values.

us in uniquely identifying the node as shown in Fig. 2. In Fig. 2 we have a node
(X,Y), which has three access points (AP1, AP2 and AP3) in its range. The
RSSI values from these three access points can uniquely identify node (X,Y),
and hence we store their corresponding Mac addresses and RSSI values.

Using the *WifiManager* API provided by the Android operating system, our
application is able to find out the Mac addresses and RSSI values of each access
point detected by the smartphone at any given point of time. These acquired
Mac addresses and signal strengths are then compared with the existing database
to find the location of the user. This function runs every 2 ms to update the
localization information of the user.

The floor map information was provided to the application in the form of
a graphical data structure [14], where each node represents a grid cell in our
reference coordinate system. Using this graphical data structure we were able
to generate the shortest path between the user's starting location and chosen
destination, by applying the BFS algorithm [15].

2.2   Graphical Interface and Voice Navigation

The current location of the user and the generated path is depicted on the screen
of the Android device by using various classes provided by the Android API
such as *Canvas, Drawable, Bitmap*, etc. Figure 3 shows the user interface of the
developed application. Since the application is targeted for individuals suffering
from visual impairments, direction's to traverse the path were provided in the
form of voice instructions by using textitPico, Android's Text-To-Speech (TTS)
module.

Fig. 3. Images showing screen-shots of graphical interfaces in the application.

2.3 Crisis Response

Our next step was to implement an Emergency and Non Emergency Response module in the application. This module can be invoked by using android gestures, such as a left to right swipe. When the user invokes this module, their location is sent as an SMS to the emergency or non-emergency response team along with a floor map, indicating the user's current location. Figure 4 shows the Emergency module implemented. The floor map sent along with the text message includes all the possible path's from each entrance point of the building to the users location and the shortest path among them will be represented by using a red line as shown in Fig. 4.

3 Result and Analysis

The application was validated using an Android based Samsung galaxy S6 phone on the fourth floor of the Wang Hall at Purdue University. Android API 22 was used for developing the application and *Ubiquiti Nanostation* [16] routers were used as access points in the study.

As neither localization accuracy nor navigation was the priority of our project, to verify accuracy we set our margin of error to 22 percent and using normal distribution we derived the sample size to be 60. The application was test run 60 times and the results acquired varied from 1.5 m to 3.5 m with Wi-Fi signal fluctuations playing a major role in determining location accuracy. Figure 5 shows the bar chart indicating percentage accuracy at different locations. As shown in the figure, an accuracy of 1–2 m in approximately 70 percent in the most locations and 2–3 m in approximately 30% of the test runs could be achieved. Since the localization accuracy of the application was in the range of 1.5 m to 3.5 m, as it was completely dependent on Wi-Fi signal strengths, it might not be an ideal solution for indoor navigation considering the visually impaired people would require higher accuracy of localization for their independent navigation. Nonetheless it can serve the purpose of emergency or non-emergency

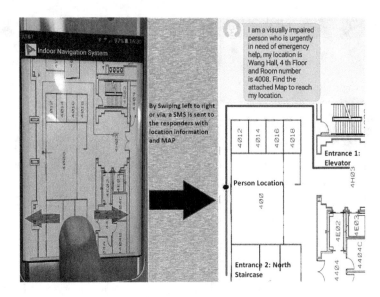

Fig. 4. MMS with text and an image of the current map (right) are sent to responders when performed a gesture (left).

response for people with visual impairment well as the first responders would have to search for the person only within a 3 m radius rather than through the entire building.

4   Conclusion and Future Works

4.1   Conclusion

This paper presents the prototype of a navigation system that helps the visually impaired to navigate within indoor environments. The results of the preliminary tests indicate that the solution is feasible and useful and can guide the user in indoor environments. However, it is important to conduct more rigorous experiments and involve visually impaired people to understand the true effectiveness of our system and improve upon it further.

4.2   Future Works

Our main motivation while developing this application was to create a platform on which we can add more features and hence develop a highly personalized piece of software that could help the visually impaired community in leading an independent and better quality of life.

To achieve this aim, we are currently working on developing a system that allows the smartphone camera to detect the presence of any stationary or moving

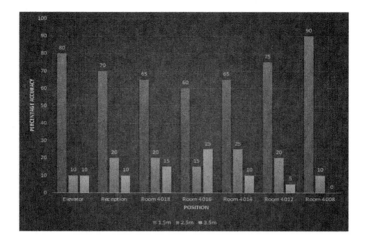

Fig. 5. A Bar chart indicating percentage accuracy at different locations.

obstacle and provide voice feedback to the user so that the user can take appropriate measures. Also, we intend to deploy RFID tag readers that would allow any users to scan the RFID tag, and then be able to obtain all the necessary details such as the various access points, their signal strengths at various points on a floor plan, and all the other requisite data that are necessary for using the application to provide localization and navigation features when a user enters a new building.

References

1. Li, N., Yang, Z., Ghahramani, A., Becerik-Gerber, B., Soibelman, L.: Situational awareness for supporting building fire emergency response: information needs, information sources, and implementation requirements. Fire Saf. J. **63**, 17–28 (2014)
2. Kane, S.K., Jayant, C., Wobbrock, J.O., Ladner, R.E.: Freedom to roam: a study of mobile device adoption and accessibility for people with visual and motor disabilities. In: Proceedings of the 11th International ACM SIGACCESS Conference on Computers and Accessibility, pp. 115–122. ACM (2009)
3. Jayant, C., Ji, H., White, S., Bigham, J.P.: Supporting blind photography. In: The proceedings of the 13th International ACM SIGACCESS Conference on Computers and Accessibility, pp. 203–210. ACM (2011)
4. Bigham, J.P., Ladner, R.E., Borodin, Y.: The design of human-powered access technology. In: The Proceedings of the 13th International ACM SIGACCESS Conference on Computers and Accessibility, pp. 3–10. ACM (2011)
5. Bigham, J.P., Jayant, C., Ji, H., Little, G., Miller, A., Miller, R.C., Miller, R., Tatarowicz, A., White, B., White, S., et al.: Vizwiz: nearly real-time answers to visual questions. In: Proceedings of the 23rd Annual ACM Symposium on User Interface Software and Technology, pp. 333–342. ACM (2010)
6. Elfes, A.: Sonar-based real-world mapping and navigation. IEEE J. Robot. Autom. **3**(3), 249–265 (1987)

7. Ran, L., Helal, S., Moore, S. Drishti: an integrated indoor/outdoor blind navigation system and service. In: Proceedings of the Second IEEE Annual Conference on Pervasive Computing and Communications, PerCom, pp. 23–30. IEEE (2004)
8. Sim, R., Dudek, G.: Learning and evaluating visual features for pose estimation. In: Proceedings of the Seventh IEEE International Conference on Computer Vision, vol. 2, pp. 1217–1222 (1999)
9. Farshad, A., Li, J., Marina, M.K., Garcia, F.J.: A microscopic look at WiFi fingerprinting for indoor mobile phone localization in diverse environments. In: International Conference on Indoor Positioning and Indoor Navigation, pp. 1–10, October 2013
10. Evennou, F., Marx, F.: Advanced integration of WiFi and inertial navigation systems for indoor mobile positioning. EURASIP J. Appl. Sig. Process. **2006**, 164 (2006)
11. Ahn, J., Han, R.: An indoor augmented-reality evacuation system for the smartphone using personalized pedometry. Hum.-Centric Comput. Inf. Sci. **2**(1), 18 (2012)
12. Li, N., Becerik-Gerber, B., Soibelman, L., Krishnamachari, B.: Comparative assessment of an indoor localization framework for building emergency response. Autom. Constr. **57**, 42–54 (2015)
13. Wada, T., Takahashi, T.: Evacuation guidance system using everyday use smartphones. In: International Conference on Signal-Image Technology & Internet-Based Systems (SITIS), pp. 860–864. IEEE (2013)
14. Hardwick, M.: Graphical data structures. ACM SIGGRAPH Comput. Graph. **15**(4), 376–404 (1981)
15. Rose, D.J., Tarjan, R.E., Lueker, G.S.: Algorithmic aspects of vertex elimination on graphs. SIAM J. Comput. **5**(2), 266–283 (1976)
16. Ubiquiti networks - wireless networking products for broadband and enterprise. https://www.ubnt.com/. Accessed 17 Mar 2017

Human Algorithm

How Personal Reflection of Data Agents Improves Crowdsourcing Data Collection in a Smart City Planning Study

Jue Ren[1](✉), Youyang Hou[2], Tat Lam[3], and Yang Yang[3]

[1] Harbin Institute of Technology, ShenZhen, GuangDong, China
2284164@qq.com
[2] School of Information, University of Michigan, 105 S State Street,
Ann Arbor, MI, USA
youyangh@umich.edu
[3] ShanZhai City, 501, Rykadan Capital Tower 135 Hoi Bun Road,
Kwun Tong, Hong Kong
tat@shanzhai.city, sunnie.joeng@gmail.com

Abstract. Crowdsourcing is widely used in smart city/community study, but the research on cooperating pattern among participants is limited. In order to find the methods to speed up crowdsourcing data collection and refine collected data quality, this study uses mixed methods to trace the methods that 13 data agents used to overcome cultural and technical barriers doing crowdsourcing data collection in an ongoing community based smart city planning study. We find the personal reflection is accompanied throughout the data collection process, which we called Human Algorithm, a cultural critical reflective evaluation mechanism to the data collection purpose, data collection tools and methods, and relation between data agents and community member. We argue that human algorithm would be helpful to improve crowdsourcing data in quality and collecting speed in community crowdsourcing studies. We conclude with the design implications of personal reflection mechanism of human algorithm in crowdsourcing data collection for the community based Smart City planning systems. We noted the importance of pre data processing on social impact evaluation among data collection with instantly feedback from end users for the Smart City systems.

Keywords: Smart city · Human sensor

1 Introduction

For the Smart City planning system of urban reconstruction design for historical urban landscape communities, it is important to leverage crowdsourcing data platforms. These platforms would help understand community members' real time opinions about planning, which serves as a social impact evaluation of the effect of urban reconstruction project and help urban planners to do more subtly design for sustainable urban development with historical landscape protection and community integrality.

© Springer International Publishing AG 2017
C. Stephanidis (Ed.): HCII Posters 2017, Part II, CCIS 714, pp. 405–412, 2017.
DOI: 10.1007/978-3-319-58753-0_58

Increasingly, big data has been used for social and economic developmental issues [1]. Many studies explore how to use human sensors, such as social media users, to investigate and understand society and community reactions of social issues such as natural disaster management [2], poverty alleviation, education development, and urban development. Digital humanitarian research [3] focuses on investigating how to leverage crowdsourcing and social media data to create real time crisis map and implement machine learning algorithms for analytics. Interactions among volunteers are also necessary during the sensing process but usually absent in most existing crowd human sensing systems [4].

However, due to the lack of technical skillset, data literacy and local cultural constrain, community members in historical urban landscape communities find it hard to share their opinions online to social media and crowdsourcing platforms by themselves directly. Data agents who help to collect community members' opinions play a crucial role as intermediaries in filling the gap between these end users and technical smart city planning system. This intermediaries' role has been increasingly recognized revealed in recent study of community health service in e-government system [5].

We are specifically concerned about data agents' working pattern as an intermediated human sensor during their data collection to prove high quality data could be collected within limited time. This paper presents a case in which data agents are explored to use Human Algorithm, recognized by us to be a personal reflective evaluation mechanism to "debug", find the solution, when they face the cultural and technical barriers in encountering community members with digital devices and cloud application. By exploring these human sensors experience, we could improve crowdsourcing data collection in the smart city planning in historical community projects.

2 Background

In this paper, we focus on the project of Impact Learning cloud analytics platform developed by ShanZhai City presented in Beijing Design Week 2016 during September, 2016. During this project, we used a cloud computing system combining online survey and instant mapping on a television screen to present grassroots community members' opinions on the Beijing Design Week 2016 held in these two historical landscape community, Baitasi (BTS) and Dashilar (DSL), as a part of BeiJing urban reconstruction project.

As a real-time cloud impact analytics computing system with data collection, data analysis and mapping insightful results to the audience, it is a big challenge to make data agents collecting high quality data within limited time and human resources (see Figs. 1 and 2).

13 student data agents started to collect data, after one-day field research training workshop and one-day field pilot visiting, using face to face interviews with community members to collect data, and then uploaded data through an mobile survey form on their mobile phone, tablet and laptop computer. There are one field advisor, one project manager and one team assistant work with student data agents in the 11 working days (see Figs. 3 and 4).

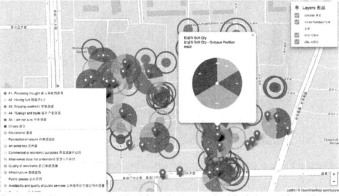

Real time dashboard system providing information to general public during social event in Beijing in September, 2016

Fig. 1. Real time dashboard system providing information in general public during Beijing Design Week 2016, local resident's attitudes to the social even held in the event are labeled in different colors. (Color figure online)

Fig. 2. The toolkit of data agent: a bag with mobile wi-fi, tablet for data collecting and uploading, canvas folding stool

During 9 days, the 4 data agents divided in 2 groups, and 99 respondents' opinion data was collected in BTS. Another team of 9 people into 3 groups and collected 103 respondents' opinion data in DSL. The data was first collected through the online questionnaire application called Jinshuju[1]. Then via APIs, the data was stored and

---

[1] https://jinshuju.net/.

Fig. 3. Data agent interview community grassroots elder members alone with her own mobile phone

analyzed at a cloud computing platform, and subsequently displayed through a real-time impact map web application shown on a television screen located in event site of BeiJing Design Week 2016 in BTS.

3   Research Approach

In this case study, with mixed methods, such as semi-structured online survey, group discussion, and participant observation, data agents personal working pattern is traced during the data collection processing,

13 student data agents are all female, aging from 21–27 years old. 8 data agents are undergraduate students and 5 are postgraduate. 6 students' majored in urban planning, 3 majored in anthropology, 2 majored in foreign language, 1 majored in architecture and 1 majored in psychology. They are all recruited from internet with the purpose to contribute to a project to give voices to grassroots community members to the urban reconstruction planning.

One researcher worked along with student data agent to be one of the data agent team taking half time in BTS, and the other half time in DSL, to follow up how data agent work during their data collection and joined data agents everyday group meeting after daily data collection.

Other researchers held two group discussions with the data agents, and a semi-structure online survey were collected after the data collection work. Both researchers joined the one mid-term and one final presentation for data agents held by data collection team leaders as observers.

4   The Findings

By examining the day to day work of student data agents, we find that both technical and cultural barriers interfere their data collection work, and they would find their alternative way after self-reflective evaluation to solve the unexpected situations and keep going the data collection, also their personal value to the community development would influence their emotion and trust to the work they are doing, which will influence the questions they prefer to ask, write down and to submit into the crowdsourcing data pool.

4.1 Technical Barriers of Data Agents Work

The most critical technical barriers reported by data agents are trouble in submitting survey form online due to the functional bugs and the lack of mobile wi-fi signals. For example, we set a page break in the survey to separate different kind of questions at first,However, in the interview with community members, data agents need to follow informants' talking logic to catch the main data we need to collect, so they have to jump the questions up and down, and the page break restricts their checking action with all questions needed in the field work.

Another challenge is that it is hard to do speech recognition of the interview instantly, and interview recording transcription defer the data submission. As a result, the data agent prefers to write down the main data they think are mostly related to the data we need to collect into the survey form and submit instantly. Paring working design is to make the 2 person or 3 person working team could interview by one data agent, and input the choices and answers into survey form and to submit online.

In addition, the mobile wi-fi card we used is pre-paid with daily limited flow rate, which would cause losing mobile internet connection without any warning. It makes data agent depress to find that all texts they have input in the form, which is a long discussion of community members' opinion are lost when they press the submit button but could not access to the internet. They could not recall all text and have no enough time to rewrite again to try the second submission.

In order to save time and minimize the risk of lost internet connection again, most data agents choose to record the interview as a backup solution, and write down the key sentences by hand on their own notebook and recall the main opinions of informants so that they could submit it when they go back to home at night. At the same time, they ask for adding wifi flow rate in the all data agent working wechat group from the team assistants. Team assistant's online support could help data agent's working tablet connected to the internet, but could not provide instantly help any time since assistant would do another work to do. Some data agents have to use their own mobile phone and laptop with their own wifi flowrate.

And for the mobile wifi card would have opportunity to lost signal to give the wrong GPS location in the survey form, we change the location info of interview site from mandatory to optional, and ask data agent to take pictures or write down the interview site info and to correct the GIS info in the online form after their daily work. This functional bug of digital data collection tools gives technical anxiety and additional workload to data agent, which reduce the trust the data agents trust to the all cloud computing system and change to use handy tools such as notebook and pen with their own evaluation on time and workload saving, their Human Algorithm prefer to make a decision to choose low risk tools to save the collected data at real time, and then submit them into online survey form later.

Fig. 4. The blue dot pointed by red arrow is the wrong GIS info mapping on the Impact Learning dashboard occurred wifi signal error. (Color figure online)

4.2 Cultural Barriers of Data Agents Work

The main cultural barriers happen in their interactions with community members. Their identity of outsiders and a lack of local knowledge causes to community members to worry about their purposes and their capacity of data collection. They need to construct trust with community members using their own field skills and personal experiences. Data agent all report their identity of young female students conducting an academic research contribute more trust to community members.

Community members' attitudes towards data agents, whether they welcome them or excluding them, affect the quantity and quality of the data collection. One student data agent report that she was yelled by a resident in a building in which is a building with few new outsider to come into, to warning her to exit.

On the other hand, after days of interaction among community members, the young, female data agent are more accepted than the first day they come in, and they find the main gathering sites of community members is a good place to look for more informant, which could save time and reduce workload. When they come to a gathering point to interview one informant, the other community members gather around will share their opinions with data agents. The data supplied by a number of informants is overloaded to data agents' affordance, they could not talk with the informants one by one, what would hurt informants enthusiastic and lost their trust. And data agent could write down that all conversation with different informants by hand or input into online survey. Data agents have to make the decisions without any hesitate to catch up the communication rhyme with informants and choose the most important data to keep in mind. Any buffering produced by their feedback action or technical errors would make the interview processing.

In addition, the sympathy to community members' bad living and housing situation in one side to add data agents' responsibility to do more contributions to the community reconstruction through the data collection, on the other side willing to make them lost trust to their own capability.

More importantly, data agents Human Algorithm would collapse, when they facing value conflict during the data collection. One data agent lost her temper to tears after seconds silence when she could not get possible feedback of team advisor's concern about living situation of community members in her final presentation, which is disaccording to her original understanding of the project, she lost her trust to the data collection project. Her Human Algorithm could not find an alternative solution as they work during the data collection, and she chooses an emotional way to express the all pressure she facing when her Human Algorithm works.

5 Conclusion

In this case study, we find out Human Algorithm works in three type of mutual interaction during the crowdsourcing collection processing:

- 1 mutual interactions with technical system;
- 2 mutual interactions with community members
- 3 mutual interactions among the crowdsourcing team members.

The crowdsourcing data collection processing is linearity working scenario in which the Human Algorithm, agents' personal reflective evaluation, working with technical tools in each mutual interaction approaches, to keep the processing going on.

We also explore the real time scenarios in crowding sourcing data collection in the community to find that the data collected is technically and culturally constructed.

Real-time data mapping is not that real time. The data collection processing would be interrupted by the online survey functional errors, mobile internet accessibility and online survey formation design when using mobile device to record and upload community member's opinion. Data agent would ask for help from team member in the field or online backup team members. When they cannot get help to solve the technical problem remotely, they would choose low cost and low risk and high efficient way in her personal offline context.

Data agents in the field is not isolated by the technical tools, but cooperate with technical tools, their team members and community member as their informant to finish the task of data collection. Crowdsourcing agents are not only the 13 data agents in this case, but also all stakeholders involved.

Data Agents need to trigger their Human Algorithm to find a solution to solve each unexpected emerging technical and cultural errors instantly.

Human Algorithm also works as a safety valve to ensure data agents works well under the limited social supports during their data collection work.

For an agent-based data collection in the Smart City planning system, we need to construct an affordable working scenario for data agents. And the Human Algorithm make a victual role in crowdsourcing data collection, and with more attention on the research of Human Algorithm can help to trace the source of data constructed through the data collection processing.

With the data preprocessing with Human Algorithm by data agent during the data collection period, we can accelerate the crowdsourcing data collection and get more refined and insightful data for planning design for Smart City.

Acknowledgements. We would like to thank all the student data agents and the project team of Shan Zhai City.

References

1. Ali, A., Qadir, J., ur Rasool, R., Sathiaseelan, A., Zwitter, A.: Big data for development: applications and techniques (2016)
2. Aulov, O., Halem, M.: Human sensor networks for improved modeling of natural disasters. Proc. IEEE **100**(10), 2812–2823 (2012)
3. Meier, P.: Digital Humanitarians: How Big Data is Changing the Face of Humanitarian Response. CRC Press, Boca Raton (2015)
4. Lane, N.D.: Community-aware smartphone sensing systems. IEEE Internet Comput. **16**(3), 60–64 (2012)
5. Dombrowski, L., Voida, A., Hayes, G.R., Mazmanian, M.: The labor practices of service mediation: a study of the work practices of food assistance outreach. pp. 1977–1986. ACM Press (2012)

Face Recognition Based on Adaptive Singular Value Decomposition in the Wavelet Domain

Jing-Wein Wang[1]([✉]) and Tzu-Hsiung Chen[2]

[1] Institute of Photonics and Communications, National Kaohsiung University of Applied Sciences, Kaohsiung 813, Taiwan, ROC
jwwang@cc.kuas.edu.tw
[2] Department of Computer Science and Information Engineering, Taipei City University of Science and Technology, Taipei 112, Taiwan, ROC
thchen@tpcu.edu.tw

Abstract. Face recognition is challenging because of lighting variation. This paper proposes a wavelet-based method combined with singular value decomposition (WSVD), which can be used to enhance face images, to overcome this problem. With the designated Gaussian template, the three color channels of the face image were next transformed to the discrete wavelet domain. By multiplying the singular value matrices of these frequency subband coefficient matrices with their corresponding compensation weight coefficients, the frequency subband coefficients of the three color channels were automatically adjusted. The 2D inverse discrete wavelet transform was then performed to obtain the WSVD-compensated color face image. The public color face databases confirmed that our proposed method can be efficiently applied in real applications.

Keywords: Face recognition · Lighting variation · Compensation coefficients

1 Introduction

Face recognition has been widely used in the real world and become a mature research field while the amount of approaches published every year is high. One may state that the recognition problem is already well solved but it is not true. It holds only for the cases when the faces are sufficiently well aligned and have limited amount of lighting variations. The performance of a face recognition system is considerably affected by the pose, expression, and illumination variations in face images. As discussed in [1], illumination treatment for image variation has been considered as one of the most critical preprocessing steps in face recognition. Variation in illumination conditions can make the appearance of a face in an image change greatly. Lighting causes larger differences in facial images compared with pose variations [2]. There has been much researches about how to overcome the illumination problem. As a rule, these methods can be separated into two main categories of methods for processing grayscale face images and processing color face images, respectively.

The methods used for color images can be divided into three subcategories. Illumination normalization-based methods [3] that are used to perform illumination

© Springer International Publishing AG 2017
C. Stephanidis (Ed.): HCII Posters 2017, Part II, CCIS 714, pp. 413–418, 2017.
DOI: 10.1007/978-3-319-58753-0_59

normalization in face images captured under different lighting conditions. Reflectance model-based methods [4] extract illumination invariant components and then use these components as features for face recognition. Methods of modeling faces [5] under varying illumination as a low-dimensional linear subspace in the face space require a large amount of both training data and constraints in real applications. Accordingly one can argue that compensation of illumination on faces can not only improve the face recognition performance but also prove to be very useful for the improvement of face color quality. While most of the methods attempt to resolve the problem of illumination variation for grayscale face images, a few methods have processed color face images recently [6–8].

In this paper, a novel illumination compensation method called wavelet-based method combined with singular value decomposition (WSVD) is proposed for reducing the effect of light on a color face image when there is insufficient light, and improving the capability of recognition systems. The method first transforms a color face image to the two-dimensional (2D) discrete wavelet domain and then adjusts the magnitudes of the three color channels automatically by multiplying singular value matrices of the three magnitude matrices of the RGB color channels with corresponding compensation weight coefficients. The experimental results obtained by using the known color face database show that our method can render color face images more clear, natural, and smoother, even if the face image is under lateral lighting. Therefore, it is very useful for the color face recognition task.

The rest of this paper is organized as follows. Section 2 presents the proposed method for a color face image. Experimental results are reported in Sect. 3 and concluded in Sect. 4.

2   Wavelet-Based Method Combined with Singular Value Decomposition (WSVD)

In order to reduce the effect of illumination on color, we propose the method of lighting variation compensation based on wavelet subbands, where the compensation value varies dynamically with the ratio of the average individual RGB values. The singular value decomposition of the color image Ξ_A can be expressed as

$$f_A = U_A \sum\nolimits_A V_A^T, \tag{1}$$

where $A = \{R, G, B\}$, representing the employed RGB color space; Σ_A is a matrix containing the sorted singular values on its main diagonal; and U_A and V_A are orthogonal square matrices. Daubechies wavelet characterized by a maximal number of vanishing moments for some given supports is applied to decompose the face image. The first-level coarse resolution is adopted to reduce the computation complexity and computing time. The size of the color image f_A is assumed to be $M \times N$ and the 2D discrete wavelet trasnsform is applied to decompose the three RGB color channels into their four subbands at scale level 1. The matrices are denoted as the LL, HL, LH, and HH wavelet subbands, and their mean values are μ_{LL}, μ_{HL}, μ_{LH}, μ_{HH}, respectively; the matrices G_LL, G_HL, G_LH, and G_HH are also denoted as the associated Gaussian templates, respectively.

$$\text{Max}(\mu_{LL}, \mu_{LH}, \mu_{HL}, \mu_{HH}) = \varpi, \tag{2}$$

$$\xi_{LL} = \left(\frac{\varpi}{\mu_{LL}}\right) * \frac{\text{Max}\left(\sum_{G\_LL}\right)}{\text{Max}\left(\sum_{LL}\right)}, \tag{3}$$

$$\xi_{HL} = \left(\frac{\varpi}{\mu_{HL}}\right) * \frac{\text{Max}\left(\sum_{G\_HL}\right)}{\text{Max}\left(\sum_{HL}\right)}, \tag{4}$$

$$\xi_{LH} = \left(\frac{\varpi}{\mu_{LH}}\right) * \frac{\text{Max}\left(\sum_{G\_LH}\right)}{\text{Max}\left(\sum_{LH}\right)}, \tag{5}$$

$$\xi_{HH} = \left(\frac{\varpi}{\mu_{HH}}\right) * \frac{\text{Max}\left(\sum_{G\_HH}\right)}{\text{Max}\left(\sum_{HH}\right)}, \tag{6}$$

where the mean and standard deviation of the synthetic Gaussian intensity matrix Σ_G are 0.5 and 1, respectively. Based on the maximum mean vale ϖ, LL, HL, LH, and HH wavelet subband coefficients of the RGB color channels are updated by multiplying the singular value matrices of each color channel wavelet subband with their corresponding compensation weight coefficients ξ_{LL}, ξ_{HL}, ξ_{LL}, and ξ_{LL} to adjust the image contrast caused by illumination variation. After compensation, the equalized image f_{EA} can be derived as follows:

$$f_{EA} = U_A(\xi \sum\nolimits_A) V_A^T. \tag{7}$$

The face contrast was adaptively adjusted by multiplying the singular value matrix of each subband coefficient matrix by the corresponding compensation coefficients.

3 Results and Discussions

In this research, we used the color FERET database [9]. The database provides the standard testing subsets that constitute one gallery set fa and one probe set fb. The set fb has face images with different facial expressions, taken seconds after the corresponding fa. The images show variation in terms of pose, expression, illumination, and resolution. We made use of 100 fa images as gallery set, while 100 fb images were used as probe set. To remove the effect of background and hair style variations, the face region is cropped by excluding background and hair regions. The images are taken at resolution 512 × 768 pixels and were rescaled to 100 × 100 in pixels. The recognition rate is defined by the ratio of the number of correct recognition to the size of the probe set. In the experiments on recognition, we used projection color space (PCS) [10] to transform and process images after WSVD illumination compensation by using the following equation

$$H_{C,R} \cdot H_{C,G}^T \cdot H_{C,B} = I_H, \tag{8}$$

where $I_H \in R^{m \times n}$ is the PCS transformed image, where "·" stands for the dot pro-duction. $H_{C,R}$, $H_{C,G}$, and $H_{C,B}$ are respectively the R, G, and B color channels with WSVD illumination compensation. PCS transformation involves enabling a linear analysis in analyzing the nonlinear characteristics of image processing and using the linking information between color and image. Moreover, the elevated dimensions can obtain the correlation among image information. The automatic detection technique proposed in [11] is adopted to obtain T-shape face regions comprising eyes, nose, and mouth. Then, the T-shape regions were restored to matrix form. The compensated T-shape results are shown in Fig. 1, where column (a) shows the original images, column (b) shows the recombined T-shape faces with lighting compensation, and column (c) shows the PCS images of (b).

(a)   (b)   (c)

Fig. 1. Example images taken from the color FERET database. (a) Original images. (b) Recombined T-shape region images of (a) with WSVD compensation. (c) PCS images of (b).

In order to analyze the clustering performance of raw faces and compensated faces, we used the leading ten eigenvectors derived from principal component analysis (PCA) [12] to examine the capability of collecting similar objects into groups. The trained and tested face images are classified using 1-NN. We conducted 10 experiments to evaluate the performance of the proposed method. In the experiment, we used 5 images from each subject as the training images and the other 5 images as the probe images. The comparisons of original images, SVD compensation (without wavelet decomposition), and WSVD compensation are shown in Table 1 to confirm that the proposed method can be applied in the real applications.

Table 1. Recognition rates for original (Ori), SVD, and WSVD images, obtained by applying eigenfaces, fisherfaces, and proposed methods to the color FERET database images (rate in %)

Method	Ori	SVD	WSVD
Eigenfaces	82.5	85.3	91.5
Fisherfaces	84.9	88.8	96.4
Proposed	87.1	92.9	98.9

4   Conclusions

In this work, we present the WSVD method for efficient face recognition. The proposed face recognizer is robust to large lighting variation. Experiments show that the proposed method can efficiently recognize a face in a short time less than 1 s. The presented framework was implemented with Microsoft Visual C++ 2010. The experiments were run on a PC with Intel Core i7-6700 (3.4 GHz) (4 GB RAM, Windows 7 operating system).

Acknowledgments. This study was funded by the Ministry of Science and Technology under project code MOST 104-2221-E-151-026.

References

1. Hsu, R.-L., Abdel-Mottaleb, M., Jain, A.K.: Face detection in color images. IEEE Trans. Pattern Anal. Mach. Intell. **24**, 696–706 (2002)
2. Luo, J., Crandall, D.: Color object detection using spatial-color joint probability functions. IEEE Trans. Image Process. **15**, 1443–1453 (2006)
3. Luo, Y., Guan, Y.P., Zhang, C.Q.: A robust illumination normalization method based on mean estimation for face recognition. ISNR Mach. Vis. **2013**, 1–10 (2013)
4. Baradarani, A., Wu, Q.M.J., Ahmadi, M.: An efficient illumination invariant face recognition framework via illumination enhancement and DD-DTCWT filtering. Pattern Recognit. **46**, 57–72 (2013)
5. Chen, T., Yin, W., Zhou, X.S., Comaniciu, D., Huang, T.S.: Total variation models for variable lighting face recognition. IEEE Trans. Pattern Anal. Mach. Intell. **28**, 1519–1524 (2006)
6. Wu, Y., Huang, T.S.: Nonstationary color tracking for vision-based human-computer interaction. IEEE Trans. Neural Netw. **13**, 948–960 (2002)

7. Wang, Y., Xu, Z.: Image retrieval using the color approximation histogram based on rough set theory. In: IEEE International Conference on Information Engineering and Computer Science, pp. 1–4 (2009)

8. Ikeda, O.: Segmentation of faces in video footage using HSV color for face detection and image retrieval. In: IEEE International Conference on Image Process, vol. 2, pp. 913–916 (2003)

9. Phillips, P.J., Moon, H., Rizvi, S.A., Rauss, P.J.: The FERET evaluation methodology for face recognition algorithms. IEEE Trans. Pattern Anal. Mach. Intel. **22**, 1090–1104 (2000)

10. Wang, J.-W., Lee, J.S., Chen, W.-Y.: Face recognition based on projected color space with lighting compensation. IEEE Sig. Process. Lett. **18**, 567–570 (2011)

11. Li, H., Lin, Z., Shen, X., Brandt, J., Hua, G.: A convolutional neural network cascade for face detection. In: IEEE Computer Society Conference on Computer Vision and Pattern Recognition. pp. 1–10 (2015)

12. Turk, M.A., Pentland, A.P.: Face recognition using eigenfaces. In: IEEE Computer Society Conference on Computer Vision and Pattern Recognition, pp. 586–591 (1991)

Biometric Identification Using Video of Body Silhouette Captured from Overhead

Hiro-Fumi Yanai$^{(\boxtimes)}$ and Shunsuke Kouno

Department of Media and Telecommunications,
Ibaraki University, Hitachi, Ibaraki, Japan
`hfy@ieee.org`

Abstract. One of the most actively studied natural user identification methods would be the ones that use the gait. Although gait-based methods are quite promising, their applications often require rather large open space for implementation. We wanted to propose methods that are appropriate for home or small office. We used video data of a user captured by a camera installed right overhead of the user. We obtained image sequences while users were pushing a button and return to the initial position without moving the feet placement. From the image sequences, we obtained users' silhouette and the bounding box of the silhouette that change in time. We defined 26 features from the silhouette itself and length and width of the bounding box, then selected six features through the analysis of principal components. We achieved recognition accuracy of 99% for 12 users using a nearest-neighbor classifier.

Keywords: Biometrics · Body · Silhouette · Video · Action · Doorbell · Security

1 Introduction

Lots of natural user identification methods have been proposed for replacing or supplementing existing identification techniques. One of the most actively studied methods would be the ones using the gait [1–3]. Although gait-based methods are quite promising, their applications often require rather large space to be implemented. We wanted to evaluate methods that are appropriate for home or small office. We were inspired by the seminal Active Floor [4] and the Smart Floor [5] that are based on force pressure profile curve obtained by a load cell embedded in the floor, where only a single footstep is sufficient for identifying a user. The Smart Floor relied on ten features (mean, standard deviation, two peak values, times of peaks, etc.), and recognition accuracy of the method for 15 users were 93% [5]. Note those two methods have a common limitation that the footstep has to be single (users have to step on the sensor with just one foot, thus requiring users somewhat unnatural behavior). If right and left footsteps overlap, force pressure profile curves from the right and left foot merge into an essentially different curve, so that features for the case of single footstep may

© Springer International Publishing AG 2017
C. Stephanidis (Ed.): HCII Posters 2017, Part II, CCIS 714, pp. 419–423, 2017.
DOI: 10.1007/978-3-319-58753-0_60

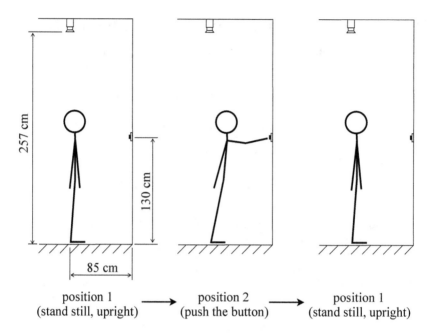

position 1 $\longrightarrow$ position 2 $\longrightarrow$ position 1
(stand still, upright)   (push the button)   (stand still, upright)

Fig. 1. Experimental setup. Users do actions (position 1 → position 2 → position 1) as natural as possible. The height 130 cm of a button was chosen based on the de facto standard of this sort of buttons in Japan. The distance between the face of the wall and users' heels was determined from preliminary experiments by ourselves; 85 cm scored best in the accuracy of user identification.

not effective any more. To overcome those limitations, a new methodology was proposed by which ground reaction force merged from both feet can be used [6].

In the present study, we used video data of users captured by a camera installed right overhead of the user at 257 cm above the ground. We instructed the user to push a button (this mimicked pushing an electronic doorbell) and return to the initial position without moving the feet. By subtracting the background and binarizing the image, we obtained image sequences at the rate of 20 fps. From an image sequence, we got two curves, width and length curve, of the bounding box of a user's body viewed from overhead. We defined 26 features from the curves and the silhouette, then selected six features through the analysis of principal components. We reached recognition accuracy as high as 99% for 12 users using a classifier based on Nearest Neighbor.

There is a study in which top-views of users are used for user identification [7]. The study investigates static images and depth data of users, whereas we only use image data and utilize sequences of user actions (movements).

2   Experiment and Results

In this section, we describe experimental procedures, how to select usable features, then we summarize the results.

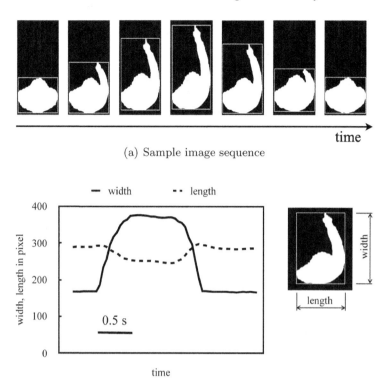

(a) Sample image sequence

(b) Sample curves of width and length of the bounding box

Fig. 2. Sample image sequence and sample data

Procedures. Twelve undergraduate or graduate students participated in the experiment (10 males and 2 females; 22 years old on average). The participants were instructed to

1. Stand still maintaining upright posture,
2. Push the button on the wall,
3. Then return to the original position.

While doing the above action, the participants were instructed not to move their feet position; otherwise, they could make arbitrary, natural movements if only they are consistent. A straight line was drawn on the floor at the distance of 85 cm from the wall and in parallel to the face of the wall. The participants placed their heel on the line. The button (a small electronic doorbell) was placed at 130 cm from the ground. Figure 1 illustrates the experimental setup. Figure 2 is to show samples from image sequences and obtained data.

Feature Selection. Features, say x, were normalized like $(x - \bar{x})/\sigma_x$, where $\bar{x}$ is average and σ_x standard deviation of the feature x over all participants, action samples and opportunities. Of all 26 features we defined from the silhouettes

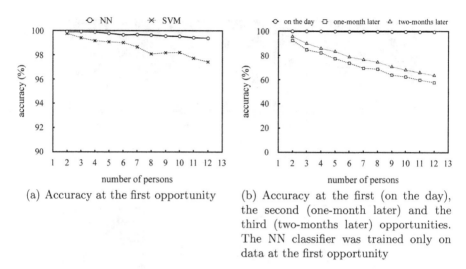

(a) Accuracy at the first opportunity

(b) Accuracy at the first (on the day), the second (one-month later) and the third (two-months later) opportunities. The NN classifier was trained only on data at the first opportunity

Fig. 3. Classification accuracy. Classifiers are Nearest Neighbor (k-NN with $k = 1$) and SVM (kernel: linear).

and the corresponding bounding box (see Fig. 2), 6 features were selected based on the amount of component loadings via principal component analysis. For the analysis of principal components, 360 samples of image sequences were used, where the samples consisted of 12 participants × 10 actions × 3 opportunities (opportunities with one-month interval each). Selected features were (in descending order of component loading values; values are given in ( )):

1. Maximum area of the bounding box (0.88)
2. Average length of the bounding box (0.86)
3. Minimum length of the bounding box (0.86)
4. Maximum area of the silhouette (0.86)
5. Initial area of the bounding box (0.85)
6. Initial length of the bounding box (0.83)

Results. Results are summarized as follows from two points of view. First, accuracy of user classification is evaluated for the samples on the first opportunity, i.e. 10 action samples acquired in the first day for each of 12 participant. Second, we tracked the stability of classification across time; the same 12 participants' actions were sampled three times in total with the interval of about one month.

For classifiers we used the method of Nearest Neighbor (k-NN for $k = 1, 3, 5$) and Support Vector Machine with different kernels. Evaluation was done through the procedure of 2-fold cross validation over 10 action samples. Of all NN and SVM, 1-NN achieved the highest accuracy of 99.4% for classification of 12 persons (see Fig. 3 (a)). Accuracy of 1-NN classifier, as trained by the data of the first opportunity, after one month and two months is shown in Fig. 3 (b). After one or two months, the classifier is unable to achieve as high accuracy as for the first-day data. However, degradation of the accuracy seems to stop within a month (compare results for one-month later and two-months later of Fig. 3 (b)).

3   Summary and Discussion

We showed that a sequence of actions viewed from overhead of a person that mimics pushing a doorbell contains information with which 12 persons could be classified with the accuracy of 99%. The actions took typically only ~ 2 s. Image processing procedures required were rather simple; background subtraction and binarization. Here background subtraction was easier since the background in the present case is the floor or the ground beneath a person.

We have to note that the above mentioned high levels of accuracy was achieved only within the data sampled in one day, to be precise, within a set of actions in a row (the results in the present study were based on 10 successive actions with the interval of a minute or so). In spite of this instability issue, it is interesting to note that the accuracy for 12 persons is about 60% after two months using only 6 features. So it would be worth mentioning that, by selecting other sets of features, we might be able to keep higher accuracy after several months.

References

1. Foster, J.P., Nixon, M.S., Prügel-Bennet, A.: Automatic gait recognition using area-based metrics. Pattern Recogn. Lett. **24**, 2489–2497 (2003)
2. Wang, L., Tan, T., Ning, H., Hu, W.: Silhouette analysis-based gait recognition for human identification. IEEE Trans. Pattern Anal. Mach. Intell. **25**(12), 1505–1517 (2003)
3. Iwama, H., Okumura, M., Makihara, Y., Yagi, Y.: The OU-ISIR gait database comprising the large population dataset and performance evaluation of gait recognition. IEEE Trans. Inf. Forensics Secur. **7**(5), 1511–1521 (2012)
4. Addlesee, M., Jones, A., Livesey, F., Samaria, F.: The ORL active floor. IEEE Pers. Commun. **4**, 35–41 (1997)
5. Orr, R.J., Abowd, G.D.: The Smart Floor: a mechanism for natural user identification and tracking, GVU Technical report GIT-GVU-00-02 (2000)
6. Seki, S., Fujii, S., Sawada, A., Minoh, M.: Person identification using ground reaction force during walking. IEICE Trans. Inf. Syst. **J90–D**(2), 441–449 (2007)
7. Kouno, D., Shimada, K., Endo, T.: Person identification using top-view image with depth information. In: 13th ACIS International Conference on Software Engineering, Artificial Intelligence, Networking and Parallel/Distributed Computing, pp. 140–145 (2012)

Mobile Interaction

Interaction Modalities for Augmented Reality in Tablets for Older Adults

Ana Georgina Guerrero Huerta[1(✉)], Erika Hernández Rubio[1],
and Amilcar Meneses Viveros[2]

[1] Instituto Politécnico Nacional, SEPI-ESCOM, Mexico City, DF, Mexico
`aguerreroh1600@alumno.ipn.mx, ehernandezru@ipn.mx`
[2] Departamento de Computación, CINVESTAV-IPN, Mexico City, DF, Mexico
`ameneses@cs.cinvestav.mx`

Abstract. Augmented reality can recreate scenes with where users interact. Tablets are suitable devices for working in this environment. Augmented reality applications have been developed for treatment health problems in older adults. Older people are willing to use this application if they are usable. However, augmented reality interfaces don't consider the seniors impairments. This paper presents an analysis of different interaction modalities in augmented reality applications in tablets for older adults.

Keywords: Augmented reality · Older adults · Interaction modalities · Tablets

1 Introduction

Augmented reality is a technology that combines the real world with virtual objects [9]. Virtual objects can be manipulated by the user and controlled by specialists, in some applications it is a safe environment for users [13]. Augmented reality can be used in various devices, such as lenses [28], automatic virtual environments [15], volumetric visualization [12] and computers [27]. Some authors have suggested that tablets are suitable devices to work in augmented reality [3,23,29]. In recent years, augmented reality applications have been developed to support the medical area [3,13], for treatment health problems in older adults [16,28]. If augmented reality medical environments are useful and usable by older adults, they will be more likely to use them, as older people do not reject the technology; instead, they are willing to learn how to use it [25]. However, there area augmented reality interfaces that don't consider the impairments of the elderly, such as loss of vision and hearing, and alterations in cognitive and motor functions. Although older people have an receptivity attitude when starting to use new technology, they may present anxiety and frustration when using it if the technology doesn't have adequate interaction [12].

In this document, we analyze the different interaction modalities in augmented reality applications in tablets for older adults. The main objective of

© Springer International Publishing AG 2017
C. Stephanidis (Ed.): HCII Posters 2017, Part II, CCIS 714, pp. 427–434, 2017.
DOI: 10.1007/978-3-319-58753-0_61

this analysis is to provide recommendations for usable software development. Next section presents the related work to this area. The third section explains the topic of augmented reality, as well as and the technology that use it. Next, the physical and cognitive impairments of older adults are discussed. Fifth section describes the analysis of interaction modalities in augmented reality, with each impairment of elderly people. Sixth and seventh sections discuss the results and conclusions, respectively.

2   Related Work

The design of interfaces for older adults has been a necessity for some years so, they have been creating lines of design and applications oriented to health that consider the physical deteriorations that have people over 65 years as shown below:

Design lines for the tactile interaction modality for older adults [2]: Analysis of design recommendations contemplating a tactile interaction modality for the elderly, in order to facilitate the development of interfaces in mobile devices.

Luria test in mobile devices to analyze memory [23]: Memory tests were applied to a population of older adults on mobile devices, providing a tool in the area of neuropsychology. These applications have graphic user interfaces oriented to the elderly.

Augmented Reality for performing Otago exercises to improve balance and gait, as well as reduction of falls in 21 older adult women [28]: This is a study that determines the effects of augmented reality in the performance of exercises that Help in the balance and in the gait of the elderly. This study uses augmented reality lenses and a camera computer to work with augmented reality. The result was increased speed, improved stride and stride length, as well as reduced falls.

3   Augmented Reality

Augmented reality is a technology that integrates images of virtual objects into real-world images [7]. The main elements to achieve this are: Marker to identify objects, an element that captures the images (could be the camera of the mobile device) and the software to processes the images captured and overlays the virtual objects [6].

Augmented reality, as well as other virtual environments, are used in the medical area. Some applications are used for the simulation of medical procedures and others for the rehabilitation of patients [12]. The augmented reality allows to recreate scenes in which the patient receives the stimulation that generates his problem in the specialist's office [13, 20].

Several devices have been used to present the virtual information, for example, augmented reality lenses [28], computers [27] and automatic virtual environments [15]. However, these devices have disadvantages, such as image distortions in curved screens, limited volume, low resolution or adverse effects in patients [12].

Some authors suggest that tablets are suitable devices to work in augmented reality [3,23,29]. The interaction is the way the user works on the tablet, i.e. the action that a user performs and receives feedback. There are different ways to do it, they called interaction modalities. The possible interaction modalities in a tablet are:

Speech recognition that allows communication between the mobile device and the user through dialog; Keyboard input [21]; Tactile (when the tablet is able to feel the location of a finger pressing the screen and react to this) [4]; Haptic interface allows the user to interact with a real or simulated object in a tactile way, through a computer or mobile device, giving a feedback by vibration [24]; Interaction by vision is when the device can acquire information from the user and its environment through a camera [22].

4   Physical and Cognitive Impairments in the Elderly

Natural physical and mental deteriorations appear in the human from the 65 years of age, which make it difficult their daily activities [1]. These problems are divided into four groups: vision, hearing, cognitive and movement [25]. Vision problems appear when some of the parts that make up the eye decrease their ability to move and flex, resulting in visual restraints on visual acuity, the ability to focus on nearby objects, and to rapidly adapt to light conditions in their environment, color vision, contrast detection and low susceptibility to glare [11,25].

The aging-related hearing loss is due to the softening of the cilia within the ear, so that the sound signals are attenuated and it becomes difficult to detect the sound, determine the location of the sound in a horizontal space, and the Ability to inhibit background sounds [11,25].

Also, older adults have decreases in mental functions or cognitive impairment. Cognitive abilities refer to the way people perceive, understand and act on information in their environment [25,26].

Loose of control of motor skills is common in older people. This loose of control can be even higher when diseases such as Parkinson's or arthritis occur, resulting in an increase of about 25% in response time in people over 65 years, as well as deterioration in fine motor skills, such as accuracy [11,25].

5   Analysis

Literature on Application Development for Seniors on Mobile Devices include tactile, voice and haptic interface interaction [2,5,17], but the applications developed do not consider the use and Manipulation of virtual objects, as well as interaction based on vision.

Table 1 shows the analysis of the different interaction modalities for direct manipulation of virtual objects in tablets for older adults. The modes of interaction contemplated are those that can be implemented in a tablet.

5.1   Vision

Voice interaction is viable when the user presents visual impairment. This modality of interaction works from small problems to total blindness. Furthermore, an auditory signal lets the user to know that he is pressing small targets [2,14,19]. For the tactile interaction a technique called "eyes-free" was developed, this technique interprets the tactile gestures in a predefined way and with an auditory signal, the user knows what action he is doing [14]. For keyboard input, it is recommended that the keys be large [17]. The haptic mode provides feedback to the user and indicates the status of the action being performed [21].

5.2   Hearing

Voice interaction should consider the following recommendations: Use of female voice [25]; Measure the ambient noise of the context in which the user will perform the task, because the sound that the application is to emit must be much larger than the ambient noise [25]; Use 85 dB so that users can perceive the sound without increasing the impairment, however, it's possible consider use more than 90 dB depending on the hearing damage [25]; The user should be familiar with the language, in addition, the language should be concise, brief and pronounced with the necessary stress [5,25]; For instructions that are issued by voice, it is necessary to consider giving 4 options or less and the instructional depth structure should be maximum of 2 depth levels [25]; Sound alerts should be short and paused [25].

5.3   Cognition

Voice interaction is not recommended for people with acute cognitive problems [25]. Vision based interaction is not recommended for people with space ability problems. In case of using it, the virtual objects must have the behavior of a real object [25].

5.4   Movement

People with loss of precision ability have difficulty calculating the movement produced by a device, so tactile interaction is advisable. There are tasks that do not produce the desired result for people with movement difficulties, such as "double click". For tactile, haptic and vision-based interactions, it is recommended not to put too many targets on the screen; Set large objects; Do not use scroll bars [25]; And avoid dragging objects [2,25]. Keyboard interaction should be avoided [17]. Haptic interfaces are recommended for older adults to give them

Table 1. Comparison between interaction modalities and older adults impairments

Older adults impairments/ interaction modalities	Vision	Hearing	Cognition	Movement
Voice. (Input/ Output)	Auditory signal	Use female voice; Measure ambient noise; Recommended to use 85 dB or more; Use prosody; Use familiar language; Menu of 4 options or less; Short, paused sound alerts	Loss of ability to express and understand language; Menu of 4 options or less	Some people with Parkinson disease don't understand language
Tactile	Technique called "eyes-free"			Low accuracy; Direct interaction; Use of physical barriers; Inconvenient response time; Big targets; Don't use scroll bars; Objectives on screen; Dragging objects
Based on vision			Navigation problems; Real object behavior	Difficult to differentiate between voluntary and involuntary movements; Do not put too many targets on the screen; Dragging objects
Keyboard	Deterioration increases typing time; Easily visible keys			Low user accuracy
Haptic	Provide feedback to the user			Feedback of the action they are doing; Do not put too many targets on the screen; Dragging objects

feedback about the action they are performing [25]. Parkinson's disease may hinder the understanding and expression of language [10], so voice interaction is not advisable.

6   Discussion

Using the appropriate interaction mode for the interaction of augmented reality applications with older adults does not ensure their acceptance and usability. The application must comply with interface design requirements appropriate to the deterioration of the elderly users.

6.1   Design Guides for Augmented Reality

For users with visual impairment it is recommended: Do not make large variations of light on the screen; Use very contrasting colors in virtual figures; Use representative figures that the user is able to distinguish and differentiate; Virtual objects must be large; To consider the laws of Gestalt for the perception and visualization of objects [25]; Highlight the main objects so that they are easily reachable by the user [5,25].

For users with difficulty of movement: Use Fitt's law to calculate the difficulty and response time of the elderly; Use words instead of icons [25]; Prevent the quickly screen lock [18];

Finally, if patients have vision problems, t is convenient to think on implement multimodal interactions [25]. To improve their hearing, some older adults use ear-molded headphones with which they can control the volume of what they hear. It is possible to create a multi-user interface, so that the volume is adjusted according to the needs of each patient, but it is advisable to provide extra information in writing [25]. Parkinson's disease in an advanced state is a limiting. Device must be protected with a rubber coating, for safety [8].

7   Conclusion

The choice of interaction modalities for Augmented Reality applications, depends on functionality and its target population. From the analysis in this work, the following recommendations are presented:

The keyboard is a mode of indirect interaction that may generate cognitive conflicts. In most of the impairments is not feasible to use it, so its use is not recommended.

The interaction based on vision has several problems with movement and cognitive problems. However, this interaction modality has not been proven enough to recommend or discard it. Further studies are recommended.

Voice interaction is recommended for vision and movement problems. It is important to ensure that all the necessary criteria are implement so that this interaction modality may be usable by people with hearing and cognitive impairments.

Haptic and tactile interaction modes are appropriate for people who have auditory and cognitive impairments. If you have a good design, these modes may be usable by people who have vision problems. However, these are not advisable with movement impairment. Apparently the haptic and tactile interactions reduce the workload for cognitive impairments, it is important to carry out studies about it.

Acknowledgment. A.G.G.H., E.H.R. and A.M.V. thanks section of research and graduate studies (SEPI) of ESCOM-IPN, CINVESTAV- IPN, Agencia Espacial Mexicana, project number 2015-262756 and Institutional stimulus scholarship for researchers training program (BEIFI) of IPN by the resources provided and the facilities for this work.

References

1. Estadísticas a propósito del día internacional de las personas de edad. Technical report, Instituto Nacional de Estadística, Geográfica e Informática (2005)
2. Al-Razgan, M.S., Al-Khalifa, H.S., Al-Shahrani, M.D., AlAjmi, H.H.: Touch-based mobile phone interface guidelines and design recommendations for elderly people: a survey of the literature. In: Huang, T., Zeng, Z., Li, C., Leung, C.S. (eds.) ICONIP 2012. LNCS, vol. 7666, pp. 568–574. Springer, Heidelberg (2012). doi:10.1007/978-3-642-34478-7_69
3. Behringer, R., Christian, J., Holzinger, A., Wilkinson, S.: Some usability issues of augmented and mixed reality for e-Health applications in the medical domain. In: Holzinger, A. (ed.) USAB 2007. LNCS, vol. 4799, pp. 255–266. Springer, Heidelberg (2007). doi:10.1007/978-3-540-76805-0_21
4. Buxton, W., Hill, R., Rowley, P.: Issues and techniques in touch-sensitive tablet input. ACM SIGGRAPH Comput. Graph. **19**(3), 215–224 (1985)
5. Díaz-Bossini, J.M., Moreno, L.: Accessibility to mobile interfaces for older people. Procedia Comput. Sci. **27**, 57–66 (2014)
6. Fernández Sánchez, N.: Sistema de realidad aumentada para aplicaciones android. Master's thesis, Escuela Politécnica Superior (2012)
7. Figueroa Angulo, J.: Desarrollo de un sistema de realidad aumentada basado en la colocación de objetos virtuales en escenas reales a partir de la obtención de nubes de puntos en una secuencia de imágenes. Master's thesis, Universidad Nacional Autónoma de México (2009)
8. Gao, J., Koronios, A.: Mobile application development for senior citizens. In: PACIS, p. 65 (2010)
9. González, C., Vallejo, D., Albusac, J., Castro, J.: Realidad aumentada. un enfoque práctico con artoolkit y blender (2013)
10. Grossman, M., Carvell, S., Stern, M.B., Gollomp, S., Hurtig, H.I.: Sentence comprehension in Parkinson's disease the role of attention and memory. Brain Lang. **42**(4), 347–384 (1992)
11. Holzinger, A., Searle, G., Nischelwitzer, A.: On some aspects of improving mobile applications for the elderly. In: Stephanidis, C. (ed.) UAHCI 2007. LNCS, vol. 4554, pp. 923–932. Springer, Heidelberg (2007). doi:10.1007/978-3-540-73279-2_103
12. Jacko, J.A.: Human Computer Interaction Handbook: Fundamentals, Evolving Technologies, and Emerging Applications. CRC Press, Boca Raton (2012)
13. Juan, M.C., Alcaniz, M., Monserrat, C., Botella, C., Baños, R.M., Guerrero, B.: Using augmented reality to treat phobias. IEEE Comput. Graph. Appl. **25**(6), 31–37 (2005)

14. Kane, S.K., Bigham, J.P., Wobbrock, J.O.: Slide rule: making mobile touch screens accessible to blind people using multi-touch interaction techniques. In: Proceedings of the 10th International ACM SIGACCESS Conference on Computers and Accessibility, pp. 73–80. ACM (2008)
15. Keshner, E.A., Kenyon, R.V.: Postural and spatial orientation driven by virtual reality. Stud. Health Technol. Inform. **145**, 209 (2009)
16. Kim, S., Dey, A.K.: Simulated augmented reality windshield display as a cognitive mapping aid for elder driver navigation. In: Proceedings of the SIGCHI Conference on Human Factors in Computing Systems, pp. 133–142. ACM (2009)
17. Kobayashi, M., Hiyama, A., Miura, T., Asakawa, C., Hirose, M., Ifukube, T.: Elderly user evaluation of mobile touchscreen interactions. In: Campos, P., Graham, N., Jorge, J., Nunes, N., Palanque, P., Winckler, M. (eds.) INTERACT 2011. LNCS, vol. 6946, pp. 83–99. Springer, Heidelberg (2011). doi:10.1007/978-3-642-23774-4_9
18. Kurniawan, S.: Mobile phone design for older persons. Interactions **14**(4), 24–25 (2007)
19. Lacey, G., Dawson-Howe, K.M.: The application of robotics to a mobility aid for the elderly blind. Robot. Auton. Syst. **23**(4), 245–252 (1998)
20. Loomis, J.M., Blascovich, J.J., Beall, A.C.: Immersive virtual environment technology as a basic research tool in psychology. Behav. Res. Methods Instrum. Comput. **31**(4), 557–564 (1999)
21. Love, S.: Understanding Mobile Human-Computer Interaction. Butterworth-Heinemann, Oxford (2005)
22. Manresa-Yee, C., Amengual, E., Ponsa Asensio, P.: La usabilidad de las interfaces basadas en visión. FAZ **7**, 12–31 (2014)
23. Miranda, J.A.H., Rubio, E.H., Viveros, A.M.: Analysis of luria memory tests for development on mobile devices. In: Duffy, V.G. (ed.) DHM 2014. LNCS, vol. 8529, pp. 546–557. Springer, Cham (2014). doi:10.1007/978-3-319-07725-3_54
24. Monroy, M., Oyarzabal, M., Ferre, M., Cobos, S., Barrio, J., Ortego, J.: Dispositivos hápticos: Una forma de realizar la interacción hombremáquina. Domótica, Robótica y Teleasistencia para Todos, p. 39 (2007)
25. Pak, R., McLaughlin, A.: Designing Displays for Older Adults. CRC Press, Boca Raton (2010)
26. Pérez, M.: Deterioro cognoscitivo. Technical report, Instituto de Geriatría (2010)
27. Shema, S.R., Brozgol, M., Dorfman, M., Maidan, I., Sharaby-Yeshayahu, L., Malik-Kozuch, H., Yannai, O.W., Giladi, N., Hausdorff, J.M., Mirelman, A.: Clinical experience using a 5-week treadmill training program with virtual reality to enhance gait in an ambulatory physical therapy service. Phys. Ther. **94**(9), 1319 (2014)
28. Yoo, H., Chung, E., Lee, B.H.: The effects of augmented reality-based Otago exercise on balance, gait, and falls efficacy of elderly women. J. Phys. Ther. Sci. **25**(7), 797–801 (2013)
29. Zhou, F., Duh, H.B.L., Billinghurst, M.: Trends in augmented reality tracking, interaction and display: a review of ten years of ISMAR. In: Proceedings of the 7th IEEE/ACM International Symposium on Mixed and Augmented Reality, pp. 193–202. IEEE Computer Society (2008)

ElectAR, an Augmented Reality App for Diagram Recognition

Abián Hernández Mesa[1(✉)], M. Peña Fabiani Bendicho[2],
and Jorge Martín-Gutiérrez[2]

[1] Faculty of Engineering and Technology, University of La Laguna, Avda
Astrofísico Francisco Sánchez sn, 38201 San Cristóbal de la Laguna, Spain
abihermes@hotmail.com
[2] Faculty Communication Sciences, University of La Laguna,
Avda Cesar Manrique sn, 38071 San Cristóbal de la Laguna, Spain
{mfabiani,jmargu}@ull.edu.es

Abstract. Object recognition (detection and identification) is one of the most
challenging problems that computer vision needs to face nowadays. Paradoxi-
cally, recognition becomes harder the simpler the object is, specially with
handwritten symbols. In this context, we have focused on solving this problem
for "computers" that everybody has got into his/her pocket: smartphones and
tablets. In this poster we present an augmented reality app for Android systems,
capable of identifying symbols on normalized electrical diagrams; besides,
virtual information is provided.

The app has being applied to standardized electrical hardwired logic diagrams
and has been used with educational purposes in practical scenarios. Its usability
and efficiency have been tested on university and upper grade educational cycle
students, showing very good results. However, this study reveals the limits of
these apps in common engineering environments, where the simplicity of
standardized symbols makes their recognition difficult.

Keywords: Augmented reality · Mixed reality · Self-learning · Electrical
diagram · Object recognition · Diagram recognition

1 Introduction

In the era where cutting-edge technologies and hyper-connectivity is our everyday life,
Virtual Reality (VR) and Augmented Reality (AR) have become a popular technology
and will increase in importance over the next 10 years (Ezawa 2016).

Virtual and Augmented Reality are becoming an important tool in several fields
(Craig 2013) and their application to an educational context will allow to the "Classroom of the Future" (Cooperstock 2001). We can already find some examples of its
application in very different educational contexts (Kaufmann and Meyer 2008; Cheng
and Wang 2008; Jarmon et al. 2009; McKerlich et al. 2011; Parton and Hancock 2012;
Connolly and Hoskins 2014; Ibañez et al. 2014; Fonseca et al. 2014; Gutiérrez et al.
2015; Billinghurst and Kato 2002).

© Springer International Publishing AG 2017
C. Stephanidis (Ed.): HCII Posters 2017, Part II, CCIS 714, pp. 435–440, 2017.
DOI: 10.1007/978-3-319-58753-0_62

Software applications for mobile devices with AR help to learn difficult subjects and abstract concepts (Kotranza et al. 2009; Martín-Gutiérrez et al. 2010; Bujak et al. 2013), more than outdated methodology does. They can also give students a better motivation (Sotiriou and Bogner 2008; Di Serio et al. 2013; Martín-Gutiérrez and Meneses Fernández 2014) and improve their procrastination (Fabiani Bendicho et al. 2017).

Our work is focused to promote new educational experiences in engineering higher education (Martín-Gutiérrez et al. 2012, 2015) but we are just starting to generate didactic material for permanent use. In this context we present a new AR app to be used in a technological educational context to understand complex concepts and to encourage students to an autonomous exploration and learning.

2 Technical Description

The name of the developed app is ElectAR and its main objective is to serve as a learning tool in electricity practices at laboratory, helping students in the following fields:

- Better understanding of specific hardwired logic diagrams, with the help of graphic information such as images, texts, videos and interactive 3D elements.
- Being capable of accomplish practices' goals, such as wiring, commissioning and testing of hardwired logic circuits, only with the information obtained through the app.
- Provide students with a self-learning tool.

Software development has been characterized by the following key points (Behr et al. 2011):

- An application focused to work on mobile devices.
- Real-time processing capacity.
- Virtual elements superimposed over real elements.
- Targeting user-friendliness, achieved through graphic elements that ensure information can be understood easily.
- High interaction with user.

To achieve these goals, app development has been done using Android Studio Integrated Development Environment (IDE), specifically for Android applications. The Software Development Kit (SDK) used for the Augmented Reality Engine is Metaio SDK. To improve the recognition of very simple marks (standardized electrical symbols are usually difficult to detect) we have included more complex intermediate symbols to define the environment.

Graphic design of the application has been done in a way that permits an attractive layout at the same time that uses a relatively low amount of resources. This allows the system to be used in a wide range of devices. The type of graphic elements used in real-time by the app can be divided into two categories:

- Reference images, that need to be rich in details such as color contrast and non-symmetrical, to permit the software to be able to detect them in a robust way. The position of the information about electrical elements of the circuit are calculated relative to the position of reference images.
- Images, 3D models and videos with optimum quality to be run in real time by the application and present augmented information about the circuit to the student.

On the main screen of the application, the user can choose from a list of available electrical practices, which one of them he/she wants to perform. After loading, the app will identify, through the camera device, the position of different symbols shown in the diagram and will help the student to understand how the specific circuit works, with the aid of 2D and 3D images, theoretical contents and videos (Fig. 1).

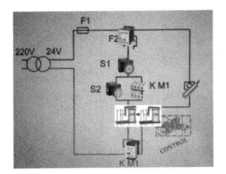 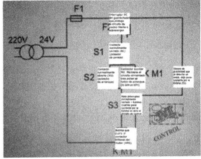

Fig. 1. Basic diagram with AR information: left 3D models and right theoretical contents.

Once the practice is selected, the development of a specific practice to be added to the application can be divided into four parts:

- Direct access button added to the main screen of ElectAR, with a unique name.
- A loading screen, where the user can see which circuit is needed and also can read information about the practice before it starts.
- A resource extraction activity, invisible to the user.
- Main augmented reality activity, where the camera is activated and can detect reference images in the specific electricity circuit related, showing augmented information to the user.

Different functionalities have been added to the app, to allow a higher level of interaction with users. A list of them includes but are not limited to:

- The screen captured frame can be stopped through a freeze button, allowing users to interact with AR elements in a more comfortable way.

- Different actions can be performed on interactive elements like: dragging, changing size, changing orientation, and clicking on them to swap between graphic information and theoretical one.

3   App Validation

Test validation was done with upper grade educational cycle students. The test location was Upper Grade Educational Institute "Marítimo Pesquero", in Santa Cruz de Tenerife, Spain. Test characteristics were the following:

- It was a mandatory test.
- The number of participants were 26.
- 26 students were from two different courses of the institute, one with previous knowledge and the others without any prior knowledge about electricity and hardwired logic diagrams.

App tested had three different hardwired logic diagrams on it:

- Motor commissioning with stop button.
- Motor commissioning with stop button and also stopping through a metal proximity sensor.
- Motor commissioning with star-delta configuration starting.

After the students were gathered, an explanation of the test was done, with the following description:

- Students had a defined time to do the test.
- No explanation was given about the practices included in the app. Diagrams themselves were given in paper format.
- After a defined time, usability and satisfaction tests were given to them, in order to take the students' first impressions.

To evaluate the product we have used a SUS usability and satisfaction questionnaire with a scale ranging from completely disagree (1) to totally agree (5). The questions and results are gathered in Table 1. We don't see any significant difference between the two groups of students (with different previous knowledge level), so we present all students results together.

Results obtained showed that ElectAR app had a very high acceptance. From testers feedbacks we have select the followings as the most relevants:

- Software extension with more tools and more circuits.
- To expand the app to other topics.
- To enable real-time simulation of current and circuit logic (e.g. switches).
- Generic recognition (e.g. normalized symbol recognition).

Table 1. Validation Test

	Usability and efficiency	Average	Variance
A1	*Do virtual contents showed coincide with related images?*	4.88	0.13
A2	*Are 3D-models correctly implemented?*	4.18	0.44
A3	*Do virtual models coincide with the ones used in lab.?*	4.65	0.22
B1	*Is the app able to quickly show elements?*	3.71	1.02
B2	*Is virtual contents resolution appropriate?*	4.29	0.95
B3	*Are virtual models stable?*	4.30	0.53
C1	*Evaluate 3D-models quality*	3.94	0.53
C2	*Evaluate videos quality*	3.82	1.26
C3	*The app is easy to use*	4.47	0.42
C4	*This app can be useful for teaching theoretical concepts*	4.29	0.95
C5	*This app would be useful in other environments*	4.18	1.36
C6	*This app helps to understand abstract concepts*	4.59	0.26
C7	*The app has portability: it can be used everywhere and anytime*	4.12	1.46
	Satisfaction	*Average*	*Variance*
P1	*I would like to use this system frequently*	3.53	1.49
P2	*I found the system unnecessarily complex*	2.06	1.52
P3	*I needed external assistance for being able to use it*	2.18	1.30
P4	*The system is easy to use*	4.47	0.57
P5	*Diverse system functions are well integrated*	3.94	0.59
P6	*There are inconsistencies in the system*	2.76	1.79
P7	*Most of the people can learn to use the system quickly*	4.18	0.42
P8	*The system is complex to use*	1.76	0.99
P9	*I felt confident using the system*	4	1.08
P10	*I had to learnt a lot before being able to use the system*	1.82	2.13

4   Conclusions

We present ElectAR, a new AR app to interpret complex electrical diagrams. This app initially has an educational objective, but may also have practical applications in the field of engineering.

As observed with usability and satisfaction tests results ElectAR obtained mostly high results. A generalized opinion stated that the app is easy to use and may help in teaching of theoretical contents and abstracts subjects. Regarding self-teaching, screen pop-ups, when app opens for the first time, can help students to be completely autonomous.

One of the critical points is stability of contents in real time detection of very simple marks. This topic is much related to the recognition methods that Metaio SDK includes and needs to be improved. The complexity of the system can be reduced if software could detect circuit diagram symbols directly and not via intermediate more complex symbols.

References

Bujak, K., Radu, I., Catrambone, R., MacIntyre, B., Zheng, R., Golubski, G.: A psychological perspective on augmented reality in the mathematics clasroom (2013)

Behr, J., et al.: Instantreality - a framework for industrial augmented and virtual reality applications. In: Ma, D., Fan, X., Gausemeier, J., Grafe, M. (eds.) Virtual Reality & Augmented Reality in Industry, pp. 91–99. Springer, Heidelberg (2011)

Billinghurst, M., Kato, H.: Collaborative augmented reality. Comput. Support. Coop. Work (CSCW) **24**, 515–525 (2002)

Cheng, S., Wang, X.: An empirical study on tangible augmented reality learning space for design skill transfer (2008)

Connolly, E., Hoskins, J.: Using iPads to teach year 7 induction with Aurasma (2014)

Cooperstock, J.: The classroom of the future: enhancing education through augmented reality (2001)

Craig, A.: Augmented Reality Application (Understanding Augmented Reality edn.) (2013). (Craig, M- Kauffmann, Edits.)

Ezawa, K.: Virtual & augmented reality. In: Investment Themes in 2016. Citi Global Perspectives & Solution. Citigroup Inc. (2016)

Di Serio, A., Ibañez, M., Kloos, C.: Impact of an augmented reality system on students motivation for a visual art course (2013)

Fabiani Bendicho, P., Efren Mora, C., Añorge-Díaz, B., Rivero-Rodríguez, P.: Effect on academic procrastination after introducing augmented reality (2017)

Fonseca, D., Martí, N., Redondo, E., Navarro, I., Sánchez, A.: Relationship between student profile, tool use, participation and academic performance with the use of augmented reality technology for visualized architecture models (2014)

Gutiérrez, J., Domínguez, M., González, C.: Using 3D virtual technologies to train spatial skills in engineering (2015)

Ibañez, M., Serio, A., Villarán, D., Delgado, C.: Experimenting with electromagnetism using augmented reality: impact on flow student experience and educational effectiveness (2014)

Jarmon, L., Traphagan, T., Mayrath, M., Trivedi, A.: Virtual world teaching, experiential learning, and assessment: an interdisciplinary communication course in Second Life (2009)

Kaufmann, H., Meyer, B.: Simulating educational physical experiments in augmented reality (2008)

Kotranza, A., Lind, D., Pugh, C., Lok, B.: Real-time in-situ visual feedback of task performance in mixed environments for learning joint psycho-motor-cognitive tasks (2009)

Martín-Gutiérrez, J., Meneses Fernández, M.: Applying augmented reality in engineering education to improve academic performance and student motivation (2014)

Martín-Gutiérrez, J., Fabiani, P., Benesova, W., Meneses, M., Mora, C.: Augmented reality to promote collaborative and autonomous learning in higher education (2015)

Martín-Gutiérrez, J., Fabiani, P., Meneses-Fernández, M., Pérez-López, D.: Adaptation of electrical laboratory systems through augmented reality for optimization of engineering Teaching University (2012)

Martín-Gutiérrez, J., Saorín, J., Contero, M., Alcañiz, M., Pérez-López, D., Ortega, M.: Design and validation of an augmented book for spatial abilities development in engineering students (2010)

McKerlich, R., Riis, M., Anderson, T., Eastman, B.: Student perceptions of teaching presence, social presence and cognitive presence in a virtual world (2011)

Parton, B., Hancock, R.: Animating the inanimate using aurasma: applications for deaf students (2012)

Sotiriou, S., Bogner, F.: Visualizing the invisible: augmented reality as an innovative science education scheme (2008)

Explore the Differences Between Iphone7 Camera Interaction and User Habits

Bin Jiang and Tongtong Liu[✉]

School of Design Arts and Media, Nanjing University of Science
and Technology, 200, Xiaolingwei Street, Nanjing 210094, Jiangsu, China
jb508@163.com, 15620625528@sina.cn

Abstract. With the continuous development of science and technology, mobile phone develops many interactive forms, and at the age which ties close with information, people show themselves and their lives by taking pictures and sharing with friends. This paper takes Iphone7 as an example, using the Likert scale form, the subjects and experimental questions, and investigates the difference in mobile phone camera gesture to influence people to use mobile phone camera behavior habits, and the preference of people interaction in the mobile phone camera. This article only research the phone with a camera to take pictures of this gesture to conduct experimental research, excluding all types of mobile applications and other additional features.

Keywords: Mobile phone camera · Interactive gesture · Otherness

1 Introduction

When taking pictures and browsing pictures occupy most of our lives, It becomes a trend that how to design the mobile phone to adapt to the behavior of people to take pictures [1]. According to the famous social media FACE BOOK revealed in the white paper, till the middle of September 2013, the company's daily average of 1 billion 150 million users upload photos, the total number of photos uploaded to the site is 250 billion. Facebook's photo sharing site Instagram upload million photos a day, that means 16 billion mobile phone cameras or digital cameras will become the mainstream of photography. In Chinese mobile phone market, mobile phones that take cameras as selling point has become popular For example, Ipone6s has launched a very attractive camera function, and press the volume key on the left side can take photos quickly, without this function, taking photos by one hand is not convenient. This is an upgrade in man-machine interaction.

In this paper, we take the Iphone7's camera as an example, to explore the interaction between the mobile phone camera and the relationship between the user, in this study, these following research questions are put forward: (1) The difference of user's interaction in the use of mobile phone camera. (2) Whether there is a change in the use of mobile phone camera gestures to user habits? (3) The problem when users use the camera to take pictures. (4) Whether users can solve the existing problems by using a variety of interactive gestures. (5) What kind of gestures that users would like adopt to take photos by phones.

© Springer International Publishing AG 2017
C. Stephanidis (Ed.): HCII Posters 2017, Part II, CCIS 714, pp. 441–447, 2017.
DOI: 10.1007/978-3-319-58753-0_63

This paper selected 20 young people aged 20–30 as experimental subjects, and they have different occupations, different genders, ask them to take photos by Iphone7, and fill the questionnaires [2].

2 Mobile Camera Operation Process

Use the Iphone7's camera general operating process is divided into three steps:

1. Click on the phone camera APP (Fig. 1).
2. Click on the photo icon (Fig. 2).
3. Click the Home button to return to the interface (Fig. 3).

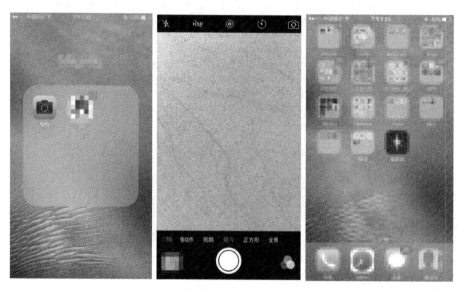

Fig. 1. APP   **Fig. 2.** Photo icon   **Fig. 3.** Return to the interface

Use the Iphone7's camera from the up and down tuning keys to take photos is divided into three steps:

1. Click on the phone camera APP.
2. Press the any one of the right side on Iphone7 can take pictures.
3. The third step: click the Home button to return to the interface.

Use the Iphone7's mobile camera shortcut to take camera is divided into four steps:

1. Slide the up menu (Fig. 1), the phone camera has the fixed position in the upper right corner of the menu.
2. Click on the phone camera App.
3. Click the Home button to return to the interface.

Before release the instructions, to ensure that 20 people in the same laboratory, age between 20–30 years old, to ensure in the experimental there has 10 males and 10 females, and choose the subjects who are familiar with the Iphone7 (Fig. 4).

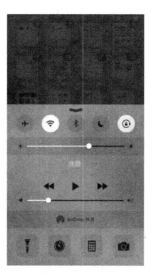

Fig. 4. Up menu

Instruction 1: use a single hand to open the phone7's camera application, to complete the whole process of taking picture, and then change another hand to open the camera application, record the time required to complete the process.

Instruction two: use single hand by shortcuts to open the mobile phone camera application, to complete the whole process of taking picture, then change another hand to open mobile phone camera application, record the time required to complete the process.

Instruction three: use the Iphone7 to Press the any one of the right side on Iphone7, then record the time have to spent.

The experimental results are as follows:

In the first instruction, under the single hand to use the mobile phone camera applications to complete the photo process, It took 4.87 s on average, the longest time is 6.31 s, the least time is 3.96 s. Use the both hands to complete the whole process of taking photos, it has spent 4.29 s on average, the longest time is 6.6 s, the least time is 3.35 s.

In the second instruction, use the single hand to complete the process of Iphone7's shortcuts, it has spend 3.91 s on average, the longest time is 5.63 s, the least time is 2.56 s. Use the both hands to complete the process of taking photos with shortcuts, it spent 3.42 s on average, the longest time is 4.11 s, and the least time is 2.98 s.

In the third instruction, using a singer hand to complete the photo process by mobile phone's tuning key, it spend 4.37 s on average, the longest time is 5.81 s, the least time is 2.81 s. Use the both hands to complete the process of taking photos with tuning key it spent 3.32 s on average, the longest time is 5.26 s, the least time is 2.36 s. Among the whole experiment, it has two errors in one hand operation of the camera to take pictures of that two experimental process is not recorded in the results.

The experimental results are as follows form (Fig. 5):

The first instruction/second 1	2	3	4	5	6	7	8	9	10
one hand 4.18	4.9	6.31	4.6	4.8	6.18	5.63	4.91	5.1	4.56
two hands 6.6	4.23	4.91	3.6	4.31	3.58	4.83	4.08	3.71	4.11
The first instruction/second 11	12	13	14	15	16	17	18	19	20
one hand 4.7	5.34	5.8	4.76	6.12	4.32	4.96	3.96	4.52	5.71
two hands 4.63	3.81	4.21	3.9	3.35	3.11	4.21	3.48	3.55	3.8

The second instruction / second	2	3	4	5	6	7	8	9	10
one hand 2.56	3.09	3.55	3.75	3.29	3.6	4.23	3.53	4.73	3.81
two hands 4.11	3.68	3.86	4.11	3.21	3.01	3.26	3.31	2.98	3.65
The second instruction / second	12	13	14	15	16	17	18	19	20
one hand 3.88	3.75	4.5	4.08	4.18	3.56	3.73	5.63	4.59	4.05
two hands 3.48	3.66	3.43	3.51	3.45	3.49	3.75	3.01	3.2	2.88

The third instruction / second	2	3	4	5	6	7	8	9	10
one hand 4.81	4.71	4.61	5.85	5.65	5.81	4.88	4.55	3.88	5.69
two hands 5.26	3.16	3.58	3.78	3.91	3.48	3.1	3.46	3.33	3.55
The third instruction / second	12	13	14	15	16	17	18	19	20
one hand 3.38	4.43	3.91	3.38	3.48	4.86	3.7	3.61	2.81	3
two hands 2.65	2.91	3.09	3.7	2.93	2.86	3.16	3.16	3.15	2.36

Fig. 5. Form

According to the experimental instruction one, two and three of the results, on the one hand operation in the process of the instruction, an open mobile phone application process complete spend 4.87 s on average, in the second instruction, using tuning keys on the Iphone7's left side are spend 3.91 s on average, use the shortcut in the third instruction complete are spend 4.37 s on average. When use two hands of the operating process, open the mobile phone application instruction process complete are spend 4.29 s on average, the second instruction using the tuning keys on the Iphone7's left side are spend 3.42 s on average, use the shortcut in the third instruction to take photo complete spend 3.32 s on average.

We can acquire this conclusion, use the single hand to operation, use the turning keys in the Iphone7's left side this interactive way is faster than using open the application icon and use shortcut keys, in one hand operation than the other two more convenient. When use two hands to take operation process, the use of shortcuts to complete the process of taking pictures is faster than open application icon and tuning function keys are faster, may be faster than the other two hands.

In contrast to the one hand and two handed operation can be seen in the instruction of a single hand operation than the 0.5 hands to spend more than two seconds, in the second command, hands to operate more than one hand to spend more than 0.38 s. In order three, single hand operation time than hands operation time spend more than 1.05 s, the experiment results show that the interaction, regulating function in use on the side of the volume, single hand operation can be faster than hand operation, but in the interactive mode and instruction in instruction at a third, hands than a single hand use the results show use less time.

3 When Using a Mobile Phone Camera May Appear Gestures

In the course of the experiment, the 20 people recorded in the experiment using a mobile phone camera to take pictures of possible gestures [3].

1. In the first instruction, a single hand to open the phone camera application for a complete picture of the process of hand gestures and gestures (Fig. 5).

The operation is closely related to the size of the phone and the size of the hand, and the Iphone7 is 4.7 inches in size, Iphone7 size is 4.7 inches, in this size, use two hands will be more stable, but single hand operation may laborious, especially for women.

2. Instructions two, a single hand using a mobile phone shortcut keys to open the camera application for a complete picture of the process of hand gestures and gestures (Fig. 6).

Fig. 6. The first instruction's gestures

While in the experimental second 2 with single hand did not succeed disposable. Description of a single hand because of the strength of the sideslip or finger on the phone's surface area is not enough, or the size of the hand may affect the sideslip effect. While the hands will be more stable operation, no cases of sideslip unsuccessful (Fig. 7).

Fig. 7. The second instruction's gestures

3. Instructions, a single hand press the phone up and down the left and right tuning function keys, a complete picture of the process of gesture and hand gestures.

From the experiment the process of instruction in three, one finger in the left hand to operate the tuning key, when right hand operation will generally use two or three fingers, in the operation process, a reference to the two and three fingers are more likely to force, and when both hands, ten fingers and hand the dispersion of power and potential enough to support formed shape, the operation will be more stables (Fig. 8).

Fig. 8. The third instruction's gestures

From the use of gestures can be concluded that, according to different people's behavior habits or camera needs, will create more and more suitable for interactive gestures for camera service, with the appearance of the phone is also a big problem. And for the 4.7 inch size with Iphone7, both hands will be more comfortable than the use of a single hand.

4 Users in the Use of Mobile Phone Camera Will Produce Problems

There are several problems in the course of the experiment. (1) The finger could not touch the specified position of the user single hand operation; (2) Users may not hold the mobile phone with single hand when operating; (3) slip operation may fail with single hand. (4) When a single hand press the upper and lower keys, the finger may not have enough strength complete the whole process. (5) The newest version like Iphone7 change shortcut pull gesture to the mobile phone sliding mode, while some of the subjects are unable to adapt quickly [4].

5 Users of Mobile Phone Camera Shooting Look Interactive Gestures

In the course of the experiment, the interactive mode of the mobile phone camera which is expected to be improved can be inquired and recorded. (1) In the mobile phone interface can appear a slide camera icon, you can slide to any location in the interface of the user in a single hand operation. (2) Can be considered in the open cell phone application, without the use of fingers, you can accurately take pictures of things. (3) Under the condition of beautiful appearance, the width of the mobile phone can be more suitable for the proportion of the human hand.

6 Conclusion

In this paper, from a single cluster of mobile phone camera this aspects to study the interaction using a mobile phone camera, with a questionnaire from one or two hands respectively on the mobile phone application icon camera and the left button to adjust the volume and shortcut operation respectively to test, to provide certain data analysis for interactive mobile phone camera, in the analysis of the Iphone7 mobile phone camera interaction problems but also for mobile phone camera provides user demand.

Iphone mobile as a beacon in the mobile phone market, constantly in the innovation and development, to bring convenience to our lives at the same time also quietly changing our way of life. The interaction has become a hot topic in many aspects of today's society of science and technology and design in the field of mobile phone has already become an important partner in our daily life, can reflect the importance of mobile phone in all aspects of basic necessities of life, make life better interaction with our mobile phone, for our service.

References

1. Ballagas, R., Memon, F., Reiners, R., Borchers, J.: iStuff mobile: rapidly prototyping new mobile phone interfaces for ubiquitous computing. In: CHI 2007: Proceedings of the SIGCHI Conference on Human Factors in Computing Systems, pp 1107–1116. ACM, New York (2007)
2. Ahn, S.J., Bailenson, J., Park, D.: Felling a tree to save paper: short- and long-term effects of immersive virtual environments on environmental self- efficacy, attitude, and behavior. Paper presented at the Annual Meeting of the International Communication Association. London, UK (2013)
3. Lippa, Y., Adam, J.J.: An explanation of orthogonal S-R compatibility effects that vary with hand or response position: the end- state comfort hypothesis. Percept. Psychophys. **63**, 156–174 (2001)
4. Bock, B.C., Marcus, B.H., Pinto, B.M.: Maintenance of physical activity following an individualized motivationally tailored intervention. Ann. Behav. Med. **23**, 79–87 (2001)

Design of Tangible Programming Environment for Smartphones

Yasushi Kambayashi[1(✉)], Kenshi Furukawa[1],
and Munehiro Takimoto[2]

[1] Department of Computer and Information Engineering,
Nippon Institute of Technology, 4-1 Gakuendai, Miyashiro,
Minamisaitama, Saitama 345-8501, Japan
yasushi@nit.ac.jp, cl115416@cstu.nit.ac.jp
[2] Tokyo University of Science, Department of Information Sciences,
2641 Yamazaki, Noda, Chiba, Japan
mune@is.noda.tus.ac.jp

Abstract. This paper proposes a tangible programming environment which the user uses on a smartphone. Our goal is to provide those who possess only a smartphone for a programming environment so that they can start learning programming without any preparations. Visualization requires certain region, i.e. big screen, but people do not have personal computers as commonly as smart phones. In order to address this problem, we propose a tangible programming environment where the user can program not in a screen but on a table by using physical cards. The users place cards on a table by hand and combined them to create programs. Each card has a QR code, which the user makes their smartphone read. After reading all the codes, the users make them execute on the smartphone and validates the results on the tiny screen. In addition, the user can draw arbitrary animation characters on a paper, which they input as a photo into their smartphones and use it in their programs just as the Scratch user can manipulate characters called sprits. Thus, the user of our programming environment can construct any program as the Scratch user can without using personal computers.

Keywords: Tangible · Visual programming · Smartphone

1 Introduction

Recently, the programming is getting popular and integrated into the grade school's curriculum. The programming is said to be effective to cultivate the thought process that is so called "logical thinking." Ministry of Education, Culture, Sports, Science, and Technology is now promoting the programming education in the elementary school [1]. We can expect the programming is a common practice for everyone.

This paper proposes a tangible programming environment which the user uses on a smartphone. Our goal is to provide those who possess only a smartphone programming environment so that they can start learning programming without any preparations. It is well known that visual programming languages are suitable for young programmers.

© Springer International Publishing AG 2017
C. Stephanidis (Ed.): HCII Posters 2017, Part II, CCIS 714, pp. 448–453, 2017.
DOI: 10.1007/978-3-319-58753-0_64

The most famous one is Scratch that Mitchel Resnick developed [2]. The user manipulates visual joining blocks that represent syntax elements to construct programs. Visualization requires certain region, i.e. big screen. This may be a restriction for providing programming experience for those who do not have personal computers. Today, almost everybody has a smartphone and it has significant computing power. On the other hand, what hinders users from widely using it in programming is its small screen. It is not suitable for fine operations because of the poor operability, which causes frequent recognition errors.

In order to address this problem, we propose a tangible programming environment where the user can program not in a screen but on a table by using physical cards in this paper. Each card used in the environment represents a certain command of an abstract imperative programming language. The user places cards on a table by hand and combined them to create programs. Each card has a QR code, which the user makes his or her smartphone read. After reading all the codes, the user makes them execute on the smartphone and validates the results on the tiny screen. In addition, the user can draw arbitrary animation characters on a paper, which they input as a photo into their smartphones and use it in their programs just as the Scratch user can manipulate characters called sprits. Thus, the user of our programming environment can construct any program as the Scratch user can program without using personal computers.

2 Programming Environment

The user of this application program can learn programming while producing programs such that they can construct them in Scratch. The user can use up to three arbitrary images in the programs by taking their photos into their smartphones. When the user starts the application, first, the user is asked to take drawings called sprites as shown Fig. 1. A sprite must be identified by the identification marker.

Fig. 1. The identification marker and a marked sprite

A program is constructed by combining command blocks that instruct a sprite how to move. A command block has a label that shows what the command block represents, and a QR code that represents a command for the corresponding sprite. Figure 2 shows a part of a program that uses five command blocks and how they are read though the camera on the smartphone. A command block consists of three items, namely ID, the explanation, and the command. ID is a six digit integer that is used for identifying each block to avoid reading the same command block more than once. The explanation is a short description showing what the block does. When the user read a command block by the smartphone, the explanation appears on the screen so that the user can confirm its read. The command is the instruction given to the sprite. This is corresponding to one statement of an ordinary procedural programming language. The commands are stored in an array in the system, and picked one by one during the execution.

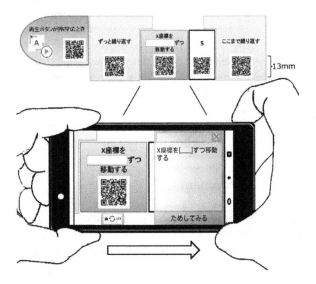

Fig. 2. Command blocks and how they are read

There are eight kinds of command blocks the programming environment provides; they are start blocks, instruction blocks, numeral blocks, variable blocks, wait/terminate blocks, repetition blocks, conditional branch blocks and cloning blocks. We describe them in the next sections.

2.1 Start Blocks

Each program begins with a start block. Since the system can handle three sprites, and they can behave concurrently, there are three start blocks. Each start block starts the corresponding sprite in action when the user pushes the "play" button. Also a sprite can be cloned as described later. Therefore there are three more start blocks to indicate at where the cloned sprite starts its action.

2.2   Instruction Blocks

Instruction blocks instruct how the corresponding sprite acts on the screen, such as moving in specified distance horizontally or vertically, rotation in specified degree, bouncing, expanding and reducing its size, making transparent (invisible), and making opaque (visible).

2.3   Numeral Blocks

Some instruction blocks need some numerical values such as moving distance and rotation degree. Numerical blocks provide the values. The system provide a feature for the user can input numerical values on the screen, but our experiments reveal that numerical blocks are more convenient than screen inputs.

2.4   Variable Blocks

Our programming environment is designed to produce ordinary procedural programs. Therefore we need variables to be defined with certain values and to be used them later. Variable blocks are used in such occasions. They are used with instruction blocks in the place where numerical blocks are allowed as well as in the assignment instructions.

2.5   Wait/Terminate Blocks

In a multi-thread environment, the functionalities of suspending and terminating an action is required for each sprite. Wait block and terminate block do the works. A wait block stops the corresponding sprite's action for the specified period and resumes its action after that. It takes a numerical block or a variable block as the argument. Terminate block simply kill the corresponding concurrently running thread.

2.6   Repetition Blocks

A pair of repetition blocks provides repetition structure. Repetition-start block indicates where it starts repetition and takes a numerical block or a variable block as the argument as the number of iterations. Repetition-end block indicates where it stops. The sequence of actions the user want the sprite performs is placed between the repetition-start block and the repetition-end block. The system also has a pair of infinite repetition blocks.

2.7   Conditional Branch Blocks

In order to construct the conditional branch structure, the environment provides a triple of branch blocks and three condition blocks. Each of three branch blocks corresponds to the "if," "else," and "end-if" components of ordinary if-then-else structure, and three condition blocks represent =, <, and > respectively.

Since our programming environment mainly produces moving sprites' actions, we provide special condition "when this sprite bump into the other sprite" construct. Since each thread represents one sprite's action, "this sprite" is implicitly known. Therefore this structure simply specifies the sprite into which the current thread's sprite bumps and what actions the current thread's sprite takes.

2.8   Cloning Blocks

Our system allows a sprite to clone itself. The cloned sprite looks like the same as the original one, but has its own thread. Therefore it behaves independently from the original sprite's thread.

3   Discussion and Conclusions

We have proposed a programming environment that provides enough features so that the users of this system can construct any program as the Scratch users can construct. Using QR codes is the key of our success because our system suppresses users' operations on the screen. When using numerical blocks, the user can construct a program only placing various blocks on a table, and taking the blocks as images by his or her smartphone. Figure 3 shows an example program that imitates the "Pong Starter" published by a Scratch team (https://scratch.mit.edu/projects/10128515/). Figure 4 shows the execution screen on a smartphone.

Current system requires the user to scan the entire program at once. This requirement hinders the user from constructing a large scale complex program. Also current programming environment lacks of extensibility. The user cannot add new constructs to the environment. As the next steps, we plan to address these problems.

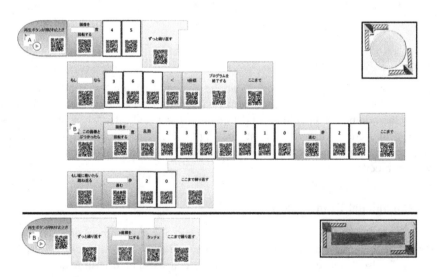

Fig. 3. Example program imitating "Pong Starter"

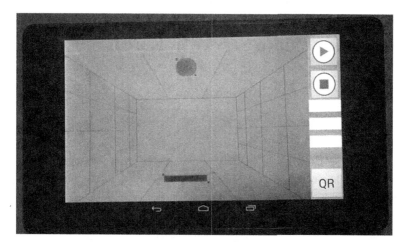

Fig. 4. Executing the Pong Starter like program

Since one QR code can contain considerable amount of information, we plan to add the subprogram feature. By using this feature, the user should be able to collapse into a subprogram block. Then, the user could archive such subprograms as library functions. Also we plan to provision this programming environment so that the user can add new program constructs.

There are only a few tangible programming environment inspired by Scratch. Yashiro et al. extended the instruction blocks of the Scratch to physical blocks, designing a tangible interface where users can program the behaviors of physical robots by composing the blocks by hands as well as the behaviors of the images of robots on a display [3]. Matsuzaki et al. constructed an environment that composes graphical representations of programs with a tangible environment through the augmented reality technique [4]. Through studying related works, we would like to make our programming environment complete.

References

1. Ministry of Education, Culture, Sports, Science, and Technology: On programming education in the stage of elementary schools (2016). (in Japanese). http://www.mext.go.jp/b_menu/shingi/chousa/shotou/122/attach/1372525.htm
2. Resnick, M., Maloney, J., Hernández, A., Rusk, N., Eastmond, E., Brennan, K., Millner, A., Rosenbaum, E., Silver, J., Silverman, B., Kafai, Y.: Scratch: programming for all. Commun. ACM **52**(11), 60–67 (2009)
3. Yashiro, T., Kazushi, M.: Material programming: a visual programming development environment with material. In: IPSJ Interaction (2014). (in Japanese)
4. Matsuzaki, S., Takimoto, M., Kambayashi, Y.: Design of tangible procedural programming of robots based on augmented reality. In: Proceedings of the 10th International Conference on Computer Graphics Theory and Applications, vol.1, pp. 492–497 (2015)

An Analysis of Usage and Attitude for Mobile Video Service in Korea

Min-Jeong Kim[✉]

Sookmyung Women's University, Seoul, Korea
min-jeong.kim@sookmyung.ac.kr

Abstract. Recent mobile phones offer mobile video services which provide TV or video contents. However, the total paid subscribers of mobile video services are still not many. The purpose of this paper is therefore to examine Korean consumers' mobile video service usage and attitude from a behavioral perspective. We conduct an empirical study including usage situation, factors affecting to behavioral intention, mainly used content, and willingness to pay amount under paid subscriptions for premium content.

Keywords: Mobile video services · Usage and attitude · Willingness to pay

1 Introduction

The world media environment, which has been centered on traditional TV, is changing rapidly to internet video services based on the competitiveness of major internet video services such as Netflix, Hulu, and YouTube. In addition to having provided PC and laptop-based internet video services, service providers began to launch their video services on mobile phones thanks to the evolution of mobile technologies. Even if the PC and laptop remain the most used device for viewing video contents over the Internet, viewing online video on a mobile phone is growing dramatically [1].

As the number of people who select mobile phones for viewing TV or video contents is rapidly growing, domestic IT companies are also providing mobile video services competitively. There are many types of mobile video services in Korea, which include mobile internet protocol television (IPTV) services provided by mobile service providers, TVing offered by a cable TV broadcaster, pooq provided by joint terrestrial broadcasters, the Web TVs of large portals, and Africa TV focused on real-time broadcasts. In addition, mobile TV service which generally refers to the digital video broadcasting-handheld (DVB-H) and digital multimedia broadcasting (DMB) may be one of the mobile video services. However, in this paper, mobile TV service is excluded from the mobile video services because mobile TV service is different from mobile video services in terms of services, contents, user access, and charges. Most of mobile video services have paid subscribers paying a monthly fee. Paid subscribers of mobile IPTV are estimated to total 10.6 million people and the total paid subscribers of mobile video services exceed 11 million people when TVing and pooq are also taken into consideration [2]. Considering TVing, mobile IPTV and pooq launched in 2010, 2011 and 2012, respectively, the figure of 11 million paid subscribers indicates that

© Springer International Publishing AG 2017
C. Stephanidis (Ed.): HCII Posters 2017, Part II, CCIS 714, pp. 454–460, 2017.
DOI: 10.1007/978-3-319-58753-0_65

domestic markets are still being formed mainly around mobile video services provided free of charge even if the number of people who select mobile phones for viewing TV or video contents is rapidly growing. Because the need for the activation of mobile video services by mobile video service providers has been raised, research for the activation of mobile video services is very useful. However, many researchers have sought to understand user acceptance of mainly mobile TV. Few research results of studies that sought to examine consumer acceptance of mobile video services have been reported to date. Therefore, there is a need to investigate usage and attitude for mobile video services.

This study aims to analyze the current usage and attitude for mobile video services. In this paper, the actual usage behaviors of mobile video service are examined. We investigate usage situation, factors affecting to behavioral intention, mainly used content, and willingness to pay (WTP) amount under paid subscriptions for premium content.

2 Background

Studies on mobile media use have mostly focused on mobile TV. Zhou [3] noted that perceived ease of use, access speed and content quality of mobile TV positively affected flow experience, which further affected perceived usefulness and usage intention. Jung et al. [4] examined that flow experience and content had a significant role on users' acceptance of mobile TV. However, price value was reported to be insignificant with behavioral intention. Kaasinen et al. [5] studied user acceptance of mobile TV services through field trial of commercially available mobile TV services. Thus far, although previous studies on user acceptance of mobile TV have led to a range of findings, the study of mobile video services has not yet been fully addressed.

Survey results revealing the increasing trends of video viewing through mobile phone have been released continuously [1, 6]. From these results, experts judge that mobile video services can attract a considerable portion of demand from consumers who have enjoyed terrestrial DMB broadcasts since mobile video services provide the feature of high-definition (HD) and extract a WTP from subscribers who are interested in live broadcasts such as sports and news since mobile video services support a variety of functions, including replays [7]. However, as mentioned above, the figure of 11 million paid subscribers of mobile video services implies that the acceptance rate is not at the diffusion stage, considering service launching year. In addition, because of the lack of agreement over the contents pricing terms between terrestrial broadcasters and mobile video service providers supplying the broadcasting contents, if the paid subscribers are not be able to utilize the terrestrial broadcasting contents in mobile video services, the market situation of paid subscribers is expected to worsen [8]. Therefore, studies are necessary to analyze the actual usage and attitude of mobile video services because there are limits in identifying reasons for not diffusing rapidly.

3   Analysis

The data for this study were obtained from online survey methods with 500 people using LTE smartphone in Korea. The target population consisted of men and women between the ages of 19 and 49. It should be noted that age group of 19–49 was selected in this study because we assumed that this group is very likely to use the mobile video services and core target group for the mobile service market as economically active population and mobile power user. Sampling was conducted for 1 month during August 2016. For the main sampling conditions, the significant allocation was made first according to mobile service brand's market share in Korea, after which the proportional allocation was applied taking into account the population distribution by age. All the analyses of this study were done using SPSS 23.0 version. The demographic information of respondents by mobile service brand is described in Table 1.

Table 1. Demographic information of respondents by mobile service brand

Mobile service brand	Total	Gender		Age		
		Men	Women	20s	30s	40s
A	273	185	88	54	137	82
B	143	81	51	40	60	32
C	93	56	39	17	46	32
Total	500	322	178	111	243	146

A survey results on when mobile video service users use mobile video services are shown in Table 2. This survey was conducted only for mobile video service users (414 persons). Similar to earlier study [5], the main usage situations took place when commuting and at home. Especially, for usage situation at home, we classified two situations including mobile video service use before sleeping at home. It was found that women group uses the services at home the most frequently. We used Chi-square test to examine the difference by gender and age. A significant difference was shown in both gender and age groups.

Table 2. Usage situation of mobile video services

Classification	Total	Gender		Age		
		Men	Women	20s	30s	40s
Commuting	121	78	43	26	72	23
Home	76	42	34	22	34	20
Short break	62	44	18	8	25	29
School/workplace	59	47	12	13	27	19
Home (before sleep)	41	19	22	11	19	11
Wi-Fi	33	20	13	11	10	12
Restroom	19	18	1	3	13	3
Others	3	1	2	0	2	1
χ^2 test		24.981***		28.590*		

*p < .05, **p < .01, ***p < .001

Factors affecting to behavioral intention of mobile video services are shown in Table 3. The most influential factor was diverse channels and the second influential factor was charging scheme. Table 3 also shows that Wi-Fi installation, additional charges, and data volume were considered in use of the services. These factors are related to charges and the total percentage for charges is higher than the percentage for diverse channels. Therefore, the findings indicate that charges are a meaningful consideration factor in mobile video services use. These results are consistent with the previous study results [9–11].

Table 3. Factors affecting to behavioral intention of mobile video services

Classification	Total	Gender		Age		
		Men	Women	20s	30s	40s
Diverse channels	85	52	33	15	44	26
Charging scheme	58	28	30	15	29	14
Streaming quality	54	34	20	17	23	14
No.of VODs	50	35	15	10	24	16
High definition	35	28	7	8	18	9
VOD update	27	17	10	5	14	8
Wi-Fi installation	20	14	6	7	5	8
No. of users	17	12	5	5	8	4
Exclusive contents	16	14	2	3	9	4
Additional charge	15	8	7	1	10	4
User convenience	14	12	2	1	8	5
Data volume	12	7	5	3	6	3
Same brand as TV	4	2	2	3	0	1
Diverse information	3	2	1	0	2	1
Diverse services	2	2	0	0	2	0
Others	2	2	0	1	0	1
$\chi 2$ test		22.168		26.995		

*p < .05, **p < .01, ***p < .001

Our finding that diverse channels have a significant role in consumers' behavioral intention of mobile video services may be consistent with the findings in consumer adoption of mobile TV [3–5] because diverse channels imply contents. The study analyzed the presence of a difference in factors affecting to behavioral intention of mobile video services depending on gender and age, but no statistically significant difference was observed.

Next, we investigated mainly used contents by mobile video service users, as shown in Table 4. The results show that the mainly used contents in the area of broadcasting are different from the mainly used contents in the area of VOD. However, the top three contents mainly used by mobile video service users were broadcasting contents. This shows that broadcasting channels provide the users of mobile video services the immediacy of content and the users appreciate easy and continuous access to TV contents [5]. Chi-square test was conducted to identify the difference in mainly used contents used depending on gender and age difference. A statistically significant difference was observed between men and women and among different age groups.

Table 4. Mainly used contents by mobile service users (B:Broadcasting, V:VOD)

Classification	Total	Gender		Age		
		Men	Women	20s	30s	40s
B(sports)	106	99	7	14	49	43
B(dramas)	68	28	40	9	34	25
B(entertainment)	48	23	25	20	21	7
B(movies)	16	15	1	3	10	3
B(music)	13	8	5	2	8	3
B(animation)	7	4	3	3	1	3
B(education)	4	4	0	1	3	0
B(economy)	3	2	1	0	1	2
B(documentary)	2	0	2	0	2	0
B(travel)	2	1	1	0	1	1
V(entertainment)	25	12	13	8	13	4
V(dramas)	24	11	13	9	12	3
V(music)	23	11	12	7	12	4
V(movie)	20	10	10	4	8	8
V(sports)	9	9	0	1	6	2
V(documentary)	4	3	1	0	0	4
V(animation)	3	2	1	0	2	1
V(economy)	2	2	0	0	2	0
V(education)	1	0	1	0	1	0
V(travel)	0	0	0	0	0	0
UCC	28	20	8	10	13	5
Others	6	5	1	3	3	0
χ^2 test		94.169***		69.828**		

*$p < .05$, **$p < .01$, ***$p < .001$

We investigated the monthly WTP amount of the existing mobile video service users for premium services if released paid premium content channels in the near future. The WTP amount for premium services is analyzed in Table 5. The WTP amounts in Table 5 imply the monthly WTP amount for those using the mobile video services free of charge and the additional month WTP amount for those already using paid mobile video services. From the results, more than half of the mobile video service users expressed no WTP. These results are similar to the survey results found by Venturini et al. on the WTP amount for YouTube premium services [1]. That is, the existing mobile video service users are reluctant to pay additional charges even for the premium services. The monthly average WTP amount was 2,230 KRW. From the results of conducted for the monthly average WTP amount using t-test for gender groups and one-way ANOVA for age groups, no statistically significant differences were observed between the two genders or among any of the age groups.

Table 5. Monthly WTP amount by mobile video services

Classification	Total	Gender		Age		
		Men	Women	20s	30s	40s
0 KRW	264	181	83	55	131	78
~3,000 KRW	71	37	34	21	33	17
~5,000 KRW	38	23	15	9	20	9
~10,000 KRW	23	15	8	6	12	5
~30,000 KRW	17	13	4	3	6	8
~50,000 KRW	1	0	1	0	0	1
Average WTP	2,230.20	2,202.61	2,281.39	2,308.51	1,858.92	2,803.39
Standard deviation	5155.68	5020.74	5414.53	4946.55	3745.14	7050.48
t-value		-0.148				
F-value				1.266		

$p < .05$, $p < .01$, $p < .001$

4 Conclusion

In this paper, we analyzed the current usage and attitude of mobile video services. We first analyzed when mobile video service users use the services most often, which factor is affecting to behavioral intention, and which content they use mainly. We also examined monthly WTP amount for premium mobile video services when the existing services would be release paid premium content channels. The major results are as follows.

First, the mobile video service users utilized the services most commonly in "pure mobile" situations such as commuting. In immobile situations, men used the services at school or workplace most frequently while women used the services at home most frequently, showing that smartphones are used for viewing outside, but act as secondary devices to the TV at home. For factors affecting to behavioral intention of mobile video services, the availability of diverse channels was the highest factor for the use of the services, followed by charging scheme. However, considering other factors related to charges, charges are a meaningful consideration factor in mobile video services use.

Second, the results show that sports broadcasting was the most frequently used content, followed by dramas and entertainment broadcasting. These results show that consumers perceive mobile video services as a handheld TV. In addition, some differences were observed in the most frequently used content depending on gender and age. From the results of the survey investigating the monthly WTP amount when premium mobile video services are launched on a paid subscription basis, the respondents desired average WTP of less than 3,000 KRW, which is lower than the paid scheme currently operating domestically. The respondents who were not even willing to pay the charges, at 63.8%, accounted for the highest proportion. This result demonstrates that the mobile video service users are reluctant to pay the additional charges and that the charges are confirmed as a key factor affecting the use of mobile video services.

Although this paper conducted a usage and attitude analysis of mobile video service users, there is a limitation regarding the general applicability of results. As mobile video services are used worldwide, the survey needs to be conducted throughout various international user groups with consideration of cultural differences. For this purpose, a cross-country comparison is a potential direction for future research.

Acknowledgements. This study was supported by the Sookmyung Women's University Research Grants [1-1603-2002].

References

1. Venturini, F., Carlier, B., Mishra, B.: Multi-tasking and Taking Control. Accenture, Dublin (2013)
2. Lee, S.Y.: Mobile Service Providers, Mobile IPTV competition as a New Business Model. http://www.fnnews.com/news/201606161718254169
3. Zhou, T.: The effect of flow experience on user adoption of mobile TV. Behav. Inf. Technol. **32**(3), 263–272 (2013)
4. Jung, Y., Perez-Mira, B., Wiley-Patton, S.: Consumer adoption of mobile TV: examining psychological flow and media content. Comput. Hum. Behav. **25**(1), 123–129 (2009)
5. Kaasinen, E., Kulju, M., Kivinen, T., Oksman, V.: User acceptance of mobile TV services. In: 11th International Conference on Human-Computer Interaction with Mobile Devices and Services, p. 34 (2009)
6. Vernocchi, M., Venturini, F., Patel, D.: Consumers of all Ages are Going Over-the-Top. Accenture, Dublin (2011)
7. Hwang, J.H.: Mobile IPTV has its day. http://news.mk.co.kr/newsRead.php?year=2014&no=233046
8. Sung, Y.K.: Mobile IPTV without terrestrial channels, who has advantage? http://www.mt.co.kr/view/mtview.php?type=1&no=2015062213531142967&outlink=1
9. Seol, J.A., Bong, M.S.: A study on the IPTV usage and service satisfaction. Korean J. Commun. Inf. **46**, 485–510 (2009)
10. Jang, E.J., Kim, J.K., Sin, Y.H.: Exploring antecedent of mobile IPTV satisfaction: focusing on aesthetic simplicity and moderating role of network quality. J. Inf. Syst. **21**(4), 133–153 (2012)
11. Kim, M.J.: A study on consumers' perception and attitudes for market promotion of mobile. J. Inst. Internet Broadcast. Commun. **14**(5), 45–53 (2014)

The 60 Seconds Guestbook – An Auditory Place Media for Guesthouse Residents

Chia-Lung Lee[1(✉)] and Katsuhiko Ogawa[2]

[1] Graduate School of Media and Governance, Keio University, Minato, Japan
twcannonlee@hotmail.com
[2] Faculty of Environment and Information Studies,
Keio University, Minato, Japan

Abstract. In recent years, travelers have demonstrated a preference for guest-houses as their form of accommodation to enable them to make friends or have good interpersonal interactions. Travelers may record their experience and the interactions they had in the guesthouse by writing and drawing in the guestbook. However, the traditional guestbook has several shortcomings. Besides, compared to the visual sense, the auditory sense allows travelers to recall the atmosphere more impressively.

"The 60 seconds guestbook" is proposed as an auditory place medium that enables travelers to record their reviews and memories by using a vocal and auditory method in the guesthouse in 60 s. "The 60 seconds guestbook" enables residents to communicate with others who visited before and will be visiting after them, a to inform themselves about various aspects of the guesthouse and the area. This contributes to making travelers' stay not only interesting but also more meaningful.

Our research for this article also included two experiments: First, we tested and identified the shortcomings of the "The 60 seconds guestbook v1.0," by developing a prototype to allow residents to use it by themselves. Second, we produced a camera and voice recording of a BBQ party to verify that people derive more joy from listening to a recording than by looking at a photo of the same event.

Keywords: Guesthouse · Auditory sense · Place media · Guestbook · Travel

1 Introduction

In recent years, besides beautiful landscapes and culinary delicacies, travelers have increasingly focused on meeting people on their journeys. These travelers usually choose a guesthouse (or a hostel) for their accommodation.

The reason is not only the relative affordability of a guesthouse, but also the opportunity to make friends or have interesting encounters with other travelers, staff members, and local people. Travelers may record their memories of the experience and the interactions they had in the guesthouse by writing and drawing in the guestbook (Fig. 1): the greater the number of stories, the greater the value of the place. Although the readers can relate to other guests' feelings by reading what they wrote, a traditional guestbook has several shortcomings:

© Springer International Publishing AG 2017
C. Stephanidis (Ed.): HCII Posters 2017, Part II, CCIS 714, pp. 461–468, 2017.
DOI: 10.1007/978-3-319-58753-0_66

- Travelers cannot read the guestbook once they have departed from the guesthouse.
- The guestbook can easily become soiled.
- People who are not good at writing and drawing may find the guestbook difficult to use.
- Past messages are difficult to review.
- Writing or reading while others are using the guestbook is difficult.

In order to solve the problems and provide a special recording experience in a guesthouse, "The 60 seconds guestbook" is proposed as an auditory place medium, which enables travelers to record their reviews and memories via voice and sound in the guesthouse in 60 s. This contributes to making the travelers' stay not only interesting but also more meaningful.

Fig. 1. A guestbook

2   What Is a Guesthouse?

A guesthouse is a place that offers accommodation similar to that of a hostel. Different from the usual hotel, a guesthouse operates on the principle of "sharing." It typically provides a common relaxed space for socializing, as well as a dormitory (shared room), shared kitchen, and shared bathroom. Because they "share" these facilities with others, travelers find it easy to open their minds to new perspectives and they have more opportunities to communicate with others.

Besides, a guesthouse typically has a café or bar as its common space. Travelers can also meet local people, as well as members of staff and others. In Japan, some guesthouses also play important roles in community building [1].

3   Concept

3.1   Web Media Services

Hotels and guesthouses usually use web media services as follows:

Homepage: Since the homepage is created by the guesthouse, the contents might be subjective. Besides, constructing a homepage is sometimes difficult for the staff. They eventually enter basic information such as the concept, location, rooms, and prices only.

Social Networks Services (SNSs): Since it is easy to use these services to upload information, guesthouses usually use Twitter, Facebook, or Instagram to upload text and photos. Travelers can also learn more about the atmosphere of the guesthouses from SNSs or by communicating with each other.

Booking Site: Compared with the homepage and the pages on SNSs, both of which are created by the guesthouse, a booking site (for example: Agoda, or Booking.com) places emphasis on objective reviews and ratings from previous guests.

A traveler's relationship with a guesthouse and the web media can be divided into three parts (Fig. 2):

- Before traveling
- While traveling
- After traveling

Travelers are known not to use the web media when they are traveling. Therefore, it may be possible to create an online medium for travelers' to use while they are staying at a guesthouse to enable them to record and ensure that their experience becomes more enjoyable.

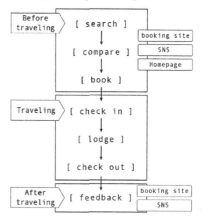

Fig. 2. Traveler's interaction with the guestbook before, during, and after traveling

1. To remember a touching experience in the guesthouse.

2. The user can use "the 60 seconds guestbook" to record it.

3. Every one can hear and feel the touching experience via the recall.

Fig. 3. How to use "The 60 seconds guestbook"

3.2 The 60 Seconds Guestbook

Travelers usually use photos and handwritten descriptions to record their memories. Compared to the visual sense, the auditory sense allows travelers to recall the atmosphere more impressively [2].

The core concept of place media is to link the web space and real space by allowing the spatiotemporal feeling of a place to be experienced [3]. "The 60 seconds guestbook" (Fig. 3) aims to apply this concept to guesthouses, so that people can communicate with others before and after their stay. Because staff members, travelers, and local people have different viewpoints, listening to "The 60 seconds guestbook" would inform the listener about various aspects of the guesthouse and the area.

As for the visual sense, we can look through the text at our own pace. However, the auditory sense is restricted by the time limit of the music, melody, or recording. The recording might be boring if it is too lengthy. In view of that and the copyright law of Japan, this design sets 60 s as the time limit for every recording.

4 Experiment I: Using the 60 Seconds Guestbook v1.0

4.1 Method

This experiment was run at the Guesthouse Hakone Tent [4] from December 24, 2016 to January 8, 2017, "The 60 seconds guestbook" was set on an iPad to allow users to record their messages by themselves. In addition, instructions were printed on two A4 pages to allow users to use their own mobile device by scanning the QR code.

The guestbook is designed to enable users to easily and quickly upload their recording and data, i.e., the homepage of "v1.0" is also the upload page (Fig. 4). Except for the recording and name, this experiment also requested the user to provide their age, gender, nationality, comment, and e-mail address. Besides, with regard to the recording programming, "v1.0" uses the original iOS camera application to help users to record and upload their recording; however, it only uses voice data.

Fig. 4. Structure, flow, and interface of "The 60 seconds guestbook"

4.2 Result

During the 16 days of this experiment, 14 data entries were recorded; furthermore, only five groups recorded their messages (the others only left comments). The contents (Table 1) are mostly simple words of thanks or self-introductions. Since the users usually are unsure what to say when they are recording, it sometimes also felt awkward listening to the recordings.

4.3 Review

The results we obtained with "The 60 seconds guestbook v1.0" suggested that we would need to solve the following problem in the next version: 1. Attracting more guests of the guesthouse to use this service. 2. Simplifying the upload procedure. 3. Decreasing the number of awkward recordings and make the recordings more interesting to encourage guests to make more recordings.

Table 1. Contents of the recordings

Date	Identity	Age	Recording length	Recording contents	Language
2016/12/26	J from Germany	20	0:15	Yo～ konichiwa～ I am in Hakonetent. I am very tired so i could not study! I loved here so much. Hot spring is the best	Japanese Germany
2016/12/27	M from France	28	0:15	In Japan～ You have this pop corn. It's got fried chicken favor. Ya	English
2016/12/29	A from Canada	28	0:59	Really good time. Comfortable. Friendly people. Onsen is very good temperature. Next time come to Takamatsu!	English Japanese
2017/1/6	N from Japan	16	0:09	We came to Hakone! We are very happy in these two days! Ye～	Japanese
2017/1/8	C from China	20	0:20	(Self-introduction * 3)	Japanese

Furthermore, from the viewpoint of the guesthouse, as this experiment used one iPad to allow customers to make their recordings, staff members need to be prevented from losing the device. This means they need to take care of the iPad and store it in a safe place every night when the lounge closes, and need to remember to replace the device in the morning. Therefore, we would need to find a way to prevent their work from being disrupted.

5 Experiment II: Comparison Between Recording and Photo

5.1 Method

According to Tauchi, compared to the visual sense, the auditory sense can allow travelers to recall the atmosphere more impressively [2], but we also need to be concerned about the feeling obtained by the user (audience/reader). This experiment tried to determine whether people derive more joy by listening to a recording than viewing photos of the same event.

In this experiment, we recorded the BBQ party of a crewmember of Guesthouse Hakone Tent by using a camera and voice recorder. After one week, we separated the members into a recording group and a photo group, both of which contained four people, asked them to complete a questionnaire and recall their memories by producing a 5-min recording (Fig. 5) or 100 photo frames by using the following steps:

Step1. Questions about the mentation and the characteristics of subjects.
Step2. Exam questions about details of the BBQ party.
Step3. Listening to the recording or viewing photos group by group respectively.
Step4. Further exam questions about details of the BBQ party.
Step5. Further questions about the mentation.

5 mins Recording

length	45 seconds	59 seconds	60 seconds	17 seconds	57 seconds	52 seconds
episode	Prepare in kitchen	Chatting	New staff coming	Takes group photo	Cheers	Say good-bye

Fig. 5. Episodes of the 5-min recordings.

In the case of questions about the mentation, we used 24 adjectives from the UWIST Mood Adjective Checklist (UMACL) [5], giving them not only a 5-rated evaluation, but also positive and negative values to judge the mentation of the subjects (positive: 12, negative: 12). We also probed the characteristics of subjects by asking the subjects to provide some information about themselves and their prior experience with media and memory.

5.2   Result and Discussion

We devised a "Mentation Value" (MV) to quantize the mentation of the subjects. The formula of the MV is:

$$MV = \sum positive\ adjective\ points - \sum negative\ adjective\ points''$$

Observing the change in the user's MV as a result of using the medium, i.e., between the time at which they started using it and again after they finished using it (Fig. 6), it is clear that listening to recordings can increase the MV even though it was negative before, whereas viewing photos decreases the value in 3/4 of the cases.

Besides, in terms of the exam questions about the details of the BBQ, subjects are allowed to answer 50%–80% of the questions before touching the media; however, even after touching the media, no subjects were able to obtain more than 90% (Fig. 7). All questions that are answered are corrected by more than three people.

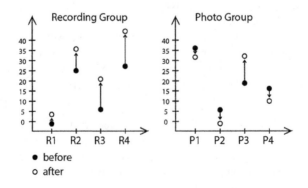

Fig. 6. Variation in the MV before and after using the media.

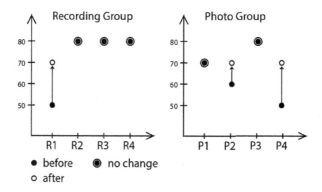

Fig. 7. Variation in the MV before and after using the media.

We also asked subjects about their favorite and most impressive episode/photo. All of the members of a group photo usually selected the group photo as their favorite; the two most impressive photos are those showing food, one for showing funny gestures, and the other being the group photo.

On the other hand, all of the members of the recording group chose their most impressive episodes from situations in which they were spectators, which means they were not the main actors in the recordings but that felt strong emotions in those episodes. Two of the members chose the same favorite as their most impressive episodes. Compared to the attention the member of the photo group paid to the group photo, only one member of the recording group referred to the scene in which members were greeting each other upon departure from the guesthouse (as the group episode).

This experiment enabled us to discover that recording is a valuable medium with potential. Out discovery that people's mentation, which was lower even when viewing photos of happy memories increased after listening to recordings, is interesting.

6 Conclusion

According to Oldenburg [6], "The great third place can let residents have the same feelings of warmth, possession, and belonging as they would in their own homes." A guesthouse, in its capacity as a place where travelers can interact with other residents, is always fresh and fascinating. Our attempts to record these kinds of interaction and emotion involved using a vital auditory place medium to save the recordings in an interesting and dynamic way.

Although this was not successfully achieved in the experiment we carried out with "The 60 seconds guestbook v1.0," we nevertheless tested and verified the advantages of making the recordings in the compared experiment.

Currently, our aim is to allow residents to record the auditory emotion and information by themselves and to enhance their enjoyment of using the media. Thus, we are designing a new version of "The 60 seconds guestbook." This time, the objectives of "The 60 seconds guestbook v2.0" are: First, to obtain more inspiration from and to

Fig. 8. Design of the user interface of "The 60 seconds guestbook v2.0"

communicate more easily with others than before, the user will be able to listen to a random recording before they start their own recording. On the other hand, in terms of conducting the experiment, we decided to avoid troubling the staff by only providing instructions that are easy to understand with a QR code rather than using an iPad. We plan to carry out this experiment during April for two weeks as before (Fig. 8).

References

1. Hayashi, Y., Fujihara, T.: Guesthouses as a field where travelers interact with other travelers: social psychological study of interactive tourism. Dep. Bull. Pap. **120**, 79–87 (2015)
2. Tauchi, H., Jo, H.: The effects of audio information on function of imagination. Bull. Grad. Sch. Hum. Dev. Environ. **7**(1) (1999). Kobe University
3. Ogawa, K.: Future of Place: Information Technologies and Place Media Grow New Relationship between Human and Place. The Institute of Electronics, Information and Communication Engineers Society Magazine (2008)
4. Guesthouse Hakone Tent. http://hakonetent.com/. Accessed 19 Mar 2017
5. Matthews, G., Jones, D.M., Chamberlain, A.G.: Refining the measurement of mood: the UWIST mood adjective checklist. Br. J. Psychol. **81**, 17–42 (1990)
6. Oldenburg, R.: The Great Good Place: Cafes, Coffee Shops, Bookstores, Bars, Hair Salons, and Other Hangouts at the Heart of a Community. Da Capo Press, Cambridge (1999)

Investigation of Smartphone Use While Walking and Its Influences on One's Behavior Among Pedestrians in Taiwan

Jun-Ming Lu[✉] and Yi-Chin Lo

Department of Industrial Engineering and Engineering Management,
National Tsing Hua University, 101, Section 2, Kuangfu Road, Hsinchu, Taiwan
jmlu@ie.nthu.edu.tw

Abstract. While bringing about convenience, using smartphones while walking may distract the users, leading to potential hazards for both the user him/herself and other road users. In recent years, the number of accidents resulting from smartphone use while walking keeps growing. It hence becomes urgent to develop countermeasures to solve this problem. Therefore, this study aims to investigate the current status of smartphone use while walking in Taiwan, as well as analyzing its influences on the user's behavior.

On the one hand, a structured questionnaire was administered to 100 participants ranging from 20 to 64 years old, in which one's experience of and attitude toward smartphone use while walking being surveyed in detail. On the other hand, behavioral data were collected and analyzed among three male and three female adults in their 20 s by an eye tracking system and a motion capture system. The performance and strategies of foot-eye coordination were compared among conditions including free walking, walking while holding a smartphone, and texting on a smartphone while walking.

Results showed that most people are aware of the risks associated with smartphone use while walking, but they somehow fail to follow the recommendations for not doing so. The findings also suggest that distracted walking caused by smartphone use did slow down the pedestrian, limit his/her visual attention, and impair the stability of walking. Therefore, countermeasures would be necessary to help reduce the associated risks.

Keywords: Smartphones · Distracted walking · Foot-eye coordination

1 Introduction

According to the Institute for Information Industry (2015), the possession rate of smartphone in Taiwan is now approximately 73.4%. In addition, it seems that smartphones have also gradually become one part of middle-aged and older adults' daily lives, with the possession rate reaching 26.6%. However, the dependence on smartphones may lead to problems such as phone/Internet addiction, increased stress, poor social relationship, and musculoskeletal disorders (Lanaj et al. 2014; Hassanzadeh and Rezaei, 2011; Eom et al., 2013). Further, as more and more people keep using smartphones while walking, the associated cognitive or physiological changes in one's behavior can reduce risk awareness of potential hazards.

© Springer International Publishing AG 2017
C. Stephanidis (Ed.): HCII Posters 2017, Part II, CCIS 714, pp. 469–475, 2017.
DOI: 10.1007/978-3-319-58753-0_67

Fox and Duggan (2012) reported that 53% of smartphone users have the experience of colliding with others due to distracted walking, in which the majority is the young people aging from 18 to 24 years old. In the United States, hospital statistics indicated that the number of patients sent to the ICUs due to phone-use issues reached 1,152 in 2011 (Pew Charitable Trusts 2014). In Japan, there were 122 pedestrians sent to hospitals because of accidents associated with phone use (Tokyo Fire Department 2014). The Road Traffic Authority of Korea found that the growth rate of phone-related emergency services is 1.7 times more than that of the countries in OCED (Molko 2016). The case is similar in Taiwan, but there were very limited studies or surveys addressing related issues.

In addition to the statistics of preferences and accident histories, behavioral changes due to distracted walking while using smartphone are also of great concern. For example, Haga et al. (2015) invited participants to walk clockwisely along a 3 m-by-3 m square, during which a smartphone was used for texting, watching video clips, and playing games. Their observations suggest that distracted walking with smartphones may lead to greater deviations from the walking route and reduced attention to unexpected visual stimuli. Nevertheless, the participant's gaze behavior was not analyzed, and quantitative data of the lower-limb movements were limited. Further, how auditory attention is affected was also not studied.

Therefore, this study aims to investigate the experience of and attitude toward smartphone use while walking among Taiwanese people, as well as analyzing the effects of such distracted walking on one's gaze behavior, performance and strategies of foot-eye coordination, and residual capacity of both visual and auditory attention.

2   Investigation of Users' Preferences

A structured questionnaire covering the demographics, experiences of smartphone use, attitude toward distracted walking with a smartphone, and the acceptance of few countermeasures against smartphone use while walking was administered to 100 participants ranging from 20 to 64 years old and collected in one month. All of them own a smartphone and agreed with the consent statement for the questionnaire.

78% of the participants are under 50 years old (23 are between 20 and 24 years old; 23 are between 25 and 29 years old; 10 are between 30 to 34 years old; 10 are between 35 and 39 years old; 8 are between 40 to 44 years old; 4 are between 45 and 49 years old), while 22% are over 50 years old (10 are between 50 and 54 years old; 11 are between 55 and 59 years old; 1 is between 60 to 64 years old). In addition, there are 57 males and 43 females.

Considering the time spent with the smartphone, 49% of the participants are frequent users who spent more than 4 h per day. In the cases of smartphone use while walking, 78% of the participants have had such experiences. Among these 78 participants who have used smartphones while walking, only 14% of them did this frequently. Further, 36 out of these 78 participants used their smartphones while walking with social media applications (e.g. Facebook, LINE), followed by talking on the phone (14 out of 78), reading text messages (6 out of 78), listening to music (6 out of 78), and so forth. As for those 22 participants who never used smartphones while walking, their reasons include "feeling it's dangerous" (33%), "avoiding collision with other road users or obstacles" (21%), "avoiding trips or falls" (21%), and so on.

Despite the high percentage of the experience of smartphone use while walking, only 22% of them have hence got involved in accidents such as collision with other road users or obstacles. This is probably one of the major reasons that encouraged them to keep doing this, even though 78 out of the 100 participants disagree with the use of smartphones while walking. From this point of view, people's attitude toward smartphone use while walking may conflict with how they actually behave, which hinders the promotion of corresponding countermeasures.

Moreover, in the questionnaire, the participants were asked to rate from 1 (strongly unacceptable) to 5 (strongly acceptable) about their attitude toward each of six countermeasures designed for preventing smartphone use while walking. The most acceptable countermeasure (with the average of 3.66 out of 5.00) was the introduction of a transparent screen that allows the user to see through the screen for keeping attention to the information around his/her feet. Following that, the simplified design of user interface (requiring less time and attention) also received a rating than 3.50 (out of 5.00). On the contrary, pop-out windows warning that "stop using smartphones while walking" was least acceptable (with the average of 2.82 out of 5.00), followed by auto-locking of the screen as the users is detected as walking (with the average of 3.15 out of 5.00). In short, people tend to prefer technologies that improve one's attention and allow smartphone use while walking, rather than those prohibit them from such a multitasking behavior.

3 Behavioral Changes Associated with Distracted Walking

In order to quantify the behavioral changes associated with distracted walking due to smartphone use, six participants (3 males and 3 females) ranging from 22 to 26 years old were recruited to perform simulated tasks in the laboratory environment. The body height is 168.3 ± 1.5 cm for males and 158.7 ± 7.0 for females, whereas the body weight is 62.0 ± 2.0 for males and 46.7 ± 4.2 for females. All of them have the experience of smartphone use while walking and signed the informed consent prior to the experiment.

Each participant was asked to wear a mobile eye-tracking system, the standard suit for motion capture with 37 reflective markers attached, and a pair of standard shoes that fits his/her feet. First, the participant was allowed to get used to walking along the 5.1 m by 3.6 m square, in which the route width was set at 0.3 m. There was a monitor placed 1.6 m away from the end of each longer side (5.1 m), which was prepared for presenting unexpected stimuli (pure colors of red, yellow, or green, lasting for 60 ms) as the measure of the participant's residual capacity of visual attention when walking on any of the two longer sides. In addition, a wireless speaker was placed at the center of the square, so that the sound recorded in a crowded street (with the loudness of 65 dB) can be played while the participant performs the task. Once the participant is on any of the two shorter sides (3.6 m), a horn (with the loudness of 70 dB) might appear for 0.5 s to test his/her residual capacity of auditory attention. Further, a digital video recorder was placed at the corner opposite to the starting point. The layout is shown in Fig. 1.

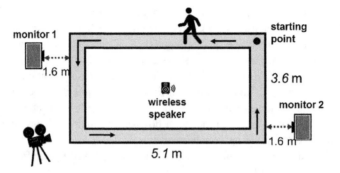

Fig. 1. Layout of the simulated route (Color figure online)

After practicing walking along the route shown in Fig. 1 with and without the use of the standard smartphone, there were six sessions assigned for each participant. In each session, the participant needs to walk along the route for four laps in his/her preferred pace while the corresponding tasks are performed. In the first session, the participant was required to keep standing on the starting point and use a social media application to interact with a chatting robot through texting. In the second session, the participant also kept standing on the starting point while playing games on a typing test application. These two sessions were designed as controls to see how the participant's performance may change as he/she was required to complete the same tasks while walking. In the third session, free walking along the route for four laps was required, as shown in Fig. 2 (left). This is considered as the baseline of one's behavior under such an environment. In the fourth session, the participant walked along the route while holding a smartphone without really using it for four laps. This is used to clarify whether the behavioral changes are purely due to smartphone operation, or the fact that one is holding it as well (Fig. 2; right). The fifth session is similar with the first session, except that the participant had to walk along the route for four laps. Finally, in the sixth session, the participant did the same smartphone task as in the second session, but

Fig. 2. Free walking (left) and walking while holding a smartphone (right) (Color figure online)

he/she was required to walk along the route for four laps. In sessions 3 to 6, the participant's gaze data and motion capture data were collected throughout the four-lap movement. Meanwhile, the behaviors were videotaped using the digital video recorder, while the operations on the smartphone were recorded using a remote control application. Further, the participant's responses to the visual/auditory stimuli were collected in terms of response time (from the appearance of stimulus to the beginning of the participant's verbal reaction) and percentage of correct responses (whether the participant spoke out the correct color or the presentation of the horn).

When there was smartphone operation involved while walking (session 5 and session 6), the participants generally moved the gaze away from the smartphone only as turning at the four corners (Fig. 3; left), whereas the gaze was mostly on the smartphone no matter whether they walked on the longer or shorter sides (Fig. 3; right). In the case of walking on the longer sides, the participants tended to look at a higher level, which seems to be prepared for capturing the upcoming visual stimulus. However, while performing the chatting task, the participant usually spent some time thinking about what to communicate with the chatting robot. So, at these moments, some of the participants moved their gaze away from the smartphone slightly longer, allowing more residual capacity of visual attention.

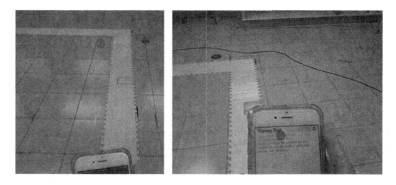

Fig. 3. Gaze away from (left) and on (right) the smartphone (Color figure online)

As illustrated in Fig. 4, considering the stability of walking (along the center line of the route), conditions while performing the typing task or the chatting task showed greater lateral deviations. This conforms with the assumption that distracted walking may increase the difficulty of walking as the attention is drawn to the tiny screen of the smartphone. In addition, it was found that the lateral deviation of walking while holding a smartphone is quite similar with that of free walking. In other words, it is very likely that gait changes associated with smartphone use while walking were purely due to the decreased attention caused by smartphone operation.

Moreover, the walking speed (measured in terms of task completion time throughout the four laps) was found to be significantly reduced as the smartphone was used while walking ($p = 0.049$). The mean completion time for four laps was 77.1 s, 79.1 s, 99.1 s, and 103.9 s for holding, free walking, chatting, and typing, respectively.

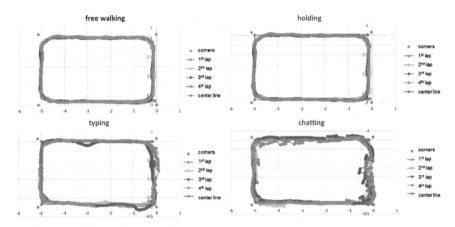

Fig. 4. Lateral deviation from the center line of one participant (Color figure online)

Post-hoc analysis revealed that the participants walked significantly more slowly while performing the typing task than in holding and free walking conditions. Obviously, it is very likely that the high level of the participant's attention on the smartphone changed his/her gait pattern in terms of both accuracy and efficiency.

Generally speaking, the use of smartphone requires more visual attention than auditory attention. Thus, following the multiple resource model (Wickens, 1980), one should be more sensitive to unexpected auditory stimuli than visual ones. However, surprisingly, the increase of response time to auditory stimulus ($p = 0.049$) was found to be as significant as that to visual stimulus ($p = 0.033$), while comparing between conditions with and without smartphone use. In the case of visual stimulus, the mean response time was 0.665 s, 0.715 s, 0.895 s, and 0.969 s for holding, free walking, chatting, and typing, respectively. Post-hoc analysis showed that the response time was significantly longer in chatting and typing tasks than in holding and free walking tasks. As for auditory stimulus, the mean response time was 0.619 s, 0.655 s, 0.808 s, and 0.886 s for holding, free walking, typing, and chatting, respectively. Post-hoc analysis indicated that the response time was significantly longer in the chatting task than in holding and free walking tasks.

Nevertheless, on the other hand, the percentages of correct response to visual stimuli were found to be significantly different among conditions ($p = 0.001$), whereas there was no difference in the percentage of correct response to auditory stimuli ($p = 0.422$). Post-hoc analysis showed that there were significant differences for visual stimuli between any pair of conditions, except for holding versus free walking and typing versus chatting. In other words, though it took a longer time to respond to auditory stimuli as one uses smartphone while walking, it doesn't affect how accurately the response is. As for visual attention, both capacity and accuracy were impaired.

4 Conclusion

In this study, the investigation of the experience of and attitude toward smartphone use while walking was conducted among 100 Taiwanese people ranging from 20 to 64 years old. Statistics showed that most people tend to behave in this way, even though they are aware of the risks associated with it. Hence, countermeasures that both allow people to do so and improve the safety would be required. On the other hand, findings of the experiment suggested that distracted walking due to smartphone use did make the user walk more slowly and less stably, as well as limiting the visual attention. Further analyses on gaze behavior and lower-limb kinematics will be continued, so as to highlight the importance of corresponding countermeasures and to identify reliable measures for testing and evaluation.

References

Institute for Information Industry: Innovative Service Experience Ecosystem Research and Development Project (3/4) (2015, in Chinese). http://www.find.org.tw/market_info.aspx?k= 2&n_ID=8482/

Lanaj, K., Johnson, R.E., Barnes, C.M.: Beginning the workday yet already depleted? Consequences of late-night smartphone use and sleep. Organ. Behav. Hum. Decis. Processes **124**(1), 11–23 (2014)

Hassanzadeh, R., Rezaei, A.: Effect of sex, course and age on SMS addiction in students. Middle-East J. Sci. Res. **10**(5), 619–625 (2011)

Eom, S.H., Choi, S.Y., Park, D.H.: An empirical study on relationship between symptoms of musculoskeletal disorders and amount of smartphone usage. J. Korea Saf. Manag. Sci. **15**(2), 113–120 (2013)

Fox, S., Duggan, M.: Mobile Health 2012. Pew Internet & American Life Project, Washington, DC (2012)

Pew Charitable Trusts: Distracted walkers are major concern for cities and states (2014). http://www.pewtrusts.org/en/research-and-analysis/blogs/stateline/2014/12/11/distracted-walkers-are-major-concern-for-cities-and-states

Tokyo Fire Department. Mind Smartphoning!, Tokyo Fire Department (2014). http://www.tfd.metro.tokyo.jp/lfe/topics/201403/mobile.html

Molko, D.: Smartphone zombies have taken over Seoul, CNN News (2016) http://edition.cnn.com/2016/08/14/south-korea-smartphone-zombie/

Haga, S., Sano, A., Sekine, Y., Sato, H., Yamaguchi, S., Masuda, K.: Effects of using a Smart Phone on Pedestrians' attention and walking. Procedia Manuf. **3**, 2574–2580 (2015)

Wickens, C.D.: The structure of attentional resources. Attention Perform. VIII **8**, 239–257 (1980)

Understanding Modern Audience
in Traditional Settings

Asreen Rostami$^{(\boxtimes)}$, Christoffer Cialec, and Gabriel Werlinder

Stockholm University, Stockholm, Sweden
asreen@dsv.su.se, {chci6046,gawe4669}@student.su.se

Abstract. While audience members of theatre productions are generally discouraged from using their mobile devices, as mobile technology is interwoven
into our daily lives use in theatres still goes on. Some of this use is encouraged
by the artists and built into the performance, however the furtive use by audience members during non-interactive performances has not been studied. In this
poster we report on our work-in-progress consisting of preliminary analysis of
in-situ observation and video analysis of four out of seven performances currently recorded to understand when and how mobile devices are used. This
analysis is supported by interviews of selected audience members to better
understand why and for what purpose these devices are used in this setting.
These preliminary results draw attention to the correlations between (i) the
audience's distance from the stage, (ii) the engagement of the current scene, and
(iii) the audience's personal connection to the art work or the performers, and
frequency of mobile phone use.

Keywords: Audience interaction · Mobile phone use · Performance

1 Introduction

There has been a growing interest in using technology in interactive performances to
support storytelling [1] and audience participation [4, 5]. The mobile phone has been
one of the first devices to be used by curators and artists as part of the narrative,
creating dialogue between the audience and the performance or allowing audience to
contribute to the performance. This practice however, is different in traditional theatre
settings, where audience is strongly encouraged to stay quiet during the performance
and warned that they will be evicted if they cause disturbance or distraction [8]. Yet,
audience members are still using their mobile devices during the performance to record
a scene, take a photo of their favourite actor, secretly answer a call, or reply to a
message. While the use of mobile phones in interactive performances have been
explored extensively in HCI [4, 6, 7], studies on how audience members are using their
devices while watching a traditional performance has been relatively absent.

This study sets out to understand the current behaviour of modern audiences and
their motivations for using mobile phones while in a traditional theatre like setting. We
conducted this study using in-situ observation, video recordings and analysis, and
interviews of selected audience members at seven performances. The results draw
attention to (i) the correlation between the audience's distance from the stage and

© Springer International Publishing AG 2017
C. Stephanidis (Ed.): HCII Posters 2017, Part II, CCIS 714, pp. 476–480, 2017.
DOI: 10.1007/978-3-319-58753-0_68

frequency of mobile phone use, (ii) the engagement of the current scene, and (iii) the audience's personal connection to the art work or the performers.

2   Research Methods

The empirical material was collected during seven performances. These performances were: one theatre based live music concert, two runs of a play and four performances of improvisational theatre. We collected data through observations, note-taking, and multi-angle video-recordings.

More than 400 people were observed over 13 h of performance, resulting in a total of 26 h of video data. The recording was done in collaboration with the venue; the venue informed the audience before the start of the performance. At this point if no objections were raised, we started the recording. One camera was set up behind the audience, point down towards the stage, and the second camera angle from the near the back of the audience, stage right (Fig. 1). The videos were combined and synchronised to provide the data or analysis. These angles, combined with the relative brightness of a mobile phone screen in comparison to the overall darkness of the auditorium provided an estimated 80% coverage of audience members' mobile device usage.

When the play was over, we approached those audience members who had been observed using their mobile phone during the play for an interview. The goal of the interviews was to gain an understanding of audience members' reason of using their mobile phones.

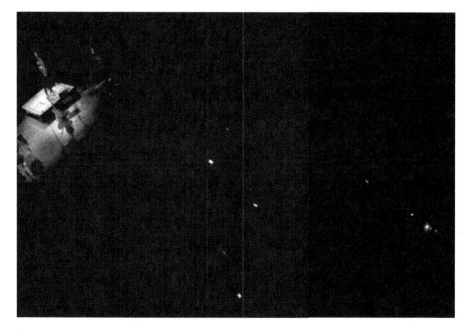

Fig. 1. Screenshot of a single camera angle showing 6 mobile phones in use plus the stage lighting controller on the far right

This poster reports the analysis of the first four of these performances, all of which were different improvised theatre productions at the same venue.

3   Findings

Table 1 provides an overview of the mobile device uses seen in our video. Of note the high interaction time shown in performance C, here a young child was in the audience and had been given the mobile device by the adults with her in order to watch cartoons. This was observed not only to distract the parents, but at times also to draw the attention of others in the vicinity. The interaction time not including that child is shown in brackets.

Table 1. Overview of mobile device uses during the four performances.

Performance	A	B	C	D
# Device uses	23	19	60	33
Total interaction (seconds)	1017	765	5042 (2571)	1332
# of people interacting	5	10	15	6
Avg. length of interaction	44,21	40,26	84,03 (42,85)	40,36

Interestingly, the average length of interaction in this time is similar to the 38 seonds shown in [2], however the number of interactions per person is much less than the 8 per hour detected by the Wagner et al. in [9]. This can be understood by the observed use that the mobile device was put to in this context, that of a recording device. While there were shorter interactions recorded that appeared to be checking the time or checking and answering messages, the majority of the use was in taking photographs and videos. This was supported by our interview participants.

> *"You do not really use your phone during a performance, you can use it as a camera, I think it is a bit rude to have to phone receive a call or sit there and talk." – A3*

Table 2 shows a clear correlation between distance from the audience and the amount of mobile device use in performances A through C. In performance D we can see a stark reversal of this trend. From our observations and discussion with the theatre staff this performance had a large number of friends and family of the performers in the

Table 2. This table shows the split of use between those near the stage, and those at the back of the auditorium.

Performance	A	B	C	D
# Device uses	23	19	60	33
Front audience uses	5	1	11	29
Back audience uses	18	18	49	4

front row. This provided them with a larger motivation for taking pictures and video, as those on stage were close to them, and could be seen to have removed some of the barriers in place of using mobile devices in such contexts. One interview subject described his taking of a photo as a communicative act between himself and his spouse on stage.

'I wanted [her] to see me taking the photograph at that bit, it was a really good scene I had seen in another run, and I wanted her to see me enjoying it.' - A6

Another interesting point drawn from the interviews was that the level of engagement with the performance was reported as influencing the use of mobile devices. While the personal engagement described in the quote above can be seen to influence, and increase, mobile device usage by the audience more general engagement with the performance, plot, and pacing of what is happening on stage has the opposite effect.

"I think that uhm if it is very intensive and you are following you probably not going to use it but when it becomes a bit slow and drawn-out maybe you start peeking at something else." – A1

This ability of the mobile phone to be used in down-time, or moments when you are disengaged from the flow of conversation or interaction around you has been documented [2], yet the situations described in as candidates for this type of use were far removed from the theatre context under investigation here. This shows that while down-time use may be a more prevalent design opportunity on public transport, while waiting in line, or during commercial breaks such opportunistic software design could be seen to be engaging in a much wider range of circumstances.

4   Conclusion

In this preliminary analysis of video recording and interviews on the topic of mobile device use we have presented three factors determining the frequency of mobile use by audience members. Interestingly we have also shown that use in this context is generally longer, centering around photo and video composition, in comparison to previous works on mobile device use in other contexts [3].

Our continued work in this area will compare different types of performance, and focus on gaining a deeper understanding of the interaction with, and around, the mobile device. In our current data we can see that the mobile device is not always used individually in this context, with the composition of photos particularly eliciting gestural and whispered input from those around the user of the device. In order to analyse how this interaction differs from co-located use as seen in, for example, we plan to include an infra-red camera in our recording set up. This will allow us to perform moment-by-moment video-analysis of these interactions before and after the light of the mobile phone screen illuminates the audience members.

This understanding will provide design opportunities for mobile applications and services tailored to fit both the context of audiencehood and the current practice of audience members.

References

1. Barkhuus, L., Rossitto, C.: Acting with technology: rehearsing for mixed-media live performances. In: Proceedings of the 34th Annual ACM Conference on Human Factors in Computing Systems, CHI 2016 (2016). https://doi.org/10.1145/2858036.2858344
2. Brown, B., McGregor, M., McMillan, D.: 100 Days of iPhone use: understanding the details of mobile device use. In: Proceedings of the 16th International Conference on Human-computer Interaction with Mobile Devices & Services (MobileHCI 2014), pp. 223–232 (2014). https://doi.org/10.1145/2628363.2628377
3. Brown, B., McGregor, M., McMillan, D.: Searchable objects: search in everyday conversation. In: Proceedings of the 18th ACM Conference on Computer Supported Cooperative Work & Social Computing (CSCW 2015), pp. 508–517 (2015). https://doi.org/10.1145/2675133.2675206
4. Cerratto-Pargman, T., Rossitto, C., Barkhuus, L.: Understanding audience participation in an interactive theater performance. In: Proceedings of the 8th Nordic Conference on Human-Computer Interaction: Fun, Fast, Foundational (NordiCHI 2014), pp. 608–617 (2014). https://doi.org/10.1145/2639189.2641213
5. Rashid, O., Mullins, I., Coulton, P., Edwards, R.: Extending cyberspace: location based games using cellular phones. Comput. Entertain. **4**(1) (2016). https://doi.org/10.1145/1111293.1111302
6. Rossitto, C., Barkhuus, L., Engström, A.: Interweaving place and story in a location-based audio drama. Pers. Ubiquitous Comput. **20**(2), 245–260, (2016). https://doi.org/10.1007/s00779-016-0908-x
7. Sheridan, J.G., Bryan-Kinns, N., Bayliss, A.: Encouraging witting participation and performance in digital live art. In: Proceedings of the 21st British HCI Group Annual Conference on People and Computers: HCI. But Not As We Know It - Volume 1 (BCS-HCI 2007), pp. 13–23 (2017). http://dl.acm.org/citation.cfm?id=1531294.1531297. Accesed 15 Jan 2017
8. Simkins, M.: Alas, poor Benedict! Fans filming isn't the only peril that could throw Cumberbatch. The Guardian (2015). https://www.theguardian.com/culture/2015/aug/10/benedict-cumberbatch-hamlet-barbican-fans. Accessed 29 Mar 2017
9. Wagner, D.T., Rice, A., Beresford, A.R.: Device analyzer: understanding smartphone usage. In: Stojmenovic, I., Cheng, Z., Guo, S. (eds.) MindCare 2014. LNICST, vol. 131, pp. 195–208. Springer, Cham (2014). doi:10.1007/978-3-319-11569-6_16

Development of a User Participatory Mobile App to Promote a Local Tourist Attraction: The Okayama Korakuen Navi App

Wangmi Seok[✉] and Akihiko Kasw

Okayama Prefectural University of Faculty of Design, Soja Shi, Japan
{seok,kasw}@dgn.oka-pu.ac.jp

Abstract. Users planning to visit tourist attractions find a lack of information on websites, which are not updated in real-time. This study develops a user-participating app that sustains the interest of users towards tourism resources, so as to attract more tourists to regional tourist destinations. The proposed app focuses on Okayama Korakuen, one of Japan's three great gardens, and allows anyone to contribute information. An analysis of visitors after distributing the app showed that there was an increase in the number of returning locals to the garden.

Keywords: Develops a user-participating app · Tour contents

1 Purpose of Study

With the launch of various smart devices, many compatible apps have also been released. Apple, one of the leading tech companies, runs its own app store, and Google also runs an app store offering products tailored to the Android operating system, where people can download a variety of apps for free or for a fee. The widespread consumer embrace of the Web 2.0 environment enables almost anyone to produce and share content, instead of a few privileged people monopolizing or exclusively owning information. Now, consumers of information are able to share their experiences through the Internet anytime and anywhere, and some regular users even suggest improvements to the services available.

The results of this study indicate that a mechanism that allows users to utilize and produce information will play a positive role in revitalizing local tourism. Domestic organizations, including tourism companies, are the parties primarily in charge of the promotion of local tourist attractions, but in general the descriptions of these attractions that they provide have hardly changed over the years. Since the relevant websites always display the same information, there is no reason to visit them regularly.

To overcome the difficulty involved in constantly providing information that reflects new developments, this study suggests a system that allows users to participate in the production of information on local tourist attractions. Based on a literature review, reviews of several tourism related apps, and surveys of visitors to Korakuen in Japan, the Korakuen Navi app, a mobile app designed to promote tourism in the area, was developed.

© Springer International Publishing AG 2017
C. Stephanidis (Ed.): HCII Posters 2017, Part II, CCIS 714, pp. 481–488, 2017.
DOI: 10.1007/978-3-319-58753-0_69

2   The State of Tourism Related Content

In order to promote tourism, local organizations participate in various activities such as creating websites, planning events, distributing leaflets, and creating apps. In Japan, there are 363 tourism related apps for IOS and 229 for Android (as of March 2016). However, most have not been widely downloaded. The exceptions are apps with frequent updates that have been developed by large tourism companies. Based on the preliminary survey of this study, it is clear that many people deleted or stopped using apps created by local organizations after downloading them, because they did not receive user feedback, and most of the information that these organizations provided was also available from other sources on the internet or in other media.

This study examined the specific contents, user participation methods, user interfaces (UIs), and frequency of information updates of the top 10 most frequently downloaded apps among the total of 592 Japanese tourism apps. Since the top 10 apps offered by tourism companies all enabled the reservation of hotel rooms and tourism packages, two more apps created by local organizations were also included in the analysis. Specifically, apps detailing the attractions of Kenrokuen in Kanazawa city, one of the top three landscaped gardens in Japan, and Kairakuen in Mito city were examined, in order to analyze how apps created by such local organizations fared, in accordance with the purpose of this study (Fig. 1).

Fig. 1. Top 10 tourism apps and local organization apps

2.1   Contents, UIs, and Information Updates of Apps

The top 10 tourism apps originally enabled the reservation of hotel packages and tourist itineraries, rather than providing information on tourist attractions. Currently, these apps also provide information about nearby tourist attractions by making a search function available. Although they primarily offer tourist information that is also available from other media, updates on any changes in local amenities and circumstances are available immediately. In terms of encouraging user participation, many of the top 10 apps allow recent visitors to review and rate tourist attractions.

In the case of the app for Kenrokuen in Kanazawa, if a user scans a certain location in Kenrokuen with her smart device, a detailed description using the augmented reality (AR) system is displayed on the device screen. In the case of Kairakuen in Mito, tourist information is provided not via its own app but in the tour section of the official Mito city app, which does not allow any user participation such as the writing of comments. Both of these apps are semi-regularly updated by the information provider.

In the case of the user interface (UI) of the Rurubu app, which is the 3rd most frequently downloaded, if a user selects "tourist attractions" for a local area on a list, related sites in that area appear, their order depending on their user rating. Since the app offers the same data as internet sites, it is updated in real time in order to gain an advantage. It also provides more practical and specific information by allowing users to leave reviews. As a result, the rankings of tourist attractions are highly reliable because they are determined by users. However, the writing ability of a user greatly affects the quality of their review, and there is no mechanism that encourages users who have left comments to do so again (Fig. 2).

Fig. 2. UI of the Rurubu app

2.2 Mapping in Terms of the Level of User Participation and the Update Interval

In Fig. 3, an ideal Korakuen app is presented in 2 × 2 matrix form in terms of the user participation level and the information update interval. This study focused on the issues of user participation and rapid feedback in order to develop an app that people will continue to use without losing interest.

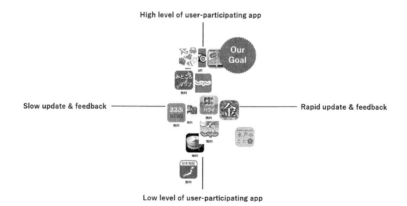

Fig. 3. Attributes of an ideal app

3 User Generated Content

3.1 Concept and Form of User Generated Content

User generated content (UGC) designates online digital content created by individuals using computers or smart phones. Kaplan and Haenlein (2010) defined user generated content as content created without the need for professional processes and training. User generated content was born in the Web 2.0 environment. With the spread of Internet technology and the resulting ease of information production and distribution, users have been increasingly able to produce content easily, and this has led to the significant development of user generated content. O'Reilly (2005) defined collective intelligence, an attribute of Web 2.0, as the collective ability that results from the intellectual capacity created through cooperation and competition among many individuals. The forms of user generated content created in the Web 2.0 environment vary because the phrase "user generated" has very broad meaning. The basic elements of UGC include text, photos, videos, and location information, and the degree of their respective uses varies depending on the basic attributes of various platforms such as blogs or SNS hubs.

3.2 Features and Functions of User Generated Content

With the advent of Web 2.0, users of various platforms began to share their thoughts and experiences with others by uploading posts to their blogs or SNSs, which have provided opportunities to learn from others' experience. In other words, content containing personal experiences and feelings or thoughts are now seen to constitute valuable data. In addition, the creation of user generated content is mostly voluntary. The motivation for content generation is personal and varies according to the circumstances and motives of the users in question. Smadja (2009) categorized the impetus behind information generation in terms of direct motivation, which involves material rewards, and indirect motivation, which involves a sense of accomplishment or satisfaction. Despite this fundamental difference, both forms of motivation promote the sharing of voluntary information. This suggests that information sharing can be induced by situation-specific factors. In the course of being exposed to and consumed by others on various platforms (blogs or SNSs), this content sometimes comes to be regarded as valuable. When content has high value, immediate sharing occurs and the information is widely propagated. In this process, the originator of this information achieves the satisfaction of creating such popular content, because the recognition of content is considered to be coterminous with the recognition of its creator (Goodchild 2007; Smadja 2009).

   This study deals with the information generation of users who are focused on tourist attractions. One example of such user generated content is OpenStreetMap, a map service launched by a non-profit organization in the U.K., the OpenStreetMap Foundation. All geographic information in this map service is created by ordinary individuals. It is well-known that, at the 2014 Sochi Olympic Games, it was not Google Maps but OpenStreetMap that provided the best information on the athletic village and its surrounding environment. During the two months of the Olympics, including the preparatory period, there were more than 1.5 million people who posted helpful information about the event online and more than 2,000 cases of information provision and supplementation.

Another example of interesting user generated content is the Love Clean Streets app created in the U.K. However, this app was not created to share tourist information. The Love Clean Streets app sends pictures of environmental problems in towns and cities where people reside directly to responsible agencies, along with location information. This app is so popular that over 820,000 urban problems have been reported in the U.K. since the app's creation. There is a similar app in Korea, the Life Inconvenience Report app, with which people send pictures and videos of various problems in their everyday lives to relevant organizations in order to encourage them to resolve these issues.

User generated content constitutes a huge information warehouse consisting of information provided by individuals. These people are motivated to gain recognition, and others are motivated to obtain good information, and thus, over time a system that assimilates this flow of useful information is created.

4 Planning of a User Participatory App for Korakuen

With a total area of 133,000 m^2, Korakuen in Okayama, one of the top three landscaped gardens in Japan, is three times larger than the Tokyo Dome and welcomed 700,758 visitors in 2015. According to the Okayama Tourism Action Plan devised by Okayama prefecture, approximately 700,000 foreigners visited Okayama in 2012. Korakuen is in all probability the number one tourist attraction among foreign tourists visiting Okayama. It is easy to visit Korakuen because it is not far from the downtown area, Okayama Castle, and other parks. It is also a good year-round place to see many plants and flowers. Through surveys on the awareness and use of Korakuen, it was found that although it was visited by many people from outside Okayama, its footfall mostly consisted of repeated visits by local residents. Many people used the route to Korakuen as a walking trail because it is near the downtown area, and they can also view nearby parks and Okayama Castle while walking. In addition, in these surveys many people said that it is a great pleasure to see the well-maintained plants and flowers in Korakuen. In this study, the qualities of "participation and sharing" were the criteria used to evaluate the Korakuen Navi app, and its continuous use by tourists and local residents were examined. The study also analyzed ease of use, since the age range of visitors was very wide, from teens to people in their 60s or older.

4.1 Design Concept of the Korakuen Navi App

Concept of the App: My Photos of Korakuen's Flowers and Trees.

The Korakuen Navi app aims to be an optimal system through which users participate and create content. After examining a variety of attributes that encourage user participation, I chose to incorporate into this app a photo-centered information sharing system that allows the high quality transmission of images and convenient user participation. In addition, data updated by users can be shared via the app or other SNS hubs.

Since cameras are pre-installed in smart phones, anyone with a smart phone can upload images with a few taps of the screen. In addition, photos uploaded by other users are displayed in the order of their upload date, so people can see the latest Korakuen images even if they do not upload images themselves. This ubiquity of images has a stronger impact than any text could.

The Korakuen Navi app is usable in five languages—Japanese, English, French, Korean, and Chinese—because these are the languages of most of its users. The main menu on the home screen is vertically arranged in the Japanese version but is horizontal in foreign language versions. This is because it is natural to read vertically from the top right to bottom left in Japan, while it is natural to read horizontally from the left to the right in other countries.

4.2   Designing Workflow for the Korakuen Navi App

The Korakuen Navi app does not require any training in order to use it. New information is always on the home page, and users can easily access it by tapping the screen a few times. The menu consists of four sections: Submitting Photos; Viewing Others' Photos; Events; and Hot Spots. The upper part of the home page is comprised of a real time slideshow of updated photos, while the lower part is divided into four global menus. Photos can be uploaded by specifying the locations where they were taken, which is accomplished by selecting a specific site in the park on Google Maps. Photos can also be uploaded accompanied by their category, for example plants, flowers, or hot spots. Photos submitted by other users are displayed in thumbnail format, and can be zoomed in on upon selection. Users can return to the home page at any point (Fig. 4).

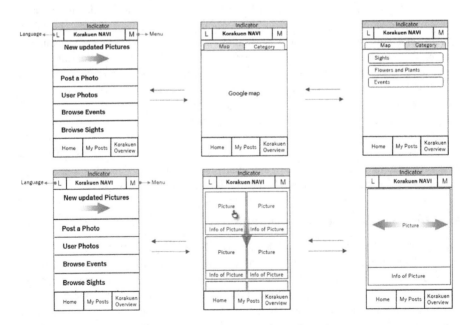

Fig. 4. Task Workflow on the main menu

4.3   Production of GUI

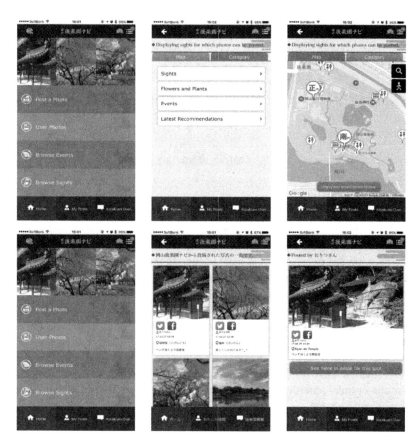

Fig. 5. Working model

5   Conclusion

The Korakuen Navi app can be downloaded for free from the iPhone App Store, the Android Google Play Store, and its own website. It is an app for Okayama Korakuen Park which incorporates a visual element to induce user participation (Fig. 5).

From the analysis of user log data dating from the release of the Korakuen Navi app in May 2015 to February 2016, the age of the 3,331 recorded users ranged from the teens to the 60 s, but middle-aged users in particular were heavily represented. Users from all across Japan accessed the app, but the majority, numbering 1,238 users, were living in the central region of Japan where the Okayama prefecture is located. A total of 128 users uploaded 975 photos. Of these users, those living in Okayama uploaded more than half of all photos. These figures indicate that most users of the Korakuen Navi app are local residents. Of the foreign users, 114 were from Taiwan, 81 were from Hong Kong, and 16 were from China (Fig. 6).

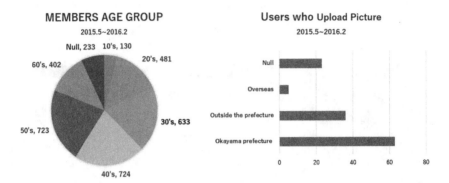

Fig. 6. Analysis of user log data

The quality of information contained in user generated content can be improved by increasing the level of user participation. Many media provide similar local tourist information, which is also true for Okayama Korakuen. Although Korakuen boasts different flowers and scents each season, its promotional information is rarely updated, with the exception of news related to local events. In this context, we have proposed an app that makes user participation more enjoyable by letting users take pictures of developments in the park and upload and share them. This provides fresh information to other users and ultimately motivates them to visit the park. It is also important to demonstrate that the app is being well managed by providing news or event updates in good time, which is the app manager's responsibility.

The study showed that the number of active users who uploaded photos was relatively small relative to the overall number of users. More research is needed to discover the optimal parameters that can ensure the continuous and active use of the Okayama Korauken app.

Acknowledgments. We received user log data from City-Planning team of Okayama Prefecture.

References

Goodchild, M.F., Li, L.: Assuring the quality of volunteered geographic information. Spat. Stat. **1**, 110–120 (2012)

Kaplan, A.M., Haenlein, M.: Users of the world, unite! The challenges and opportunities of social media. Bus. Horiz. **53**, 59–68 (2010)

Smadja, F.: Mixing financial, social and fun incentives for social voting. In: Proceedings of the First International Workshop on Motivation and Incentives on the Web (in the 18th International WWW Conference). Madrid (2009)

O'Reilly, T.: What is Web 2.0, 30 September 2010. http://www.oreilly.com/pub/a/web2/archive/what-is-web-20.html

http://android.app-liv.jp/hobbies/traveling/0738/

Evaluation of Information Presentation with Smartphone at History Museum by Eye Tracking

Honami Take and Kiyoko Yokoyama[(✉)]

Graduate School of Design and Architecture,
Nagoya City University, Nagoya, Japan
yokoyama@sda.nagoya-cu.ac.jp

Abstract. Our aim in this study was to evaluate the effect of information presented via smartphones on the behavior of visitors to a history museum and to propose appropriate website content for use with smartphones. We used eye-tracking data to analyze the behaviors of visitors. Of the 18 study participants, six were male and twelve were female. The participants wore head-mounted Eyemark Recorders (EMR-9, NAC Image Technology, Inc.) to view the exhibit. We recorded eye-tracking data for about an hour of the subjects' whole viewing time. The website content of the smartphones provided a series of four exhibit materials from which participants could obtain information. In the first part of the experiment, the participants viewed these four materials for about 10 min. Then, they viewed about a thousand exhibit materials at their own pace. The viewing times ranged from about 40 to 60 min. We analyzed the eye-tracking data from three perspectives: (1) object gaze time, (2) whether or not the participant was using the smartphone, and (3) the effect of the website content. There was no significant difference between the gaze times of exhibit materials and explanatory board with or without smartphone information presentation. This suggests the potential for smartphone information presentation in exhibits having a large amount of information to be presented as well as for exhibit materials such as those found in history museums. Based on our results, we see potential for increasing interest in material content by inducing visitors to view exhibit materials.

Keywords: QR code · NFC tag · History museum · Web content · Smartphone · Eye-tracking data · Behavior analysis of museum visitor

1 Introduction

With the ongoing development of information technology, museum exhibits now also feature displays of pictures and images on tablets or on museum materials and the presentation of interactive explanations by touch-screen technology [1]. In addition, some museums display exhibit descriptions on smartphones and at multifunctional terminals, using QR codes and IC tags as input [2]. Others utilize the latest information-expression technologies such as virtual reality, augmented reality, and projection mapping [3].

© Springer International Publishing AG 2017
C. Stephanidis (Ed.): HCII Posters 2017, Part II, CCIS 714, pp. 489–496, 2017.
DOI: 10.1007/978-3-319-58753-0_70

We have found few studies in the literature that have evaluated how these technologies affect the behavior of museum visitors. To evaluate a museum's exhibit plan, museums have long conducted analyses of visitor behavior. The general method is to analyze observations of visitor behavior, the time spent viewing exhibits, and viewing flow lines [4, 5]. The results of these analyzes are useful for planning layouts of display shelves and materials in display cases. However, they are not suitable for detailed analyses regarding which material in an exhibit case is receiving the most attention, which materials are looked at for longer periods of time, and so on. For this type of detailed analysis, tracking the gazes of visitors can be useful [6].

In this research, we analyze the effectiveness of providing explanations of displayed materials on smartphones or multifunctional terminals in changing visitor behavior in history museums. The purpose of the evaluation is to determine whether the content of the displayed explanation affects the visitors' "observing exhibit materials" behavior. Based on the results, we determine whether it is possible to promote "viewing the exhibit" actions by providing exhibit explanations on smartphones or multifunctional terminals at historical museums. Furthermore, we consider the potential of content to effectively promote "viewing the exhibit." First, we measured the gaze time of visitors standing in front of exhibits. Then we determined whether and for how long they gazed at the "smartphone," "explanatory board with text information," and "exhibit materials."

2 Experiment Outline

Of the 18 participants in our study, six were male and twelve were female. The study target exhibit was a permanent exhibit of the Nagoya City Museum which houses roughly a thousand historical items.

As shown in Fig. 1(a), while viewing the exhibit, participants wore head-mounted Eye Mark Recorders (EMR-9, NAC Image Technology, Inc.). We recorded eye-tracking data for about an hour during the participants' entire viewing time.

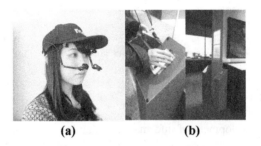

(a)   **(b)**

Fig. 1. Image of measurement

There were four exhibit materials for which participants could obtain information via the website content of their smartphones. In the first part of the experiment, the participants viewed these four materials for about 10 min. Afterwards, they viewed the entire exhibit at their own pace. The total participant viewing time was between 40 and 60 min. We described the experiment to the participants before they entered the exhibit and did not accompany the participants.

The EMR-9 device records the direction of the participant's head with a view camera, and uses an eyeball camera to record the eye position indicating where the participant is looking in the field of view, known as the eye mark. By superimposing the eye mark on the visual-field video, we can analyze the participant's line of sight. In this experiment, the view camera used a lens viewing angle of 62° and detected the eye mark with its binocular eyeball camera.

2.1 Measurement of Gaze at Exhibit While Utilizing Smartphone Information Presentation

We selected the content of four exhibit materials to be presented on smartphones and prepared one web page for each of the four exhibit materials. These four materials had a common "animal" theme. The selection of a common theme made it is easier to compare and draw interest to the exhibit materials. Figure 2 shows a view of the layout of these materials.

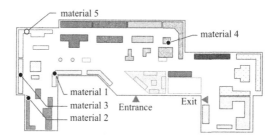

Fig. 2. Schematic map of the target museum and layout of materials 1 to 5.

We prepared two types of Web contents. The first one was "to show gaze points and induce positive viewing of the exhibit." The other was "to show only objective information such as attributes and eras, and positive viewing of the exhibit is not induced." The contents for materials 1 and 4 had the former characteristics and the contents for materials 2 and 3 had the latter characteristics.

Web content can acquire URLs from QR codes and NFC tags. We set the QR code and NFC tag on the reading table, as shown in Fig. 1(b), and located it near the exhibit materials.

The participant was instructed to view these four materials in the order of 1 to 4 while referring to information on the smartphone. In addition to the materials targeted by the Web content, the participant was free to read exhibit materials in the vicinity and any related explanatory panels.

2.2   Measurement of Gaze During Normal Viewing

After measuring participant gaze while they were using the smartphone, we measured the freely viewed gazes of participants throughout the whole exhibit. The 18 participants viewed the exhibit in about 40 to 60 min at their own paces.

For the time analysis, our target was material 5 (Fig. 2), for which it was easy to determine the participant's gaze because there was sufficient distance from the surrounding material.

3   Analysis Method

Of the 18 measurement data, 8 data included one male and seven females with high eye mark detection accuracy were selected and analyzed. Gaze time series was detected by the d-factory, which is the software for image processing of eye tracking movie. The statistical parameter calculated from the gaze time series were analyzed. Furthermore, participants' behavior analysis was performed using view camera image, while recorded the video camera wearing the participant.

3.1   Gaze Time Calculation Method

Here, we define "gaze time" as the "duration of the state of gazing to obtain detailed information." We describe the judgment criteria for this state in Sect. 3.2 below. In d-Factory videos, eye marks are superimposed on the visual-field video recorded by the EMP-9. While watching the video, we tag gaze items such as "sp (to indicate smartphone)" in every 2/60 sec frame and thereby generate a gazing time series.

3.2   Criteria for Judging the Gazing State to Obtain Detailed Information

We know that there are two search states in the gazing process, known as "diffusion search" and "specific search" [7]. In this analysis, we paid particular attention to the "state in which detailed information is obtained," which corresponds to "specific search."

When utilizing gaze detection, to identify the materials and interests toward which the participants direct their searches, we used a method for detecting the gazing and fixation points based on the characteristics of the eye movements [8].

Based on these characteristic eye movements, we acquired visual information from the point on which the line of sight rested.

Therefore, to detect "the state of obtaining detailed information," we must discriminate between the eye movement fixations.

To define the range of eye movement fixations, we use the two elements of time and distance. As a feature of the duration of eye fixation during the specific search activity of painting appreciation, the retention of a participant's gaze is reported to most often tend to have an eye fixation duration of 300 ms [7].

In this analysis, we defined the staying times of eye marks of 300 ms or more as "fixations in eye movement." In addition, to obtain detailed and clear information, we recorded participants visually examining many images from which we judged their states of gazing, and found the variations of their lines of sight to be within about 80 × 80 [pixel] on field images of 640 × 480 [pixel]. Hence, when this condition was satisfied, we defined "fixations in eye movement" to have occurred. When tagging gazed items, we used a visual observer to judge whether this occurred within about 80 × 80 [pixel] or less.

However, in this experiment, there were three gaze items categorized as "the state of obtaining detailed information." In Sect. 3.3, we describe our judgment criteria for "the state of obtaining detailed information".

3.3   Gaze Items

Figure 3 indicates a typical participant's gaze behavior, including "gazing at smartphone (sp)," "getting information from explanatory board with text information (read)," "gazing at the exhibit materials (material)," "movement of line of sight (jump)," "search for gaze target (search)," and so on. Of these, "sp," "read," and "material" are gazing objects categorized as states of obtaining detailed information.

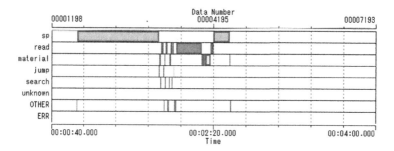

Fig. 3. Pattern diagram of viewing exhibit

The gaze item "sp" indicates the state of gazing at the smartphone, when the eye mark has remained there for more than 300 ms. "Read" indicates the state in which information is obtained from an explanation board on which there is text information, when the "lateral direction movement" of the eye mark follows a character from left to right for more than 300 ms. "Material" indicates the state of gazing at the exhibit materials when the line of sight remains within the range of 80 × 80 [pixel] at the exhibit material or its vicinity and the dwell time is 300 ms or more.

3.4   Regarding the Analysis of Participant's Behavior

The web page content for materials 1 and 4 have the characteristic "show gaze points and induce positive viewing of the exhibit." The web page content of materials 2 and 3 have the characteristic "show only objective information such as attributes and eras and no positive viewing of the exhibit is induced." Specifically, the content for material 1 states that "there is a dog's bone near the chest of the skeleton" and reference 4 states that "it is for warming the hand and there is a hole at the back." We conducted a behavior analysis in response to this material 1 text using the index "Were there any participant behaviors of gazing at the chest part of the human bones?"

With respect to material 4, we performed a behavior analysis with the index "Were there gazing behaviors from other than the front, such as going around and behind the material or looking into the back of the material?"

4   Results

We analyzed eye-tracking data from three perspectives: (1) object gaze time, (2) whether or not the smartphone was used, and (3) the effect of the website content.

4.1   Results Regarding the Proportions of Gaze Times of "Sp," "Read," "Material" of Entire Gaze Time When Viewing Exhibit with Reference to a Smartphone

From Fig. 4, we can see that for cases where participants viewed exhibits while referring to a smartphone, the proportion of time spent looking at the smartphones was the greatest at around 70%. In addition, the average percentage of gaze time for the state in which participants obtained information from the explanation board with text information was 14%, and the average of the gaze time for the state of gazing at the exhibit materials was about 14%, which is almost the same rate.

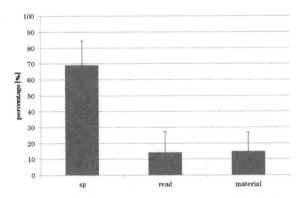

Fig. 4. Percentages of gaze times of "sp", "read", and "material" with respect to the entire gaze time for materials 1 to 4.

4.2   Comparisons of Whether or not Smartphones Were Used

Figure 5 shows a graph comparing the absolute gaze times of "read" and "material" with and without the use of a smartphone. We analyzed the difference between them

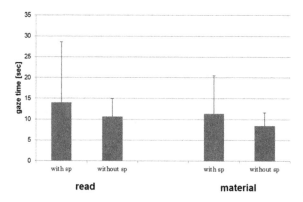

Fig. 5. Gaze time durations of "read" and "material" when using and not using smartphone

and the results indicate that the difference was not at a 5% significance level. As such, we found there to be no potential for participants not to see materials due to their viewing information while referring to a smartphone. Also, even when presenting information via a smartphone, we found panels and captions to be viewed as much as when participants had not referred to smartphones.

When comparing the gaze times spent when using and not using a smartphone, the average time when used was about 80 sec and when not used was about 20 sec. The difference between these average values is at the 5% significance level. Therefore, we can conclude that referring to smartphones while viewing exhibits provides opportunities for visitors to stop in front of exhibit materials and spend time looking at them.

4.3   Effect of Web Content on Participant's Behavior

In our behavior analysis for material 1, we used the index "Were there participant gazing behaviors at the chest part of the human bones?" In that of material 4, we used the index "Were there gazing behaviors other than at the front, such as going around and behind the material or looking into the back of the material?"

The behavioral analysis results for both materials 1 and 4 confirmed the presence of the above behaviors for more than half the participants. As such, we can confirm that information presented by the smartphone led to active appreciation behavior by the participants.

5   Conclusions

In this experiment, we found the gaze time of "sp" to constitute the longest proportion of the gaze time with respect to information presentation by smartphones when viewing the exhibit. On the other hand, there was no significant difference between the gaze times of "material" and "read" with or without smartphone information presentation. This suggests the potential for smartphone information presentation in exhibits having a large amount of information to be presented as well as for exhibit materials such as those found in history museums. Enabling the selective acquisition of information that cannot be conveyed by panels and captions utilizing terminals only, such as by smartphones, does not influence gaze behaviors toward exhibit materials and text information. Enhancement of the exhibit by promoting active information acquisition by interactive content-utilizing terminals such as smartphones can leading to increased learning. Furthermore, utilizing the learned information to induce viewing of actual exhibit materials can facilitate the appreciation of the museum experience. Although the subject of the experiment was a history museum, we believe that this result can be applied to science and natural history museums with similar characteristics that have visitor learning as a goal. However, other considerations arise with exhibits such as those in art museums that do not require a lot of information presentation in order to appreciate their worth.

In future work, we will increase the accuracy of the detection of participant interest. In this analysis, we used as criteria the judgment of participant time and distance. We did not consider the possibility that a participant may not be interested but simply gazing at a random single point. As such, when judging participant gaze, we must consider not only the time but also the eye fixation frequency and the pupillary response to improve the detection accuracy of participant interest.

References

1. Economou, M.: The evaluation of museum multimedia applications: lessons from research. Mus. Manag. Curatorship **17**(2), 173–187 (2007)
2. Di Rosa, E., Benente, F.: Excavate and learn: Enhancing visitor experience with touch and NFC. In: Digital Heritage International Congress, Accession No. 14143981 (2013)
3. Wojciechowski, R., Walczak, K., White, M., Cellary, W.: Building virtual and augmented reality museum exhibitions. In: Proceedings of Ninth International Conference on 3D Web technology, pp. 135–144 (2004)
4. Bitgood, S.: An analysis of visitor circulation: movement patterns and the general value principle. Curator Mus. J. **49**(4), 463–475 (2006)
5. Sandifer, C.: Time-based behaviors at an interactive science museum: Exploring the differences between weekday/weekend and family/nonfamily visitors. Sci. Educ. **81**(6), 689–701 (1997)
6. Eghbal-Azar, K., Widlok, T.: Potentials and limitations of mobile eye tracking in visitor studies - evidence from field research at two museum exhibitions in Germany. Soc. Sci. Comput. Rev. **31**(1), 103–118 (2013)
7. Yoshitaka, A., Nishida, K., Hirashima, T.: Detection of the state of attention based on temporal frequency of eye fixation in painting appreciation. IPSJ J. **50**, 1467–1476 (2009)
8. Sakata, M., Harada, J., Tokuka, M.: An attempt to process KANSEI information focused on eye movements in dance appreciation - analysis of their gaze using eye mark recorder - IPSJ Symposium series, pp. 167–172 (2006)

Wrist Watch Design System with Interactive Evolutionary Computation

Hiroshi Takenouchi[1]([⊠]) and Masataka Tokumaru[2]

[1] Fukuoka Institute of Technology, Fukuoka 811-0295, Japan
h-takenouchi@fit.ac.jp
[2] Kansai University, Osaka 564-8680, Japan

Abstract. We propose a wrist watch design system with Interactive Evolutionary Computation (IEC) using Winner-based Paired Comparison (WPC) method. Some companies have developed various product design customization systems. However, in most of these systems, users must choose each design component from multiple design components. Consequently, it is difficult for users to create a favored design because there are many design elements. In this study, we propose a system that can automatically generate product designs based on users' subjective evaluations. We employ an IEC method to develop the system and the WPC method to reduce user evaluation loads. The WPC method passes the winning design in the current competition to the next competition. We demonstrate the effectiveness of our system by an evaluation experiment for real users. The experimental results show that the proposed system can create designs that satisfy users in a short time.

1 Introduction

People enjoy shopping on the Internet with their computers or smart phones. Some shopping sites provide functions to customize products, such as shoes, wrist watches, shirts, and sports uniforms. Users create their favorite design by selecting a color, shape, and design elements. However, it can be difficult for users to select an appropriate design for each part of the product. Moreover, in the process of creating the products, users may not notice some good design elements.

Therefore, we use an Interactive Evolutionary Computation (IEC) method to customize products and create a product that satisfies the user. The IEC method creates products based on user subjective evaluations and Evolutionary Computation (EC) technique [1]. Previously proposed systems that apply IEC include various image processing filter designs [2], music generation [3–5], and image retrieval systems [6]. However, IEC has a problem that user evaluation loads of candidate solutions are large.

To address this problem, IEC researchers have discovered that simple evaluation processes are more effective [1]. Previously, we proposed a tournament-style evaluation to evaluate candidate solutions by paired comparison [7]. We confirmed that this tournament-style evaluation is more effective for reducing user

© Springer International Publishing AG 2017
C. Stephanidis (Ed.): HCII Posters 2017, Part II, CCIS 714, pp. 497–504, 2017.
DOI: 10.1007/978-3-319-58753-0_71

evaluation loads than a 10-stage evaluation method for music, animations, and images. However, with tournament-style evaluations, it is difficult for users to find relationships among candidate solutions between the current and previous paired comparison evaluations. Therefore, a user may not be motivated to use the system because paired comparisons where relationships are unknown must be repeated. To address this problem, it is effective to ensure that the previous competition's winning candidate solution matches new solution.

Then, we propose a Winner-based Paired Comparison (WPC) method whereby a winning candidate solution reaches the next competition. The WPC method performs paired comparisons between the winner candidate solution of the previous competition and new solution. Therefore, a user can find the relationship between competitions and will be motivated to continue the evaluations. Additionally, the number of evaluations per one generation is $(n-1)$ when the number of candidate solutions is n. We create a wrist watch design system with WPC method and verify the effectiveness of the proposed system with real users. Many people are interested in wrist watch design, and design is an important factor in the fashion of each user. The wrist watch design of our system consists of four parts: hand, dial, dial edge, and strap. We employ a Genetic Algorithm (GA) as the evolutionary algorithm in the IEC method. We examine the effectiveness of the proposed system for real users relative to satisfaction level for the generated design, usability, and evaluation time.

2   Proposed System

2.1   Winner Based Paired Comparison Method

Figure 1 shows the schematic of the proposed system. First, the system randomly generates initial candidate solutions and presents them to the user. The user evaluates the presented candidate solutions with the WPC method. When the user has evaluated all candidate solutions, the system generates new solutions with a GA operation and presents new candidates to the user. The system repeats these operations and creates objects that user can satisfy.

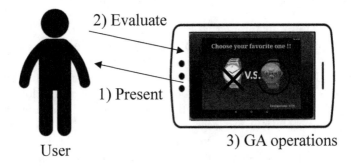

Fig. 1. Outline of the proposed system

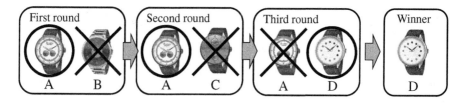

Fig. 2. Candidate solution evaluation method of WPC

Figure 2 shows candidate solution evaluation method of WPC. First, WPC assigns an evaluation value of 1 to all generated candidate solutions. Then, the system generates a pair of candidate solutions randomly and presents it to the user for evaluation. When the user selects their favorite candidate, the WPC method adds the evaluation value of the losing candidate solution to the evaluation value of the winning candidate solution. In Fig. 2, as A wins the first round, WPC adds the evaluation value of B to the evaluation value of A. Then, the evaluation value of A is 2. A also wins in the second round; thus, the WPC adds the evaluation value of C to evaluation value of A. Then, evaluation value of A is 3. Since D wins in the third round, the WPC adds the evaluation value of A to the evaluation value of D. Thus, the evaluation value of D is 4. Finally, the evaluation values of each candidate solution are $A = 3, B = 1, C = 1$, and $D = 4$. The proposed system uses these evaluation values for the GA operations.

2.2   Evaluation Interface

Figure 3 shows evaluation interfaces of the proposed system. We create the proposed system as an Android application. When the user starts the application, the application shows the start interface (Fig. 3(a)). If the user taps the start interface, the application shows the evaluation interface (Fig. 3(b)). Here, the user evaluates two designs. The winning candidate solution is passed to the next competition. The user can confirm the number of the current evaluation by the number in the lower-right of the interface. When the user completes the evaluations, the application shows the created best design (Fig. 3(c)). If the user taps the "Good bye!!" button, the application is closed.

2.3   Wrist Watch Design

Figure 4 shows the gene coding of the wrist watch design. The wrist watch design consists of four parts: hand, dial, dial edge, and strap. Each part has eight or sixteen designs, which are expressed by 3 or 4 bits. Then, the system can create 16,384 designs because the gene length is 14 bits. Figure 5 shows the design elements of the wrist watch design. We determined the bit patterns of each design part by considering the similarity between the appearance of each design part and bit pattern.

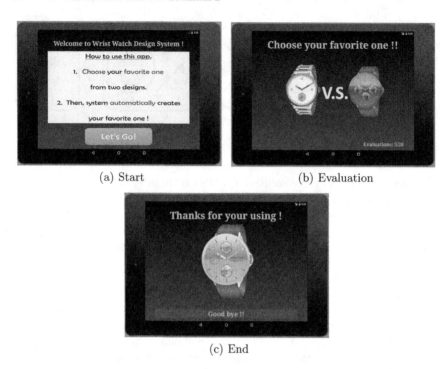

(a) Start   (b) Evaluation

(c) End

Fig. 3. Evaluation interfaces of the proposed system

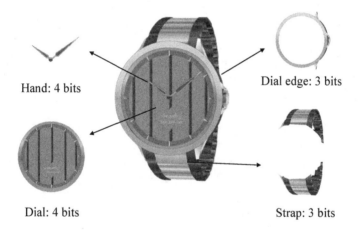

Hand: 4 bits   Dial edge: 3 bits

Dial: 4 bits   Strap: 3 bits

Fig. 4. Gene coding of wrist watch design

3   Evaluation Experiments

3.1   Outline of the Experiment

Here, we investigate the effectiveness of the proposed system for real users using
the wrist watch design system. Twenty subjects (twelve men and eight women)

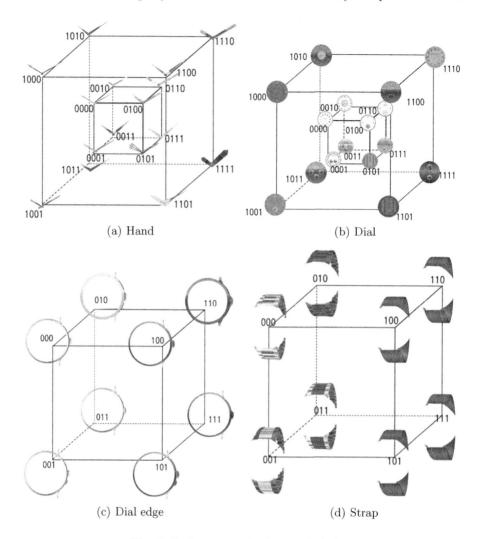

(a) Hand

(b) Dial

(c) Dial edge

(d) Strap

Fig. 5. Design parts of wrist watch design

in their twenties participate in the evaluation experiment. The men subjects used the proposed system based on the concept that customers will select the wrist watch design that they want to wear to enjoy fashion. The women subjects used the proposed system based on the concept that they want men of a friend to wear.

Table 1 shows the experimental parameters. We set the number of generations and candidate solutions to 10 and 8; thus the subjects evaluated seven paired comparisons per generation and 70 paired comparisons for all generations. The mutation operation flips each gene locus without the current elite candidate solution according to a predetermined mutation rate. We set the mutation rate to

Table 1. Experimental parameters

Gene row	Bit pattern
Gene length	14 bits
Generations	10
Candidate solutions	8
Selection	Roulette selection + Elite preservation
Crossover	Multiple points crossover
Mutation rate	20%

20%. After the experiment, the subjects evaluated satisfaction level for the generated design and the usability of the proposed system in a five-stage evaluation.

3.2   Experimental Results

Figure 6 shows the satisfaction level for the generated designs. More than half of all subjects assigned a value of greater than 4 to the generated design. The average satisfaction level was 4.15. Therefore, we confirmed that the proposed system can create designs that satisfied the subjects.

Figure 7 shows the usability of the proposed system. More than half of all subjects assigned a value of greater than 4 for the usability. The average usability was 3.75. Therefore, we confirmed that the proposed system can be used easily and can create designs that satisfied the subjects. However, 35% of all subjects assigned a value of less than 3 for usability. They commented that they wanted response visual effects when using the application because they may not understand which design has been selected.

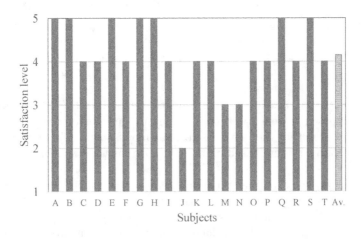

Fig. 6. Satisfaction level for the generated design

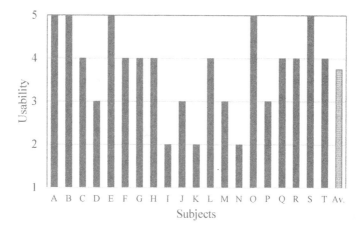

Fig. 7. Usability for the proposed system

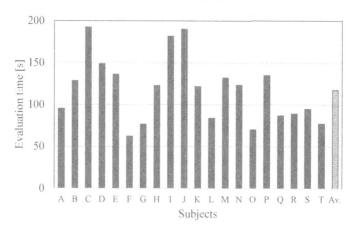

Fig. 8. Evaluation time for the proposed system

Figure 8 shows the evaluation time for the proposed system. The longest (shortest) evaluation time was three minutes and thirty-one seconds (one minute and four seconds). The average evaluation time was two minutes and thirteen seconds. More than 85% of all subjects finished evaluating the designs because the proposed system employs paired comparisons as a simple evaluation interface.

From the experimental results, we confirmed that the proposed system can create a wrist watch design that can satisfy the user without increasing user evaluation loads. Therefore, the proposed method is effective at creating wrist watch designs in a simple manner.

4   Conclusions

We have proposed a wrist watch design system with an IEC method that employs the WPC method. We performed an evaluation experiment with real users to verify the effectiveness of the proposed system. The experimental results showed that the proposed system can create wrist watch designs that satisfy user preference in a simple manner. In future, we will improve our system in consideration of the subjects' comments and compare the effectiveness of the proposed system to other IEC algorithms.

References

1. Takagi, H.: Interactive evolutionary computation: fusion of the capabilities of EC optimization and human evaluation. Proc. IEEE **89**(9), 1275–1296 (2001)
2. Ono, S., Maeda, H., Sakimoto, K., Nakayama, S.: User-system cooperative evolutionary computation for both quantitative and qualitative objective optimization in image processing filter design. Appl. Soft Comput. **15**, 203–218 (2014)
3. Jeong, J.H., Ahn, C.W.: Automatic evolutionary music composition based on multi-objective genetic algorithm. In: Handa, H., Ishibuchi, H., Ong, Y.-S., Tan, K.-C. (eds.) Proceedings of the 18th Asia Pacific Symposium on Intelligent and Evolutionary Systems - Volume 2. PALO, vol. 2, pp. 105–115. Springer, Cham (2015). doi:10.1007/978-3-319-13356-0_9
4. Marques, V.M., Reis, C., Machado, J.A.T.: Interactive evolutionary computation in music. In: IEEE International Conference on Systems Man and Cybernetics (SMC), pp. 3501–3507 (2010)
5. Ianigro, S., Bown, O.: Plecto: a low-level interactive genetic algorithm for the evolution of audio. In: Johnson, C., Ciesielski, V., Correia, J., Machado, P. (eds.) EvoMUSART 2016. LNCS, vol. 9596, pp. 63–78. Springer, Cham (2016). doi:10.1007/978-3-319-31008-4_5
6. Dass, M.V., Ali, M.R., Alio, M.M.: Image retrieval using interactive genetic algorithm. In: International Conference on Computational Science and Computational Intelligence (CSCI), vol. 1, pp. 215–220 (2014)
7. Takenouchi, H., Tokumaru, M., Muranaka, N.: Tournament-style evaluation using Kansei evaluation. Int. J. Affect. Eng. **12**(3), 395–407 (2013)

Towards Prediction of User Experience from Touch Interactions with Mobile Applications

Carola Trahms[✉], Sebastian Möller, and Jan-Niklas Voigt-Antons

TU Berlin, Institute of Software Engineering and Theoretical Computer Science,
Quality and Usability Lab, Ernst-Reuter-Platz 7, 10587 Berlin, Germany
{carola.trahms,sebastian.moeller,jan-niklas.voigt-antons}@tu-berlin.de
http://www.qu.tu-berlin.de

Abstract. In this work a first attempt is made to model user experience ratings with recordings of touch interactions. To measure the user experience the AttrakDiff Mini questionnaire is used providing three quality dimensions: pragmatic quality, hedonic quality and attractiveness. The feature selection for linear models shows that it is possible to predict the pragmatic quality for a test set with an r^2 of up to 0.64. The hedonic quality and attractiveness, however, seem not to be reflected in these touch interactions in a linear way. Still, the results from this work constitute a promising direction for future research on assessing or even optimizing the user experience for apps automatically in real time.

Keywords: Touch interaction · User experience estimation · Quality estimation · Mobile applications · AttrakDiff

1 Introduction and Related Work

A satisfying user experience is one of the main objectives for any mobile application. However, assessing user experience is no trivial task at all. It depends mainly on subjective opinions, earlier experiences or preferences of the single users [6]. To this end, several questionnaires to rate the user experience or the usability of an application by real users have been created over the years, such as AttrakDiff [5], SuS [2] or UEQ [10]. Traditionally, real users are asked to rate their experience with a system using such questionnaires, typically in laboratory test situations. This can be a tedious and expensive procedure. Thus, in recent years several approaches have been developed to formally describe and predict user behavior and ratings for a given system without having to ask real users [3,9,11]. It is, however, not an easy task either, to model user behavior reliably. There is always the challenge of capturing cultural, gender or even only dexterity differences in the ratings of the users.

In recent years touch interface devices such as smartphones and tablets found a wide distribution in all parts of the world. Most recently it has been shown that it is possible to predict the emotional state of users by analyzing their touch interaction [12]. These findings indicate that touch interaction seems to be a

C. Stephanidis (Ed.): HCII Posters 2017, Part II, CCIS 714, pp. 505–512, 2017.
DOI: 10.1007/978-3-319-58753-0_72

much more intuitive interaction modality than the previous examined desktop point-and-click interaction [7].

In this work we propose a combination of both the above approaches: Using the ratings from the AttrakDiff Mini questionnaire [4] and real user's touch interaction traces to train a model that can predict the user experience ratings. The AttrakDiff Mini questionnare yields three quality dimensions: pragmatic quality (PQ), hedonic quality (HQ) and attractiveness (ATT). The pragmatic quality is connected to the usability of the application and gives insight in whether the application's interface is suited to fulfill a task. The hedonic quality describes whether the user felt that his or her individual needs (identification or stimulation) were met by the application. Attractiveness is a synthesis of PQ and HQ. We expect that at least the pragmatic quality aspects of user experience should be predictable from touch interactions as touches are a direct consequence of how easy an application is to use.

2   Methods

As a first step towards predicting user experience ratings from touch interactions, a study with 31 test participants was conducted. The test participants were 16 females (15 right-handed, 1 left-handed) and 15 males (all right-handed). The test participants were asked to use a mobile application and rate it. To this end, we used the AttrakDiff Mini questionnaire [4]. It has only 10 items und such is more likely to yield a high quality on repeated subjective measures.

The mobile application used in this study [1] provides a tracking framework that allows to log interactions with the application. Two games were presented to the test participants through the mobile application: *Spell* and *Quiz*. We chose games to get meaningful contributions from functional as well as non-functional aspects of user experience. In *Spell* a word of varying length needs to be spelled. The letters are spread over the screen and the user has to drag them to target tiles in the correct order. In *Quiz* questions are asked and four possible answers are provided. The user chooses between them by tapping on one of them.

These two games provide solely single-touch interactions. In *Spell* mainly swipe interactions are performed while spelling a word by dragging and dropping the letters. This will be referred to as *drag and drop interaction*. In *Quiz* mainly taps were performed while answering questions in the quiz game by tapping on the answers. This will be referred to as *point and tap interaction*. To cover a variety of user experiences and corresponding ratings three versions of the app were presented: *Normal* (the app was presented as it was originally intended to work and look like), *TinyIcons* (the app's look and control was degraded by providing too small control elements) and *Freezing* (the app's response time was slowed down with delayed interaction feedback).

This resulted in six different test conditions for the study: (1) *Quiz-Normal*, (2) *Quiz-Freezing*, (3) *Quiz-TinyIcons*, (4) *Spell-Normal*, (5) *Spell-Freezing* and (6) *Spell-TinyIcons*. These six conditions were presented to each test participant in two sets each containing only one game. In each set all three degradation versions were randomly presented and rated twice resulting in six sessions per set. Each of these sessions lasted two minutes. Between the sets a five minutes break was granted. The starting game was alternated between all test participants. This resulted in 372 ratings for each quality dimension in total.

To be able to extract features, the interaction intervals within a session were subdivided into tasks and interactions. A task consists of choosing the correct answer or dragging the correct letter to the target tile. One task can be composed of several interactions such as choosing any answer or moving any letter anywhere but the correct target tile.

The features that were chosen to be extracted from the tracking can be grouped into touch counts, touch measures and performance related features. The touch counts features are counts of number of times the screen was touched, a control element was missed or hit during an interaction, a task or a session. The touch measures are calculated from the positions and timestamps of the tracking points, such as swipe length and speed, duration of a single touch, interaction or task, duration between two touches or the distance between a touch and the center of a control element. The performance related features are defined by the task logic and these are number of correct answers and number of completed tasks per session. The latter two feature types were aggregated for each session by calculating descriptive statistics on them. This resulted in 107 features in total for the modeling of AttrakDiff's quality dimensions.

A closer look at the data revealed that for the condition *Freezing* some touches were lost for the first 20 test participants. Thus, in the analysis, we will concentrate on predicting the quality dimensions on the data containing only the conditions *Normal* and *TinyIcons*.

As a first step, appropriate features for the linear regression model need to be selected. This is done with forward selection [8], which starts with one feature and successively adds more features that provide the best *residual sum of squares* (RSS). To measure the goodness of the linear models using different numbers of features, adjusted r^2 and the *Bayesian information criterion* (BIC) were used. The adjusted r^2 relates to the fraction of the data's variance that is explained by the linear model (r^2), but takes the number of features selected for the model into account. It punishes overfitting using too many features. The BIC is another measure that penalizes too many features in the model. In model selection, a model with high adjusted r^2 and low BIC is preferred. An additional information on the expected prediction performance of a linear model is given by the *residual standard error* (RSE). It gives insight into how much the real outcomes deviate in average from the regression line of the model. The quality dimension ratings range from 1 to 7, so a RSE at approximately 1 or below should be sufficient to estimate a user rating.

After analyzing the whole data set, the prediction performance of the linear models containing different numbers of features were tested. To this end, the data set was divided into a training and test set at a ratio of two thirds to one third. The feature extraction was done on the training set and the best trained model was evaluated using the *mean squared error* (MSE) on the test set. The

MSE is the average deviation of the outcomes predicted by the model and the real outcomes from the test set. Following the reasoning for the RSE, a value of approximately 1 indicates a good performance for the MSE as well.

3   Results

The top of Fig. 1 shows the different ratings for the quality dimensions pragmatic quality (PQ), hedonic quality (HQ) and attractiveness (ATT) for the conditions *Normal* and *TinyIcons* for both games and *Spell* and *Quiz* separately. The normal versions of the apps were rated better and with less variation than the diminished versions in all three dimensions. The small icons lessened the ratings of all three quality dimensions in *Spell* (drag and drop interaction). For *Quiz* (point and tap interaction) only the ratings for the attractiveness are especially distinct.

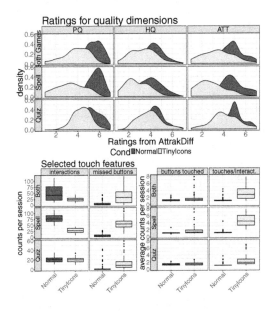

Fig. 1. Top: distribution of the ratings for pragmatic quality (PQ), hedonic quality (HQ) and attractiveness (ATT) for the conditions Normal and TinyIcons. The first row shows the ratings for both games, the second for Spell and the last for Quiz. Bottom: exemplary features that were extracted from the touch interaction tracking.

The extracted touch interaction features differ as well for the two app versions. This is shown in the bottom of Fig. 1 for four exemplary features. The number of interactions performed in one session is higher for the undisturbed versions while the number of missed control elements is higher for too small

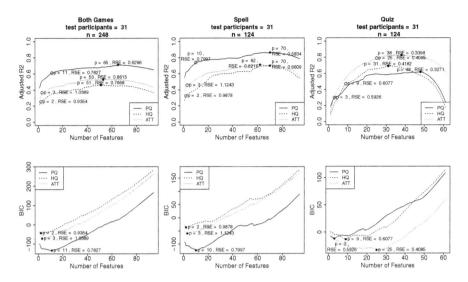

Fig. 2. First row: the adjusted r^2 for linear regressions against the number of selected features for pragmatic quality (PQ), hedonic quality (HQ) and attractiveness (ATT). The first column shows results for both games combined, the second for Spell and the last for Quiz. Second row: the Bayesian information criterion (BIC) for the three quality dimensions. The black dots indicate the optimal number of features selected and the resulting RSE. The empty circles in the upper plots indicate the corresponding adjusted r^2 for the number of features selected by minimizing the BIC.

control elements. The number of control elements that were touched per interaction in average per session do not differ very much. The touches per interaction, however, are higher for the diminished condition.

The findings presented in Fig. 1 suggest indeed that it should be possible to predict the quality ratings from the touch interactions. Figure 2 shows the results from the feature selection for linear regression models.

In the upper row the adjusted r^2 values for PQ, HQ and ATT are plotted against the number of features used for the linear model. The black dots indicate the number of features (p) that lead to a maximum for the adjusted r^2 and the residual standard error (RSE) for the corresponding model. The number of features that are selected maximizing the adjusted r^2 is very high (between 31 and 70 features on 124 and 248 data points). This could lead to an overfitting of the data. Thus, to determine a smaller number of features, the Bayesian information criterion (BIC) was minimized. As the lower row of Fig. 2 shows, the minima of the BIC indicate much less features for the models while still having an acceptable RSE between 0.41 and 1.12. The empty circles in the upper plots indicate the corresponding adjusted r^2 for the number of features selected by minimizing the BIC. It can be seen that the adjusted r^2 is still quite high as the adjusted r^2 is flattening at that point such that the gain in adjusted r^2 is not big from this point on compared to the danger of overfitting by adding more and more features.

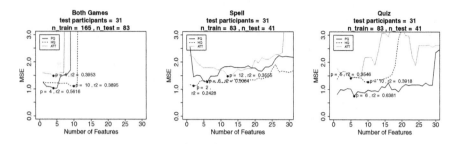

Fig. 3. Mean squared error (MSE) for test outcomes predicted by a model trained on training data. The first column shows results for both games combined, the second for Spell and the last for Quiz.

Overall, it can be seen that for *Spell* and both games combined the pragmatic quality can be modeled best. For *Quiz* the attractiveness is modeled best. To get an impression on whether the prediction performance can be generalized, the data set was split into a training and a test set. Figure 3 shows the mean squared errors (MSE) for the prediction of test outcomes from models trained with different numbers of features. The smallest MSE indicates the best model. This approach, too, suggests a small set of features for prediction for all three quality dimensions. The black dots indicate the best model and the fraction of variance of the test data that is explained by the trained model, r^2. For HQ and ATT it is very low - about 0.4 and lower - for all apps. For PQ, however, it is between 0.51 and 0.64.

4 Discussion

The ratings for *Quiz* (Fig. 1, top) indicate that diminishing an interface that is mainly used for pointing and tapping with much too small control elements reduces the attractiveness, but it does not influence the mean values of the pragmatic or hedonic quality ratings much. This could lead to the conclusion that the small control elements do not reduce the pragmatic quality of a point and tap game, but only its attractiveness, e.g. through reduced readability. For a drag and drop game (e.g., *Spell*) this disruption reduces the pragmatic quality as it is much harder to perform a task.

To verify this, the results from the *Freezing* condition should be viewed at least for the last 10 test participants where the recording worked.

The linear models trained on the *Quiz* data yield the highest values of the adjusted r^2 for attractiveness (Fig. 2) while on the other data sets the pragmatic quality is modeled best. This, too, could be explained by the differences in the ratings from Fig. 1. Looking at the prediction performance on a new data set (Fig. 3), however, only the variance in the pragmatic quality ratings can be predicted to a satisfying fraction, $r^2 = 0.64$ and an MSE of below 1. This tendency can also be seen for *Spell* and both games combined. Whether this is due to the model simply guessing between the highest peaks of the rating's distributions

(Fig. 1) or that the touch features used in this work can be used to predict pragmatic quality needs to be examined further. These features, however, seem not to be suited to model hedonic quality and thus, attractiveness. It will be interesting to define and extract further touch features from the recorded interactions that might lead to a better model of hedonic quality and attractiveness. The linear regressions for both games seem to "follow" the outcomes for the linear regressions for the spell game. This could mean that the features predicting best for *Spell* also predict well for *Quiz*.

The features that actually *were* selected for the different models presented above were quite different. It was not possible to find any features that seemed more connected to predicting especially PQ, HQ or ATT. However, there were tendencies to which features seem to be more connected to a certain quality dimension, such as the number of interactions per session known from Fig. 1 (bottom, first column), which counts how often the user had to interact with the system until a task was completed seems more connected to pragmatic quality. The number of missed control elements (bottom, column 2) seems to be slightly more connected to the attractiveness. The average number of control elements touched per task (bottom, column 3) are more relevant to hedonic quality and attractiveness and finally the average number of interactions per session (bottom, column 4) seems to be connected to all three quality dimensions.

5   Conclusion and Outlook

This work demonstrated that it might be possible to assess the pragmatic quality of a user interface degraded by too small control elements from the recorded touch behavior of the users. It yielded a r^2 of up to 0.64. It also showed that the user experience of different interaction methods are more (drag and drop) or less (point and tap) sensible to small control elements.

The results presented in this work indicate an interesting direction for future research. They strengthen the hypothesis that it is possible to predict subjective opinions from user touch interaction. It is, however, subject to future research to determine which kind of disruption of a user interface influences which kind of interaction methods. It was found that for a point and tap interaction (*Quiz*) the small control elements influence the attractiveness dimension. For a drag and drop interaction (*Spell*) it influences all quality dimensions. Another future research question is which features can reflect this rating differences best in the predictions. As shown in Fig. 3, the features selected for this work have a good performance for predicting the pragmatic quality for both interaction methods. They perform poorly on predicting the other dimensions. The range of the ratings, however, was limited and their distribution peaked at similar ratings. Further research should strife to collect more uniformly distributed user ratings.

To enhance the prediction performance for the quality ratings, other prediction methods, such as non-linear regressions, neural networks or support vector machine regression could be applied.

Still, it should be addressed which features are good predictors for hedonic quality and attractiveness.

References

1. Antons, J.N., O'Sullivan, J., Arndt, S., Gellert, P., Nordheim, J., Mller, S., Kuhlmey, A.: Pflege Tab: enhancing quality of life using a psychosocial internet-based intervention for residential dementia care. In: Proceedings of International Society for Research on Internet Interventions, p. 1. International Society for Research on Internet Interventions, Sanford (2016)
2. Bangor, A., Kortum, P., Miller, J.: Determining what individual SUS scores mean: adding an adjective rating scale. J. Usability Stud. 4(3), 114–123 (2009)
3. Byrne, M.D.: Computational cognitive modeling of interactive performance. In: The Oxford Handbook of Cognitive Engineering, pp. 415–423. Oxford University Press (2013)
4. Diefenbach, S., Hassenzahl, M.: Handbuch zur Fun-ni Toolbox - User Experience Evaluation auf drei Ebenen (2011). http://fun-ni.org/wp-content/uploads/Diefenbach+Hassenzahl_2010_HandbuchFun-niToolbox.pdf
5. Hassenzahl, M., Burmester, M., Koller, F.: AttrakDiff: Ein Fragebogen zur Messung wahrgenommener hedonischer und pragmatischer Qualitat. In: Szwillus, G., Ziegler, J. (eds.) Mensch & Computer 2003, pp. 187–196. Springer, Heidelberg (2003). doi:10.1007/978-3-322-80058-9_19
6. Hassenzahl, M., Tractinsky, N.: User experience a research agenda. Behav. Inf. Technol. 25(2), 91–97 (2006)
7. Holzinger, A.: Finger instead of mouse: touch screens as a means of enhancing universal access. In: Carbonell, N., Stephanidis, C. (eds.) UI4ALL 2002. LNCS, vol. 2615, pp. 387–397. Springer, Heidelberg (2003). doi:10.1007/3-540-36572-9_30
8. James, G., Witten, D., Hastie, T., Tibshirani, R.: An Introduction to Statistical Learning: With Applications in R. Springer Publishing Company, Incorporated, Heidelberg (2014)
9. Kieras, D.: Model-based evaluation. In: Human-Computer Interaction Handbook, pp. 1299–1318. Human Factors and Ergonomics, CRC Press, May 2012
10. Laugwitz, B., Held, T., Schrepp, M.: Construction and evaluation of a user experience questionnaire. In: Holzinger, A. (ed.) USAB 2008. LNCS, vol. 5298, pp. 63–76. Springer, Heidelberg (2008). doi:10.1007/978-3-540-89350-9_6
11. Quade, M.: Automation in model-based usability evaluation of adaptive user interfaces by simulating user interaction. Ph.D. thesis, TU Berlin (2015)
12. Shah, S., Teja, J.N., Bhattacharya, S.: Towards affective touch interaction: predicting mobile user emotion from finger strokes. J. Interact. Sci. 3(1), 1–15 (2015)

Research on Interactive Design of Mobile Payment Based on Embodied Cognition

Qi Wang and Zhao Hui Huang[✉]

Department of Industrial Design, Huazhong University of Science
and Technology, Office no. 403, C9 Building, 1037 Luoyu Road, Wuhan, China
573308070@qq.com, 1210796075@qq.com

Abstract. The purpose of interactive design is to achieve good usability and user experience, that is to say a good interactive design not only to help users achieve the basic operation, but also in the interactive process allows users to have a positive emotional experience. Because the usability and user experience focus on the direction is not consistent. Definition and evaluation criteria are different, which in many cases, the interaction design is difficult to meet the consistency of the two. Thus, the theory of Embodied cognition theory in psychology can provide an opportunity to establish a unified usability and user experience. Based on the current cognitive psychology of new orientation of Embodied cognitive research progress, combined with the development trend of mobile payment in recent years. The relationship between usability, user experience, and Embodied cognition is analyzed experimentally by interacting with the payment form. The discovery of usability and user experience is based on the cognitive orientation of the implicit measurement method and the traditional assessment of the design method of continuous iterative design evaluation. According to the idea of cognitive design, combined with people-centered design ideas, proposed to build a process based on specific cognitive payment form interaction. The biggest characteristic of this process is to unite the evaluation criteria of usability and user experience for the purpose of cognitive design, which lays the foundation for the establishment of systematic and scientific cognitive mobile interactive design method. Finally, our practical experiment applies the theoretical method of mobile interactive design based on cognitive knowledge and proves the availability of the method.

Keywords: Interactive design · Embodied cognition · Mobile payment · User experience · Usability assessment

1 Introduction

1.1 Hand-Held Mobile Payment Development

With the use of mobile phones as the representative of the mobile terminal more and more widely used, people in the mobile side to complete the complex payment opportunities are more and more, the payment form of the mobile side is more important than the design of the payment form at the web end. At the same time, due to the limitation of the screen size, the mobile payment form is more complicated than the

© Springer International Publishing AG 2017
C. Stephanidis (Ed.): HCII Posters 2017, Part II, CCIS 714, pp. 513–520, 2017.
DOI: 10.1007/978-3-319-58753-0_73

design of the web-side payment form. It is necessary to study the actual needs and difficulties of users when interacting and interacting with the interface design. In the process of developing software, a large amount of payment form pages did not do well in the transformation between needs and demands. The theoretical research and application of the interactive design of payment form does not keep up with the changes and development of consumer psychology and behavior. There is a lack of experience in interaction and user operation, therefore even with ultimate product functionality and visual richness, the product is still not qualified in terms of ease of use and order volume.

1.2   Forms of Interaction and Embodied Cognition Links

This article will proceed from the Embodied cognition point of view, to explore the use of people in the process of behavior and cognitive relationship. The core of Embodied cognition is the integration of perception, action and thinking process, cognitive thinking can not be separated from the sensory and behavioral processes, and behavior is the one that constitutes the understanding and cognition of the product, only from the user's needs, user-centric, through the analysis and study, improve the user experience, allowing users to use the product in the process of pleasure and value, in order to allow mobile payment really into the user's life. Embodied cognition emphasizes the importance of the body in the process of human cognition and gives the pivotal role and decisive significance of the body in the process of human cognition.

2   Analysis of User Requirements for Offline Payment Forms

The APP called "Illegal search assistant" is a necessary illegal information query tool. It helps owners check the violation record easily. To avoid overdue processing of illegal penalties caused by unnecessary losses. Payment form is the most important part in this APP, directly related to the query function behind the conversion of the order transaction is completed, so use APP as the carrier, to do research of form user requirements.

Analysis of user requirements was conducted through a questionnaire survey, understand the user distribution group, establishment of user model. First, segment the overall target market to identify the target audience, and conduct qualitative research.

User Research. In order to qualitatively study, we divided the age, professional, education, occupation, vehicle life, online proficiency and so on, and then integrated the data to find out the most closely related groups. The questionnaire was distributed in 100 cases, the age group is mainly divided between 18–25, 26–35, 36–45, 45–55, 56–65, 20 copies of each age level, 96 questionnaires and 96 valid questionnaires. According to the questionnaire results, we found that the use of specific categories of APP category of people mainly concentrated in the 26–45 year-old crowd, the age group of people using the product frequency was significantly higher than other age groups. According to the frequency of product use and related products familiarity. 67% of users have their own clear needs to pay proficiency on the Internet, They are our main target groups; About 21% of users have a certain frequency of use and to meet their use of the scene will produce a corresponding payment behavior, optimize the potential users of products that can attract them; Leaving 12% of the users are independent users, the product associated with the use of low frequency. The target age in our target group is distributed at 25–45 years of age. The target age in our target group is distributed at 25–45 years of age. According to the age distribution, the target user occupies mainly for the enterprise white-collar workers, business organizations, private owners. The user model is clear and established, 25–35 year old enterprise white collar, 36–45 year old business staff and private owners.

3 Body-Based Assessment and Research Based on Embodied Cognition

Embodied cognition theory holds that physical experience is the basis of human cognitive activity. The body schema theory studies the unconscious adaptation of body posture and body movement. Human body structure and perceived behavior will affect and shape their cognition. Hand-held mobile terminal for the user is outside the body of things, people through their own body to understand the hand-held mobile terminal, but also by it to influence and shape their own, resulting in new cognitive and emotional. Accordingly, I have done the following experiment, observe the interaction between body schema and form interface.

3.1 Evaluation of the Experiment

The main elements of the form include the label text, pop-up window and the process of three buttons, before the experiment, according to the mobile side of the form of the arrangement to establish three different elements of the model. Set up five forms of labels that are different but have the same content. The category is "Top alignment", "Right alignment", "Left alignment", "Input box alignment", "Mixed alignment" five models (as Fig. 1); Create three button prototypes (as Fig. 2), the category is "prototype of suspending the middle button", "prototype of buttons appearing at the bottom of the right", "prototype of buttons appearing at the bottom of the right". Establishment three kinds of shells prototype (as Fig. 3), "Centered modal pop-up", "top discoloration

Fig. 1. Five models

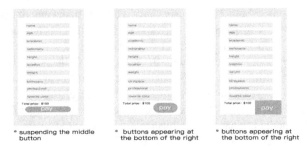

* suspending the middle   * buttons appearing at   * buttons appearing at
  button   the bottom of the right   the bottom of the right

Fig. 2. Three button prototypes

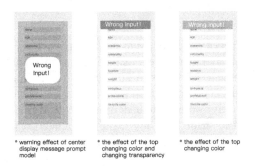

* warning effect of center   * the effect of the top   * the effect of the top
  display message prompt   changing color and   changing color
  model   changing transparency

Fig. 3. Three kinds of shells prototype

pop", "top discoloration and transparency pop". According to the experimental data collection comparison, to find the relationship between Embodied cognition and form interaction.

1. Number of tests: 30
2. Personnel requirements:

- Owners of vehicles with private owners, corporate white-collar workers and staff
- Age between 25–25 years old
- Users who have had access to the experience of illegal operations, including those who have experience with others and those who have no fee experience.

3. Test method:

- The first part of the test fill out the form, five form prototypes appear in turn;
- The second part of the test button click, the three button prototype in turn;
- The third part of the test window message, three kinds of pop-up prototype in turn;
- Record the time taken by each prototype to complete the steps and user steps to interact with the prototype.

3.2   User Interviews and Questionnaires

The interview was conducted on five prototype prototypes, three button prototypes, and three pop-up prototypes. The author creates a questionnaire based on the steps of the user's operation and collects the data for statistics.

3.3   Data Collection and Analysis

Test Part. The first part of the test length data shows operation part, the longest time consuming of adjusted data is 01:11. 45, which is form model aligned with the label entry box. The shortest is 00:55. 71, which is form model top-aligned with label. The reverse order of the reverse type is the most serious when the user enters the in-put box alignment and mixes the alignment form, the number of non - continuous fillings up to 4 times and 2 times. Test the first part of the synthesis of two indicators to give users a clear view of the line and efficient filling experience is mainly the top alignment and right-aligned label form prototype.

The second part, the longest time consuming is 00:01. 51, which is prototype of suspending the middle button. The shortest is 00:00. 37, which is prototype of buttons appearing at the bottom of the right. Invalid clicks of suspending the middle button is the most which up to 2 times. The third button–prototype of buttons appearing at the bottom of the right is the shortest time-consuming and the most precise.

The third part, the longest time-consuming of pop-up box is 00:03. 13. this model of pop-up box is top discoloration message. Middled modelized window consumes the shortest time—00:00. 81.

Interview and Questionnaires. In the course of interview and questionnaires, according to Interview information and questionnaire data, we have the following findings:

In the first test part, testers show satisfaction with the indicators are relatively high of the left alignment label model. 63% of the testers considers the longest time-consuming part is top alignment model. Testers think the form information is more than others (in fact, the content is the same, just the labels appear in different order). 53% of the test considers that right-aligned prototype is the most uncomfortable arrangement of the vision. 56% of the testers considers that input box label model repeat the highest number of clicks. Most of testers think that the label content will disappear to increase the memory burden after clicking on the input box. The testers mentions less of the description of mixed label model.

In the second test part, 56% of the testers think that suspending the middle button is the most usable. The given reason is more recognizable. 26% of the testers suggest that buttons full appearing at the bottom of the right is easier click. Few testers refer to the second button prototype.

In the third test part, 76% of the testers think warning effect of center display message prompt model is strongest. But most of them suggest that model presentation

Q. Wang and Z.H. Huang

will make people do not know how to close the tips and believe that the interface jumps mistakenly. 16% of the testers think that the effect of the top changing color and changing transparency is strong. 7% of the testers think that the effect of the top changing color is strong. In the course of interview, one of the testers indicates that he found the prompt message by looking for tips in the test of only color changing on the top. after further inquiries, we recognized that this tester is hypochromatopsia who can not distinguish similar colors.

Data Comparison. By comparing the two parts of the data, we find that most of the two parts of the data is consistent, but also a small part of the difference.

In the first part of the test data, testers' cognition about "aligned label entry box form model" are basically same in the interview and after interview, reflecting the problem of poor availability. The top-aligned label model is quite different which is the least one in the test, But because of its label arrangement led to the form is too long, resulting in the examination of the differences in testers' judges. Reverse to fill the situation is more serious in mixed alignment form, and users haven't realized the problem about complex browsing line reflected in the test.

In the second part of the test data, prototype of button suspended in the middle which is the most time-consuming and invalid clicks in the test is the most usable button in questionnaires. The ease of use reflected from actual operation and subjective feedback have a big difference.

In the third part of the test data, feedback data in the test and after the test are basically same. But feedback data from the second and third model which just differ from transparency have a difference. We also find the existence of hypochromatopsia in qualified test crowd during the latter part of the interview. Distinguishing these groups in prototype will make it more usable, and this is what we haven't take into consideration before test.

Summary. According to a comparative analysis of the data before and after the test, we discover that using implicit measurement method based on embodied cognition to assess increased reliability of design evaluation. Traditional design evaluation methods such as Observation, interview, copywriting, heuristic evaluation, usability test, questionnaire survey, card collection, and etc., can only assess the explicit behavior based on consciousness and hardly touch the embodied cognition in the interaction process between user and system. embodied cognition evaluates cognition behind behaviors by implicit measurement method, and explore the users' embodied cognition processing process. Comparing with traditional explicit behavior measurement, it increased reliability of design evaluation and provided an new interactive design process from user research to embodied test to awareness - based explicit assessment. The new interactive design process of payment form based on embodied cognition increased availability of mobile payment forms.

4   Optimization and Evaluation on Interactive Design of Mobile Payment Based on Embodied Cognition

Based on the cognitive-based implicit test combined with traditional knowledge based explicit behavioral data analysis mentioned above, the form tag is positioned and sort as "left alignment, supplemented by mixed arrangement", the process button is selected as "bottom right button", and message prompt mode is selected as "center dialog box".

4.1   Optimization Design

We have evaluated the original form interaction based on the above-mentioned cognitive approach, applied new analysis on the comparison of data and information, improved the way of interaction for different scenarios, also combined with the above test on the mobile payment form positioning thinking, and then deigned a new form of interaction.

4.2   Experiment Evaluation

Re-evaluate the new form with a method based on cognitive method of implicit measurement and traditional assessment design, combined with the two assessments, information for pre-test and post-test feedback is collected to visualize the integration. Re-compare the original form interface and optimize the page information data, we have clearly found that iterative design optimization of the form through the cognitive-based interactive design process, two assessments of availability data and information, significantly has more positive response than the original interface.

5   Conclusion

Overall, the cognitive and interactive cognitive design theory of the unified usability and user experience evaluation criteria provide a new direction for the interactive design of the system to establish the scientific theory and methods. In any one of a individual-centered interactive design process, design evaluation is the most significant element. In the past, usability and user experience was examined through measuring user's explicit behavior, thus often lead to inconsistencies and even contradictory conflict between multiple evaluation criteria.

Based on the theory of cognitive design, our paper puts forward the evaluation process of comprehensive evaluation standard with explicit index and explicit consciousness for users, we then accomplished and set standards to implement the harmonization of usability and user experience evaluation, and then build upon this core element to create a specific cognitive interaction design process. Finally, improve the design process through the mobile side of the illegal query payment interface, through a iterative design process for comprehensive evaluation of hand movement trajectory data and user's explicit awareness data. Effectively, not only improve the availability of mobile payment forms and provide a more objective basis for judgments on its availability, but also brought a new vision to the payment form of interactive design research, which makes the validity of the theory and method of cognitive design.

In the future, we will also use the theory and method of cognitive interaction design to more applications, and strive to achieve continuous improvement and development in real practice.

References

1. Preece, J., Rogers, Y., Sharp, H.: Interaction Design Beyond Human Computer Interaction. Wiley, New York (2002)
2. ISO: Guidance on usability: ISO FDIS 9241211 [S]. [S. l.]: ISO (1997)
3. Nielsen, J.: Usability Engineering. Academic Press, Boston (1993)
4. Sloman, S.A.: The empirical case for two systems of reasoning. Psychol. Bull. **119**, 3–22 (1996)
5. Kahneman, D.: A perspective on judgment and choice: mapping bounded rationality. Am. Psychol. **58**, 697–720 (2003)
6. Dijksterhuis, A., Nordgren, L.: A theory of unconscious thought. Perspect. Psychol. Sci. **1**, 95–109 (2006)
7. Evans, J.S.: In two minds: dual-process account of reasoning. Trends Cogn. Sci. **7**, 454–459 (2003)
8. Goel, V., Dolan, R.J.: Explaining modulation of reasoning by belief. Cognition **87**, 11–22 (2003)
9. Nessler, D., Mecklinger, A., Penney, T.B.: Perceptual fluency, semantic familiarity and recognition-related familiarity: an electrophysiological exploration. Cogn. Brain. Res. **22**, 265–288 (2005)
10. Wang, X.T.: Emotions within reason: resolving conflicts in risk preference. Cogn. Emot. **20**, 1132–1152 (2006)
11. Berlin, H.A.: The neural basis of the dynamic unconscious. Neuropsychoanalysis **13**, 5–31 (2011)
12. Nick, B., Gellatly, A.: Cognitive Psychology. Oxford University Press, Oxford (2012)

Visual Design and Visualization

Exploring of the Barrier-Free Design for Visual Impairment in Graphical User Interface Design

Yilin Chai and Ying Cao[(⊠)]

Huazhong University of Science and Technology,
Wuhan, People's Republic of China
150110363@qq.com

Abstract. According to the China Disabled Persons' Federation statistics, by 2015 China's low vision and the number of blind people had up to 31.475 million; and color blindness in China is about 5.5% to 9%. While the red-green blind population accounts for about 8.5% of the global population. Of which 6% of the population suffered from color weak, and about 2% of the population is color blindness. Visually impaired people can not compete with ordinary people in the living environment of information access. In this situation, as the rapid expansion of network information, visual barriers are more hard to access to information from the network and had some obstacles that the amount of information obtained they get is more limited than before compared with present ordinary people. The mainly way people who suffer from visual impairment cognitive world are tactile, auditory, olfactory, taste, a certain vision of the obstacles may be the color of cognitive problems. That means when those people browsing the graphical interface they may have some problems if the design not humane enough.

Graphical User Interface is a main way to expression in the human-computer interaction interface, but its main form of interaction is visual. Even ordinary people in daily life in case of excessive information will encounter problems, which will lead to inconvenience when visually impaired people accepted Information in the Graphical User Interface such as machine operation interface. For example, people with color blindness, green blindness is the most common form of color blindness, green blind and red blind can not see what we call the red line and green line of color. Blue blindness do not see the colors we call blue line and yellow line because of the lack of cone cells. If designers use these kinds of colors, then in the eyes of these special people, there will be a lot of mistakes, which will badly affect the user experience. As a result, although the rapid development of the network and the popularity of intelligent devices had opened a new door for these people, because of such kind of imperfect graphical user interface design for those special people, that can not play a key role.

Actually in the last century, the concept of barrier-free design has been put forward by the United Nations in order to achieve the concept of equality for all that people who have trouble visually in society can eliminate obstacles and lead to a cheerful life. After that, there are many people had made efforts in some fields, for instance, product design, architectural design, interior design and other aspects of the design has a more robust design specifications. In the design of virtual products, also has progress. However, over the years the domestic

© Springer International Publishing AG 2017
C. Stephanidis (Ed.): HCII Posters 2017, Part II, CCIS 714, pp. 523–533, 2017.
DOI: 10.1007/978-3-319-58753-0_74

visual impairment of people in the improvement of quality of life has not been greatly improved, the attention of interface design for the special groups is relatively small. This requires pay more attention to barrier-free design in the Graphical User Interface. At the same time, at the international level, thanks to the introduction of the United States's Section 508, Accessibility Guidelines by W3C web-side, IOS systems and Android system, so that foreign designers in the barrier-free interface design has a more comprehensive design guidance, which are worthy of the domestic interface designers learn and assimilates.

In the first stage, the author summarizes the potential problems in the use of visual barriers and explores the need for the design of barrier-free graphical interface. The second stage is to obtain the information through the disabled. The way of analysis and interface color, the interface of information acquisition ways to study the two aspects, and finally hope to visually impaired people such as color blindness, visual disabilities can make a positive help.

Keywords: Barrier-free design · Visual impairment · Graphical User Interface design

1 Background

In this paper, we focus on the need for the graphic interface design needs of the elderly with visual impairment.

To begin with, we will provide a brief background on the paper. With the acceleration of the aging society, the proportion of the older in the social population is getting bigger and bigger, according to recent research. The world's elderly population will reach 480 million by 2050. At the same time, there are more than 400 million elderly people who are over 60 years old in China. Taking good care of the old becomes a salient society problem. And Epidemiology of people with disabilities presents that the prevalence of disability increases with age, self-care ability will decline, and a variety of disability, visual disability is the second one.

WHO has reported that almost 50% of blind patients in the world have cataract patients, and senile cataracts is among the most common types. According to the relevant survey, 41 years old to 60 years old group of people have an inherent law with age and degree of their high myopia morphological.

(1) 40 years of age are the critical age of pathological myopia changes.
(2) Myometrial changes in high myopia showed a continuous trend between 41–60 years old. It might be the result of superimposed with the body aging process, or influence by other parameters or the impact of the high incidence in the elderly.

In addition to vision disability, people will have obstacles to the daily life of color blindness; according to the China Disabled Persons' Federation, the incidence of color blindness in our country is about 5.5% to 9%. According to the random sampling which has been conducted by members of the Statistics Department from author's province, a total of 16,919 elderly people were investigated for color vision disorder, including male 13912, female 2419. The result indicates that male color blindness 86, female color blindness 12, color perception of a total of 98 people, the prevalence rate of 0.70%, male:female = 6:1.

But unfortunately, in addition to some of our community and social support, there is no corresponding policy for those huge amount of the aging of the physiological status or pathology of the elderly caused by visual impairment.

Paganini D and Mariotti SPM of the World Health Organization (WHO) published the latest estimates of global visual disability in 2010, published in the British Journal of Ophthalmology (BJO) in December 2011.

The main causes of visual impairment were uncorrected refractive error (43%), cataract (33%), glaucoma (2%), age-related macular degeneration (1%), diabetic retinopathy (1%), trachoma %), Corneal opacity (1%), can not determine the reasons for 18%. The main causes of blindness were cataract (51%), glaucoma (8%), age-related macular degeneration (5%), blindness (4%), corneal opacity (4%), uncorrected refractive error (3%), Trachoma (3%), diabetic retinopathy (1%), and the cause of uncertainty was 21%. In all blind people, 50 years old accounted for 82%.

His results show that visual impairment is still a major global public health problem, the prevalence of visual impairment between the uneven distribution of the region, but 80% of which is preventable.

In addition to visual disability, the international community has also made statistics on the color blindness group. According to Colblinder, roughly 8% of men and 0.5% of women are affected. Deuteronomy is by far the most common color vision deficiency regarding red-green color blindness. The most common three types of color blindness are occurring at nearly the same ratio and do affect about one out of 100 persons each.

2 Review

2.1 Definitions

Design for those with physical or other disabilities, involving the provision of alternative means of access to steps with ramps and lifts for those with mobility problems. It is also called universal or barrier-free design.

Barrier-free is a very informative word. Macroscopically, including the accessibility of the physical environment, accessibility of the human environment, information and communication barrier. Through the Internet to access to information has become an important part of people's daily life.

The initial barrier-free design was for the user's accessibility. As a result of the Second World War, the number of veterans and the number of disabled people increased, such people return to the community is facing greater difficulties, in order to eliminate obstacles in the lives of people with disabilities proposed a barrier-free design.

The concept of barrier-free design first appeared in the 1974 United Nations Expert Group Meeting on Barrier Free Design, the main purpose is to eliminate obstacles in the urban environment, to create an equal and harmonious social environment.

Now the barrier-free design gradually from the initial disabled to the elderly, including the elderly and the poor vulnerable groups. It's more attention is the physical and psychological needs, is for all to provide convenient, safe, equal survival and living rights.

2.2   The Efforts of Various Disciplines

Architecture. Barrier-free design is the first application in the construction of public space and other places. At present, each country has introduced barrier-free design regulations, from the city road to the indoor ground, provides a very detailed specific requirements for facilities for disabled people in public places, including specific channels, auxiliary handrails, blind road facilities, Material, size, slope. The construction sector has made great efforts in decades to improve the travel of people with disabilities.

Products. About product design, barrier-free experience gradually transferred to the universal design or inclusive design. The term "universal design" was coined by the architect Ronald L. Mace to describe the concept of designing all products and the built environment to be aesthetic and usable to the greatest extent possible by everyone, regardless of their age, ability, or status in life [1]. It is an extension of barrier-free design, a concept of standardization. In the product design of this aspect, people also summed up a set of universal design rules, which in Japan's product design in the implementation of universal design and implementation of the most prominent.

Graphic. Graphic is a huge area. It is a visual means to communicate and way to express the emotion or idea. It includes identification, publications, websites, mobile devices, and so on. With the development of the information age, people will be able to get a lot of resources to expand the horizon of thinking when stay at home. But most of the information is presented in a graphic interface that may cause distress to people with visual impairments. This makes people pay attention to the design of the graphical interface for those disables. Gradually appeared in the law, for example: the United States's Section 508, Accessibility Guidelines by W3C web-side, IOS systems and Android system. Domestic in 2008 also drafted the website design barrier-free technical requirements. In this request mainly related to the interface of the text and non-text content of the design requirements, multimedia processing, auxiliary equipment, technical requirements and so on.

About Design Guidelines. The mainstream system IOS and Android's accessibility guide, also known as the Accessibility Programming Guide. Take the barrier design guidelines published by the China Association for the Blind as an example to summarize the main contents of the accessibility guide. The guidelines required specific technical requirements for disables surf the internet. Including the perceived requirements of web content, the operational requirements of the interface components, the understandability of content, control, support for existing and future possible technical requirements. Besides, the guidelines also specifies the text color contrast of the graphic interface, and give requirement about the link, auxiliary technology, multimedia, subtitles, text, non-text content; alternative text, pure decoration, video playback, color relative brightness, brightness, contrast ratio, user agent, viewport, context-sensitive help, focus, Web section, Voice information and other aspects of the development of the corresponding requirements. These requirements can be summarized for the optimization of the user's operating habits. Users can skip the dialog box, and directly into the system, with auxiliary equipment, when the people listening to the website, if they clicked hyperlinks it will have a corresponding voice prompt. For vision barrier people, they can also adjust their own text. Barrier-free service provides "attribute" descriptions of selected messages, such as headings, pictures, buttons, so that users can quickly understand some of the functional properties of the "text". Barrier-free service can also provide overall information situation of the page, like which page is the users's in, how many elements in the pages and other information. After receiving this information, the user can form the organizational framework of the interface information in the brain. Barrier-free service needs to help users understand the functionality and structure of the entire website [2].

3 Research

The difficulty is different because vision disabled from different stages of the age has different time contact with the modern society. At present, product development for the order is still in a relatively backward stage in our country. The specific study is also focused on the theoretical level. So it's easy to find out that elderly industry in the market is in short supply. Due to lack of funds to pull the market, less than 10% of the elderly products were provided to the market. Because of low production, high prices, the elderly even don't care about these things, companies can't get enough profit lead to the industry lag. We can only see medical equipment or cell phone which is not beautiful provider on the market aimed at older people.

For the elderly, the development of elderly market, can satisfy the growing consumer demand for the elderly better, is positive to solve the problems in the elderly's life, improve the living standards of the elderly. For enterprises, it can open up new markets for enterprises to bring market opportunities, which bring economic benefits. So in this study, we chose the elderly in the visual decline and suffering from eye diseases as the object of study.

3.1 Physiological Characteristics of the Elderly

Visual is the main way for human to obtain information, the human perception system mainly constitutes in the eyes, ears, nose, skin and other sensory organs, sensory organs will get the information transmitted through the nerve signal to the brain.

In addition to human beings' 12 kinds of senses. In accordance with the principle of contact with the body, sense can divided into feeling of the outside world (including: visual sense, sense of hearing, language, semantic sense, self-consciousness, temperature perception) and the feeling about ourselves (including: taste, smell, touch, balance, sense of movement and sense of life.).

In these senses, visual, auditory and touching are the main sensory channels for people to enter outside information. In human cognition, about 80% of the information is obtained through the visual system.

Aging is the natural law of the life process of the body. Elderly people have a significant decline in the physiological function of the trend, the human body system is also accompanied by varying degrees of signs of aging. With the increase of age, the sensory capacity of the elderly is reduced, which directly affects the elderly activities and the slow response to environmental stimuli.

We use the questionnaire survey to do part of our research, and we find out:

- The elderly memory capacity declined significantly, they often forget things that the first ten minutes or twenty minutes ready to do but which was interrupted, take one elderly who is participants in our survey for example, he suggests that when a family member sent photos to their account, they need to think about it for a long time to recognize the step to open the electronic album.
- The elderly lack the motivation to learn new things, when we asked whether they are willing to try to set their own desktop layout, about 51.2% of the elderly refused.
- Ability to understand becoming lower, when we carry out the experiment, we need to explain many times the subjects for those older to understand what we want to do.

3.2   Psychological Characteristics of the Elderly

With the physiological changes, the elderly psychological changes with the age growth and physiological change. According to our survey we find that elderly become hard to accept fresh things. They began to miss the past life and time. After the loss of the original social role, they suffered a hard time to adapt to the new life, they are still eager to get social attention. While the degradation of physical function so that they began to worry about illness and death. They sometimes become pessimistic, depressed, etc., in this contradiction, the elderly suffered. During elderly, the children become busy, the days spent together become shorter, then if widowed, the negative emotion will be increasing. Alone for a long time, will lead to negative emotions, talking and activing less. Even worse, some of the elderly will be accompanied by depression, they can not judge thing properly.

3.3   The Way How Poor Vision Elderly Gets Information

In our survey, the way in which the visually impaired elderly have access to information depends mainly on five categories, as follows: (1) Electronic products such as computer, TV, mobile phone, tablet; (2) Chatting with friends during play cards to get information; (3) Reading books, newspapers; (4) Tourism; (5) Community organization activities.

3.4   Research of GUI Design for the Elderly

This section summarizes some of the interface design needs, suitable for the elderly who are suffer from reduced vision. We selected 173 adults in several community of Wuhan to conduct an inquiry into. Screening out 152 people over the age of 50.

We counted from the age of 50. Respondents' basic data illustrates that the frequency of the use of electronic products basically did not change much before the age of 70. And it is not much related to education level before this age group. The result can also confirm that visual acuity decreased with age. When it's come to the use of habits, we find that the older ones do not like typing. There are four main reasons:

- People older than 70 are less educated due to historical reasons.
- The older has slower typing speed, because the joints become inflexible.
- The higher the age, the lower the accuracy of pinyin.
- Typing habits related to career, the older was engaged in civilian is more accustomed to typing Fig. 1.

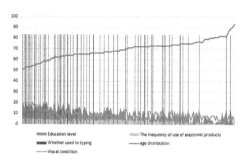

Fig. 1. Respondents' basic data

Font Size Mobile reading has slowly become one of the mainly ways for people get the most information, whether it is the network of debris information or news reports depends on words. The recognition of words becomes particularly important, for the elderly to better read the information on the graphical interface, we choose font size as an important point in our research. According to ergonomics, research data for more than 60 years old people's visual condition showed that: Vision degradation of the phenomenon began at the age of 40, 60 years of age fell more than 74% of the proportion of vision. According to domestic research, the best font size for more than 60 years old people easy to read on paper media is 15pt, followed by 12pt, according to the complexity of Chinese characters [3], the more complex the lower the word can be recognition. Based on the study, we narrowed the measurement range to 15pt to 36pt due to differences in the graphical interface and the way the paper was read. Converted to pixels is 21px–48px. According to the questionnaire, we divided 250–300 degrees of hyperopia between 65–70 years old respondents into four groups, each group of 20, no one wear corrective equipment. According to the reaction rate, the survey results as showed below Fig. 2:

Through the data analysis, we can find that in identifying the same complex Chinese characters, the recognition speed of more than 36px tends to be the same, and less than 36px, the smaller the characters the lower recognition degree.

Color. Objective conditions, from the physiological to psychological factors will affect the color of identification. We sort out the identification conditions are as follows:

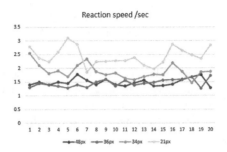

Fig. 2. Reaction speed of different font size

- High lightness is better for distinguishing.
- Lightness and Hue need great difference.
- Clean surroundings are better than a complex one.
- The size of the graphics, shape and other issues will affect the situation to identify [4].
- Natural light or artificial light environments can lead to different identification situations [4].
- Integral and orderly layout makes good discrimination.

Because the structure of the retina is very low sensitivity to blue light, only 2% light can be distinguished, we need to avoid the use of pure blue in the text, on the contrary, the blue primary color is very suitable as a background color. In addition, when design a graphic user interface, we need to avoid putting extreme saturated colors on the same screen at the same time.

Avoid using saturated colors in low-chroma. Avoid using proximity colors. Due to elderly's needs, design with high-contrast image. Thus, we designed the background color recognition experiment. Use the font size picks up from the previous experiment with better identification, through different hue of color combination. By testing the elderly for the different color combinations of text recognition rate, analyze and sort out the basic color of the interface design for the elderly Table 1 and Fig. 3.

Table 1. Experiment detail

Color combination	Black White Red Yellow Blue Green
Test text	拨号 (means dial)
Font	Round hand which can distinguish better

After color proofing, we exclude colors that may cause difficulty in resolving colors: red and blue, red and green, yellow and white, and these colors may cause trouble to make the difference Table 2 and Fig 4.

According to the statistical results, we can find that without considering about the old man's visual condition, black combine with white are always the highest degree of recognition of the color. Followed by white background with red text and black background with yellow text.

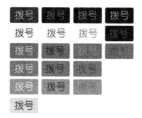

Fig. 3. Part of test picture

Table 2. Statistical results

Text color / Background color	White	Black	Red	Blue	Green	Yellow
White		152	148	122	115	
Black	144		111	8	108	137
Red	97	65				11
Blue	93	83				121
Green	85	87				128
Yellow		139	13	49	129	

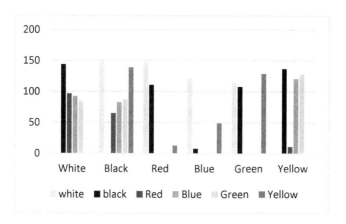

Fig. 4. Statistical results (Color figure online)

Interface Layout. By collecting a large number of elderly mobile phone, the elderly model, the layout of the elderly website, we summed up the following layout Fig. 5:

Through the questionnaire, the following statistical results are obtained Fig. 6:

We can find the 3*3 square layout has high degree of acceptance obviously.

Humanistic Care. Through interviews in the survey, we found that the elderly often encountered problems in dealing with electronic equipment at home, and did not like to

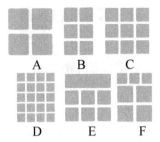

Fig. 5. Layout

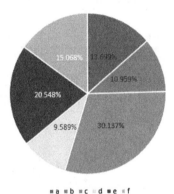

Fig. 6. Statistical results

ask their families for help because they thought they would disturb their families. According to those interviews, we summarized some experiential needs are as follows:

1: 94 of the 152 elderly people who participated in the survey did not like the shift of the desktop icon due to false touch, 30 thought it did not matter.
2: 127 people who are involved in the investigation do not like the daily reminders of mobile phone/computer garbage cleanup and software update iteration.
3: 73% of elderly people surveyed believe that the old model/simple model of the smartphone now used is not beautiful at all.

4   Conclusions

Through our questionnaires and experiments, we confirmed that the elderly will appear obvious visual impairment with age, and life has been troubled by those visual problem. We found that the lives of the elderly tend to be stable, not used to change. The main use of electronic products is the computer and television, and the younger elderly are, they spend more time with cell phones. Among them, the elderly like a fixed layout, and prefer a regular interface layout design. According to our experimental results, the interface font size is not the bigger the better, the poor vision of the elderly use orthopedic facilities for a better sight, and even didn't use the correction in the experiment can also clearly distinguish 36px size of the font. In our collected questionnaires, we can find that the higher the level of knowledge culture, the more attention to the beauty of the graphic interface. They are not satisfied with the existing mobile phone model, the general model cannot meet the vision requirements, and special mode cannot meet the aesthetic needs, it's an urgent need for designers to improve. Our experiments and surveys have made some effort for the graphical interface design, giving us the design requirements that can provide a reference to the aesthetic value of the interface for the elderly who are constantly degenerating and even the serious pathological degeneration. Which is summarized below:

1. The main way for the elderly to obtain information is now gradually changing to electronic products.
2. The font size 36px is more suitable for the elderly in the graphical interface
3. Base on the layout of the 3*3 square format is suitable for the graphical interface provided to the elderly.
4. Older people like a simple operating process, refused pop-up notice or advertising services, which makes them very uncomfortable.
5. Older people prefer a colorful combination of the graphical interface color rather than black and white because they believed that can't bring good luck. But they have the highest recognition rate of combination of black and white, followed by red text on the white background.
6. Most of the elderly believe that the graphical interface which is frequently used should not change much, which is related to the changes in the personality of the elderly.
7. Most elderly are not accustomed to typing, which is related to the age and education, the lower the level of education, the more exclusion of typing operations.

In the visually impaired population, the elderly users have an urgent need for the need for network interaction, and based on the special physiological and psychological characteristics of the elderly, the current universal interface design in the use of the elderly have produced a lot of unnecessary obstacles. With the increasing of the elderly population and the need of product development for this special group, is a vast market.

References

1. Ronald, L.: Mace on NC State University, College of Design. https://design.ncsu.edu/. Accessed 26 July 2013
2. Reed, P., Holdaway, K., Isensee, S., Buie, E., Fox, J., Williams, J., Lund, A.: User interface guidelines and standards: progress, issues, and prospects. Interact. Comput. **12**(2), 119–142 (1999). Published by Elsevier Science B.V.
3. Yang, Z.: A review of studies on text, color and layout design for the elderly. Decoration **5**, 86–87 (2012)
4. Wang, L., Sato, H., Rau, P.L.P., et al.: Chinese text spacing on mobile phones for senior citizens. Educ. Gerontol. **35**, 77–90 (2009)

Research on the Experiential Communication of Digital Humanities and Information Visualization: A Case Study of Iconography Measurement

Zhigang Chen[1](✉) and Jing Ma[2]

[1] Studio of Information and Interaction, College of Fine Arts,
Shanghai University, Shanghai 200444, People's Republic of China
410432675@qq.com
[2] Department of Landscape Design, Shanghai Xian Dai Architectural
Design Group, Shanghai, People's Republic of China

Abstract. The purpose of digital humanities and information visualization in culture heritage preservation is the inheritance of values and dissemination of culture. The introduction of digital technologies strengthened the importance of transmitting the value of heritage. This dissertation proposes applied theoretical framework for the digitization, preservation and communication of cultural heritage, from the perspective of design thinking and based on experiential communication prototyping methodology. It proposes an "Information-Value-Experience" heritage communication framework. By examining "experience as a medium" and "experience as communication," the author presents an experiential communication concept and a prototyping methodology for experiential communication of digitized cultural heritage.

This paper defines experiential communication in the context of digitization and preservation of cultural heritage as a set of communication design methods and guiding principles. Based on the analyzing the evolution of cultural heritage and of heritage preservation philosophy. It proposes the concept of a cultural heritage experience and analyzes its attributes and the process of the experiential communication of heritage. The analysis of "digital heritage" and "digitization of cultural heritage" clarified for digital humanities; the scope of technology application, the main form, and the basic process. There are four basic principles that are proposed for the process of the digitization of cultural heritage. By comparison of the communications transmission model and the rituals model clarified basic characteristics of the communication of digitized of cultural heritage. Visualization used the book Iconography Measurement to validate the application of the experiential communication prototype and visualization method. The digital and visualization of this book illustrated the value and meaning of experiential communication prototype for digital humanities.

Keywords: Digital humanities · Information visualization · Experiential communication

C. Stephanidis (Ed.): HCII Posters 2017, Part II, CCIS 714, pp. 534–542, 2017.
DOI: 10.1007/978-3-319-58753-0_75

1 Introduction: Cultural Heritage and Context

Cultural Heritage, also named as cultural capital, cultural property or cultural wealth, is the traditional culture that equipped by architectures, historical relic, historical sites and various non-materials with prominent humanity history, arts and scientific values. It can be divided into "material cultural heritage" and "non-material cultural heritage" in concept. The "material cultural heritage" is the traditional "cultural heritage". In accordance with the definition in "Convention Concerning the Protection of the World Cultural and Natural Heritage", historical relics, historical buildings, human cultural sites are included. The "non-material cultural heritage" refers to various practices, performances, presentation forms, knowledge, skills and related tools, objects, artworks and cultural places etc., which are regarded as cultural heritage by various groups, teams and sometimes individuals.

With the rapid development of society and economy, the survival and development environment of cultural heritage is increasingly severe. A large amount of cultural heritages are ruined or over explored, have vanished or close to vanishment; besides that, the social humanity environment which cultural heritage lives by also disappears and vanishes. Therefore, under the background of post-industrial era, Barbara Kirshenblatt-Gimblett (1995), American anthropologist, proposes that as a past culture production mode exists in modern time and a kind of "added-value" industry is formed through the presentation of differences between the past and the present and some local value supplementary elements of heritage. Therefore, the protection of heritage should return to the actual social environmental requirements and modern elements can be added conditionally with the insistence of tradition and the balance between different related-benefits. Originated from the concept of language discipline, context was divided into context of situation and cultural context by an anthropologist named Malinowski for the first time and consisted of three elements: cultural background, emotional scenes and time and space environment. Extending into cultural heritage area, especially the gradual process in digital technology, In the environment culture heritage is in and the crossing of human society from industrial time to information time, the connection function should be adjusted in accordance with the development of culture background, emotions and space environment etc. Therefore, with the combination of digital technology, the putting forward of the context cultural heritage is an important topic from the post industry society to information society.

2 Context Interpretation of Digital Dilemma and Construction Strategy

The development of digital technology not only provides technical means for the protection and presentation of cultural heritage, but also changes the traditional way of protecting cultural heritage, it has made indelible contributions to the conservation and inheritance of cultural heritage. However, its effectiveness is still not fully developed; it shows some shortcomings in the protection and presentation of material and non-material cultural heritage, and the dissemination of cultural information. Meanwhile, it may bring adverse effects to cultural diversity and ecological balance.

2.1 Digital Dilemma

Compared with the digital technology represented by computer and the Internet, the constitution of Cultural heritage has fundamental differences. Cultural heritage mainly comes into being, develops and spread in the form of "atom", while the digital technology is mainly based on "bits"; the conventional protection of cultural heritage does not involve the transform of "mode to state", but data collection and conversion is the first step of digital protection. The integrity and fidelity of stored information will be influenced by different storage patterns, which are mainly reflected in the following aspects:

Digital Preservation Outweighing the Intrinsic Value Heritage Protection. Digital protection came into existence to transform the material and non-material cultural heritages into digital forms that can be widely used and easily spread on computers and the Internet with the aid of technical means, so as to achieve the permanent preservation and wide dissemination of cultural heritages. However, currently the domestic digital data of cultural heritage mainly include picture, audio, video, three-dimensional data, texture data, etc. The process of digitization focuses on the recording, collection and preservation of data, and the so-called "heritage protection" is to store the data collected by computer into the hard disk, just like "specimens" to be stored in the museum. Therefore, most of the digital protection work still stuck in the data "save" stage, data are used for relevant research on heritage, but the "protection" of heritage is not yet in full swing.

Media Outweighing Content Mining. The major difference between "bit" and "atom" is that bit cannot be touched, smelled, seen or heard, it can only demonstrate its feature and function with the aid of other carriers, so digitized cultural heritage also face such problem, the characteristics of media can directly affect people's cognition on the characteristics of cultural heritage. Therefore, the ultimate goal of cultural heritage digitization is to choose the right media and restore the original cultural heritage truthfully, including the natural environment, social environment and humanistic environment.

Digital Content Becoming "Heritage". Digital technology is a multidimensional media performance means, which integrates sound, image, text, virtual reality, video animation and other performance methods. However, the replacement cycle of computer technology is very short, as described by Moore's Law that computer power would be doubled every 18 months. Therefore, with the improvement of information technology, the data derived from the digitization of present stage need be "migrated" continuously, converting into new format and replacing new storage media. In this process, the digitized cultural heritage becomes "heritage" again, sucking in the circle of ceaseless iterative update.

The "Homogenization" of Digitalized Heritages Interpretation. The protection of cultural heritage is based on the universal consensus of preserving "cultural diversity", diversity and difference precisely reflect the value of cultural heritage, its traditionality, artistry and scientificity also demonstrate that it is based on quests of originality of various nations and ethnics under the trend of globalization. However, the biggest advantage of digital technology is that it can break the constraints of time and space, and all the data are saved into different combinations of 0 and 1. The storage formats of different heritages are exactly the same, its display and transmission methods are much the same, too. Thus, "homogenization" is a serious phenomenon in the display and dissemination process of contemporary digital preservation of cultural heritage, which fails to meet the original goal of protecting cultural diversity, and is currently the plight of the digital heritage protection.

2.2   Context Interpretation and Construction Methods

Digital technology is a computer "language" of the information age. With the development of modern technology and the improvement of social and humanistic environment, it will inevitably encounter the above-mentioned "digital dilemma" when describing "cultural heritage", which represents the traditional history and culture. The discussion on the dilemma existed in the digital protection of cultural heritage is not to stop the "digitization" progress, but to avoid the bad effects rising from the technical defects of digital technology, restore the original appearance of cultural heritage more truthfully, and create a more natural experience of digital heritage. Currently, context construction is a new approach in the digital protection of heritages, using digital technology as the computer "language" of "information age", and regarding the "cultural heritage" as the target "sentence". In order to fully express the "meaning" of mass digital survival condition, and experience the cultural values behind the cultural heritage more naturally, I think we should take measures from the following aspects:

Combining Synchronic Context with Diachronic Context. Heritage is the art of time. Therefore, the historical context and realistic context of cultural heritage cannot be ignored in the process of digital expression of cultural heritage. The historical context of cultural heritage provides answers to its formation, development and decline. By restoring history, the essential connotation of cultural heritage can be found and interpreted as the focused value of art performance at later stage, reflecting the implied meaning of those "heritages" under the given historical backgrounds, rather than simply presenting the artistic level of heritages from the perspective of visual arts. Synchronic context can enable cultural heritage to find an expression method that is in line with the cognition of modern people in the realistic context, and interpret the realistic context without violating the original intention of protecting cultural heritage. This process always exists, because modern people cannot judge things if they give no consideration to their economic, social and cultural environments, and they will inevitably ignore elements beyond their perceived values in the process of interpretation. Therefore, in the process of digitization of cultural heritage, we should interpret the Synchronic context of the heritage under the premise that we have fully understood its historical context.

Combining the Virtual World with the Real World. With the development of information technology, the digitization of modern society has been gradually strengthened. Negro Ponty, a Professor from MIT, said that: We are digitized at a rapid pace; all the things that can be digitized will be digitized by us. However, at the junction of the virtual world and real world, people have not changed their favor for "materials", they still needs carriers that can be felt, touched, smelled and seen to provide basic sense of existence. The two features of cultural heritage are very similar, which are tangible and intangible. Both of the material cultural heritage and intangible cultural heritage have tangible and intangible characteristics, which are not isolated from each other. In the digitization process, especially in the interpretation, dissemination and presentation processes, we should give even consideration to the tangible and intangible elements of heritages, making the intangible Social and cultural customs and rituals go along with the tangible cultural heritage; making intangible cultural heritages have "tangible" subjects that can be felt, touched, smelled, heard and seen.

Artistic Interpretation and Scientific Presentation. The purpose of cultural heritage protection is to protect the artistic value, heritage protection starts from the protection of its artistic value. Therefore, how should we describe, restore and present the artistic value of cultural heritage in the process of digitization? Digitalized heritages are different from those original heritages, original heritages have powerful "self-explanatory feature", in no needs of other media-assisted self-presentation. Digital heritages have changed the "format" of their existences, their status in space and time dimensions are analogs of heritages. Therefore, we should give full play to the characteristics of the artistic value of the cultural heritage in such "context", make reasonable interpretation of art on this basis, set appropriate guidance and expansion of art, bring the audience into the atmosphere created by artistic interpretation, and present and disseminate them in a scientific, rational and natural way.

Online Demonstration and Offline Validation. The virtual environment created by computers and the Internet is the main arena of digital cultural heritage, and digital interactive experience can attract the audiences' curiosity about the real collections. Amit Sood, who is born in India, holds a similar view: "The more images of collection you see, the stronger desire for face-to-face contacts with them you will have". Amit Sood had no chance to go to museums for many years, and such regret became the driving force for him to start the Google Art Project. "Digitization cannot replace the physical museums. Conversely, when people acquire a certain understanding and knowledge of the museum and its collections, they will be more interested to visit the museum." Therefore, the online culture heritage shaped by digital technology has demonstration effects, promoting its publicity and encouraging more people to have personal experience in reality.

3   Case Study of Experiential Communication of Digital Humanities and Information Visualization

It is involved to present the information of the heritage itself, to design the exhibition space of the heritage and the interaction design while the expressing of the information and experience during the design of experiential communication of Digitized Cultural Heritage. Generally speaking, "Experiential Communication" is to figure out the relationships between information, interaction and experience. Two examples are shown in this article, one is the Buddha statues in the 45th and 159th cave of Mogao

Grotto at Dunhuang, while another one is the painting call Iconography Measurement drawn in the 18th century which showed roughly same as in the iconography measurement classics.

The so-called "Iconography Measurement" is the proportion of the Buddha figure and the ruler of the statue. It could be the reference standard to draw the figure of Buddha in Tibet and Nepal district in the 18th century, which contains 36 detailed drawings. Since the figures of the Buddha are not fabricated, their physical proportion, appearance, postures and decorations were rigorously stipulated. Meanwhile the figures were recorded in the books like "Iconography Measurement" in the style of line drawing. The unit of the measurement is called "one finger" (the width of the figure's middle finger).

First of all, the most important task of the design of experiential communication of Digitized Cultural Heritage is to accurately express the information of the cultural heritage itself and to transmit basic information of the artistic and scientific value of the cultural heritage. Whether the information are accurate and scientific can directly influence the deep excavation of the concealed humanity, art, history and etc Fig. 2.

Fig. 1. Information collection of the Buddha statues

Fig. 2. Million-level pixel statue display

The 45th and the 159th caves in Mogao Grotto are the representatives of the caverns digged at the same time whose types of caves, statues and murals possessed really high historical and artistic value. The preservation of them are comparatively integrated. On the processing of the Buddha statue at the left side of the shrine in the 45th cave, not only the "original appearance" is shown to the spectators, even the beyond-the-real visual angles are provided because of the advantages of digitization (Fig. 1). Million-level-pixel photograph can distinctly show the linetype, brushwork, and even the tiny dust dropped on the Buddha statues for the past thousand years. (P.2) The "beyond-the-real" details could be shown in the digitized scenes. When the statue of Sakyamuni was found missing and only left his lotus throne, the original statue was virtually reconstructed by the means of digitization, allowing spectators to transform their mobile terminals to digital display device (Figs. 3 and 4).

Fig. 3. Mobile terminals enhancing display   **Fig. 4.** Digital restored missing Buddha statue

Secondly, from the perspective of communication, the interaction design of Digitized Heritage is not merely technical considerations, but overall considerations of the textural environment and the relationship between human and digitized heritage and the installation of the interaction points. Opposite to the management of the content of the heritage, interaction techniques provide a kind of hidden existence and initiatively discover the spectator's need of the experience in the virtual space, providing a interact participation way which could be naturally responded on the processing of the design of the organization, presentation and transfer mode of the information. Such as in (Fig. 5), on the settlement of the digitization and interaction of the different pictures,

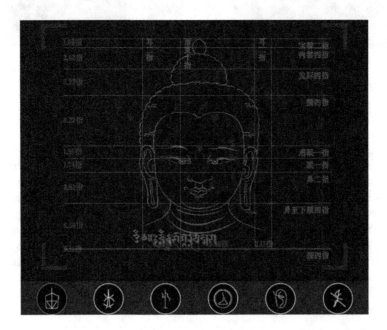

Fig. 5. The mural Iconography Measurement full of media interaction installation

the proportion, appearance, decoration are reconstructed according to the separation of the stories, forming a Multi-Sensory experience which gathers different media formats such as voice, video and pictures.

Finally, Digitized Heritage is the experience at the dimension of time and space, so the society, history and cultural foundation of the time should be considered during the intact Digitized Cultural Heritage experience. Just as Confucius wrote in The Analects of Confucius, "See what he is, find what he did, observe what he is content with". The Cultural Heritage is similar to that. "See what he is"-know exactly what the heritage is; "Find what he did"- explore why and how it became a heritage; "Observe what he is content with"- dig out why the heritage has located that place for so many years, finding out the constant rules among the transformations, thus answer the questions occurred in the practical environment. There are three progressive levels in the designing of the whole picture - picture explanation, scripture interpretation and art deduction. (Figure 6) Level 1: reconstruct the images in the Iconography Measurement by the means of digital techniques, restoring its original environment and building the relatively real experiencing environment. Level 2: scientifically interpret the acquirement and presentation of all the elements at the back of the images, illustrating the meaning of the frames, Buddha sculpture, color, texture and contents. Level 3: deduce the art guided by the experiential communication at the foundation of the research result of the first and second level. By the means of data visualization, the spectators can drag the proportion line to judge the level of similarity of the scales and Iconography Measurement. On the one hand, it can provide the ordinary spectators a basic rule to learn Buddhist statues; on the other hand, it helps to provide the professionals a digitized auxiliary tool.

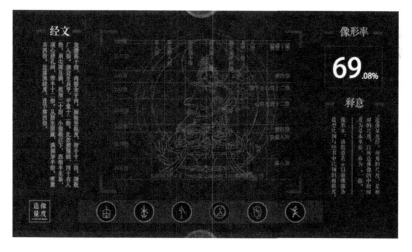

Fig. 6. Interface design of Iconography Measurement

4 Conclusion

As another existence form of heritage, Digitized Cultural Heritage is the products of technology evolution and the social and economic development. It is the construction to the existence of the Heritage Digitization. It helps to avoid the "Digitized Predicament" by bringing in the conception of experiential communication, gathering up the information presentation, interaction techniques and environmental construction involved in the field of heritage digitization design. It provides different spectators proper textual environment of heritage experiential communication, creating a new way for the communication, interaction and expression between different cultures. Digitized Cultural Heritage provides some available theories, methods and tools for the protection of the cultural heritage, exhibition, museum management, cultural creative industry and many other fields.

In summary, the cultural heritage exists naturally and can sustain for a long history, so its traditional foundation will inevitably be affected by the huge differences of humanistic and social environments between modern society and the era of heritage. Staring from the digital dilemma, the author proposes the construction strategy for the digital protection of cultural heritage from the contextual perspective of time dimension, combines the positive and negative impacts of information technology with that of interactive techniques, analyzes the multidimensional features of cultural heritage in the process of digitization, avoids attaching too much emphases on the limitations of the digital media, uses digital technology as the "language" and the modern expression of cultural heritage as its "sentence meaning", explores cultural connotation and essences behind culture heritage from experiences, and provides new methods and direction for the preservation, protection and dissemination of cultural heritage from the construction of context.

References

1. Howard, P.: Heritage: Management, Interpretation, Identity. Continuum International Publishing Group, New York (2003)
2. Hems, A., Blockley, M.: Heritage Interpretation. Routledge in Association with English Heritage, Abingdon (2006)
3. Schofield, J., Szymanski, R.: Local Heritage. Global Context. Ashgate, Farnham (2011)

Optimal Design of the Front Face of Minicars Based on Analytic Hierarchy Process

Wenjie Deng[1(✉)], Xinhui Kang[2], and Congru Zhang[1]

[1] Faculty of Humanities and Arts, Theory and Practice of Art Design,
Macau University of Science and Technology,
Avenida Wai Long, Taipa, Macau 999078, China
117274871@qq.com, avmichelle@sina.com
[2] School of Art, Design and Media, East China University of Science
and Technology, No. 130, Meilong Road, Xuhui District,
Shanghai 200237, China
nbukxh@163.com

Abstract. Faced with the pressure of market competition, the minicar manufacturers need to the design of the front face effectively. The paper will collect the samples of appearances of existing minicars and adopt the analytic hierarchy process (AHP) to explore the optimal design of the front face of minicars in China's automobile market. The research results will provide useful reference for the initial stage of the development and optimal design of minicars' front faces. The appearances of the minicars' front faces are divided into 7 factors and 32 levels. The weight of each factor is obtained by using AHP, and the optimal design of the front face of minicars is analyzed. AHP will effectively simplify the complex and irregular factors, and make the final decisions of the front face design of minicars, through various experimental analyses, to provide effective quantitative criteria. Our quantitative criteria can help the products to be put on the market be easily recognized by consumers, thereby increasing the market value of this product in China.

Keywords: Kansei engineering · Analytic hierarchy process · Minicar

1 Introduction

Nowadays, the consumers' demand for minicars changes from the functional requirements to the symbol of the consumers' own value, so the minicar styling will become an important factor that must be taken into account. Due to the characteristic of minicar styling that it is the front face of car that is easily noticed, the front face design of minicars has a direct impact on the purchase of cars by the consumers. However, the creative ability of most of China's self-owned enterprises on the automobile appearance design is still to be improved. In fact, many designs are suspected of copying, over-imitation or outsourcing to design companies with foreign capital, etc., such as Lifan 320 to MINI, Landwind X7 to Range Rover Evoque, Shuanghuan SCEO to BMW X5 and so on. Therefore, China's automobile industry needs a method to make an optimal design of minicars' front face originally and aesthetically.

© Springer International Publishing AG 2017
C. Stephanidis (Ed.): HCII Posters 2017, Part II, CCIS 714, pp. 543–549, 2017.
DOI: 10.1007/978-3-319-58753-0_76

In this paper, we adopt analytic hierarchy process (AHP) to analyze the factors of minicars' front face design in China's automobile market. Based on the above description, the purpose of this study is as follows: It adopts the document research and comparative analysis, to find the optimal methods and related technologies suitable for the front face design of minicars; it compares the factors in the optimal design of minicars' front face through questionnaire; it uses the analytic hierarchy process as the analysis tool, to analyze the elements and standards needed by the early development and research of the optimal design of minicars' front face; it finally carries out the sorting of factors in the optimal design of minicars' front face, to help develop decision-making during the initial development.

2 Literature Review

2.1 Kansei Engineering

As a new subject that combining with social science and natural science, kansei engineering is rigorous and scientific. By means of engineering technology, it tries to quantify the various feelings of people (temporarily called "amount of sensibility"), and then it finds out the functional relation between the amount of sensibility and the various physical quantities used in engineering technology as the basis of engineering analysis and research [1]. Kansei engineering effectively quantifies the abstract problems, so as to help the researchers develop relevant quantitative criteria. The research on the application of kansei engineering in the car-related design has also achieved some progress. For example, based on the research on the appearance design of off-road vehicles with kansei image, the design reflects the integrity, coordination, balance, toughness and other kansei images of the off-road vehicle modeling [2]. Through the study on the matching of the shape and consumers' emotional intention, it finds out the products that accord with the customers' intention. For kansei assessment of the constituent elements and the overall interrelations in car steering wheel design [3], it design more intelligent and convenient vehicle-mounted steering wheel; based on the kansei engineering and TRIZ theory, it designs the car seat taking into account visual comfort [4], in order to meet the consumer's requirements for the comfort of the car seat; the above studies all have used the method of kansei engineering, which provides decision-making conclusions for its related questions of design.

2.2 Analytic Hierarchy Process

Analytic hierarchy process (AHP) was formally proposed in the mid-1970s by Saaty, a US operational research expert. It is a qualitative, quantitative, systematic and hierarchical analysis method. Because of its practicality and effectiveness in dealing with complex decision-making problems, it has gained great attention all over the world [1]. Saaty [5, 6] and Vargas [7] pointed out that AHP can also be further applied to the analysis of thirteen categories of problems, including: prioritization, alternation, selection of preferred plans, requirements, resource allocation, predicting results, performance measurement, system design, system stability, optimization, planning, conflict resolution and risk assessment [8].

AHP is mainly to distinguish the complexity of the study, through a variety of different ways of simplified definition, to from a simple and clear hierarchical relationship. The factors to be studied are compared one by one, and the quantified values represent the weights of the factors at each level and are evaluated synthetically. The basic process of the analytic hierarchy process is as follows: (1) It simplifies the experimental object and constructs it into a hierarchical model; (2) It creates a quantization table of the comparison array; (3) It calculates the weight value and checks it, which is only effective after meeting the consistency; (4) It calculates the comprehensive weight value and carries out the consistency test of comprehensive weight. Then the decision is made through the use of the results.

Saaty and Vargas [9] proposed four approximate solutions to the eigenvectors in the AHP matrix, and the large eigenvalues were obtained by multiplying the pairwise comparison matrix A (hierarchy X) by the eigenvector W to obtain the new vector W'. Each large value (λ_{max}) can be obtained by dividing each vector value of the vector W' by the vector value of the original vector W, and then calculating all the values obtained. After the calculation of the large eigenvalues (λ_{max}) of the pairwise comparison matrices, the consistency index (C.I.) is used as the indicator of whether the consistency is achieved and consistency ratio (C.R.) is used as the indicator of whether the degree of consistency is satisfactory. C.I. and C.R. are calculated as follows. $C.I = \lambda_{max}-x/(x-1) \leq 0.1$; $C.R. = C.I./R.I. \leq 0.1$. In the above formula, R.I. is the random consistency index corresponding to the matrix; namely, according to the size of the normalization matrix (hierarchy) it selects the appropriate random consistency index [8].

2.3 Front Face Design of Cars

The front face design of cars has also made a lot of related achievements, such as the bionics design of the front face [10]. Through the discussion on the application of design bionics in the front face design of cars, it reveals a new design form of "bionic conceptual design", which will lead the front face design of cars to the new trend. Based on the kansei engineering of the optimal design of cars' front face shape [11], through the neural network structure and eye movement experiments, it provides product designers with reference for kansei design.

To sum up, it is not common to study the optimal design of the front face of cars by using the AHP to analyze the weight of the front face of many vehicle models. Therefore, there is much space for studies on this topic.

3 Experimental Process

According to the front face of more than 70 minicars, it draws the chart of shape affected by relevant factors; and then according to the chart, it develops the questionnaire of shape; the age of the participants of the questionnaire is between 18 and 40 years old. The sample questionnaire is taken. Among 30 candidates who have the intention of buying a car or have a car, it chooses 7 women and 7 men randomly to conduct a detailed questionnaire survey. The results of the questionnaire are analyzed by AHP analysis and the weight is obtained. It also obtains the comprehensive weight values, and then develops the product chain to which consumers pay attention. The following is the analysis process (all the values in the table are the weight value according to the questionnaire, so there is no unit of quantity), taking the seven factors of the front face of cars as an example.

First of all, it constructs the hierarchical model, including the formation of two hierarchical relations (see Table 1); the first layer is on behalf of the seven factors that consumers pay attention to when considering the front face of minicars, which are air-inlet grille of engine, knuckle line of the bonnet, front windshield, bumper, rearview mirror, frame of automotive lighting and fog light. The second layer chooses a single factor for overall comparison, according to the principle of AHP, to determine the weight relationship of each factor in the front face of minicars among seven elements. Then, it develops the description of the questionnaire evaluation scale (see Table 2) and designs the questionnaire (see Table 3).

Table 1. Hierarchical model

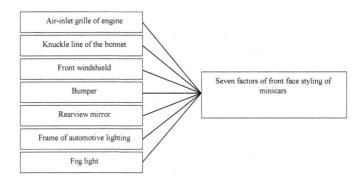

Table 2. AHP evaluation scale description

Evaluation scale	9	7	5	3	1	2, 4, 6, 8
Definition	Absolutely important	Extremely important	Very important	Slightly important	Equally important	Median
Description	Absolutely like	Extremely like	Like very much	Slightly like	Equally important	Striking an average

Table 3. Questionnaire design

Factor 1	Relatively important ← Equally import → Relatively important																		Factor 2
	9	8	7	6	5	4	3	2	1	2	3	4	5	6	7	8	9	
Air-inlet grille of engine																			Knuckle line of the bonnet
Air-inlet grille of engine																			Front windshield
....																			....

4 Experimental Results and Conclusions

4.1 From the Above Experimental Data, We Can Draw the Following Experimental Results

Because the validity of the questionnaire should meet the consistency of the questionnaire results, it is determined by the overall consistency ratio CI, RI, CR value. In this study, supposing that CR < 0.1 is the effective research result, 12 questionnaires (5 women, 7 men) are identified as valid reference questionnaires among the 14 questionnaires collected, and the data are calculated and analyzed according to the results of the study. After the normalization of the results, 8 copies are obtained. One of the survey results is shown in Table 4.

In this study, according to the above analysis of the results, can further develop the sorting of attention when the enterprise or design agencies conduct optimized combinational design of minicars' front face, as in Table 5. Therefore, it can optimize the existing products accurately and efficiently, thereby enhancing the consumers' desire to buy the products.

Table 4. Results of the weight of 7 factors in the car shape and of the consistency test based on the questionnaire survey results

No.	Air-inlet grille of engine	Knuckle line of the bonnet	Front windshield	Bumper	Rearview mirror	Frame of automotive lighting	Fog light	Consistency (CR=CI/RI) <0.1
Shape								
Interviewee1	0.082	0.028	0.157	0.071	0.050	0.394	0.218	CI(0.130)/RI(1.320)<0.1
Interviewee 2	0.292	0.024	0.208	0.087	0.067	0.279	0.044	CI(0.122)/RI(1.320)<0.1
Interviewee 3	0.088	0.432	0.058	0.237	0.056	0.079	0.050	CI(0.131)/RI(1.320)<0.1
....								....
Integrated weights	0.15011	0.07851	0.10006	0.09755	0.06468	0.17111	0.10839	

Table 5. Comparison results of effective experimental comprehensive weight value

Preferred design grade	Factors of front face	Factors of styling							
1	Frame of automotive lighting	Diamond-shaped	Narrow	Parallelogram	Teardrop-shaped	Triangular	Irregular rounded rectangle	Irregular rectangle	Round
0.17111		0.17543	0.13057	0.12345	0.08374	0.08294	0.07104	0.06542	0.05448
Preferred design grade	Factors of front face	Factors of styling							
2	Air-inlet grille of engine	Double symmetrical	Narrow	Arched	Irregular triangular	Trapezoidal	Oval	Irregular shape	
0.15011		0.20074	0.11995	0.11355	0.09182	0.08358	0.08079	0.07387	
3	Fog light	Irregular shape		Irregular rectangle		Irregular trapezoidal		Round	
0.10839		0.27932		0.22037		0.20084		0.09615	
4	Front windshield	Wide or irregular trapezoidal				Higher trapezoidal			
0.10006		0.50194				0.29933			
5	Bumper	Concave		Irregular trapezoidal		Rectangular		Trapezoidal	
0.09755		0.46594		0.14577		0.13203		0.10122	
6	Knuckle line of the bonnet	Irregular shape		Inner arc octagon		Octagonal shape		Funnel-shaped	
0.07851		0.38922		0.18791		0.12755		0.11042	
7	Rearview mirror	Irregular ellipse		Square arc			Oval		
0.06468		0.38958		0.22561			0.1691		

4.2   Conclusions of the Analysis

This study will provide useful reference for the early stages of the development and design of minicars' front face. Taking the AHP as the analytical tool, the quantitative elements of the development strategy of minicars' front face design should be established to determine the objectives when designing. Through the process and results of the analysis, it can be found in this study that the analytic hierarchy process can effectively reduce the complexity of many elements of irregular structures, to develop the quantitative criteria which are helpful for final decision, judgments and reference.

With the process of gradual decomposition from high level to low level, it improves the existing procedure of decision that relies on the previous experience, and obtains the preferred weighted value of each factor index, providing a sufficient basis for the final decision-making program. The bigger the integrated weighted value is, the higher the priority of adoption is, and thus the risk of decision error reduces to some extent. Through this experiment, we can design the front face of minicars according to the results of the experiment so that the products to be put on the market will be recognized by consumers as much as possible, thereby increasing the market value of this product.

5 Conclusion

The paper takes the front face design of minicars as an example, with the basic principles of kansei engineering and simplifies the shape of front face of minicars through the experimental study by analytic hierarchy process. After the analysis and demonstration, it achieves the quantification of consumer's desire for the factors in the front face styling of minicars. Finally, it designs and justifies the factors of shapes with the quantitative relationship.

Through this experiment, in addition to intuition and experience, it can also carry out mini-car design and research from another point of view which is more scientific and more effective; car design itself is of more complex relationship, so it is necessary to start from the consumers' own demand and to find the quantitative criteria that accords with the actual situation; this analysis method of quantitative criteria not only meets the needs for minicars' front face design decision-making, but also can be applied to any part of the minicars' design decision-making. As the decision-makers of enterprises, it is necessary to use a more scientific and reasonable way to make decisions for providing the majority of consumers with better experience services.

References

1. Li, Y., Wang, Z., Xu, N., Kansei Engineering, Maritime Press, October 2009
2. Hu, W., Zhang, M., Xie, W., Li, H., Yang, Y.: Mach. Des. **31**(11) (2014)
3. Chang, Y.-M., Chen, C.-W.: Int. J. Ind. Ergon. **56**, 97–105 (2016)
4. Sun, L., Kong, F.: Jilin Univ. J. (liberal arts ed.) **44**(1) (2014)
5. Thomas, L., Saaty, A.: Scaling method for priorities in hierarchical structures. J. Math. Psychol. **15**(3), 234–281 (1977)
6. Saaty, T.L.: How to make a decision: the analytic hierarchy process. Eur. J. Oper. Res. **48**(1), 9–26 (1990)
7. Vargas, L.G.: An overview of the analytic hierarchy process and its applications. Eur. J. Oper. Res. **48**(1), 2–8 (1990)
8. Xu, N., Guo, Z., Lin, W.: Rainfall pattern design through analytic hierarchy process. J. Chin. Inst. of Civ. Hydraul. Eng. **22**(2) (2010)
9. Saaty, T.L., Vargas, L.G.: The Logic of Priorities. KluwerNijhoff, Boston (1982)
10. Fang, H., Zhou, X., Yuan, J.: Packag. Eng. **29**(2) (2008)
11. Guo, F., Zhao, L., Cao, Y., Zhang, X.: Ind. Eng. Manag. **17**(6) (2012)

A Visualization System for Traffic Violation Using H2O Random Forests

Chyi-Ren Dow$^{(\boxtimes)}$, Zhe-Rong Lin, and Kuan-Chieh Wang

Department of Information Engineering and Computer Science,
Feng Chia University, Taichung, Taiwan
{crdow,M0406352,M0522977}@fcu.edu.tw

Abstract. Traffic violation is one of the major reasons of road safety preventions and traffic accidents, but the data is too large and complex. Thus, it is important to find useful information, build analysis models, and use interactive tools to understand the relevance, trends, and driving behaviors from the traffic violations data. In this paper, we will establish a traffic violations data analysis model and interactive and visualization platform for users by using historical traffic violation data of Taiwan in recent four years. First, we will focus on using the traffic violations data to understand the definitions and data types of violation attributes in order to exclude the data abnormality, including formatting errors and over-range. Second, we remove the attributes that have no effect on the classification through the violation data analysis and classification which were performed by using the random forest scheme on the H2O platform for those attributes with the most critical impacts. We also performed the spatial, temporal, and behavior analysis to find the features of serious violations. Analysis of violation discrepancy is performed for different time, space, and ages, and different traffic penalty rules for cars and motorcycles. By comparing the information from Taiwan's northern, central, and southern regions, we also investigate in the regional differences in violations. After the analysis, we do the visualization to show the variety with the number of violations or the differences of violations rules. We use Highcharts and C# development tools to show the results of the analysis, and emphasize on the obvious differences of data such as Heatmap and PivotTable report. Finally, based on the analysis results, users can use the platform to find critical traffic violations, for examples, providing governments or police with information which strengthens the law enforcement and road construction of road safety in the future.

Keywords: Traffic violations · Visualization systems · Data cleaning · Data classification · Random forest

1 Introduction

Traffic violation is one of the major reasons of road safety preventions and traffic accidents. Almost 300,000 cases of total traffic accidents occurred in Taiwan each year. Some of the major causes are drivers violating traffic violations, such as drunk driving, speeding, running a red light, etc. By analyzing traffic violation data, it can increase the crackdown for enhancement in traffic violation and improve the road safety.

© Springer International Publishing AG 2017
C. Stephanidis (Ed.): HCII Posters 2017, Part II, CCIS 714, pp. 550–554, 2017.
DOI: 10.1007/978-3-319-58753-0_77

Data visualization is the data image by referring the database of each data item as a single element representation and building up a large number of data sets. This approach facilitates an effective way when individuals or organizations want to disseminate some information to the public. The observers can find useful information from the visualization of the data and can develop guidelines for the terms to reduce the number of casualties associated with transportations. For example, spatial analysis can be used to observe violations at high incident areas. Behavioral analysis can be used to identify age-specific violation that strengthens road safety advocacy.

The paper is organized as follows. Section 2 describes the recent research related to this work. Section 3 discusses how we can effectively analyze information about traffic violations. Section 4 presents the experimental results. Finally, Sect. 5 summarizes our conclusions.

2 Related Work

Babič and Zuskáčová [3] performed predictive mining on road accident data. Lu et al. [9] used accident data to do the regression analysis and find the road prone to accident. Flores et al. [5] used the onboard data storage system to find traffic hotspots from vehicle data. Ji et al. [7] detected the vehicle violation by video image detection technology. Tong et al. [10] analyzed the DMV accident data to find the collision.

Jahangiri et al. [6] used the machine learning method to predict the red light violation. Ahn et al. [1] used the support vector regression and the naive Bayesian classifier for highway traffic flow forecasting. Alencar et al. [2] used K-means and random decisions databases for pedestrian judgment and classification. Cruz and Machado [4] presented traffic flow changes in a pulsed manner. Joshi et al. [8] used GIS to show timely vehicle tracking status.

3 Data Analysis Model and Visualization System

In order to develop our proposed traffic violation visualization system, we will establish and use certain ways to complete it, including data collection, data preprocessing, data analysis and data visualization techniques. The first step of data prepocesing is data cleaning such as checking and identifying incorrect information. The part of the typo check is to delete the typos or irrelevant data such as violation place code and other fields to collect such as the violation place code and other fields and delete the data which is not complete. The style comparison check is carried out to identify whether the data in accordance with the provisions of the format input. In the steps of the scope check, we will find out the unreasonable data beyond the default value of the field to delete. Data conversion needs to be organized into a format that is easily performed in the data analysis as well as to define the severity of the violation. We use the random forest algorithm to model various violation features.

For the analysis model, we will preprocess the data and organize it into the sparking water platform. As shown in Fig. 1, we use the C# CsvHelper which is used to analyze and export from the database to C# CSV format file and import to H2O [11]. By using H2O Spark to create a Resilient Distributed Dataset (RDD), the RDD data can be stored in memory for each subsequent result of the operation of the RDD dataset. The next operation can be directly applied from the memory input to eliminate the need for a large number of disk write operations. In the calculation process, we can use the hard disk for data exchange, if the machine's memory is not enough.

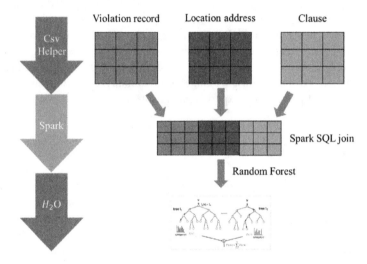

Fig. 1. H2O data analysis

4 Experimental Results

In order to find out the changes in the high-risk areas at different time, we further use the violation date field in the violation data to determine the violation year and season. As shown in Fig. 2, we can identify hot zones and road segments prone to violations in Taipei, Taiwan.

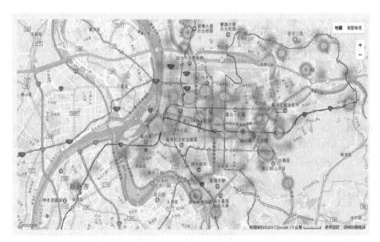

Fig. 2. Violation hot zones

Figure 3 shows the distribution of traffic violations in three cities of Taiwan, Taipei, Changhua and Tainan. We further identify the violation distribution for cars and motorcycles in terms of violation data from 2012 to 2015. Figure 3 also demonstrates that Tainan's average penalty fee of each violation is much higher than that of other cities. Thus, Tainan's law enforcement to ban on serious traffic violations is more strict than other cities.

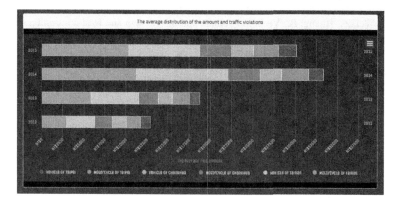

Fig. 3. Distribution of traffic violations

5   Conclusions

In this paper, we propose a visualization system for traffic violation. Data cleaning techniques are used to delete the outliers of the violation data and present the data in a graphical manner. The violation hot spots can be identified for different time periods and violation terms for different age groups. The violation data was analyzed by using random forest algorithms. Our visualization system can be used to render trends and identify specific violation information to help the government to make the right decision.

References

1. Ahn, J., Ko, E., Kim, E.Y.: Highway traffic flow prediction using support vector regression and bayesian classifier. In: Proceedings of the International Conference on Big Data and Smart Computing (BigComp), pp. 239–244, January 2016
2. Alencar, F.A.R., Filho, C.M., da Silva, D.G.: Pedestrian classification using K-means and random decision forests. In: Proceedings of the Joint Conference on Robotics: SBR-LARS Robotics Symposium and Robot Control (SBR LARS Robot Control), pp. 103–108, October 2014
3. Babič, F., Zuskáčová, K.: Descriptive and predictive mining on road accidents data. In: Proceedings of the 14th IEEE International Symposium on Applied Machine Intelligence and Informatics (SAMI), pp. 87–92, January 2016

4. Cruz, P., Machado, P.: Pulsing blood vessels: a figurative approach to traffic visualization. IEEE Comput. Graphics Appl. **36**(2), 16–21 (2016)
5. Flores, V., Mata, M., Fernandez, J.: A multi-agent, in-vehicle database recorder system for supporting traffic hotspots detection, geographical representation and analysis view document. In: Proceedings of the IEEE International Conference on Information Fusion (FUSION), pp. 1–6, July 2014
6. Jahangiri, A., Rakha, H.A., Dingus, T.A.: Adopting machine learning methods to predict red-light running violations. In: Proceedings of the 18th IEEE International Conference on Intelligent Transportation Systems (ITSC), pp. 650–655, September 2015
7. Ji, X., Wei, Z., Huang, L.: Violation vehicle automated snap and road congestion detection. In: Proceedings of the 4th International Conference on Cloud Computing and Intelligence Systems (CCIS), pp. 16–20, August 2016
8. Joshi, N., Tripathy, A.K. Sawant, S.: Near real time vehicle tracking using GIS. In: Proceedings of the International Conference on Technologies for Sustainable Development (ICTSD), pp. 1–6, February 2015
9. Lu, T., Dunyao, Z. Lixin, Y.: The traffic accident hotspot prediction: based on the logistic regression method. In: Proceedings of the International Conference on Transportation Information and Safety (ICTIS), pp. 107–110, June 2015
10. Tong, W., Cherian, P., Liu, J.: Statistical analysis of DMV crash data. In: Proceedings of the IEEE International Congress on Systems and Information Engineering Design Symposium (SIEDS), pp. 113–117, April 2016
11. H2O. http://www.h2o.ai/

Transportation CMF Design Strategy Based on Regional Culture

Bin Jiang[(✉)] and Bin Geng

School of Design Arts and Media,
Nanjing University of Science and Technology,
200, Xiaolingwei Street, Nanjing 210094, Jiangsu, China
jb508@163.com, 1920940469@qq.com

Abstract. In order to cater to the aesthetic needs, value orientation and individual requirements of the target consumer groups in different regional cultures, the method of CMF design for geography culture is studied in order to meet the needs of CMF. The First of all, the level and connotation of the CMF design of the vehicle are analyzed rationally, and the coincidence points of the regional cultural elements and the vehicle CMF design are needed. Secondly, the methods of group culture, analogical reasoning, deductive reasoning and behavior analysis are used to study how this paper analyzes the design method of the local culture in the vehicle CMF design, emphasizes the extraction, abstraction, transplantation and variation of the regional cultural symbols, and carries on the transportation means CMF design. Results: The method of CMF design for traffic from regional culture was proposed from the horizontal and vertical routes. At the same time, the consumption physiology, psychology and behavior of the target consumers in the region were studied, and the experiment was carried out according to the preference experiment. Conclusion: The expression of cultural characteristics is an important means to enhance the value of the product, and the CMF design for the regional culture is an effective way to develop the regional cultural and creative industries and to improve the CMF design level of the vehicle. How to integrate the regional culture into the vehicle CMF design, so that the regional cultural connotation and the target population in the region's aesthetic tendencies to coordinate, and for modern product design into the regional cultural connotation to enhance the design quality, is the current direction of the development of CMF.

Keywords: Regional culture · Transport · CMF design

1 Background

CMF (Color, Material & Finishing), belonging to the category of industrial design, the color, material and surface treatment process of the product design, and the vehicle CMF design is to study the color, material and surface treatment technology of the vehicle. With the rapid development of social economy, culture and information technology, consumers in the purchase of products is no longer simply to product features as the main measure, personalized, beautiful, affinity and other characteristics gradually become the impact of whether consumers buy the product Of the important reference indicators. The consumer's focus on the product gradually from the "material" to the

© Springer International Publishing AG 2017
C. Stephanidis (Ed.): HCII Posters 2017, Part II, CCIS 714, pp. 555–560, 2017.
DOI: 10.1007/978-3-319-58753-0_78

"spirit" level, "form to follow the function" design style has not meet the needs of the times, designers need to find new ways to interpret the product design and emotion [1].

The CMF design of traffic in different regions needs different methods. In order to cater to the aesthetic needs of the consumer groups in the region, we must analyze the regional culture rationally, as shown in Fig. 1. In the vehicle CMF design into the regional culture can play a very good creative effect, at the same time to enhance the transport of cultural heritage, color and other aspects can provide a great help.

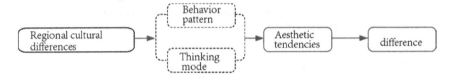

Fig. 1. Regional cultural differences

2   Research on the Extraction of Regional Cultural Elements

To build a home culture based on the home car CMF design system, we must fully tap the cultural elements and design elements of the commonality, while collecting and summarizing the characteristics of cultural symbols used in product design methods, first from a regional culture to extract Characteristics of the typical cultural symbols, the symbol can be the region's classic architectural forms, ethnic costumes, handicraft products, religious art, and then from the horizontal and vertical two ways to extract elements [2].

At present, there are few researches on the design of CMF design elements from the regional culture. CMF designers are more from the current fashion elements to extract the design elements, designers are more concerned about the trend, but rarely involved in cultural connotations, The spirit of the elements, so from the user's own cognitive and psychological aspects of CMF design trends more and more important, as shown in Fig. 2. The following is a summary of the methods of CMF design elements extracted from our regional cultural elements:

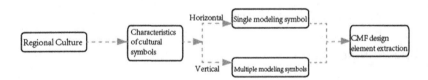

Fig. 2. Method of extracting regional cultural elements

1. traditional religious culture: "Dao" and "doctrine" it deeply affects you I am now aesthetic tendencies, and this aesthetic tendencies are Europe and the United States and Japan and other regions of the aesthetic confirmed, so we can extract a few keywords: Simple, bright, pure, but also for abstract expression and emotional sublimation.

2. traditional buildings: Huizhou architecture and Jiangnan Water Village, can be refined, black and white walls, clear lines
3. traditional art: ink painting, Chinese painting stresses, freehand, "to shape God", the pursuit of a "wonderful and not like" between the feeling.
4. the traditional performance art: Chinese martial arts, Tai Chi, pay attention to rigid and soft and forward (Fig. 3).

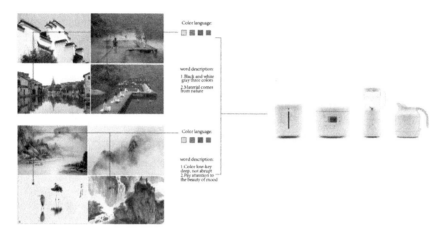

Fig. 3. Cultural element extraction method

The same foreign excellent design can not be separated from their own regional culture, Finland Fiskars, is a world-class tool design brand, the brand almost to the extreme play orange [3]. Orange become his brand mark, then why is this color? How did you choose this color?

Through the study, Fiskars orange handle scissors was born in 1967, belong to the last century 70's, 70s of last century what is it? Through the extraction of elements we get the following answer (Fig. 4).

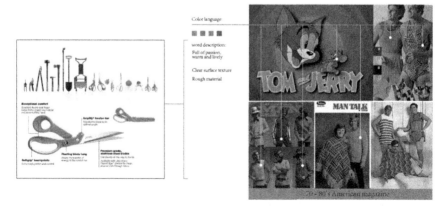

Fig. 4. Finnish product design element extraction (Color figure online)

3   The Regional Cultural Elements in the Vehicle CMF Design of the Use of Analysis

China's traditional culture in the masculine beauty and feminine beauty, carrying the unique aesthetic implication of Chinese culture. Masculine beauty and feminine beauty in the car design as a design element, in the form of interpretation of a wide range of artistic creativity, showing the masculine beauty of the structure of the re-creation of the United States. Emphasizing the extraction, abstraction, transplantation and variation of regional cultural symbols, taking into account the relationship between markets, products and consumers (Fig. 5).

Fig. 5. Products, consumers and the relationship between the market

3.1   "Brought"

Strictly speaking, it is not innovative, but for the relevant areas of information collection and extraction, in a similar cultural areas to make innovations, such as from our social culture to extract the traditional Chinese red, can be combined with the design of the product, At the same time it needs to pay close attention to industry dynamics [4].

3.2   "Combination"

Will be different areas of cultural elements with each other, combined with each other at the same time combined with the characteristics of transport industry, cultural elements and international trends combined with each other, both to meet the target consumer groups have a sense of belonging and highlight the consumer's pursuit of fashion.

3.3   "Subversion"

On the subversive design, we need to understand the future direction of development of cultural elements but also to predict the trend. Such as Apple's CNC technology, Apple used before, only for the Shouban, but Apple put the process used in mass production, the products made of crafts, and then we see a subversion process brought about by the industry whirlwind, plastic injection Spraying down [5].

4   The Use of Regional Cultural Elements in the Vehicle CMF Design Analysis

4.1   Adapt to the Geographical Environment

The geographical environment for the car in addition to the ground conditions, but also the region's urbanization, population density, environmental quality and so on. The impact of ground conditions on the car model is obvious, different ground conditions, people's needs on the car there is a fundamental difference.

4.2   Highlight the Regional Culture

Regional culture includes life philosophy, social sentiment and regional system and other human factors. People living in different regions in life philosophy, lifestyle, way of thinking, social and other aspects of a significant difference (Fig. 6). These differences are reflected in the car is the difference between people's understanding of car styling.

Fig. 6. Car interior with regional culture

4.3   Consistent with Regional Aesthetic

Color and shape is the car design of the two basic elements, people on the color and shape of the understanding is very different, especially in the car performance [6]. The influence of geographical customs and geographical aesthetics on the design of auto-mobile is also reflected in the nationalization of automobile design to a certain extent.

5   Summary

Through the in-depth study of different regional culture, to find out the key factors influencing the development of CMF in different cultural backgrounds, and to analyze the popular elements of automobile CMF development among different regional cul-tures, and to explore how to add the connotation of local culture to automobile CMF design, And the correct use of extraction, abstraction, transplantation and mutation design methods, (Fig. 7) the geographical elements of the application to the vehicle CMF design.

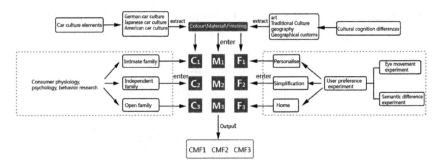

Fig. 7. Analysis of CMF design method for vehicle

6 Conclusion

Regional environmental conditions will almost affect people's preferences for the model, the same model in different regions to adapt to adjust to meet the functional requirements of the car, so the geographical environment changes will affect the design of the model. The cultural conditions of the area affect the user's recognition of the car shape, and the user's deep psychological needs have a direct relationship. Geographical aesthetic affect the car body lines, block surface and steam color, material, processing technology. Therefore, the system, a comprehensive understanding of the geographical environment, culture and aesthetics can clearly design direction, to grasp the design trends, the formation of a nationalized car style has a certain reference value, more targeted to meet the psychological needs of the car.

References

1. Sun, H.: The research on sign elements used in auto-body modeling design. Zhuangshi **11**, 98 (2010)
2. Hai, Y., Zhou, X., Yuan, J.: Discussion on bionic design of automobile's face. Packag. Eng. (2008)
3. Hasher, L., Zacks, R.T.: Working memory,comprehension, and aging: a review and a new view. In: The Psychology of Learning and Motivation, pp. 193–225. Academic Press, San Diego (1988)
4. Salthouse, T.A.: The processing-speed theory of adult age differences in cognition. Psychol. Rev. **103**, 403–428 (1996)
5. Lu, B.: The two methods of design element in culture of chinese taste. Contention Lit. Art **4**, 66 (2011)
6. Peng-cheng, K.: Four paradigms and their fate of chinese aesthetic modernity. J. Southwest Univ. **1**, 159 (2010). (Social Sciences Edition)

Development and Evaluation of an E-picture Book System Using Multi-directional Scrolling and Illustrations with Visual Guidance

Negar Kaghazchi[1(✉)], Azusa Yoshii[2], Sachiko Kodama[2], and Masakatsu Kaneko[2]

[1] Graduate School of Informatics and Engineering Sciences, The University of Electro-Communications, Tokyo, Japan
negar.kaghazchi@uec.ac.jp
[2] Department of Informatics, The University of Electro-Communications, Tokyo, Japan

Abstract. This study is about the development and evaluation of a new e-picture-book (electronic picture book) system designed for touch screen devices. The narration method of this e-picture-book is inspired by the Japanese old paintings in which the whole story was happening in a single page. The artists were using visual elements as navigation method on the page for their story telling propose.

For this project, we have made an edgeless single-page picture book with many images (story scenes), which are arranged in several columns and rows. Each scene has illustrated images with visual guidance (e.g. pointing finger, gaze point, arrow shape composition, animation movements and sound effects), which indicates a certain direction to make the user able to find the story line. A multi-directional scrolling (similar to the scrolling method in the Google map) interface has been designed to enable the user to navigate freely between the story scenes and find the story line. Kaghazchi created an original story "The Cloudy Lady" for this e-picture book.

For evaluating and verifying the effectiveness of each scene and also the guidance ability of the elements to navigate the user through the story line, we performed two types of experiments (eye tracking camera and video recording). Analyzing data from the experiments, we discussed which visual elements and expressions in each illustration have affected the user navigation considering the percentage of successful scrolls toward the target area(s) per each scene. Our future goal is to improve and complete the user navigation method for this e-picture-book.

Keywords: E-picture book · GUI · Multi-direction scrolling · Eye navigation

1 Introduction

Although picture books continue to be published in print-based formats, many are now offered in digital formats for reading and viewing on computers, tablets, and smartphones [1]. How picture-books are digitized varies from simply scanning print-based

© Springer International Publishing AG 2017
C. Stephanidis (Ed.): HCII Posters 2017, Part II, CCIS 714, pp. 561–568, 2017.
DOI: 10.1007/978-3-319-58753-0_79

picture-books to make them available on digital reading devices to the creation of sophisticated software applications, or apps, that offer interactive features that alter the original format of the picture-e-book, provide new options and content for the reader, and move these digital narratives closer to the gaming or entertainment industry [2].

The main idea of this e-picture-book is originated from the old Japanese narrative paintings. In the old Japanese paintings, the story was experienced throughout a piece of horizontal paper by scrolling. This scroll of paper is called "Emaki-mono" in Japanese (Fig. 1). Emaki-mono is read by exposing an arms-length of the scroll at a time, from right to left. By scrolling and following illustrations with visual expressions indicating the next direction, the user can experience the story.

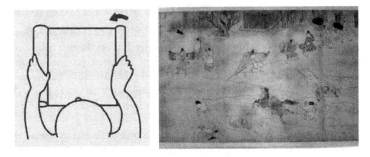

Fig. 1. A typical and old Japanese narrative painting and its scrolling method [3]

In our e-picture-book "the Cloudy Lady" we have developed a system for a one-page, and none-edge picture book with 25 scenes. Each scene has illustrated images with visual guidance, like the Japanese old Emaki-mono, which indicates a certain direction. A multi-direction scrolling (similar to the scrolling method in Google) interface has been designed to enable the user to navigate freely between the stories scenes and find the story line. The aim was to determine the accuracy of user navigation to specific directions by referring to visual expressions.

Development of visual guidance of this picture book was designed according to our previous experiment results using a gaze tracking system[1] for "Hokusai Manga"[2] which has many visual elements to navigate the reader (Fig. 2).

---

[1] The camera and software used for the experiment with elements of Hokusai-Manga were EYETECH Digital Systems-TM3, QG PLUS Ver2.0.

[2] Hokusai-Manga is a collection of sketches of various subjects by a Japanese artist Hokusai. Subjects of the sketches include landscapes, flora and fauna, everyday life and the supernatural. The word manga in the title does not refer to the contemporary story-telling manga, as the sketches in the work are not connected to each other. Block-printed in three colors (black, gray and pale flesh) [4].

Element		Average Percentage	Element		Average Percentage
• Pointing Finger 		57%	• Gaze direction 		50%
• Pointing finger character 		72%	• A group of sequential objects 		45%
• Movement 		42%			

Fig. 2. Elements of visual guidance in "Hokusai Manga" and the average percentage of scrolling in the expected direction

2 System

We developed the system using Xcode 8.1 environment, Swift 3.0.1 language and the execution device was the iPad with the operation system iOS 10.1.1.

2.1 Navigation Method

In this e-picture-book, we have 25 images (story scenes), which are arranged in five columns and five rows[3]. When opening the book, the user can see an image in the center of the display and a small piece of neighbor images on the right, left, up, bottom and corners of the display frame (Fig. 3).

Since the multi-direction scrolling is possible in this e-picture-book, the user can scroll to move to any image by touching and dragging an image. The system automatically adjusts the intended image to the center of the display after dragging the image. The animation and sound effects start to be played once the translocation of each scene in the center part.

Each scene has been designed and illustrated to indicate a certain direction in which the author would expect the reader to follow by the expression of the illustrations, animation movements, and sound effects. We have built sphere architecture to avoid any inconvenient edge and help the user to move smoothly between the scenes (Fig. 4), Thus, a reader can follow a story in the e-picture-book with multi-direction scrolling (Fig. 5).

---

[3] Each image size is 420 * 420 (px), arranged in a square of 5 * 5 with the margins of 100 (px) by 40 (px).

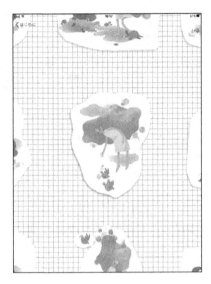

Fig. 3. User can see an image in the center of the display and a small piece of neighbor images

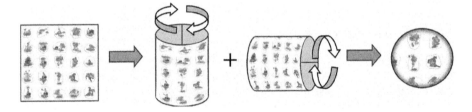

Fig. 4. Toroidal architecture to avoid any inconvenient edge and help the user to move smoothly between the scenes

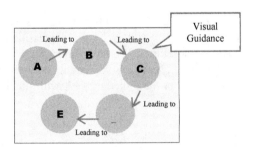

Fig. 5. The orange circles are the illustrations (scenes) which are dependent partially and also one sequence in the whole story line

2.2   Illustrations with Visual Guidance

For illustrating the story of this book, we considered the composition, colors, texture, size, space, and other visual elements to make a strong visual guidance, based on the results of the experiment with the elements of "Hokusai Manga" as our reference. Figure 6 shows samples of illustrations used in our e-picture-book.

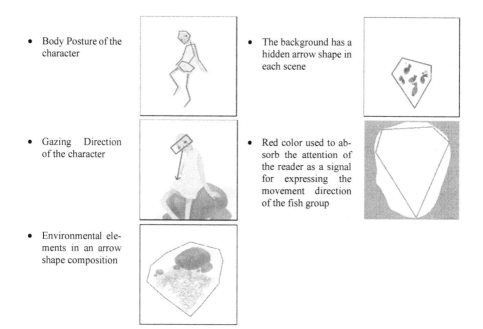

- Body Posture of the character

- The background has a hidden arrow shape in each scene

- Gazing Direction of the character

- Red color used to absorb the attention of the reader as a signal for expressing the movement direction of the fish group

- Environmental elements in an arrow shape composition

Fig. 6. Visual elements in each illustration (scene) (Color figure online)

2.3   Story "The Cloudy Lady"

The story of this book is exclusively written and designed for the presented book format. It is an ethnic story with the theme of dedication and nature conservation. The story revolves around a character called the cloudy lady, who lives in the sky and has hair made of clouds. A lake is about to dry out and A group of animals that want to save the lake and asking the cloudy lady to come down and help the lake. Each scene of this book contains pictures of the lady as well as the environment and animals and also animation and sound effects which have guiding value. The cloudy lady comes to earth following the birds and with the help of a rabbit a horse and a turtle finds the drying lake and starts to rain until the lake gets full of water, she loses her cloudy hair and becomes so sad but finally with the help of butterflies she goes back to the sky.

3   Evaluation

For evaluation of the effectiveness of each image and also the guidance ability of the elements to navigate the user through the story line, we performed two types of experiment.

3.1   Experiment 1

The first experiment, was conducted with Tobii studio eye tracking camera (Tobii Pro X2-30). Six participants (three females and three males, between 20 and 30 years old) took part in this experiment. On a PC screen, each participant observed the visual information which was changing with the following order as shown in Fig. 7.

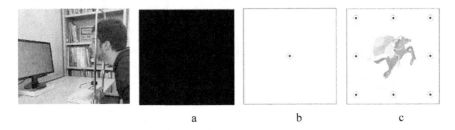

a   b   c

Fig. 7. Experiment with eye tracking camera (left) and the configuration of illustrations in the experiment using eye-tracking camera. a: blackout, b: cross mark at the center, c: object (illustration) at the center, 8 cross marks in 8 directions

3.2   Experiment 2

For the second experiment, we asked the same six participants to use the e-picture-book application on the iPad and recorded the video while they were using the application in order to analyze their screening direction (Fig. 8).

Fig. 8. Recording experiment of a user exploring the picture book on the iPad

3.3   Analysis

In the experiment with the eye-tracking camera, we used AOI (area of interest) data analyses method. In AIO method, we defined 8 areas of interest which one or two of them are aimed to be the target areas(s). We calculated the percentage of successful scrolls toward the target area(s) per each scene (Fig. 9).

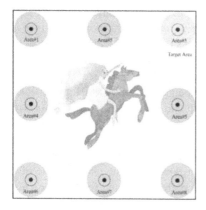

Participants	Target area which partic-ipant gazed after watch-ing the center image
Female A	3
Female B	3
Female C	3
Male A	3
Male B	3
Male C	3
Percentage	100%

Fig. 9. AOI (area of interest) data analyses method

Additionally, with the gaze map pictures see Fig. 10 (left), we observed the direction of eye movements, order of the eye fixations and the fixation duration of each participant. We also made a diagram of each user's scrolling direction by analyzing the recorded videos of the second experiment and compare them with the pre-determined storyline (Fig. 10).

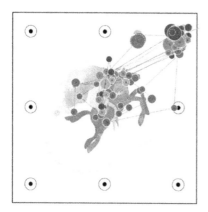
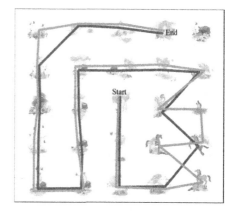

Fig. 10. In gaze direction map each color represents the gaze direction of each participant and numbers are the order of eye movements on the picture and the circles' size increases according to the gaze fixation duration (left). Diagram of predetermined story line (red) and the blue line is the example path traveld by a study (right) (Color figure online).

4   Conclusion

In this project, the authors developed an e-picture book system for the iPad. The authors conducted an experiment by using images from "Hokusai Manga" to evaluate the effect of the illustrations for navigation and to determine the accuracy of user's navigation to specific directions by referring to visual expressions. Considering the experiments result, a new e-picture book content for "the cloudy lady" was designed.

Analyzing the data of the experiments, we observed and obtained a unique result. According to the experiment with the eye tracking camera, the possibility that user navigated in the intended direction by images with strong visual expressions is so high (it could be 100% successful). However, the successful percentage in the experiment by using the e-picture book on the intended device (the iPad) is different. The resulted ratio shows that the users' curiosity to check the neighbor scenes which are visible on the iPads' screen effects on the scrolling direction and leads the user to go to a wrong direction. In this case the user can find her/his own original story line by connecting the various possibilities of interactions between the characters and illustrations in the picture book. Therefor the next stage of this research will be analyzing the effects of two or more images, and to understand how to make the unique reading style of this e-picture-book more attractive and enjoyable for both creator and reader. The creator will design storyline(s), and the reader can find many story lines in the book. We will continue the development and improvement of this picture book system to create a new and enjoyable experience of story narration with illustrated materials.

Acknowledgement. We thank Mana Asada and Professor Takeshi Ito laboratory (department of computer and network engineering, the university of electro-communications) for supporting us during the experiments with the eye tracking camera and analysis system.

References

1. Yokota, J., Teale, H.: Picture books and the digital world: educators making informed choices. Read. Teacher **67**(8), 577–585 (2014)
2. Juul, J.: Games telling stories? a brief note on games and narratives. Game Stud. 1(1) (2001). http://www.gamestudies.org/0101/juulgts
3. KIDAI SHORAN (CD-ROM) (2000). ISBN 3-88375-466-8
4. Sadao, T., Wada, S.: Discovering the Arts of Japan: A Historical Overview. Kodansha International, Tokyo (2003)

Humanizing the Machine

Basic Communication for Unskilled Operators

Robert Lightfoot$^{(\boxtimes)}$, Bruce Gooch, and Robert Michael Fowler

Computer Science and Engineering, Texas A&M University,
College Station, TX, USA
{rob.light, rmichaelfowler94}@tamu.edu,
brucegooch@gmail.com

Abstract. This paper discusses the problem associated with sophisticated computer controlled machines that achieve 100% accuracy in the lab and far less accuracy in the field because they are typically operated by unskilled, illiterate, or a non-native speaking person. A particular case study is described, in which the typical LCD screen with cryptic messages showing the status of the machine or the steps necessary to complete the task at hand often left the operators guessing the next step, which led to incorrect inputs, resulting in incorrect outputs.

These machines are capable of doing the work of several people with high levels of accuracy if the machine is operated by someone of sufficient skill in reading and understand the machine's interface. The typical operator often lacks the skill in reading or understanding to produce the accuracy or output desired by the machine's owner. Adding languages or making less cryptic messages appear on the machine's interface is not solving the inaccuracies seen when the machine is operated by the unskilled worker.

This problem can be solved with simple visual cues that quickly inform the operator the status of the machine and then the machine's expectation of the operator's input. With these simple changes to the Human Computer Interface (HCI), the operator quickly, without guessing, knows if the machine is operating correctly and if their inputs are correct.

To improve the accuracy, two sets of lights were added; the first set of lights showed the status of the machine itself, quickly informing the operator if the control circuits of the machine were operational and if the additional physical requirements of the machine were met, e.g. compressed air, three phase power, chilled water, etc. The second set of lights communicated to the operator the status of their operations, i.e. scan accepted, load item, item accepted, or operation stopped due to error.

With the addition of two sets of status lights and two audio signals, our change to the HCI allowed the same accuracy in the field that were produced in the design and testing labs. Users of any skill level were now able to know immediately if the machine was up, ready, and if their inputs were accepted and correct.

Keywords: Unskilled · Illiterate · Cryptic · Non-native speaking

© Springer International Publishing AG 2017
C. Stephanidis (Ed.): HCII Posters 2017, Part II, CCIS 714, pp. 569–574, 2017.
DOI: 10.1007/978-3-319-58753-0_80

1 Introduction

Portibiti is dry cleaner conveyor system developed by Metalprogetti, a leading company based in Italy, that designs and manufactures automated systems for moving, sorting, and handling hanging and folded garments as well as a range of other light items. The innovation of mixing computer systems with mechanical conveyor systems was and still is leading the industry in capability. Unfortunately, as the product gained popularity from the time and cost savings its owners experienced, installations and features started growing quickly. The "early adaptors" of this technology were eager to get, use, and understand the machine and its capability. As the product became more widespread, and the decision to purchase a machine in the $60,000 to $450,000 range became more of a business decision, machines were placed in plants, stores, and operations where the manager and employees often did not want them, or did not understand how to use and benefit from them.

The group of engineers and designers at Metalprogetti are highly innovative and dedicated to the work they do. Their testing lab looks more like the showroom of a Ferrari dealership than the workshop of a machine manufacturing operation. They are well educated and some of the top engineers. As new machines are designed, they arrive in the testing lab, are operated as designed, and made to perform as designed. To add to the initial success, the "early adaptors" of the product were a group of well-educated business owners that understood the workings of the machine and how to make it perform as expected. In fact, many of the new owners would take a trip to Perugia, Italy to see their machine being built and tested. These owners had a personal interest in using the latest technology and making it work for them.

Metalprogetti gained lots of attention. It was the star of trade shows for the textile industry, and the testimony of the "early adaptors" was very beneficial to the company; however, as the product customer base grew, the accuracy many newer customers achieved fell dramatically. The research into these problems dealt with the human computer interface and not the design of the machine itself. Metalprogetti's lab results, as well as those first customers, was more than a proof of concept, it verified the system worked well when used as designed. The following paragraphs discuss the causes of this decline and the steps taken to bring the desired accuracy to all the users.

2 Lab vs. Field, Different Results

The accuracy observed with the machine operated by skilled workers was everything the designers and developers wanted. Unless there was a mechanical failure, the machine operated as expected with near perfect results, and with the checks in the software system, the machine would give the operator enough information to find the problem if one did occur. Then, with the largest single day sale of machines from a trade show, Metalprogetti sold twenty-four systems to be built and installed in rapid succession. A new type of customer started purchasing and using the machine, and for the first time, the system was not performing as expected. It was imperative to find the issues and resolve them.

Testing in a laboratory differs from studying that same item in the real world. Many things shape what actually happens in the real world that can be taken out of the environment in a lab. Progress happens when some piece of research adds new knowledge to or corrects other knowledge [1]. Our field consisted of nineteen different locations throughout the United States. Of these locations, fifteen were seeing far too many failures to make this a viable product to use. Four locations were seeing the expected results, and the results consistent with those "early adaptors" that created much of the desire in Metalprogetti's products.

Our first observations in Orlando Florida were strictly from the point of view that the machine was not performing in the same manner. The owners described how the employees had been trained, and they were certain the machine was the culprit of the high failure rate. After two days of observation and interaction with the development and support staff in Italy, it was quite clear the machine was working as it was intended. This shifted our efforts to finding the problems with the use of the machine. Our first field observation was a location that had a failure rate of 20%. In real numbers, this was over 400 garments not being returned to their rightful owner. The majority of the problem at this first location was not the users of the machine, but the method of entering the items into the Point of Sale (POS) software was not correct. Therefore, the machine simply did not know about certain items and could not successfully sort them. The message was simply "NOT FOUND" and gave the user no context to continue. We observed some users did not understand the message displayed and would either load the item anyway or scan another barcode to get the machine to accept the prior item.

To operate a Metalprogetti conveyor, a user scans a barcode attached to a garment. The conveyor records the item number and is ready to accept the item if it is in its database. Then continues to accept additional items until all pieces of the order are collected. In a different location, the conveyor deposits the complete order to the exit rail, giving space for more garments to be added. Ideally, when all garments have been loaded onto the conveyor, all orders are complete and delivered to the exit rail, and the conveyor is empty. Initially, short cryptic messages from a small display was the only communication from the machine to the user.

The development team was unable to understand this use of the machine and offered almost no help, simply stating the employees were causing the problem. While this location was having the largest problem, our initial thoughts were to correct the problems we observed and move on to the next few locations having similar problems. We identified corrective actions for two major problems:

1. Correct the process being used to enter the items into the system at the beginning, eliminating the "NOT FOUND" error that was encountered most often.
2. Correct the process employees used when a "NOT FOUND" message did appear so the problem would not spread to other garments and compound the issue.

Our initial findings were relayed back to the owners and the Metalprogetti development team that more comprehensive training and better processes were needed at this location. We were still concerned that the number of locations that were experiencing problems was growing at about the same rate as installations. Something was very different about the first thirty machines and the results those owners were seeing versus the second thirty. Later we would return to this location to find we solved only part of the problem.

Our next location, Jacksonville Florida, showed an entirely different aspect of the problem. The items were entered into the Point of Sale (POS) software correctly and consequently, the Metalprogetti conveyor recognized the item. The rate of failure at this location was just under 10%, which represented nearly 100 garments going to the wrong order. As we observed these employees, they appeared confident and knowledgeable about their job, yet they often would read the display and take what seemed to be random actions based on the same message. As we discussed the issues with the employees, we quickly learned they spoke different languages and usually just pretended they understood. With more observation and more pressing questions about the actions being taken, we found out this particular location had thirteen different languages spoken by the employees, with only a few translators in the group. The simplest of messages were not understood and the prevailing culture was not to ask questions and show you didn't understand English. To resolve the first level of issues found at this location, as series of post-it notes and a chart of common messages with translations was located at each loading station to help the users understand the messages appearing on the screen. We also noticed many users did not understand the difference between machine status messages versus messages about the item to be sorted.

To solve this issue of understanding the two message types, we installed a yellow light and a small buzzer to inform the user that there was a machine issue and not a problem with the garment or items being sorted. This allowed the user to find the problem with the machine if they knew how, or find another employee that could help them. Just knowing it wasn't something they did or should have done allowed them the knowledge of what to do next.

We then visited two locations with new conveyors, one in Las Vegas and one in Nashville, where both operations were achieving the results they expected. At both locations, we added the yellow light and buzzer and asked them to report back in a week about what they thought of the addition. The responses were identical: it helped to quickly realize when there was a machine problem so they could resolve it.

In both Chicago and Boston, we ran into a new problem. The operators of the machines could speak English, but it took a while for us to realize that a few of them were illiterate. The operators who were illiterate were not willing to disclose this information freely, but a few of their confidants informed us of the issues without letting anyone know they had told us. We learned this is common with many illiterate people [2]. In 2014, 47% of Chicago's residents cannot read [3] and many of the lower skilled and lower educated people were the types of employees that ended up working on Metalprogetti conveyors. These locations achieved 95% accuracy overall. This was due to some operators being able to read and understand the messages and other operators making their best guess at what they should do when a message appeared that they did not understand.

3 Results from the Field

During the short term, we continued working with the nineteen installations, to improve training and processes, but we knew the long term solution was to design the machine to communicate better with the users to achieve the desired outcome across the board.

New displays were developed to further communicate with the operator so they were aware of the next step. See Fig. 1. The text-based display is still present, but depending on the system two to four lights and up to two audio signals can now be added to communicate with the operator. In most cases, the lights added are a green light telling the operator it is now ready to accept the item to be sorted and a red light alerting the operator that an issue has occurred with their previous action. The audio signals allowed another form of communication.

Fig. 1. New user interface with additional lights for enhanced communication.

The audio signals we added were two piezo buzzers attached to the display: a soft chime for when the scan was accepted, notifying the operator to continue with loading the machine, and a slightly harsher buzzer to alert a problem with the either the last action or the status of the conveyor.

The conveyor is now shipped with many more lights than those early days, including lights to display the status of compressed air and certain electrical inputs. This simple form of communication allows almost any level of employee to use the machine as effectively as the early adaptors and almost as well as the development team itself. During the installation of the machine, customers are offered the additional communication of the chime and buzzer.

> In one location, during a particularly bad day of employee absences, the ten-year-old daughter of the owner was allowed to load the conveyor. Her instructions were to continue only if she saw a green light. She was successful during her four-hour shift on the conveyor with the lights and buzzers installed.

4   Conclusion

The Metalprogetti conveyor was originally designed and initially deployed in the most desirable atmosphere for a sophisticated machine. Developers and initial users were not only impressed with the accuracy and ability of the machine but excited about using the new technology. When the success of the machine became known in the industry, many machines were installed in a much less desirable atmosphere for the same level of success. With a better understanding of the new conditions in which the machine was being used, better forms of Human Computer Interface elements were added. Metalprogetti now installs over 700 systems per year.

References

1. Koskinen, I.: Design Research Through Practice: From The Lab, Field, and Showroom. Elsevier, Amsterdam (2011)
2. Riekmann, W.: Functionally illiterate adults and their confidantes – results of the qualitative study, January 2014. https://www.researchgate.net/publication/279920222_Functional_Illiterates_and_their_confidants.pdf.ResearchGate, <https://www.researchgate.net/>
3. Karen Lewis and Chicago's Illiteracy Problem. Union Watch. N.p., 20 Nov. 2016. Web, 23 March 2017. <http://unionwatch.org/karen-lewis-and-chicagos-illiteracy-problem/>

An Investigation into the Key Factors to Improve the Attractiveness of Modular Furniture in the Living Environment of China's Metropolitan Migrants

Miao Liu, Zhaoyang Sun[✉], Xinming Guo, Xue Chen, and Ziwei Liu

East China University of Science and Technology, Shanghai, China
{183787975,775660337,534495190,
375325551,865911201}@qq.com

Abstract. Against the background of rapid urbanization, metropolises in China such as Beijing, Shanghai and Guangzhou are under intense pressure housing enormous waves of young migrants from all parts of the nation, also known as the "metropolitan new migrants" who expect better living environment, but faced with meagre paychecks, which was addressed by means of furniture design here. In this study, potential customers' pain points were identified by field researches and questionnaire. A simplified model was also proposed. A modular product system was divided into 3 dimensions: (1) Form, (2) Behavior, (3) Emotions, which were represented by (1) Structure and framework, (2) Linkage, (3) Individualization in a specific modular furniture system. An attempt was also made to innovate online shopping interface in order to enhance user experience. To make sure that the customers' solution space doesn't affect issues of safety, strength, ergonomics etc., a series of mechanical analysis was also done in reference to China's current standards for furniture strength. The simplified model proposed in this paper engages the customers in the process of design and planning, which ultimately promotes the users' sense of self-worth and and the feeling of being respected. One of the key factors to improve the attractiveness of modular furniture was identified—to meet users' emotional needs, which was finally confirmed by feedbacks of respondents revisited.

Keywords: Modularity · Furniture design · Emotional design · User experience · Interaction

1 Background

Emonormous waves of young people are flooding into metropolitan cities such as Beijing, Shanghai, Guangdong etc. with the speeding up of urbanization, and they are defined as "metropolitan new migrants". Different from "migrant workers" who migrate from rural areas to cities to earn a living by laboring physically, the "new migrants" mainly include poorly paid college graduates and white-collar workers. This group bears two hallmarks: First, mostly born after 80s or 90s, they are of young ages; Second, most of them are not of rural origins, instead from other cities or towns, and

© Springer International Publishing AG 2017
C. Stephanidis (Ed.): HCII Posters 2017, Part II, CCIS 714, pp. 575–582, 2017.
DOI: 10.1007/978-3-319-58753-0_81

they are migrating to more developed cities for better life conditions. Thus, their ways of life are neither similar to native metropolitan citizens nor manual workers—they live in neat and compact rented apartments and are subject to occasional relocation; On the other hand, due the the the facts that they are generally highly educated and tend to pursue cultural pluralism and individualism, which is typical of Chinese "post-90s", moreover they have already been accustomed to urban life, they are in need of individualized and higher living quality. However, researchers found in preliminary researches that it's typical of them to settle for a single compact room in a department shared with other tenants, and have to use second-hand furniture owned by landlords, which are worn and obsolete in appearance. This enormous population's living condition is far from expectations and can not be ignored. This study is aimed at improving their living environment through innovation in furniture design.

Modular furniture is seen as an opportunity of making breakthrough in this issue, because of its advantages over traditional furniture. A modular product (system) is composed of a series of units with allocated functions and standardized linkage structures. Modular furniture is economical in manufacture, time-saving in lead-time, environmentally friendly in recycling, and efficient in management, storage and transportation. Besides, modules are interchangeable and highly adaptable, which makes it possible to gain unlimited results (solution area) with limited units. There have been many attempts in modular furniture development, but surveys found that popularity and customers' satisfaction are low as for modular furniture products available on the market. Most of the respondents don't like the second-hand furniture in the rented apartments, but hardly any of them are willing to purchase modular furniture available on the market, because of their flaws in design, usability and prices. Preliminary surveys also showed that it's an urgency to reverse customers' negative impressions and conventional ideas about what modular furniture is, and furthermore to identify key factors to improve the attractiveness of modular furniture.

Based on the difference in the process of construction, modular furniture can be divided into two types: Type 1 and Type 2. There are 3 stages to construct a modular furniture product (system):

- Overall form design. The product as a whole is planned and designed at the outset.
- Deconstruction and module formation. The product as a whole is deconstructed and modules are separated out with different forms, functions, dimensions and structures etc. allocated to them.
- Modular product design. The modules are orchestrated and integrated into a product again with efficient linkage, usablility and feasibility and the design process is therefore completed.

In the second stage, parts of the whole product are reduced and simplified, for example a set of furniture can be divided into varied parts–desktops, table legs, chair legs etc., which are subsequently reduced and simplified to modules such as supporting modules, enclosure modules and surface modules. But not all pieces of so-called modular furniture are designed this way. So two types of modular furniture are therefore divided depending on whether there is a process of reduction and simplification.

Type 1: modular furniture without modular reduction and simplification. Surveys found that users' conventional ideas about modular furniture are what IKEA (Swedish furniture retailer) is like. But most products of IKEA are pre-designed, dismantled to pieces before transportation and re-assembled in customers' home. The customers can't individualize a certain piece of product. IKEA products belong to Type 1.

Type 2: modular furniture with modular reduction and simplification. For example, desktop and seat of a chair can be reduced to one single kind of module—surface module, and in this way, different modules are formed. The more simplified it is, the more advantages it have over traditional furniture. Customers can individualize their products as their wishes under certain instructions, in this way participate in product design and furthermore customers' needs for individualization are better satisfied.

By dividing the numbers of all possible solutions (S) with numbers of modules (M) (of the same one product or system), we have a value, which is defined as modular ratio (R). A higher modular ratio means bigger solution area and more simplified modules.

$$modular\ ratio = \frac{numbers\ of\ all\ possible\ solutions}{numbers\ of\ modules} \ or\ R = \frac{S}{M}$$

Take an IKEA product (A) and a modular furniture system (B) for comparison, $MA = n$, $SA = 1(n > 1)$, so $RA = 1/n$; $MB = 1$, $SB = m(m > 1)$, so $RB = m$. $1/n < 1 < m$, $RA < RB$. A belongs to Type 1 and B belongs to Type 2. Type 1's modular ratios are generally more than those of Type 2's. The studies hereafter exclusively deals with **modular furniture of Type 2**.

2 Pain Point Identification and Analysis

Preliminary surveys indicated that in contrast to the scarcity of modular furniture in customers' everyday life, conceptual designs of modular furniture are increasing in numbers, which implies development of modular furniture are backward in application. In order to seek out the key factors to improve the attractiveness of modular furniture (if not specifically explained, all "modular furniture" hereafter mentioned is referred to modular furniture of Type 2), a survey will be carried out from two perspectives: the perspective of retailers and that of customers. Modular furniture is a relatively avant-garde idea for an average Chinese, so most of them are sold online in e-shopping stores of Taobao or Tmall (both affiliated to Alibaba), the most influential e-commercial platforms in China. As for the potential customers the study was carried out by questionnaires.

2.1 A Survey on Retailers

Researchers searched on Taobao/Tmall for modular furniture products and the first 30 items were recorded as samples, among which 26 items belonged to Type 1 and only 4 of them belonged to Type 2. The 4 Type 2s' monthly sales fall between 0–3, total sales fall between 0–5, and statistics showed 0 users had added them to "favorites". Researches randomly chose one of the popular furniture retailers in China as a comparison, and found that monthly sales of all of the items in its Tmall official online store fell between 100–200, total sales 1000–7000, and numbers of users who had added any one of the items to "favorites", 50,000–200,000. The sharp contrast illustrated the unpopularity of modular furniture.

2.2   A Study on Potential Customers

By the definition of metropolitan new migrants, 300 potential customers were chosen as the subjects. They are from 3 districts: Xuhui, Minhang and Fengxian in Shanghai. Questionnaires were done either offline or online by the assistance of researchers, 298 questionnaires were retrieved and 280 qualified as valid. The respondants' personal information such as age, gender, income is shown in Table 1.

Table 1.   Respondents' personal information.

Age (years old)	18–22	22–26	26–30	31–35	36–40
Percentage	9%	32%	36%	21%	2%
Annual income ($\times 10^4$ yuan)	$(1/\infty, 5)$	$[5, 10)$	$[10, 20)$	$[15, 20)$	$[20, \infty]$
Percentage	16%	29%	26%	15%	14%
Gender	Male	Female			
Percentage	56%	44%			
Residence	Rented apartments	Private apartments	Others		
Percentage	82%	3%	15%		

100% of the respondents hold non-Shanghai "household registration"(aka Hukou system, which indicates where a citizen is native to), among whom males and females are of similar proportion, and mostly are youths aging between 22–35, earning 50,000–20,000 Chinese yuan annually. They were questioned in terms of their living conditions, attitudes towards modular furniture and tendencies in furniture-purchasing. 75% of the respondents had moved more than twice over the past 5 years. 82% didn't like their landlords' furniture in the rented apartments but hardly any of them are willing to buy new furniture they liked in order to improve their living environment. The main reason of the hesitation is the furniture is too heavy and would add to the ordeal of moving from one place to another.

When asked about their attitudes toward modular furniture, 92% of them tended to think the perfect archetype of "modular furniture" was IKEA, and there was nothing special about them in comparison with traditional furnitures, only they were dismantled in transportation and re-assembled in customers' home, therefore 7% of them didn't believe that "modular furniture" had the potential to be the solution to meet customers' needs of individualization and improve their living environment. Also, they mentioned "modular furniture" was difficult to assemble for non-professionals. And by then the concepts of two types of modular furniture was explained to respondents.

When asked about their attitudes towards modular furniture of Type 2, respondents expressed their concerns about technical problems such as safety, strength, ergonomics etc., which implied modular furniture of Type 2 would bring not only larger freedom of individualization, but also raise concerns about technical problems.

Chinese youths are becoming more and more dependent on Internet in every aspects of life including shopping. When asked about they preferred whether online shopping or offline shopping as to furniture-buying, 84% of the respondents preferred online shopping, 13% would accept both ways, while only 3% of them preferred offline shopping, or to say, physical stores. Many respondents also suggested that to be able to preview the effects visually would be a incentive to encourage consumption.

2.3   Summarize

A few pain points were identified through the previous studies, which are as follows:

- The furniture products available on market are generally too heavy and inconvenient to carry around.
- A modular furniture product or system consists of individualizable area and non-individualizable area. Non-individualizable area includes elements that affect safety, strengh, ergonomics etc. Individualizable area may include textures, colors, appearance which have no negative feedbacks on non-individualizable area. Modular products of Type 1, such as IKEA products, leave barely no individualizable area to customers.
- Modular furniture products of Type 2 give significantly larger individualisable area to customers but will also raise customers' concern about problems of safety and strengh etc. To dissolve their concern, and encourage them to construct their furniture reassuredly, elements that affect safety, strengh, ergonomics should be strictly confined within non-individualisable area, and at the same time individualisable area sould be enlarged to its extreme.
- Customers can't preview visually what it's like to arrange the furniture in their homes, which is of no help to customers' making purchasing decisions effectively and accurately.

3   Model Construction

3.1   Hypothesis Proposing

In this section, an attempt will be made to seek out the key factors to improve the attractiveness of modular furniture by hypothesis proposing, analyzing and constructing a simplified modular furniture system. Take the typical modular furniture system of Type 2—"Junction T" for example. From the aspects of form and operation, it's delicate and convenient. But from the perspective of emotions, it has an air of primitiveness due to its scaffolding-like, emotionless appearance. It can perfectly fit in some scenes but not in our target users' apartments. The importance of emotional factors were reiterated in Donald A. Norman's theory of emotional design. It is suspected that failure to take emotional factors into consideration is one of the reasons why modular furniture has failed to gain popularity. A modular furniture product (system) is divided into 3 dimensions, namely Form, Behavior and Emotion: The dimension of Form deals with modules' structure and framework; The dimension of Behavior deals with the way of construction, in specific, the linkage and its convenience, effectiveness and furthermore, the overall user experience; The dimension of Emotion deals with users' emotional needs, by offering more attractive product semantics, larger individualizable area, wider range of optional accessories etc. A hypothesis was made that one of the key factors to improve modular furniture's attractiveness is to meet users' needs on the third dimension, namely emotional needs.

The simplified model was completed with 3 sequential stages, namely (1) form and structure, (2) linkage, (3) individualization, which correspond with the 3 dimensions.

3.2   Three Stages to Construct Modular Furniture

The simplified model was constructed with reference to the pain points previously identified and users' emotional needs. Four major goals were set at the outset.

- To improve convenience in operation and to enhance portability.
- To enlarge the individulaizable area.
- To define the non-individualizable area by confining the factors of safety, strength and ergonomics within the non-individualizable area, and to dissolve users' concerns about these issues.
- To design online shopping interface including functions such as customerization, real-time preview, online paying and web-based tool-kits etc.

Stage One: Structure and Framework
4 types of furniture were the most commonplace in the target users' apartments, which are desks, chairs, beds and storage furniture including closets and drawers etc. Ergonomically acceptable dimensions are shown in reference []. Also, the difference between heights of a desk and chair is supposed to be within 280 mm–320 mm, the height of the space for thighs to fit in is supposed to be larger than 580 mm and etc. In order to make sure by combining the modules users can get all dimensions ergonomically desired, 3 kinds of modules shaped like cubes with different dimensions were proposed.

Stage 2: Linkage
To ensure a barrier-free experience, the linkage should be as simple as possible. Butterfly bolts are therefore employed in this system, so that users can screw up and down the bolts with bare hands, which ensures easy and efficient assembling, and also adds more fun to the experience.

Stage 3: Individualization
Full range of individualization options will be availble in order to satisfy users' emotional needs. Users can customize the furniture's material, texture, color and

surface treatments according their own preferences and tastes. Users will also be provided with optional accessories such as matresses, cushions and all kinds of drawers.

A prototype of web-based user interface was designed to visualize functions such as customization, preview and online paying etc. The interface includes four main functional zones: (1) Modules and Accessories: to display all available modules, accessories and decorations; (2) Preview: where all the units can be dragged to a previously built room (according to the real-life room's dimensions) and assembled in a way the users prefer, and where the users can preview the rendering effects, like trying on clothes in a shop before a mirror. Users can click on any part of the model to customize the material, color and texture of this part. (3) Total price: where users can see the names, numbers and prices of all the units they have chosen. (4) Online paying.

The new interface gives the users the opportunity to "try on" the products in their living space and see the effects real-timely, and therefore make wiser purchasing decisions.

3.3 Packaging

The traditional modular furniture of Type 1 was usually disintegrated to flat boards in order to save space. But to ensure the integration and stability of the product, modules will not be reduced to smaller parts, instead, a new way of packaging was employed. Smaller modules can be fitted inside larger ones. After we set them this way, we top them with a square panel with slots shaped as enclosed squre, so the modules' positions can be stabilized. Packaged this way, modules are more convenient to store, manage and transport, and the package panels can also be made use of in furniture assembling.

3.4 Mechanical Analysis

By mechanical analysis and referring to national standards in China, the product's usability, strength and safety were proved valid. Non-individualizable area was defined.

4 Conclusions and Prospects

The potential users were revisited, and 68% of them were "willing to try" the new model. In comparison with the previous proportion of 7% (who welcomed the idea of modular furniture of Type 2), the improvement can be confirmed.

Many of the respondents have indicated that the model managed to satisfy the needs of the metropolitan new migrants. It's simple, customizable, portable, recyclable, cost-saving, environment-friendly and highly adaptable to different living environments. It gives the users a larger individualizable area, within which the users can put their creative ideas in practice. Also, the interface of online shopping is convenient and quite favorable by the youths, and was thought to be able to facilitate the transportation.

However, there were a few of respondents who criticize the modules' "uniformity", which might result in dullness. "Uniformity" is the cost of modularity, and higher level of modularity results from higher level of uniformity, which is inevitable in modular design. To buffer the negative effects brought about by uniformity, breakthroughs were made in the third stage—or in the dimension of Emotion, though there are still some users call for more variation on products' form. It was also found that males and females' opinions on the model diverged significantly, specifically, more females showed interest in the model than males, which might be a new focus of study in the future.

The innovative aspects of this study are as follow: (1) The target users are metropolitan new migrants in China, which is symbolic of our time and who require more attention. The study is aimed at how to improve their living environment by furniture design. (2) From the perspective of design process, Type 1 and Type 2 were defined. *Modular ratio* and the formula of *modular ratio* was also proposed, which indicated the level of modularity. (3) In consideration of the unpopularity of modular furniture, Type 2 was seen as an opportunity to rejuvenate the modular furniture. The research question was raised—how to improve the attractiveness of modular furniture. (4) Users' pain points were identified by field researches and questionnaires. In reference to Donald A. Norman's theory of emotional design. The hypothesis was made that one of the key factors to improve the attractiveness of modular furniture is to satisfy users' needs in the emotional dimension. (5) By the construction of a simplified model and web-based user interface, and mechanical analysis, the study was carried out by theoretical deduction and design practice. The respondents revisited helped confirm the validity of the hypothesis—one of the key factors to improve the attractiveness of modular furniture (of Type 2) is to meet users' needs in the emotional dimension.

In the background of China's rapid urbanization, the conflict between metropolitan new migrants' rising demand for living conditions and the shrinking living space in cities, and that between the diversity of customers' needs and relatively tight budgets are addressed in this paper by means of modular furniture design. Modular furniture can not only be a promising solution, but can also cater for the new migrants' needs for pluralism, individualization and quality living environment. Further studies will be focus on how to refine modular furniture system, the difference between different groups of users, how to applicate the concepts to mass-produced furniture products, and how to produce guidelines for the design of modular products.

References

1. Holle, M., Straub, I., Roth, M.: Customer individual product development methodology for product architecture modification. In: IEEE Systems Conference (2016)
2. Norman, D.A.: Emotional Design. Basic Books, NewYork (2005)
3. Xu, S., Tao, Y.-B., Li, P.: Research on application of modularity in cabinet design. For. Mach. Woodwork. Equip. **11**, 016 (2011)
4. Norman, D.A.: The Design of Everyday Things. Basic Books, New York (2002)
5. GB/T 10357-2011 Experiment of furniture's mechanical property: Part 5–strength and durability of cabinets (2011)

The Interaction of Casual Users with Digital Collections of Visual Art. An Exploratory Study of the WikiArt Website

Lucia Marengo$^{(\boxtimes)}$, György Fazekas, and Anastasios Tombros

Queen Mary University of London, London E1 4NS, UK
l.marengo@qmul.ac.uk

Abstract. As many cultural institutions are publishing digital heritage material on the web, a new type of user emerged, that casually interacts with the art collection in his/her free time, driven by intrinsic curiosity more than by a professional duty or an informational goal. Can choices in how the interaction with data is structured increase engagement of such users? In our exploratory study, we use the WikiArt project as a case study to analyse how users approach search interfaces for free exploration. Our preliminary results show that, despite the remarkable diversity of artworks available, users rely on familiarity as their main criterion to navigate the website; they stay within known topics and rarely discover new ones. Users show interest in heterogeneous datasets, but their engagement is rarely sustained, while the presence of slightly unrelated artworks in a set can increase curiosity and self-reflection. Finally, we discuss the role of the database's perceived size on users' expectations.

1 Introduction

In the past 20 years, prominent museums have published their collections online, SFMOMA, Musei Vaticani and Rijks Museum, among others. Other projects collate data from smaller institutions and make them available as a single, larger collection, like Europeana, Google Cultural Institute and Wikiart. These projects aim to open, democratise and make cultural heritage more accessible, and have the potential to reach and engage a wide audience of casual users, beyond professionals and scholars, which research on exploratory interfaces mostly concentrated on.

How can we support exploration of casual users with digital collections of artworks? Our research adopts a user-centred approach and analyses the interaction of casual users with existing interfaces to extract how relevant features influence the user experience.

The paper is organised as follows. In the next section, we introduce our theoretical framework that draws from research on information seeking behaviours, and we describe previous studies in the design of exploratory interfaces for casual users. We then illustrate the exploratory study we conducted by observing ten participants freely exploring the Wikiart website [1]. Self-reported data

© Springer International Publishing AG 2017
C. Stephanidis (Ed.): HCII Posters 2017, Part II, CCIS 714, pp. 583–590, 2017.
DOI: 10.1007/978-3-319-58753-0_82

about the experience were collected through an interview and behavioural data were collected by logging their activity on the website (clicks). We analysed the choices and motivations of the participants following theories in information seeking behaviours.

2 Theoretical Framework and Related Works

Casual users interacting with digital collections are driven by intrinsic motivation in that they voluntarily expose themselves to information. They have no obvious task, information need or specific knowledge gap to bridge. Instead, casual-leisure behaviours can have a wide range of motivating factors, including a desire to change mood or physical state, to kill time, to further personal knowledge, often with no requirement for a specific topic, or to interact socially [6].

Previous studies have discussed the design of interfaces for casual users and have proposed design recommendations. According to Falkowski, the use of a search bar can limit exploration when it dominates the interface. While some search algorithms can isolate users from ideas and opinions different from their own, a phenomenon known as *filter bubble*, browsing gives the user an idea of the breath of contents and expose him/her to all the options, helping the discovery of new perspectives [7]. Walsh and Hall's propose the use of textual summaries of the content to expose the casual users to the overall potential collection. Other suggestions are providing semantic maps of the topics and subtopics, and highlighting contents with high "interestingness" (based on other users' behaviours) [9]. Björneborn introduces dimensions across digital physical and social interfaces to support divergent exploratory behaviours. Examples include, diversity and richness of topics, genres and modalities, use of contrast and imperfections to trigger curiosity, cross contacts between dissimilar areas of the collection, interfaces that invite the user to move, but also to stop and look closer [3].

Following a prototype-based research, Whitelaw developed an interesting framework based on visual representation specifically addressing accessibility of users with casual browsing behaviours [10]: in his *generous interfaces* visual weight is used to show the relative number of artifacts each category contains, or the home page is used to offer a full view of the whole collection.

Finally, Coburn run a design and evaluation study of an experimental interface for the Tyne & Wear online collection [4]. The interface is designed to foster serendipity and it presents the user with a random section of artworks and a dynamic infinite scroll: if the user scrolls frequently and fast the contents s/he encounters will be randomised, if s/he scrolls slowly the contents displayed will keep a close semantic with current ones. Users appreciated the interaction concept, express the need for a search bar for a better navigation control, while sustained immersive behaviours were at times perceived as addictive.

Behavioural psychology, specifically works by Berlyne [2] and Loewenstein [8], provide rich insights into exploratory behaviours and curiosity. Berlyne associated curiosity with the recognition and pursuit of novelty and challenge. Exploratory behaviours are described along two dimensions: on one axis curiosity ranges between *sensory*, seeking for novel sensation and stimuli, and *cognitive*, seeking for knowledge; on the second axis it ranges between *diversive*, seeking various sources of novelty, and *specific*, seeking in-depth experience with a stimulus. Moreover, behaviours move along both dimensions and curiosity can dry out and revive during a single experience. As described by Loewenstein, curiosity happens when we perceive a gap in our knowledge and, as we seek out to resolve the gap, we engage in exploratory behaviours. The theory proposes that curiosity is more likely to be triggered by information gaps that are significant yet not too big: finding a missing piece is more interesting when we are aware of the greater picture. A small gap is likely to be perceived as not worth any action, while a big one is usually perceived as an impossible goal, the user does avoid exposing him/herself to new information and the gap is not resolved.

3 The Study

For our first, exploratory study we selected Wikiart as a case study to observe the interaction of casual users. WikiArt is an online visual art encyclopedia. It collects more than 75000 digital reproductions of paintings from around the world and allows users to edit information about the pieces, much like what Wikipedia does. For this reason, some items are carefully annotated and enriched by textual information and others are not. The website was also chosen for the variety of works it displays, from popular masterpieces to works of less known artists, because it focuses on one type of contents only - visual art, and because it has a simple graphics and limited search options. The interface includes a home page that displays random artworks (changed daily), a search bar and a menu with predefined categories to browse. Whenever the user selects a single painting s/he is led to a detail page that also shows all other paintings from the same artist.

We designed two modalities for the user to interact with, free and topic-based exploration - FE and TE. In the free exploration the participant is able to navigate the website without any constraint; in the topic based exploration the participant chooses a topic and explore it using the database. Whilst they could propose a topic of their choice, a list of topics was available for participants to choose from.

3.1 Method

The study was conducted in one of the Labs at Queen Mary University of London. No compensation was offered and participants were thanked with some drinks and snacks. Each subject signed a consent form for the collection and use of the data. The study design follows a mixed-method (similar to [4,5,11]): we collected both quantitative and qualitative data during a one-hour session. At the beginning, participants were given a short introduction to the interface, including the main navigation options, as we were not interested in evaluating Wikiart's learnability nor we wanted the participant to spend time figuring out the navigation structure. The study was divided into two parts: in each part the participant explored the website using one of the two modalities for ten minutes and then answered a post-experience questionnaire. This included open and closed-ended questions, the former were answered in person and recorded. Table 1 shows the basic structure of the interview. The order of the modalities was randomised. At the end of the second part, the participants answered a final questionnaire about demographics, personal skills and past experience with digital collections. To analyse exploratory behaviours we collected all actions of click the participants performed; for each 'click' we saved the object that was clicked on and the time stamp.

Table 1. Examples of questions used during the interview

	Behaviour	Feedback
Main	How did you start?	What was positive during the experience?
	What happened?	What was negative?
Follow-up	Why did you select it?	What would you change?
	Was a painting your favourite?	

Participants were recruited via email among students of Queen Mary University of London. Ten people took part in the study individually, 9 of which were females; participants' age ranged between 19 and 47 years old, with 80% being in the 19–27 age group. All participants are students or ex-students in the Humanities Department. 50% were non-British and had other cultural backgrounds (Italy, China, India, Japan). 9 out of 10 indicated they have a medium to high interest in art, and none of them had professional training in the art field, 3 people had self-taught knowledge and 5 people studied art in high school.

3.2   Analysis and Results

Answers to the questionnaire have been plotted and analysed in a qualitative way; data collected during the interviews were transcribed and analysed thematically. In most cases data were analysed in a complementary way: interviews helped highlight motivations and emotional responses of the participants, while activity logs and results of the questionnaire gave us a quantitative measure of the reported behaviours and a reality check. The analysis focused on exploratory strategy, what the user was looking for, what the user did as first step of its exploration and on how and why it was attracted to a specific area of the collection (or single item). We are not discussing other aspects, such as how people changed their interest and modality.

On average participants were equally satisfied with the two modalities (3.8/5 FE and 3.4/5 TE). During the interview, all participants but two preferred the free exploration setting - P9: "that is why I preferred free exploration, cause it is kinda, well free".

Familiarity. Familiarity guided most participants in their free exploration. P1, P6 and P8 searched straight-away for a specific painting, artist or style they knew well in advance. They used both the search bar (P8 and P1), both the category menu (P6). P1: "I went straight back to that page that I liked from last time [during topic exploration]" P8: "I already had artists in my head that I like, I went straight searching for them. That is how I started". Familiarity was also a way to structure the exploration around a topic - P8: "my topic was, stuff that I like" - or to initially judge the collection and getting to know it - P6: "the first thing I did was I had a look at category which I know well to see what was in it, then I searched for my favourite artist". Participant were often attracted to a specific painting by familiarity, either with personal experiences, backgrounds or tastes - P5 picked the picture of a letter that reminded him/her of a movie s/he recently saw, on another occasion was guided by his/her cultural background - "it is a special Japanese style, is my language, is very special for me". P1 picked an artwork whose title reminded him/her of a character from a book and later selected a painting related to his/her assignment at QMUL. Personal tastes also related to the participants' choices. P9: "it makes me think to when I was younger and I used to really enjoy looking at this kind of paintings". Participants selected familiar topics also while using browsing tools that give them an overview of many other options, like the menu of categories - P5 selected impressionism because "I know the topic a little bit from before".

Attraction to the Unknown. The home page was a good attractor to novelty: P2, P4, P9 and P10 started by looking at random artworks. P4 and P9 likes the idea of random artworks, while P10 used it to have an overview of the contents of the website. All the participants quickly moved to other, less random modalities, the maximum time spent on random artworks is 1'06". Only one participant returned to use the home page - P2: "I followed the work of that artists, and then I came back to the home page [and picked another random artwork]. That happened once or twice". The interface seems not to support random exploration: when selecting one random artwork WikiArt displays artworks from the same author that have a semantic connection, while this might not match the user's intentions. P9: "it does not let you carry on, the randomness, so I had to go back and pick it again and that is when I started to go to the styles instead". The menu was used to find novelty (P2, P6, P3), though often people chose categories that *ring a bell* in their mind and they were not completely sure about (P9, P6). P9 never selected totally unknown categories, instead s/he picked those s/he had an expectation about, and enjoyed testing whether her/his assumption was correct. The lack of information about what the name of the categories mean sometimes discouraged people from selecting totally unknown options (P9). Finally, visual information gaps also worked as attractors: P2 was intrigued by the thumbnail of a painting that contained text s/he could barely read (because of the size). Attraction to novelty and diversive exploration seemed also related to personal inclination (P2, P3, partly P6) - P3: "[I select one style], but I always go back to see another type, another art movement I never saw before."

Heterogeneity. In many occasions, participants noticed artworks that were slightly different from those they were grouped with and followed this serendipitous encounter. P1 was looking at paintings of people reading books but picked the only one where the subject was looking straight at the painter - P1: "she is not even holding a book, so I do not know why it was in *reading*, I just though that face was interesting". Unrelated painting helped to independently learn about unknown themes: P1 compared paintings from the 18th century to less recent ones that also appeared in the results, and was able to talk about how the depicted subjects changed over time. P5 was able to compare the artist skills with different techniques as the interface displayed sketches and oil paintings together. An overview of the categories can also help the user to formulate an idea of the overall contents of the website and of the work of a single artist, and can give a sense of clarity and order that is appreciated (P5, P8, P10).

Information and Missing Information. People often mention the experience could have been better if they had more information about the paintings or the categories: information would help to connect and understand an artwork beyond a first, superficial look (P10, P4, P1, P8). Some people, however, did not like written information that was perceived intrusive to their personal experience and interpretation of art (P2, P6, P9). P6 said s/he did not look at any text, for P9 little information about the painting technique could be valuable, but "I wouldn't be too bothered to read reviews about paintings, because when you look at art, it is so, subjective [...] I see what I see, you see what you see". Similarly P2: "you do want some background, but not so much that the explanation takes over the artwork. [...] I think it takes away from the art a little when it requires so much explanation". Incomplete information also triggered imagination: P1 created a story about the girl in the painting after reading a short description of her relationship with the artist.

Size and Completeness. The huge number of items available was a positive feature (P5, P8, P9) and something that differentiate the website from a physical gallery with limited space (P5). P8 "it is quite impressive [...] they literally have maybe every piece of work that I would want to see". However, the richness of contents seems not balanced across categories, specifically between Western and Asian artist (P3, P10). The website might be perceived as being bigger than it is because its name suggests all known artworks are included (P6). The perceived size can influence the participants' expectations, they can be disappointed if they cannot find a specific artist they were looking for - P6: "I am sure it would be in there, I am sure they aim to put everyone in there". The size of the collection was also inferred from the number of styles in the category menu, and this sometimes led participants into a state of information overload. P9: "it was confusing, I was like wow, gosh that is without an information, like I do not know what any of these means either. 300 styles there were just so many". P10: "after I use [the filter tool] there is still a large collection to see, it is still too much for me."

Engagement. We evaluated how participants were engaged and whether their behaviours and feedback were due to active interest or passive browsing. Figure 1 shows the ratings from 1 to 5 for the engagement-related dimensions of satisfaction, boredom, interest, relaxation, fun, perception of the passing of time and of the physical context. Participants reported the experience to be a positive one, during both modalities (FE and TE), with the dimensions of boredom and non-interest having a low average (1.1 FE/TE, 1.2 FE and 1.1 TE), and fun and relaxing state having high rating (3.8 and 4.1 FE and 3.7 and 4.2 TE). People reported that they would be open to repeating the experience (3.8 FE and 3.7 TE). We found no significant difference comparing the rating for 1st and 2nd activity. The analysis of qualitative interviews highlighted that P10 was nervous because s/he was not given a specific task and did not feel useful to the research and that P6 was nervous because s/he thought the study was meant to evaluate his/her skills using the interface.

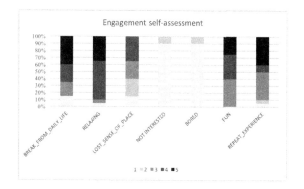

Fig. 1. Self-assessment of engagement-related dimensions

Usability. Participants reported on the usability and on any bugs they encountered. All subjects rated the usability with a score of 3 out of 5 or higher and 60% rated it 5. We judged the bugs as non-relevant in the scope of the study.

4   Discussion and Conclusion

We presented an exploratory study of casual users' interaction with the search interface of the WikiArt website. Participants' behaviours can be described according to curiosity dimensions proposed by Berlyne: some people seemed to be guided by diversive curiosity, using the category menu and jumping from one item to another, while others focused on few artists or styles (*specific curiosity*). The interface seems to be better suited for the latter group: to engage in diversive exploration users need to "go back" to the menu multiple times, or to open separate tabs, possibly associated with a higher cognitive load. We can also distinguish elements that might support *perceptual curiosity* (grid of thumbnails used to present search results) from elements that relate to *cognitive curiosity* (textual information and sections with heterogeneous artworks. Insights from the interviews revealed that users used familiarity as a main criteria to navigate the interface and, while serendipitous encounters still happened, people mostly explored areas of the collection they were already somewhat familiar with. These results support the information gap theory, while also suggesting that the current search interface does not encourage extreme curious behaviours, possibly leading to the information bubble phenomenon.

It should be considered that the study was run in a Lab and cannot fully mimic the experience in real context. The session could reflect behaviours during the first interaction with a website, but might not reflect subsequent interactions. Finally, participants were mostly females.

Acknowledgments. This research was funded by EPSRC and AHRC Centre for Doctoral Training in Media and Arts Technology (EP/L01632X/1).

References

1. Wikiart.org - visual art encyclopedia. https://www.wikiart.org/
2. Berlyne, D.E.: A theory of human curiosity. Br. J. Psychol. **45**(3), 180–191 (1954). General Section
3. Björneborn, L.: Design dimensions enabling divergent behaviour across physical, digital, and social library interfaces. In: Ploug, T., Hasle, P., Oinas-Kukkonen, H. (eds.) PERSUASIVE 2010. LNCS, vol. 6137, pp. 143–149. Springer, Heidelberg (2010). doi:10.1007/978-3-642-13226-1_15
4. Coburn, J.: I don't know what im looking for: better understanding public usage and behaviours with tyne & wear archives & museums online collections. In: MW2016: Museums and the Web 2016 (2016)
5. Dörk, M., Williamson, C., Carpendale, S.: Navigating tomorrow's web: from searching and browsing to visual exploration. ACM Trans. Web (TWEB) **6**(3), 13 (2012)
6. Elsweiler, D., Wilson, M.L., Kirkegaard Lunn, B.: Chapter 9 understanding casual-leisure information behaviour. In: New directions in Information Behaviour, pp. 211–241. Emerald Group Publishing Limited (2011)
7. Falkowski, J.: Custom collections content and generous interfaces. In: MW2016: Museums and the Web 2016 (2016)
8. Loewenstein, G.: The psychology of curiosity: a review and reinterpretation. Psychol. Bull. **116**(1), 75 (1994)
9. Walsh, D., Hall, M.M.: Just looking around: Supporting casual users initial encounters with digital cultural heritage (2015)
10. Whitelaw, M.: Generous interfaces for digital cultural collections. Digit. Humanit. Q. **9**(1), 38 (2015)
11. Zhang, J., Marchionini, G.: Evaluation and evolution of a browse and search interface: relation browser++. In: Proceedings of the 2005 National Conference on Digital Government Research, pp. 179–188. Digital Government Society of North America (2005)

Interactive Image Search System
Based on Multimodal Analogy

Kosuke Ota, Keiichiro Shirai, Hidetoshi Miyao, and Minoru Maruyama[✉]

Computer Science and Engineering, Shinshu University, Nagano, Japan
`maruyama@cs.shinshu-u.ac.jp`

Abstract. We propose an image search system based on multimodal analogy, which is enabled by using a visual-semantic embedding model. It allows us to perform analogical reasoning over images by specifying properties to be added to/subtracted with words such as *[a image of a blue car] - 'blue' + 'red'*. The system mainly consists of the following two parts: (i) an encoder that learns image-text embeddings and (ii) a similarity measure between embeddings in a multimodal vector space. As for the encoder, we adopt a CNN-LSTM encoder proposed in [1], which was reported that it can learn multimodal linguistic regularities. We also introduce a new similarity measure based on the difference between additive and subtractive query. It gives us reasonably better results than the previous approach at qualitative analogical reasoning tasks.

Keywords: Multimodal learning · Neural networks

1 Introduction

Most of the modern image search systems only determine images that have properties specified by a given query. They still work most of the time. However, it is often the case that search results are not quite right for our need. Suppose, for example, we have an image that is perfect except for the color of one object. In this case, it is desirable that we can perform arithmetic operations such as *[a image of a blue car] - 'blue' + 'red'* so that we can get the ideal image. Such a system could extend the possibilities of image searching. This could lead to a more interactive system, for instance, which can search for images through verbal interactions with voice assistants.

To address this problem, we propose an image search system based on multimodal analogy. A visual semantic embedding model, which forms the core of the system, enables us to perform analogical reasoning over images by specifying properties to be added to/subtracted from the current results with words.

Additionally, in order to search for an image specified by the aforementioned arithmetic operation, it is necessary to introduce an appropriate similarity measure. We therefore propose a measure based on the difference between additive and subtractive queries. We show the effectiveness of the measure by experiment.

© Springer International Publishing AG 2017
C. Stephanidis (Ed.): HCII Posters 2017, Part II, CCIS 714, pp. 591–596, 2017.
DOI: 10.1007/978-3-319-58753-0_83

2   Multimodal Learning

2.1   Visual-Semantic Embedding Models

To operate arithmetic between images and text, they need to be represented in a shared vector space. Much research has been done on learning joint embeddings of images and text. A well-known approach is to learn a function that maps both image and word embeddings into a common vector space [1–3]. The learned image-text embeddings are often called *visual-semantic embedding* since semantic relationships between images and text can be obtained through its training process.

2.2   Multimodal Linguistic Regularities

Kiros et al. [1] reported that multimodal linguistic regularities were found in an image-text embedding space, while the main focus of their work is on image captioning. They qualitatively investigated properties of the multimodal vector space and the results indicate that linguistic regularities [4] carry over to the joint space.

They also proposed the visual-semantic embedding learned on the image-text encoder. The image-text encoder (Fig. 1) consists of convolutional neural network (CNN) [5] and long short-term memory (LSTM) [6]. The CNN and LSTM take images and sentences as input, respectively. In the training phase, the network is optimized to minimize a pairwise ranking loss:

$$
\min_{\theta} \quad \sum_{\boldsymbol{X}} \sum_{k} \max\{0, \ \alpha - S(\boldsymbol{X}, \boldsymbol{V}) + S(\boldsymbol{X}, \boldsymbol{V}_k)\} + \\
\sum_{\boldsymbol{V}} \sum_{k} \max\{0, \ \alpha - S(\boldsymbol{V}, \boldsymbol{X}) + S(\boldsymbol{V}, \boldsymbol{X}_k)\}, \tag{1}
$$

where $\max\{\cdot, \cdot\}$ returns the larger value, θ denotes the model parameters, α is a margin, and cosine similarity is used as a scoring function $S(\cdot, \cdot)$. $\boldsymbol{V}_k$ and $\boldsymbol{X}_k$ are, respectively, contrastive embeddings for image embeddings $\boldsymbol{X}$ and sentence embeddings $\boldsymbol{V}$. Intuitively, the loss function trains the network to assign high scores to correct pairs of images and text, while it gives incorrect pairs low scores.

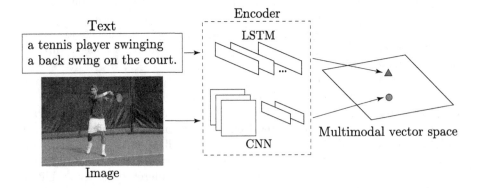

Fig. 1. Image-text encoder of the visual-semantic embedding model

3 Similarity Measure Based on the Difference Vector

Given a base query image and words that specify additive/subtractive properties, Kiros et al. [1] uses the following similarity measure:

$$S(\boldsymbol{X},\ q_{\text{img}} - q_{\text{sub}} + q_{\text{add}}), \tag{2}$$

where q_{img}, q_{add}, q_{sub} are vector representations of queries in the multimodal vector space and $S(\cdot, \cdot)$ is cosine similarity. With the similarity measure (2), we try to find vector $\boldsymbol{X}$ that is closest to $q_{\text{img}} - q_{\text{sub}} + q_{\text{add}}$, with respect to cosine similarity.

A desirable target $q_{\text{img}} - q_{\text{sub}} + q_{\text{add}}$ can be represented as "$q_{\text{img}} + \text{difference}$." The difference vector is specified by direction and magnitude. The similarity measure in (2) constrains both the direction and the magnitude of the difference from the base image. However, the arithmetic "base $-$ sub $+$ add" is just a qualitative one. Usually, it could be hard for us to specify the magnitude of the difference vector by only giving additive/subtractive words.

In our method, instead of (2), we use the following measure:

$$S(\boldsymbol{X} - q_{\text{img}},\ q_{\text{add}} - q_{\text{sub}}). \tag{3}$$

With this similarity measure, we try to find $\boldsymbol{X}$ such that the difference from the base image is similar to "add $-$ sub" (see Fig. 2).

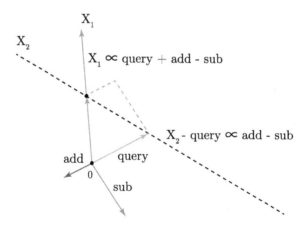

Fig. 2. Relations among our similarity measure and the previous one

4 Experiments

We conduct experiments in the same manner as [1] to compare our results to the previous method [1]. We used the Microsoft COCO dataset [7] to train the encoder.

---

[1] We reproduced their results using code available on https://github.com/ryankiros/visual-semantic-embedding.

594   K. Ota et al.

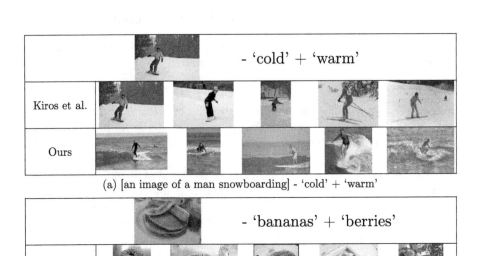

(a) [an image of a man snowboarding] - 'cold' + 'warm'

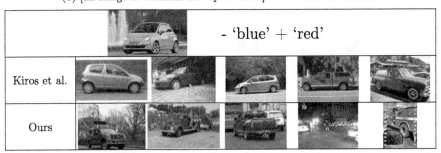

(b) [an image of bananas on top of cakes] - 'bananas' + 'berries'

(c) [an image of a blue car] - 'blue' + 'red'

(d) [an image of a dog] - 'dog' + 'cat'

Fig. 3. Examples that our measure performs better than the previous method

The dataset contains about 83,000 images and each image is accompanied by 5 descriptive sentences.

Figures 3 and 4 both shows (2) vs. (3) comparison on multimodal analogical reasoning tasks. Figure 3 illustrates some examples that our measure performs better than the previous one in terms of ranking order. Note that our measure also performs well when query words are not visually obvious as shown in the first example in Fig. 3, while the previous approach struggles to find plausible images.

On the other hand, Fig. 4 shows cases of our poor results. The system gives us irrelevant images. We speculate this is most likely due to the insufficiency of training data and it prevents the network from learning semantic relationships. However, we still need to investigate the cause further.

Taking all these results into consideration, we consider our measure to be more suitable to search for images based on multimodal analogical reasoning.

(a) [an image of cats in a cup] - 'bowl' + 'box'

(b) [an image of pancakes with bananas] - 'sweet' + 'salty'

Fig. 4. Examples that our measure shows irrelevant images

5   Conclusion

We proposed an image search system based on multimodal analogy that allows us to perform analogical reasoning over images and text. Our difference-based similarity measure gives us reasonably better results than the previous method at qualitative analogical reasoning tasks. The system provides us flexibility that would be useful when searching for images through verbal interactions with voice assistants, which is gaining more and more attentions recently, as well as traditional web image search systems.

Acknowledgement. M. Maruyama was supported by JSPS Kakenhi Grant Number JP26330249.

References

1. Kiros, R., Salakhutdinov, R., Zemel, R.S.: Unifying visual-semantic embeddings with multimodal neural language models. arXiv preprint arXiv:1411.2539 (2014)
2. Dong, J., Li, X., Snoek, C.G.M.: Word2visualvec: cross-media retrieval by visual feature prediction. arXiv preprint arXiv:1604.06838 (2016)
3. Frome, A., Corrado, G.S., Shlens, J., Bengio, S., Dean, J., Ranzato, M.A., Mikolov, T.: Devise: a deep visual-semantic embedding model. In: Advances in Neural Information Processing Systems (NIPS) (2013)
4. Mikolov, T., Yih, W.T., Zweig, G.: Linguistic regularities in continuous space word representations. In: Proceedings of Conference of the North American Chapter of the Association for Computational Linguistics (NAACL) (2013)
5. Simonyan, K., Zisserman, A.: Very deep convolutional networks for large-scale image recognition. In: Proceedings of International Conference on Learning Representations (2015)
6. Hochreiter, S., Schmidhuber, J.: Long short-term memory. Neural Comput. (1997)
7. Chen, X., Fang, H., Lin, T.-Y., Vedantam, R., Gupta, S., Dollar, P., Zitnick, C.L.: Microsoft coco captions: data collection and evaluation server. arXiv preprint arXiv:1504.00325 (2015)

Preliminary Survey for Multigraph Integration and Visualization Framework

Ryosuke Saga[✉]

Graduate School of Humanities and Sustainable System Sciences,
Osaka Prefecture University, Sakai, Japan
saga@cs.osakafu-u.ac.jp

Abstract. This study presents a preliminary survey on treating multiple graphs in visualization tasks. Preprocessing and visualization are involved in visualizing graphs. However, to treat multiple graphs, related viewpoints, such as graph skeletons, graph summarization, and graph drawing, should also be considered. This study describes approaches based on these viewpoints and presents their limitations.

Keywords: Visualization · Graph integration · Graph drawing · Co-occurrence network

1 Introduction

Graph visualization has recently given importance to the areas of visualization and data analysis. Graph visualization is commonly shown as a node–link diagram that enables observers to recognize data as the relationships among data are shown by connected links [1, 2].

To reduce visual clutter in graph visualization similar to other visualization techniques, changing the layout of the graph was initially proposed [3]. By re-arranging the nodes correctly, the visibility of the graph increases to a certain degree. However, this approach cannot address the problem of a graph having large edges. To solve this problem, a new approach called edge bundling was suggested [4, 5]. This method enables observers to recognize the main stream of edges through bundle edges based on some rules. The mechanical bundling method proposed in related works has succeeded in improving the visibility of graphs by clarifying the bundle of edges.

In a comparison analysis, multiple graphs are compared to determine the features among them. For example, graphs that show topics in each newspaper can be compared, and their elements, such as node, link, label, and cluster, among others, are verified. However, the cost of verifying these elements is massive, and understanding the features through this process is difficult. To solve this problem, Saga et al. proposed a method called FACT-Graph to analyze the two integrated graphs [6]. Although FACT-Graph can be used for comparison analysis, it mainly targets trend visual analysis by integrating two graphs. Therefore, the process of generating FACT-Graph is not generalized for general-purpose visual analysis.

© Springer International Publishing AG 2017
C. Stephanidis (Ed.): HCII Posters 2017, Part II, CCIS 714, pp. 597–601, 2017.
DOI: 10.1007/978-3-319-58753-0_84

This study aims to build a framework to integrate not only two but also multiple graphs and more methods for general-purpose problems. The overall framework consists of three components: graph skeleton, graph summarization, graph drawing. This study describes the state of the art of the technologies and discusses the possibility of building this framework.

2 Graph Integration Strategy

2.1 Graph Representative

A graph is based on graph theory in mathematics. It consists of vertices and edges, which also possess attributes. The vertex set is V, the edge set is E, and the graph G_i is presented as $G_i = (V_i, E_i)$. V and E are also known as graph elements, and V_i and E_i are elements of graph G_i. Each vertex $v_i \in V_i$ and each edge $e_i \in E_i$ has n and m attributes, that is, $v_i = (v_{i1}, v_{i2}, \ldots, v_{in})$, $e_i = (e_{i1}, e_{i2}, \ldots, e_{im})$. Additionally, each vertex and edge has a label as its identifier. The edge between two vertices A and B is expressed as $e_{A \to B}$ (note that $e_{A \to B}$ is equal to $e_{B \to A}$ in an undirected graph).

We also assume that graphs derived from datasets $D_1, D_2,\ldots, D_n$ are shown as $G = \{G_{Di}, G_{D2,\ldots} G_{Dn}\}$ and $G_{Di} = (V_{Di}, E_{Di})$ ($i = 1, 2, \ldots, n$), and the integrated graph is $G' = (V', E')$.

2.2 Graph Skeleton

A graph skeleton is a template of overall graphs, and it aids in integration and summarization. If an element can be observed in one graph but not in others, then the integration and summarization processes may not work because of missing elements.

To express the skeleton as a formula, the graph skeleton G_s is shown as formula (1):

$$G_S = (V_S, E_S) = set(G), \tag{1}$$

where the *set* function is a selection function of the elements from the graphs. The union function (formula (2)), intersect function (formula (3)), and probabilistic approaches (formula (4)) can be used. Formula (2) is adopted in studies such as [7] and called a super graph. The graph frequency pattern can also be employed to extract useful vertices and edges [8].

$$set(G) = \left(\bigcup_{i=1}^{N} V_i, \bigcup_{i=1}^{N} E_i \right) \tag{2}$$

$$set(G) = \left(\bigcap_{i=1}^{N} V_i, \bigcap_{i=1}^{N} E_i \right) \tag{3}$$

$$set(G) = \left\{ (V_p, E_p) | v \in V_p, e \in E_p, S(v) \geq t_v, S(e) \geq t_e \right\} \tag{4}$$

We suppose that the graph G_A has three vertices labelled "A," "B," and "C" and that graph G_B has "B," "C," and "D." Furthermore, G_a has two edges, $e_{A \to B}$ and $e_{B \to C}$, and

G_B has three edges, $e_{B \rightarrow C}$, $e_{B \rightarrow D}$, and $e_{C \rightarrow D}$. The integrated graph has four vertices and four edges as shown in Fig. 1.

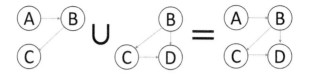

Fig. 1. Example of two graphs by a union operation

2.3   Graph Summarization

After generating the graph skeleton, each attribute in each element is integrated and summarized. The summarized attribute values are based on visualization. The function called *integrate function* is generally expressed as formula (5):

$$\text{Integrate}(G) = (f_v(v_{si}), f_e(e_{ei})), \tag{5}$$

where f_v and f_e are aggregated functions like sum and average. When the integration function obtains the maximum elements of a certain attribute, each vertex and each edge are applied as follows:

$$\text{Integrate}(G) = (\max(v_{D1}, \ldots, v_{Dn}), \max(e_{D1}, \ldots, e_{Dn})). \tag{6}$$

If the graphs are temporary graphs based on a time-series dataset, integrate functions can become weight attributes. To summarize attributes, the principle component analysis (PCA) and clustering can be utilized. Specifically, PCA can reduce the number of attributes, but the meaning of the principal component is difficult for a computer to comprehend. Clustering is similar to PCA. It naturally finds the common causality and hidden relationships behind the multivariable data treated in this study. Consequently, clustering leads to summarizing the multivariable data and reducing the number of vertices.

2.4   Graph Drawing

An integrated graph is visualized on screen. Graph layout algorithms, such the Kamada-Kawai layout, are important and useful in drawing graphs. Compounding vertices can also be adopted using clustering algorithms. Note that each element layout based on the attribute value, relationships, and aesthetic criteria should be considered. However, these approaches cannot treat massive edges. Recently, edge bundling has become attractive in the field of graph drawing. Several approaches for edge bundling were proposed by Saga and Yamashita [9] and Yamashita and Saga [10]. Presentation, that is, how vertices and edges based on multivariable data are expressed, should also be considered. The visualization of a graph drawing is summarized in [11] according to the perceptions of group-only, group–vertex, group–edge, and group–network.

3 Limitation and Conclusion

This study described a preliminary survey for treating multiple graphs in visualization tasks. We discussed three viewpoints, namely, graph skeletons, graph summarization, and graph drawing. Similar to other studies, this work has its limitations.

Evaluation. Several criteria, such as Data-ink and the criteria proposed by Saga [12], can be used. However, building complete evaluation criteria for integrated graphs is difficult because much information and multiple viewpoints are embedded in an integrated graph. Therefore, developing an experimental design for qualitative evaluation is challenging, thus leading to the difficulty in building a quantitative evaluation model.

Massive and Messy Data. Originally, messy and massive data must be disclosed, as it is an important task for visualization. However, an integrated graph may become more complex through the integration and summarization processes. Finding hundreds of categories/classes is possible in massive data, but traditional representation methods that attributes, such as color and shape, to graph elements are not sufficient and solutions for visualization are expected. Nevertheless, effective methods are now developing through filtering and interaction.

Acknowledgement. This work was supported by JSPS KAKENHI Grant Numbers 16K01250 and 25420448.

References

1. Ward, M., Grinstein, G., Keim, D.: Interactive data visualization. A. K. Peters, Natick (2010)
2. Herman, I., Melançon, G., Marshall, M.S.: Graph visualization and navigation in information visualization: a survey. IEEE Trans. Vis. Comput. Graph. 6(1), 24–43 (2000)
3. Mueller, C., Gregor, D., Lumsdaine, A.: Distributed force-directed graph layout and visualization. In: Proceedings of the 6th Eurographics Conference on Parallel Graphics and Visualization, Lisbon, vol. 6, pp. 83–90 (2006)
4. Zhou, H., Xu, P., Yuan, X., Qu, H.: Edge bundling in information visualization. Tsinghua Sci. Technol. 18(2), 145–156 (2013)
5. Holten, D.: Hierarchical edge bundles: visualization of adjacency relations in hierarchical data. IEEE Trans. Vis. Comput. Graph. 12(5), 1077–2626 (2006)
6. Saga, R., Terachi, M., Tsuji, H.: FACT-graph: trend visualization by frequency and co-occurrence. Electron. Commun. Jpn. 95(2), 50–58 (2012)
7. Beck, F., Burch, M., Diehl, S., Weiskopf, D.: The state of the art in visualizing dynamic graphs. In: EuroVis – STARs, pp. 83–103. Eurographics Association (2014)
8. Inokuchi, A., Washio, T., Motoda, H.: An apriori-based algorithm for mining frequent substructures from graph data. In: Zighed, D.A., Komorowski, J., Żytkow, J. (eds.) PKDD 2000. LNCS, vol. 1910, pp. 13–23. Springer, Heidelberg (2000). doi:10.1007/3-540-45372-5_2
9. Saga, R., Yamashita, T.: Multi-type edge bundling in force-directed layout and evaluation. Procedia Comput. Sci. 60, 1763–1771 (2015)

10. Yamashita, T., Saga, R.: Edge bundling in multi-attributed graphs. In: Yamamoto, S. (ed.) HIMI 2015. LNCS, vol. 9172, pp. 138–147. Springer, Cham (2015). doi:10.1007/978-3-319-20612-7_14
11. Vehlow, C., Beck, F., Weiskopf, D.: Visualizing Group Structures in Graphs: A Survey. Computer Graphics Forum (2016)
12. Saga, R.: Quantitative evaluation for edge bundling based on structural aesthetics. In: Isenberg, T., Sadlo, F. (eds.) EuroVis 2016 - Posters. The Eurographics Association (2016)

A Study on the Relationship Between Form Features and Images of Concept Bicycles Using the Theory of Archetype

Meng-Dar Shieh[1(✉)], Fang-Chen Hsu[2], and Chi-Wei Huang[1]

[1] Department of Industrial Design, National Cheng-Kung University, No. 1, University Road, East District, Tainan City 701, Taiwan, R.O.C.
mdshieh2016@gmail.com
[2] Department of Multimedia and Entertainment Science, Southern Taiwan University of Science and Technology, No. 1, Nan-Tai Street, Yungkang District, Tainan City 710, Taiwan, R.O.C.
id9lelva@gmail.com

Abstract. Two-wheel electric vehicles have gradually attracted people's attentions in recent years, thus more designers focus on styling designs to satisfy consumers' psychological demands. A product need to satisfy consumers' expectation with not only nice appearance and functions, but also a good image. A product with its definite image can create its segment in the marketplace. This study applies the archetype theory in product form design, and takes the concept bicycle as a case study. The classification of morphological features is carried out by a great deal of concept bicycle images. Then 60 samples made according the morphological chart are used for image evaluation. Finally, the relationship between form features and image perceptions is built by back-propagation artificial Neural Network (NN). According to the results, the pattern of the Innocent archetype has a similar condition as the Jester archetype. Both of them correspond to the styling with a strong sense of volume and perfectly round form. For the Explorer archetype, the riding posture has a large effect on subjects' image perceptions. Meanwhile, the handlebar and drive system have enormous effects on image perceptions as well. The image perceptions of the Sage, Outlaw, Lover, and Ruler archetypes are conducted to be different by colors, materials, and curved surfaces on the image cognition map. But, those three factors above cannot be recognized by the samples drawn in gray. Moreover, the form features for each archetype have been carried out. These would be useful for the designs of concept bicycle.

Keywords: Archetype theory · Form feature · Concept bicycle · Image perception · Neural network

1 Introduction

Design is an instrument applied to develop customer's faith in product and brand, facilitate the positioning of product and brand (Berkowitz 1987; Bitner 1992; Bloch 1995), and a means of great significance to raise product's competitiveness (Bloch 1995;

© Springer International Publishing AG 2017
C. Stephanidis (Ed.): HCII Posters 2017, Part II, CCIS 714, pp. 602–611, 2017.
DOI: 10.1007/978-3-319-58753-0_85

Kotler and Alexander Rath 1984). Apart from meeting customer's expectations of appearance and function, a product with a clear image is able to separate itself from others in the market, which is beneficial to marketing and the building of brand image (Mark and Pearson 2001), while the product design with aesthetics awareness receives positive comments on brand (Kreuzbauer and Malter 2005). In the context that the bicycle sports recreation prevails across the world, a growing number of consumers are willing to buy a bicycle at a higher price instead, which drives quite a few businesses to promote brands and to be dedicated to the design and development of high-end products. Having knowledge of the relationship between image feature and customer's cognition of image can help designers on the style design. In the sector of industrial design, adjective vocabulary in Kansei engineering is most used as a method for product's image description (Guo et al. 2016; Su and Li 2007; Wang 2011; Wang and Yeh 2015). Woodside et al., however, argue that a product with record may linger in people's minds (Woodside et al. 2008), finding favor with a consumer. A consumer may have a particular psychological archetype image according to the research on the bicycle of Triathlon. The image is just the idea which a designer expects to reflect in the product style design (Shieh et al. 2016). In this research, archetype theory is used to probe into the cognition of product images, so as to determine the impact of form features on the product image, and acquire consumer's image cognitions of concept bicycles. Back-propagation artificial Neural Network (NN) is applied to analysis the relationship between the form features and archetype images, thereby helping a designer with the style design.

2   Background

2.1   The Descriptions of Form Features

Style design comprises three essential factors, i.e. morphology, color and texture, of which, morphology is the first used by a consumer to know a product. Two ways, qualitative and quantitative, are normally employed for the description of morphology. In terms of the former, a product's deconstruction generally depends on the experienced expert. For example, morphological analysis features a wider range of morphology, with the disadvantage presented by subjectivity and inaccuracy. While the latter, thanks to precise description of morphology, is more used in the quantitative research on morphology. For example, curve description. The appearance demonstrated with point coordinates, however, may lead to the failure of an interviewee to have direct association with the morphology.

Morphological analysis was originated by Zwicky, a Swiss astronomer working with California Institute of Technology (Zwicky 1948). Based on structure analysis, the form features of object are listed and all variable factors can be combined in any possible manner in the morphological chart. Thanks to the objective and various combinations of product appearance, morphological analysis is seeing an extensive in the industrial filed. In the research on the appearance of bicycle, Hsiao and Ko adopted morphological analysis to establish the morphological factors table in accordance with parts of bicycle, including "handlebar", "saddle", "frame", "wheel set", and "chainwheel set an crank", and the combination of the features mentioned above may enable a large number of design schemes (Hsiao and Ko 2013). Lai, Lin, and Yeh divided a mobile into nine design factors of shapes and outlines by morphological analysis in the research on the mobile design, totaling 27 types (Lai et al. 2005). Yang divided the design of digital camera into factors under 16 types by morphological analysis (Yang 2011). Due to the feature of the analysis in the systematic deconstruction of product form, the combination of possible solutions may offer several design ideas or proposals, which makes possible the simple and objective of handing of problem particulars, so as to understand and analyze the problem in a more correct way (Cross and Roy 1989; Jones 1992).

2.2   The Application of Neural Network in Form Design

Back-propagation artificial NN is a most universal and typical network in the NN for the structure of Supervised Learning Network. Many scholars use NN to conduct the research related to the association between product form features and images. Chen and Chang held that the network, compared with conventional statistics and analysis technology, boasts priority in the independent and dependent variables. As a result, it used to establish the predication model of "design feature of cutter" and "consumer's image cognition" (Chen and Chang 2014a). In terms of decreased independent variable, the model still delivers a good performance by the combination of back-propagation NN and multiple linear regression (Chen and Chang 2014b). Lai et al., by the combination of grey prediction and NN to establish the predication model, which enables the best combination of design factors for an ideal product image. Apart from allowing a designer to put more focus on the design factors of product itself by a simplified NN, it can deliver a better performance in predication than those of conventional NN (Lai et al. 2005).

2.3   Archetype Theory

To explain the personality and motivations, Carl Jung, a psychiatrist, proposed the concept of archetypes. People thought that Jungian archetypes were collectively and unconsciously hidden in an individual's deeper gradation of sub-consciousness. It was shown in various "symbols", such as dreams, myths, arts, religions, etc. In many ancient myths, tribal legends and primitive art, the common symbols were found existing in different civilizations and nationalities repeatedly. These symbols were combining with instinct, archetypes, and archetype images commonly and widely. The archetype was a kind of tendency to form various meanings and appearances, which kept the basic pattern yet transformed the details. Campbell, the myth pundit, had found that the contents of hero stories in different cultures were not always the same but the story plots could follow the same archetype. Hence, every type of archetype has its own symbols to present the specific images in different situations (Campbell 2008).

Based on Jungian psychology, twelve kinds of archetypes, including "Hero", "Ruler", "Sage", "Creator", "Magician", "Explorer", "Lover", "Caregiver", "Innocent", "Jester", "Outlaw", and "Regular Guy", have been defined by Mark and Pearson. They pointed out the possibility of applying the archetypes on products' brand designs.

Brands could have distinctive images by making appropriate marketing strategies through the archetypes to arouse consumers' brand recognition and then deepen and strength the meaning of brands. When a brand has a strong meaning, it could be more distinguished than other brands, and it could even affect the decision making and self-development of consumers (Mark and Pearson 2001). Take two worldwide famous brands for examples: "Explorer" is a brand image of a famous jeans, Levi's, and it creates the concept of maintaining independence; "Hero" is a brand image of a famous sports brand, NIKE, and it conveys the concept of acting courageously.

The relationship between the extended self and possessions had been proposed by Belk. Consumers would regard products as one part of themselves, and then products could help build their self-identities. "Ownership" could symbolically extend the self, so that individuals are convinced that they are more unique than the others who do not own this possession (Belk 1989). When a consumer owns a product of a brand, the meaning of the product or the brand could bring him some feeling. The further extension of the meaning of a brand cannot only produce the identification, objects, and behavior of the personal, but also help him achieve his goals and get the spiritual power to symbol himself.

3 Proposed Approach

3.1 Form Analysis and Features Coding of Concept Bicycles

Thanks to the demonstration of most design features, the lateral view of bicycle is determined as the object to be probed into in this research. Meanwhile, a total of 146 lateral view pictures of concept bicycles released by manufacturers, works wining award in the design contest and works of designer are collected. In this research, such structure systems with distinctive features of a bicycle as frame, drive, wheel and control are used as bases for the selection of representative parts. The design feature of a bicycle is subject to the function. The conventional bicycle employs gear disc and chain as the drive system, while part of concept bicycle integrates the drive system and frame, which makes it not easy to identify in terms of appearance, or the spoke-less wheel, which leads to the great difference in form. As a result, the appearance of a concept bicycle is discussed in the three parts as follows: "**Frame**", "**Wheel set**" and "**Handlebar**", of which, due to great variation of concept bicycle in form, the "**Frame**" is divided into 25 categories. In terms of the "**Drive system**" of concept bicycle, the form of gear disc unit and spoke is an important factor having a direct bearing on the design of appearance and an impact on the product image. It comes into four categories of "Chain drive", "Shaft drive", "Gear-to-gear drive" and "Shaft drive(Spoke-less)", of which, the latter two are in spoke-less form. In terms of "**Riding-posture**", the category of bicycle normally reflect the function hereof. For example, the tracing bicycle differs greatly from the leisure in appearance. By the rider's demands for the speed of bicycle, the riding postures may be divided into four categories from low to high as follows: "Aerodynamic", "Aggressive", "Relaxed", and "Very-Relaxed", the first two require higher tilt while the latter call for lower one. As the "**Wheel diameter**" and "**Wheel base**" of a bicycle have a direct bearing on the interval between the handlebar and the rider, the diameter of the front wheel also have an impact on the height of the handlebar, thereby determining the riding posture. As a result, the diameters of front and rear wheel and the distance between the two wheels can be divided into three grades separately: "Small" (12–16 in.), "Medium" (18–22 in.) and "Large"(24–29 in.) and "Small", "Medium" and "Large" respectively. Catalano proposed that the positions of "**Volume**" and "**Barycenter**" have a great impact on the product style (Catalano 2004). As the research on bicycle design is normally based on a lateral view, despite the influence on weight imposed by the adopted material, this research is not to focus on the detailed size of frame and the bicycle area indicated in the view are used a condition for volume. In this research, work out the area of bicycle frame following the outlined bicycle by AutoCAD, and then, divided the volumes of all samples into three degrees: "Small", "Medium" and "Large". The distance of "**Barycenter**" between the front and rear wheels is divided into three grades: "Front", "Medium" and "Tail".

According the morphological analysis, the form features of concept bicycles are listed as the above ten elements, and their categories are shown in Table 1. Sixty

Table 1. The morphological chart of concept bicycle.

Item	Elements	1	2	3	4	5
1	Frame					
		6	7	8	9	10
		11	12	13	14	15
		16	17	18	19	20
		21	22	23	24	25

Item	Elements	1	2	3	4	5
2	Handlebar					
3	Wheel set					
4	Drive system	Chain drive	Shaft drive	Gear-to-gear	Spoke-less	
5	Riding-posture	Aerodynamic	Aggressive	Relaxed	Very-relaxed	
6	Front wheel diameter	Small	Medium	Large		
7	Rear wheel diameter	Small	Medium	Large		
8	Wheelbase	Short	Medium	Long		
9	Frame volume	Small	Medium	Large		
10	Barycenter	Front	Middle	Tail		

concept bicycle samples are decoded by this morphological chart. Let's take sample S1 for example. S1 is combined with category 1 of feature "Frame", category 2 of feature "**Handlebar**", category 1 of feature "**Wheel set**", category 1 of feature "**Drive system**", category 2 of feature "**Riding-posture**", category 2 of feature "**Front wheel diameter**", category 2 of feature "**Rear wheel diameter**", category 2 of feature "**Wheelbase**", category 1 of feature "**Frame volume**", and category 2 of feature "**Barycenter**". Therefore, the form features of sample S1 are coding as 1211222212. These codes are the input data for NN models.

3.2 Samples of Concept Bicycle

In this research, a total of 146 pictures of concept bicycle are collected, and three product designers with practical experience are invited to help classify the collected samples according to the 10 features planned above and design 60 combinations as the samples for the research following the principle that each category shall be used once at least, of which, 25 concept bicycles are originated by the designers. In order to ensure the unified system and size of the sample pictures, such 60 samples are drawn once again by Adobe Illustrator, and the surface coating is removed with gray colors. In addition, add paper-cut silhouette into them to help the interviewee understand the actual size and riding posture of a bicycle.

3.3 Image Perceptions of Concept Bicycle Samples

Twelve senior graders majoring in design, who have finished the fundamental design courses, are selected to conduct the focus group method. Members in the group collect related material and discuss mutually, so as to probe into the application of 12 archetypes in product design, and attempt to describe the association between the form features applied to a product and the archetypes with design technique of archetype image by the drill of front end engineering. The contents of group are scheduled to be performed in three phases, which is conducted for around three hours per week within months. **Phase I** mainly covers the outline of the features of 12 archetype theory and images, and provides the adjective vocabulary and image cognition map used by Shieh et al. to describe the archetypes (Shieh et al. 2016), so as to allow the members to know the archetypes in a faster manner. **Phase II** is aimed at extracting the features of cognition or emotion from the material of archetype images, and describing such relatively abstract archetypes by concrete vocabulary or things. The members collect the materials concerning the archetype images of non-product, which features visual forms such as picture or film, and then discuss the material by referring to the features and the vocabulary (Shieh et al. 2016). In **Phase III**, to conduct the image cognition maps with pictures for archetypes. The members discuss in groups, collect the pictures or films of the products related to the archetype and make an analysis of the cause of particular archetype feature, and then mark it with slogan or noun and adjective and raise such other features that the product has. Finally, to sort out the form features that the product shows in the appearance, including line, curve surface, construction form, color, material, surface preparation and texture.

The image of concept bicycle are evaluated with Likert scale, which requires the interviewee to rate the 60 samples with archetype recognition, which comes in seven levels, with the highest of 7, and lowest 1. The 30 interviewees are of the background related to design, with male 17, and female 13. This study only targets at the impact of form on the images. The identification of materials and non-color samples are difficult for none design-background people. Hence, the interviewees are limited to senior grades of design-background students Ahead of the questionnaire, the researcher briefs the interviewee the 12 archetypes and the related image cognition maps got in focus group method, so as to raise their understanding of the archetype for a better performance in the evaluation.

3.4   Using NN Models to Build the Relationship Between Form Features and Archetypes

NN is applied to the analysis of the association between the design features and archetypes. Its basic structure comprises input, conceal and output layer. In the input layer of NN are the sample codes of the classified form and form features, and output layer offers a rate of each archetype responding to the particular sample. The Mean Square Error (MSE) are used to verify NN models with several drills. Following the interviewee's image evaluation of the 60 concept bicycle samples, standardization of the questionnaire's results are conducted so as to allow the values to be between 0 and 1. These codes are the output data for training NN models. Fifty out of the 60 samples are used for drill, while the rest 10 for verification. Then NN models for each archetype are built and verified. In order to allow the MSE to be a reasonable range, the weighted value and partial weight value offered each time are determined at random in the training of NN models. Follows couples of training, choose the minimum value as the optimum convergence value. After the completion of the drill of all 12 NN models, take 10 out of them for verification, so as to work out the average error and accuracy rates shown in the Table below (Table 2).

Table 2. The accuracy rates of NN models for 12 archetypes.

Num.	Type	Average of MSE	Average of correct rate
1	Innocent	13.6%	86.4%
2	Explorer	14.7%	85.3%
3	Sage	6.1%	93.9%
4	Hero	13.6%	86.4%
5	Magician	10.0%	90.0%
6	Outlaw	11.8%	88.2%
7	Lover	7.4%	92.6%
8	Regular guy	10.5%	89.5%
9	Jester	15.6%	84.4%
10	Caregiver	16.8%	83.2%
11	Creator	9.4%	90.6%
12	Ruler	11.2%	88.8%

3.5   The Image Perception and Form Features of Archetypes

After the rating of the 60 samples by the interviewee, take a sample with the highest average evaluation of each archetype and use them as the representative samples of 12 archetypes. See the Table below for the representative samples of these archetypes and the form features hereof (Table 3).

Table 3. Representative samples and their form features of each type of archetype.

Archetype	Representative sample	Image evaluation	Frame	Handlebar	Wheel set	Drive system	Riding-posture	Front wheel diameter	Rear wheel diameter	Wheel-base	Frame volume	Bary center
Innocent	9	0.78	9	1	5	4	3	1	3	1	3	3
Explorer	54	0.83	15	3	5	4	1	2	2	2	2	1
Sage	41	0.68	3	1	5	3	2	3	3	1	1	2
Hero	2	0.74	2	3	1	2	2	2	2	2	2	3
Magician	11	0.72	11	1	1	2	3	1	1	2	3	2
Outlaw	2	0.65	2	3	1	2	2	2	2	2	2	3
Lover	14	0.61	14	1	2	1	3	2	2	2	1	2
Regular guy	48	0.89	1	2	3	1	2	2	2	2	1	2
Jester	9	0.87	9	1	5	4	3	1	3	1	3	3
Caregiver	8	0.76	8	1	1	2	3	1	1	2	3	1
Creator	11	0.78	11	1	1	2	3	1	1	2	3	2
Ruler	34	0.69	2	3	4	2	2	2	2	2	2	3

As the 60 samples cannot cover all the sample combination of morphological chart, the possible solutions for samples are up to 1,458,000(= 25 × 3 × 5 × 4 × 4 × 3 × 3 × 3 × 3 × 3), of which, the feasible is 317,844, from which, obtain the highest rate of each archetype, and these solutions with the highest rates are deemed as the optimum sample combination. Analyze and break the combinations above in terms of form. See Table 4 for morphological chart to understand the image cognition of each form combination.

Table 4. The highest evaluation of samples for each archetype and their form features.

Archetype	Image evaluation	Frame	Handlebar	Wheel set	Drive system	Riding-posture	Front wheel diameter	Rear wheel diameter	Wheel-base	Frame volume	Barycenter
Innocent	0.98	1	1	4	2	4	1	1	1	1	3
Explorer	0.94	5	3	5	4	1	3	1	1	2	3
Sage	0.85	5	1	5	4	1	3	1	1	1	3
Hero	0.91	4	1	4	1	1	3	1	3	3	2
Magician	0.92	3	1	5	4	2	1	1	3	3	3
Outlaw	0.98	5	3	5	3	1	3	1	3	2	1
Lover	0.83	1	1	4	1	1	3	3	1	1	3
Regular guy	0.99	1	1	1	1	4	1	3	3	1	1
Jester	0.87	4	1	1	2	4	3	1	1	1	3
Caregiver	0.98	1	1	1	1	4	3	1	2	1	3
Creator	0.9	2	3	1	2	1	3	1	2	3	3
Ruler	0.97	2	3	1	2	1	1	1	3	3	1

4   Results of Form Design

Comparing the conclusions reached by focus group method and the results of the questionnaire, it can be found that: (1) the form features summarized by "Innocent" archetype comprise: the outline of product is prone to smooth curve, and the sense of "Innocent" archetype is likely to raise with the "variation" and "dissymmetry" of the basic geometric shapes. The "dissymmetry" may raise to the extent that falls into the image of "Jester" archetype. In the result of image evaluation, the images of "Innocent" and "Jester" archetypes all correspond to this design feature. As a result, the form features of "Innocent" archetype are small-diameter front wheel, big-diameter rear wheel, large wheel base, big volume and visual focus titling to the rear. (2) all the image evaluations of "Sage", "Outlaw", "Lover", and "Ruler" archetypes are less than 0.7. These might be caused by that the effective factors of these four archetypes are color, texture, surface composing factors of "overlap of surfaces" or "projected or cut prism surface". As a result, the presence of only outline discourages the interviewee from showing strong image sense.

According to the comparison the results of the questionnaire and the form analysis of sample: (1) samples S54 and S15 differ from features only in terms of "**Ridding-posture**", but the gap of rate is up to 0.46. As the sample S54 can most represent "Explorer" archetype, "**Ridding-posture**" can be deemed as the key to influence the image cognition of "Explorer" archetype. (2) "**Handlebar**" poses an extremely great influence on the archetype image. For example, the forms of sample S3 and S11 differ from the form features only in terms of "**Handlebar**", while the gap between the evaluations by "Sage" archetype is up to 0.31. As a result, the change in the form of "**Handlebar**" affects the image as a whole. (3) among the form features of "**Drive system**", the frame featuring spoke-less wheel is relative concise and its evaluation result may be prone to the image perceptions of "Magician", "Sage", and "Creator" archetypes.

5   Discussion and Conclusion

In this research, form analysis and NN models are used to establish the association between the form features of concept bicycle and image. Apart from the result mentioned in the previous section, the 12 archetypes analyzed in focus group method and the design factors of image cognition maps are good references to a designer, who may combine the categories for the ten elements of the form analysis, and obtain the image evaluation value by the predication models, or fix a particular form feature, conduct the design image evaluation of concept bicycle by alteration of local form features, thereby helping the designer to conduct the design in a diversified and more correct manner. The archetype image cognition maps obtained in focus group method are not confined to concept bicycle. Although the local design depends on product function under some circumstance, for example, drive system of concept bicycle, styles for other parts still make possible good image designs. As a result, designs of other products may still refer to the image cognition maps in this research for the establishment of product image.

References

Belk, R.W.: Extended self and extending paradigmatic perspective. J. Consum. Res. **16**(1), 129–132 (1989)

Berkowitz, M.: Product shape as a design innovation strategy. J. Prod. Innov. Manag. **4**(4), 274–283 (1987)

Bitner, M.J.: Servicescapes: the impact of physical surroundings on customers and employees. J. Mark. **56**(2), 57–71 (1992)

Bloch, P.H.: Seeking the ideal form: product design and consumer response. J. Mark. **59**(3), 16–29 (1995)

Campbell, J.: The Hero with a Thousand Faces, vol. 17. New World Library, Novato (2008)

Catalano, C.E.: Feature-based methods for free-form surface manipulation in aesthetic engineering. Unpublished doctoral dissertation, University of Genoa, Italy (2004)

Chen, H.-Y., Chang, Y.-M.: Development of a computer aided product-form design tool based on numerical definition scheme and neural network. J. Adv. Mech. Des. Syst. Manuf. **8**(3), JAMDSM0033 (2014a)

Chen, H.-Y., Chang, Y.-M.: Incorporating the multiple linear regression with the neural network to the form design of product image. Paper Presented at the Natural Computation (ICNC), 2014 10th International Conference on Natural Computation, pp. 174–180 (2014b)

Cross, N., Roy, R.: Engineering Design Methods, vol. 2. Wiley, New York (1989)

Guo, F., Liu, W.L., Cao, Y., Liu, F.T., Li, M.L.: Optimization design of a webpage based on Kansei engineering. Hum. Factors Ergon. Manuf. Serv. Ind. **26**(1), 110–126 (2016)

Hsiao, S.-W., Ko, Y.-C.: A study on bicycle appearance preference by using FCE and FAHP. Int. J. Ind. Ergon. **43**(4), 264–273 (2013)

Jones, J.C.: Design Methods. Wiley, Hoboken (1992)

Kotler, P., Alexander Rath, G.: Design: a powerful but neglected strategic tool. J. Bus. Strategy **5**(2), 16–21 (1984)

Kreuzbauer, R., Malter, A.J.: Embodied cognition and new product design: changing product form to influence brand categorization. J. Prod. Innov. Manag. **22**(2), 165–176 (2005)

Lai, H.-H., Lin, Y.-C., Yeh, C.-H.: Form design of product image using grey relational analysis and neural network models. Comput. Oper. Res. **32**(10), 2689–2711 (2005)

Mark, M., Pearson, C.S.: The Hero and the Outlaw: Building Extraordinary Brands Through the Power of Archetypes. McGraw Hill Professional, New York (2001)

Shieh, M.-D., Hsu, F.-C., Tian, J.-S., Chen, C.-N.: A study of product form design using the theory of archetypes. In: Antona, M., Stephanidis, C. (eds.) UAHCI 2016. LNCS, vol. 9737, pp. 327–339. Springer, Cham (2016). doi:10.1007/978-3-319-40250-5_32

Su, J., Li, F.: Research of product styling design method based on neural network. Paper Presented at the Natural Computation, ICNC 2007, Third International Conference on Natural Computation (2007)

Wang, K.-C.: A hybrid Kansei engineering design expert system based on grey system theory and support vector regression. Expert Syst. Appl. **38**(7), 8738–8750 (2011)

Wang, T.-H., Yeh, Y.-E.: A study on extraction of consumer affective factor for Kansei engineering. J. Interdisc. Math. **18**(6), 667–679 (2015)

Woodside, A.G., Sood, S., Miller, K.E.: When consumers and brands talk: storytelling theory and research in psychology and marketing. Psychol. Mark. **25**(2), 97–145 (2008)

Yang, C.-C.: A classification-based Kansei engineering system for modeling consumers' affective responses and analyzing product form features. Expert Syst. Appl. **38**(9), 11382–11393 (2011). doi:10.1016/j.eswa.2011.03.008

Zwicky, F.: Morphological astronomy. Observatory **68**, 121–143 (1948)

Study of Color Emotion Impact on Leisure Food Package Design

Tian-yu Wu$^{(\boxtimes)}$, Ya-jun Li, and Yan Liu

School of Design Art and Media, Nanjing University of Science and Technology,
Nanjing, Jiangsu, People's Republic of China
1031063471@qq.com

Abstract. *Objective.* This paper seeks to provide an objective evaluation of how consumers of leisure food perceive package color visually and psychologically by analyzing color emotions and drawing on Kansei Engineering. It offers theories and methods for color design of food package in the future. *Method.* Semantic Differential and HSV color quantization are used here, and questionnaires and Likert scale are adopted to extract participants' satisfaction for package color and recognition of color emotional semantics. Data correlation is analyzed to clarify the potential relation between satisfaction and recognition. That enable package color design "centered on users' emotional demand". *Conclusion.* After collecting experimental data and mathematical evaluation, we have obtained theme colors that leisure food consumers are highly satisfied with, as well as scores for recognition of color emotional semantics. Objective data prove that there is an inner connection between color satisfaction and recognition of color emotional semantics.

Keywords: Color emotion · Kansei engineering · Leisure food · Package design · User experience

1 Color Emotion Design in Leisure Food Package

Today, people's daily life is intertwined with leisure food. Increasing income and better living quality add to requirements on the forms of food packages. In addition to meeting basic packing requirements, package should also be funny, interactive and agreeable. In other words, it should meet consumers' emotional demands. Color design is the major visual language for package, and sets the keynote for the emotional design of leisure food package. As indicated by statistical data of psychology, people are more easily to resonate with and pay visual attention to colors of package, rather than its shape, pattern, and structure [1]. Kansei image, mental preference and emotional demand for package color deliver a number of benefits: adding to the emotional resonance that consumers have for food package, stirring up consumers' desire to buy, thus promoting food sales, and shaping and communicating the brand image for the leisure food.

"Color can reflect human emotions faithfully, and this is an irrefutable fact," said American educator Rudolf Arnheim [2]. Color is more than just visual perception of objective things, but also emotional expression of people's subjective awareness. Color

C. Stephanidis (Ed.): HCII Posters 2017, Part II, CCIS 714, pp. 612–619, 2017.
DOI: 10.1007/978-3-319-58753-0_86

emotion is actually a kind of psychological state generated by associating the color information received by people's visual organs and transmitted by optic nerve with past memories, lives and personal experience. It can be perceived and obtained by any people with normal vision and common sense.

When buying leisure food, consumers normally measure three criteria: food attribute, brand scale, and price, which are all closely related to package color. In global design competitions like Pentawards and iF, the majority of outstanding package designs give priority to visual color (as shown in Fig. 1). For modern enterprises, reasonable color matching for food package is necessary for successful marketing. When selecting leisure food, consumers are first attracted visually by colors; after confirming the basic information about food, consumers would choose to pay based on their own preferences and brand awareness. Correspondingly, color design is meant to improve the emotional experience of consumers in buying and add to the correlation between satisfaction for package color and consumers' emotional demand. In that, color design can drive a positive cycle of food buying.

Fig. 1. Outstanding leisure food package designs from Pentawards and iF (Color figure online)

2 Research on Relation Between Leisure Food Package and Color Emotional Semantics

Color semantic can best reflect the expression of people's mental feelings and emotional effects. By nature, color semantics describe in words the connotative meaning of color expression using textualism [3]. It mainly studies the physical sensory stimulation generated by color vision and experiential psychological association. This experiment aims to analyze and conclude the potential relation between theme colors for leisure food package and consumers' color emotional semantics, and to prove the factual correlation between them. There are mainly three phases: 1. Gaining leisure food package theme colors preferred by consumers; 2. Testing and integration of emotional semantics for leisure food package colors; and 3. Correlation analysis of leisure food package colors and color emotional semantics. Specific procedures are shown in Fig. 2.

Considering the frequent buying groups of leisure food and the difference in semantic cognition of color emotions, a total of 30 college students and teaching and administrative staff from a college in Nanjing Xuanwu District are selected for the experiment. They are all good in physical conditions, and free from any visual exceptions. Men and women are divided by 50/50, with age distribution: 40% for 18–21; 40% for 22–25; 15% for 26–30; and 5% for 31–35. Screening for participants

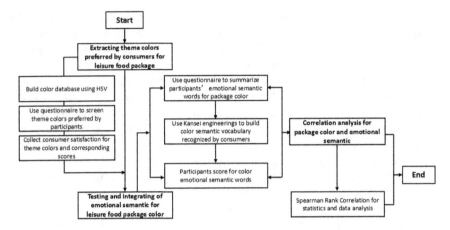

Fig. 2. Experiment flowchart

guarantees that they have common recognition for the semantic expressions of package colors, thus ensuring that color information transmitted by leisure food package is correct.

Spearman Rank Correlation from socioeconomic statistics is adopted for studying the relationship between young consumers' color satisfaction for leisure food package and recognition for color emotional semantics. Spearman's correlation coefficient for ranked data is used to assess the correlation between two variables X and Y, and their correlation can be expressed by monotone function [4]. Spearman Rank Correlation has wide application, and requires less on data compared to that of coefficient of production-moment correlation. As long as the observation thresholds of two variables are pairing, they can be analyzed by Spearman Rank Correlation irrespective of distribution pattern and sample size.

2.1   Obtaining Consumer Preferences for Package Colors

Following Munsell Color System, quantitative color data is used to build HSV package theme color database for the initial phase. The database includes color numbers and all attributes. Based on three attributes of each color, they are combined to present matching package colors [5]. The Munsell Color System presents Hue (H), Saturation (S) and Value (V) for each color. These three basic attributes have different value ranges, with 0–360 for H, 0–100 for S, and 0–100 for V.

Where, x, y, and z correspond to H, S, V respectively, thus the value ranges are $0 \leq x \leq 360$; $0 \leq y \leq 100$; $0 \leq z \leq 100$. In consideration of the actual operability and color vision features of participants, the three attributes are valued by segment, specifically: 10 segments for H: 0, 36, 72, 108, 144, 180, 216, 252, 288, 324; 5 for S: 20, 40, 60, 80, 100; and 5 for V: 20, 40, 60, 80, 100. Due to the fact that achromatic packages are not covered in the experiment, the achromatic part (0–20) for S and V is eliminated; while segments 324–360 and 0–36 of H show the same color, and are therefore eliminated. This means that there are totally 250 (10 * 5 * 5) theme colors of leisure food package generated by the color database, and some of the colors and their attributes are shown in Table 1.

Table 1. Part of package theme color and their attributes

No.	H, S, V	No.	H, S, V	No.	H, S, V	No.	H, S, V	No.	H, S, V
1	0.20.20	51	72.20.20	101	144.20.20	151	216.20.20	201	288.20.20
2	0.20.40	52	72.20.40	102	144.20.40	152	216.20.40	202	288.20.40
3	0.20.60	53	72.20.60	103	144.20.60	153	216.20.60	203	288.20.60
...	...	...	...	...	...	...	...	...	...
50	36.100.100	100	108.100.100	150	180.100.100	200	252.100.100	250	324.100.100

A total of 30 young people are invited to select from 250 theme colors for leisure food package. For easy observation and selection, the 250 original colors are grouped into 10, with 25 colors for each group. The experiment is totally done on PC, and visual colors corresponding to the color values from the database are extracted from Adobe Photoshop. In other words, 250 HSV colors are converted into RGB colors, and color cards are made on PC, enabling participants to quickly and accurately select package theme colors they prefer (as shown in Fig. 3).

Fig. 3. Part of leisure food package color cards and participant select preferred package color (Color figure online)

Food package colors are the target in this experiment, and package colors belong to spray paint. Therefore, formula (1) is used to convert RGB colors obtained into CMYK colors to guarantee color recognition and effectiveness.

$$(C, M, Y, K) = \begin{cases} K = 0 \\ C = 100\text{-}R^*100/255 \\ M = 100\text{-}G^*100/255 \\ Y = 100\text{-}B^*100/255 \end{cases} \tag{1}$$

The visual preference experiment delivers theme colors samples preferred by 30 participants, and these samples in each group are ranked by the number of participants preferred such colors in descending order. There are totally 10 tables. Two groups of theme colors favored by most participants are selected, and thus 20 colors (10 for each group) are confirmed for the experiment. The participants are invited to rate the 20 theme colors in "1–5", corresponding to "Dissatisfied - Satisfied". After computation, the satisfaction scores for the 20 themes colors by 30 participants are obtained, and then the averages are calculated for the final ranking of color satisfaction scores in descending orders. Figure 4 shows the 10 leisure food package theme colors obtained, and these samples would be used in phase 3.

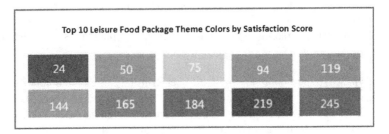

Fig. 4. Top 10 leisure food package theme colors by satisfaction score (Color figure online)

2.2 Kansei Comments for Color Emotional Semantics

A combination of literature theory method, questionnaire and interview is used to screen semantic vocabulary for color emotions by participants. Out of 30 questionnaires issued to respondents, 22 valid questionnaires are obtained, and the rest 8 questionnaires are invalid. A principle of "the majority" is used. In details, only semantic words mentioned in at least 50% of questionnaires would be selected as the final samples of color emotional semantics. There are 22 valid questionnaires, and semantic words selected less than 11 times would be eliminated. In that, 10 words are rejected. After data code formatting, 12 semantic words are obtained with respect to theme colors (Table 2).

Table 2. List of semantics words for leisure food package theme colors

No.	Semantic adjective	No.	Semantic adjective	No.	Semantic adjective
V_1	Quiet	V_5	Clean	V_9	Refreshing
V_2	Passionate	V_6	Relaxing	V_{10}	Comfortable
V_3	Natural	V_7	Magnificent	V_{11}	Excited
V_4	Simple	V_8	Elegant	V_{12}	Mysterious

In a relatively stable environment, 30 participants are required to select by visual preference from 10 groups of theme colors obtained in phase I on mobile PC. And they would rate the 12 semantic words by satisfaction. Image scale in Kansei engineering is adopted, and Likert scale is used to build satisfaction scale. Scoring measures for semantic word recognition are the same as those in Phase I. With the top 10 theme colors by satisfaction score, we can get the satisfaction scores for each group from C_1 to C_{10} and for 12 semantic words.

2.3 Spearman Rank Correlation

If the significance for the correlation coefficient on statistical is less than 0.05, i.e. $p < 0.05$, there is significant correlation between recognition of semantic words and satisfaction for theme color; if $p < 0.0.1$, such correlation is highly significant; and if $p > 0.05$, there is no significant correlation between the two. In this phase, satisfaction scores for 10 theme colors and recognition scores for 12 semantic words are analyzed for Spearman's correlation coefficient for ranked data. The correlation coefficients between each color satisfaction and all 12 semantic words are calculated, shown in Table 3. (Only part of SPSS statistical data is presented due to limited space.)

Table 3. List of correlation coefficients between theme color satisfaction and semantic recognition

	Spearman		
	Correlation coefficient	Sig. (2-tailed)	N
Spearman rank correlation			
V_1	·	·	30
V_2	0.896**	0.006	30
V_3	0.000	1.000	30
V_4	−0.328	0.398	30
V_5	0.000	1.000	30
V_6	0.418	0.350	30
V_7	0.000	1.000	30
V_8	0.354	0.437	30
V_9	−0.850	0.172	30
V_{10}	−0.316	0.490	30
V_{11}	0.816*	0.025	30
V_{12}	−0.418	0.350	30

2.4 Data Analysis and Results Discussion

After analyzing the correlation for the 10 groups, the correlations between theme colors of C_1–C_{10} and color semantics of V_1–V_{15} are shown in Table 4. Data indicate that correlation coefficients between color satisfaction and semantic recognition differ for the 10 groups (C_1–C_{10}). Take C1 for example, V_2 (passionate) and V_{11} and (excited) have the highest correlation with the color satisfaction. Correlation coefficient for V_2 is 0.896, and significance is 0.006; while that for V_{11} is 0.816 and 0.025 respectively. Since 0.006 < 0.025, V_2 has a higher correlation to C_1 theme colors compared to V_{11}.

Table 4. List of correlation between theme color satisfaction and semantics words

C_1	V_2 (passionate), V_{11} (excited)
C_2	V_{10} (comfortable)
C_3	V_3 (natural)
C_4	V_5 (clean), V_9 (refreshing)
C_5	V_3 (natural), V_5 (clean)
C_6	V_1 (quiet), V_4 (simple), V_{10} (comfortable)
C_7	V_1 (quiet), V_{10} (comfortable)
C_8	V_4 (simple), V_8 (elegant)
C_9	V_{12} (mysterious)
C_{10}	V_7 (magnificent)

In this color experiment, 8 of all 10 groups show significant correlation by Spearman's correlation coefficient for ranked data, and all of them are positive. V1 and V10 have the highest correlation coefficients with 10 theme colors. Correlation data obtained indicates that there is positive correlation between theme color satisfaction for leisure food package and emotional semantic recognition. The higher the recognition for the color semantic, the higher the satisfaction for the theme color. This also implies a close inner connection between package colors and color emotional semantics.

3   Conclusion

In face of fierce market competition, leisure food can only arouse consumers' emotional appeal if the package color can accurately reflect good information [6]. This thesis screens theme colors for leisure food package and confirms matching color semantics. Through mathematical analysis, the factual correction is explored between color emotional semantics and package colors. Research into the relation between leisure food package color and color emotional semantics can offer beneficial guidance in the color emotional design of leisure food package. By using such potential connection in a reasonable way, designers can more accurately obtain the color demands of consumers and gain a deeper understanding of consumers' color preference. Guided by color emotional semantics, color emotional design for leisure food package offers a number of benefits: adding to consumers' awareness for perceptive consumption and emotional resonance for package color; enabling emotional interaction between consumers and product packages, and creating spiritual experience for consumers.

References

1. Luke Jr., R.H.: Psycho-physiological influences of color as related to package design. In: Bellur, V.V. (ed.) Marketing Horizons: A 1980's Perspective. DMSPAMS, p. 322. Springer, Cham (2015). doi:10.1007/978-3-319-10966-4_75
2. Na, N., Suk, H.J.: The emotional characteristics of white for applications of product color design. Int. J. Des. **8**(2), 61–70 (2014)

3. Liu, J., Li, J., Guodong, A.L.: Color scheme design through color semantic and interactive genetic algorithm. J. Comput. Aided Des. Comput. Graph. **24**(5), 669–676 (2012)
4. Zhang, W.Y., Wei, Z.W., Wang, B.H., Han, X.P.: Measuring mixing patterns in complex networks by Spearman rank correlation coefficient. Phys. A Stat. Mech. Appl. **451**, 440–450 (2016)
5. Cochrane, S.: The Munsell color system: a scientific compromise from the world of art. Stud. Hist. Philos. Sci. **47**(2), 26 (2014)
6. Zhang, S.: Efficient color design scheme of children food packaging. In: Du, W. (ed.) Informatics and Management Science IV. LNEE, vol. 207, pp. 493–499. Springer, London (2013). doi:10.1007/978-1-4471-4793-0_61

Social Issues and Security in HCI

Hacking the Body 2.0: Ethics in Wearable Tech, Etextiles Design and Data Collection in Performance

Camille Baker[1($\boxtimes$)] and Kate Sicchio[2]

[1] School of Communication Design,
University for the Creative Arts, Epsom, UK
CBaker10@uca.ac.uk
[2] New York University Tandon School of Engineering, Brooklyn, NY, USA
Sicchio@nyu.edu

Abstract. The technology fervour over the last 2–3 years around wearable technology that collects user's personal body data, under the pretense of medical or fitness monitoring, highlights that it is time to raise critical questions. The ethics of corporate data collection has only begun to be discussed outside media arts forums and the fine print for wearable sports and health devices and corresponding mobile apps. More public awareness and education about body data mining is critical, everyone should have the right to access, own, explore, and use their own body data. Wearable companies should be required to provide users open access and ownership of their own body data, as well as to grant rights it, to enable them new ways to express their personal identity, as well as to interpret or reinterpret this data however they choose – which is presently not easy since the companies hold it as proprietary and only sell it to insurance or medical companies (Forrester 2014). *Hacking the Body 2.0 (HTB2.0)* is an on-going practical investigation, by media artist/choreographer/researcher Kate Sicchio and Camille Baker, which explores the issues of personal data collection and data as identity. The focus of *HTB 2.0* has been in interpreting inner processes in order to try define them as part of one's personal identity, which may (or may not influence) one's movement and interaction with others. The issues of data collection other ethical issues of using wearable tech, etextiles and electronics in general will be discussed, specifically how *HTB 2.0* has been addressing these issues in our garment creations, choreography, interaction design and in our final performances.

Keywords: Wearable tech and e-textiles · Performance · Personal identity · Ethics of data collection

1 Bodies, Technology and Performance

Over 15 years of digital media and performance practices incorporating mobile media, wearable sensors and devices embedded in garments for interactive and participatory performances, have witnessed substantial numerous changes unfold in technological development, bringing wearable devices into the mainstream corporate, sports, fitness

© Springer International Publishing AG 2017
C. Stephanidis (Ed.): HCII Posters 2017, Part II, CCIS 714, pp. 623–627, 2017.
DOI: 10.1007/978-3-319-58753-0_87

and medical technological development. Yet, as Ryan noted in her book Garments of Paradise (Ryan 2014), few have explored the full potential of wearable technology in performance. She writes:

'Wearables in the context of performance present opportunities for exploring our relationships with our bodies and how we move them… [Or how] communications interfaces, and other soft and sensory technologies allow us to experience or transcend our bodies, and how the concept of theatrical performance can be expanded in virtual space'. (2014:8)

Conceptually, *Hacking the Body and HTB 2.0* started by examining rhetoric within the online computing community on code, hacking, networks, the quantified self, and data as a new approach to examining inner and outer states of the human body, measured by sensing devices within performance. By using modern DIY wearable electronics and smart materials alongside hacked corporate fitness tech, we explore issues of data identity and data ethics that are adding a new dimension to the evolution of technology in performance. As researchers and artists, we question corporate and government agendas, and explore ways to access body data locally (not 'in the cloud'), to uniquely demonstrate who we are, our physiological changes, movement, and interaction-like language. While examining these issues, can we create new forms of non-verbal interaction and communication, and empower ourselves through access to our own body data, to enable us to express and perform our identity, outside the cloud?

The participatory performance activities and choreography developed for *HTB 2.0* are informed by physiological code and data collection as a means for performers to interact with their own body data, through experiential, sensual, haptic engagement with the custom-made garments on their bodies and those of other performers as such, they become co-creators in the work. But *HTB 2.0* is not only focused on the making of physiological sensing and actuating garments, but also on how to enable performers to understand, express and perform their 'data-as-identity', as a means to reclaim control over it and as another technique to devise movement and interaction to co-create performance. And as with other forms of data, body-as-information can be hacked and re-purposed, and re-physicalised, but we argue this should only done by the owner of that body. The project aims to highlight ethical issues by putting the concept of data ownership back literally back into the hands of the body from which it originates and is collected from.

2   Research to Performance

In practical terms, *HTB 2.0* is as much a performance investigation as a conceptual research endeavour, and its instantiations have developed our hands-on making skills in DIY electronics, soft-circuits and smart textiles, while unearthing the greater unethical data collection issues. In response, we have created non-data-collecting technology garments that trigger expression and portray personal identity through movement responses and haptic interaction. In the process, performers invited to express their own body code during several performance 'hacks' or experiments based on the concept of physiological code ownership.

In our more recent iterations the focus has been on garment aesthetics, ethical used of fabrics, housing for the electronics, as well as the interaction design of the sensing and actuation of the electronics, as well as a focus on the movement vocabulary and gestural responses of the dancers triggered by the actuation and how this could be made into dance performance phrasing. This was intended to allow dancers to interact and respond to touch, the sensors and their response to actuation or output through vibration, to develop new movement 'dialogue' between performers, exploring their identities.

HTB 2.0 took to the public stage in 2016. We hacked into off-the-shelf devices to enable the dancers to interact directly with the embedded electronics in the garments on their bodies, to trigger the dancers to move in conversation with each other, with an added feature that allows the choreographer, or indeed the audience, to intervene directly with the dancers' bodies and their movement responses. Two pieces were developed for the performances: (1) *stutter/flutter* – costumes with haptic garments and motor actuation 'tickles'; (2) *feel me* – costumes with custom etextiles breath sensors and vibe actuation. *feel me*, the piece with the hacked corporate devices, is a very structured piece of choreography that had a strict form of repetition, so that when one dancer exhales, the other dancer stops moving for the duration of that breath. The movement is forced to become stagnant rather than follow the expected patterns (Fig. 1).

Fig. 1. Images from performance of the piece in February 2016 in London, UK - the dancers interacting with the textile touch sensors embedded in the pink pleated fabric.

The ultimate goal is that performers engage with their own and other's body code to create new forms of 'live data performance', with the performer initiating the inter-action, using these skin interfaces to aid their performance interaction. The performers interact or respond to the smart garments and each other through movement, enabling code-based movement phrases or 'dialogue' to emerge, reacting to each other's unique gestures representing their data identities. This may then allow them to interact or respond to biosensing to create new movement 'dialogue' or interaction with other performers and explore identities. In this way, the performers have one way to directly reclaim their data sensing, expression and collection and the technology, as another tool or collaborator to devise movement and co-create performance works. This circum-vents, and puts ownership back into the hands of users, and in turn becomes another critical act of making and a small confrontation of surveillance and data control. This is intended to challenge the power and control of patented/copyrighted body data collecting tools, versus personal body rights, and expands concepts of the body as part of greater social, political and the (open-source) technological network (Fig. 2).

Fig. 2. Image from Feel Me performance still from February 18, 2016 in Sheffield

3   Reflections and Directions

Part of our aim in *Hacking the Body 2.0*: to explore the body, movement, nonverbal communication with the collaboration of the technology as a resistance to the modes of working with wearable technologies and etextiles through making, performing and public debate. We are more concerned in what a body can do, but first we must sublimate the technology, rather than conform to its inherent limitations. We recognise that we cannot actually reclaim the ownership of our private physiological data automatically or on a substantial global level through performance experimentation and its debate alone, but with additional interventions and the development disruptive technologies, we hope to add to the increasing voices and resistance to such control. We can also initiate more collaboration between artists and performers with wearable technologists and companies, to find a mutually satisfactory way forward, demonstrating how art and performance can influence the research and development of Human Computer Interaction, interfaces and data collection, not to mention creating more ethical, environmental and sustainable technologies and interfaces for the future.

Endnotes

[1] This concept is unpacked well by Slavoj Zizek in his book *How To Read Lacan*, especially the about the concept of unknown knowns, which he states, *"...Lacan's claim that the subject is always 'decentred'. His point is not that my subjective experience is regulated by objective unconscious mechanisms that are decentred with regard to my self-experience and, as such, beyond my control (a point asserted by every materialist), but rather something much more unsettling: I am deprived of even my most intimate subjective experience, the way things 'really seem to me', deprived of the fundamental fantasy that constitutes and guarantees the core of my being, since I can never consciously experience it and assume it."* (2006:52–53).

[2] Our methods are based on Thecla Schiphorst's methods which I learned working for her as a research assistant in 2002–2005 on her wearable performance project *whispers* in Vancouver Canada.

[3] Such as *Transmediale Festival 2015 Capture All* in Berlin, where the topic for the festival was focused on critical examining these issues.

Acknowledgements. This work was supported by the University for the Creative Arts research funding scheme in 2015; Arts Council England Grants for Artists Scheme 2015.

References

Forrester, I.: Quantified self and the ethics of personal data, (IN BBC R&D blog), June 2014. http://www.bbc.co.uk/rd/blog/2014/06/qs-ethics-ofdata. Accessed 26 Nov 2014

Ryan, S.E.: Garments of Paradise. MIT Press, Cambridge (2014)

I Am Ok, the Material's Not: A Transactional Analysis of Information Security Education Material for Swedish Elementary School Students

Stewart Kowalski[1](✉), Tina Andersson[2], and Sabina Windahl[2]

[1] Norwegian University of Science and Technology, Gjøvik, Norway
stewart.kowalski@ntnu.no
[2] Stockholm University, Stockholm, Sweden
klistret@gmail.com, sabina.windahl@gmail.com

Abstract. Thirty-two Swedish teacher responded to online survey of their qualitative judge of an Information Security teaching package to be used in Swedish K-12 classrooms. Self-reported results of Transactional analysis questionnaire indicate that are significant correlations between ego state and how the material is perceived, where teachers having the dominant ego state Parent and Adult have a better opinion regarding the material than teachers having the dominant ego state Child. Also, Parent and Adult consider the material motivating while Child considers it authoritative.

Keywords: Information security education · Transaction analysis

1 Introduction

In this study we analyzing education material produced by the Swedish Civil Protection Agency to be used by teacher in elementary school to educate child about information security problems and solutions. In particular, two aspect of the educational material were studied. The first aspect was what are the success factors for the adoption and use of material and second aspect, was does different teachers' transactional ego state correlates with the perception and use of a tuition material.

The lack of competence for information security within the Swedish society is agreed upon by several parties. Since children using the internet are getting younger and younger it's of great importance that the schools start educating early to provide possibility for the children to be able to handle the information securely. In the curriculum for the Swedish elementary school information security is vaguely addressed which gives a large room for interpretation and there are no expressed requirements to educate in information security. Since the teaching time is valuable it is of great importance that the tuition material produced for the teachers is of high quality. The tuition material produced for the teachers can be perceived differently depending on the personality of the teacher, hence the aim with this study is to use the ego states from transactional analysis in order to investigate whether teachers' different ego states affects how the tuition material is perceived, and if perception differs depending on the ego state of the teacher.

© Springer International Publishing AG 2017
C. Stephanidis (Ed.): HCII Posters 2017, Part II, CCIS 714, pp. 628–631, 2017.
DOI: 10.1007/978-3-319-58753-0_88

The basics of transactional analysis is that every person, which in our case that would be the teachers of the educational package designers and the students themselves belongs to a dominant ego state – Parent, Adult or Child. Communication is frictionless and effective when the parties transmitting the communication directs it towards the ego state the receiver is predominatelyin.

2   Terminology of Transaction Analysis

According to the transaction the founder, Eric Berne individuals can have communicate using the three different ego states - Parent, Adult and Child, as describe in Fig. 1 below:

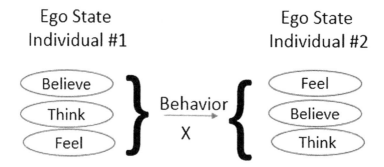

Fig. 1. Parent like behavior to X to perceived as childlike.

These ego states and behavior of an individual is driven by an order sets of their, beliefs, thoughts and feelings [1]. In Fig. 1 above we have to individuals 1 which has an order set of ES1 = {believes, thoughts, feelings} communicating and or transacting with individual 2 about or using a certain behavior X. This individual has an order set = {feeling, believes, thoughts}. The individual 1 is acting parent like and the individual 2 is perceives the behavior as being childlike.

These order set are dynamic and in some situations can change depending on a number of factors however, over time a dominate ordering of the set develops in and individual and can be characterized has have one dominate ego state of adult, parent, or child. It is this simplistic model this study aims to use - to examine participants' dominant ego. Standard self-reporting questionnaires have been developed to determine an individual's dominate ego state [2].

Figure 2 gives a rough schematic model over this type of communication between the main stakeholders in the socio-technical educational system in focus for this study. Here we see the groups or type of persons in the systems and the education material modeled a communication channel. When communication is transmitted to an ego state different from the one the receiver is in a conflict can occurs. Put in a context of a tuition material, the teacher is likely to react in a negative way if the tuition material is transmitting its information towards a different ego state than the teacher dominate state.

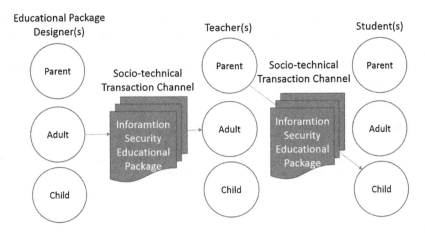

Fig. 2. Socio-technical communication schematic

3   Results and Conclusion

A web survey was published in two Facebook groups containing teacher profiles to collect data. The web survey contained an ego state questionnaire developed by Loffredo et al. [2] and a series of questions regarding the teacher's opinions and use of the education material. Thirty-two teachers participated in the survey. How the material was perceived and how or if it was used was analyzed with t-tests, correlation- and regression analysis.

Figure 3 gives an overview of the relative strength of the correlations observed between measured variables. In Fig. 2 ovals are used for descriptive variables, round rectangles for perceptions of the pedagogical material diamonds for actions that that teacher would take i.e. read more and or use the material.

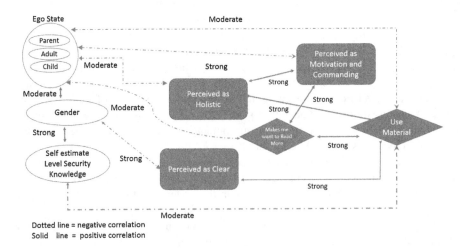

Fig. 3. Significant variable correlation diagram

The results show that there are significant correlations between ego state and how the material is perceived, where teachers having the dominant ego state Parent and Adult have a better opinion regarding the material than teachers having the dominant ego state Child. Also, Parent and Adult consider the material motivating while Child considers it authoritative.

References

1. Loffredo, D., Harrington, R.: Ego state differences in university students by gender, race and collage major. J. Psychiatry Psychol. Ment. Health **2**(1), 1–9 (2008)
2. Heyer, N.R.: Development of a questionnaire to measure ego states with some applications to social and comparative psychiatry. Trans. Anal. J. **9**(1), 9–19 (1979)

The Rise and Proliferation of Live-Streaming in China: Insights and Lessons

Jinglan Lin(✉) and Zhicong Lu

Department of Computer Science, University of Toronto, Toronto, Canada
{cjlin,luzhc}@cs.toronto.edu

Abstract. The $5 billion dollar live streaming industry has a tremendous impact on the social behaviours of internet users in China. However, despite early appearance of the technology in the North America, live streaming has yet to reach the level it has in China. Using observations from the rise and proliferation of live streaming services in China, we identify some culture and social insights about the phenomenon as well as some lessons that we can apply to North America.

Keywords: Live streaming · Social computing

1 Introduction

Man seeketh in society comfort, use and protection.
– Sir Francis Bacon, *The Advancement of Learning, 1605*

As early as 2005, live-streaming culture began in China when public video chat room services such as YY were repurposed by users to host public performances [3]. Continuous growth has resulted in millions of viewers watching the anchors (主播 -zhǔ bō) perform live each night on China's most popular live-streaming platforms [2], creating an estimated $5 billion dollar industry [10]. However, despite the early appearance of the technology through gaming live-streams like Twitch.TV [7] in North America, it has only recently expanded into mainstream culture with Facebook Live and mobile applications like Periscope.

Breaking off from the traditional advertisement or pay-per-view model that many streaming platforms have adopted, these live-streaming services use a reward-based system where viewers buy gifts for streamers. Once streamers receive these gifts, they can then exchange them for cash. Chinese live-streams also differ greatly in content, style and form (Fig. 1) where various live pan-entertainment live-streams like sports, e-commerce, variety shows and concerts are popular [3]. A unique category of live-streams is one the Chinese call showroom live-streaming (秀场直播 - xiù chǎng zhí bō) where streamers, mostly beautiful girls, sing and dance in front of a webcam. As its popularity grew, live-streaming sessions have shifted to become a new form of social media, allowing the creation of social connections between the streamer and viewer. Viewers who have difficulty or are reluctant to integrate into traditional social settings are provided with a new means of seeking "comfort, use and protection".

© Springer International Publishing AG 2017
C. Stephanidis (Ed.): HCII Posters 2017, Part II, CCIS 714, pp. 632–637, 2017.
DOI: 10.1007/978-3-319-58753-0_89

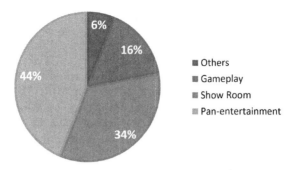

Fig. 1. Live-streaming content composition [3]

2 Related Works

There has been a lot of research in mobile live video chatting, online video sharing, and specialized video streaming services, which relate closely to live-streaming.

Video chatting apps on mobile devices have enabled users to share their experience with remote friends or even strangers. A study by O'Hara et al. [11] has showed that more than half of video calls on mobile devices occurred outside the home or work environment. Procyk et al. [12] found that video streaming shared activity created a strong tie between remote people and improve social interaction. Some other study focused on how strangers communicate using live video chat. Tian et al. [16] studied a mobile app which randomly connected strangers to chat. Their study shown that video chat among strangers tended to be short and only appealed to super users. Many of the live-streamed contents in China are in the form of communications between strangers, however, they tend to be lengthy and attracts both super users and occasional users. By investigating streamer motives, live-stream content and streamers' interaction with the audience, we can gain some preliminary insights of this.

While large-scale online video sharing services such as Youtube enable people to share video contents, comment on videos and follow other uploaders' sharing, it has been shown that 63% of the most frequent uploaders often uploaded copied content from other sources [5]. Live-streaming, on the other hand, enables streamers to perform improvisational self-produced content without the lengthy process of post-editing.

There have been a number of works that focused on various aspects of game live-streaming using platforms such as Twitch. In particular, studies have been done on the development of live-streaming online communities [7] and how it affects users' behavior [14]. Tang et al. [15] conducted a mixed methods of study to understand how people use the live-streaming apps and their data provided insights about early live streaming use practices. However, the platforms they studied were vastly different from what is currently popular in China, and the usage patterns of such apps are also vastly different. We will highlight these differences and discuss about why these differences have resulted in different levels of popularity and social influence.

3   Discussion

3.1   The Rise of Live Streaming

In China, the various forms of live streaming began when netizens began to re-purpose the public video chat room service, YY. By 2013, the live streaming ecosystem had completely matured and involved large guilds that trained and managed streamers. The early release of user-friendly live streaming infrastructure and platforms made it easy for regular internet users to broadcast from their bedrooms with just a webcam and a microphone.

Mobile live streaming was limited by the high bandwidth requirement of watching live streaming (48 Mbps). The advancement and penetration of mobile 4G networks in 2015 allowed for users to watch live streams from their mobile devices whenever and wherever [3]. Improvements of mobile hardware,i.e. increase in camera resolution, made it easier for users to capture live videos thereby further lowering the barrier for anyone to be a live streamer.

3.2   The Proliferation of Live Streaming

An analysis of the live-stream user base in China showed that nearly 70% of its users are under the age of 30 of which 74.7% are male [13]. In this demographic, the majority of individuals categorizes themselves as a (diǎo sī (屌丝 - plebeian), an ordinary person born in an ordinary family, with a mediocre look, and having a humble job [9]. At night, 59.3% of them kill time on the internet at home alone [13]. This aligns with statistics that show live-streaming traffic peaks during lunch breaks and after work hours. Through watching and interacting with live-streamers and their communities, this demographic seeks to satisfy their need for social contact and entertainment. In addition, the live comment and gift visualization streams encourages immediate responses from streamers thereby allowing viewers to create a more personal relationship with the streamer.

Geographically, only 11% of viewers are in Tier 1 cities (i.e. Beijing, Shanghai, Guangzhou), 34% in Tier 2 cities and 55% in Tier 3 cities [13]. For viewers in Tier 1 cities, a reason for watching live-streaming is rooted in loneliness, since many of them are living away with their parents and childhood friends; for viewers in lower-tier cities, live-streaming provides a window to previously unseen experiences, and gifting allows them prestige that they can't have in real life. For instance, a guy who comes from less developed areas can get the same amount of attention and interactions from celebrities as a guy from Tier 1 cities, as long as he gives decent amount of gifts to streamers.

3.3   Cultural Parallels

In an environment where piracy and counterfeiting run rampant, what is it about live-streaming that makes viewers willingly pay for something that they can watch legally for free? Beginning from the Han Dynasty (202 B.C.–220 A.D.), "rewards" was the main source of income for most authors, performers, and artists in ancient China [4]. The act of rewarding artists and performers historically indicated that the person was in a high societal position with prestige or wealth. Street performers in ancient China often began their performance by shouting "有钱的捧个钱场，没钱的捧个人场" (If you have money, please donate. If you don't have money, please make the crowd bigger.) To some degree, popular live streaming platforms have emulated that environment by including some key elements in their interface (Fig. 2).

Fig. 2. YiZhiBo app interface

By displaying the profile pictures of some of the fellow live stream viewers in addition to the number, viewers are placed in a digital crowd and therefore are more inclined to participate. The steady visualization of gifts in the form of real life objects also give users instant gratification in the form of pride. For instance, a higher price gift may be in the form of a yacht or a sports car. This is further enforced with gamification components like leaderboards, allowing users to grow "face"- a Chinese concept of maintaining a public image of one's prestige or reputation.

Although the majority of live-streaming viewers are male, female anchors make up 73% of the streaming population [1]. In a survey by Baidu, the top reason given for watching live-streams is because of "beautiful streamers" [6]. This is similar to ancient Chinese brothels where more often than not, beautiful girls were performers rather than prostitutes – giving rise to the phrase "卖艺不卖身"

(sell entertainment but not body - mài yì bú mài shēng). Historians have confirmed that these brothels were often cultural centers in historical China and adopted a similar business model of "rewarding" the performance [8].

3.4 Effects on Mainstream Media

Live-streaming in China also makes up an important component of the one-person media concept that gained popularity with the proliferation of social media. Similar to the rise of internet celebrities with the invention of YouTube, live-streaming has created a new road to fame that breathed new life into the Chinese entertainment circle. For example, it has bred unique categories of music like 喊麦 (a form of rapping - hǎn mai) and 古风 (pop interpretations of ancient Chinese music - gǔ fēng). More recently, live-streaming has become a paying profession with some companies paying their streamers a fixed salary in addition to a cut of whatever they receive as gifts.

Mainstream media in China has also embraced live-streaming as an innovative way of connecting with their audience and a new way of discovering talent. In addition, the focus on viewer interaction methods enabled by the "rewards" system has replaced the need for talent thereby lowering the barrier to entry for these streamers.

4 Insight and Lessons

The live-streaming market has thrived in China because it capitalized on the social needs for people living in the social media era. By providing a novel way to create and maintain social connections, live streaming services have replaced, in modern China, social environments that have existed since ancient China. The live-streaming ecosystem has further morphed from an cheap and wide-reaching stage for showcasing talent to one that encouraged social connections between strangers in real life. Live-streaming services from Facebook, YouTube and Snapchat differ greatly in interface design and interaction methods and often do not encourage interactions between the streamer and the viewers in the way that popular Chinese live-streaming applications like YiZhiBo, YingKe and YY do. It is important that we take cues from more successful platforms about new ways that satisfy human beings' need to seek "comfort, use and protection" from societal connections.

References

1. 2016 Live Stream Industry Insights Report, September 2016. http://data.weibo.com/report/reportdetail?id=328
2. Barboza, D.: Lucrative stardom in china, using a webcam and a voice, April 2014. http://www.nytimes.com/2014/04/18/business/media/lucrative-stardom-in-china-using-a-webcam-and-a-voice.html

3. Cao, T., Ren, R.C.: Live stream industry research report, 36KR Research. Technical report, June 2016. http://36kr.com/p/5048270.html
4. Chen, R.: Study of self publishing media platform "reward" model, Journalism and Copyright, no. 5 (2016)
5. Ding, Y., Du, Y., Hu, Y., Liu, Z., Wang, L., Ross, K., Ghose, A.: Broadcast yourself: understanding youtube uploaders. In: Proceedings of the 2011 ACM SIGCOMM Conference on Internet Measurement Conference, ser. IMC 2011, pp. 361–370. ACM, New York (2011). http://doi.acm.org/10.1145/2068816.2068850
6. Feng, W.: Baidu Zhidao big data: Exposing development history of online live streaming, June 2016. http://software.it168.com/a2016/0617/2719/000002719135.shtml
7. Hamilton, W.A., Garretson, O., Kerne, A.: Streaming on twitch, : fostering participatory communities of play within live mixed media, In: Proceedings of the 32nd Annual ACM Conference on Human Factors in Computing Systems, pp. 1315–1324. ACM (2014)
8. Huang, G.: Prostitutes and poets, November 2013, http://www.theworldofchinese.com/2013/11/prostitutes-and-poets/
9. Kan, K.: 'Diaosi': understanding China's Beijing 2013. http://online.thatsmags.com/post/diaosi-understanding-chinas-generation-x
10. Moshinsky, B.: Chinese millennials have created a $5 billion industry in their search for 15 minutes of fame, September 2016. http://www.businessinsider.com/credit-suisse-note-on-chinese-livestreaming-industry-2016-9
11. O'Hara, K., Black, A., Lipson, M.: Practices with mobile video telephony. In: Proceedings of the SIGCHI Conference on Human Factors in Computing Systems, ser. CHI 2006, pp. 871–880. ACM, New York (2006) http://doi.acm.org/10.1145/1124772.1124900
12. Procyk, J., Neustaedter, C., Pang, C., Tang, A., Judge, T. K.: Exploring video streaming in public settings: shared geocaching over distance using mobile video chat. In: Proceedings of the SIGCHI Conference on Human Factors in Computing Systems, ser. CHI 2014, pp. 2163–2172. ACM, New York (2014) http://doi.acm.org/10.1145/2556288.2557198
13. A. B. D. Research: Mobile live stream industry research report, Aurora Big Data Research, Technical report, July 2016
14. Seering, J., Kraut, R., Dabbish, L.: Shaping pro and anti-social behavior on twitch through moderation and example-setting. In: Proceedings of the 2017 ACM Conference on Computer Supported Cooperative Work and Social Computing, ser. CSCW 2017, pp. 111–125. ACM, New York (2017). http://doi.acm.org/10.1145/2998181.2998277
15. Tang, J.C., Venolia, G., Inkpen, K.M.: Meerkat and periscope: i stream, you stream, apps stream for live streams. In: Proceedings of the 2016 CHI Conference on Human Factors in Computing Systems, ser. CHI 2016, pp. 4770–4780. ACM, New York (2016) http://doi.acm.org/10.1145/2858036.2858374
16. Tian, L., Li, S., Ahn, J., Chu, D., Han, R., Lv, Q., Mishra, S.: Understanding user behavior at scale in a mobile video chat application. In: Proceedings of the 2013 ACM International Joint Conference on Pervasive and Ubiquitous Computing, ser. UbiComp 2013, pp. 647–656. ACM, New York (2013). http://doi.acm.org/10.1145/2493432.2493488

How Are Social Capital and Parental Mediation Associated with Cyberbullying and Cybervictimization Among Youth in the United States?

Johanna Sam[1](✉), Pamela Wisniewski[2], Heng Xu[3],
Mary Beth Rosson[3], and John M. Carroll[3]

[1] Department of Educational and Counselling Psychology and Special
Education, Vancouver, Canada
johanna.sam@alumni.ubc.ca
[2] College of Engineering and Computer Science, Orlando, USA
Pamela.Wisniewski@ucf.edu
[3] College of Information Sciences and Technology, State College, USA
{hxu,mrosson,jcarroll}@ist.psu.edu

Abstract. Introduction: Past evidence suggests parental mediation may influence their children's online exchanges with others; for example, parental mediation of adolescents' technology and internet use buffers against cyberbullying (Collier et al. 2016). Yet, no research has investigated how parental mediation and adolescents' social capital relates to cyberbullying. The present study explores the associations between social capital and parental mediation with cyberbullying and cybervictimization. **Methods:** 215 adolescents (56% female) aged 13 to 17 in a parent-teen diary study were recruited across the United States via a Qualtrics panel. Two Hierarchical Linear Regression analyses were conducted with cyberbullying and cybervictimization as the outcome variables while taking into consideration sex, age, ethnicity (Block 1) and internet use (Block 2). Social capital variables were entered into Block 3 and parental mediation variables were entered into Block 4. **Results:** Both internet use and social capital positively predicted cyberbullying and cybervictimization ($p < 0.05$), suggesting trade-offs between frequency of internet use and the ability to bond with others online in direct relation to the risk of engaging in or exposing oneself to cyberbullying. As shown in Table 1, social bonding, internet use, and device use monitoring are significantly associated with cybervictimization ($p < .05$). Social bonding and online monitoring were significantly associated with cyberbullying ($p < .05$). **Conclusions:** Our research highlights the complex relationships between adolescent internet use, the benefits of engaging online with others, and the potential risks of cyberbullying. However, parental mediation linked to these cyber risks indicates that caregivers mediate when there are online concerns.

Keywords: Online aggression · Adolescence · Parental mediation · Social capital

C. Stephanidis (Ed.): HCII Posters 2017, Part II, CCIS 714, pp. 638–644, 2017.
DOI: 10.1007/978-3-319-58753-0_90

1 Background

Internet and digital media have created novel and innovative pathways of communication for adolescents to connect with others in a meaningful way. Social media sites and instant messaging services have grown in use and popularity among adolescents (Lenhart et al. 2015). For example, posting updates on various social media sites, such as Snapchat, Facebook, or YouTube, has become part of day-to-day life for many young people. As such, online platforms have the potential to promote interpersonal bonds because digital media offers a way in which adolescents share with others. *Social capital* extends beyond simply sharing with others, but consists of having relationships with others whom one can count on to provide support in the future (Williams 2006). Putnam (2000) described two distinct categories of social capital, specifically bridging and bonding, to reflect different types of interpersonal bonds. For instance, *bridging* refers to the formation and maintenance of weak social ties to others, possibly in large social networks (Liu et al. 2016). Therefore, bridging may expand social networks to include other worldviews or create opportunities for information or resources in the future (Williams 2006). Contrastingly, *bonding* is considered to occur when strongly tied individuals (e.g., adolescents with family and peers) provide each other with emotional support. The reciprocity observed in bonding social capital promotes strong emotional bonds that enables mobilization of support and resources (Williams 2006). Past research revealed a link between internet use and social capital highlighting that electronic devices help to promote and strengthen relationships among adolescents (Liu et al. 2016). Yet, social capital generated by engaging in online social networks by adolescents may be influenced to the extent in which caregivers provide their teens with access to technology and digital media.

Researchers have started to explore the role of caregivers in relation to their children's media use (Livingstone et al. 2011). Key aspects of parental mediation include distinct strategies that are implemented by caregivers, specifically active mediation, restrictive mediation, and monitoring mediation. First, *active mediation* refers to the parent discussions regarding online content, such as interpreting and critiquing, to support adolescents' consumption of digital media (Livingstone et al. 2011). Next, *restrictive mediation* refers to when the caregiver sets rules that restrict the adolescent's use either by time or activities (Livingstone et al. 2011). Lastly, *online monitoring* considers when the caregiver checks available records of the adolescent's internet use afterwards whereas *device use monitoring* considers the use of software to filter, restrict or monitor the adolescent's use of technologies and digital media (Livingstone et al. 2011). As a result, parental mediation may influence their children's online exchanges with others; for example, parental mediation of adolescents' technology and internet use buffers against cyberbullying (Collier et al. 2016).

This shift towards online communication has provided an opportunity for potentially harmful online interactions, such as, cyberbullying and cybervictimization incidents. *Cyberbullying* refers to an intention by a group or individual to repeatedly send hurtful messages or posts to an individual through electronic devices or digital media (Tokunaga 2010). Relatedly, *cybervictimization* refers to being a target of online aggression that occurs through technology (Shapka and Maghsoudi 2017). Empirical evidence indicates that cyberbullying as well as cybervictimization prevalence rates range from 5% to 74% among adolescents (Hamm et al. 2015; Tokunaga 2010). Furthermore, Pelfrey and Weber (2013) found in a nationally representative sample involving 3,400 United States adolescents that approximately 3% reported cyberbullying others every day. As such, it appears that cyberbullying is a widespread concern that impacts a substantial proportion of young people. Yet, no research has investigated how parental mediation and adolescents' social capital relates to cyberbullying and cybervictimization. The present study addressed this gap by investigating the link among social capital and parental mediation with cyberbullying and cybervictimization. The main research question that guides the present work is:

RQ: What are the associations between social capital and parental mediation on cyberbullying and cybervictimization, while taking into consideration sociodemographic background (e.g., age, ethnicity, and gender)?

2   Methods

2.1   Data Collection

The sample included 215 adolescents from the United States (56% female) aged 13 to 17 who participated in a web-based survey with their parent or legal guardian. This study received post-secondary institutional approval from their behavioral review ethics board. After the adult participants provided their informed consent for themselves and their child, teens were also given the opportunity to assent to be a part of the study. Teen participants who did not provide their assent were not included in the analysis. Parents completed their surveys first then were asked to leave the room so that their teens could complete their portion of the survey. In this paper, we only analyzed data collected from teen participants. To recruit a nationally representative sample of participants, we leveraged a Qualtrics panel[1]. Qualtrics compared data collected with regional demographics to prevent over sampling from a particular population. Attention screener questions were used to filter out low quality data. The data collection was completed by the end of August 2014.

2.2   Measures

Cyberbullying and Cybervictimization. Participants' cyberbullying and cybervictimization experiences were measured with an online harassment scale (Wisniewski et al. 2017). This behavioral-based measure consists of 6-items with two subscales: cyberbullying (3 items) and cybervictimization (3 items). Items are scored on a 5-point Likert scale ranging from 1 = *not at all*, 2 = *one to a few times this past year*, 3 = *a few times a month*, 4 = *a few times a week*, to 5 = *almost every day*. A higher score

---

[1] https://www.qualtrics.com/online-sample/.

represents greater involvement in cyberbullying or cybervictimization. The measure asks respondents about their online interactions between self and others. The cyber-victimization items are grouped together, followed by the set of cyberbullying items. The measure asks respondents about their online interactions between self and others. Sample cybervictimization items include "Based on your experiences within the past year, please indicate how frequently you were subjected to online interactions between you and others that involved someone treating another person in a mean or hurtful way, making rude or threatening comments, spreading untrue rumors, harassing, or other-wise trying to "cyberbully" another person" and "online interactions between you and others that involved sharing personal or sensitive information either without the owner's consent or that otherwise breached someone's personal privacy." A sample of cyberbullying item include "Based on your experiences within the past year, please indicate how frequently you sought out online interactions between you and others that involved exchanging sexual messages (i.e. "Sexting"), sexually suggestive text-based messages or revealing/naked photos, or arranging to meet someone first met online for an offline romantic encounter." The cybervictimization measure has a Cronbach's α of 0.93 and cyberbullying has a Cronbach's α of 0.94.

Social Bonding. Participants' bridging and bonding social capital were measured with the Internet Social Capital Scale (ISCS; Williams 2006). This measure consists of 20-items with two subscales: bridging (10 items) and bonding (10 items). Items are scored on a 5-point Likert scale ranging from 1 = *strong disagree, 2 = disagree, 3 = neutral, 4 = agree,* to 5 = *strongly agree.* A higher score represents higher social capital. Sample bonding items include "the people I interact with online would put their reputation on the line for me" and "there is someone online I can turn to for advice about making very important decisions." Sample of bridging items include "interacting with people online makes me feel connected to the bigger picture" and "Interacting with people online makes me interested in things that happen outside of my town." The ISCS measure had been shown to have a Cronbach's α of 0.90 (Williams 2006).

Parental Mediation. Parental mediation strategies measured were active, restriction, and monitoring (Livingstone et al. 2011). The measure consists of 20-items with three subscales: active (5 items), restriction (6 items) and monitoring (11 items). Items are scored on a 5-point Likert scale ranging from 1 = *not at all, 2 = rarely, 3 = sometimes, 4 = often,* to 5 = *almost all of the time.* Next, sample active item includes "Do either of your parents currently do any of the following things with you? Talk to you about what you do on the Internet." Sample of restriction item includes "For each of these situations, please specify how restrictive your parents usually are: Upload photos, videos or music to share with others." Lastly, examples of monitoring item include "Does either of your parents sometimes check any of the following things - which websites you visited based on your Internet browsing history" and "Use parental control technologies to keep track of the websites you visit." The parental mediation measure had been shown to have Cronbach's α of 0.75 for active mediation, 0.94 for monitoring mediation, and 0.88 for restriction mediation.

Demographics. Self-reports of age and ethnicity were used to determine demographic characteristics of participants. Age was determined by asking participants to select their current age from categories of 13 years old, 14 years old, 15 years old, 16 years old, and 17 years old. Participants identified their gender as either male or female. Participants were also asked "Choose the category which best describes you" Respondents endorsed one response that they most closely identify with: White/Caucasian, Black/African-American, Hispanic/Latino, Asian, Native Hawaiian or Other Pacific Islander, American Indian/Alaska Native, Other. The ethnic descriptions were collapsed into the following four categories: White, Black, Hispanic/Latino, and Other (Asian, Native Hawaiian or Other Pacific Islander, American Indian, Alaska Native, Other).

2.3   Data Analysis

Two Hierarchical Linear Regression analyses were conducted with cyberbullying and cybervictimization as the outcome variables while taking into consideration sex, age, ethnicity (Block 1) and internet use (Block 2). Social capital variables were entered into Block 3 and parental mediation variables were entered into Block 4.

3   Results

As shown in Table 1, both internet use and bonding social capital positively predicted cyberbullying and cybervictimization ($p < 0.05$). Parental mediation strategies were also positively associated with cyber-risks; online monitoring predicted cyberbullying

Table 1. Summary of hierarchical multiple regression examining the influence of social capital and parental mediation on cyberbullying and cybervictimization.

	DV = Cyberbullying				DV = Cybervictimization			
	Block 1	Block 2	Block 3	Block 4	Block 1	Block 2	Block 3	Block 4
R^2	0.07	0.23	0.38	0.45	0.07	0.28	0.40	0.45
Adj. R^2	N/A	0.16	0.31	0.36	0.00	0.22	0.34	0.37
Variables - β								
Female	0.11	0.04	0.05	0.04	0.13	0.08	0.06	0.05
Age								
17 Years Old	(ref)	--	--	--	--	--	--	--
16 Years Old	-0.18	-0.22	-0.21	-0.19	-0.10	-0.13	-0.15	-0.17
15 Years Old	0.08	-0.03	0.01	0.04	0.03	-0.07	-0.06	-0.07
14 Years Old	-0.03	-0.04	0.02	0.05	-0.07	-0.06	0.00	0.01
13 Years Old	-0.03	-0.05	0.02	0.06	-0.07	-0.06	0.00	0.01
Ethnicity								
White	(ref)	--	--	--	--	--	--	--
Black	0.03	-0.01	0.00	0.02	-0.03	-0.06	-0.07	-0.08
Hispanic	0.08	0.01	-0.04	-0.06	0.18	0.10	0.05	0.00
Other	0.01	0.01	0.02	0.00	-0.02	-0.01	-0.01	-0.03
Internet Use		0.43***	0.32***	0.18		0.47***	0.37***	0.29**
Social Capital								
Bridging			-0.16	-0.11			-0.22*	-0.18
Bonding			0.48***	0.36**			0.46***	0.35**
Parental Med.								
Active				-0.11				-0.14
Restrictive				0.21				0.17
Monitoring				0.26*				0.05
Dev. Monitor				0.09				0.24*

Note. *$p < 0.05$.   **$p < 0.01$ ***$p < 0.001$.

while device monitoring by parents was significantly associated with cybervictimization. Internet use became a non-significant factor for cyberbullying once parental mediation (Block 4) was added to the model. The main effects of demographic factors, specifically age, ethnicity, and gender, did not significantly contribute to the models.

4 Discussion and Conclusion

Our research highlights the complex relationships between adolescent internet use, the benefits of engaging online with others, and the potential risks of cyberbullying. Study findings indicate that there is a significant association between cyberbullying experiences, social capital, and parental mediation. Our results suggest trade-offs between frequency of internet use and the ability to bond with others online in direct relation to the risk of engaging in or exposing oneself to cyber-related risks. Interestingly, parental mediation did not seem to have an effect on reducing cyber-risks. Instead, our results are consistent with prior work (Wisniewski et al. 2015) that suggests parents may take more reactive approaches to mediate teens' online risk experiences once they occur. Yet, a limitation of our findings is that cross-sectional data is not best suited to confirm causal relationships. Therefore, longitudinal studies are needed to investigate the dynamic relationship between social capital and parental mediation as adolescents develop and encounter stressful online situations, such as cyberbullying and cybervictimization. Future studies examining the interplay between parental mediation techniques, adolescent internet use, online risks, and online benefits would serve to further disentangle these effects.

Acknowledgements. This research was supported by the U.S. National Science Foundation under grant CNS-1018302. Part of the work of Heng Xu was done while working at the U.S. National Science Foundation. Any opinion, findings, and conclusions or recommendations expressed in this material are those of the authors and do not necessarily reflect the views of the U.S. National Science Foundation.

References

Collier, K.M., Coyne, S.M., Rasmussen, E.E., Hawkins, A.J., Padilla-walker, L.M., Erickson, S.E., Memmott-elison, M.K.: Does parental mediation of media influence child outcomes? A meta-analysis on media time, aggression, substance use, and sexual behavior. Dev. Psychol. **52**(5), 798–812 (2016)

Hamm, M.P., Newton, A.S., Chisholm, A., Shulhan, J., Milne, A., Sundar, P., Ennis, H., Scott, S. D., Hartling, L.: Prevalence and effect of cyberbullying on children and young people. JAMA Pediatrics **169**(8), 770–777 (2015). http://doi.org/10.1001/jamapediatrics.2015.0944

Lenhart, A., Smith, A., Anderson, M., Duggan, M., Perrin, A.: Teens, technology and friendships, Pew Research Center (2015). http://www.pewinternet.org/2015/08/06/teens-technology-and-friendships/

Liu, D., Ainsworth, S.E., Baumeister, R.F.: A meta-analysis of social networking online and social capital. Rev. Gen. Psychol. **20**(4), 369–391 (2016)

Livingstone, S., Haddon, L., Görzig, A., Ólafsson, K.: Risks and safety on the internet: the perspective of European children: full findings and policy implications from the EU Kids online survey of 9–16 year olds and their parents in 25 countries (2011). http://doi.org/2045-256X

Pelfrey, W.V, Weber, N.L.: Keyboard gangsters: analysis of incidence and correlates of cyberbullying in a large urban student population keyboard gangsters: analysis of incidence and correlates of cyberbullying in a large urban student population. Deviant Behav. **34**(1), 68–84 (2013). http://doi.org/10.1080/01639625.2012.707541

Putnam, R.D.: Bowling Alone: The Collapse and Revival of American Community. Simon & Schuster, New York (2000)

Shapka, J.D., Maghsoudi, R.: Examining the validity and reliability of the cyber-aggression and cyber-victimization scale. Comput. Hum. Behav. **69**, 10–17 (2017). http://doi.org/10.1016/j.chb.2016.12.015

Tokunaga, R.S.: Following you home from school: a critical review and synthesis of research on cyberbullying victimization. Comput. Hum. Behav. **26**(3), 277–287 (2010). http://doi.org/10.1016/j.chb.2009.11.014

Williams, D.: On and off the 'net : scales for social capital in an online era. J. Comput.-Mediated Commun. **11**, 593–628 (2006). http://doi.org/10.1111/j.1083-6101.2006.00029.x

Wisniewski, P., Jia, H., Xu, H., Rosson, M.B., Carroll, J.M.: 'Preventative' vs. 'reactive:' how parental mediation influences teens' social media privacy behaviors. In: The Proceedings of the 2015 ACM Conference on Computer Supported Cooperative Work (CSCW 2015), Vancouver, BC, Canada (2015)

Wisniewski, P., Xu, H., Rosson, M.B., Carroll, J. M.: Parents just don't understand: why teens don't talk to parents about their online risk experiences. In: Proceedings of the 2017 ACM Conference on Computer Supported Cooperative Work and Social Computing (2017)

Parental Controls: Oxymoron and Design Opportunity

Diane J. Schiano[(⊠)] and Christine Burg

Strategic Family Therapy Clinic, Mental Research Institute (MRI),
Palo Alto, CA, USA
Diane.Schiano@springernature.com

Abstract. This paper summarizes a set of findings from an extended research project on family dynamics around digital media use, and in particular, on parental concerns and practices in managing their children's media use. Here we focus primarily on qualitative results from a nationwide online survey and follow-up interviews that enrich and extend previously published quantitative findings, and permit a more nuanced understanding of this important yet often neglected socio-technical landscape. We then challenge the design community to re-imagine parental control technologies (PCLs) as collaborative self-regulation training tools.

Keywords: Parents · Children · Parental controls · Media use · Technology use

1 Introduction

Most American kids spend more time on digital media each day than they do in the classroom [1]. Moreover, in the past 5 years there's been an explosion in mobile devices, games and apps marketed to very young children, extending the potential for chronic media immersion to infants and toddlers. In 2015, the American Academy of Pediatrics (AAP) published remarkable findings on digital media use by low-income children aged 6 m–4 yrs. [2]. Use of smart mobile devices was "almost universal"; proficiency in device usage was surprisingly widespread among toddlers, and almost a third of these very young children were regularly put to bed with a mobile device. After over 3 decades of calling for no screen time at all for kids under two, and no more than 1–2 h per day after that [3, 4], the AAP abandoned its guidelines in 2016. Instead, parents are now offered an online "toolkit" with extensive information around technology health risks, references to media resources, and various tips and tools (e.g., a time-use calculator) intended to help parents make decisions in their role as family media managers [5]. Struggling with family media management has been called a challenge of "unprecedented proportions" [4] and "one of the most difficult parenting issues we've ever faced" [6]. Yet parents—and families, for that matter—are already "busier than ever", thank you very much [7, 8]. So what are parents to do when—as one parent we interviewed put it—"even the experts can't keep up with the new technology"? And how can we help them?

This paper summarizes a set of findings from an extended research project on family dynamics around digital media use, and in particular, on parental concerns and

© Springer International Publishing AG 2017
C. Stephanidis (Ed.): HCII Posters 2017, Part II, CCIS 714, pp. 645–652, 2017.
DOI: 10.1007/978-3-319-58753-0_91

practices in managing their children's media use. Here we focus primarily on qualitative results from a nationwide online survey and follow-up interviews that enrich and extend previously published quantitative findings [9], and permit a more nuanced understanding of this major yet neglected socio-technical landscape. We then challenge the design community to re-imagine parental control technologies (PCLs) as collaborative self-regulation training tools.

2 Methods

A wealth of data was generated for this project between 2014–2017, primarily from a nationwide online survey and from formal follow-up interviews with survey participants.

The online survey explored parenting styles, family dynamics, family media use and parental concerns and practices around managing media use by their children. It consisted of: (1) 50 rating-scale (1–7) items, (2) a large comment box, where parents were asked to discuss specific concerns, approaches and experiences at some length; and (3) ~15 demographic items. English and Spanish versions of the survey were posted on Surveymonkey; recruitment was primarily through Craigslist ads posted nationwide between Sept 2014–Dec 2015. The survey was completed by over 472 parents, ~30% of site visitors. Almost 77% were female; median age was 41 years. Over 64% were partnered, ~11% were "single"; divorce/separation rate was 35%. Median number of children was 3; their median age was 12 yrs. Annual household income ranged widely, with a median of $65 K. Straightforward quantitative analyses were performed on survey rating-scale items. Content analyses of open-ended survey comments involved both qualitative thematic analysis [10] and quantitative analysis of the frequency of keyword/topic mentions. Keywords were both pre-determined (e.g., media types, parenting style, parental control technologies (PCLs)) and derived from themes emerging from the data itself (e.g., addiction, lack of control).

Formal follow-up interviews were conducted with 18 survey participants, in person at home (if local) or via Skype or phone (if remote). Interviews were conversational and semi-structured, lasted 1–1.5 h. and were audio-recorded. Other family members were included in the interviews (sometimes together, most often separately) whenever possible. Interviewees were primarily recruited via email; all survey respondents who indicated an interest in participating were contacted. Eight interviewees participated as volunteers without pay; 10 more were randomly selected for paid participation. Most interviewees were mothers, 3 were fathers; 13 were white and 5 were Hispanic, black or mixed-race. Other demographics were similar to those of the survey as a whole. The interviews were analyzed primarily through thematic analysis, informed by the survey findings.

We note that our work on this project was also informed by the following: 1. Both authors are psychotherapists who have worked for years with children and families, largely from disadvantaged households. 2. Both authors are also mothers, who engaged in a wide variety of informal, ethnographic-style experiences, interactions and conversations with other parents, children and educators on the topic of family media management, in our local communities (in Northern California and Bamburg, Germany) and elsewhere.

3 Findings

Our survey results document the increasingly predominant use of smart mobile devices from infancy through young adulthood. The mobile phone was by far the primary device parents said their kids used overall, and across childhood age spans. Tablets have also become quite common, at home and increasingly at school, especially for younger children and in more advantaged households.

3.1 Parental Concerns

When survey respondents were asked to describe specific concerns around media use, the topics of sex and violence came up, but also such issues as commercialism, poor role modelling and disparagement of women. Parents, especially those with very young children, said they occasionally look up media ratings (e.g., using Common Sense Media), though admittedly not as often as they might. Easy—and sometimes inadvertent–access to pornography is troubling. One mother complained that kids do not come to parents for information around sexuality anymore; instead, "pornography is the new Sex Ed". Fears of sexting, cyberbullying and sexual predators were mentioned in comments and interviews, but fairly rarely and largely in the abstract. Interestingly—though with notable exceptions–most parents seemed to feel that their own children were made aware of online identity, privacy, and safety risks both at school and at home, and for the most part were fairly confident that their preteen and teen children "have pretty good heads on their shoulders". Still, taking some steps to protect children from these risks was seen as a part of their job as parents. This largely included discussing with their kids the "digital trail" left by all online interactions, and encouraging them not to post identifying information online, to use privacy settings on social media and to avoid online interactions with strangers. Some "checking up" on texts and Facebook posts was reported, most often for tweens upon first obtaining a smartphone (typically between 10–12 yrs.), or when they started using social media. Otherwise, and as reported elsewhere, most parents, especially with teens and from more advantaged households, tended—with some ambivalence–to try to respect their kids' "right to privacy" [8].

The primary parental concern, voiced across all demographics, and for children of all ages, was around excessive use of, or so-called "addiction" to, media/technology use. (Note that—with a few notable exceptions–the term "addiction" is used here colloquially, not as a clinical diagnosis; a discussion around clinical addiction and excessive technology use is provided in our previous paper). Concerns were voiced around the effects of "too much technology" on kids' physical wellbeing—e.g., eyesight, brain development, quality of sleep; their cognitive development—e.g., focused attention, reading, executive functioning; and, increasingly, their social/emotional development—e.g., emotional regulation, empathy, conversational skills and deep connections to family and friends. Half of our survey respondents' ratings characterized one or more of their children as "addicted to technology". (As expected, for males, addiction was associated primarily with games (and later—and to a lesser extent, porn); for females, overwhelmingly with social media). Still, the same percentage viewed their kids' media use as "pretty much like that of most kids of their age and gender." Moreover, almost as many parents also rated themselves—and/or their partner—as addicted. The qualitative data confirm and extend these results, strongly supporting the notion that this focus on addiction—again, with some exceptions–reflects a vague but deep unease with the degree to which media and technology in general intrude into our lives these days. How much is too much? Not even the AAP will say anymore! Consistent with previous reports [8, 11], many of the parents we encountered felt that the pervasive pull of technology is "out of control" yet "inevitable"—in their kids' lives, in their own lives, and in the culture at large.

Three-quarters of survey comments and many of the interviews reflect a palpable sense of lack of control in a heavily demanding and burdensome role. Parents feel strong social pressure to be "good parents" (not too permissive, not too strict) around media management, and to pass on "family values" around technology use, but they are also "overwhelmed", "stressed out" and unable to devote the time and energy that due diligence requires. The march of technology diffusion in our society appears relentless, and fighting it is an "uphill battle". One mother noted that she "didn't want to lend my child to this giant social experiment", but added that "resistance is futile."

The demands and burdens parents described include keeping informed about constantly changing media and media content, making and revising limits and other discipline decisions, maintaining constant vigilance and consistent modelling and discipline despite other responsibilities and their children's persistent whining, tantrums, battles and "get-arounds". Lower-income parents may take on multiple jobs to make ends meet, while higher-income parents might be required to work long hours, travel extensively, and—most commonly–to have an online work presence even during "off hours." Other challenges include being a single parent, limited financial or family resources to help with childcare, strong differences between parents on appropriate media management and parenting styles, child vulnerabilities/co-morbidities such as ADHD, autism or anxiety and depression, and the increasingly online nature of schooling (from posting assignments and grades online to providing tablets for students).

One father of teen boys complained that parental media management requires "too much responsibility with too little authority—just like my job!" This then negatively impacts family dynamics, especially around issues of trust (that kids are following the rules and not taking huge risks) and respect (for parental authority and teens' "supposed rights" to privacy and self-determination). Parents complain of the inability to "really tell" what their kids are doing online (especially as mobiles are often used behind closed bedroom doors), a sense of exclusion from what their kids are "really doing" and a feeling of being left out, left behind and even disrespected if not "tech-savvy" enough. One fairly prototypical devolving dynamic, especially in more advantaged households, starts out with a preteen begging for a smartphone and arguing that "everyone has one and they'll be left out", parents recognizing the usefulness of a phone for "emergencies" and schedule "co-ordination", parents then giving the child a phone with initial warnings and admonitions around its use, followed by the child assuming sole ownership, and vehemently asserting privacy and "always on" "rights", especially in the teen years.

3.2   Parental Controls and Media Management Strategies

The media management strategies most frequently mentioned by parents in the survey involved the use of time limits and filtering/blocking of specific content, sites or apps (i.e., forms of monitoring and restriction). Parental control (PCL) software to implement these strategies is now available on most devices, and some, like Microsoft Family Safety, are cloud-based and intended to work across devices. Wifi routers are the most typical PCL hardware. Analyses of survey results by age of first child shows that PCL use at home begins early, with 27% of children aged 0–2 yrs. Use peaks at 62% for 9–11 year olds, then falls to 46% by ages 15–17. A similar pattern is found for mobile device-based PCLs, although peak PCL use for mobiles occurs somewhat earlier (ages 6–8), and declines rapidly thereafter. Satisfaction with PCLs dramatically declines across the age span, as addiction ratings rapidly rise. Overall, the quantitative trends suggest that many parents—especially in more advantaged households where there are at least some older children–adopted PCLs fairly early on, but over the teen years, PCL use became so unsatisfactory (with battles, backfiring, etc.) that they "gave up", at least on controlling devices used by those teens [12–14]. Of course, these are not longitudinal data and, in part, must reflect cohort effects. Still, this interpretation is strongly supported by comments and interviews characterizing experiences over time with children that are currently older teens or young adults. PCLs—especially cloud- and router-based controls–were described as extremely cumbersome to use, inflexible, unintegrated, and noticeably slowing performance. They were also seen as frustratingly unreliable and with poor customer support. Inherent difficulties in filtering (e.g., "you can't block everything") were noted, as were innumerable logistical problems. For example, turning off cellphone data access or implementing revised PCL settings on laptops and tablets typically requires restarting the device.

In addition, simple technical solutions such as absolute time limits easily become complex and problematic when, say, game companies penalize players who must leave the game when timed-out before completing a battle. And does downloading a game update "count" as time online? It is also noteworthy that in many households, the PCLs are effectively controlled by one parent (often the father) while the other tends more often to be at home, "in the trenches". Several mothers confessed in the interviews to wanting to "soften" or be "more flexible" on rigid rules implemented via PCLs. Moreover, many less technical parents do not fully understand how their PCLs on their kids' devices work. Indeed, most interviewees who said they used PCL restrictions on their children's smartphone access could not accurately describe how they work. Several did not appreciate that their smartphone restrictions did not apply to wifi use. All of this can lead to inconsistencies in parenting, and disappointing dynamics of deception, manipulation and mistrust between parents and children.

By far the most common complaint against PCLs placed on devices used by teens concerned how easy it is for kids to learn to get around them; that is, they "backfire". For example, one interviewee said "there's not a single [PCL] my 12 yr. old son can't get around—easy-to-follow instructions are posted on YouTube!" Passwords can be changed (or figured out), phones can be reset, and kids can "flip between tabs" to pretend they are working. Then there's "incognito mode" search, history clearing, hidden accounts, "stealth mode" vpns and emulators, and so much more. Some parents resorted to physically removing wifi routers to limit surreptitious gaming. The tweens and teens we interviewed fairly uniformly—and cheerfully–reinforced the notion that their parents "have no idea" of the real extent of their media use. While some parents viewed PCLs as a way to "de-personalize" discipline around media management, their kids increasingly saw them as a challenge to work around.

The parents we interacted with tended to view media management in the larger parenting context of promoting increasing maturity through self-regulation [15, 16]. Analogies to "childproofing" [17] are often made, but the task is far more complex, dynamic and uncertain in the digital environment. Parents may feel misgivings about courses taken when problems arise, and principles all-too-often yield to pragmatics. Still, most parents—and families–seem to muddle through. The obvious "pull" of digital media has made access control (imposing or relaxing restrictions, sometimes with PCLs) a core discipline tool for both offline and online behaviors. Access control is not only used to punish excessive media use, but also to reinforce desired activities (e.g., high grades, completing homework or chores, participation in sports, reading, music practice, in-person socializing), and even to promote family cohesion (e.g., media off for family dinners, on for movie nights; videogames for father-son bonding; increased access to reinforce more—or more consistent–family communication). Other common approaches include modelling, conversational advice and guidance (active mediation), co-use (e.g., friending on Facebook, watching TV together), participatory learning (e.g., programming together), and various forms of parental awareness, supervision and monitoring (e.g., using timers to "keep track and make sure he doesn't play forever"; locating game consoles or TVs in a public space for casual oversight; reading texts and posts; using PCLs to track phone locations or monitor online activities.)

A wide variety of other values-based parenting strategies were also mentioned, some quite common ("keep them busy!", "homework first!" grades-based approaches and "the _not_ rules" (e.g., not at dinner/restaurants/in the car/with relatives/in your room after bedtime) and others, more family-specific ("drop everything and read!", "media Sabbaths", "TV is toxic!"). The "keep them busy!" strategy might involve anything from occasional coercion to "go outside and play" to collaboratively creating alternative activities. A common version of this approach, especially in more advantaged households, is to indirectly limit time available for media use through intensive scheduling of more "worthwhile" enrichment activities and sports pursuits. While this can generate a "calendaring and co-ordination nightmare", especially for mothers, it has the advantage of being fairly effective without the need for parents to explicitly "come down too hard" and appear strict or authoritarian—i.e., "not a good parent." In fact, several mothers we talked with who relied on this approach saw themselves as rather "laissez faire" about their kids' media use, despite phone tracking and continuous texting around co-ordinating schedules, etc.

In short, parents bring to bear a panoply of concerns and practices, both on- and offline, on the challenging task of media management. This is done in the more general parenting context of promoting self-regulation, and approaches may vary as resources, creativity, specific kids and situations and the complexities of modern family life allow. Methods simplistically classified in earlier work as inherently "preventative" or "reactive" [8] are in practice customized, blended together and applied flexibly for the purposes at hand. This is most obvious when parents, in effect, try to use PCLs as behavioral training tools—providing clear limits and rewards, and fairly immediate, targeted reinforcements contingent on the performance of desired behaviors [18]. Of course, tools should be effective, usable and useful. And even the best tools and rules require some buy-in and collaboration to be effective, especially with teens. (Joint media contracts are often recommended, but success can be short-lived; this can be attributed to insufficient "scaffolding", or targeted, immediate and feedback and persistent, adaptive support [18, 19].) As our results demonstrate, the widespread need for better media management tools is palpable.

4 Implications for Design

Attracting and retaining users is a digital media design requirement, and PCL design isn't exactly sexy. As one engineer, father and interviewee put it:

> *[Digital media] is addictive by design...of course it's hard to resist! [PCLs] make parents feel like they're in control, but kids soon learn the truth... Parental controls are an afterthought at best at worst, an oxymoron!*

As members of the design community, we share some responsibility for the social effects of our products. Some authors have called for improving the design of our technologies to promote social values [8, 11, 16]. For example, Sherry Turkle [16] suggests promoting more intentional transitions and interactions, "unitasking" (as opposed to multi-tasking), and increased time offline (to reflect and converse). We applaud these efforts. We also recognize the importance of ongoing work to incrementally enhance the usability and usefulness of PCLs. But beyond this, and more fundamentally, we challenge the PCL design community to recognize and respond to the creative opportunity our results suggest. Parents are concerned about excessive technology use by their children, but feel a sense of burden and lack of control in managing media use. Better PCL tools could help. Especially if PCL functionality were re-imagined beyond simple surveillance and control (and battles and backfiring).

Here's one blue-sky scenario: PCLs could become integrated, adaptive, and increasingly collaborative self-regulation training tools, instantiating best practices—perhaps even via AI agents. Helping parents become more effective media mentors and managers, and supporting their kids in the process of becoming aware of, discussing and learning to manage their own media use as they mature. Perhaps featuring collaborative construction of media contracts, with revisions based on feedback over time. Kid-friendly graphical activity–even bio- and neuro-feedback–displays with immediate, targeted feedback to promote awareness, self-reflection and self-regulation. Collaborative co-creation and gamification to promote engagement and partial opacity to respect teen privacy [20]. More targeted behavioral training (e.g., star charts and token economies) as needed to motivate and reinforce progress. Easy connection to communication and calendaring tools, with appropriate alerts, warnings, reminders, count-down timers, etc. Voice-control and thumbprint security. Maybe even links to CommonSenseMedia reviews, or games and apps designed to train specific skills. Self-regulation apps and related technologies have been called "the wave of the future" [20]. Application to media management for and by kids will be a challenge, but the need is real and the promise is clear.

References

1. Common Sense Media: The Common Sense Census: Media Use by Tweens and Teens. https://www.commonsensemedia.org/research/the-common-sense-census-media-use-by-tweens-and-teens
2. Kabali, H.K., et al.: Exposure and use of mobile media devices by young children. Pediatrics **136**(6), 1044–1050 (2015). doi:10.1542/peds.2013-2656
3. American Academy of Pediatrics Council on Communications and Media: Policy statement: children, adolescents and the media. Pediatrics **132**(5), 958–961 (2013). doi:10.1542/peds.2013-2656
4. Shifrin, D., et al.: Growing up digital: media research symposium. American Academy of Pediatrics (2015). doi:10.1016/j.jadohealth.2014.07.012.22
5. American Academy of Pediatrics. Media and Children Communication Toolkit. https://www.aap.org/en-us/advocacy-and-policy/aap-health-initiatives/pages/media-and-children.aspx
6. Ruston, D.: Screenagers: Growing up in the Digital Age. Film (2016). http://www.screenagersmovie.com
7. Darrah, C.N., Freeman, J.M., English-Lueck, J.A.: Busier than Ever!: Why American Families Can't Slow Down. Stanford University Press, Stanford (2007)
8. Clark, L.S.: The Parent App: Understanding Families in the Digital Age. Oxford University Press, New York (2013). doi:10.1080/08838151.2013.875025
9. Schiano, D.J., Burg, C., Smith, A.N. Moore, F.: Parenting digital youth: How now?' In: Extended Abstracts of ACM 2016 CHI Conference on Human Factors in Computing Systems, pp. 3181–3189. ACM, New York (2016). doi:10.1145/2851581.2892481
10. Braun, V., Clarke, V.: Using thematic analysis in psychology. Qual. Res. Psychol. **3**(2), 77–101 (2006). doi:10.1191/1478088706qp063oa
11. Turkle, S.: Reclaiming Conversation: The Power of Talk in a Digital Age. Penguin Press, New York (2015)
12. Wisniewski, P., Jia, H., Xu, H., Rosson, M.B., Carroll, J.M.: "Preventative" vs. "reactive:" how parental mediation influences teens' social media privacy behaviors. In: Proceedings of the 18th ACM Conference on Computer Supported Cooperative Work & Social Computing, pp 302–316. ACM, New York (2015). doi:10.1145/2675133.2675293
13. Byrne, S., Lee, T.: Toward predicting youth resistance to internet risk prevention strategies. J. Broadcast. Electron. Media **55**(1), 90–113 (2011). doi:10.1080/08838151.2011.546255
14. Kerr, M., Stattin, H.: What parents know, how they know it, and several forms of adolescent adjustment: further support for a reinterpretation of monitoring. Dev. Psychol. **36**(3), 366–380 (2000). doi:10.1037/0012-1649.36.3.366
15. Bronson, M.B.: Self-Regulation in Early Childhood: Nature and Nurture. Guilford, New York (2000)
16. ConnectSafely. Less parental control, more support of kids' self-regulation: study. http://www.connectsafely.org/less-parental-control-more-support-of-kids-self-regulation-study/
17. Rosemond, J.: Teenproofing: Fostering Responsible Decision-Making in Your Teenager. Andrew McMeel, Kansas City (2000)
18. Graziano, A.M., Diament, D.M.: Parent behavioral training: an examination of the paradigm. Behav. Modif. **16**(1), 3–38 (1992). doi:10.1177/01454455920161001
19. Yardi, S., Bruckman, A.: Social and technical challenges in parenting teens' social media use. In: Proceedings of the 14th ACM Conference on Human Factors in Computing Systems, pp 3237–3246. ACM, New York (2011). doi:10.1145/1978942.1979422
20. Tran, J., Mandal, T.: Self-Regulation and Technology – The Wave of the Future. http://www.snow.idrc.ocad.ca/node/255

Establish Security Psychology – How to Educate and Training for End Users

Katsuya Uchida[(⊠)]

Institute of Information Security, Yokohama, Japan
uchidak@gol.com

Abstract. Social engineering that attacks human psychological weakness is becoming mainstream. Attackers and methods of attack have been published from the old age for countermeasure of individuals. However, we need comprehensive defense methods for individuals and the organization. I propose "security psychology" and believe that it is important for the theory of Sun Tzu which is "know the enemy and know thyself". The "to know the enemies" part is almost the same as social engineering, so I focus on the "to know thyself" part and considered it. And I will describe the result of training of "To know thyself".

Keywords: Security psychology · Social engineering

1 Introduction

This paper discusses a practical approach to cyber security education, training and awareness.

This approach based on a human activity perspective, that is, the cognitive psychology, Human factor, and Criminal psychology perspective and so on.

The definition of Security psychology is the research and practice based on human security such as cyber security areas, human factor, and security management of organization, mainly.

Security education, training, and awareness in security psychology are divided into two areas, namely Social engineering and CSEAT.

Figure 1 is the bird's-eye view of Security Psychology.

Social engineering has practical social engineers' books, hands-on education & training and research papers [1, 2].

CSEAT is defined in this paper and is a comprehensive education, training and awareness system, not only targeting individual users but also education and training considering organizations.

2 Essential Knowledge of Security Training

It is important to clarify what to protect and it is important to think about the risk of assets to protect.

© Springer International Publishing AG 2017
C. Stephanidis (Ed.): HCII Posters 2017, Part II, CCIS 714, pp. 653–657, 2017.
DOI: 10.1007/978-3-319-58753-0_92

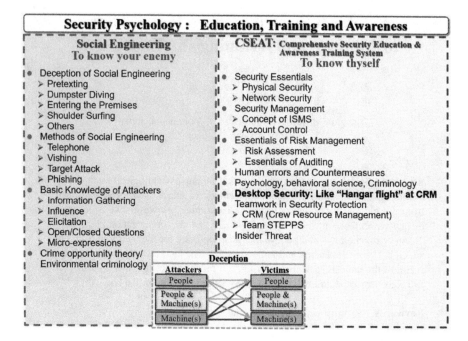

Fig. 1. Bird's-eye view of security psychology

2.1   Definition of Information Assets

The following are definition of the information assets which are classified with the four groups [3].

- People are those who are vital to the expected operation and performance of the service. People may be internal or external to the organization.
- Information is any information or data, on any media including paper or electronic form.
- Technology describes any technology component or asset that supports or automates a service and facilitates its ability to accomplish its mission. Some technology are specific to a service (such as an application system) and others are shared by the organization (such as the enterprise-wide network infrastructure).
- Facilities are the places where services are executed and can be owned and controlled by the organization or by external business partners. In general, any of the information assets are targeted attackers and many of the cyber-attacks use the findings of psychology and behavioral science as well as the technical knowledge.

2.2   Security Incident

One of the security survey shows that the top four patterns.account for nearly 90% of all incidents.is people (Fig. 2) [4].

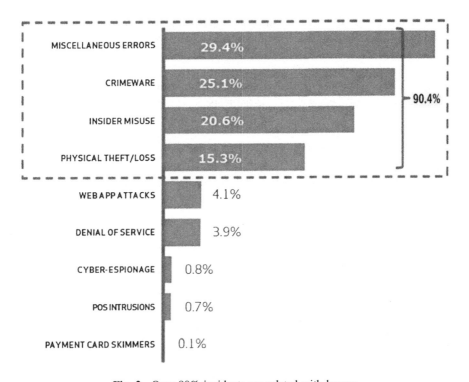

Fig. 2. Over 90% incidents are related with human

Also, July, 2002, Howard Schmidt is vice chairman of the president's Critical Infrastructure Protection Board speaks about cyber security issues.

Q: What kinds of technology will be needed to stave off electronic attacks? Do we need bigger anti-virus programs?

A: The common misconception is this is a technology issue. But it's not a technology issue. For example, the DOD did an analysis last year and it's somewhere in the high 90s, like 97 [percent] to 98% of things that have hit the DOD systems have been the result not of some new piece of technology but exploitation of people that have not had processes in place to install patches or to configure their systems properly.

Kevin Mitnick, most excellent social engineer, said in his book,

**As noted security consultant Bruce Schneier puts it, "Security is not a product, it's a process."
Moreover, security is not a technology problem - it's a people and management problem.**

3   Practical Security Training for End-Users

3.1   Training Background

Private information about a woman who was stalked and killed by her former boyfriend a year ago is thought to have been leaked by the local government in Japan.

Senior officials of the firm are suspected of obtaining her address from the local government within hours of receiving the request and giving it to the detective agency.

It seems that the detective used the elicitation technique which is technique used to discreetly gather information [5].

In accordance with this incident, three-hour training was conducted for staff of a local government and there were 37 participants.

3.2   Contents of the Training

Outline of the training is as follows

- The importance of confirmation (Fig. 3A)
- The importance of experience (Fig. 3B)
- How to memorize (Fig. 3C)
- Human Element: Importance of organizing communication

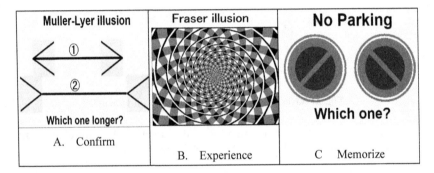

Fig. 3. The importance of confirmation [A] The importance of experience [B] How to memorize [C]

- – CRM: Crew Resource Management [6]
- – Team STEPPS
- – The invisible gorilla

3.3   Results of the Training

The result of the training was as follows

- Almost all attendees are satisfied
- The questionnaire is done just after training (Fig. 4).

Training Satisfaction											

Training Satisfaction
- ➤ Very useful: 57% (21 people)
- ➤ Somewhat: 43% (16 people)
- ➤ Not very useful /
      not useful at all: 0%

Recommend the training to others?
- ➤ Definitely recommend: 19% (7)
- ➤ Recommend: 43% (16)
- ➤ Somewhat recommend: 19% (7)
- ➤ Can not say either: 8% (3)
- ➤ Rather not recommend: 3% (1)
- ➤ Not to recommend: 3% (1)
- ➤ No answer: 5% (2)

0:Low <-------------->10:High	0	1	2	3	4	5	6	7	8	9	10
Understanding of the contents	0	0	0	0	0	4	2	6	12	8	5
Utilization of Business	0	0	0	0	0	5	3	6	11	6	6
Same as attendance motivation	0	0	0	1	0	6	3	7	9	6	5

Fig. 4. Evaluation of the training

4   Conclusion

This education/training can be used for other security incidents.

It is said that the evaluation of the municipal officials in Japan is severe, but the result of this time was a relatively good evaluation.

Since the questionnaire is done just after training, it has not been verified whether it will be useful at an actual incident occurs.

References

1. Christopher, H.: Social Engineering: The Art of Human Hacking. Wiley, Hoboken (2010)
2. Mitnick, K.D.: The Art of Deception: Controlling the Human Element of Security. Wiley, Hoboken (2003)
3. Caralli, R.A., et al.: CERT Resilience Management Model, version 1.0, pp. 4–5. Software Engineering Institute, Carnegie Mellon University, Pittsburgh (2010)
4. Verizon, 2015 Data Breach Investigations Report (2015). http://www.verizon.com/about/news/2015-data-breach-report-info/
5. Federal Bureau of Investigation, Elicitation. https://www.fbi.gov/file-repository/elicitation-brochure.pdf/view
6. Crew Resource Management. http://www.crewresourcemanagement.net/
7. Agency for Healthcare Research & Quality, Team STEPPS. https://www.ahrq.gov/teamstepps/index.html
8. The invisible gorilla. http://www.theinvisiblegorilla.com/videos.html

Decision Tree Analysis on Environmental Factors of Insider Threats

Michihiro Yamada[✉], Koichi Niihara, and Hiroaki Kikuchi

Meiji University Graduate School, Meiji University,
Tokyo 164-8525, Japan
jam_1934@yahoo.co.jp

Abstract. In information security management, insider threat is one of the biggest threats. Since there are too many involved factors, it is not clear which factor plays the most significant role in malicious activities. Hence, this study aims to identify the factors of insider threat for security management viewpoint. We conduct an experiment from that a total of 198 subjects work to review sample web search engine and observed what they behaved. Our decision tree analysis reveals the typical characteristics of malicious ideas.

1 Introduction

In information security management, insider threat is one of the biggest threats. Since there are too many involved factors, it is not clear which factor plays the most significant role in malicious activities. Hence, this study aims to identify the factors of insider threat for security management viewpoint. Classifying behaviors into two classes, positive and negative, Hausawi conducted interviews with security experts [1]. This survey-based study is very useful for understanding insider's behaviors and collecting all possible features for malicious activities. However, survey and interview are not always true, e.g., subjects pretending to be honest and unintentionally protecting their organization. Moreover, it is not feasible to observe potential insider's every steps to perform malicious action.

In order to overcome the difficulties, in observation, we propose an experiment that subjects are employed to work to given task and observe the number of malicious activities of subjects.

We conduct an experiment from that a total of 198 subjects work to review sample web search engine and observed what they behaved. Our decision tree analysis reveals the typical characteristics of malicious ideas.

2 Experiment

In our experiment, we focus on an assignment of identities to users. If users share some common ID such as "administrator" with others, they tend to be malicious more often than users with individual IDs. Since it is impossible to figure out who makes misbehavior, the ID sharing user may think the malicious activities

C. Stephanidis (Ed.): HCII Posters 2017, Part II, CCIS 714, pp. 658–662, 2017.
DOI: 10.1007/978-3-319-58753-0_93

never be exposed. To verify how much malicious activities are increased when ID is shared, we divided a set of subjects into two groups; the first half assigned to a common ID, and the other half assigned to individual IDs.

The flow of experiment is as follows. First, all subjects login to a registration site by using the IDs of the crowdsourcing service. At that site, subjects are assigned the word list to be studied in a trial search service. Second, at the search site, subjects are divided into two groups; individual-IDs users and ID-sharing users groups. The individual-IDs users need to input their IDs of crowdsourcing site before login to the search site. While, the ID-sharing users are allowed to login without any information for access. At the search site, they tested the given 50 search words, and evaluate the quality of results as well as the performance of the search function.

If subjects complete the test with less than 50 words, we regard them as a malicious activity.

3 Experimental Results

3.1 Malicious Subjects

Table 1 shows the summary of experimental result. We show the numbers of malicious subject for their demographic attributes, e.g., sex, age, and affiliations.

Table 1. Maliious subjects with respects to demographic groups

Group	Shared IDs Malicious	N	Individual IDs Malicious	N	Total Malicious	N
Sex male	13	51	11	58	24	109
Sex female	7	47	4	42	11	89
Age –19	1	1	0	0	1	1
Age 20–29	2	15	2	8	4	23
Age 30–39	9	35	4	41	13	76
Age 40–49	2	30	4	38	6	68
Age 50–59	2	12	2	10	4	22
Age 60–	4	5	3	3	7	8
Job office worker	5	22	5	26	10	48
Job public servant	1	1	0	0	1	1
Job self employed	7	28	3	29	10	57
Job parttime worker	1	9	0	10	1	19
Job houseworker	2	19	2	18	4	37
Job students	1	1	1	1	2	2
Job unemployment	1	9	3	12	4	21
Job others	2	9	1	4	3	13
Total	20	98	15	100	35	198

As a result, we observed that 20 ID-sharing users (out of 98) played malicious activity. The number of malicious users who shared a common ID is greater than that of individual-IDs users. Based on the experimental result, we analyze the set of malicious subjects in some methods, (1) Decision tree, and (2) Association rule mining, and (3) Logistic regression analyses.

3.2 Decision Tree Analysis

By a decision tree, node "Age" is chosen as the best classifier, which is at the root of tree, and plays a significant role for insider.

A decision tree reveals the logical conditions for determining a target attribute. Figure 1 shows the decision tree of malicious users, learned in R package "rpart". The target attribute is whether the subject is malicious or not. In this tree, nodes are logical conditions to classify subjects and the left branch means satisfied. By labels "Malicious/Honest", we denote the numbers of subjects in the node. For example, if user's age is over 55 (at the left sub tree of the root node) then 7 subjects are malicious except 1 honest (at Sex = b).

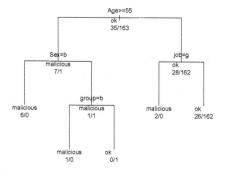

Fig. 1. Decision tree of malicious subjects

3.3 Association Rules Mining

To reveal the typical characteristic of insider related with combination of attributes, we extract some association rules by using R package, "arules". Table 2 shows the selected association rules. By Support and Confidence, we denote a joint probability $Pr(lhs, rhs)$, and a conditional probability $Pr(rhs \mid lhs)$, respectively. For example, No. 1 rule means that "If users use individual IDs and they are self-employed worker, then they are legitimate with 89% confidence. No. 5 means that "ID-sharing users sometimes (20% confidence) have played malicious activity".

The association rule shows "If individual-IDs users are 30's, they are legitimate".

3.4 Logistic Regression Analysis

A logistic regression is an analysis method to predict a conditional probability of event given conditions in a logistic model. We applied the logistic regression to the dataset of malicious subjects of some demographic attributes. Our model is of the form

$$\log \frac{Pr(malicious \mid x)}{1 - Pr(malicious \mid x)} = -1 - 0.05x_1 + 0.048x_2 + \cdots + 0.064x_{10}$$

where the coefficients of variables are given in Table 3.

Table 2. Assosiation rules

No	lhs	rhs	support	confidence	lhs.support	lift
1	{group = individual IDs, job = self-employed} =>	{Judge = ok}	0.1313131	0.8965517	0.1464646	1.089063
2	{group = individual IDs, Age = 40's} =>	{Judge = ok}	0.1717172	0.8947368	0.1919192	1.086858
3	{group = individual IDs, Age = 30's} =>	{Judge = ok}	0.1868687	0.902439	0.2070707	1.096214
4	{group = individual IDs, Sex=Male, job=self-employed} =>	{Judge = ok}	0.1111111	0.9166667	0.1212121	1.113497
5	{group = shard IDs} =>	{Judge = malicious}	0.1010101	0.2040816	0.4949495	1.154519

Table 3. Logistic regression analysis

	Estimate	Pr(>|t|)	Odds
(Intercept)	−0.107074	0.384287	2.41E-02
Group individual IDs	−5.42E-02	0.306387	6.78E-01
Sex male	0.048906	0.465707	1.41E+00
Age	6.49E-03	0.023689 *	1.05E+00
Job self-employed	0.031873	0.735564	1.38E+00
Job office worker	0.097586	0.297715	2.18E+00
Job other	0.087399	0.476033	1.86E+00
Job part-time worker	−0.06025	0.566693	4.41E-01
Job public servant	0.668873	0.082308	2.90E+07
Job student	1.012411	0.000336 ***	3.37E+08
Job unemployment	0.06497	0.558746	1.74E+00

4   Conclusions

We studied the factor analysis of malicious insider in total of 198 subjects with some conditions. Our experiment showed that sharing ID and Password could increase a risk of malicious insider by $\frac{1}{0.68}$ times than without sharing.

References

1. Hausawi, Y.M.: Current trend of end-users' behaviors towards security mechanisms. In: Tryfonas, T. (ed.) HAS 2016. LNCS, vol. 9750, pp. 140–151. Springer, Cham (2016). doi:10.1007/978-3-319-39381-0_13

Evaluation of Accessibility of University Websites: A Case from Turkey

Zehra Yerlikaya[1,2,4(✉)] and Pınar Onay Durdu[3,4]

[1] Department of Computer Engineering, Graduate School of Natural and Applied Sciences, Kocaeli University, Izmit, Kocaeli, Turkey
zehra.yerlikaya@kocaeli.edu.tr
[2] Computer Center, Kocaeli University, Izmit, Kocaeli, Turkey
[3] Department of Computer Engineering, Faculty of Engineering, Kocaeli University, Izmit, Kocaeli, Turkey
pinar.onaydurdu@kocaeli.edu.tr
[4] Human Computer Interaction Research Laboratory, Kocaeli University, Izmit, Kocaeli, Turkey

Abstract. In this study, the accessibility of Turkish public universities website was analyzed to find the common accessibility issues that might detriment the users' interaction. 20 public universities were randomly selected based on their URAP (University Ranking by Academic Performance) scores. Automated assessment was conducted by SortSite testing tool.

According to the results, it was revealed that all of the websites have a number of accessibility conflicts with WCAG 2.0 criteria. It is worthy to note that there is no single university that fully satisfies the accessibility criteria. Most violations can be listed as missing text alternatives for non-text contents, missing helpful and clear page titles, unclear links, unassigned document main language, contrast violations or unclear labels.

Keywords: Accessibility · Accessibility evaluation · Universal design · University websites · WCAG · W3C

1 Introduction

Nowadays, websites gain much more importance due to rapidly increasing amount of information. Websites become main mechanism to disseminate information to a variety of audiences for a wide spectrum of organizations from commercial to governmental. The universal design of this communication medium becomes an important issue for all these organizations [1, 2]. Universal design enables usable web pages that will be accessible to all people without defining any target group including people with disabilities, elderly or kids [3, 4].

Millions of people have disabilities that affect their use of the Web and currently many of the websites have accessibility barriers that make it difficult for many people [5]. In order to provide equal access and equal opportunity to all people, some guidelines and recommendations have been developed by Web Accessibility Initiative (WAI) [6] which was founded by World Wide Web Consortium (W3C) [7]. W3C and

© Springer International Publishing AG 2017
C. Stephanidis (Ed.): HCII Posters 2017, Part II, CCIS 714, pp. 663–668, 2017.
DOI: 10.1007/978-3-319-58753-0_94

WAI have developed two sets of guidelines, which were WCAG 1.0 [8] and WCAG 2.0 [9]. There are also other organizations that focus on the accessibility issues in some countries and developed some web accessibility national laws. For example United States' Section 508 standard was mandated for all federal agencies' websites to comply with it [10]. Similar accessibility requirements were determined in other countries such as United Kingdom, Australia, Switzerland, Finland, France, Spain and Romania [11]. Furthermore, Turkey also signed United Nations' Convention on the Right of Person with Disabilities in 2008 [12] and with this convention accepted to ensure the accessibility issues for all people.

Web Accessibility Content Guidelines (WCAG) developed by WAI is much more comprehensive [13]. The first set, WCAG 1.0, included a set of guidelines and principles to make web content accessible with disabilities and WCAG 2.0 extended the first version by broadening the range of people as well as the range of web technologies [8, 9]. WAI organized these guidelines around four principles, which were perceivable, operable, understandable and robust. For each principle, technology-independent success and conformance criteria were defined. WCAG 2.0 [9] has divided success criteria into three levels of conformance which are A, AA and AAA. Level A means that website conforms to guideline items at minimum level, while AA is an extension of level A and AAA is an extension of level AA.

In order to assess the accessibility of a website there are two approaches, one of them is assessing by a human evaluator and the other is by using an automated tool. Previously, there were several studies conducted for the evaluation of web accessibility of university websites in some countries. Many of these studies applied automated evaluation methods [1, 2, 11, 14–20] while a few applied manual [21] or both methods [22, 23]. Thomson et al. [22] compared the results of automated tool and expert review and they reported that although there were some limitations with automated tools, it was sufficient to assess the accessibility of an organizations' website. In many of the automated tool based studies, more than one tool was used [1, 2, 14, 17–19] and their results were consolidated.

On the other hand, there is not any accessibility study conducted for Turkey's university websites. However, Menzi-Çetin et al. [24] conducted a usability evaluation of a university website with visually impaired students. They reported problems on the need for a search tool and a text version for all pages, the use of tabs for navigation links and more information for visuals on the pages.

In this study, the website accessibility of Turkish public universities was analyzed in order to find the common accessibility issues that might detriment the users' interaction. The main aim of this study was to increase awareness of these issues rather than providing a categorization of the selected universities based on their accessibility.

2   Method

In this study, web sites of public universities in Turkey were analyzed in terms of accessibility. 20 public universities were selected based on their URAP (University Ranking by Academic Performance) scores [25]. Universities were grouped into five groups based on their URAP scores and four universities were selected from each group randomly. Automated assessment was conducted.

WAI listed 88 tools in its "Complete List of Web Accessibility Evaluation Tools" [26]. Free edition of SortSite [27] automated tool was selected for this study since it could analyzes 100 pages of an organization's websites starting from homepage according to WCAG 2.0 accessibility standard in its A, AA and AAA levels. Although Nielsen [28] stated that the homepage determined the tone of an entire website, he also focused on that would not be adequate.

All the assessments of university web sites were conducted during September 2016. Analysis took average of 20 min for each university website.

3   Results

The results of the accessibility analysis of 20 Turkish public university websites showed that each university websites had some problems in all levels of WCAG 2.0. The frequency of problems in each level were reported.

Based on the results of the analysis, universities were grouped into four groups based on the total accessibility problems in all levels. There were not any university website, which had less than 10 problems. On the other hand, many of the university web sites had either 10–15 errors or 16–20 errors while only one of the university websites had more than 25 errors as can be seen in Table 1. In addition, a Pearson product-moment correlation was run and it was found out that there was no statistically significant correlation between them regarding their URAP scores.

Table 1. Categorization of university web sites based on total problems

# of accessibility problems	# of university web sites
10–15	7
16–20	7
21–25	5
26–30	1
Total	20

Level A of WCAG 2.0 consisted of 21 criteria. 15 violations were detected in at least one of the 20 university web sites. These problems and their frequency can be seen in Fig. 1. For level A, the problems that were encountered across all university websites could be listed as missing text alternative for non-text content, unclear link purpose from its context, and missing name, role, value for elements on the site.

Level AA of WCAG 2.0 consisted of 13 criteria. 3 violations were detected in at least one of the 20 university web sites and these can be seen in Fig. 2. Mostly detected problem was contrast violations between text and background of the website which was detected in 18 of these web sites. Unclear headings and labels and inability to resize text without loss of content or function were the other problems.

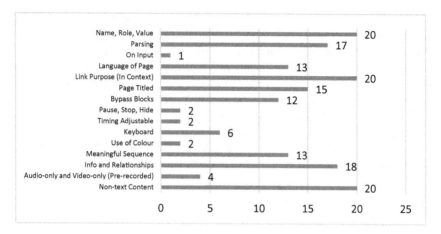

Fig. 1. Problems at level A of WCAG 2.0

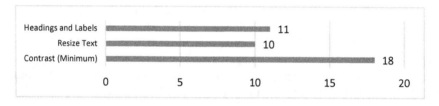

Fig. 2. Problems at level AA of WCAG 2.0

Finally, Level AAA of WCAG 2.0 consisted of 23 criteria. The results showed that there were seven problems and these can be seen in Fig. 3. The problems that were encountered across all university websites could be listed as initiation of changes on websites without user request and unclear link purpose.

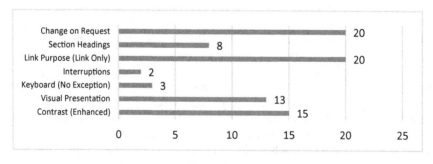

Fig. 3. Problems at level AAA of WCAG 2.0

4   Conclusion

In the scope of this study, 20 Turkish public universities' web sites were analyzed with SortSite automated tool. All of the examined websites have been reported having a number of accessibility conflicts with WCAG 2.0 criteria. Most violations can be listed as missing text alternatives for non-text contents, missing helpful and clear page titles, unclear links, unassigned document main language, contrast violations or unclear labels.

In order to overcome these problems; textual alternatives to content should be provided; links should be meaningfully named as consistent with the content they are related to and define its goal; names, roles and values must be assigned for all items on the site; text and visual items must have appropriate contrast values and automatic changes can only be initiated or stopped with the user request.

As a conclusion, the findings from this study have a practical implication for web developers of universities. It showed that universities in Turkey should consider the accessibility issues to ensure the right to access the website for people. The limitation of this study is that it did not include all universities, rather just a sample of public universities. As a future work, this study should be extended to evaluate all public and private universities' web sites in order to reveal the complete picture. In addition, other available automated tools could also be employed to get more detailed results.

References

1. Zaphiris, P., Ellis, R.D.: Website usability and content accessibility of the top USA universities. In: WebNet, pp. 1380–1385, October 2001
2. Ismail, A., Kuppusamy, K.S.: Accessibility of Indian universities' homepages: an exploratory study. J. King Saud Univ.-Comput. Inf. Sci., 1–11 (2016). doi:10.1016/j. jksuci.2016.06.006
3. Laux, L.: Designing web pages and applications for people with disabilities. In: Human Factors and Web Development, pp. 87–95 (1998)
4. Kamis (2016). http://kamis.gov.tr/?page_id=23. Accessed 20 Sept 2016
5. W3C. Introduction to Web Accessibility (2005). https://www.w3.org/WAI/intro/acces sibility.php. Accessed 5 Sept 2016
6. WAI. https://www.w3.org/WAI/. Accessed 5 Sept 2016
7. W3C. http://www.w3.org/. Accessed 5 Sept 2016
8. WCAG 1.0. http://www.w3.org/TR/WAI-WEBCONTENT-TECHS/. Accessed 12 Sept 2016
9. WCAG 2.0. http://www.w3.org/TR/WCAG20/. Accessed 12 Sept 2016
10. Section 508 Standards. https://www.section508.gov/summary-section508-standards. Accessed 8 Sept 2016
11. Cojocar, G.S., Guran, A.M.: Evaluation of Romanian academic websites accessibility: a Case Study. Stud. Univ. Babes-Bolyai Inform. **58**(4), 26–34 (2013)
12. Engellilerin Haklarına İlişkin Sözleşme (2009). http://www.ttb.org.tr/mevzuat/index.php? option=com_content&view=article&id=686:engeller-haklarina-k-slee&Itemid=36. Accessed 20 Sept 2016

13. Abou-Zahra, S.: Web accessibility evaluation. In: Harper, S., Yesilada, Y. (eds.) Web Accessibility, pp. 79–106. Springer, Heidelberg (2008). doi:10.1016/j.iheduc.2008.06.007

14. Harper, K.A., DeWaters, J.: A quest for website accessibility in higher education institutions. Internet High. Educ. **11**(3), 160–164 (2008). doi:10.1016/j.iheduc.2008.06.007

15. Aziz, M.A., Isa, W.A.R.W.M., Nordin, N.: Assessing the accessibility and usability of Malaysia higher education website. In: 2010 International Conference on User Science and Engineering (i-USEr), pp. 203–208. IEEE (2010). doi:10.1109/IUSER.2010.5716752

16. Hashemian, B.J.: Analyzing web accessibility in Finnish higher education. ACM SIGACCESS Access. Comput. **101**, 8–16 (2011). doi:10.1145/2047473.2047475

17. Adepoju, S.A., Shehu, I.S.: Usability evaluation of academic websites using automated tools. In: 2014 3rd International Conference on User Science and Engineering (i-USEr), pp. 186–191. IEEE, September 2014. doi:10.1109/IUSER.2014.7002700

18. Ahmi, A., Mohamad, R.: Web accessibility of the malaysian public university websites. In: Proceedings of International Conference on E-Commerce, pp. 171–177 (2015)

19. Kesswani, N., Kumar, S.: Accessibility analysis of websites of educational institutions. Perspect. Sci. **8**, 210–212 (2016). doi:10.1016/j.pisc.2016.04.031

20. Alahmadi, T., Drew, S.: An evaluation of the accessibility of top-ranking university websites: accessibility rates from 2005 to 2015. In: DEANZ Biennial Conference, pp. 224–233 (2016)

21. Aizpurua, A., Harper, S., Vigo, M.: Exploring the relationship between web accessibility and user experience. Int. J. Hum.-Comput. Stud. **91**, 13–23 (2016). doi:10.1016/j.ijhcs.2016.03.008

22. Thompson, T., Burgstahler, S., Comden, D.: Research on web accessibility in higher education. J. Inf. Technol. Disabil. **9**(2) (2003)

23. Kane, S.K., Shulman, J.A., Shockley, T.J., Ladner, R.E.: A web accessibility report card for top international university web sites. In: Proceedings of the 2007 International Cross-Disciplinary Conference on Web Accessibility (W4A), pp. 148–156. ACM, May 2007. doi:10.1145/1243441.1243472

24. Menzi-Çetin, N., Alemdağ, E., Tüzün, H., Yıldız, M.: Evaluation of a university website's usability for visually impaired students. Univ. Access Inf. Soc. **16**, 1–10 (2015). doi:10.1007/s10209-015-0430-3

25. University Ranking by Academic Performance (2016). http://tr.urapcenter.org/2016/2016_t9.php. Accessed 20 Sept 2016

26. Web Accessibility Evaluation Tools List (2016). http://www.w3.org/WAI/ER/tools/. Accessed 20 Sept 2016

27. SortSite. http://www.powermapper.com/products/sortsite/. Accessed 20 Sept 2016

28. Nielsen, J.: Designing Web Usability: The Practice of Simplicity. New Riders Publishing, San Francisco (1999)

Author Index

Printed in the United States
By Bookmasters